Manual of Pediatric Therapeutics

DR. B. A. SPILKER

Manual of Pediatric Therapeutics

Department of Medicine
Children's Hospital Medical Center, Boston

Edited by
John W. Graef, M.D.
Thomas E. Cone, Jr., M.D.

Little, Brown and Company   Boston

To our patients

Foreword

The *Manual of Pediatric Therapeutics* should prove tremendously useful to the busy practitioner of family medicine or pediatrics, to the house officer beginning his career, and to the physician in emergency medicine. In it they will find in clear, outline form a scientifically based approach to the diagnosis and management of most of the major syndromes and diseases of infants, children, and adolescents, and rational therapeutic procedures for the basic pediatric emergencies that are life threatening and demand prompt action.

This volume is the product of the combined efforts of many of the house officers and fellows in training at the Children's Hospital Medical Center, with the assistance of certain members of its senior staff. It could be called *The Pocket House Officer* because it contains so much of the specific information that becomes second nature to the experienced pediatric resident—dealing daily with serious illness—information that is easily forgotten by those of us who use it less frequently but who must know what to do when faced with what for us is an unusual emergency. The *Manual* is a team effort in the best sense of the word. We hope that it will help physicians on the firing line feel confident in their essential roles of protecting children's lives and health and in supporting the parents of their patients in moments of stress.

Charles A. Janeway, M.D.
Physician-in-Chief

Preface

Throughout the preparation of the *Manual of Pediatric Therapeutics* our intent has been to provide a broadly based and authoritative guide to the medical care of children in both the ambulatory and inpatient setting. Our goal is to provide for pediatricians a reference manual with the usefulness the *Manual of Medical Therapeutics* has provided for internists.

To assure a general pediatric perspective, we decided that, with few exceptions, this manual would be written by house staff and fellows and not necessarily by those with specific subspecialty training in the subjects discussed. While not intended to be encyclopedic, it covers the major areas of concern to the *general* pediatrician.

Second, entities for which no known therapy could be agreed upon as useful are excluded, with the exception of some for which relief of symptoms or complications could be described.

Next, we left out ubiquitously available reference standards (growth charts, etc.), but provided some information that is either uniquely available from our institution, hard to find in other texts, or essential to accurate management.

Finally, we felt that some evaluative and diagnostic information *would* be essential to proper intervention. Overall, this information is kept to a minimum. Since some presenting complaints trouble pediatricians so frequently as to warrant comment, we chose ten of these and devoted one chapter (Chapter 8) to short discussions of their differential diagnosis and to an approach to the evaluation of children with these complaints.

The first part of the manual deals with general pediatric problems, the balance with specific subspecialty areas, of which most are represented. Although there is no separate chapter on allergies, the most important allergic problems are in other related sections (e.g., anaphylaxis in the chapter on emergencies, asthma and environmental control in the pulmonary chapter, allergic rhinitis in chapters on eye disorders and ear, nose, and throat disorders, and urticaria in the chapter on dermatology; serum sickness is discussed in the section on inflammatory disease). The material on emergencies was the most difficult to organize. Some entities are included in their own subspecialty chapter: epiglottitis and meningitis, for example, although true emergencies, are to be found in the chapter on infectious diseases. Extensive cross references, particularly to Chapters 4, 9, 11, 14, and 19, should permit the reader to find readily the information needed in an emergency situation.

On the subject of meningitis, particular attention should be drawn to the new recommendation for the treatment of meningitis of unknown etiology in age groups susceptible to *Hemophilus influenzae*. This recommendation reflects recently observed changes in the antibiotic sensitivity of *Hemophilus* in some areas of the country and the recommendation of the Committee on Infectious

Diseases of the American Academy of Pediatrics as well as the opinion of our own infectious disease group. We are further indebted to the "Red Book" of the AAP for the material on immunization in Chapter 1.

This manual was conceived four years ago as a work to be written by house staff for house staff. It attempts to answer questions that all of us have encountered in our pediatric training, drawing on current literature, practice at the Children's Hospital Medical Center, and our own experience. We are especially grateful to Dr. Charles A. Janeway, whose patience and support permitted us to mobilize the help we needed. We also thank that singularly gifted group of teachers, our senior staff; the Medical Foundation, Inc., under whose fellowship support the bulk of the editorial work was done; Drs. Jan Breslow, Harvey Markovitch, and Paul Mueller for invaluable editorial assistance; Mrs. Anne N. Merian and Mrs. Lin Richter of Little, Brown and Company for their patience and guidance in the organization and copyediting of the manual; Miss Dee Atkinson for indexing expertise; Mss. Cinny Thorndike, Annette Cardillo, Judy Fiott, and Linda Gilman for their help with the preparation of the manuscript; and, finally, the wives and families of all the house officers and fellows who contributed to this book. Their husbands spent many hours stolen from already scarce family time in working and reworking this material.

This book is meant to fill a need for the many pediatricians, house officers, and others who care for sick children. We hope they find it useful.

J. W. G.
T. E. C.

Contents

Manual of Pediatric Therapeutics

NOTICE

The indications and dosages of all drugs in this Manual have been recommended in the medical literature and conform to the practices at Children's Hospital Medical Center, Boston. The medications described do not necessarily have specific approval by the Food and Drug Administration for use in the diseases and dosages for which they are recommended. The package insert for each drug should be consulted for use and dosage as approved by the FDA. Because standards for usage change, it is advisable to keep abreast of revised recommendations, particularly those concerning new drugs.

1 General Care of the Patient

I. CARING FOR CHILDREN Illness can be a frightening and unpleasant experience, particularly for children. Concern for the child's needs has helped to foster understanding of the impact of hospitalization on the child's growth and development. Hospital personnel are learning to consider how the child matures and learns, how he uses imagination and make-believe, the meaning of his toys and other possessions, and his capacity for adaptation to others.

Children can feel and react even at times when they might appear uninterested or are absorbed by fear about their illness and the attendant hospital procedures. For this reason care must be taken to respect the modesty, integrity, and privacy of each child. And because children are likely to be afraid of situations they do not understand, they need to be told about their illness and its treatment in terms they can comprehend. Insincerity is a quality children quickly recognize, and deceiving a child is an abuse of trust that only serves ultimately to alienate him.

It should not be surprising if a child reacts angrily to painful procedures or is frustrated at his own lack of progress. An understanding physician views this anger as a normal reaction and should not feel threatened by it. It is the quiet and passive infant or child who may be a cause for concern. Older children, particularly, understand pain and even death and can be made unnecessarily anxious by bedside staff conversations that may be misinterpreted or misunderstood.

Both parents, but particularly a child's mother, are seen by the child uniquely, especially when the child is sick. The parents, in turn, know their child far better than those trying to help care for him. Listening to parents, carefully noting their observations, putting them at ease, and hearing out their worries even if they appear unrelated can help to provide them with the emotional resources needed to help their child. Impatience or misunderstanding with parents can impede their inclusion in the therapeutic process, particularly because parents will continue to have caring responsibility for the child after his illness—a point easily overlooked during the time of acute intervention.

To make their meaningful participation easier, parents need objective advice from the physician. While they should not be asked to make medical judgments, parents have a legal and ethical right to be properly informed of the attendant benefits and risks of therapy and to be included in the decision-making process.

Finally, a pediatrician's responsibility to a child does not end when the child has been cured of his physical illness. It is the unique role of those who care for children to help them fulfill their potential worth and take their rightful place as responsible adults. This may require the pediatrician to go far beyond traditional medical intervention into the area of schools, environment, and economic circumstances in his efforts to assist the child.

II. THE HOSPITALIZED PATIENT

A. **Medical orders** Written medical orders are the physician's instructions to the nursing staff concerning the care and treatment of the patient. They should be written clearly and accurately, with special consideration to dosage calculation and decimal points. Orders are the legal responsibility of the physician and should be correctly dated and signed. Unusual orders should be discussed with the nurse at the time they are written and individualized for each patient. Properly written orders should cover diagnosis and treatment and provide for the patient's comfort and dignity. The following schemes may be utilized:

1. **Diagnosis** List the diagnostic findings in order of significance. Indicate the condition of the patient, whether critical, fair, or satisfactory. When a patient's condition is listed as critical, the family should be informed by the physician to avoid misunderstanding.

2. **Disposition** This includes the frequency of monitoring vital signs and weighing the patient, permitted activities, special observations, isolation procedures, and environmental conditions.

   a. Unnecessarily frequent determination of vital signs overburdens the nursing staff and may unnecessarily discomfit the patient.

   b. Bed rest for an ill child is often more constraining than limited activity, and the social environment will also affect the degree of activity. Hospitalized children, particularly those in isolation, should not be denied social interaction.

3. **Diet** Choose the diet with the following considerations in mind: age, caloric needs, ability to chew, and special nutritional requirements necessitated by problems of absorption, intestinal irritation, residue, and transit time (see Chap. 16, Sec. II).

4. **Diagnostic tests** Group in logical sequence (e.g., blood, radiographic). List all tests and the dates they are to be done. Before ordering tests, consider their necessity and *cost*.

5. **Drugs** Include generic name, dose, route, frequency, and length of time to be administered. Review orders for narcotics *daily*. In general, separate drugs for specific therapy from drugs for symptomatic relief. Orders for respiratory or physical therapy must also be explicit as to duration, frequency, type, anatomic site of administration, and associated medication.

B. **Common pediatric procedures**

1. **Venipuncture and intravenous infusion**

   a. **Indications** To withdraw venous blood or for continuous administration of solutions or drugs.

   b. **Site** Hands, feet, scalp, or antecubital veins.

   c. **Technique**

      (1) Restrain the hands, feet, or arm with an armboard, or shave scalp aseptically.

      (2) Place a tourniquet proximal to the puncture site. A rubber band with a small adhesive tag (for release) may be placed around the forehead to distend scalp veins in infants. Palpate the vein desired.

(3) Attach a short-beveled scalp vein needle, #21 or 23, to a small syringe filled with sterile saline solution. If the puncture is to be used for blood collection, attach an empty syringe.

(4) Prepare the skin with 70% alcohol. (This does not sterilize. To prepare a sterile area for blood culture, iodine or thimerosal [Merthiolate] must be applied, then washed with alcohol.)

(5) Palpate the target vein with one hand and grasp the plastic "wings" of the needle with the other. Pierce the skin slightly to one side and 0.5 cm distal to the entry site. Infants' veins, especially on the scalp, are usually superficial, and a deep thrust may cause distal wall penetration and a hematoma. If venipuncture is for blood sample only, *reverse* the direction of the thrust by the needle.

(6) Draw back on the syringe.

(7) If blood returns, confirming venipuncture, *slowly* inject 1 ml of saline and observe the site for swelling. If swelling occurs, saline is infiltrating, and a new site must be selected and prepared.

(8) If saline enters the vein smoothly, tape the wings of the needle securely to the skin and attach the infusion set.

(9) Protect the infusion from accidental dislodging by taping an inverted paper cup or dish over the site with a "door" cut in one side to permit tubing to pass.

2. Arterial puncture

a. Indications   Oxygen concentration determination; blood culture in endocarditis if venous blood cultures are negative; in cases of venous collapse.

b. Site   Femoral or brachial or radial artery.

c. Technique

(1) Prepare the skin with iodine solution.

(2) No tourniquet is used.

(3) The needle must be sharp and without burrs.

(4) Locate the vessel by palpation.

(5) Infiltration with procaine is optional but may obscure the vessel.

(6) Puncture the skin and push the needle *through* the arterial site. Withdraw it slowly until blood is seen in the tubing.

(7) Blood will flow into syringe without suction if the artery is punctured.

(8) After the needle is withdrawn, maintain compression at the puncture site for 3–5 min.

3. Gastric gavage

a. Indications   When infants with normal gastrointestinal function are slow to accept or cannot accept oral feeding.

b. Site   Preferably the nasal route.

c. Technique

(1) Wrap the child.

(2) Insert a lubricated, cooled, 10–14F feeding catheter into either nostril and pass into the stomach.

(3) Observe respiration. If the trachea is entered, coughing will usually occur.

(4) Inject *2–3 ml* of air and listen over the stomach for an air rumble.

(5) Attach the funnel and pour the feeding *slowly*.

(6) Pinch the tube while withdrawing to avoid aspiration.

4. Lumbar puncture

a. Indications   Diagnostic evaluation of spinal fluid or as a route for therapy or part of testing procedure. Funduscopic examination is a prerequisite.

b. Site   The 3rd or 4th lumbar interspace (at the level of the iliac crest in infants).

c. Technique

(1) Have an assistant hold the child in the lateral recumbent position on a flat table with one arm around the back of the child's neck and the other arm in the back of the knees. *The success of the pediatric lumbar puncture is in the technique of holding.*

(2) Scrub the hands and wear surgical gloves.

(3) Prepare the back with iodine solution and wash with alcohol. Iodine can cause dermatitis.

(4) Drape the area with sterile towels.

(5) In older children, infiltrate to the dura with a 1% procaine solution (with or without epinephrine).

(6) A 20- or 21-gauge needle with a stylet is used in children. A 22- or 23-gauge needle (short) may be used in infants.

(7) Placing your finger or thumb on the third or fourth lumbar vertebra, insert the needle below the vertebral spine in the midline.

(8) A click is usually felt as the dura is entered.

(9) Remove the stylet to watch for fluid.

(10) If blood returns in the needle, replace the stylet and *leave the needle in place.*

(11) Repeat the procedure one interspace above.

5. Thoracentesis

a. Indications   Diagnostic evaluation of pulmonary diseases with pleural effusion; occasionally therapeutic in patients with empyema; to instill irritant chemicals in patients with recurrent pneumothorax who are not candidates for pleurectomy.

b. Site   In free pleural effusion, 7th posterolateral intercostal space. If effusion is loculated, fluoroscopy should be utilized to locate site of puncture.

c. Technique

(1) Always try to have the current chest x-ray film in the treatment room, and recheck the physical findings (especially dullness to percussion) to assure correct site of puncture.

(2) Explain the procedure to the patient if he is old enough.

(3) Have an assistant hold the patient so that the most dependent site to be tapped is easily accessible to the instruments. The best position is usually sitting upright. If the patient is under traction or in decubitus for other reasons, he can be positioned on two chairs or small tables with the chest area exposed between the chairs. If the patient is in sitting position and is old enough, he can rest his head and arms on a pillow placed on top of a bedside table raised to the proper height.

(4) Prepare the skin as in lumbar puncture.

(5) Palpate the ribs and count with the index and middle finger.

(6) In older children, infiltrate the parietal pleura with 2% lidocaine (Xylocaine).

(7) Insert the needle (gauge 20, or preferably 18) over the upper edge of the lower rib (to avoid the intercostal vessels).

(8) Place a hemostat or Kelly clamp across the needle approximately 1 cm from the tip, so that the needle will not be inadvertently thrust too far into the lung parenchyma.

(9) In the majority of patients with fluid in abundance and some degree of pleural reaction, there is a feeling of "going through leather." If a syringe is attached, a gentle pull of the plunger will aspirate fluid into the barrel.

(10) A three-way stopcock can be attached to facilitate removal of aliquots of fluid and to help prevent air leaks while changing syringes. If the fluid is clear, a new syringe is rapidly substituted for the syringe in use, until enough material is withdrawn for studies or until the area is "dry." This maneuver of rapidly utilizing clear fluid will avoid interference with the differential diagnosis encountered in cases of "bloody" tap, since it is at the end of the procedure that trauma to the lung tissue is more likely.

(11) In many cases a pleural biopsy can be obtained at the same time. This should be done while there is enough fluid to keep the lung away from the needle.

(12) Remove the needle while maintaining negative pressure on the syringe. A plain bandage will suffice.

(13) Check vital signs and, if satisfactory, a control chest x-ray film should be taken in which the presence or absence of pneumothorax and associated parenchymal disease, previously obscured by fluid, may be seen.

(14) Complications

(a) Intercostal vessel bleeding usually is not significant unless biopsy needles are used. Its occurrence should be followed with vital signs every 15 min for the next 2 hr and then hourly.

(b) Pneumothorax See Chap. 19, Sec. **VII.**

(c) Air embolism This rarely occurs with thoracentesis, but could occur with the accidental aspiration of lung "juice."

C. Analgesia and sedation

1. Analgesia

a. General principles The following guidelines may be helpful (see also Table 1-1) :

(1) If pain is present in multiple sites, only the *single* most severe source will be recognized by the patient.

(2) Although it is sometimes assumed, particularly in small infants, that pain is not felt, or is easily forgotten, local anesthesia should be provided for diagnostic procedures whenever feasible.

(3) True analgesics such as morphine may mask pain, while sedatives such as phenobarbital will not. For this reason sedatives may be helpful in elucidating pain and tenderness, particularly in the acutely disturbed abdomen.

(4) Postoperative pain, while generally of shorter duration in children than in adults, may still be severe enough to require medication for several days.

b. Specific therapeutics

(1) Nonnarcotic analgesics See Table 1-1.

(a) Acetylsalicylic acid (aspirin) is the most frequently used analgesic and has antipyretic properties as well (see Sec. **III.B.2.c** for dose and route of administration).

   i. Its analgesic properties are most suitable for the pain of headache, arthralgia, or muscular ache. Doses for acute rheumatic fever and juvenile rheumatoid arthritis are considerably higher (see Chap. 20, Sec. **I.A.4.d.**) than for simple analgesia.

   ii. Enteric-coated preparations are available to reduce gastric irritation, but absorption of these preparations is variable.

   iii. Toxic effects include salicylism (see Chap. 3, Sec. **II.D.**), gastrointestinal bleeding, iron deficiency anemia, abnormal clotting, altered thyroid function tests, decreased fasting blood sugar in diabetes, and increased

Table 1-1.   Narcotic and Nonnarcotic Analgesics and Dosages for Pediatric Use

Name	Dose
Nonnarcotic:	
Acetylsalicylic acid (aspirin)	65–100 mg/kg/24 hr in 4–6 doses
Acetaminophen (Tempra, Tylenol)	Under 1 year 60 mg 1–3 years 60–120 mg 3–6 years 120 mg over 6 years 240 mg
Propoxyphene (Darvon)	32–65 mg q3–4h PRN
Pentazocine (Talwin)	30 mg q3–4h PRN in adults. Not for children under 12
Narcotic:	
Codeine phosphate	3 mg/kg/24 hr in 6 divided doses. Antitussive: 1 mg/kg/24 hr
Meperidine (Demerol)	6 mg/kg/24 hr
Methadone	0.7 mg/kg/24 hr
Morphine sulfate	0.1–0.2 mg/kg/dose
Camphorated opium tincture (Paregoric)	0.25–0.5 ml/kg/dose

cardiac load, which can aggravate incipient congestive heart failure and hemolysis in patients with G-6-PD deficiency (see Chap. 15, Sec. **III.B.2**).

(b) Acetaminophen (Tempra, Tylenol)

    i. Although this drug (see Table 1-1) is more valuable for antipyresis than analgesia, it has the advantage of availability in liquid form. It is also more expensive. Peak blood levels are achieved in 2 hr (see Sec. **III.B.2.c**).

    ii. Toxicity effects include methemoglobinemia, anemia, and liver damage, but it does not cause hemolysis in G-6-PD deficiency.

    iii. Phenacetin, a sister drug, has similar properties, although it is probably more toxic. It is often used with aspirin and caffeine (Empirin compound), but there is no evidence that this combination is more effective than aspirin alone.

(c) Propoxyphene (Darvon) (see Table 1-1) is a slightly stronger analgesic than aspirin and is similar to codeine. It is available in combination with aspirin and is sometimes effective when aspirin alone is not. Toxic reactions include gastrointestinal upset, vertigo, and drowsiness, as well as pruritus and skin eruptions. Severe reactions include cyanosis, convulsions, coma, and respiratory depression. **It is not approved for use in children under 12.**

(d) Pentazocine (Talwin) (see Table 1-1), a morphine-related drug, produces weak morphine antagonism, and morphine-like subjective effects. **It is not approved for use in children under 12,** and because of adverse effects on the CNS, **its use should be reserved for hospitalized patients.** For an extensive discussion of this preparation, see *Medical Letter*, vol. 14, no. 13, June 23, 1972.

(2) Narcotic analgesics   See Table 1-1.

(a) Codeine, a morphine derivative, is more effective than aspirin but less so than morphine itself. It is also less addictive than morphine and causes less disturbance of gastrointestinal function, although seizures have been reported with its use. Its antitussive properties are well known, and it is frequently used for this purpose.

(b) Meperidine (Demerol) is probably a more effective analgesic than codeine, partly because higher doses are tolerated.

i. Highly addictive, it is less constipating and less depressing to the respiratory center than morphine.

ii. It is widely used as an obstetrical analgesic.

iii. *Because it does not constrict smooth muscle,* it can be used in the presence of asthma.

iv. In combination with promethazine (Phenergan) and chlorpromazine (Thorazine), it can be used as a "lytic cocktail" to produce rapid sedation with analgesia for painful diagnostic procedures (see **3.a**).

(c) Methadone is included because of its widespread use in antiaddiction programs.

i. Its analgesic potency is roughly equivalent to that of morphine, and it is effective PO.

ii. Its respiratory depressant effect is considerable, but it causes less gastrointestinal disturbance than morphine.

iii. When an addict can substitute it for morphine or heroin, withdrawal may ultimately be easier, if more prolonged. Nevertheless, *methadone is addictive*. It merely produces less euphoria; thus the psychological component of addiction is undermined by its use.

(d) Morphine is perhaps the most important and widely used narcotic analgesic and is effective in any age group. It has little sedative property and produces concomitant euphoria, with risk of addiction.

i. Because PO and PR preparations are somewhat unreliable in absorption and metabolism (although effective), parenteral use is generally advised, either SQ (20 min), IM (20 min), or IV (immediate but dangerous).

ii. Its excretion is via the liver, and caution should be used when it is administered to a newborn or a patient with liver disease.

iii. Paregoric or **camphorated opium tincture** makes use of the constipating properties of morphine to aid in relieving symptoms of diarrhea with spasm of the colon. **Camphorated opium tincture should never be confused with tincture of opium, which is 25 times more powerful.**

iv. Because morphine is so addictive, its administration in the pediatric age group should be limited to patients with pulmonary stenosis and infundibular spasm, congestive heart failure, severe visceral pain of known origin, intractable pain, severe postoperative pain, and pain in the patient with terminal disease. While up to 14 days of administration is usually required to produce addiction, some adolescents may become addicted on only 1 or 2 doses.

v. Tolerance to morphine includes its CNS depressive properties, so that increasing the dose does not increase the likelihood of respiratory toxicity. The physician should remember that when a patient's dose is missed, a smaller amount might suffice. Death frequently occurs in addicts who administer their *usual high dose* after a few days off the drug, when tolerance is less.

vi. Toxic effects include respiratory depression, increased intracranial pressure, arterial hypotension, nausea and vomiting, hyperglycemia, antidiuresis, addiction, and constipation.

vii. A unique problem is the treatment of newborn infants of morphine-addicted mothers. Chlorpromazine, 0.7–1.0 mg/kg q6h, and paregoric, 2–4 qtts/kg q4h, have been used effectively to prevent withdrawal symptoms in the infants (Chap. 5, Sec. **VIII**).

2. Sedation

a. General principles   Among the most important characteristics of childhood are curiosity and the drive to explore and learn. Sedation can interfere with the child's capacity to interact with and learn from his environment. It narrows his experience which, like childbirth for the mother, may be painful, but with help and support, can be rich and memorable.

(1) Indications for sedation in children are few. They include preanesthesia (Table 1-2); painful diagnostic procedures such as bone marrow aspiration; agitation that contributes to morbidity, as in respiratory diseases such as asthma or croup (in which sedation should be used only with **extreme caution**); intubation or tracheostomy for respiratory assistance; intractable pain; and, occasionally, in the evaluation of severe visceral pain, e.g., as in acute appendicitis. In this last case, sedation short of general anesthesia does not mask pain but permits its elucidation by reducing surrounding anxiety and factitious tenderness. In children, sedation is *not* the treatment of choice in insomnia or hyperactivity, and is only used as a last resort.

(2) The reaction of children to sedatives, particularly barbiturates, is unpredictable. At the toddler stage, sedatives may cause a child to become agitated. In addition, children have a higher

Table 1-2.   Directions for Preoperative Medication for Infants and Children[a]

Age	Average Weight (lb)	Pentobarbital (Nembutal[b,d]) (mg)	(grains)	Morphine (mg)	(grains)	Atropine or Scopolamine (mg)	(grains)
Newborn	7	None	None	None	None	0.2	1/300
6 months	16	30 PR	½	None	None	0.2	1/300
1 year[e]	21	45 PR	¾	1.0	1/60	0.2	1/300
2 years	27	60 PR	1	1.5	1/40	0.3	1/200
4 years	35	90 PR	1½	3.0	1/20	0.3	1/200
6 years	45	90 PR	1½	4.0	1/15	0.4	1/150
8 years	55	100 PO	1½	5.0	1/12	0.4	1/150
10 years	65	100 PO	1½	5.0	1/10	0.4	1/150
12 years	85	100 PO	1½	6.0	1/8	0.6	1/100

[a] For average, well-developed patients. Reductions must be made in dosage for subnormal patients.

[b] For rectal use Nembutal is given in the form of a suppository; dosage form is 30, 60, 90 mg.

[c] Meperidine (Demerol) or morphine and atropine are to be given hypodermically 45 min before operation.

[d] To be given as indicated, before ether, cyclopropane, or thiopental anesthesia. Give pentobarbital, morphine, and atropine as suggested by table.

[e] Approximate dosage:

Under 8 years: pentobarbital, 2.5 mg/lb PR; morphine 0.75 mg per year of age.

Over 8 years: pentobarbital, 100 mg PO; morphine, 0.5 mg per year of age up to a maximum of 8 mg.

incidence of idiosyncratic reactions to sedatives than do adults. For most purposes, the *weakest* effective sedative, such as hydroxyzine, is safe and least liable to cause unwanted side effects.

b. Specific therapeutics   See Table 1-3.

(1) Alcohol is an old-fashioned sedative, especially useful in infants; 10 ml brandy in 30 ml water, PO or by gavage, is usually effective.

(2) Chloral hydrate is probably the safest sedative and is inexpensive. It has a wide margin of safety, with the acceptable dose from 20–40 mg/kg/24 hr. Although the aftertaste is bitter, it is also available in PR form and seems to be well tolerated by children, particularly if offered in a small glass of juice. Peak activity usually occurs within 30–60 min of dose. Caution should be used in patients with liver disease.

(3) Paraldehyde   (See Chap. 2, Sec. **III.4.**) This drug has the advantage of rapid action and is relatively safe. Used primarily for alcohol withdrawal in adults, it is particularly valuable in the management of seizures in children. Caution should be exercised in patients with liver disease, but it can be used in those with renal insufficiency.

(4) Antihistamines   (For a more complete discussion of these

Table 1-3. Sedatives and Dosages for Pediatric Use

Name	Dose
Alcohol	6 ml/kg brandy in 30 ml/H_2O in infants
Chloral hydrate	15–40 mg/kg/24 hr in 2–3 divided doses
Paraldehyde	0.15 ml/kg/dose
Antihistamine	Diphenhydramine 5 mg/kg/24 hr
	Promethazine 0.5 mg/kg/dose
	Hydroxyzine 2 mg/kg/24 hr
Chlorpromazine	2 mg/kg/24 hr
Barbiturates:	
Amobarbital (Amytal)	6 mg/kg/24 hr in 3 divided doses
Secobarbital (Seconal)	6 mg/kg/24 hr in 3 divided doses
Pentobarbital (Nembutal)	6 mg/kg/24 hr in 3 divided doses
Phenobarbital	6 mg/kg/24 hr in 3 divided doses
Demerol compound:	
25 mg meperidine	1 ml/15 kg IM, not to exceed 2 ml
6.25 mg chlorpromazine	
6.25 mg promethazine	
in one ml	

agents, see *Medical Letter*, vol. 13, no. 25, Dec. 10, 1971.) Antihistamines have a variety of clinical uses which have varying degrees of success.

  (a) Antihistamines with the most effective sedative properties include promethazine (Phenergan), diphenhydramine (Benadryl), and hydroxyzine (Atarax). Cyclizine, meclizine, and promethazine are also clinically useful as antiemetics. Trimeprazine and diphenhydramine may reduce pruritus, possibly due to their sedative properties. Promethazine, chlorpromazine, and meperidine form a lytic cocktail (see **3**), which produces rapid analgesia with sedation and is particularly useful for painful diagnostic procedures.

  (b) **Serious adverse effects** are few and the drugs are well tolerated PO.

  (c) Because of the occasional stimulating effect of barbiturates in children under 2, antihistamines may be used in this age group. Nevertheless, the dose must be titrated to achieve sedative effect, and in many children no effect at all is seen.

(5) Tranquilizers With the exception of the phenothiazines, these drugs have little use in pediatrics. (See Dobkin, *Can. Anaesth. Soc. J.* 5:177, 1958.) Chlorpromazine (Thorazine) is the most widely used phenothiazine and is the third component of the lytic cocktail. It has a relatively wide margin of safety and can be used effectively in agitated adolescents. It is one of the effective agents in the management of the infant of the heroin-addicted mother in a dose of 0.7–1.0 mg/kg q6h IM.

(6) Barbiturates are true hypnotic agents.

(a) Phenobarbital is used most widely in the control of seizure disorders and to antagonize stimulants such as caffeine or amphetamines (see Chap. 14, Sec. **I.A.2.b**).

(b) Secobarbital and pentobarbital are probably more useful sedative hypnotics because of their rapid action and are widely used as preoperative medication. They are not analgesics, so that pentobarbital in particular can be helpful in evaluating abdominal pain in the anxious small child.

(c) All three agents are available for use PO, PR, or parenterally.

(d) For PR administration of barbiturates, a suppository should be used; even then, effective absorption is variable. IM or IV injection is more reliable, but the individual reactions to a given dose preclude prediction of its effect.

(e) **Because of respiratory depression, extreme caution should be used in administering barbiturates IV,** although pentobarbital produces relatively little respiratory depression for the hypnotic dose used.

3. Combined analgesia and sedation (lytic cocktail, Demerol compound) To supply rapid analgesia and sedation, a compound preparation of meperidine, chlorpromazine, and promethazine has found wide acceptance at our institution. Ampules of 10 ml are made up in which each milliliter contains 25 mg meperidine hydrochloride, 6.25 mg chlorpromazine hydrochloride, and 6.25 mg promethazine hydrochloride. The IM dose is 1 ml/15 kg of body weight, up to 2 ml maximum.

D. Transfusion therapy Blood transfusion involves a significant risk. Absolute compatibility of blood is seldom met; the possibility of sensitization by subgroup factors is much more common than is appreciated by most physicians.

Donor blood is now routinely screened against the hepatitis associated antigen either by counterelectrophoresis or radioimmunoassay. However, these methods are not sensitive enough to detect all infectious units of blood.

1. Blood banking procedures

a. It is a universal practice for both donors and recipients to be separated into A, B, O, and AB groups and Rh_0 (D) positive and Rh_0 negative types. The incidence of isoimmunization to the subgroups of the Rh factor and subsequent hemolytic reactions is not negligible. It is desirable that all Rh_0 (D) negative bloods be tested for the Rh′ (C), Rh″ (E), and Rh^u (Du) factors.

b. The saline crossmatch detects complete antibodies and is a check on the donor's and patient's ABO grouping; however, neither this nor a serum crossmatch will detect a majority of the immunizations to the subtypes of Rh or other factors. The best assurance of at least in vitro compatibility includes the utilization of the indirect Coombs (antihuman globulin) technique, which detects incomplete antibodies.

2. Blood components

a. Fresh whole blood Fresh whole blood is beneficial in massive transfusion or hereditary or acquired coagulation defects if there is associated blood loss. Platelet viability decreases after 6 hr storage as whole blood at 0–6° C; factor VIII is at maximal level within the first 8 hr after collection; and factor V is present in adequate levels in blood stored less than 3 days.

b. Blood component therapy

(1) Packed (sedimented) red cells Packed red cells are the therapy of choice in anemic and chronically debilitated patients. Some febrile reactions, especially in patients who have had repeated transfusions, may be due to the recipient's leukocyte antibodies. In such instances, leukocyte-poor red cells can be prepared by differential centrifugation or filtration or both.

(2) Platelets

(a) One unit of a platelet concentrate (the amount of platelets obtained from 500 ml whole blood) for every 10 lb of the recipient's body weight should raise the platelet count 50,000/mm^3 above the baseline level. Platelet concentrates can now be stored at room temperature for 48 hr with normal viability and hemostatic effect.

(b) In children who have idiopathic thrombocytopenic purpura or have had multiple platelet transfusions, platelet survival time is markedly shortened because of the formation of platelet antibodies.

(3) Factors VIII (antihemophilic factor) and IX See Chap. 15, Sec. V.A.

(4) Fibrinogen A deficiency in production of fibrinogen occurs as a rare congenital defect and in some patients with severe liver disease. Acute hypofibrinogenemia can also result secondary to disseminated intravascular coagulation (DIC) or fibrinolysis. The critical level of fibrinogen for normal blood coagulation is 100 mg/100 ml. At the present time, the therapy of choice is cryoprecipitated antihemophilic factor which contains, on the average, 300 mg/U.

(5) Plasma expanders One of the most urgent therapeutic emergencies is the treatment of shock associated with acute blood loss, severe burns, acute dehydration, or toxemia of infections (see Chap. 2, Sec. II.C, and Chap. 4, Sec. II). The immediate need is to expand the circulating blood volume until whole blood (in cases of hemorrhage) is available. The agents of choice are:

(a) A 5% solution of human albumin or other 5% fractionation derivatives.

(b) A 25% albumin solution diluted to 5% concentration with normal saline. **Note that undiluted concentrated 25% albumin is contraindicated in a dehydrated patient.**

3. General considerations A figure of 5 ml/lb packed red cells and 10 ml/lb whole blood certainly represents a maximal pediatric transfusion in a nonbleeding patient. Although many children can withstand this increase in blood volume, some will demonstrate signs of cardiac decompensation. Since severe anemia is often associated with borderline cardiac failure, elevated temperature, or infection, these children are least tolerant of such a load. The following principles of transfusion therapy are general guidelines that the physician must tailor to fit the specific circumstance.

a. Chronic anemia

(1) Patients who may be helped by adequate medical therapy should *not* receive transfusion unless specific conditions coexist, such as cardiac insufficiency, need for an operative procedure, or infection.

(2) In general, a child in whom iron deficiency or other anemia has gradually developed will rarely manifest symptoms unless the hemoglobin concentration is 5.0 gm/100 ml or less.

(3) The more anemic the patient, the more likely that cardiac decompensation will be precipitated or aggravated by a rapid increase in blood volume in transfusion. In such instances, a modified exchange transfusion is necessary.

(a) Determining transfusion requirements To determine the volume of sedimented red blood cells required to reach the hemoglobin concentration desired, the following simple equation may be used:

$$\text{Volume of cells} = \frac{\text{Wt} \times \text{V} \times (\text{Hb}^{\text{b}} - \text{Hb}^{\text{a}})}{\text{Hb}^{\text{s}}}$$

where Wt = patient's weight in kilograms
V = patient's blood volume (80 and 69 ml/kg are considered normal in infants and adults respectively)
Hb^{a} = hemoglobin level before transfusion
Hb^{b} = desired hemoglobin level
Hb^{s} = hemoglobin concentration of sedimented red blood cells (22 to 24 gm/100 ml, depending on the degree of packing

(Posttransfusion survival of blood stored less than one week is 92 percent; 7 to 14 days 85 percent; and 15 to 21 days, 78 percent.) Thus if it is desired to attain a hemoglobin level of 10 gm/100 ml in an infant weighing 12 kg with an initial hemoglobin of 5 gm/100 ml, one would substitute in the above equation as follows:

$$\text{Volume of cells} = \frac{12 \text{ kg} \times 80 \text{ ml/kg} \times (10 \text{ gm/100 ml} - 5 \text{ gm/100 ml})}{23 \text{ gm/100 ml}}$$

Volume of cells = 218 ml

Since this child's initial hemoglobin was 5 gm/100 ml, one would accomplish this with two transfusions of 110 ml each.

(b) Recommendations The following recommendations are based on the practical application of this equation:

   i. The adoption of 10 ml/lb of whole blood or 5 ml/lb of packed red cells as a maximal pediatric transfusion in the absence of acute blood loss.

   ii. If the initial hemoglobin level is less than 5 gm/100 ml, the volume of transfusion should be 3 ml per pound.

   iii. If cardiac decompensation exists, a modified exchange transfusion should be performed, using packed or sedimented red cells.

b. Massive transfusion   The rapid infusion of blood in amounts approaching the patient's blood volume within a short period of time introduces several potential hazards.

   (1) Biochemical changes depend on the anticoagulant solution and the duration of storage, as shown in Table 1-4.

   (2) The transfusion of a large amount of stored blood can cause temporary thrombocytopenia and deficiencies of factors V and VIII.

   (3) Rapid infusion of large quantities of cold blood can result in cardiac irregularities or arrest. Bringing the temperature of the blood to 30°–37° C from its normal of 1°–6° C is an acceptable alternative.

c. Special situations

   (1) Emergency transfusions   When there is not time for a complete crossmatch, the choices in order of preference are:

   (a) Group and type-specific blood

   (b) Group O, Rh negative red cells suspended in AB negative plasma or 5% albumin

   (c) Group O, Rh negative whole blood

   (2) Exchange transfusion   Duration of storage depends on the anticoagulant used.

   (a) Heparin   Blood should be no more than 24 hr old.

Table 1-4.   Biochemical Changes in Anticoagulant Solutions

Storage (days)	ACD Solution[a]			CPD Solution[b]		
	pH	Potassium (mEq/L)	DPG[c]	pH	Potassium (mEq/L)	DPG[c]
0	7.0	9.5	Normal	7.2	4.2	Normal
7	6.80	19.6	35% of normal	7.0	9.5	Normal
14	6.75	27.2	10% of normal	6.89	20.1	40% of normal
21	6.72	34.5	Negligible	6.85	24.5	Negligible

[a] Acid, citrate, dextrose
[b] Citrate, phosphate, dextrose
[c] Diphosphoglycerate

  (b) ACD   Blood should be no more than 48 hr old.

  (c) CPD   Blood should be no more than 5 days old. (ACD and CPD bloods can be converted to heparinized blood by initially adding 22.5 mg heparin to one unit of blood. After complete mixing, 5 ml of a 10% calcium gluconate solution should be added.)

 (3) Neonatal thrombocytopenia Platelets from random donors often do not survive because of a maternal isoantibody. In such instances, platelets suspended and washed in AB plasma should be used.

d. Complications of transfusion

 (1) Hemolytic transfusion reactions occur when red cells are destroyed by antibodies in the plasma of the recipient or donor. Signs of a reaction may follow administration of as little as 25–50 ml of blood.

  (a) Signs and symptoms   Chills, headache, chest or back pain, nausea, vomiting, a rapid rise in temperature, and a fall in blood pressure. There is also concomitant hemoglobinemia and hemoglobinuria.

  (b) Treatment   Stop treatment. Attempt to provoke a diuresis; 50–100 ml of 20% mannitol is given in 5 min, followed by an infusion containing 25 mEq sodium bicarbonate to produce a urine flow of 1–3 ml/min. The mannitol should be repeated, with hydration adequate to maintain a urine output of 100 ml/hr. If urine flow is unsatisfactory, tubular necrosis may be presumed.

 (2) Febrile (nonhemolytic) reactions

  (a) Signs and symptoms may vary from mild chilliness and slight temperature rise to severe chills and high fever. There may also be muscular aches and pains, flushing, nausea, and vomiting. Often this cannot be distinguished from a hemolytic reaction except that there is *no hemoglobinemia or hemoglobinuria*.

  (b) Treatment   Stop transfusion and administer antipyretics if necessary (see Sec. **III.B.2.c**).

 (3) Allergic reactions occur in approximately 2 percent of transfusions and are seldom severe.

  (a) Signs and symptoms are hives, itching, or a diffuse rash. Facial and periorbital edema with mild laryngospasm may sometimes occur.

  (b) Treatment   Stop transfusion. Give antihistamines, or steroids, or both.

III. COMMON MANAGEMENT PROBLEMS

A. Feeding

 1. General considerations Nutritional requirements (Table 1-5) vary according to general health, activity states, growth rate, intestinal absorption, and the presence of metabolic disturbances. Normal growth and development is the best measure of adequate nutritional intake.

Table 1-5. Recommended Daily Dietary Vitamin
Allowance for Infants 0–1 Year

Calories	100–130/kg
Protein	2–3 gm/kg
Calcium	700 mg
Iron	1 mg/kg
Vitamin A	1500 IU
Vitamin D	400 IU
Ascorbic Acid	30 mg
Thiamine	0.4 mg
Niacin	6 mg equivalents[a]
Riboflavin	0.6 mg

From *Handbook of Infant Formulas*, revised 6th
ed., Feb. 1969, J. B. Roerig. By permission.
[a] Niacin equivalents include both niacin and its
precursor, tryptophan. 60 mg tryptophan represents 1 mg niacin.

No values are given for fat, carbohydrate, phosphorus, trace minerals, or vitamins B_6, B_{12},
and E.

Table 1-6. Nutritional Requirements

Type of Patient	Calories (per kg)	Water (ml/kg)	Protein (gm/kg)
Infants	110	150	2.0–3.5
Children, age 2–6 years	90	100	2.8
Children, age 7–9 years	80	75	2.8
Undernourished infants	150	150	3.5

a. Protein requirements are proportionately higher during childhood because of rapid growth rates (Table 1-6). If protein
sources are largely vegetable, foods must be more varied to insure an adequate intake of amino acid and vitamins.

b. Cooking, in general, increases the digestibility of protein foods,
but prolonged heating reduces protein availability.

c. The frequent and often unjustified changing of formulas for
children with feeding problems may only serve to increase
anxiety in both mother and child.

d. Parents of infants with family histories of allergy should be
aware of the more troublesome foods in the first year of life
(orange juice, nuts, fish, strawberries, chocolates, and egg
whites).

e. Obese parents should be given long-term dietary instructions for
their infants, as there is a tendency for obesity to be familial
(see Chap. 17, Sec. **I.A**).

f. A child's food intake is seldom constant and varies daily in
quantity and quality.

Table 1-7. Approximate Electrolyte Content of Standard, Soy, and Special Formulas (milliequivalents per liter)

	(Na) Sodium	(K) Potas- sium	(Ca) Cal- cium	(P) Phos- phorus	(Cl) Chlo- ride	Total Electro- lytes
Standard formulas:						
Baker's Infant Formula	17	23	42	37	19	151
Bremil	13	22	35	18	11	117
Carnalac	18	25	42	37	20	165
Cow's Milk	25	36	61	53	34	219
Enfamil	11	18	32	32	11	121
Evaporated 1:2	18	25	42	37	20	165
Formil	13	18	31	28	14	118
Human Milk	7	14	17	9	12	70
Lactum	17	28	50	48	23	194
Modilac	16	26	40	35	18	147
Purevap	18	25	44	40	20	165
Similac	11	23	34	30	15	120
SMA S-26	7	14	21	21	12	89
Soy formulas:						
Isomil	13	18	35	28	15	114
Mull-Soy	16	40	60	46	16	210
Neo-Mull-Soy	17	25	42	24	6	123
ProSobee	24	28	47	42	7	175
Sobee	22	33	50	32	14	186
Soyalac	14	23	21	21	10	119
Special formulas:						
Alacta	22	44	70	65	31	258
Dryco	30	42	75	58	35	285
Lofenalac	25	37	47	47	23	202
Nursette Premature	20	33	50	52	23	212
Nutramigen	17	26	50	45	23	181
Olac	22	41	60	58	28	236
PM 60/40	7	14	17	10	12	65
Similac with Iron 24	13	27	41	36	18	144

From *Handbook of Infant Formulas*, revised 6th ed., Feb. 1969, J. B. Roerig. By permission.

Table 1-8.   Calcium and Phosphorus Content

	% Protein	Ca:P Ratio	mg/qt Ca	mg/qt P
Standard formulas:				
Baker's Infant Formula	2.2	1.3:1	825	615
Bremil	1.5	1.5:1	630	420
Carnalac	2.4	1.3:1	804	615
Cow's Milk	3.5	1.3:1	1300	1004
Enfamil	1.5	1.3:1	615	473
Evaporated 1:2	2.4	1.3:1	804	615
Formil	1.65	1.3:1	590	455
Human Milk	1.25	2.2:1	320	146
Lactum	2.7	1.3:1	946	710
Modilac	2.15	1.3:1	800	605
Purevap	2.3	1.3:1	830	635
Similac	1.7	1.3:1	662	473
SMA S-26	1.5	1.3:1	400	310
Soy formulas:				
Isomil	2.0	1.4:1	662	473
Mull-Soy	3.1	1.5:1	1200	800
Neo-Mull-Soy	1.8	1.3:1	800	600
ProSobee	2.5	1.4:1	750	600
Sobee	3.2	2.0:1	946	473
Soyalac	2.1	1.1:1	392	343
Special formulas:				
Alacta	3.4	1.3:1	1200	900
Dryco	4.0	1.3:1	1440	1100
Lofenalac	2.2	1.3:1	897	690
Nursette Premature	2.84	1.3:1	940	750
Nutramigen	2.2	1.3:1	887	683
Olac	3.4	1.3:1	1135	850
PM 60/40	1.5	2.0:1	320	165
Similac with Iron 24	2.12	1.3:1	800	610

From *Handbook of Infant Formulas*, revised 6th ed., Feb. 1969, J. B. Roerig. By permission.

Table 1-9. Approximate Analyses of Commonly Used Infant Formulas

	Normal Dilution	Cal/Oz	Percentage			Per qt @ Normal Dilution			
			Fat	Pro-tein	CHO	Units A	Units D	mg C	mg Iron
Standard formulas:									
Baker's Infant Formula	1:1	20	3.3	2.2	7.0	2500	400	50	7.5
Bremil	1:1	20	3.5	1.5	7.0	2500	400	50	Trace
Carnalac	1:1	20	2.7	2.4	8.2	1035	400	80	Trace
Cow's Milk (undiluted)	—	20	4.1	3.5	5.0	946	38	17	Trace
Enfamil	1:1	20	3.7	1.5	7.0	1500	400	50	1.4
Evaporated 1:2	1:2	15	2.7	2.4	3.4	800	265	—	Trace
Formil	1:1	20	3.5	1.65	7.0	2500	400	50	Trace
Human Milk	—	20	3.8	1.25	7.0	1419	95	40	Trace
Lactum	1:1	20	2.8	2.7	7.8	400	400	2	Trace
Modilac	1:1	20	2.7	2.15	7.7	1500	400	45	10
Purevap	1:2	20	2.6	2.3	8.0	800	400	—	Trace
Similac	1:1	20	3.4	1.7	6.6	2500	400	50	Trace
SMA S-26	1:1	20	3.6	1.5	7.2	2500	400	50	7.5
Soy formulas:									
Isomil	1:1	20	3.6	2.0	6.8	1419	378	47	11.4
Mull-Soy	1:1	20	3.6	3.1	5.2	2000	400	40	5
Neo-Mull-Soy	1:1	20	3.5	1.8	6.4	2000	400	50	8
ProSobee	1:1	20	3.4	2.5	6.8	1500	400	50	8
Sobee	1:1	20	2.6	3.2	7.7	1500	400	50	8
Soyalac	1:1	20	4.0	2.1	5.9	1500	400	30	10
Special formulas:									
Alacta (powder only)	†	†	1.2	3.4	10.8	—	—	—	Trace
Dryco (powder only)	1:2	16	1.5	4.0	5.7	2500	400	—	Trace
Lofenalac (powder only)	1:2	20	2.7	2.2	8.5	1500	400	50	15
Nursette Premature	Premixed	24	3.7	2.84	9.1	1500	400	50	Trace
Nutramigen (powder only)	1:2	20	2.6	2.2	8.5	1500	400	30	9.5
Olac	1:1	20	2.7	3.4	7.5	2500	400	—	Trace
PM 60/40 (powder only)	1:2	20	3.4	1.5	7.2	2500	400	50	2
Similac with Iron 24	Premixed	24	4.2	2.12	8.0	3000	480	60	15

Adapted from *Handbook of Infant Formulas*, revised 6th ed., Feb. 1969, J. B. Roerig. By permission.

g. New foods may be refused initially due to unfamiliarity.

h. Forced feedings are never useful at any age.

2. Infant feeding

a. Breast Although in most of the world there are no adequate hygienic alternatives to breast milk, breast-feeding in our society has become a matter of personal preference by the mother. Mothers on well-balanced diets who have sufficient fluid intake and adequate rest can, with minor additions, supply the full nutritional requirements of infants for the first 4 months of life. Adequate instruction and encouragement is the key to successful breast-feeding.

(1) Feeding schedule The normal infant can begin feeding 8 hr after birth and may be fed q3–4h. For the first few days, the breasts secrete colostrum, which is low in fat and carbohydrate but thicker and richer in protein than milk. Early in the first 2 weeks of feeding, a source of vitamin D, vitamin C, and fluorides should be added. The largest amount of milk is obtained in the first 10 min; 20 min should be sufficient total feeding time on each breast.

(2) Feeding problems Breast-feeding failures may occur when infants suck poorly because of oral malformations or nasal obstruction. This in turn results in diminished lactation. Sore, infected, or depressed nipples may also create feeding difficulties. However, the most common causes of failure are the mother's worries about quantity of intake, the unsatisfied infant, and lack of adequate instructions.

b. Formula Formula-feeding is the method chosen by the majority of women in North America and Europe. Products commercially prepared for this purpose contain full protein, fat, and carbohydrate nourishment and added vitamin supplements. (For formulas and analyses of their caloric, vitamin, and electrolyte content, see Tables 1-7 through 1-9.) The most important principle in formula-feeding is flexibility in amount and schedule. Mothers may be guided by this rule: *not less than 2 oz/lb* daily. The American Academy of Pediatrics Committee on Nutrition has recommended that all infants not breast-fed receive a commercial formula supplemented with iron.

c. Introduction of solids The infant fed by formula or with human milk does not need solid foods prior to 4 months of age. Although the early introduction of solids provides pleasure and change for

Table 1-10. Ages at Which Solids Are Introduced

Age (months)	Solid
2–4	Cereals
3–5	Vegetables and fruits
4–5	Meats

both mother and infant, strained foods and cereals have fewer calories per unit volume than does a formula. Table 1-10 lists the usual ages at which solids are introduced.

B. Fever control

1. General considerations Fever is a cardinal and often the first sign of illness in many children. Yet its pattern may be even more important than its presence (see Chap. 8, Sec. **IX**). Attempts to reduce a fever should *never* interfere with efforts to ascertain its cause. In addition, there is evidence that the presence of fever may be of biologic value in some cases. The following suggestions for management of fever may prove helpful.

a. Clinical correlation The height of the fever does not necessarily correspond directly to the severity of its cause. Newborns with sepsis may have subnormal temperatures.

b. Dehydration Because dehydration can be associated with fever (see Chap. 4, Sec. **III.E**), adequate amounts of fluid must be administered either PO if tolerated, or IV if necessary. If dehydration *is* present it may contribute to the potential toxicity of aspirin, particularly in infants.

c. Skin exposure Children can lose excess heat through their skin and should be lightly clothed when febrile.

d. Sponging A number of antipyretics are available, but all have undesirable side effects and toxicities. Sponging, on the other hand, is safe and effective *if done properly.*

e. Aspirin is the most widely used antipyretic, but remember that it can mask fever and signs of acute rheumatic disease and should never be used carelessly.

2. Specific measures

a. Hydration See Chap. 4, Sec. **III.**

b. Sponging Only tepid water should be used. Alcohol or ice water, while lowering temperature more rapidly, are associated with increased morbidity, particularly in small infants and should be avoided. The skin may be rubbed briskly to increase skin capillary circulation and heat loss. Sponging may be done no longer than a half hour every two hours.

c. Antipyretics See Table 1-11.

(1) Acetylsalicylic acid (Aspirin) The most widely used medication available, aspirin still has side effects and toxicity that necessitate caution in its use. Cumulative levels occur, and the half-life of the drug is fairly long. Because of insolubility, it is available only as a tablet or suppository. Children's preparation are flavored tablets of 75 mg each and are now limited by law to bottles of 36 tablets. Ordinary dosage for fever in children is 60 mg per year of age q4h. Doses in inflamatory disease are discussed elsewhere (see Chap. 20, Sec. **I**). Side effects and toxic reactions include GI upset, GI bleeding, depression of platelet activity, and prolongation of prothrombin time. The rectal preparation can irritate the mucosa, and a toxic reaction is known to occur from this route due to variable absorption.

Table 1-11.   Some Antipyretics Useful in Pediatrics[a, b]

Drug	Analgesic	Anti-inflammatory[c]	Suggested Antipyretic Oral Dose (mg/kg q6h)
Aspirin and other salicylates	+	+	10–20
p-Aminophenols	+	−	
Phenacetin			5–10
Acetaminophen			5–10
Acetanilid			. . .[d]
Salicylamide	±	−	10–20

[a] Reprinted with modifications and by permission from Done, A. K., and Done, D. D. Symposium on Pediatric Pharmacology *Pediatr. Clin. North Am.* 19: 171, 1972.
[b] The phenylpyrazoles, including aminopyrine, dipyrone, phenylbutazone, and oxyphenbutazone, are excluded from this list because their adverse potential precludes their use for simple antipyresis.
[c] Specifically, antirheumatic.
[d] Not recommended for general antipyretic use in children.

(2) Acetaminophen, a widely used liquid alternative to aspirin, has the advantage of somewhat greater accuracy of dosage and less gastric irritation. It lacks antirheumatic properties, but is equal to aspirin in effectiveness as an antipyretic. The dose is 5–10 mg/kg q4–6h.

(3) Phenacetin, because it is more toxic than aspirin or acetaminophen, has no advantage over either.

(4) Salicylamide is unrelated to aspirin, does not have antirheumatic properties, and is not so effective an antipyretic as aspirin or acetaminophen. It is well tolerated PO and produces few toxic reactions. Because it is a liquid, it is often used in infants but is probably rarely useful and has little to recommend it.

C. Constipation

1. Diagnosis

a. Constipation may be diagnosed by history with the finding of fecal contents on abdominal or rectal examination. Abdominal pain may suggest it.

b. Although constipation may accompany many syndromes (see Chap. 16, Sec. **II**), it more often represents too little free water in the diet, inadequate intake of high-residue food, disruption of the child's daily habits, or a painful anal fissure that causes withholding of the stool.

2. Treatment   A stepwise approach follows:

a. To assist the child to pass a hard stool:

(1) Glycerine or bisacodyl (Dulcolax) suppository (one only).

(2) Fleet's enema (may be repeated once).

(3) Mineral oil, 15 ml PO. Magnesium sulfate or sodium sulfate may help in passing a hard stool and softening a forming stool.

(4) Manual disimpaction, which is unpleasant for both child and physician, but may be necessary. There is no known simple or pleasant way to perform this time-honored physician's chore.

b. To increase bulk and soften the stool:

(1) An increase in intake of free water.

(2) Natural dietary lubricants (e.g., prune juice, olive oil, tomatoes, and tomato juice).

(3) High-residue foods (e.g., green vegetables and fruits).

(4) Pharmacologic stool softeners such as dioctyl sodium sulfosuccinate (Colace), 5 mg/kg/24 hr, malt soup extract (Maltsupex), or Senna concentrate (Senokot). Dosage of stool softeners is as follows: age 1 month–1 year, ½ tsp bid; 1–5 years, 1 tsp bid; 5–15 years, 2 tsp bid. Large initial doses are essential; when the stools become soft, dosage can be reduced. Regular daily dosage is continued for about 2–3 months and slowly reduced as bowel tone and regular bowel habits are acquired. Relapses are common, and prolonged follow-up is advisable.

c. To assist the child with anal fissures:

(1) A glycerin or bisacodyl suppository may be necessary (1 only).

(2) Soften stool as described.

(3) Sitz baths tid for small children.

d. If anatomic lesions have been ruled out:

(1) Establish a pattern of bowel movement after meals (gastrocolic reflex) or other times but at the same time each day by sitting the child on the toilet whether or not a bowel movement results.

(2) Be sure emotional stress and anxiety have been carefully excluded as causes.

(3) Relax.

e. If constipation persists and encopresis occurs, a psychiatric evaluation is indicated, and long-term management by the pediatrician will be required.

D. Acute nonspecific gastroenteritis

1. Etiology   This common condition is most often attributed to a viral source (see Chap. 9, Sec. **IV.P,** and Chap. 16, Sec. **II.B**).

2. Evaluation   This condition is often manifested by a sudden onset of vomiting, followed by diarrhea. It is most often self-limited. Fever may or may not be present, but with a reduction of fluid intake, dehydration may occur.

a. History   In evaluating the patient with gastroenteritis, record the following: weight loss, duration, presence of blood or mucus, type and frequency of stools, type and amount of feedings, frequency of urination, presence or absence of tears, and associated symptoms such as fever, vomiting, localized abdominal pain, current family illnesses.

b. Physical examination should include a description of the skin turgor, mucous membranes, fontanelles, eyes, presence or absence of tears, activity state, irritability, and associated rashes.

c. Laboratory tests While these can be minimized in the milder clinical states, stool cultures and Wright's stain for polymorphs may be helpful, and urinary specific gravity is a useful sign of early dehydration. (For further work-up in cases of diarrhea, see Chap. 16, Sec. **II.B.**)

3. Therapy

a. Children with diarrheal disease and minimal dehydration are treated most efficiently with clear fluids which include water, Coca Cola, ginger ale, and Jell-O. In the initial vomiting stage in infants or small children, large-volume feedings should be avoided. Small amounts (1–2 oz) qh as tolerated are initially sufficient.

b. Water may be sweetened with sugar or a 5% glucose solution can be used.

c. Oral electrolyte solutions (Table 1-12) may be administered for up to 24 hr.

d. *Boiled skim milk has a very high solute load and can cause hypernatremia.*

e. Frequent feedings increase the gastrocolic reflex and may aggravate the problem.

Table 1-12. Electrolyte Content[a]

Approximate content of solutions useful for fluid replacement or when oral administration of electrolytes is desired.

Milliequivalents per Liter	(Na) Sodium	(K) Potassium	(Ca) Calcium	(P) Phosphorus	(Cl) Chloride	(Mg) Magnesium
Lytren	25	25	4	5	30	4
Pedialyte[b]	30	20	4		30	4
Ready 4-Bouillon[c] (Range)	(30–40)	< 5	< 5	< 5	(20–30)	< 5
Ready 4-Cola[c]	< 5	< 5	< 5	< 5	< 5	< 5
Ready 4-Gelatin[c]	< 5	< 5	< 5	< 5	< 5	< 5
Ready 4-Tea[c]	< 5	< 5	< 5	< 5	< 5	< 5

[a] Approx. content of solutions available in Disp. Hospital Systems.
[b] Plus 28 mEq per liter in the form of lactate.
[c] In severe dehydration cases, these solutions should be supplemented with additional electrolytes.
From *Handbook of Infant Formulas*, revised 6th ed., Feb. 1969, J. B. Roerig. By permission.

f. Clear fluids alone should not be continued more than 48 hr, or reactive loose stools may occur. Bland solids can then be added such as rice cereal, banana flakes, saltines, Ritz crackers, dry cereal, or toast with jelly for older children.

g. The value of drugs such as kaolin and belladonna-containing compounds remains unproved, and their usage should probably be discouraged. In the rare case when an antispasmodic is considered, diphenoxylate (Lomotil[1]) or camphorated opium tincture (paregoric; 0.2 ml/kg/dose) may be used sparingly.

h. Anti-emetics such as promethazine (Phenergan), dimenhydrinate (Dramamine; 6–12 years, 12.5–25 mg tid; over age 12, 50 mg tid) or trimethobenzamide (Tigan; 100–200 mg tid) suppository or capsule in one or two doses are useful adjuncts when simple gastroenteritis is established as the cause of vomiting. Side effects of these drugs preclude their chronic use. If vomiting persists, more vigorous evaluation and management is indicated.

i. Close follow-up including daily weights is most imperative, particularly in smaller infants who may rapidly become dehydrated.

IV. IMMUNIZATION[2] See Table 1-13.

A. Routine smallpox vaccination in the United States The United States Public Health Service (USPHS) recently recommended that routine vaccination against smallpox be discontinued in the United States. The USPHS Advisory Committee on Immunization Practices (ACIP), which developed the original recommendation, included a regular liaison member from the Committee on Infectious Diseases of the American Academy of Pediatrics who participated in all deliberations and consulted regularly with members of the Academy Committee.

The full Committee on Infectious Diseases of the American Academy of Pediatrics reviewed the USPHS position at its meeting on October 16–17, 1971, and unanimously supported it. The Committee emphasizes four essential points:

1. The risk of smallpox in the United States is now insufficient to justify continuing the *routine* primary vaccination of infants and children. Smallpox vaccination occasionally results in severe adverse reactions, some fatal.

2. Current state or local regulations and statutes may conflict with the immediate implementation of the new policy. Physicians and health officials should collaborate to facilitate this change.

3. Smallpox vaccination is still recommended for certain persons:

a. Medical and hospital personnel should be vaccinated regularly. They are principally at risk if a smallpox importation occurs.

b. Travelers to those few areas where smallpox remains endemic or where vaccination is required must be immunized.

---

[1] Children:
  (2–5 years) 6 mg daily
  (5–8 years) 8 mg daily
  (8–12 years) 10 mg daily

[2] Adapted from American Academy of Pediatrics, *Report of the Committee on Infections,* 17th Ed. (Red Book), 1974.

Table 1-13. Revised Schedule for Active Immunization and Tuberculin Testing of Normal Infants and Children in the United States

Age	Vaccine	
2 months	DTP[a]	TOPV[b]
4 months	DTP	TOPV
6 months	DTP	TOPV
1 year	Measles[c]	Tuberculin Test[d]
1–12 years	Rubella[c]	Mumps[c]
1½ years	DTP	TOPV
4–6 years	DTP	TOPV
14–16 years	Td[e]	Td[e] (and thereafter every 10 years)

[a] DTP = diphtheria and tetanus toxoids combined with pertussis vaccine.

[b] TOPV = trivalent oral polio virus vaccine. The recommendation in the table is suitable for breast-fed as well as bottle-fed infants.

[c] May be given at 1 year as measles-rubella or measles-mumps-rubella combined vaccines.

[d] Frequency of repeated tuberculin tests depends on risk of exposure of the child and on the prevalence of tuberculosis in the population group.

[e] Td = combined tetanus and diphtheria toxoids (adult type) for those over 6 years of age, in contrast to diphtheria and tetanus (DT), containing a larger amount of diphtheria antigen.

From American Academy of Pediatrics, *Report of the Committee on Infectious Diseases*, 17th Ed. (Red Book), 1974.

Tetanus toxoid at time of injury: For clean, minor wounds no booster dose is needed by a fully immunized child unless more than 10 years have elapsed since the last dose. For contaminated wounds, a booster dose should be given if more than 5 years have elapsed since the last dose.

4. All vaccine recipients should be screened carefully for the known contraindications. These precautions can reduce complications to an absolute minimum.

B. **Rubella vaccines** More than 40 million doses of live attenuated rubella virus vaccines have been distributed in the United States since licensure in June 1969. The Committee is encouraged by the data on continuing persistence of vaccine-induced immunity. Having reviewed the theoretical risk of transmission of vaccine-virus, the occurrence of joint manifestations following vaccination, and questions related to reinfection, the Committee reaffirms its previous recommendation for the use of rubella vaccine. Vaccine is recommended for all children between the age of 1 year and puberty, with the priority given to children in elementary school (Table 1-13). To date, more than two-thirds of school-age children have received vaccine.

At present, the Committee emphasizes the importance of administration of vaccine to:

1. Unvaccinated school children, *particularly girls approaching puberty.*

2. Seronegative women of childbearing age who are not pregnant and who are on an acceptable regimen of pregnacy prevention for 2 months following vaccination. To extend vaccine use to this group, it will be essential to establish additional serologic testing programs.

3. Preschool children, especially those attending kindergarten, day care centers, and other similar groups.

V. DEATH OF A CHILD When a child has a fatal disease, the parents face an extended period of sadness and the loss of all their expectations for the child. After learning the diagnosis, parents usually cannot absorb the detailed information they are given about the disease and its clinical course. They need sufficient time and privacy to formulate their questions, and require guidance to establish realistic expectations, especially if referral to a large medical center is to be made. Parents need information they can grasp about the disease and its course, so that they can feel comfortable in caring for their child. Often their questions are repetitious, and sometimes they completely avoid certain topics. If possible, the same physician should communicate with the parents about the child's progress, and an awareness of the parents' anxiety should continue.

Parents react to the death of their child in a manner that reflects their family life, emotional structure, individual attachment, and the specific circumstances associated with the loss. The severest of all grief reactions occur in parents who have lost a child. In the first week of life, more deaths occur than in any subsequent period of childhood. Although they occur mainly in the hospital, and the parents have had little physical contact with their child, they have experienced pregnancy, have formulated plans, and have had expectations that are suddenly ended with the death of their infant. Often, mothers recall incidents during pregnancy that they feel could have influenced the eventual outcome. These parents, then, need guidance and information about the death to deter guilt feelings. The loss of a child may produce severe guilt in parents, making readjustment especially difficult. Medical personnel can share the family's burden of grief. Following a child's death, the physician's first responsibility is to inform the parents in a direct, sensitive manner; warmth and understanding provide a closeness with the family. Unless there are exceptional circumstances, a parent should *never* be informed of a child's death by telephone.

It may be important to provide sedation or a quiet place for the parents, who may prefer to be alone. The hospital staff can help parents with funeral arrangements, inform other family members, or arrange transportation.

An important prerequisite in talking to parents about their child's death is knowledge of the circumstances in which it occurred. Not being given this information may serve to reinforce the parents' doubts and guilts.

After the first week of life, the Sudden Infant Death syndrome is the most common cause of death. Because the cause is unknown, parents often blame themselves or relatives or babysitters. Although none of the numerous explanations proposed has been proved, families of infants who die from this syndrome need strong assurance that it is an actual disease entity, which is neither predictable nor preventable and for which they are not responsible. They should also be told that the cause is not suffocation, aspiration pneumonia, bacterial infection, or central nervous system damage. When a child dies unexpectedly, it is important to provide the parents with autopsy information.

When a child dies, the healthy siblings at home should not be neglected. Children react to the loss of siblings, and they should be given an explanation of the death. Parents who are able to talk about their feelings of loss will help their other children to accept the same feeling in themselves. A child needs to be assured that nothing he did or thought was responsible for the death and that he himself is healthy and will not die of the same illness. Children will very often show behavior changes after the loss of a sibling and may require counseling.

The pediatrician must be aware of and deal with his own feelings about the death of a patient. A feeling of failure is often present, particularly when complicated management did not suffice. There may be a desire to "make it up" to the family because of possible uncertainty surrounding the physician's participation. There is nothing wrong with feeling a sense of loss at the death of a patient or with the need to grieve, but it is the physician's hard task to put his own grief aside until the needs of the parents and family have been met.

2 Management of Emergencies and Child Abuse

This chapter includes only the most commonly encountered problems in emergency management. Others may be found in chapters dealing with specific types of pathology.

I. **CARDIAC ARREST** The diagnosis of cardiac arrest must be rapid (absent pulse and respirations, cyanosis, dilated pupils).

A. **Equipment**

1. Drugs: sodium bicarbonate, epinephrine 1:1000, 50% glucose, 10% calcium gluconate, atropine.

2. Needles (19–23 gauge), syringes, scalpels.

3. Pediatric-size laryngoscope, airways, endotracheal tubes (see **B.4**), and tracheotomy tube.

4. Pediatric-size mask and Ambu bag.

B. **Ventilation**

1. Clear the oral cavity of secretions. Insert an oral airway.

2. Begin bag-to-mouth or mouth-to-mouth ventilation at a rate of 20/min.

3. Insert an O_2 tube into the patient's mouth or attach to Ambu bag.

4. If ventilation is unsuccessful, perform intubation with an endotracheal tube (see Table 2-1 and p. 455).

C. **Circulation**

1. While beginning ventilation, start external cardiac massage by sternal compression. Place the patient on a solid surface.

2. Do not attempt to ventilate at the same time as the sternum is compressed; rather, alternate one breath and four sternal compressions; 60–80 compressions/min is adequate.

Table 2-1. Endotracheal Tubes Used in Children of Various Ages

Age of Child	Tube Specifications	
	Number (French)	Size (mm)
Premature–3 months	12–14	2.5–3.0
3–18 months	14–18	3.5–4.0
18 months–5 years	18–22	4.0–5.0
5–12 years	22–28	5.0–6.5
12 years or more	28–34	6.5–8.0

3. Determine the effectiveness of circulation by palpating the femoral pulse.

4. Do not attempt an IV infusion until help arrives.

D. ECG monitor When help arrives, attach an ECG monitor and start an IV infusion (central line if possible) ; (see Sec. **II.B**).

E. Drug administration See Table 2-2.

1. Administer $NaHCO_2$, 2 mEq/kg IV push, to correct acidosis.

2. If asystole is present, administer epinephrine (0.5–2.0 ml of 1:10,-000 in infants, or 0.1–1.0 ml of 1:1000 in older children) as a direct IV or intracardiac injection.

3. If QRS complexes are observed without adequate pulse, 10% calcium gluconate, 10 mg/kg (0.1 ml/kg), are administered IV or as an intracardiac injection. **Be sure the infusion is not intramyocardial.**

Table 2-2. Indications for the Use of Various Drugs in Cardiac Arrest

Indication	Drug	Intravenous Dose
Hypoglycemia	50% Glucose	1 ml/kg
To decrease secretions prior to intubation; bradycardia	Atropine	0.01 mg/kg
Ventricular tachycardia	Lidocaine (Xylocaine)	1 mg/kg
Acidosis	Trimethamine (Tham) (1 mg/ml)	1 ml/kg
Pulmonary edema	Ethacrynic acid (Edecrin)	1 mg/kg
	Furosemide (Lasix)	1 mg/kg

F. Defibrillation See also Chap. 11, Sec. **I.C.**

1. If ventricular fibrillation is present, defibrillate, placing one electrode over the apex and one over the sternal notch (see Table 2-3).

2. If there is no response, two shocks of the same magnitude in rapid succession may be given.

Table 2-3. Defibrillation Values

Type of Patient	Weight (kg)	Watt-Sec
Infant	12	25–50
Small child	12–25	100
Large child	25	100–200

G. Blood pressure Following resuscitation, isoproterenol (Isuprel) may be a useful adjunct in maintaining cardiac output (0.1 mg/100 ml 5% D/W IV). The drip should be titrated to the patient's response (see Sec. **II.C.2.a**).

H. The cause of the cardiac arrest should be diagnosed and treated as soon as possible.

II. SHOCK The various causes of shock in children are detailed in Table 2-4.

A. The aim of therapy is to restore circulation to peripheral vascular beds, thereby breaking the cycle in which metabolic dysfunction results in extravasation and pooling of blood and further loss of circulatory volume.

B. Evaluation Infants in shock are usually hypotonic and have a weak or absent cry. Older children may be disoriented or stuporous. The skin may be mottled, gray or pale in color, and cool. Capillary filling in the fingers and toes is poor. Respirations may be shallow. The pulse is rapid and weak and sometimes cannot be obtained by palpation of the radial or femoral arteries. Blood pressure is diminished or unobtain-

Table 2-4. Causes of Shock in Children

Etiology	Common Preexisting Conditions	
	Newborn	Older Child
Hemorrhage	Via placenta or cord	Trauma to abdominal
	Intracerebral	organs, liver, spleen
	Fetomaternal,	Thrombocytopenia
	twin-twin	DIC
Fluid loss	Gastroenteritis	Gastroenteritis
		Severe burn
		Diabetes mellitus and
		insipidus
Gram-negative sepsis	Congenital pneumonia	Pyelonephritis
	Amnionitis	Meningococcemia
	Infected umbilical	Immunologic deficiency
	catheter	
Cardiogenic and	Hypoplastic left	Coxsackie myocarditis
vascular	ventricle	Rheumatic heart disease
obstruction	Coarctation of aorta	Pulmonary embolus
	Endocardial fibro-	Thrombotic thrombocyto-
	elastosis	penic purpura
Neurogenic	Cord injury following	Spinal cord transection
disturbance	breech delivery	Epidural hematoma
		Other causes of acutely in-
		creased intracranial
		pressure
Anaphylaxis	(Rare)	Allergy to food or drugs
Adrenal disorder	Adrenogenital syn-	Adrenogenital syndrome
	drome	Pituitary insufficiency
	Adrenal necrosis fol-	
	lowing breech	
	delivery	
Respiratory disorder	Diaphragmatic hernia	Pneumothorax
	Severe hyalin mem-	Severe pneumonia
	brane disease	
	Neonatal pneumonia	
	Pulmonary atresia	

able. Urine output is decreased or absent. Hemorrhage from veni-puncture sites or from the gastrointestinal tract may be present if shock has been complicated by disseminated intravascular coagulation (DIC) (see Chap. 15, Sec. **V.B**).

1. Pulse Continuous ECG monitoring is indicated for the patient in shock as a check on heart rate and rhythm. Silver-chloride elec-trodes are convenient in the newborn because of their small size.

2. Blood pressure

   a. In the newborn Accurate arterial blood pressure measurements should be obtained even in the smallest of premature infants. Auscultation and palpation methods are usually ineffective in newborns. However, the flush method provides a good measure of mean arterial blood pressure, especially in the absence of methods for the direct measurement of arterial pulse pressure via an arterial cannula.

   (1) Flush blood pressures in the newborn are obtained with a 5.0-cm cuff applied to the wrist or ankle. The corresponding hand or foot is then compressed by wrapping with a soft rubber drain or bandage 3.5 by 50 cm, beginning at the tips of the digits and working proximally to the edge of the cuff. The cuff is inflated to 300 mm Hg, the wrap is released, and pressure is decreased at the rate of approximately 5 mm Hg/sec while the extremity is maintained at the level of the heart.

   (2) During the first week of life, mean flush blood pressure at the wrist is 41 ± 8 (± 2 standard deviations) mm Hg, and flush pressure between 1 and 12 months is 72 ± 10.5 mm Hg. *Changes in the trend of successive pressure recordings are more significant than are individual recordings.*

   (3) A 3½F, 5F, or occasionally 8F Argyle catheter may be passed via the umbilical artery into the thoracic aorta proxi-mal to the diaphragm for blood gas determinations and arterial blood pressure measurements via a pressure trans-ducer (see Chap. 5, Sec. **II.C**).

   b. In older children Blood pressure measurements in the older child are obtained with a cuff of a width ⅔ the length of the upper arm. Mean systolic blood pressure is 65 mm Hg at 1 day of age, 90 mm Hg at 1 year, 100 mm Hg at 6 years, and 113 mm Hg at 12 years.

3. Central venous pressure (CVP)

   a. In the newborn

   (1) An umbilical vein catheter is positioned in the superior vena cava at a level above the diaphragm. **Never insert a catheter unless the free end is attached to a closed syringe,** since a low CVP combined with negative intrathoracic pressure may drain air from the catheter into the vena cava, resulting in air embolism.

   (2) CVPs are measured from the midaxillary line to the top of the column of liquid while the child is in the supine position. The fluid column should vary with respiration and pulse.

Pressures of 4–7 cm of water are usually within the normal range in premature and full-term newborns.

b. In infants and older children

(1) Catheterization of the external jugular vein may be used in infants, while in older children the preferable site is in the antecubital fossa via the median basilic vein into the superior vena cava.

(2) Silastic is the material of choice for catheters inserted from a peripheral vein because it is pliable, radiopaque, and inert.

(3) A CVP of 0–6 cm H_2O is low in children and should be corrected with plasma expanders (see Sec. **II.C.1.a**). A pressure of 6–15 cm H_2O is within the range of normal; a pressure greater than 15 cm H_2O is **dangerously high.**

4. Urine output   In newborns and infants, urine is measured hourly. While unnecessary catheterization of the bladder is usually avoided in children, shock is one clinical situation in which the advantages of accurate hourly measurements of urine output usually outweigh the disadvantages of catheterization. The closed urinary drainage system is relatively effective in preventing bladder infection. Urine output should be maintained at a minimum of 8 ml/kg/24 hr.

5. Airway and oxygen

a. In the newborn   Even if there is no gross pulmonary or cardiac disease, children in shock should be given the benefit of an increased inspiratory O_2 concentration.

(1) Added O_2 should be warm and moist.

(2) Isolettes maintain high O_2 concentrations poorly; a hood should be used. Hoods similar to the Olympic Oxyhood are satisfactory, providing inlets for intravenous tubing, nebulized oxygen, monitoring probes, and a thermometer. Hoods are available in three sizes, for infants ranging in weight from 2½–18 lb. The tops may be removed for suctioning.

(3) Inspired O_2 concentration is monitored by serial arterial blood gas determinations and kept below 100 mm Hg.

b. In older children   Infants and older children frequently do not tolerate nasal O_2, and O_2 via face mask is usually indicated. An oral airway is especially helpful, and orotracheal intubation may sometimes be necessary.

6. Temperature   The mortality of sick newborns is significantly increased if the temperature is allowed to fall below 95° F (see Chap. 5, Sec. **II.D**). Skin temperature should be relatively constant. Isolette temperature should be maintained by a servomechanism activated by the infant's skin temperature. A continuous record of Isolette temperatures should be maintained.

7. Blood gas measurement and correction of acidosis   See also Chap. 4.

a. A severely asphyxiated infant may have a base deficit of 25 mEq/L in the cord blood. Ventilation can lower this to 16 mEq/L, and the remaining metabolic component of the acidosis can be corrected by infusing bicarbonate. If blood gas determinations are not available, 5–10 mEq $NaHCO_3$ solution can be given to the full-term newborn over 2–5 min intravenously.

b. *Before infusion, bicarbonate must be diluted 50% with 5% D/W to reduce its hypertonicity.* (Rapid infusions of hypertonic bicarbonate solution have resulted in seizures, and hepatic necrosis may occur if the solution is given directly into the liver through a malplaced umbilical catheter.)

c. As a rule of thumb in older children with suspected severe metabolic acidosis in shock, $NaHCO_3$, 2 mEq/kg of body weight, can be given slowly IV. However, acidosis should be managed on the basis of arterial blood gas determinations whenever possible.

8. Other parameters Evaluation for infection, electrolyte imbalance, and renal function should be done as the patient is stabilized.

C. Treatment The key to successful treatment of shock is rapid correction of circulatory insufficiency and its causes. A physician should be in attendance until the critical stages are passed, and *attention to detail is of the utmost importance, especially when treating the premature or full-term newborn infant.* Maintenance of temperature can make the difference between survival and death in a newborn. Even excessive handling can contribute to stress experienced by the newborn, and manipulations and procedures should be kept to a minimum in any child.

1. Volume expansion Rapid expansion of the intravascular volume is critical in patients with shock in whom the CVP is low (less than 6 cm H_2O in older children, less than 4 cm H_2O in the newborn) and in whom there is evidence of poor peripheral circulation. Intravascular volume should be expanded *before* pressor agents are given.

a. Fluids for volume expansion See also Chap. 4.

(1) Albumin Five percent albumin (salt-poor albumin, human) in isotonic saline is probably the best volume expander in shock. Albumin does not carry the risk of hepatitis, does not have to be crossmatched, and does not cause allergic reactions so often as does blood or plasma; 25% albumin can be obtained in units of 20, 50, and 100 ml and can be stored at room temperature; 5% albumin solutions are obtained in 250-ml aliquots.

(2) Plasmanate Plasmanate, which may be used as an alternative to 5% albumin, is a 5% solution of plasma protein fractions containing 88% normal human albumin, 7% alpha globulin, and 5% beta globulin. Electrolyte concentrations of plasmanate are as follows: sodium, 110 mEq/L; potassium, 0.25 mEq/L; and chloride, 50 mEq/L. *Blood group agglutinins and coagulation factors are absent from plasmanate.* Plasmanate has the same effective volume expansion as 5% albumin.

(3) Blood If albumin or plasmanate is not available, whole blood crossmatched against the patient's blood may be used, although the risk of hepatitis is therefore increased (see Chap. 1, Sec. **II.D**). Freshly drawn heparinized blood is best because of its low acid and potassium content. **Avoid in-**

fusing **unmatched type O negative blood** during the early stages of shock because this leads to errors in crossmatching at a later time. In severe exsanguination, however, the use of unmatched type O negative blood may be unavoidable. If fresh blood is not available, acid-citrate-dextrose (ACD) blood not more than 6 days old should be given.

(4) Isotonic solution   Saline is not the treatment of choice for shock because the absence of colloid fails to prevent loss of saline from the intravascular space. However, in progressive shock, there is probably loss of extracellular, extravascular fluid in addition to intravascular fluid; thus some saline may be given in addition to the colloid necessary to expand intravascular volume, improve urine flow, and provide for ongoing fluid losses. When albumin, plasma, or blood is unavailable, saline is given as a stopgap measure to restore circulation.

(5) Fresh frozen plasma   Plasma is also less desirable as a volume expander because of the risk of hepatitis, especially in pooled plasma preparations. Fresh frozen plasma can be used in shock when clotting factors are needed, such as in hemophilia.

b. Rate of administration   In general, plasma expanders should be given as rapidly as possible until a blood pressure can be obtained and the CVP increases.

(1) In the newborn   An initial volume of 5% albumin in isotonic saline may be given at a dose of 10 ml/kg over ½ hr. If the blood pressure is still low and the CVP is still less than 4.0 cm H_2O, the dose may be repeated.

(2) In infants and older children   Give 10–15 ml/kg 5% albumin in isotonic saline over ½ hr. Repeat if there is no response in pulse, blood pressure, and CVP. Higher rates of infusion through more than one venous line are indicated in cases of severe hemorrhage.

2. Drugs   See Table 2-5.

a. Isoproterenol hydrochloride   The value of pressor agents in shock is unproved. Only after failure of adequate attempts to restore circulation by volume expansion may pressor agents be used.

(1) Isoproterenol is titrated as a drip until the heart rate begins to increase, and the blood pressure just begins to fall.

(2) Do not give isoproterenol and epinephrine concurrently because of the risk of arrhythmias.

(3) Continuously monitor ECG during isoproterenol infusions.

b. Levarterenol and metaraminol   These agents **should probably not be used except in cases of impending cardiac arrest.** No attempt should be made to bring blood pressure to normal values with these agents, because excessive doses cause severe renal arteriolar constriction and reduce urine output.

c. Corticosteroids   High doses of corticosteroids have been used in patients with severe hypovolemic shock as well as gram-negative sepsis, but their use is still experimental.

Table 2-5. Drugs Used for the Treatment of Shock in Children

	Mechanism of Action	Dose

Isoproterenol hydrochloride (Isuprel)	Beta adrenergic
	Increases
	  Inotropic heart action
	  Chronotropic heart action
	Decreases
	  Arteriolar resistance
	  Venous capacitance
	  Airway and pulmonary vascular resistance
		Use a solution of 1.0 μg/ml
		Give by IV drip at a rate of 0.05–4.0 μg/min

Levarterenol bitartrate (Levophed)	Alpha adrenergic stimulator
	Increases
	  Inotropic heart action
	  Chronotropic heart action
	  Peripheral resistance
		0.1 μg/kg/min; not to exceed 1.0 μg/kg/min

Metaraminol bitartrate (Aramine)	Alpha adrenergic	0.04–0.2 mg/kg IM or SQ or 0.3–2.0 mg/kg to 500 ml IV Adjust IV drip rate to patient's responsiveness

Methoxamine (Vasoxyl)	Alpha adrenergic pressor amine
	Increases
	  Peripheral resistance
	Decreases
	  Renal blood flow
		0.25 mg/kg as a single IM dose, up to maximum dose of 15 mg IM
		Effective over 60–90-min period

Phenylephrine hydrochloride (Neo-Synephrine)	Increases Smooth muscle arteriolar tone	0.10 mg/kg as a single IM dose Maximum dose 7.0 mg IM
Vasopressin (Pitressin)		0.125–0.50 ml (20 U/ml) given as a single IM dose

Hydrocortisone (Solu-Cortef)	Increases
	  Cardiac output
	  Enzyme synthesis
	  (use in shock is controversial)
		25 mg/kg IV initially, followed by 12 mg/kg/24 hr in divided doses

Dexamethasone (Decadron)	Decreases
	  Peripheral resistance
	  Lactate production
		2 mg/kg IV initially, followed by 1 mg/kg/24 hr in divided doses

Mannitol	Osmotic diuretic	1 gm/kg IV

d. Heparin Heparinization may be indicated if there is evidence of DIC (see Chap. 15, Sec. **V.B**).

e. Mannitol If CVP is adequate, blood pressure has been restored, and urine output is still less than 8 ml/24 hr, a single IV dose of mannitol may be given in an attempt to establish adequate urine flow. Mannitol is supplied as a 25% solution containing 250 mg/ml. **Mannitol should not be given when the serum is hyperosmolar,** as in children with hypertonic dehydration or diabetes mellitus with extreme dehydration and hyperglycemia.

3. Treatment of specific shock syndromes

a. Cardiogenic shock See also Chap. 11, Sec. **II.**

(1) Oxygen, diuretics, digoxin, morphine, upright positioning, and aminophylline are important.

(2) CVP measurements are essential. If the CVP is low, give IV fluids; if it is high, phlebotomy may be indicated.

(3) Monitor the ECG carefully and measure urine volume hourly.

(4) Use an isoproterenol infusion for impending cardiovascular collapse. However, watch carefully for tachycardia and arrhythmias.

b. Neurogenic shock Severe injury to the spinal cord may result in loss of vasomotor tone, pooling of venous and arterial blood, and hypotension.

(1) Monitor the CVP and give plasma expanders until the CVP returns to normal.

(2) In the rare instances when volume expansion has not restored circulation in neurogenic shock, give vasopressin, or an alpha adrenergic stimulator such as methoxamine (Vasoxyl) or phenylephrine (Neo-Synephrine).

c. Bacteremic shock

(1) Obtain cultures of blood, spinal fluid, urine, and other infected sites available for culture.

(2) Begin antibiotics as soon as possible. (For treatment of meningitis and bacteremic sepsis, see Chap. 9, Sec. **IV.U**)

(3) Measure the CVP and expand the intravascular volume if the CVP is low.

(4) Give high doses of corticosteroids IV.

(5) If the CVP is normal and poor perfusion persists, start an isoproterenol drip (see **2.a**).

(6) Monitor for DIC at the beginning of treatment and at frequent intervals. If laboratory evidence suggests DIC, and restoration of blood pressure does not result in a normal coagulation profile, begin heparin (p. 340).

d. Anaphylactic shock

(1) Delay absorption of antigen from the injection site by placing a tourniquet proximal to the site so as to impede lymphatic and venous drainage, but not arterial flow.

(2) Give 1:1000 aqueous epinephrine SC at the injection site to retard absorption of antigen (0.01 ml/kg initially, followed by the same dose at 20-min intervals for a total of 3 doses).

(3) If laryngeal edema seriously impairs respirations at the time of the initial evaluation, the first dose of epinephrine may be given IV as a dilution in 5–10 ml normal saline.

(4) Measure the CVP and restore circulation rapidly with albumin if the CVP is low (see **B.3**).

(5) For bronchospasm, give aminophylline 4 mg/kg IV over ½ hr. For persistent bronchospasm, give aminophylline up to 16 mg/kg/24 hr in divided doses q6h.

(6) For severe or prolonged anaphylactic reactions, in addition, give 10 mg/kg hydrocortisone stat IV, followed by hydrocortisone, 16 mg/kg/24 hr in divided doses IV q4–6h. Dexamethasone (Decadron) may be used as an alternative to hydrocortisone.

(7) Antihistamines may be of some help. Give diphenhydramine (Benadryl) in 4 divided daily doses PO, IV, or IM. Do not exceed 150 mg total per day.

III. SEIZURES are associated with much parental anxiety and always carry the threat of hypoxic CNS damage. Thus evaluation and therapy must be a coordinated, reasoned effort by emergency room personnel (see Chap. 14).

A. Evaluation

   1. Historical events surrounding the seizure

      a. Known seizure disorder

      b. Medications child is taking

      c. Illnesses that may be associated with seizures, e.g., hypertension

      d. Acute illness prior to the seizure

   2. Description of the seizure

      a. Localized or generalized

      b. Duration

      c. Incontinence

      d. Cyanosis

B. Diagnostic studies at initial presentation should include the following: electrolytes, BUN, blood sugar, calcium, pH, Tco$_2$, toxicology screen, blood lead level, urinalysis, and lumbar puncture.

C. General evaluative and supportive measures for any patient who has a seizure

   1. Determine the adequacy of the airway; i.e., is vomitus or saliva obstructing the airway? Are the clothes too tight about the neck?

   2. Suctioning may often be necessary, and to expedite it, the child's head should be lower than his trunk.

   3. Oxygen administration is advisable whether or not cyanosis is present.

4. If the tongue is obstructing respirations, an oral airway may be tried empirically while respirations are monitored simultaneously. Use of a tongue blade is of questionable value.

5. Make certain the child will not harm himself by falling off the bed or by striking hard objects during the seizure.

6. Perform a brief but thorough physical examination with special reference to the neurologic system. Look for Medic-Alert tag or identification card in the patient's wallet and inquire about a history of seizures.

7. Monitor vital signs carefully.

8. Draw blood for appropriate chemistries and save a clot tube for anticonvulsant levels. Make a Dextrostix determination and rule out or confirm hypoglycemia with administration of 50% D/W IV, 2 ml/kg stat.

9. Intravenous infusion of 5% D in 0.25% saline is started.

10. After adequate ventilation is maintained and cardiac status is stable, drug treatment should be started to arrest the seizures. Effective therapy depends on the following information:

    a. Is there a history of epilepsy and status epilepticus?

    b. Is this the initial episode, *or*

    c. Does it accompany a known metabolic epileptogenic disorder?

11. If the patient is known to have epilepsy and is taking anticonvulsants, one may assume that he has not received them regularly, or the dose has been inadequate or ineffective, or there is a precipitating cause, often infection.

D. General treatment of status epilepticus

1. Diazepam

a. Although still investigational in children under 12, IV diazepam (Valium) is the drug of choice in doses of 2 mg q3–5 min up to 10 mg. It is supplied as 5 mg/ml and given undiluted close to the infusion site; the IV line is flushed. In many children there will be a prompt and lasting effect from this regimen.

b. **Hypotension and respiratory arrest are known complications of this therapy, and pressor agents and assisted ventilation must be available.** If the episode is terminated, then recurs 5–15 min later, another course of up to 10 mg may be given IV. *Intramuscular administration of diazepam has no place in the management of status epilepticus.* Once the seizures are terminated, treatment with diphenylhydantoin (Dilantin) should begin.

2. **Diphenylhydantoin,** 8–10 mg/kg, is given slowly IV in saline (not to exceed 25 mg/min) and also 3 mg/kg IM. If successful, this is followed by daily maintenance of 5–8 mg/kg in 3 divided doses IM or PO.

   The major cause of death in status epilepticus is cardiac or respiratory failure closely following the IV use of a hypnotic agent. *An accurate flow sheet must be kept, with vital signs recorded q5–10 min and all medications listed.*

E. Specific therapy: febrile seizures

1. Begin fever control with tepid water sponging and rectal aspirin 60 mg per year of age up to 600 mg.

2. Give 2–3 mg/kg phenobarbital IM. If this is not effective in 10 min, give an additional 2–3 mg/kg IM. A maximum dose of 120 mg is advised. If the patient has been taking phenobarbital prior to the seizure, adjust the stat dose so it will not exceed 5 mg/kg daily. The use of IV phenobarbital is not warranted.

3. As previously discussed, diazepam is also effective as an initial drug in seizures. However, as it is investigational in children and is a cardiorespiratory depressant, its use in febrile seizures, which are, by definition, self-limited, should be approached with caution. *It should not be used in conjunction with phenobarbital.* The dose is as listed in **D.1.a.**

4. **Paraldehyde**   This may be used initially or in conjunction with diazepam or phenobarbital. It is given by high rectal tube in a dose of 0.3 ml/kg, up to 6.0 ml. It is mixed with an equal volume of mineral oil injected in the tube, and 10 ml of normal saline is used to flush the mixture through the tube. The buttocks are then taped together.

5. Diphenylhydantoin is not recommended for simple febrile seizures.

F. Specific therapy: hypoglycemia

1. Provide the general supportive measures outlined previously.

2. Give 1 ml/kg IV of 50% D/W stat.

3. Then begin a drip of 15% D/W initially at a rate of 100 ml/kg/24 hr.

G. Specific therapy: hypertension

1. Provide the general supportive measures outlined previously.

2. Direct primary therapy to the hypertension (see Chap. 12, Sec. **III.C**).

3. Paraldehyde, or diphenylhydantoin, or both may be used acutely via the routes and in the dosages outlined previously.

4. Phenobarbital may also be used, with the precautions already mentioned.

H. Specific therapy: meningitis or encephalitis

1. Provide the general supportive measures outlined previously.

2. In patients with meningitis, antibiotic therapy is paramount (see Chap. 9, Sec. **IV.N**).

3. Fluids administered by the IV route should be given with caution and with a careful watch for signs of cerebral edema, in appropriate ADH or centrally mediated cardiovascular responses. The management of cerebral edema is outlined in Table 2-6.

4. Paraldehyde, or diphenylhydantoin, or both may be used acutely by the routes and in the dosages previously outlined. Phenobarbital may also be used, but be alert for respiratory depression.

I. Specific therapy: hypocalcemia

1. Provide the general supportive measures previously outlined.

2. Give 1.5 ml/kg IV of a 10% solution of calcium gluconate over a 20-min period. During this therapy, ECG monitoring is important.

3. After the 20-min infusion, start maintenance therapy with 10% calcium gluconate in a dosage of 15.0 ml/kg daily IV.

    The specific therapy for electrolyte imbalance is discussed in Chap. 4.

J. If these measures fail to control a seizure in a 1-hr period, general anesthesia must be considered. However, if ventilation and oxygenation are adequate, the risk to the patient associated with a prolonged seizure is reduced, and further efforts to end the seizure can be instituted in an orderly manner.

IV. THE UNCONSCIOUS PATIENT: A GENERAL PLAN OF MANAGEMENT

A.

1. Evaluate vital signs and level of consciousness. If shock is present, institute emergency measures (see Sec. **II.C**).

2. Smell the patient's breath for signs of ketosis, alcohol, hydrocarbons, or other substances.

3. Check for Medic-Alert tag, examine the contents of pockets, wallet, and so on.

B.

1. Institute treatment for vital functions that are compromised.

2. Draw blood for CBC, type and crossmatching of whole blood, electrolytes, BUN, glucose, SGOT, LDH, bilirubin, arterial blood gases where indicated, prothrombin time, and toxicology screen. Save two tubes of clotted blood for further studies.

3. Start an IV infusion and administer 50% glucose at 1 ml/kg.

C.

1. Be certain head trauma is ruled out by a *reliable* history. Obtain data on the chronology and progression of symptoms.

2. If the patient is unattended, assign a co-worker to contact the family by telephone.

D.

1. Perform a detailed examination to include respiratory pattern and pupillary, oculocephalic, and oculovestibular reflexes.

2. Note muscle tone and tendon reflexes.

3. Look for needle marks in older children as evidence of self-administered drugs.

E. Have a co-worker start a flow sheet of vital signs and treatment.

F.

1. Obtain a urine sample by catheter if necessary for routine urinalysis and ferric chloride determination to rule out salicylate and phenothiazine ingestion.

G. Reevaluate the patient and perform any other studies likely to yield a diagnosis.

V. CEREBRAL EDEMA (acute brain swellings)   Signs of transtentorial herniation, prolonged status epilepticus, rapidly increasing intracranial pressure, acute lead encephalopathy, and severe cerebral anoxia are present. Therapeutic measures should be undertaken as a temporizing measure until a mass lesion is ruled out. When a patient with a known posterior fossa lesion shows signs of rapidly increasing intracranial pressure, definitive surgical decompression or placement of a central ventricular drainage catheter is the preferred mode of therapy (Table 2-6).

Table 2-6.   Management of Cerebral Edema[a]

Stage of Treatment	Medication	Dosage and Method
Initial, immediate treatment	Mannitol (as Osmitrol)	20% (20 gm/100 ml) *or* 50-ml ampules containing 12.5 gm
Repeat every 4–6 hr *or* continuous infusion,[b] *or* glycerol via NG tube 2 gm/kg daily in 4 divided doses	Mannitol	
Simultaneous administration	Dexamethasone (Decadron)	Day 1: 3 mg q6h IV
Continued treatment	Dexamethasone	Each subsequent day: 2 mg q6h IV or IM

[a] Careful attention must be directed to fluid and electrolyte balance in cerebral edema patients, and an indwelling catheter should be placed. Maintenance fluid should be provided.
[b] Fluids must be maintained to avoid iatrogenic dehydration due to osmotic diureses.

VI. SEVERE ASTHMA ATTACK AND STATUS ASTHMATICUS   Status asthmaticus is a severe asthma attack that fails to respond to conservative therapy. In this condition, bronchospasm, mucosal edema, and excess mucous secretions combine to produce narrowing of airways, atelectasis, and impaired gas exchange.

An asthmatic attack is a frightening experience for a child and his parents. Reassurance is extremely important during the acute stage. Agitation can be a manifestation of hypoxemia; even if it is not, the restless, anxious child can exhaust himself from crying and purposeless resistance. Often, a parent at the bedside is the best sedative and can help the child to cooperate. (Obviously, an overly anxious parent may have the opposite effect.)

A. Evaluation

    1. History   This includes age, duration of the attack, the course and severity of previous attacks, and a list with doses of all medications previously administered.

2. Physical examination

a. Ventilatory status   Assess the quality of breath sounds, the degree of dyspnea, and the extent of retractions.

b. Mental status   Look for somnolence, confusion, combativeness, or euphoria as signs of marked impairment of gas exchange.

c. Frequently determine vital signs.

3. Laboratory tests and ancillary studies   Infection is frequently the triggering event in status asthmaticus and is often hard to recognize clinically.

a. Complete blood count   This should be obtained, if possible, before epinephrine is given; otherwise the WBC count may be unreliable and difficult to interpret.

b. BUN, sugar, and electrolytes.

c. Urinalysis; repeated determinations of specific gravity.

d. Nasopharyngeal studies include throat or sputum cultures or both.

e. Chest roentgenograms can usually be delayed until initial therapy with adequate hydration has been provided; *radiologic evidence of pneumonia may not be demonstrable until adequate hydration has been given.* Oxygenation and appropriate supervision while the child is transported and the roentgenogram taken are extremely important.

f. Blood gases

    (1) Venous pH and CO_2, obtained from free-flowing blood, without a tourniquet, will usually provide enough data to assess acid-base balance and ventilatory status at the outset of therapy.

    (2) Arterial blood gases should be measured and, in the severe attack in which the patient is unresponsive to therapy, the measurements should be repeated as necessary.

B. Therapy

1. Oxygen   *Give humidified O_2 by nasal cannula or face mask to deliver 30–40% concentration in inspired air. A mist tent can be the most convenient way to deliver O_2 to the small, uncooperative child.* Patients with severe asthma attacks will uniformly present with *some* degree of hypoxemia secondary to perfusion of nonventilated, atelectatic segments of the lung (with right-to-left shunt as a result) and maldistribution of gas within the lung.

2. Hydration and correction of acid-base abnormalities

a. Start an IV line with a scalp vein needle. In the absence of cardiac or renal impairment, it is safe to administer 20 ml/kg of 5% dextrose in 0.2 normal saline over 1–2 hr, to be followed by the same solution at 1½–2 times the maintenance rate. Fluids are essential to liquify secretions and restore acid-base balance. Most severe episodes are accompanied by dehydration due to a combination of decreased intake, increased insensible water loss, and vomiting. Forcing fluids by mouth may be adequate in the mild or moderate attack, but will usually cause more vomiting in the patient with a severe attack.

b. Use sodium bicarbonate to maintain an arterial pH over 7.25; the initial dose may be calculated as 1–2 mEq/kg over 30 min or according to the following formula:

$$\text{mEq NaHCO}_3 = 0.3 \times \text{body weight in kg} \times \text{base deficit (mEq/L)}$$

This dose can be repeated if necessary according to subsequent pH determinations.

c. The large majority of patients will present with a metabolic acidosis secondary to ketonemia of variable magnitude and accumulation of organic acid anions. If decreased alveolar ventilation supervenes, a rising Paco_2 is a potential complication of NaHCO_3 use (see *Pediatrics* 42:238, 1968).

d. The use of THAM is not recommended because of the hazard of respiratory depression.

3. Drugs

  a. Bronchodilators

    (1) Epinephrine

      (a) Give 0.01 ml/kg SQ (maximum, 0.5 ml). If a beneficial effect is obtained, the injection can be repeated once or twice at 20-min intervals. When complete clearing of the attack is achieved, give 0.005 ml/kg of Susphrine (epinephrine in a 1/200 dilution in thioglycollate suspension) 20 min after the last dose for longer-lasting action. If the patient is still in distress after 3 doses, or actually deteriorates after epinephrine administration, **do not give further doses.** *The excessive or inappropriate use of epinephrine can induce serious cardiac arrhythmias and cause increased restlessness and anxiety.*

      (b) Hypoxemia and acidosis, tenacious mucous plugs blocking the airways, and pneumothorax are among the causes of lack of bronchomotor response to epinephrine. Correction of acidosis may restore the response to epinephrine.

    (2) Isoproterenol

      (a) Use 0.5 ml of a 1/200 preparation and add 2 ml of saline (1/1000 dilution). Deliver via aerosol using a Bird respirator, Mark 8 for intermittent positive pressure breathing (IPPB) connected to a source of 100% O_2 (see Chap. 19, Sec. **IV**). Give IPPB for 5–10 min with frequent pauses and repeat q2–4h as required. It can be alternated with nebulized saline aerosol to loosen secretions further and reduce airway resistance.

      (b) Isoproterenol is a potent stimulator of beta receptors. It is frequently effective in the epinephrine-resistant patient. The age and cooperation of the child are important for its adequate administration.

      (c) *The use of IPPB with isoproterenol requires careful monitoring for the onset of serious cardiac arrhythmias.*

(3) Aminophylline

- **(a)** Give 3–5 mg/kg in 30–50 ml of IV fluids to run over 15–20 min. The dose can be repeated q6–8h, but the total daily dose should not exceed 16 mg/kg.

- **(b)** When the bronchomotor response to epinephrine has not been adequate, parenteral aminophylline may be effective in reducing the high airway resistance. Before administration, ascertain carefully the total amount of xanthine derivatives received in the previous 12 hr. If previous administration has been excessive (more than 8 mg/kg/12 hr) or in the presence of such symptoms as excitation, tremor, frequent vomiting, hematemesis, and convulsions, further use of aminophylline should be carefully considered or postponed for 6 hr after the last administered dose. *Rapid IV infusion of aminophylline can lead to cardiac arrhythmias, hypotension, and death.*

b. Expectorants   (See Chap. 19, Sec. **II.D.**) Intravenous sodium iodide (25 mg/kg daily) may be useful in loosening secretions and promoting cough. Administration may be distributed evenly over 24 hr, or it can be given in 1 dose over 4 hr.

c. Corticosteroids

- **(1)** If after the preceding measures the patient shows no improvement or actually deteriorates, give hydrocortisone IV, 5–10 mg/kg q6h, by IV push or drip.

- **(2)** Corticosteroids should be started early in the attack if the child is on long-term corticosteroid therapy, or there is a previous history of severe attacks leading to acute respiratory failure or to a complicated hospital course, or both.

d. Antibiotics   Consider their use in the presence of:

- **(1)** Significant fever

- **(2)** Elevated WBC (15,000 cu mm) and left shift obtained prior to epinephrine administration

- **(3)** A sputum stain showing purulent secretions *or*

- **(4)** Radiologic evidence of pneumonia (often difficult to differentiate from atelectasis)

e. Sedatives   Chloral hydrate may be given (15–40 mg/kg) PO or PR q6–8h as required. Opiates and barbiturates should be avoided because of the danger of respiratory depression and arrest. Other tranquilizers may pose a similar risk.

4. Physical therapy   See also Chap. 19, Sec. **I.C.**

- **a.** Encourage the patient to cough at regular intervals to help in the removal of secretions. Percussion of the chest will improve the efficiency of coughing, especially after bronchodilators have produced their effect.

- **b.** Give breathing instructions to teach the patient how to perform abdominal inspirations, followed with deeper inspirations, and finally how to expire the breath through pursed lips. These instructions are often beneficial in the child old enough to follow them.

c. Sitting in an upright position will facilitate diaphragmatic excursions.

d. When bronchospasm has ceased, therapy consisting of postural drainage, percussion, and vibration is recommended.

VII. RESPIRATORY FAILURE IN STATUS ASTHMATICUS Despite appropriate therapy, respiratory failure can develop in a few children and lead to cardiorespiratory arrest and death. The management of the patient in respiratory failure requires a team approach, specialized equipment, and intensive care facilities, which must be arranged for in advance by the child's physician so that this therapy can be instituted electively before coma and arrest occur.

A. Diagnosis

1. The clinical criteria for diagnosis of respiratory failure as outlined by Downes (*Pediatrics* 42: 238, 1968) are:

a. Decreased or absent inspiratory breath sounds.

b. Severe inspiratory retractions and use of accessory muscles.

c. Depressed level of consciousness and response to pain.

d. Generalized muscle weakness.

e. Cyanosis in 40% O_2.

2. When three or more of these criteria are present, the partial pressure of CO_2 in arterial blood ($Paco_2$) is usually $\geq$ 65 mm Hg. Some children who meet these criteria still respond well to vigorous medical therapy over one to several hours. When a rising $Paco_2$ and absence of inspiratory breath sounds appear in a child who is becoming fatigued, the need for more aggressive intervention has to be considered.

B. Monitoring

1. A **central venous line** should be started.

2. Establish an **"arterial line"** by percutaneous insertion of a plastic cannula into the radial artery (or through direct visualization of the artery by cutdown). Then connect the cannula to a "T" connector (Abbott Laboratories #4612) and then to a constant infusion pump with continuous flushing of a dilute heparin solution of 1 U/ml of normal saline at 3 ml/hr. This has to be handled with a strict aseptic technique. The arterial cannula is used in direct transducing of systemic pressure. Repeated specimens of arterial blood can be drawn as necessary for evaluation of ventilatory and acid-base status.

3. Heart rate, blood pressure, and temperature should be recorded q30 min–1h. Connect a cardiac monitor to the patient.

4. Intake and output Place a three-way lumen Foley catheter and provide catheter sterile care. Measure hourly urine output.

5. **Respirator variables** Rate, volumes, positive end-expiratory pressure (PEEP), dead space.

6. **Inspired O$_2$ concentration** (with an air O$_2$ analyzer).

7. **Chest x-ray films** as indicated clinically and by the arterial blood gases.

8. Tracheobronchial sterile **aspirates** should be smeared for Wright and gram stain and sent for culture.

9. An intensive care **flow sheet** should be used for proper recording and monitoring of all variables involved.

C. **Therapy** At present, there are two ways of aiding the child in status asthmaticus and respiratory failure:

1. **Intravenous isoproterenol** The use of this drug has been reported as a successful alternative to artificial ventilation, with lesser risks than with the latter. **This form of therapy *should not be attempted* unless proper monitoring is used and methods of dealing with the potential complications are available.** This is an experimental technique (see *J. Allergy Clin. Immunol.* 50 : 75, 1972).

2. **Mechanical ventilation** The primary aim of mechanical ventilation is to correct acidosis and hypoxemia, provide an easier way of draining tracheobronchial secretions, and gain time for medications to take effect.

a. **Induction on controlled ventilation**

(1) Use 100% O$_2$ by bag and mask with manually assisted ventilation.

(2) Aspirate upper airway secretions (10–15 sec).

(3) Aspirate the stomach with a large-size catheter (14F in an infant, 16–18F for an older child).

(4) **Myoneural blockade** After obtaining qualified help from personnel skilled in intubation procedures, provide myoneural blockade. The following drugs can be used **IV**:

(a) Tubocurarine at 0.6 mg/kg

(b) Succinylcholine by slow infusion of 10–50 mg (it has a very short duration of action)

(c) Gallamine in a dose not to exceed 1.0 mg/kg

(5) Intubate the child under direct laryngoscopy. It is best to use a Smith Porter Ivory Tube (available with a prestretched cuff in sizes over 6 mm in diameter). A clear polyvinylchloride endotracheal tube can be used satisfactorily in its place. Under emergency conditions or with lack of skill, an orotracheal tube can be placed initially. It is best if a skilled person places the nasotracheal tube.

(6) Ventilate with 100% O$_2$.

(7) Aspirate tracheobronchial secretions.

(8) Listen to both sides of the chest for breath sounds and change tube position if indicated.

(9) Prepare the skin with tincture of benzoin and fix tube with waterproof adhesive tape.

(10) Use a chest x-ray film to check the tube position and for diagnosis of pneumothorax.

b. Maintenance of controlled ventilation   See also Chap. 19, Sec. **III.**

(1) A volume preset ventilator (Emerson, Engstrom, Bennett MA 1) should be used, since a tidal volume will be delivered to the patient irrespective of airway resistance or compliance.

(2) Set inspiratory and expiratory rates. Provide a prolonged expiratory time. Tidal volume is usually calculated as 7–10 ml/kg. Initial respiratory rate should be set between 15–40/min, according to the age of the child. One must often rely on visual and auscultatory evidence of ventilation during the initial adjustments and readjust the tidal volume and respiratory rate according to serial arterial gases and pH determinations. Multiple variables such as the patient's temperature and arterial pH and the characteristics of each ventilator make the management of the patient a complicated task, involving all the principles of intensive care.

(3) In a patient with diffuse alveolar collapse, PEEP may permit reduction of inspired O_2 concentration (F_iO_2) to lower levels by substantially improving arterial oxygenation. A PEEP of 3–10 cm H_2O can be used.

(4) Humidification of the inspired air at the proper temperature is essential.

(5) When arterial blood gases have stabilized, start instillations of sterile saline (2–5 ml) at hourly intervals in the tracheal airway, followed by changes in chest position, percussion, vibration, and then sterile aspiration. The patient should not remain off the respirator for more than 15–20 sec.

(6) Institute manual hyperventilation (5–10 breaths) q30 min to prevent atelectasis, and use "artificial coughing" technique to help in drainage of secretions.

(7) Provide **continuous myoneural blockade** with:

   (a) Tubocurarine, 1 mg/kg q30 min or as required, *or*

   (b) Gallamine, 1 mg/kg q30 min or when needed

(8) If **sedation** is considered necessary:

   (a) Diazepam, 0.1–0.2 mg/kg IV prn

   (b) Pentobarbital, 1 mg/kg IV

   (c) Morphine, 0.2 mg/kg (2–10 mg IV). Monitor for hypotension

(9) Hydration is continued at 2–2½ times maintenance rate. Watch the CVP carefully. Patients on mechanical ventilation may have increased ADH secretion and impaired fluid output.

(10) Continue the use of *aminophylline, sodium iodide,* and *corticosteroids* as discussed previously. Isoproterenol via IPPB can also be used after stabilization and initial improvement in ventilatory and general status.

(11) Acid-base balance   Effective artificial ventilation will usually reduce the $Paco_2$ and increase the pH to satisfactory levels. This may not happen if there is a strong metabolic component to the acidosis. Sodium bicarbonate in the dosages discussed in Sec. **VI.B.2.b–d.** should be used then. If there is no adequate response, or in the presence of hypernatremia, THAM can be used (1–2 mEq/kg by IV infusion). With mechanical support of ventilation, the hazard of respiratory depression is avoided.

c. Discontinuance of mechanical ventilation

(1) When child is able to maintain stable arterial blood gases at 30–40% O_2 in inspired air, he is usually ready to be switched from a controlled to an assist mode, in which the patient can trigger the ventilator. Discontinue the muscle relaxant, allow spontaneous respirations to recur, and then set the ventilator to "Assist."

(2) If, after 1–4 hr of assisted ventilation, the $Paco_2$ remains under 50 mm Hg and the Pao_2, over 100 mm Hg at 50% or less F_iO_2, a program for discontinuing ventilation in stages can usually be initiated. Progressively larger intervals without mechanical ventilation, starting with 5–10 min and with arterial blood gases determined at the end, are carried out. During those periods the patient is breathing 40–60% humidified O_2 through a Briggs adaptor.

(3) Once the patient can tolerate spontaneous ventilation for several hours, consider removing the tracheal airway. The endotracheal tube is removed after careful suctioning.

(4) The patient is then placed in a high humidity oxygen tank.

(5) Provide adequate physical therapy during the recovery phase.

(6) Start oral fluids and gradually increase as the patient's condition allows.

(7) If aminophylline, iodides, corticosteroids, and antibiotics are being used, change from parenteral to oral administration.

(8) Discontinue IV fluids after oral intake is satisfactory.

(9) Remove the arterial line after the patient is extubated and arterial gases are stable.

VIII. COLD INJURY[1] may be divided into generalized injury (exposure, or accidental hypothermia) and local injury (frostbite, immersion foot).

A. Accidental hypothermia (exposure)   In this condition the body temperature is less than 95° F. The onset is insidious, with abnormal behavior, apathy, clumsiness, weakness, and cessation of shivering and

---

[1] The discussion in this section does not apply to the newborn.

may progress to profound depression with no audible heart sounds, no respiratory effort, and dilated pupils.

1. **General measures** In the moribund patient, start artificial ventilation and cardiac massage. A central venous cutdown should be placed. All patients should be placed on an ECG monitor because of the high risk of arrhythmias during rewarming. BUN, electrolytes, and pH should be taken and monitored during the course of therapy.

2. **Rewarming** Should be started as soon as possible. Several methods are possible:

   a. **External rewarming**

      (1) **Passive (slow method)** Place patient in a warm room and cover him with blankets.

      (2) **Active (rapid method)** Apply external heat to the body surface, either with a hyperthermic blanket or a warm water bath, at a temperature of 98.6° F.

   b. **Core rewarming**

      (1) **Extracorporeal** rewarming is by pump oxygenator or artificial kidney. This is rapid and avoids the problem of rewarming shock. Although it is theoretically the best method when it can be done immediately, it has the major disadvantage of the time delay involved in assembling the necessary medical-surgical team.

      (2) **Warm peritoneal dialysis** has been reported. However, this is a slow method of rewarming.

3. **Complications**

   a. **Rewarming shock** is caused by peripheral vasodilation associated with external rewarming. It is treated as hypovolemic shock (see **Sec. II.C**).

   b. **Arrhythmias** are a frequently encountered hazard (Chap. 11, Sec. I). Bradycardia, different types of heart block, "U waves," and ventricular arrhythmias may occur. Treat with external cardiac massage. If ventricular fibrillation occurs, *defibrillation cannot be effective until the patient's temperature is at least 82.4° F.*

   c. **Acidosis and electrolyte imbalance** should be treated appropriately (see Chap. 4, Sec. II).

   d. **Convulsions** may occur and should be treated appropriately (see Sec. **III.C–I**). 50% D/W, 1 ml/kg IV should be given stat because of the danger of hypoglycemia.

   e. **Frostbite** may be present (see **B**).

B. **Frostbite and immersion foot frostbite** is the result of exposure to extremely cold temperatures, usually for a prolonged time. Immersion foot occurs in the presence of moisture and at higher temperatures than frostbite. The pathologic changes of immersion foot are similar to but less severe than those of frostbite.

   1. **Rewarming** The method of choice for frostbite is rapid rewarming in hot water (104–111° F) for about 20 min. **Higher temperatures**

cause more injury and must be avoided. Meperidine, 0.5–1.0 mg/kg IM (maximum, 100 mg) may be administered for pain.

2. Avoid rubbing the skin, since it will increase tissue damage. The patient should also avoid smoking, because it causes peripheral vasoconstriction.

3. **Tetanus toxoid or antitoxin** should be given (see Chap. 9, Sec. **IV.D**).

4. **Local care**   The open method with a protective cradle is recommended. Strict asepsis (gown and mask) is advised. Gentle debridement should be done. Bullae should not be ruptured.

5. **Antibiotics** should be used if evidence of infection arises (see Chap. 9).

6. **Physical therapy** is recommended during convalescence.

7. **Amputation** should be delayed until optimal healing has occurred, which may be as long as 2 or 3 months.

8. **Malnutrition** is often present, and a high-protein diet may be beneficial.

IX. HEAT STROKE[1]   Heat stroke is a failure of the usual heat-dissipating mechanisms. The three cardinal signs are hyperpyrexia, CNS disturbance, and hot and dry skin.

A. **Hyperpyrexia**   Remove the patient's clothing and place him in ice water, with vigorous massaging of the extremities to promote vasodilation. Check rectal temperature q10 min, and discontinue the bath when the temperature falls to 100° F. Promethazine (0.5 mg/kg IM) may be used to facilitate temperature loss, but hypotension may occur.

B. **The general status** of the patient should be carefully monitored. If shock develops, a central venous line should be placed, and the shock should be treated (see Sec. **II.C**). BUN and electrolytes should be obtained and monitored and fluid losses replaced (see Chap. 4).

C. **Urine output** should be monitored closely. Acute tubular necrosis may accompany heat stroke.

D. **Convulsions** may occur and should be treated (see Sec. **III.D–J**).

E. **The ECG** should be monitored and arrhythmias treated.

F. **Liver function studies** should be followed since liver damage may occur, leading to liver failure (see Chap. 13).

G. **Watch for bleeding**, which may arise because of increased capillary fragility and decreased prothrombin levels. DIC may develop and should be treated (see Chap. 15, Sec. **V.B**).

X. BURNS   Extra fluid loss through the skin due to the denuded areas are minimized by the use of wet dressings. Urinary output is diminished, due to an increased release of antidiuretic hormone and low renal perfusion 2° to low plasma volume. Because of sequestered plasma at the burn sites, the severely burned patient has an "internal loss" of fluid.

[1] The discussion in this section does not apply to newborns.

A. Evaluation The severity of the burn will depend on its depth and the percentage of the surface area involved.

1. **First-degree burn** Vasodilation occurs. There is very little edema.

2. **Second-degree burn** Capillary damage is present. Fluid may accumulate beneath the skin (blisters, bullae). Some protein loss occurs in blistered areas.

3. **Third-degree burn** The entire skin is destroyed, and capillaries are thrombosed; edema is maximal at 48 hr after the burn, but may last for weeks.

4. The estimate of surface area burned is made by the "rule of nines" in the patient who is more than 12 years old. For the younger child, the rule must be modified and a greater area attributed to the head and face.

B. Therapy

1. **Day 1** Because of hypovolemia, an isotonic solution should be used to expand the ECV. Although isotonic saline could be used, the chloride load may cause hyperchloremic acidosis, and thus Ringer's lactate is preferred. A colloid solution (e.g., plasma or whole blood) may be substituted, but Ringer's lactate is more readily available.

    a. Replacement volume

    2 ml Ringer's lactate × % burn surface × weight (kg)

    b. Maintenance Give 1500–2000 ml/M^2/24 hr.

    c. Precautions

    (1) If the burn area involves more than 50% of the body surface, the calculation for replacement assumes only 50%.

    (2) The first 24 hr of fluid is given in two portions: the first 8 hr *after the burn occurred* comprises the *first* segment, and the remainder is given over the next 16 hr.

    d. Examination of the urine is crucial; volume and concentration should be monitored hourly; urine Na^+ and K^+ are also useful. In most cases, diminished urine volume is due to low renal perfusion, but with major burns *acute renal failure* is possible and will manifest itself as a low urine osmolality and a high urinary Na^+ content (Chap. 12, Sec. **IV**).

2. **Day 2** The patient should receive full maintenance fluid and ⅔ of the replacement volume calculated in the first 24 hr. The rate of infusion can be even over the day if the patient has a steady urine output and normal CVP.

3. **Day 3** Only maintenance fluid should be given, and careful monitoring of vital signs is mandatory. There usually is a diuretic phase as well as absorption of pooled fluid into the circulation: Observe for signs of pulmonary edema and for possible hyponatremia.

XI. DROWNING

A. Physiologic effects Most submersions are fatal after 2–3 minutes; by the third minute of submersion there is respiratory arrest and the disappearance of muscle tone. During the fourth minute there is cardiac arrest. Interruption of submersion before the third minute usually will result in spontaneous resuscitation. Animal models clearly demonstrate the differences between fresh-water and salt-water submersion, but the differences are not so readily applicable to the human being.

1. In the animal model, **fresh-water drowning** will result in hemodilution, massive hemolysis (leading to hyperkalemia, hemorrhage pneumonitis, and hemoglobinuria), and ventricular fibrillation.

2. In **salt-water drowning**, animal studies demonstrate hemoconcentration, hypernatremia, and pulmonary edema due to the local osmotic effect of the high $Na+$ aspirate in the lung.

3. When humans are submersed in either salt or fresh water, the changes observed in the animal model, with the exception of pulmonary complications, are not so apparent. The electrolyte and hematocrit imbalances are *not* easily predictable, and close monitoring of *both* is necessary. Seldom is the water free of debris and bacteria, so that antibiotics and corticosteroids must be added to the therapy. In an effort to minimize O_2 consumption, hypothermia may also be indicated.

4. The main cause of death is the pulmonary damage and edema. Thus care not to overload the patient with fluids is important and CVP and urinary output should be monitored, along with standard vital signs.

B. Therapy

1. Initial therapy

    a. **Respiratory support** Clear the airway and administer O_2 by mask or, if not available, mouth-to-mouth.

    b. **Cardiac support** Give closed chest massage if necessary. An occasional case of auricular or ventricular fibrillation has been reported.

2. Subsequent therapy

    a. Corticosteroids (see Chap. 19).

    b. Antibiotics (see Chap. 9).

    c. **Intravenous fluids** In both salt- and fresh-water drowning there is some hemoconcentration. In salt water there is a tendency toward hypernatremia; in fresh water there may be hyperkalemia (from hemolysis).

3. Maintenance therapy Because of the danger of pulmonary edema, initial maintenance is kept at insensible losses (~ 800 ml/M^2 daily) until it is clear that edema is *not* a problem or until there is good urine output ~ 1 ml/kg/hr.

4. Treatment for shock Give 10–20 ml/kg of plasma over 1 hr (use low Na plasma for salt submersion and low $K+$ for fresh water submersion). If plasma is unavailable, dextran in saline is used for fresh-water and dextran with 5% D/W for salt-water drowning. Packed cells may also be used in fresh-water drowning to combat shock.

XII. CHILD ABUSE AND NEGLECT

A. Objectives and problems

1. Recognition or suspicion of child abuse should be met by a long-range therapeutic plan, with attention to the establishment of supportive relationships. The goal of the initial process of management is protection of the child while his parents are helped through an acute family crisis.

2. Problems include parental personalities in which denial and projection serve as the principal modes of ego defense; the family's anxious confusion in facing an array of clinical specialty services and social agencies, often working in an uncoordinated manner to protect the child from themselves; and the exigencies of poverty, including mistrust of community institutions, racism, unemployment, and drugs. The clinical team may be frustrated by missed appointments, angry parental confrontations, time-consuming contacts with outside agencies, and conflicts among the responsible personnel stemming from the emotions brought forth by prolonged contact with disturbed families.

B. Diagnosis

1. **Clinical findings** Suspect child abuse or neglect whenever a child presents with any one or a combination of the following clinical findings:

   a. **Fractures** that a simple fall would be unlikely to produce.

      (1) Different stages of healing in multiple fractures

      (2) Metaphyseal fractures

      (3) Epiphyseal separations

      (4) Subperiosteal calcifications

   b. Subdural hematomas

   c. Multiple ecchymoses that may resemble purpura

   d. Intestinal injuries, ruptured viscera

   e. Burns of any kind, especially in infants

   f. Poor hygiene

   g. Inadequate gain in weight or height

   h. Marked passivity and watchfulness, fearful expression

   i. Bizarre accidents, multiple ingestions

   j. Malnutrition

   k. Developmental retardation

2. **Some frequent behavior patterns of abusive or negligent parents** They may:

   a. Use severe punishments.

   b. Give a past history of abuse in their own upbringing.

   c. Display suspicion and antagonism toward others.

   d. Lead isolated lives.

e. Make pleas for help in indirect ways, such as:

(1) Bringing the child to the physician or emergency room for no specific reason or for repeated minor medical complaints.

(2) Insisting that the child be admitted to the hospital for a minor illness and expressing anxiety if he is not.

f. Lean on their children for support, comfort, and reassurance.

g. Sample a variety of health facilities without establishing a relationship with any particular one.

h. Display poor impulse control or an openly hostile attitude toward the child.

i. Be unable to carry out consistent discipline, yet threaten or punish the child if he does not live up to an expectation or whim.

j. Understand little about normal child development and seem unable to integrate information offered about it.

C. Axioms of management

1. Once child abuse or neglect is diagnosed, the child is at great risk of reinjury or continued neglect.

2. Protection of the child must be a principal goal of initial intervention, but his protection must go hand in hand with a program to help his family through its crisis.

3. Traditional social casework cannot in itself protect an abused or neglected child in the dangerous environment. Medical follow-up is also necessary, and day-to-day contact with a child care center may help significantly to encourage his healthy development.

4. If the child is reinjured and medical attention is sought anew, the parents are likely to seek care in a facility other than that where the diagnosis was originally made or suspected.

5. Public social service agencies in both urban and rural areas do not have sufficient well-trained personnel, and the quality of administration and supervision in these agencies is not high. These factors militate against their operating effectively in isolation from other social agencies. Simply reporting a case to the public agency mandated to receive child abuse case reports may not be sufficient to protect an abused or neglected child or to help his family.

6. Early attempts by the hospital staff to identify the agent of an injury or to determine if neglect was "intentional" may be ill advised. There is rarely a need to establish *precisely* who it was who injured or neglected a child and why. Clinical experience has shown that of greater importance is the establishment of confidence and trust in the hospital personnel, which may be jeopardized by overly aggressive attempts to ferret out the specific circumstances of the injury. On the other hand, lack of evidence for parental "guilt" is not a criterion for discharge of the patient.

7. If there is evidence that the child is at major risk, hospitalization to allow time for assessment of his home setting is appropriate. Children under the age of 3 are frequent victims; infants under 1 year of age with severe malnutrition or failure to thrive, fractures, burns, or bruises of any kind are especially at risk of reinjury or

neglect. Prompt and effective intervention is vital to assure their survival.

D. Assessment of the child and his family

1. An adequate general medical history and physical examination are necessary at the time the child is brought to the physician. Photographs and a skeletal survey are made when indicated by the child's condition and the clinician's impression.

2. If a social worker is available, she is called promptly at the time of the family's visit. The physician should introduce her as someone interested and able to help them through this difficult period and then should confer with her after her interview.

3. Interviewing the parents

a. In the initial interviews and in subsequent contacts, *no direct or indirect attempt to draw out a confession from the parent is made.* Denial is a prominent ego defense in virtually all abusive parents. Their often bizarre stories of how their child was injured should not be taken as intentional falsifications. These odd accounts frequently indicate a parent's profound distress in acknowledging infliction of an injury or failure to protect a child. In the face of such a threatening reality, they repress it and may offer a blatant fabrication, which one must accept for the moment.

b. One should not accuse the parent or he may use more primitive defenses than denial; i.e., a desperate resistance to talking about the problem at all, angry outbursts directed at the interviewer or hospital, and threats to take the child home immediately. This in turn may threaten information-gathering and continuing helpful professional relationships and may endanger the child.

c. A good interview technique allows parent and child to maintain the integrity of ego and family. It is appropriate to emphasize the child's need for hospital care and protection from harm. At this time, the physician should demonstrate his concern and ability to help the *parents'* distress as well.

4. In explaining his legal obligation to report the case, the physician's compassion and honesty will go far to allay the family's anxiety.

5. The opportunity to observe parent-child interaction and the child's physical and psychological milestones that might lead to insight into the familial causes of a child's injury or neglect may not be available to a physician in an ambulatory setting.

XIII. DRUG ABUSE

A. Children and adolescents are seen by the physician for a variety of drug-related problems.

1. The state of consciousness may be altered as a result of drug overdose or unexpected effect.

2. The child may be experiencing an acute anxiety or panic reaction.

3. Secondary medical problems may be present, such as hepatitis or pneumonia.

4. Parents may request examination for real or imagined drug effects.

B. Initial approach Young people using drugs usually enter an emergency room as a last resort. The physician then has an unusual opportunity not only to give immediate help but to initiate long-term care.

1. Approach the patient in a nonthreatening manner.

2. Make him comfortable in a chair or stretcher.

3. Remove all unnecessary personnel from the room.

4. Avoid restraints.

5. Demonstrate that your knowledge, concern, and experience can help him.

6. Keep parenteral injections and blood drawing to a minimum.

C. Drug identification

1. See "Glossary of Slang Terms" (Table 2-7).

2. If necessary, send blood, urine, and gastric contents for toxicologic analysis.

3. Correlate symptoms with the known effects of commonly abused drugs (see Chap. 3, Table 3-1).

D. Therapy in specific ingestions (see Chap. 3, Sec. **II**).

1. **Barbiturates**

   a. Maintain an adequate oral airway with frequent suctioning. If necessary, intubate via endotracheal or nasotracheal tube.

   b. Give humidified O_2 as needed via catheter at 4–6 L/min or via oronasal mask at 2–4 L/min.

   c. Maintain blood pressure (see Sec. **II.C**).

Table 2-7. Glossary of Slang Terms for Various Drugs

Marihuana	Opiates	Cocaine	Amphetamines	Barbiturates	LSD
Pot	Dollies	Bernice	Bennies	Barbs	Acid
Hash	H	Coke	Blue Devils	Candy	A
Tea	Harry	Corine	Blue Velvet	Downers	D
Weed	Horse	Dust	Bombido	Goofballs	Blue Cheer
Flower	Joy-powder	Flake	Cartwheels	Nimby	Cube
Grass	Miss Emma	Gold Dust	Crossroads	Peanuts	Green Flats
Hay	Scag	Star Dust	Co-pilots	Pinks	Pink Swirls
Hemp	Gum	Cecil	Dexies	Rainbows	
Mary Jane	Morph	Girl	Footballs	Red Devils	
Griefo	Dope		Hearts	Seggy	
Reeker	Junk		Oranges	Tooies	
Rope	Thing		Peaches	Yellowjackets	
Herb	Smack		Roses	Blue Bullets	
			Truck Drivers		
			Wakeups		
			Whites		
			Browns		
			Speed		
			Uppers		

d. Introduce a central venous catheter if necessary.

e. If the patient is alert, induce emesis with 15 ml syrup of ipecac. If the patient is obtunded, endotracheal intubation may be required, using a cuffed endotracheal tube to prevent aspiration. Follow intubation with gastric lavage. Before removing the gastric tube, instill activated charcoal, 1 gm/kg per dose.

f. Avoid analeptic drugs.

g. Keep the patient's head down by elevating the feet to prevent aspiration.

h. Treat hypothermia, if present, with blankets.

i. Hemodialysis or peritoneal dialysis may be necessary.

2. Ethyl alcohol

a. Remove unabsorbed alcohol by gastric lavage or emesis.

b. If intoxication is severe (blood alcohol 0.3–0.5%), treat for aspiration hazard, airway obstruction, hypotension, and hypothermia, as in severe barbiturate intoxications.

c. Determine blood glucose. If hypoglycemic, give 50% dextrose, 1.0 ml/kg per dose, diluted ½–⅓ in an IV solution.

d. Check the ECG for evidence of cardiomyopathy.

e. Keep the urine slightly alkaline with $NaHCO_3$, 1–2 mEq/kg per dose IV, or 2 gm/250 ml water PO q2h.

f. Avoid administration of excess fluids.

g. Avoid depressant drugs.

h. Hemodialysis is indicated if the blood level is above 0.5%.

3. Amphetamines

a. Emesis with ipecac is generally preferred to gastric lavage in the alert patient.

b. For patients with mild intoxication or acute panic reactions, give emotional support.

c. Support respirations and blood pressure.

d. Acidify the urine with ammonium chloride 2–6 gm daily PO.

e. Control convulsions with:

    (1) Paraldehyde, 0.3 ml/kg PR, diluted in an equal volume of mineral oil.

    (2) Diphenylhydantoin, 2–5 mg/kg per dose, slowly IV (50 mg/min). Repeat ½ dose after 30 min if seizures continue. Do not exceed 400 mg daily.

    (3) Barbiturates should be used cautiously because of the already depressed state that may be present in amphetamine overdose.

f. Treat hypertension with phentolamine (Regitine), 5 mg slowly IV, or phentolamine hydrochloride, 5 mg/kg daily PO in 4 divided doses.

4. LSD (lysergic acid diethylamide)

    a. Induce emesis.

    b. Give emotional support. This may involve listening to the patient converse for hours, a procedure known as "talking down."

    c. For young adults, use diazepam, 5–10 mg (PO or slowly IV) for acute anxiety reactions. Do not leave the patient alone.

    d. Chlorpromazine may be helpful but is contraindicated if adulterants are present, such as strychnine, belladonna, phencyclidine, or "STP" (dimethoxymethylamphetamine).

    e. Long-term follow-up is important, since "flashbacks" and acute psychotic breaks have been known to occur after apparent recovery from the acute effects of LSD ingestion.

5. Glue-sniffing

    a. Give emotional support in the emergency and at the time of follow-up visits.

    b. Obtain blood for liver and kidney function tests.

6. Narcotics

    a. If taken orally, induce emesis or lavage.

    b. Maintain respirations, airway, and blood pressure as in patients with barbiturate overdose.

    c. Antagonize narcotic effects with naloxone hydrochloride (Narcan), 0.01 mg/kg per dose for children and 0.4 mg per dose for adults. If no response, repeat dose after 3 min. If there is no response after the second dose, narcotic overdose may not have occurred. If the patient responds to the antagonist, then relapses, give additional doses as necessary to relieve symptoms.

7. Glutethimide (Doriden)   Treatment is substantially the same as for barbiturate intoxication.

E. Medical and psychiatric follow-up   Young people abusing drugs are in need of ongoing emotional and medical support, which can be given by a physician alone or in collaboration with a school guidance counselor, clergyman, or social worker.

    1. The physician should know that young patients will often fail to keep appointments, yet will demand that the counselor be available.

    2. Common behavior characteristics of children who abuse drugs are:

        a. An unrealistic sense of trust and demand for love

        b. Denial of the reality of time

        c. Flight from their own emotions and feelings

        d. Tendency toward severe depression

        e. Isolation of physical sexuality from psychological mutuality

        f. Behavioral passivity

3. In the family history there is frequently an early lack of maternal emotional nurturance and an early and continual failure of one parent to protect the child from the irrational demands of the other.

4. Treatment attempts to bring normal activity slowly. The counselor may share his own family, thoughts, and experience with the child. Some children may require residential care or hospitalization at times of crisis.

F. Talking to parents   It is useful to ask a young patient how he plans to inform his parents that he has been on drugs. In the best of circumstances the patient will have enough rapport with his parents to discuss his problem with them, especially if he is given encouragement. Fortunately, child, parents, and physician are sometimes able to discuss together the problems common to both child and parent. Suffice it to say that difficulties arise when a counselor violates the trust placed in him by a fearful child who prefers to hide his activities from his parents.

3 Poisoning

Children under 5 years of age constitute 90 percent of recorded cases of poison ingestion. Most children ingesting poison are seen before symptoms develop. However, the clinician generally can determine the nature of the ingested substance from the history. When the nature of the ingestion is unknown the list of common signs and symptoms shown in Table 3-1 may be useful.

I. EMERGENCY MANAGEMENT

A. Identification of the poison Usually, the ingested material can be identified by a careful history. The drugs available in the home where the ingestion occurred offer helpful identifying clues.

1. The initial history should include what and how much was taken (a swallow for a 3-year-old child is approximately 4–5 ml), when the ingestion occurred, and the present condition of the child.

2. If a substance is *not* a caustic or a hydrocarbon, and if the child is *not* comatose or having a seizure, removal by emesis may be instituted.

3. The physician should accept the largest estimated amount ingested in determining therapy.

4. Physical examination will often offer supporting evidence for a particular ingestion. All vomitus and urine, as well as all containers and bottles, should be saved to assist in later identification.

B. Removal of the poison Removal prior to absorption and onset of symptoms is the primary aim. Enhancement of excretion and various methods of dialysis may be useful with the more serious ingestions.

1. **Mechanical methods** These consist of blunt objects and lavage and are less effective in inducing emesis than are chemicals.

    a. Disadvantages of the use of lavage include emotional and physical trauma, ineffectiveness in removing tablets and, to a lesser extent, liquids, and need to bring patient to the hospital.

    b. For the comatose patient, a cuffed lavage tube or prior intubation with a cuffed endotracheal tube followed by passage of a lavage tube may be indicated.

    c. **Gastric lavage procedure**

    (1) Equipment: Catheter, 8–12F; 4-oz asepto syringe; lavage with ½ normal saline.

    (2) Place the patient on his left side, with his head hanging over the table during lavage.

Table 3-1.   Common Signs and Symptoms of Toxic Ingestions

Signs and Symptoms	Drugs Involved
Disturbance of cardiac functions:	
Arrhythmias	Digitalis, quinidine
Tachycardia	Amphetamines, caffeine, ephedrine, cocaine
Bradycardia	Barbiturates, chloral hydrate, digitalis, quinine, opiates
Hypotension	Chloral hydrate, nitrites, quinine, thorazine
Nervous system symptoms:	
Depression and coma	Barbiturates, alcohols, tranquilizers, antihistamines, chloral hydrate, paraldehyde, chloroform, ether, cyanide, CO, atropine, CO_2, nicotine, phenols, scopolamine, hydrogen sulfide, insulin, bromides, benezene, zylene, morphine and its derivatives, lead
Convulsions	Strychnine, parathion and other organic phosphate esters, amphetamines, ammonium salts, camphors, picrotoxin, cyanides, chlorinated hydrocarbons, lead, barium, cocaine, belladonna group, ergot, nicotine, salicylates, CO
Delirium	Belladonna group, alcohol, cocaine, marihuana, amphetamines, antihistamines, camphor, benzene, barbiturates, aniline
Gastrointestinal symptoms:	
Nausea, vomiting, and diarrhea	Heavy metal salts, alcohol, acids and alkalis, halogens, yellow phosphorus, phenols, muscarine, digitalis, aspirin, fluoride, parathion and other organic phosphate esters, many poisonous plants
Eye signs:	
Dilated pupils	Belladonna and derivatives (atropine), alcohol, chloroform, cocaine, meperidine, nicotine, amphetamine, ephedrine, epinephrine, tripelennamine, ether, chloroform, isoproterenol, psychodelic drugs such as LSD, antihistamines
Constricted pupils	Morphine and derivatives, parathion and other organic phosphate derivatives, parasympathomimetic drugs, barbiturates, chloral hydrate, caffeine, nicotine
Blurred vision	Atropine, physostigmine, cocaine, dinitrophenol, nicotine, methyl and ethyl alcohol, indomethacin, carbon tetrachloride
Colored vision	Digitalis, quinine, CO, marihuana
Scotomas	Quinine, salicylates
Skin:	
Cyanosis (methemoglobin)	Nitrobenzene, aniline dyes, acetanilid, carbon dioxide, chloral hydrate, amyl nitrate, nitrites, methane, morphine

Table 3-1.   (*Continued*)

Signs and Symptoms	Drugs Involved
Skin (Continued) :	
Staining and coloring	Iodine, black; bromide, deep brown; nitric acid and picric acid, yellow; silver nitrite, blueish gray; CO, cyanide, pink; atabrine, yellow; methemoglobinemia, purple-brown; atropine, flushed face
Jaundice	Aniline, nitrobenzene, primaquine, benzene, arsenic, chromates, mushrooms, quinacrine, nitro compounds, phosphorus, carbon tetrachloride, phenothiazines, thiazides, diuretics
Discoloration of the gums	Lead, mercury, bismuth (usually chronic poisoning), arsenic
Tinnitus	Salicylates, quinines, streptomycin, camphor, ergot, methyl alcohol, tobacco
Alopecia	Thallium, x-rays, radium, arsenic, ergot, hypervitaminosis A
Salivation:	
Decreased salivation	Belladonna group, atropine, morphine, benedryl, ephedrine
Increased salivation	Lead, mercury, thallium, other heavy metals, mushrooms
Sweating:	
Increased sweating	Parathion and other organic phosphate esters, alcohols (acute), insulin, nitrates, muscarine, pilocarpine, mercuric chloride, arsenic, aspirin, fluoride, nicotine, ammonia
Hyperpyrexia	Atropine, quinine, zinc fumes, boric acid, dinitrophenol, phenolphthalein, atropine, salicylates
Hyperventilation	Salicylates, nicotine, aromatics, CO_2, cyanide, atropine, camphor, cocaine
Abnormal odor on breath:	
Odor of alcohol	Phenols, chloral hydrate, alcohol
Odor of acetone	Lacquer, alcohol
Odor of coal gas	CO
Odor of wintergreen	Methyl salicylate
Odor of garlic	Phosphorus and arsenic
Odor of bitter almonds	Cyanide
Odor of shoe polish	Nitrobenzene
Pearlike odor	Chloral hydrate
Other odors	Hydrocarbon, turpentine, camphor
Abnormal odor of tissues:	
Specific odor of chemical ingested	Phenol, creosote, chloroform, hydrogen sulfide, ethchlorvynol, ether, alcohol, paraldehyde

Table 3-1. *(Continued)*

Signs and Symptoms	Drugs Involved
Abnormal odor of tissues (Continued) :	
Odor of garlic	Phosphorus, arsenic, parathion
Odor of shoe polish	Nitrobenzene
Odor of violets	Turpentine in urine
Odor of pears	Chloral hydrate
Odor of bitter almonds	Cyanide
Abnormal color of gastric aspirate :	
Pink or purple	Potassium permanganate
Green	Nickel salts
Blue	Iodine if starch is present
Abnormal color of urine :	
Dark green	Phenol, resorcinol
Brown or black	Antipyrine trinol (after long use)
Yellow	Picric acid
Bright yellow, changing to scarlet on adding caustic alkali	Santonin

(3) Cool the tube with ice; use jelly to facilitate insertion.

(4) Measure the distance to the stomach, and assure entrance into the stomach by checking for bubbles under water or injecting air with auscultation over the stomach.

(5) Aspirate the gastric contents prior to lavage.

(6) Perform lavage 10–12 times or until the return is clear.

(7) If indicated, leave a specific antidote or activated charcoal in the stomach on completion.

(8) Pinch the tube on removal, to prevent aspiration.

2. Chemical methods Ipecac syrup and apomorphine are most effective chemical methods of removal.

a. Ipecac syrup is now the method of choice because it is highly effective in inducing emesis, effectively and speedily removes both pills and liquids, especially when the poisonous substance is of the type kept in the home, is available without prescription, and has a long shelf life, which allows storage at home for emergency use. It is safe when taken in the recommended dosage (less than 30 ml for patients over 1 year of age and less than 15 ml for patients less than 1).

b. Contraindications to its use include the ingestion of caustic agents or hydrocarbons, or in a patient who is comatose or having seizures. The correct method for its use follows.

(1) For the patient 1 year and older, within or outside of a hospital setting, 15 ml (1 tbsp) of ipecac syrup is given, followed by 200 ml of clear fluid. *The patient must be kept active.* If vomiting does not occur within 20 min, the same dose may be repeated once.

(2) For children age 6 months–1 year, 10 ml is given once only, followed by clear fluid and activity. If ineffective, lavage is indicated.

c. Apomorphine This causes emesis in 100 percent of patients within 2–5 min of its use. As in lavage however, the patient must come to a hospital or to a physician's office for its administration. The recommended dosage is 0.07 mg/kg per dose SQ. A respiratory depressant, its effect may be reversed with levallorphan (Lorfan), 0.02 mg/kg per dose, nalorphine (Nalline), 0.1 mg/kg per dose, or naloxone (Narcan) 0.01 mg/kg per dose. *Apomorphine is particularly effective when impending obtundation requires rapid induction of emesis.*

3. Enhanced excretion Methods of enhancing excretion should be used only in serious poisoning, as they involve some risk. Most cases are handled conservatively, allowing the patient to excrete or metabolize the ingested drug. Only a small percentage will require the following more radical forms of therapy.

a. Fluid diuresis enhances excretion by increasing the rate of glomerular filtration, so that the reabsorptive sites in the distal tubules have a shorter exposure to the ingested drug. Fluid diuresis will enhance excretion of drugs normally handled by the kidneys. A sustained diuresis of 2–3 times normal is recommended.

b. Ionized diuresis is based on the principle that excretion is favored when a drug is maintained in its ionized state. Excretion of acidic compounds such as salicylates and long-acting barbiturates is enhanced by sustained alkalinization of the urine. The more acidic the ingested drug, the more effective is alkalinization in enhancing excretion.

(1) For salicylates, a 2–3 mEq/kg dose of sodium bicarbonate ($NaHCO_3$) is given q4h. Urinary pH is monitored, and additional $NaHCO_3$ is used if a pH above 7.5 is not maintained. Serum and urinary electrolytes, calcium, and magnesium should be monitored as well.

(2) Acidification of the urine in poisoning with basic compounds (e.g., amphetamines) will also enhance excretion.

c. Osmotic diuresis Osmotic diuresis (see Chap. 4, Sec. **I.B**) is based on the principle of an osmotic load preventing reabsorption of an ingested drug in the proximal tubules, Henle's loop, and distal tubules.

(1) A diuresis of 0.1 ml/min/kg or 2–3 times the normal excretion rate is recommended.

(2) Contraindications to the procedure are cardiac disease, oliguria or anuria, hypotension, or pulmonary edema.

(3) Close monitoring of serum and urinary electrolytes, body weight, and central venous pressure (CVP) is indicated.

(4) Mannitol, 0.5 gm/kg per dose IV of a 25% solution q4–6h, may be used.

d. Diuretics Ethacrynic acid, 1 mg/kg per dose IM or IV at 2–3h intervals (or when urinary output decreases), has been used to enhance excretion. An output of 2–3 times normal in a child is sought. Furosemide (Lasix), 3 mg/kg per dose IM or IV, has also been used. Urinary and blood electrolytes should be closely monitored.

4. Dialysis Exchange transfusions, peritoneal dialysis, and hemodialysis are not part of the usual emergency management of a poisoning. Their use is reserved for the most severe cases, with the decision based on the patient's CNS involvement and his ability to maintain respiration, blood pressure, and an adequate urinary output, as well as on the drug ingested (see Table 3–2). Coma may not be an indication for dialysis if blood pressure and respiration can be maintained and the patient is not anuric.

a. Generally, exchange transfusion is effective in small children for poisoning with drugs that are tightly protein-bound and that remain in the circulation for long periods of time.

b. Peritoneal dialysis is useful in children in instances of electrolyte and acid-base disturbance and with drugs that have high dialysis clearance across the peritoneum.

c. Hemodialysis and lipid dialysis are less commonly used in children. Table 3-2 lists the drugs for which the various methods of dialysis are known to be effective.

C. Dilution and Neutralization

1. Dilution This method is relatively ineffective, its greatest effect coming from its calming influence. In the case of barbiturates, it may increase absorption by hastening transit of the ingested poison into the lower parts of the gastrointestinal tract, from which subsequent removal will be difficult.

2. Neutralization This is effective in case of ingestion of caustics. Milk of magnesia and milk can be used for acid poisoning; orange or lemon juice or vinegar (the latter diluted 1 to 4) may be used for poisoning with bases.

3. Laxatives may hasten transit through the gastrointestinal tract, thus decreasing absorption of poisons not removed by emesis. How-

Table 3-2. Currently Known Dialyzable Poisons[a]

Barbiturates[b]	Primidone–2
Barbital–1, 2	Meprobamate–1, 2
Phenobarbital–1, 2	Ethchlorvynol[b]–1, 2, 3
Amobarbital–1, 2	Ethynylcyclohexyl carbamate–1
Pentobarbital–1, 2	Methyprylon–1, 2
Butabarbital–1, 2	Methaqualone–1, 2
Secobarbital–1, 2	Heroin–1
Cyclobarbital–1, 2	Gallamine triethiodide–1
	Paraldehyde–1, 2
Glutethimide[b]–1, 2	Chloral hydrate–1
	Chlordiazepoxide–1
Depressants, Sedatives,	
and Tranquilizers	**Antidepressants**
Diphenhydramine–1, 3	Amphetamine–1, 2
Diphenylhydantoin–1, 2	Methamphetamine–1, 2

Table 3-2. *(Continued)*

Tricyclic secondary amines–1	Lead–1
Tricyclic tertiary amines–1	Lithium–1
Monoamine oxidase inhibitors–1	Magnesium–1
Tranylcylpromine–1	Mercury–1, 4
Pargyline–1	Potassium–1, 2
Phenelzine–1	Sodium–1, 2
Isocarboxazid–1	Strontium–1
Imipramine–1	

Alcohols
Ethanol[b]–1, 2
Methanol[b]–1, 2, 3
Isopropanol–1
Ethylene glycol–1, 2

Halides
Bromide–1
Chloride–1
Iodide–1
Fluoride–1

Analgesics
Acetysalicylic acid[b]–1, 2, 3
Methylsalicylate[b]–1, 2, 3
Acetophenetidin–1
Dextropropoxyphene–1, 2
Paracetamol–1, 3

Endogenous Toxins
Ammonia–1, 2, 3
Uric acid[b]–1
Bilirubin–1, 2, 3
Lactic acid–1, 2
Cystine–1
Endotoxin–1
Water intoxication–1, 2

Antibiotics
Isoniazid–1, 2
Carbenicillin–1, 2
Streptomycin–1
Kanamycin–1, 2
Neomycin–1, 2
Vancomycin–1
Penicillin–1
Ampicillin–1
Sulfonamides–1
Cephaloridine–1
Chloramphenicol–1
Tetracycline–1
Nitrofurantoin–1
Polymyxin–1
Cycloserine–2
Quinine–1, 2

Miscellaneous
Thiocyanate[b]–1
Aniline–1, 2, 3
Sodium chlorate–1, 2, 3
Potassium chlorate–1, 2, 3
Eucalyptus oil–1, 2
Boric acid–2
Potassium dichromate–1, 4
Chromic anhydride–1
Digoxin–1, 2
Sodium citrate–1
Dinitro-ortho-cresol–1
Amanita phalloides–1
Carbon tetrachloride–1
Ergotamine–2
Cyclophosphamide–1
5-Fluorouracil–1
Methotrexate–1
Camphor–1
Trichlorethylene–1, 2
CO–1

Metals
Arsenic–1, 2
Calcium–1, 2
Iron–1, 4

1 = hemodialysis, 2 = peritoneal dialysis, 3 = exchange transfusion, 4 = chelation and dialysis.
[a] Adapted, by permission, from Schreiner, G. E., *Trans. Am. Soc. Artif. Intern. Organs* 16: 544–568, 1970.
[b] Kinetics of dialysis thoroughly studied, or clinical experience extensive, or both.

ever, they cause local irritation. Enemas are effective for removing overdoses given PR.

D. **Supportive therapy**   While allowing normal renal and hepatic processes to rid the body of the ingested drug, the principles of supportive therapy must be observed. These principles include the following:

1. **Respiratory**   Assuring adequate respiratory exchange by clearing secretions, utilizing an oral airway, supplying sufficient O_2 and humidity, and turning the patient often to prevent pneumonia. Rarely, intubation and mechanical respiration will be required.

2. **Cardiac**   Correction of shock (see Chap. 2, Sec. **II.C**).

3. **Fluid homeostasis**   Replacement of previous and ongoing losses, as well as correction of electrolyte derangements (see Chap. 4, Sec. **II**).

4. **Hematologic**   Correction of hemolytic anemias with packed cell transfusions or whole blood transfusions for external losses of blood (see Chap. 1, Sec. **II.D**).

5. **Central nervous system**   CNS involvement may require control of seizures with barbiturates, paraldehyde, diphenylhydantoin, or diazepam, supportive measures for prolonged coma, adequate suctioning, and preventive measures against self-injury (see Chap. 2, Sec. **III**, and Chap. 14, Sec. **I.A.2**).

6. **Renal failure**   will require fluid and electrolyte management. Dialysis may be needed (see Chap. 12, Sec. **III.D**).

7. **Antibiotic therapy**   for bacterial superinfection. Prophylactic antibiotics are discouraged (see Chap. 9, Sec. **I.A**).

8. **General supportive measures**   include the monitoring of vital signs, avoidance of CNS stimulants, and the use of analgesics as indicated.

E. **Antidotes**   These preparations serve to inactivate an ingested poison.

1. **Local antidotes**

   a. The universal antidote (a mixture of charcoal, magnesium hydroxide, and tannic acid) is ineffective and, in fact, hepatotoxic.

   b. Activated charcoal, an odorless, tasteless black powder, is the residue from distillation of wood pulp. It forms a stable complex with the ingested toxin, thus preventing absorption.

Table 3-3.   Drugs Adsorbed by Activated Charcoal[a]

Amphetamines	Diphenylhydantoin	Penicillin
Antipyrene	Glutethimide	Phenol
Aspirin	Iodine	Phenolphthalein
Atropine	Ipecac	Propoxyphene
Barbiturates	Methylene blue	Primaquine
Camphor	Morphine	Quinine
Cantharides	Muscarine	Salicylates
Chlorpheniramine	Nicotine	Sulfonamides
Cocaine	Opium	Stramonium
Colchicine	Oxalates	Strychnine
Digitalis	Parathion	

[a] Adapted, by permission, from Corby, D. G., et al., *Pediatr. Clin. North Am.* 17: 545, 1970.

(1) **It should not be given before ipecac syrup, as it will bind the syrup and make it ineffective.** Its effectiveness depends on its small particle size and large surface area. Indiscriminate use of activated charcoal is discouraged, particularly when other effective means of removal are available. It should be used only for drugs against which it is known to be effective (Table 3-3); it is not effective against cyanide, ethyl and methyl alcohol, alkali, or acid.

(2) The ingested dose is 1 gm/kg PO or 1–2 tbsp in 8 oz of water. It may be given following induced emesis or via a nasogastric tube following lavage.

2. **Specific antidotes**   The number of ingestions for which there is a specific antidote are few. The following list includes the drugs or substances for which an antidote is available.

a. BAL, for arsenic, bismuth, chromium, cobalt, copper, iron, lead, magnesium, radium, selenium, and uranium. The dose is 12.0–24.0 mg/kg/24 hr in 6 divided doses.

b. EDTA, for lead, iron, mercury, copper, nickel, zinc, cobalt, beryllium, manganese. The dose is 50–75 mg/kg daily, IM or IV in 4 divided doses.

c. Penicillamine, for lead, copper, mercury. The dose is 25 mg/kg daily PO.

d. Amyl or sodium nitrite and thiosulfate, for cyanide. The doses are: sodium nitrite, 3% solution IV, at 2.5–5.0 ml/min, followed by sodium thiosulfate, 50 ml of a 25% solution IV, at 2.5–5 ml/min.

e. Nalorphine, levallorphan, or naloxone (Narcan), for narcotics. Doses are: nalorphine, 0.1 mg/kg per dose, levallorphan, 0.02 mg/kg per dose, naloxone, 0.01 mg/kg per dose. All are given IV.

f. Vitamin K_1, for warfarin and dicumarol. The dose is 5–10 mg/kg IM.

g. Deferoxamine, for iron. The dose is 1–2 gm or 20 mg/kg IM q4–6h.

h. Ethanol, for methanol and ethylene glycol. The dose is 0.75–1.0 ml/kg IV, followed by 0.5 ml/kg q4h.

i. Atropine sulfate and/or 2-pyridine aldoxime methiodide (PAM), for insecticides (cholinesterase inhibitors). Doses are: atropine 1–4 mg IV, with repeat doses of 2 mg at intervals of 15–30 min; PAM, 0.25 gm q12h.

j. Methylene blue, for methemoglobinemia induced by nitrites, aniline, chlorates, phenacetin, nitrobenzene, sulfonamides, quinones, dyes. The dose of methylene blue is 1–2 mg/kg IV as a 1% solution and is repeated in 4 hr.

k. Chlorpromazine, for amphetamines. The dose is 1 mg/kg IM or IV.

l. Diphenhydramine (Benadryl) for phenothiazine extrapyramidal reactions. The dose is 1–2 mg/kg IV.

m. Oxygen for carbon monoxide (100% O_2 for 30 min).

F. **Prevention**   No course of therapy, no matter how trivial the ingestion, is complete without a discussion about why the poisoning occurred and a review of ways to assure that the incident will not be repeated. Recognition that the agent, an unpredictable child, and an emotionally unstable milieu may all play a part in a poisoning is essential in such discussions.

II. **SPECIFIC INGESTIONS**   Table 3-4 lists certain common substances of low toxicity that either require no treatment when ingested or require only emesis when ingested in large quantities. The few specific ingestions listed in the following section are chosen because their management remains complex and difficult.

A. **Caustics**

1. **Etiology**   The severity of the caustic burn is related to the concentration and duration of contact rather than the amount ingested.

Table 3-4.   Common Ingestions of Low Toxicity

No Treatment Required	Removal Necessary If Large Amounts Ingested
Ballpoint Inks	Aftershave lotion
Bar soap	Body conditioners
Bathtub floating toys	Colognes
Battery (dry cell)	Deodorants
Bubble bath soap	Fabric softeners
Candles	Hair dyes
Chalk	Hair sprays
Clay (modeling)	Hair tonic
Crayons with A.P., C.P., or C.S.	Indelible markers
130–46 designation	Matches (more than 20 wooden matches
Dehumidifying packets	or 2 books of paper matches)
Detergents (anionic)	No Doz
Eye makeup	Oral contraceptives
Fishbowl additives	Perfumes
Golf balls	Suntan preparations
Hand lotion and cream	Toilet water
Ink (blue, black, red)	
Lipstick	
Newspaper	
Pencils (lead and coloring)	
Putty and Silly Putty	
Sachets	
Shampoo	
Shaving cream and shaving	
lotions	
Shoe polish (occasionally, aniline	
dyes are present)	
Striking surface materials of	
matchboxes	
Sweetening agents (saccharin,	
cyclamate)	
Teething rings	
Thermometers	
Toothpaste	

Following ingestion, a burn ensues during the first week, granulation tissue during the second week, and fibrosis during the third week. Typical **acids** ingested are toilet-bowl cleaners, metal-cleaning fluids, and some bleaching products. Typical **alkalis** ingested are powerful detergents, toilet-bowl cleaners, and dishwasher and laundry granules.

2. Evaluation and diagnosis

a. Immediate severe pain is experienced in the mouth and retrosternal area. The absence of oral burns is reassuring and is evidence against esophageal involvement. Other symptoms include vomiting, signs of vascular collapse, and coma.

b. Esophageal perforation with mediastinitis and gastric perforation with peritonitis may occur. Aspiration may lead to pulmonary necrosis or glottic edema. Bacterial superinfection is common during the first and second weeks, and esophageal stricture formation in later weeks. If a skilled surgeon is available, esophagoscopy may be performed within the first 2 days to determine the presence and extent of injury.

3. Treatment

a. Emesis and lavage are contraindicated.

b. The alkalis may be diluted and neutralized by vinegar or lemon or orange juice and the acids, by milk or milk of magnesia.

c. Opiates may be used for pain.

d. Blood, albumin, and saline are used for shock (see Chap. 2, Sec. II.C).

e. Liquids and soft foods may be given when the patient can swallow.

f. If evidence points to an esophageal burn (clinical evidence or a burn demonstrated by esophagoscopy), corticosteroids (prednisone, 2 mg/kg daily) are indicated for 3–4 weeks. Coverage with broad spectrum antibiotics is necessary throughout this period. A barium swallow is indicated following corticosteroid therapy to confirm the presence of absence of stricture formation. If present, subsequent dilatations will be necessary.

B. Hydrocarbons produce both pulmonary and CNS pathologic changes; the relative proportion of damage to each system is determined by the hydrocarbon's degree of volatility and viscosity.

1. Etiology and evaluation

a. Gasoline, lighter fluid, paint thinners, and industrial rubber solvents produce a greater degree of CNS than pulmonary damage. Furniture polishes and waxes (mineral seal oils) produce mainly pulmonary damage. Kerosene produces both (Table 3-5).

b. The type of pathologic changes in the lung will depend on the type of hydrocarbon ingested. The mineral seal oils produce low-grade chronic pulmonary inflammation, while the more volatile compounds produce a more fulminant course.

c. Central nervous system involvement is produced by all hydrocarbons as a result of absorption from the lungs, and in the case

Table 3-5. Petroleum Products: Estimation of Aspiration Hazard and Systemic Toxicity

Product	Source(s)	Systemic Toxicity	Aspiration Hazard[a]
Petroleum ether or benzine	Industrial or rubber solvents	4+	—
Gasoline	Fuel	3+	2+
Naphtha	Solvent, lighter fluid, dry cleaner, thinner	3+	3+
Kerosene	Fuel, charcoal lighter fluid, thinner, pesticide solvent	2+	2+
Mineral seal oil	Furniture polish	3+	4+
Fuel or diesel oil	Fuel, heating oil	1+	1+
Mineral oil		—	—
Lubricating oil	Motor oil, cutting oil, transmission fluid	—	—

[a] Formulations with increased viscosity have decreased aspiration hazard.

of highly volatile hydrocarbons, through gastrointestinal absorption. Pulmonary involvement is caused by aspiration either during ingestion or subsequent vomiting.

   d. The liver, kidney, spleen, myocardium, and bone marrow may all be involved as well.

2. Diagnosis

   a. Ingestion of a hydrocarbon causes mucous membrane irritation. Vomiting, bloody diarrhea, and perianal excoriation occur.

   b. Pulmonary involvement is evidenced by coughing, gagging, dyspnea, cyanosis, and rales.

   c. Central nervous system manifestations include restlessness, confusion, drowsiness, and coma. Pneumothorax and pleural effusions may complicate the pulmonary picture.

3. Treatment

   a. Removal should be deferred in the case of low-volatility hydrocarbons, the danger from aspiration being greater than the risk from gastrointestinal absorption. Compounds of higher volatility, when 30 ml or more has been ingested, will require removal.

   b. Present evidence now suggests that in the *alert* patient, emesis with ipecac syrup is a safer method of removal than lavage. In the obtunded patient, protection of the lungs with a cuffed endotracheal tube and subsequent lavage is the therapy of choice.

   c. Olive oil may be given to slow absorption.

   d. For pulmonary involvement, O_2, humidity, bronchodilators for bronchospasticity, and antibiotics (as indicated clinically) are recommended.

   e. Though use of **corticosteroids** for pulmonary involvement remains controversial, present evidence (in cases of mild to moderate severity) does not support their use.

f. Infiltrates may take 1–2 weeks to resolve fully; waxes and polishes may take even longer.

g. Central nervous system, liver, and renal involvement require supportive management.

h. Due to myocardial irritability, sympathomimetic drugs should be avoided.

C. Iron

1. Etiology Because iron tablets are ubiquitous, iron ingestion is common. Iron combined with vitamins is often present, particularly in the home of the pregnant female.

2. Evaluation and diagnosis

a. Symptoms generally occur 30 min–2 hr following ingestion and are often severe. Early symptoms include vomiting, bloody diarrhea, drowsiness, and, less commonly, shock and coma.

b. A period of improvement (6–24 hr postingestion) is followed by a recurrence of symptoms, this time including fever, metabolic acidosis, hepatic impairment, restlessness, convulsions, shock, and coma.

c. *Stricture of the GI tract* is a late complication occurring 3–4 weeks postingestion.

d. Initial laboratory studies should include a CBC, serum electrolytes, serum iron, and an x-ray film of the gastrointestinal tract for the presence of radiopaque iron tablets.

3. Treatment

a. Early emesis with ipecac syrup is indicated if 1 gm or more of ferrous sulfate has been taken.

b. Intravenous fluids, sodium bicarbonate, and volume expanders will be needed to correct fluid losses.

c. Sodium bicarbonate by mouth may relieve abdominal discomfort, prevent intestinal erosion, and decrease absorption.

d. Deferoxamine treatment

(1) Indications

(a) Coma and shock.

(b) A serum iron level > 500 $\mu g/100$ ml (there is a 35 percent incidence of shock and coma at these levels).

(c) Symptoms other than minimal vomiting and diarrhea.

(d) In any patient with a suspected overdose of ferrous sulfate of unknown quantity.

(2) Administration The parenteral route is preferable to either the PO or IV route. The IM dose is 1–2 gm q3–12h, depending on the amount ingested, the clinical state of the patient, and the serum iron level. The urine will turn burgundy-red within 2 hr of an IM dose when the serum iron level is 500 $\mu g/100$ ml or greater. In cases of hypotension, the intravenous dose is 1 gm by slow infusion, the rate not to exceed

15 mg/kg/hr. Generally, the serum iron level falls within 12–18 hr, and clinical improvement is seen in 6–12 hr. Cessation of therapy will generally be possible anywhere from 12–36 hr after beginning therapy.

(3) Dialysis Ferrous sulfate alone is not dialyzable, but is dialyzable when bound to deferoxamine and dialysis may be used in the presence of oliguria or anuria.

D. Salicylates are the most frequent cause of poisoning in children and presently account for 12 percent of all toxic ingestions.

1. Etiology Usually, the accidental ingestion of aspirin.

2. Evaluation

a. Salicylates produce an initial respiratory alkalosis due to hyperventilation secondary to central stimulation. The body compensates by excreting base via the kidneys. A state of metabolic acidosis, especially in young children, is quickly superimposed. Dehydration and worsening acidosis occur due to hyperventilation, renal solute loss, an increased metabolic rate, and vomiting. Presenting symptoms in the younger child generally include metabolic acidosis and respiratory alkalosis. The adolescent presents with respiratory alkalosis only.

b. The first symptoms seen in both alkalosis and acidosis are deep, rapid respiration, thirst, vomiting, and profuse sweating. In severe intoxication, confusion, delirium, coma, convulsions, circulatory collapse, and oliguria may ensue.

c. Salicylates increase body metabolism, prolong prothrombin times, cause platelet dysfunction, and may induce either hyperglycemia or hypoglycemia. They are first excreted in the urine within ½ hr after ingestion, and peak serum levels occur 2 hr postingestion. Of an ingested load of aspirin, 75 percent is excreted through the kidneys, and 25 percent is handled by oxidation.

d. Initial laboratory studies include a CBC, electrolytes, blood gases, serum ketones, blood glucose, prothrombin time, serum salicylate level and urine acetone, pH, protein, and ferric chloride.

3. Diagnosis Ingestion of 150–200 mg/kg will cause symptoms. A salicylate level of 50 mg/100 ml causes mild symptoms; 50–80 mg/100 ml produces symptoms of moderate severity; and 80–100 mg/100 ml produces severe symptoms. The nomogram in Figure 3-1 will be of assistance in determining the expected severity of clinical illness following a single dose ingestion of aspirin. A level of 50 mg/100 ml or any symptoms (except mild hyperventilation) will generally indicate the need for hospitalization.

4. Treatment

a. Induction of emesis with ipecac syrup is required when a toxic dose (greater than 150 mg/kg) has been ingested.

b. Intravenous fluids to replace fluid losses (see Chap. 4, Sec. II) and adequate glucose to correct hypoglycemia.

c. Lowering of temperature elevation with tepid sponging.

d. Vitamin K to combat bleeding due to hypoprothrombinemia.

e. Alkalinization of the urine (2–3 mEq/kg of $NaHCO_3$ q4–6h)

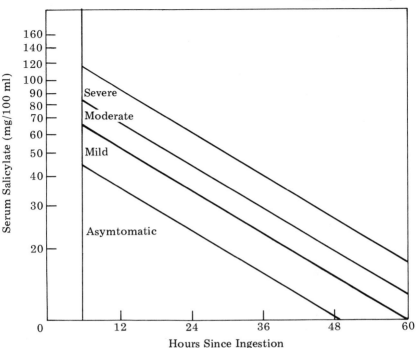

Figure 3-1. Nomogram relating serum salicylate levels to expected clinical severity of intoxications following a single dose of salicylates. (Reprinted, by permission, from Done, A. K., *Pediatrics* 26: 800, 1960.)

and monitoring of the urinary pH (keeping it above 7.5) will result in excretion of 50 percent of the ingested salicylate in 6 hr rather than the usual 24 hr. Generous amounts of potassium (3–6 mEq/kg daily) are necessary to replace potassium loss and *allow alkalinization of the urine.*

f. Potentially fatal serum levels (100–150 mg/100 ml), oliguria or anuria, and cardiac disease are all indications for dialysis. A poor response to $NaHCO_3$, coma, and seizures are *relative* indications for dialysis.

III. LEAD POISONING

A. Etiology   Lead poisoning results from the ingestion of plaster or other objects saturated or coated with lead-based paint (lead content > 0.5%); inhalation of lead vapor or fumes; ingestion of foods stored in lead-lined containers, or of ceramics coated with lead glazes and fired below 1800° F; and absorption from lead-saturated soil. Children living near highways or roadways may also have increased exposure to lead from automobile exhaust fumes, a poorly understood source of toxicity.

B. Evaluation

1. History   Data should be obtained on the size of the family, and the location, age, and condition of the home or other frequented areas.

Whether or not there is a history of pica should be determined, but pica is not a sine qua non in lead poisoning. Questions should be asked about the child's appetite, bowel habits, and general behavior as well as about signs of irritability and lethargy.

2. **Complete physical examination** This should include a complete neurologic examination, as well as the Denver Developmental Test and other psychometric tests as available.

3. **Laboratory studies**

   a. In encephalopathy, the EEG shows diffuse changes.

   b. Lumbar puncture is **contraindicated** unless it is certain that CSF pressure is not increased. Lumbar puncture adds little to the evaluation, and the findings do not affect therapy.

   c. Blood lead may be determined by a micromethod, for which several techniques are now available.

   d. A CBC, with attention to basophilic stippling of the RBC, serum iron and iron-binding capacity, serum δ-amino levulinic acid, erythrocyte δ-amino levulinic acid dehydratase, and erythrocyte protoporphyrin levels will reflect interference with hemoglobin synthesis. Urinary coprophyrins do the same, but are less well correlated with blood lead levels.

   e. Hair and teeth can be assayed for lead and reflect chronic ingestion.

   f. X-ray films of the skull for widening of sutures (encephalopathy) and of the long bones for increased metaphyseal density (chronic ingestion), and KUB for radiopacities (acute ingestion), are helpful.

   g. **Lead mobilization test (provocative chelation)** This involves a 24-hr urine collection for lead content determination during administration of ethylenediaminetetracetic acid (EDTA) up to 75 mg/kg daily in 3 divided doses or 50 mg/kg IM in a single dose. The test is positive for increased body burden if 24-hr collection yields greater than 1 μg lead/mg of EDTA injected. Note that urinary concentration of lead is *not* used. *Absolute* excretion of lead each 24 hr is measured, requiring the quantitative collection of urine. Indications for performing the lead mobilization test are listed in Table 3-6.

Table 3-6.   Indications for Lead Mobilization Test

---

1. Blood lead greater than 60 μg/100 ml whole blood
2. Blood lead 30–60 μg/100 ml whole blood *and*
   Hair lead greater than 100 μg/gm *and*
   a. Symptoms of plumbism *or*
   b. History of exposure (PICA) *or*
   c. Positive roentgenograms *or*
   d. Sibling with lead intoxication *or*
   e. Unexplained anemia and basophilic stippling *or*
   f. Positive urinary coproporphyrin or erythrocyte protoporphyrin *or*
   g. Positive urinary or serum delta ALA *or*
   h. Decreased erythrocyte delta ALA dehydratase *or*
   i. Aminoaciduria and/or glucosuria *or*
   j. Decreased osmotic fragility

C. Diagnosis   See Table 3-7.

D. Therapy   At all costs, the source of lead must be removed *despite the existence of other problems.*

1. **Chelating agents**   Commonly used chelating agents are EDTA, dimercaprol (BAL), and D-penicillamine. (For a complete discussion, see *J. Pediatr.* 73: 1, 1968, and *Pediatrics* 53: 441, 1974.)

   a. **EDTA** is the most efficient at binding lead and removes it from soft tissues and central nervous system although *not* from red blood cells. It enhances urinary excretion 20- to 50-fold, and its principal toxic effect is on the kidney. A calcium disodium salt (Versenate) can be used in a standard dose of 50 mg/kg/24 hr for the average patient and up to 75 mg/kg/24 hr in severe cases, in 3 divided doses. If given by mouth, EDTA enhances absorption of lead from the gut, and, for this reason, EDTA PO is **contraindicated** in acute plumbism.

   b. **BAL** actually removes more lead from the body than EDTA because it enhances fecal as well as urinary excretion. In addition, it diffuses well into erythrocytes. It can be administered in the presence of renal impairment because it is predominantly excreted in bile. Its disadvantages are that it must often be given IM and is toxic in lower doses than is EDTA. The usual dosage is 12 mg/kg daily and up to 24 mg/kg daily in severe cases, in 3–6 divided doses.

Table 3-7. Clinical and Laboratory Evidence of Lead Intoxication and Asymptomatic Lead Burden

Lead Intoxication	Asymptomatic Increased Lead Burden
Clinical	*Clinical*
Anorexia, constipation, irritability, clumsiness, lethargy, behavior changes, hyperactivity (sequela), abdominal pain, vomiting, fever, hepatosplenomegaly, ataxia, convulsions, coma with increased CSF pressure	History of pica Environmental lead source Positive family history
Laboratory	*Laboratory*
Microcytic, hypochromic anemia Basophilic erythrocyte stippling Increased δ-ALA in serum and urine Decreased δ-ALA dehydratase in erythrocytes Increased urinary coproporphyrin Increased free erythrocyte protoporphyrin (FEP) Decreased osmotic fragility Increased metaphyseal densities on x-ray Aminoaciduria, glucosuria	Blood lead greater than 40 μg/100 ml Hair lead greater than 100 μg/gm in proximal segment 24-hr urinary lead excretion greater than 80–100 mg Lead mobilization test greater than 1 μg/mg EDTA injected/24 hr Radiopacity in gastrointestinal tract on x-ray

c. D-penicillamine is the only available oral chelating agent, but is probably somewhat less efficient than EDTA and BAL in removing lead from the body, even when given parenterally. It does not remove lead from erythrocytes. The D-isomer has relatively low toxicity and can be given over a long period of time. The PO route apparently does not enhance lead absorption from the gut. The dose is 20–40 mg/kg daily, PO.

d. In general, all three chelating agents remove other heavy metals as well as lead from the body, and long-term iron therapy must be administered following chelation therapy. Hypocalcemia does not occur when the calcium salt of EDTA is used (although mild hypercalcemia is reported).

2. Monitoring chelation therapy   Urinary lead excretion may be used to monitor the effectiveness of chelation therapy, as the blood lead can be misleading in the presence of these agents.

a. Chelating agents are administered for up to 5 days at a time. If urinary lead excretion remains higher than 1 μg/mg EDTA injected/24 hr on the fifth day, therapy is discontinued for 48 hr and restarted. In this manner, several courses of therapy can be administered as required to deplete lead stores.

b. During chelation therapy, serum calcium, BUN, and lead in the blood and urine as well as urinalysis are monitored for evidence of hypocalcemia or renal toxicity due to EDTA. If such evidence of renal toxicity is present, EDTA can be reduced or discontinued, and renal function usually returns to normal.

c. Occasionally, a worsening of symptoms may occur during therapy. This phenomenon is not understood but removal of lead should continue with attention to changes in CNS suggestive of cerebral edema (see **E.3**).

E. Management of plumbism   Since many children with plumbism are iron-deficient, they may be receiving oral iron when the diagnosis of plumbism is made. Because iron will bind the chelating agents, **do not begin chelation therapy until iron therapy is discontinued.**

1. Asymptomatic increased absorption

a. *If* the child is asymptomatic and *if* the lead source is found and removed and *if* there is no biochemical evidence of intoxication, *no* treatment is necessary. The child may be followed by monthly blood lead determinations and, if indicated (see Table 3-6), a lead mobilization test.

b. *If* there is anemia or *if* the blood lead is increasing or *if* the child is at risk of further ingestion, a single dose of 50 mg/kg of EDTA can be given each morning for 5 days, discontinued for 48 hr, and begun again as long as the elevated lead burden persists. Hospitalization is not necessary for this purpose, and BUN, urinalysis, and blood leads can be obtained on days 1, 3, and 5.

c. *If* prolonged therapy is required, D-penicillamine, 20–40 mg/kg PO may be administered instead of EDTA. (Therapy can be continuous without 48-hr intervals.)

2. Acute lead intoxication, mild to moderate

a. Hospitalize the child.

b. Give maintenance fluids.

c. Administer EDTA *IV* if possible or IM if necessary, 50–75 mg/kg daily in 3 divided doses. If the IM route is chosen, the dose can be bid or even a single injection (with concomitant reduction of efficiency in chelation).

d. If the lead burden appears high on the basis of urinary excretion, add BAL or EDTA IM in 3 divided doses of 12–24 mg/kg/24 hr.

e. Monitor BUN, blood and 24-hr–urine lead, and urinalysis.

f. After chelation is completed, administer iron (see Chap. 15, Sec. **I.A.3**).

3. Acute lead intoxication (severe, with encephalopathy)

a. This is a medical emergency.

b. Give maintenance fluids.

c. Begin EDTA IV, 75 mg/kg daily in 3 divided doses by slow drip.

d. Begin BAL IM, 24 mg/kg daily in 3–6 divided doses.

e. Treat cerebral edema with mannitol and dexamethasone (Decadron) (see Chap. 2, Sec. **V**).

f. Continue chelation therapy at all costs, as cerebral edema will not respond to therapy until the lead burden is reduced.

g. Treat seizures with anticonvulsants (see Chap. 14, Table 14-1).

h. After 5 days, discontinue therapy for 48 hr and restart.

i. Monitor BUN, calcium, EEG, urinalysis, and blood and 24-hr–urine lead.

j. Continue with a close monthly follow-up as long as the child is at risk.

k. This syndrome produces sequelae. When the opportunity occurs, alert school officials to the child's history of lead encephalopathy.

F. Prevention *Lead poisoning is a preventable disease.* Strong laws are in effect in some states, requiring removal of lead paint from the market and strong penalties for nonremoval from houses in cases of plumbism. Intensive screening of children to identify those at risk, widespread inspection of housing, and stringent enforcement of sanitary and housing codes can reduce morbidity in this disease.

4 Fluid and Electrolyte Balance

The correct management of fluid and electrolyte problems in children demands precision as to volume replacement and solution type. The renal compensatory mechanisms are not well developed in neonates; extra insensible water loss may be found because of the high fever that is seen in childhood illness. Relatively small losses of volume or electrolytes in children can quickly cause deficiency states.

The pediatrician must therefore be familiar with maintenance therapy in different age groups and must anticipate expected deficiency states. He must familiarize himself with several basic formulas that will serve as aids in fluid and electrolyte therapy.

I. GENERAL PRINCIPLES

A. Principal electrolytes

1. **Sodium:** $Na+$ 1 mEq = 23 mg
   Normal plasma concentration = 140 mEq/L

   a. Sodium is the principal extracellular cation. With the exception of hyperglycemic, hyperlipidemic, and uremic states, it normally accounts for about 90 percent of the plasma osmolality.

   b. Sodium is readily absorbed from the gastrointestinal tract and excreted normally through the urine. Under normal conditions the urinary loss of $Na+$ is a direct function of its intake.

   c. Daily requirements are in the range of 2–5 mEq $Na+$/kg, or 50 mEq Na/M^2.

   d. An *excess* of sodium (either PO or IV) **is usually excreted** by the healthy kidney. However, edema may result if there is a concomitant increase in fluid intake or an inadequate fluid excretion. The excess sodium raises the serum osmotic pressure, and thus fluid is retained. Thirst is stimulated, and increased fluid intake lowers the $Na+$ concentration.

   e. In the newborn, the sodium and volume regulatory mechanisms are functional but limited. The newborn kidney cannot concentrate urine so well as the adult kidney, and obligatory solute excretion thus occurs at the expense of extra water loss. Moreover, the infant cannot control his intake through thirst, and care must be exercised in the administration of oral fluids that intake is adequate.

   f. Inadequate sodium leads to confusional states, restlessness, and eventually to coma and death.

2. **Chloride:** $Cl - 1$ mEq = 35.5 mg
   Normal plasma concentration 99–105 mEq/L

  a. Chloride is the principal intravascular anion and the principal anion in the gastric "juice." Chloride intake and excretion tends to parallel that of Na^+.

  b. In vomiting, Cl^- is lost from the stomach along with H^+, and a metabolic alkalosis results.

  c. Chloride in excess leads to metabolic acidosis, principally through displacement and loss of HCO_3^-.

3. Potassium: K^+ 1 mEq = 39.1 mg
     Normal plasma concentration 3.2–6.0 mEq/L
     (may be higher in neonates)

  a. Potassium is the principal *intracellular* cation and is chiefly responsible for maintaining intracellular osmolality.

  b. The normal potassium requirements are 1–2 mEq/kg/24 hr, or 40 mEq/M^2/24 hr.

  c. Since the extracellular concentration of K^+ is low, a decrease of the K^+ concentration in this compartment will produce early symptoms. The principle role of K^+ is in muscle contraction, including myocardial contraction, and in nerve conduction.

  d. K^+ deficiency states are seen in starvation, diarrhea, vomiting, diabetic acidosis, hyperaldosteronism, and during inadequate replacement in long-term IV therapy.

   (1) Symptoms are muscle weakness, cramps, abdominal distension, (paralytic ileus), and drowsiness.

   (2) The effects on the heart vary from arrhythmia to heart block, potentiated by digitalis. The ECG pattern of potassium deficit is a low voltage T wave, the presence of a U wave, and, because of the prolonged T wave, a prolonged QT interval.

  e. In K^+ excess states, such as Addison's disease, renal failure, hemolysis, or overdose, the principal manifestations are cardiac. As the K^+ concentration rises, the heart rate falls, and the conduction velocity decreases. This is especially marked at the atrioventricular node, so that hyperkalemia may produce heart block and fibrillation; depressed ST segment, peaked T wave, and/or prolonged QRS complexes are present in the ECG.

4. Bicarbonate: HCO_3^-
     Normal plasma concentration = 20 mEq/L

The bicarbonate cation, along with carbonic acid, serves as the main buffer of the extracellular fluid. The role of HCO_3^- is to maintain a normal plasma pH. (For a detailed discussion of acid-base balance, see **C**).

5. Calcium: Ca^{++} 1 mEq = 20 mg
     Normal plasma concentration 9–11 mg/100 ml
     (may be lower in neonates)

  a. The calcium anion plays a role in coagulation mechanisms, bone and teeth formation, and in maintaining neuromuscular stability.

  b. Ingested calcium is absorbed in the duodenum with the help of vitamin D and is largely excreted in the stool (10 percent is excreted in urine). The amount retained in the body is dependent on the growth rate of the individual. Calcium in the serum is in a dynamic equilibrium with skeletal calcium.

   c. Serum calcium exists in ionized form and in a nondiffusable form, which is protein-bound. In an acid pH, there is more *ionized* calcium, and conversely, in an alkaline pH, there is more *bound calcium*. Hence, in a state of alkalosis, a slight decrease in total calcium may precipitate tetany, while in acidosis, a lower total calcium is tolerated. Similarly, in a hypoproteinemic state the *total* calcium may be low but, since most of it is unbound, tetany may not be manifest.

   d. **Calcium deficiency** leads to poor dentition, osteomalacia, rickets, and tetany and contributes to osteoporosis. Hypoparathyroidism, adrenocorticosteroid use, low vitamin D intake, and hypoproteinemia are common sources of deficiency.

      (1) In the newborn infant who is bottle-fed with large quantities of a high phosphate formula (see Table 1-9), a special hypocalcemic situation may occur (see Chap. 5, Sec. **VI.B.3**). The concentration of Ca++ in cow's milk is ~ 1220 mg/L and of phosphorus, 900 mg/L, a ratio of 1.35:1. In human milk the calcium concentration is 342 mg/L and phosphorus, 150 mg/L, a ratio of 2.25:1. The high intake of phosphorus in cow's milk, coupled with poor renal excretion in the newborn, tends to raise phosphorus and lower calcium levels.

      (2) The ECG in hypocalcemia shows a prolonged QT interval due to the prolonged ST segment with a normal T wave.

   e. Excess calcium causes few problems over a short period of time (the patient may complain of nausea, vomiting, and abdominal pain). Continued high serum calcium may lead to renal stones and nephrocalcinosis.

6. Magnesium: Mg++ 1 mEq = 12 mg
Normal plasma concentration 1–2 mEq/L
(1.2–2.3 mg/100 ml)

   a. The location of Mg++ is primarily intracellular. In the serum, about one-third is protein-bound, and the pH of plasma has an effect similar to calcium. The role of magnesium is similar to that of calcium, so that a deficiency state of magnesium may simulate hypocalcemia.

   b. **Hypermagnesemia** may be seen in the newborn following magnesium administration to the mother. Symptoms are seen when the Mg++ level is greater than 4 mEq/L. Hypotension and diminished responsiveness are early signs; at a level greater than 7 mEq/L, there is a loss of deep tendon reflex. Coma is seen at levels of 12 mEq/L.

   c. **Hypomagnesemia** may be a problem in artificially fed neonates and in older children with malabsorption states. Symptoms and signs are as in hypocalcemia. Hypomagnesemia should be suspected when presumed hypocalcemia does not respond to the usual therapy.

B. Fluid compartments The average water composition of the newborn is about 70–80 percent of the total body weight. That of the adult male is about 60 percent. In the first few days of life there is a rapid loss of body water (about 7 percent of weight in full-term and 5 percent in premature infants); this loss continues gradually so that by 9–12 months of age, adult proportions are reached.

1. **Total body water** is divided into compartments, as follows:

	Newborn	**Adult**
Extracellular	40%	10–15% interstitial
		5% intravascular
Intracellular	35%	40%

From this distribution, it follows that the newborn who loses fluid from the extracellular space, e.g., through the gastrointestinal tract, will show symptoms of dehydration sooner than would an adult. In addition, the younger the patient the more critical becomes the correct fluid replacement, as there is a limit to the amount of renal regulation and hence to the capacity for fluid retention.

2. **Available mechanisms for regulation**

   a. **Osmolality** is defined as the number of particles dissolved per unit of fluid. (A **molal** represents 1 gm molecular weight of a substance dissolved in a solvent to make 1000 ml.) The dissolved osmolality of the extracellular compartment is slightly higher than that of the intracellular compartment, due to plasma protein, and normally varies little.

   (1) Water is free to move from one compartment to another to equalize the osmolality.

   (2) Since the sodium ion represents the major cation concentration, it can be used to *estimate* serum osmolality. Thus,

   $$2 \, (Na^+) = osmolality$$

   A more exact osmolality can be found by the equation:

   $$Osmolality = 2 \, (Na^+) + \frac{BUN}{2.8} + \frac{glucose \ (mg/100 \ ml)}{18}$$

   (3) The principal mechanisms in regulating the osmolality of the serum are: "thirst centers" in the hypothalamus and secretion of antidiuretic hormone (ADH). If the sodium concentration falls, there will be a compensatory decrease in the ADH secreted, so that a diuresis occurs. If the Na^+ concentration is elevated, water is retained via an increase in ADH release; in this case, thirst is also stimulated and water is taken orally.

   b. **Volume**   Through the action of aldosterone, a healthy kidney will retain fluid when there is a fall in plasma volume. This hormone causes an active transport of sodium at the distal tubule and, simultaneously, a passive transfer of water from the renal tubule back to the extracellular space. If the fall in volume also results in a rise of the serum osmolality, ADH is released and more fluid is retained.

   c. **Ionic "shifts"**   When an acid-base imbalance occurs, there are alterations of the K^+, H^+, and HCO_3^- ions. The *total body concentration* of the ions may not be reflected by the measured serum concentration.

(1) In **metabolic alkalosis** there is a loss of H^+ through vomiting or an excess of HCO_3^- given iatrogenically, or a relative excess through Cl^- loss. In alkalosis, a compensatory shift of the intracellular H^+ ion to the extracellular space occurs, in an attempt to maintain normal serum pH. Concomitantly, the extracellular K^+ moves into the cell to maintain intracellular cation balance. Hence, serum K^+ may be low, but the total body K^+ may be normal.

(2) **Hypokalemic alkalosis**   If the alkalosis persists, the kidney will excrete K^+ ions in an effort to retain H^+ ions, and eventually the total body K^+ will be lowered as well.

(3) **Paradoxical aciduria**   With diarrhea and vomiting there is a loss of all electrolytes. If all but K^+ are replaced, an alkalosis may result when H^+ ions shift into the cells, replacing intracellular K^+ and leaving an excess of extracellular HCO_3^-. Since the K^+ ion is low at the renal level in this situation, the kidney is forced to excrete H^+ ion instead of K^+, producing an acid urine.

(4) In **metabolic acidosis,** some of these shifts are reversed. There is HCO_3^- loss (as in diarrhea) or an increase in H^+. A buildup of organic acids or ketones can also cause a metabolic acidosis. With a high extracellular H^+ ion, there is a shift of H^+ ion *into* the cell and a shift of K^+ ion *out* of the cell. In this situation, the high extracellular K^+ ion concentration may be misleading in assessing the *total* K^+ ion concentration as, for example, in diabetic ketoacidosis.

C. Acid-base balance

1. Acid-base components

a. The normal pH of venous blood is 7.35–7.40 (arterial blood is usually 0.03–0.05 higher). The newborn has a lower blood pH, which is seldom necessary to correct unless it is lower than 7.25 (arterial). The pH of blood reflects a combination of available bicarbonate, buffers, and dissolved CO_2 (Pco_2), which in a reaction catalyzed by carbonic anhydrase can be converted to a weak acid.

$$H_2O + Pco_2 \rightleftharpoons H_2CO_3$$

b. Since the blood pH is derived from two variables, HCO_3^- and Pco_2, one must know which is altered. In other words, *it is not enough to know the pH* and assume that the addition of either H^+ or HCO_3^- will correct an alkalosis or acidosis.

$$pH - pK + \log \frac{base}{acid} \quad pK = 6.10 \text{ (buffer pH)}$$

$$pH = 6.10 + \log \frac{HCO_3^-}{Pco_2 \text{ dissolved}} \quad \begin{array}{l}\text{(The solubility coefficient of}\\ CO_2 \text{ is 0.03 in plasma)}\end{array}$$

$$pH - 6.10 + \log \frac{HCO_3^-}{Pco_2 \times 0.03}$$

c. The Pco_2 represents the respiratory component of the acid-base balance and is a measurement of the effectiveness of ventilation. Thus in respiratory failure the plasma Pco_2 will rise and consequently increase the acidity of the system (i.e., pH falls). If, as in hyperventilation, Pco_2 is "blown off," the Pco_2 will fall and the pH will rise.

In the former situation the increased acidity is termed *respiratory acidosis*. The latter, with a rise in the pH, is *respiratory alkalosis*. Hence the pH of the system can be altered without directly changing the bicarbonate level.

d. The HCO_3^- is not usually measured directly. It can, however, be calculated by measuring total CO_2. Since the total CO_2 is equal to the sum of the HCO_3^- and dissolved Pco_2:

$$Tco_2 = HCO_3^- + Pco_2 \; (0.03)$$

2. Compensation Although "pure" cases of metabolic or respiratory imbalances occur, it is more common to encounter the situation in which the body is attempting to compensate one imbalance with another (Table 4-1). By obtaining a good history and by knowing the pathophysiology of the disease entity, one can understand which system is affected and which is compensating.

Table 4-1. Compensation in Acid-Base Disturbances

Condition	pH	HCO_3^-	Plasma Pco_2	Compensatory Reaction
Metabolic acidosis	Decrease	Decrease	. . .	Decrease in Pco_2; acid urine
Metabolic alkalosis	Increase	Increase	. . .	Increase in Pco_2; alkaline urine
Respiratory acidosis	Decrease	. . .	Increase	Acid urine
Respiratory alkalosis	Increase	. . .	Decrease	Alkaline urine

a. A 3-week-old infant with pyloric stenosis and vomiting will lose H^+ ion (metabolic alkalosis), and the pH will rise. Compensation occurs as follows. The excess plasma HCO_3^- is converted to Pco_2 (through carbon anhydrase) and is excreted via respiration. Excretion of excess HCO_3^- by the kidney produces an alkaline urine. Concomitantly, the excess Pco_2 in the plasma lowers the pH—*compensated metabolic alkalosis.*

b. On the other hand, if the disease begins with a respiratory problem (e.g., asthma), and the Pco_2 rises (respiratory acidosis), the pH will fall. In order to return the pH to normal, the urine will become acid (excess H^+ loss) and preserve HCO_3^-, which will raise the pH—*compensated respiratory acidosis.* A fully compensated system is therefore one with a normal pH but with an alteration of both base and acid levels.

II. THERAPEUTICS

A. General principles The approach to the patient with a fluid and electrolyte problem includes consideration of:

1. Maintenance requirements, i.e., the amount of *normal* daily needs.

2. Replacement of abnormal losses already sustained.

3. Replacement of continuing extra losses.

4. Rate of administration.

5. Caloric requirement (can be ignored for short-term therapy, i.e., 2–3 days).

6. Acid-base disturbance.

B. Maintenance therapy

1. **The child**   The amount of fluid maintenance requirement (Table 4-2) during a 24-hr period is dependent on fluid losses from skin, lungs, urine, and stools. Fortunately, the kidney can compensate for moderate variations in intake. Nevertheless, guidelines are required to make reasonable estimates of how much is "usual" maintenance.

   There are three bases of estimating 24-hr maintenance fluids, namely, the meter square, caloric, and weight methods. Each has its advantages and disadvantages.

   a. The **meter square method** makes the assumption that 1500–1800 ml of fluid is required daily for each square meter of surface area. The advantage of this method is that one has to be familiar with only *one* set of numbers for *all ages*. It is reasonably accurate, but has the disadvantage of requiring a nomogram to estimate the surface area based on weight and length of the patient.

   b. The **caloric method** assumes that the usual expenditure of water is 150 ml for every 100 calories metabolized (Table 4-3).

   c. The **weight method** uses the patient's weight (in kg) alone to estimate fluid needs. This is less accurate in the patient who weighs more than 10 kg than in lighter-weight patients.

   d. The most important point is to know one method. Our preference for estimating maintenance is to use 100–150 ml/kg in the child weighing 10 kg and the M^2 method for the child who weighs over 10 kg. Table 4-4 shows average losses (and hence maintenance) for a 7-kg and a 70-kg male, using weight and using M^2.

2. **The mature and preterm neonate**   As long as the child is healthy, the ideal mode of therapy is the oral route, with either breast milk

Table 4-2.   Daily Fluid Requirements

Age	ml/kg
1–3 days	60–100
4–10 days	125–150
3 months	140–165
6 months	130–155
9 months	125–145
1–3 years	115–135
4–6 years	90–110
7–9 years	70–90
10–12 years	60–85
13–15 years	50–65
Adult	40–50

Table 4-3.   Calories Expended per 24 Hours During Fasting

Weight (kg)	Calories per kg
3	45–60
3–10	60–80
10–15	45–65
15–25	40–50
25–35	35–40
35–60	30–35
> 60	25–30

From Darrow, D., *Pediatr. Clin. North Am.* 2: 823, 1964.

or artificial formula (20–27 calories/oz; see Table 1-7). The child will invariably regulate his own needs. If the child has significant tachypnea, or is vomiting, or has insufficient oral intake, IV therapy is indicated.

a. Therapy begins with 60 ml/kg for the first 24 hr. This is gradually advanced to a total of 125/150 ml/kg/24 hr for 7–10 days. The usual solution used is 5% D/W or 10% D/W with added $NaHCO_3$ to maintain the pH at the range of 7.20 arterial in the first 24 hr and about 7.3 thereafter. By using this solution, the Na^+ requirements can be met by the addition of $NaHCO_3$ (7.5% solution: 1 ml = 0.9 mEq). In the event there is no acidosis, Na requirements can be met by using 5% D/W and ⅕ normal saline.

b. Because it is often necessary to drip in very small volumes to the neonate, it is advisable to use a continuous infusion pump. This will maintain a steady volume and minimize the possibility of sudden overloading. Obviously, **constant supervision is mandatory.**

c. Remember that the neonate under phototherapy has increased insensible loss.

C. Volume loss

1. During acute loss of fluids it is useful to assume that the total weight loss has been lost as water (1 ml = 1 gm). Thus a loss of 1 kg in weight equals an acute loss of 1000 ml of fluid. Knowledge of

Table 4-4.   Daily Fluid Losses in Males Weighing 7 and 70 Kg

Type of Loss	Average Loss		
	7-kg Male (0.36 M²)	70-kg Male (1.72 M²)	
	ml/kg	ml/kg	ml/M²
Insensible loss	45	22.5	900
Renal loss	40	20.0	800
Loss in stools	10–15	2.5	100
Average totals	95–100	45.0	1800

the exact weight loss in infants is the most accurate way of clinically assessing fluid replacement. One can resort to the method of estimating "percent of weight loss" on the basis of clinical criteria for dehydration as follows:

5% dehydration—mild	10% dehydration—severe
5–10% dehydration—moderate	15% dehydration—shock

2. The principal purpose of initial therapy is to expand the intravascular and subsequently the extracellular volume which is normally isotonic, in order to maintain the fluid in the extracellular volume and allow renal perfusion.

3. If a low osmolar solution is used as replacement and the patient's dehydration is hypotonic (i.e., salt loss is greater than water loss), free water will be distributed between the intravascular and interstitial compartments; an isotonic replacement solution, on the other hand, maintains more of the solution in the intravascular compartment.

4. It is for these reasons that initial replacement for fluid loss is best accomplished with normal saline (or at least ½ normal saline), Ringer's lactate solution, whole blood, plasma, or plasmanate (a commercial "plasma"). As an initial solution, 5% D/W is rarely indicated. Although the 5% D/W solution is isotonic before infusion, once the glucose is metabolized, it is essentially free water.

5. When dealing with a metabolic acidosis, it is best to initiate therapy with Ringer's lactate rather than "normal" saline, which has an excess chloride load. Alternatively, one can use ½ normal saline and added HCO_3-.

D. Therapy of acid-base balance Therapy is aimed at restoring a normal pH. In order to treat imbalance adequately, one must know the Pco_2 and the HCO_3- to assess whether the derangement is respiratory or metabolic and to determine the degree of compensation. If the arterial pH is so low that it is life-threatening, e.g., < 7.0 as in cardiac shock, HCO_3- must be added, even if the primary pathologic condition is respiratory.

1. **Respiratory acidosis** Therapy is directed at *improving ventilation*. A low pH will increase pulmonary resistance, and HCO_3- may be used to improve ventilation. Care must be exercised in adding HCO_3- to the patient with respiratory acidosis, as the HCO_3- can be converted to Pco_2 (through carbonic anhydrase) and add more of an *acid load* by the increase in Pco_2. Thus frequent measurements are essential. The sodium and osmotic load of IV bicarbonate must be taken into account in neonates.

2. **Respiratory alkalosis** Therapy is aimed at the underlying disorder, e.g., anxiety or hypermetabolism. If the patient experiences lightheadedness, irritability, or tetany (due to a fall in ionized $Ca++$), therapy is indicated. A paper bag over the patient's head will cause him to rebreathe CO_2, but the apprehensive child is best handled by sedation.

3. **Metabolic acidosis** The usual therapy is the addition of HCO_3- to raise Tco_2 to a low normal range of 15–18 mEq/L. Further

HCO_3^- is then added slowly as needed. Dosage is calculated by using the formula:

HCO_3 (mEq) = HCO_3 deficit × kg weight × distribution factor **(I.B)**

Besides the addition of HCO_3^-, care must be exercised to add K^+ ion as the acidosis is corrected (see p. 87).

4. **Metabolic alkalosis**   There is rarely a need to add acid per se. Since there is an excess of Cl^- ion in normal saline, it acts like a weak acid, and the extra Cl^- will displace some of the excess HCO_3^-. In the event that the alkalosis is severe, NH_4Cl can be added (75 mg/kg daily in 4 doses, or 2 gm/M^2 daily in 4 doses). NH_4Cl is supplied as a 0.9% or 2.0% IV solution and in 300-mg and 500-mg tablets.

E. **General therapy**   In all three types of dehydration (hypotonic, isotonic, or hypertonic) the aim is to expand first the intravascular and subsequently the extracellular volume (in a long-standing hypertonic state there is also an intracellular depletion with hypertonic dehydration).

1. **Initial measures**

   a. Weigh the patient.

   b. In the first hour, **if shock exists,** or if no urine is produced in ½ hr, give 20–30 ml/kg of 5% albumin *or* whole blood *or* Ringer's lactate *or* normal saline IV.

   c. After the first hour, give 10 ml/kg/hr of 5% albumin or plasma or whole blood or Ringer's lactate until shock is alleviated and actual fluid and electrolyte deficits can be accurately calculated, if needed, and precise replacement therapy planned.

   d. If the patient is asymptomatic and/or dehydration is **hyponatremic** or **isotonic,** ½ total fluids calculated for 24 hr should be administered in the first 8 hr. The remaining half should be administered in the remaining 16 hr.

   e. If **hypertonic** dehydration is present after correcting shock, correct the deficit slowly and evenly over 24–48 hr (see **III.C**).

   f. Temperature will affect the total maintenance; with fever, add 20% of maintenance amount per degree centigrade.

2. **Electrolyte loss**

   a. **Sodium loss** is calculated by the formula:

   (Na) theoretical − (Na) present × kg wt × 0.6
   = (Na) needed in mEq

   Example: Na = 120 mEq/L in an asymptomatic patient who weighs 10 kg.

   (1) The deficit in Na concentration in this patient = 20 mEq/L. Correcting slowly, add 10 mEq/L initially to obtain a serum concentration of 130 mEq/L using the preceding formula as follows:

   $$Na \text{ needed (mEq)} = Na_t - Na_p \times 10 \text{ kg} \times 0.6$$
   $$= (130{-}120) \times 10 \times 0.6$$
   $$Na \text{ needed} = 60 \text{ mEq}$$

   (2) In order to prevent an "overcorrection," it is wise to raise the Na concentration in increments of 10 mEq/L even if the deficit is greater.

(3) The patient's electrolytes are measured after 60 mEq is given and the new deficit is established. If the patient is symptomatic, the solution given and the rate will be more important (see Sec. **III**).

b. Potassium loss   Replace up to 4 mEq/kg daily even though the deficit may be greater. (Only in extreme situations of hypokalemia such as diabetic ketoacidosis should correction be faster.) The normal replacement is 1–2 mEq/kg daily, or 40 mEq/M^2 daily. Delay beginning K+ therapy in anuric patients.

c. Calcium loss   Calcium replacement in the tetanic patient is calcium gluconate 100–200 mg/kg per dose (10% calcium gluconate = approximately 100 mg elemental calcium per milliliter) given slowly over a 5-min period. **(Stop infusion if bradycardia develops.)** Calcium is not given IM or SQ, but maintenance can be given PO at 0.5 gm/kg daily of a solution not greater than 10%.

d. THAM (tris-hydroxymethylaminomethane) is an amino alcohol that is a weak base with buffering capacities. It has the advantage of raising the pH without adding excessive sodium and without adding CO_2. It is available as a 3.6% (⅓ *M*) solution with a pH of 10.2. Since hypoglycemia has been reported with a rapid administration, 5% D/W can be used to prepare the solution. (The osmolality is then raised to that of a 10% D/W solution.)

Infuse over a 3–6 hr interval and give supplementary amounts up to 25 percent of total over 5–10 min. The dose is ml (THAM) = base deficit × kg patient's weight.

III. TREATMENT OF DEHYDRATION   See Tables 4-5, 4-6.

A. Hyponatremic dehydration   Signs of hyponatremia are a result of the rate at which the Na has fallen and of the absolute Na+ concentration. If the Na+ concentration is low because of ionic *and* fluid loss, a clue may be weight loss and signs of dehydration (Table 4-7). If there is water excess and an accompanying dilution of sodium, the patient's weight may be elevated, but he can still show symptoms on the basis of hyponatremia.

Table 4-5.   Therapeutic Plans in Various Types of Dehydration

Symptoms	Turgor of Skin	Cl−	Therapeutic Plan
Hyponatremic: Asymptomatic	Very poor	Decreased	Slow correction of Na loss
Symptomatic: lethargy → coma	Poor or normal	Greatly decreased	Rapid correction: over 1 hr
Isotonic: lethargy	Poor	Yielding	Slow correction: give ½ over 8 hr
Hypernatremic: irritability, convulsions	"Doughy"	Increased	Very slow correction: give fluids over 24–48 hr

Table 4-6. Solutions Available and Concentrations of Component

Solution	Glucose	Na+	K+	Cl−	HCO₃−	Lactate	Ca++	NH₄−
5% D/W	50	—	—	—	—	—	—	—
10% D/W	100	—	—	—	—	—	—	—
20% D/W	200	—	—	—	—	—	—	—
0.85 normal saline	—	145	—	145	—	—	—	—
0.90 normal saline	—	154	—	154	—	—	—	—
3% normal saline	—	513	—	513	—	—	—	—
5% normal saline	—	856	—	856	—	—	—	—
1/6 *M* sodium lactate (1.9%)	—	167	—	—	—	167	—	—
1/6 *M* NH₄Cl (0.9%)	—	—	—	167	—	—	—	167
2% NH₄Cl	—	—	—	374	—	—	—	374
Ringer's lactate	—	130	4	110	—	27	4	—
Ringer's solution	—	147	4	156	—	—	5	—
5% D5W/NS	—	145	—	145	—	—	—	—

Additives:

10% Ca gluconate = 100 mg/ml
7.5% KCl = 1 mEq/ml
K₂PO₄ = 2 mEq/ml
3.75% NaHCO₂ = 0.45 mEq/ml
7.5% NaHCO₃ = 0.90 mEq/ml
THAM 0.3 *M* = 0.3 mEq/ml
Mannitol 25% = 1 gm/4 ml
One tsp salt/L fluid = ~ 120 mEq/L Na and Cl

Table 4-7. Clinical Signs of Dehydration

Severity	Psyche	Thirst	Mucous Membrane	Tears	Anterior Fontanelle	Skin	Urinary Specific Gravity
Mild	Normal	Slight	May be normal	Present	Flat	Normal	Slight change
Moderate	Irritable	Moderate	Dry	+/−	+/−	+/−	Increased
Severe	Hyper-irritable to lethargic	Intense	Parched	Absent	Sunken	Tenting	Greatly increased

In general:

Hyponatremia	Serum Na+
Mild	120–130 mEq/L
Moderate	114–120 mEq/L
Severe	< 114 mEq/L

Symptomatic hyponatremia may be seen with a serum Na+ concentration of 130 mEq/L if the change in concentration has been sudden. Thus the patient's symptoms, if any, must be taken into account to determine the speed of correction of the serum sodium concentration.

1. **Asymptomatic hyponatremia** Therapy requires gradual correction of the sodium deficit (see Sec. **II.E.2.a**) in increments of 10 mEq/L.

   a. **Sample calculation,** for 10-kg child with 10% dehydration and serum Na+ 130 mEq/L:

   (1) Volume deficit $= 10\% \times 10$ kg $= 1.0$ L

   (2) Volume maintenance $= 100$ ml $\times \underline{10\ \text{kg} = 1.0\ \text{L}}$
   $$2.0\ \text{L total}$$

   (3) Na needed $=$ Na deficit $\times 10$ kg $\times 0.6$
   $$= 140 - 130\ \text{mEq} \times 6$$
   $$= 10 \times 6$$
   Deficit $= 60$ mEq Na

   (4) Maintenance Na $= 4$ mEq/kg $\times 10$
   $$= 40\ \text{mEq Na}$$

   Thus: $\dfrac{\text{Total Na need} = 100\ \text{mEq/24 hr}}{\text{Total volume 2.0 L/24 hr}} = \dfrac{50\ \text{mEq Na}}{1.0\ \text{L}}$
   $$= \text{⅓ normal saline}$$

   b. Administer ½ total fluid in first 8 hr and the rest over the remaining 16 hr.

2. **Symptomatic hyponatremia** Regardless of the cause, whether Na+ loss or water excess, therapy is directed at raising the Na concentration as quickly as needed to stop symptoms. A *hypertonic* solution is infused to deliver an average of 8 mEq/kg/hr infused at 10 ± 4 ml/kg/hr.

   Sample calculation, for a patient weighing 10 kg with serum Na concentration of 130 mEq who is irritable and has diminished consciousness:

   $$10\ \text{kg} \times 0.6 \times (10\ \text{mEq deficit}) = 60$$

   (Na deficit is 60 mEq but, by using concentrated replacement solution, less free water is given.)

   3% NaCl $= 513$ Na mEq/L $= .513$ Na mEq/ml ∴ 120 ml needed
   5% NaCl $= 856$ Na mEq/L $= .856$ Na mEq/ml ∴ ~ 70 ml needed

B. **Isotonic dehydration** Since the deficit is due to an isotonic loss, the replacement solution should also be isotonic.

   1. Calculate **initial therapy:**

      20–30 ml/kg/hr Ringer's lactate or normal saline

   2. **Maintenance therapy** 1500–2000 ml/M² daily or 100 ml/kg daily (< 10-kg child).

3. **Deficit**   Replace the % loss of weight with *isotonic* fluid.

4. Calculate the total fluid loss and maintenance and infuse ½ over the first 8 hr and the remainder over the next 16 hr.

C. **Hypernatremic dehydration**   In this type of dehydration there is an initial loss from the extracellular volume (ECV). However, because of an increased osmotic load in the ECV, there is also a loss from the intracellular space.

1. The fluid deficit must be replaced slowly over 24–48 hr, or transient intracellular edema can occur, specifically, cerebral edema (water intoxication) with accompanying seizures.

2. In general, the **more severe** the hypernatremia, the *slower* the correction; similarly, the more dilute the solution being used to correct the deficit, the slower it should be infused.

3. In general, therapy should not be attempted without at least 30 mEq Na+/L in the infusion.

4. **Therapy**

   a. If a patient is in shock, give 10 ml whole blood or 5% albumin (or plasma)/kg.

   b. **First hour**   Ringer's lactate or ⅙ M Na lactate is preferred because the Cl is lower than in normal saline. This solution is used initially to expand the ECV and perfuse the kidneys. Give 20 ml/kg/hr.

   c. Calculate maintenance fluid and deficit fluid. (The deficit in a patient with severe hypernatremia is estimated at 10 percent.[1])

   d. **Solution used**

      (1) 5% D/W ½ normal saline *or*

      (2) 5% D/W ½ Ringer's lactate *or*
          (1 part Ringer's, 2 parts 5% D/W)

      (3) 5% D/W, 2 parts; 1 part ⅙ M Na lactate

---

[1] To calculate *fluid* deficit from sodium concentration:

1. Na present $\times$ ml body H_2O present = Na nl $\times$ body H_2O
2. $Na_p \times$ (kg $\times$ 0.6) p = $Na^2_{nl} \times$ (kg $\times$ 0.6)
3. Present Na = 160   Present weight = 10 kg
    160 $\times$ (10 $\times$ 0.6) = 140 $\times$ ml body H_2O.
6.85 L = normal body H_2O
6.0 L = present body H_2O
.85 L lost

The estimate of a 10 percent loss is close to the actual loss of 850 ml. For convenience, the deficit can be corrected with 1½ times maintenance volume (e.g., 150 ml/kg daily in a 10-kg child) in mild hypernatremia, or twice maintenance for severe hypernatremia, using a 5% D/W ⅕ Ringer's lactate over 24–48 hr.

5 Management of the Newborn

I. EVALUATION OF THE NEWBORN

A. Delivery room Immediate assessment of the newborn infant by the Apgar scoring system should help to identify infants with severe metabolic imbalances. At 1 and 5 min after delivery (the times at which feet and head are both first visible), the infant is to be evaluated for five signs, namely, *heart rate, respiratory effort, muscle tone, reflexes, and irritability and color,* and given a rating of 0, 1, or 2 (as defined in Table 5-1). In the extremely compromised infant, prompt and efficient resuscitation is far more important than his exact Apgar score.

Table 5-1. Apgar Score (Score Infant at 1 and 5 Minutes of Age)

Sign	0	1	2
Heart rate	Absent	Slow, less than 100	100 or over
Respiratory effort	Absent	Weak cry, hypoventilation	Crying lustily
Muscle tone	Flaccid	Some flexion, extremities	Well-flexed
Reflex irritability	No response	Some motion	Cry
Color	Blue, pale	Blue hands and feet	Entirely pink

B. Nursery

1. General

a. Activity General level of activity, movement of extremities

b. Color Cyanosis, jaundice, paleness

c. Measurements Head circumference, crown-heel length, respiratory rate, pulse rate, blood pressure (flush is most accurate), temperature

d. Respirations Rhythm, effort, rate

e. Head Head circumference $= \dfrac{\text{crown-heel length}}{2} + 10$ cm; size of fontanelles, nonfusion of sutures

f. Eyes Cataracts, red reflex; reaction to light; glaucoma; Brushfield spots; palpebral fissures

g. Ears Position: posterior rotation denotes development abnormalities; preauricular sinuses

h. Nose Patent bilaterally

    i. Mouth Size of tongue; size of mandible; cleft lip or palate

    j. Neck Broken clavicles; palpable thyroid; cysts. Pass a feeding tube to the stomach to establish that esophagus is patent

    k. Chest Retraction, auscultation

    l. Heart Point of maximal impulse (PMI); rhythm; murmurs

    m. Abdomen Liver, spleen, and kidneys are palpable in complete examination; umbilical cord: two arteries and one vein

    n. Genitalia

        (1) Male Testes descended or in canal; hypospadias

        (2) Female Vaginal discharge; enlarged clitoris

    o. Extremities Five digits on each extremity; hips; equal gluteal creases; no "click" on abduction of hip

    p. Back Spine in midline; pilonidal sinus; anus patent

    q. Neurologic Sucking; root and tonic neck reflexes; knee jerks; abdominal reflexes; withdrawal from pain; Babinski reflex present; transillumination of skull when indicated; palmar grasp; head-bobbing ability

C. Catheterization of umbilical vessel Although umbilical artery and vein catheters offer easy access to the infant's blood circulation, their placement is to be avoided when possible. The complications of their use include increased incidence of sepsis, thrombosis, and embolization. For the administration of fluids, it is preferable to use scalp vein IVs. However, when frequent arterial blood samples are required, catheterization may be necessary. The basic techniques for catheterization of the umbilical artery and vein are identical.

    1. It is best that two persons participate in the catheterization procedure.

    2. Fill a #5 radiopaque umbilical artery catheter with a dilute heparinized saline solution.

    3. Cut the umbilical cord cleanly 1–2 cm above the abdomen with a scalpel, and expose the vein or artery.

    4. Using a small iris forceps, grasp the opposite sides of the vessel while inserting the catheter into the open vessel. It is best to determine beforehand how far to insert the catheter (Fig. 5-1).

    5. When a good blood return is established, the catheter suture is placed, finishing by placing a purse-string suture around the umbilical cord. The umbilicus can be bandaged and the catheter curled so that no stress is transmitted to the catheter end of the infant's skin.

    6. X-ray films should be taken after placement of all umbilical catheters to determine their position. The tip of an umbilical *artery* catheter should be either in the lower aorta well below the diaphragm or level with T-8 to T-10, while the tip of an umbilical *vein* catheter should be in the inferior vena cava between the hepatic vein and the right atrium.

D. Temperature control Maintenance of a proper body temperature is the major concern in a normal infant's first few days. While the normal

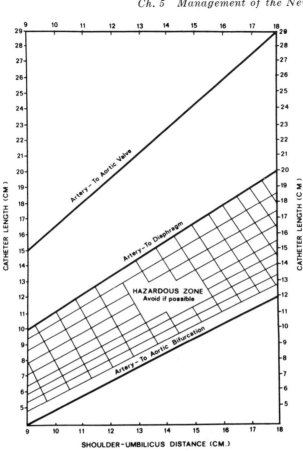

Figure 5-1. Shoulder-umbilicus distance measured from above lateral end of clavicle to umbilicus versus length of catheter needed to reach designated level. (From P. Dunn, *Arch. Dis. Child.* 41:69, 1966, by permission.)

infant can compensate for a limited amount of "thermal stress," environmental temperature extremes can overwhelm his homeostatic system.

1. Normal thermogenesis

    a. The infant's response to the environment is the adjustment of vascular tone near the body surface, an attempt to modify the effective thickness of the insulating subcutaneous tissues. Since the maximum effectiveness of this imperfect insulating layer is small, this mechanism is overwhelmed by environments under 90° F in full-term infants.

    b. The infant produces heat by increasing the metabolism of the subcutaneous **brown** fat. The brown fat can increase its O_2 consumption and its lipolysis.

2. Abnormal body temperature

a. Hyperthermia Aside from high-temperature tissue injury, heating an infant causes two major ill effects.

(1) Increased oxygen needs O_2 requirements double at 2–3° F above normal body temperature. This increase has its most important impact on hypoxic infants.

(2) Apnea Warming produces a high incidence of apneic episodes, especially among premature and compromised infants. It may also lead to cardiac arrest. Automatic apnea monitoring would be prudent. It is *not necessary to rewarm an infant,* but merely to assume responsibility for his thermal needs. He can then regain normal core temperature in several hours.

b. Hypothermia Heat losses may occur by convection of air, contact with a cooler object, evaporation of sweat or amniotic fluid, and radiation. All of these routes, except evaporation, can be reversed to warm the infant. Obvious examples are the heated air of the Isolette, the warm blanket, and the infrared heaters used daily in newborn care.

(1) Possible beneficial effect of hypothermia While several clear-cut detrimental effects of hypothermia in infants are known, neonatologists recognize only one possible beneficial effect, namely, the reduction of metabolism produced by reduced core temperature. This seems *not* to apply to full-term newborns, since brown fat supplies their heat. The ill effects of cooling, plus the great difficulty in properly controlling hypothermia, make it ill advised to "cool the baby a bit."

(2) Detrimental effects of hypothermia

(a) Death Gross survival among premature animals kept at 84° F has been shown to be lower when compared with matched controls at 89° F.

(b) Hypoxia If thermal imbalances are allowed, O_2 needs increase, and hypoxia is exaggerated. Hyperventilation also adds extra evaporative heat loss.

(c) Metabolic acidosis Acidosis is produced in the cold infant by the following:

i. Lactic acid is produced in a generally hypoxic system or in ischemic extremities and skin as a result of strong vasoconstriction.

ii. Nonesterified fatty acids (NEFA) are released as a part of thermogenesis in brown fat.

iii. Ketone bodies are formed from metabolism of lipid in a hypoglycemic infant.

3. Optimum thermal conditions

a. The ideal thermal environment is one in which O_2 and energy demands on the infant are minimal; that is, circumstances in which heat losses and the need for thermogenesis approach zero, and no warmth-induced hypermetabolism exists. In most infants this occurs at an abdominal skin temperature of 96.8°–97.7° F (and a core temperature about a degree higher). Unfortunately, the simple presence of this temperature is *not* evidence of the minimal energy situation; rather it merely indicates that the infant's compensatory temperature-regulating capacity has not been overloaded. He still could be using great excesses of fuel and O_2 or, conversely, could be sweating heavily to lose heat. There is no rapid clinical means of detecting the minimal oxygen consumption point.

b. The recognized conditions for this close-to-optimum situation are: (1) A dry baby, (2) on a surface at body temperature, with adequate foam or fabric insulation from the surface, (3) in air at $90°-93°$ F, (4) positioned near *no* large cold surfaces.

c. Humidity is also important in heat loss; a completely dry atmosphere evaporates more water from the lungs and takes significant amounts of heat with it. Thus the maximum possible inspired humidity is desirable.

4. Thermal conditions in respiratory distress syndrome   See Sec. **IV.A.**

a. For transport, the child with this syndrome should lie tilted slightly up at the head, with a rolled cloth or other soft object behind his shoulders to produce extension of the neck and improve patency of the airway.

b. The incubator will deliver $35-40\%$ O_2 (by mixture with room air) when the lower inlet is supplied with 2–4 L O_2/min. When larger amounts are needed, the upper port or a direct funnel or face hood is used.

c. The amount of O_2 used should just prevent frank cyanosis.

d. When cold O_2 is delivered directly to the face, the facial thermal receptors may stimulate thermogenesis in brown fat and consume much of the added O_2.

II. FACTORS AFFECTING NEONATAL MORBIDITY   Before delivery, a knowledge of the maternal medical and obstetrical histories is essential. Certain prenatal conditions should alert the pediatrician to possible medical problems in the newborn (Table 5-2).

A. Drugs taken by the mother may affect the fetus (Table 5-3).

B. Alterations of in utero O_2 supply   The administration of increased O_2

Table 5-2.   Factors Affecting Neonatal Morbidity

Prenatal Condition	Neonatal Morbidity
Parity primiparous	Increase in congenital malformations as compared to multigravida
Multiple pregnancies	Low birth weight, fetal-fetal transfusion, developmental delay in second-born infant
Increase of reproductive age	Postmature infants, small for gestational age infants, chromosomal abnormalities, (trisomy and Klinefelter's syndrome)
Drug addiction	Withdrawal syndrome, neonatal hepatitis, small for gestational age infants

Table 5-2. (*Continued*)

Prenatal Condition	Neonatal Morbidity
Obstetrical complications	
Premature labor and delivery	Fifty percent mortality in infants born before 30 weeks
Twins	Prematurity, depression of second child
Breech presentation	Depression due to the difficulty in delivery of the aftercoming head, possible bone fractures, transection of cervical spinal cord
"Difficult" delivery	Lacerations and fractures
Transverse presentation	Brachial plexus injury
Placental abnormalities	
Causing dysfunction and/or anorexia	
Infarctions in toxemia	Small for gestational age infants, possible CNS hypoxia
Other problems	
Choreoangioma	Small for gestational age infants, edema, hypoproteinemia
Placenta praevia	Preterm, average for gestational age infants
Placenta abruptio	Increased incidence of asphyxia, hypovolemia, and shock
Single umbilical artery	Congenital malformations
Infections	
a. Genitourinary infection	Neonatal sepsis
b. Premature rupture of the membrane longer than 24 hours	Neonatal sepsis
c. Intrauterine viral infection	Encephalitis, hepatitis, disseminated intravascular coagulopathy
Toxemia	Small for gestational age infants, increased incidence of hyalin membrane disease, increased incidence of hypoglycemia
Diabetes mellitus	Increased incidence of hypoglycemia, increased incidence of hypocalcemia. Organomegaly, large for gestational age infants, ~~HMD~~ ✓
Hyperparathyroidism	Hypocalcemic tetany, increased fractures, bone changes
Hyperthyroidism	Goiter, hyperthyroidism, jaundice, heart failure
Cretinism	Developmental retardation
Malnutrition	Small for gestational age infants
Obesity	Postterm large for gestational age infants
Idiopathic thrombocytopenic purpura	Thrombocytopenia
Neoplastic disease	Congenital malformations may be secondary to drug and/or x-ray therapy
Cyanotic heart disease	Small for gestational age infants

Table 5-3. Drugs Adversely Affecting the Human Fetus[a]

Drugs	Adverse Effect
Analgesics	
Heroin and morphine	Respiratory depression, neonatal death, addiction
Salicylates	Neonatal bleeding, coagulation defects, kernicterus
Anesthetics	
Mepivacaine	Fetal bradycardia, neonatal depression
Antibacterials	
Chloramphenicol	"Gray syndrome" and death
Nitrofurantoin	Hemolysis
Streptomycin	8th nerve damage; hearing loss; multiple skeletal abnormalities
Sulfonamides (long acting)	Hyperbilirubinemia and kernicterus, methemoglobinemia
Tetracyclines	Inhibition of bone growth, discoloration of teeth
Anticoagulants	
Warfarin	Hemorrhage, fetal death
Antithyroid Agents	
Methimazole	Goiter and mental retardation
Potassium iodide	Goiter and mental retardation
Prophylthiouracil	Goiter and mental retardation
Radioactive iodine	Congenital hypothyroidism
Depressants	
Phenobarbital	Neonatal bleeding, increased rate of neonatal drug metabolism
Thalidomide	Phocomelia, hearing defect
Diuretics	
Ammonium chloride	Acidosis
Thiazides (hydrochlorothiazide, chlorothiazide, methyclothiazide)	Thrombocytopenia, neonatal death
Sex Steroids	
Androgens, estrogens, and oral progestogens	Masculinization and labial fusion (early in pregnancy), clitoris enlargement (late in pregnancy)
Miscellaneous	
Vitamin A	Congenital anomalies, cleft palate, eye damage, syndactyly
Vitamin D	Excessive blood calcium, mental retardation
Vitamin K analogues	Hyperbilirubinemia, kernicterus

[a] Adapted from *Drugs Adversely Affecting the Human Fetus*, Ross Laboratories, Cleveland, Ohio.

to mothers in the delivery room decreases the blood flow to the fetus, producing CO_2 retention and acidosis. Interruption of the in utero oxygen supply of the fetus will lead to acidosis and fetal depression.

The fetal heart rate should be carefully monitored. To a qualified observer, abnormal heart rate response to labor contractions, i.e., less than 110 or more than 160 beats/min, and especially the disappearance of the fetal heart rate, is an indication for immediate cesarean section.

C. Diuretics The use of massive amounts of diuretics and subsequent sodium depletion in mothers with increased blood pressure may lead to infants born with markedly decreased serum sodium concentrations.

III. RESUSCITATION

A. A pediatrician should be present in the delivery room for all deliveries in which there is an increased probability that the infant will need resuscitation (e.g., in multiple births, cesarean section, decreased fetal heart rate). It is best if the pediatrician carries his own supplies.

B. Instruments These should include:

1. Umbilical artery catheters, #3 and #5.

2. Infant endotracheal tubes, #10, #12, and #14, 2.5, 3.0, and 3.5 mm internal diameter, preferably the Portex variety, to allow easy suctioning.

3. De Lee traps and catheters.

4. Infant airway.

5. Infant laryngoscope with blades for premature and newborn infants.

6. **Drugs** Levallorphan (Lorfan), naloxone (Narcan), nalorphine (Nalline), epinephrine, 50% D/W, $NaHCO_3$.

7. Needles and syringes.

8. Bulb syringe.

9. Toothed forceps.

10. Mosquito clamp.

11. Micropore surgical tape.

12. Hope Resuscitator. (This can be carried separately.)

C. Procedures

1. The delivery room should be equipped with a modern resuscitator, an *excellent* source of heat, O_2, a stethoscope, and adequate lighting.

2. The infant should be placed in a *warmed* resuscitator in a 15% Trendelenberg position.

3. The infant's nose and oral pharynx should be suctioned with a bulb syringe. In most cases, the suctioning will provide sufficient stimulation to cause the infant to breathe spontaneously.

4. If respirations have not already begun, the introduction of a catheter, 0.5–1.0 cm into the nose, will cause most lightly asphyxiated infants to take a gasp.

5. **Any infant who does not establish spontaneous respirations should be immediately assisted, or acidosis will ensue.**

6. When the upper airway is cleared, positive pressure is applied with a positive pressure mask, which should form a tight seal enclosing the infant's nose and mouth. Care should be taken that the infant's head is not flexed or hyperextended, lest the upper airway be occluded. The mask is applied for 2–3 sec, removed for an equal period, and then reapplied. To be effective, the infant's chest should expand with each inspiration. If meconium has been noted in the amniotic fluid, or especially in the oropharynx, tracheal suction before resuscitation is advised.

D. **Intubation** If the infant does not begin to breathe spontaneously after 30 sec of positive pressure, or if there is no chest expansion, the infant should be intubated.

1. The larynx is visualized, using the laryngoscope held in the left hand, and the airway and trachea cleared, using the De Lee trap and catheter.

2. An endotracheal tube of appropriate size is inserted with the right hand, using the curve of the tube to achieve easy entrance into the trachea (see Table 2-1).

3. Simultaneous auscultation of the chest will usually provide assurance that the tube is placed properly, although transmitted sounds may be misleading in this regard. Certainly, care should be taken that the tube not be inserted so far that the left lung field is bypassed.

4. An O_2 line can be placed in an experienced resuscitator's mouth and, with only the puff pressure generated by the resuscitator's cheeks, the infant's lungs can be inflated q2–3 sec. Alternatively, a Y tube, O_2 line, and pressure blowoff can be used with less danger.

5. The intubation is continued until the infant establishes respirations, or until a respirator can be attached.

E. **Drugs** In certain cases, drugs can be used to overcome the respiratory depression. However, it is usually safer to assist an infant's respiration for 2–10 min than to use drugs that may compromise an already depressed infant if an incorrect diagnosis has been made.

1. **Narcotic antagonists** Levallorphan, 0.05 mg IV; nalorphine, 0.2 mg IV; naloxone, 0.02 mg IV.

2. **Stimulants** Epinephrine 1/1000, 0.1 ml/kg for cardiac stimulation; 50% glucose, 2–3 ml IV in the umbilical *vein*.

3. Levallorphan and nalorphine can cause respiratory depression if narcotics are *not* the original cause of depression. **Therefore, they are to be avoided unless it is certain that depression is due to the narcotics.**

F. **Oxygen** After initial resuscitation or assistance, infants with decreased but spontaneous breathing should inhale O_2-enriched air as needed, usually achieved by placing an O_2 mask near the child's face while the nurses prepare the infant to leave the delivery room.

IV. **RESPIRATORY DISEASES** The most common problem in the nursery is compromise of the infant's respiratory capacity. Frequent causes of neonatal respiratory distress include hypothermia, the respiratory distress syndrome (RDS), aspiration, pneumothorax, and retained fetal lung fluid.

A. **Respiratory distress syndrome (RDS)**

1. **Etiology**

   a. The fetal lung is not fully expanded. The infant's first breath requires the expansion of the partially collapsed alveoli, which then remain expanded in fully developed infants through the action of surface active agents. Some immature infants are deficient in these surface agents, and the more immature, the greater the degree of deficiency; their alveoli do not remain expanded and require increased work for their reexpansion during successive inspirations.

   b. The combination of decreased effective lung surface and increased energy requirements leads to retention of CO_2, decreased Po_2, and respiratory and, finally, metabolic acidosis.

   c. The resultant acidosis increases the pulmonary artery resistance, decreases pulmonary blood flow, and further compromises the blood acid-base status.

2. **Evaluation**

   a. Infants with idiopathic RDS usually experience respiratory difficulties from birth. The acute onset of respiratory difficulty more than several hours after birth requires a search for other causes.

   b. The clinical evaluation of the severity of RDS includes the determination of peripheral cyanosis and evaluation of respiratory effort.

   c. The use of x-rays is imperative in all cases of respiratory difficulty. Clinical signs occasionally precede the x-ray changes.

   d. Besides frequent clinical evaluation, the most important parameters are the *acid-base* and *blood gas status* of the infant. These can be obtained either from umbilical artery catheters or arterialized venous heel stick samples.

3. **Diagnosis** The classic RDS x-ray picture is described as looking like ground glass—a diffuse haziness with an air bronchogram showing in all but the earliest films.

   a. **Mild to moderate RDS** The respiratory rate is less than 100. There is slight intercostal retraction, occasional expiratory grunt, cyanosis responding to increased O_2, and slight hypotonia.

   b. **Severe RDS**

      (1) The respiratory rate is usually greater than 100. There is expiratory grunting and seesaw respirations, and peripheral cyanosis responds poorly to increased expired O_2.

      (2) Severe RDS is associated with an increase in Pco_2, a decrease in Po_2 (in spite of O_2 therapy), and a decrease in pH. A Po_2 greater than 40 mm Hg is necessary to prevent a metabolic acidosis. A Pco_2 of less than 60 will allow for near-normal maintenance of acid-base balance, whereas a pH of

more than 7.25 will not compromise pulmonary blood flow. If the patient's values exceed these limits, appropriate therapy should be instituted.

4. **Therapy** The purpose of therapy for RDS is supportive, that is, it is designed to allow the infant to mature sufficiently to produce surface active agents so that the cycle of CO_2 retention, acidosis, decreased pulmonary blood flow, and decreased oxygen saturation can be broken. In the absence of the need for respirator assistance, all infants will begin to improve after 3 days of age.

   a. The separate physiologic parameters of the RDS can be independently treated (Table 5-4).

Table 5-4. Therapy for Respiratory Distress Syndrome

Condition	Therapy
Decreased Po_2	Adjust ambient O_2 of Isolette to a level sufficient to achieve blood Po_2 of at least 40–50 mm Hg. Values of more than 100 do not represent any significant gain for the infant. If in 100% O_2, a satisfactory Po_2 is not achieved, the infant airway pressure should be increased or the infant should be placed on a respirator
Acidosis	Base is used to correct acidosis. The base may be either TRIS buffer or sodium bicarbonate: a. Range of pH 7.25–7.15: 1 mEq of base per kilogram IV push b. In the range lower than 7.15: 1 mEq/kg/q4h as necessary by drip. Diluent should be 10% D/W
Increased Pco_2	If the Pco_2 exceeds levels of 70–80 mm Hg, the patient should be placed on a respirator

   b. **Respirators** For nursery work, respirators of the small volume (ARP or Boume) type or pressure respirators (Bird or Amsterdam) are available. Because of the small diameter of the infant's airway, high pressures may be achieved without effective ventilation with the pressure respirators.

   (1) A nasotracheal tube is placed under direct visualization of the larynx and taped in place.

   (2) Respirators are equipped with charts and nomograms, but the correct settings are usually obtained by clinical judgment. A tidal volume of approximately 10 ml/kg, a respiratory rate of 30–40 breaths/min, and a pressure of 25 cm H_2O are suggested starting values.

   (3) The oxygen concentration of the inspired air should be adjusted to *obtain a satisfactory blood Po_2.*

   (4) The tidal volume can be increased to help decrease a rising Pco_2, but hyperinflation is to be avoided. A pressure blowoff valve should be present so that the applied pressure to the infant's lung does not exceed 40 mm Hg.

   c. **Continuous positive pressure breathing** The mechanical difficulties associated with the use of respirators in the treatment of idiopathic RDS has led to the introduction of continuous positive pressure breathing (CPPB), which keeps the immature alveoli from collapsing at the end of expiration.

(1) When an infant with clinical signs of RDS is unable to maintain his arterial Po_2 in spite of breathing 100% O_2, he is intubated with an endotracheal tube (see p. 107).

(2) The endotracheal tube is connected to a T piece, the input of which is O_2-enriched air; the output is connected to a second T piece, which in turn is connected to an anesthesia bag with a screw clamp on its open tail and to a pressure gauge and water trap, where the open end of the tubing is placed 30 cm below the water surface. The water trap prevents the delivery of excessive pressure to the infant's lungs.

(3) The O_2 concentration of the inspired air is controlled, and the air is both heated and humidified.

(4) The pressure of the system can be increased to a maximum of 30 cm H_2O by adjusting the screw clamp on the anesthesia bag.

(5) Starting with 100% inspired O_2 and 6 mm Hg pressure, increase the pressure of the system until an arterial Po_2 between 50–70 is achieved.

(6) Then decrease the O_2 concentration until a decrease in the arterial Po_2 is noticed. When the system's O_2 concentration reaches 40%, direct further alterations to decreasing the pressure until the infant can maintain his arterial Po_2 without any increased pressure. Then remove the endotracheal tube and maintain ambient O_2 concentration at a level *higher* than that required with intubation.

(7) Respiratory care during the intubation Instill 0.25–0.5 ml saline into the endotracheal tube; ventilate with the anesthesia bag for 1 min, suctioning one bronchus with a sterile catheter. Ventilate again for 1 min, suctioning the other bronchus. Then repeat ventilation with the bag for 2–3 min afterwards. This procedure should be done every hour, along with percussion and vibration. The tubing connected to the endotracheal tube is changed daily, and *no* prophylactic antibiotics are used.

B. Pneumothorax See Chap. 19, Sec. **VII.**

1. Etiology Pneumothorax is never congenital, although a predisposing cause, such as a cyst, may be present.

2. Evaluation Pneumothorax most commonly occurs in association with aspiration pneumonia and hyalin membrane disease. In the latter instance, when a sudden deterioration in respiratory status occurs, especially when the patient is on a respirator, the diagnosis of pneumothorax is to be considered. Auscultation is not sufficient for diagnosis, since breath sounds from the expanded lung may be easily transmitted because of the small diameter of the infant's chest.

3. Diagnosis A chest x-ray will confirm or rule out the presence of pneumothorax.

4. Therapy

    a. A 23-gauge needle with a three-way stopcock can be inserted in the third interspace at the anterior axillary line if the infant's clinical condition demands immediate intervention.

    b. The air can be removed with a syringe and the stopcock closed until a chest tube is attached.

    c. To speed the resorption of the pneumothorax, 100% O_2 may be administered, but this requires careful monitoring of arterial Po_2 to avoid prolonged hyperoxia.

    d. A life-threatening pneumothorax (usually associated with hyalin membrane disease) should be treated by placement of a chest tube; while a minor pneumothorax (i.e., less than 10 percent collapse of lung volume), associated with aspiration pneumonia, can be watched for spontaneous resorption.

C. Pneumonia in newborn infants can be either noninfectious or infectious.

  1. Noninfectious

    a. Etiology   Aspiration of blood, amniotic fluid, or feces.

    b. Evaluation   Monitoring of respiratory rate; blood gases (arterial); x-ray studies.

    c. Diagnosis   The x-ray picture may vary from only local collapse to complete opacification.

    d. Therapy   These pneumonias do not usually require treatment with antibiotics, and the infant needs only supportive care. Corticosteroids have no proved value in the treatment of aspiration pneumonia.

  2. Infectious   See Chap. 9, Sec. **IV.M.**

    a. Etiology   Premature rupture of the membranes; overt infection in the mother.

    b. Evaluation   Same as in noninfectious pneumonia. The blood count is *not* useful. Cultures of blood, tracheal aspirate, and ear and gastric contents should be made.

    c. Diagnosis   The same as in noninfectious pneumonia. Fever *or* hypothermia may occur, and tachypnea is usually present.

    d. Therapy   Antibiotics: Oxacillin, 100 mg/kg daily in 2 divided doses and gentamicin, 6 mg/kg daily in 2 divided doses, or kanamycin, 15 mg/kg daily in 2 divided doses.

V. HEMOLYTIC DISEASE OF THE NEWBORN

A. Etiology   The lysis of infant red blood cells (RBC) due to sensitization by maternal antibody is the commonest basis of hemolytic disease in the newborn infant. The mother may be sensitized by prior immunization with red cells from an incompatible infant. Sensitization due to Rh incompatibility is the most important cause, followed in frequency by ABO incompatibility, although any blood group can be the basis of sensitization.

1. Sensitization to the Rh antigen usually occurs at the time of delivery of an Rh positive infant to an Rh negative mother. The use of anti-D gamma globulin has almost eliminated Rh sensitization where it is in general use.

2. Hemolytic anti-A and anti-B antibodies are IgG molecules, in contrast to isohemoglutinin antibodies, which are IgM. The anti-A or anti-B hemolytic antibody can be present without a prior pregnancy, and hemolysis due to ABO incompatibility thus can be present in the first pregnancy.

3. The treatment of choice for brisk hemolysis in the newborn is exchange transfusion, during which the sensitized RBC and excess bilirubin are removed to be replaced by fresh compatible blood.

B. Evaluation

1. Patients with siblings who have undergone exchange transfusion, or who have amniocentesis in high Liley zone II or III, or both, should be considered possible candidates for immediate exchange transfusion, possibly in the delivery room.

2. If an infant is born with clinical signs of edema, secondary to hypoproteinemia and congestive heart failure, anemia, hepatosplenomegaly, and jaundice, exchange transfusion should be undertaken immediately, but slowly.

3. If the exchange transfusion is not immediately necessary, serial serum bilirubin determinations should be obtained. If, after plotting the indirect bilirubin values on the graph of Allen and Diamond (Fig. 5-2), it seems probable that the serum indirect bilirubin will exceed 20 mg/100 ml despite phototherapy, exchange transfusion should be done. Otherwise, healthy premature infants, because of their less developed blood-brain barrier, should undergo exchange transfusion at a maximum serum bilirubin level of 15 to 18 mg/100 ml.

C. Diagnosis

1. To establish the diagnosis of hemolytic disease in the newborn, a positive direct Coombs test on the infant's RBC with antibody elutions is necessary. In all but the ABO incompatible group, the results of the Coombs test will usually be strongly positive. In the ABO disease, the Coombs test results may be only weakly positive.

2. Determination of hemoglobin, bilirubin, and reticulocyte counts should be done; hemoglobin of less than 15 gm/100 ml and a reticulocyte count greater than 10 percent indicate moderate to severe hemolytic disease. **Be sure to keep blood samples being sent for bilirubin determinations from long exposure to light,** either artificial or natural, because of photodestruction of the bilirubin.

D. Therapy

1. **Phototherapy** The introduction of phototherapy has decreased the need for almost all exchange transfusions not due to blood incompatibility and reduced the number of repeat exchange transfusions. In phototherapy, the toxic indirect bilirubin is converted to nontoxic compounds.

   a. Commercial phototherapy units are available. They usually consist of a number of fluorescent light bulbs. The distance the

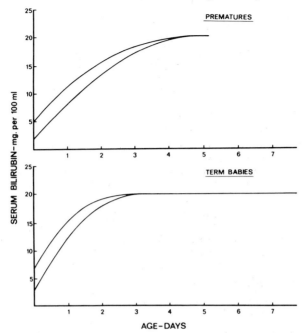

Figure 5-2.   Graph for plotting serum bilirubin values. (From L. K. Diamond, *Pediatrics* 41:1, 1968, by permission.)

       infant is placed from the light should be proportional to the number of lights in the units.

    b. The eyes of all infants undergoing phototherapy should be bandaged to prevent possible retinal damage.

2. Exchange transfusion   It is more efficient to remove sensitized RBC than to allow them to lyse and then remove the resultant bilirubin. Exchange transfusion should thus be done as soon as it is determined to be necessary.

    a. Heparinized or fresh ACD low-titered anti-A and anti-B O negative blood should be used in cases of Rh incompatibility. Blood older than 24 hr will be deficient in platelets.

    b. The patient's umbilical vein is catheterized.

    c. The total volume of the exchange should be twice the blood volume of the infant, the blood volume calculated as 8 percent of the body weight. An **accurate** record of the exchange is necessary.

    d. Depending on the size of the infant, the volume of each exchange removed should be 3 ml for infants weighing less than 1000 gm to 10–20 ml for full-term infants. As a rule of thumb, an exchange transfusion should require not less than 45 min nor more than 90 min for exchange of two blood volumes. Faster exchanges produce vascular instability, and slower exchanges increase the likelihood of sepsis.

    e. The exchange should start with the removal of blood, so that there is always a deficit to avoid cardiac overload.

f. The heart rate should be continuously monitored either by auscultation or preferably by an ECG machine or monitor.

g. If ACD blood is used, the physician should be on the alert for possible hypocalcemia, manifested by apnea, irritability, increased heart rate, and prolongation of the QT interval. Calcium gluconate, 100 mg calcium/ml, can be given *slowly* IV if these signs appear.

h. If heparinized blood is used, protamine sulfate, 1 mg/100 U heparin, should be given at the end of the procedure.

i. Blood samples for hemoglobin and bilirubin determinations should be taken before and after the exchange. If the exchange was for hyperbilirubinemia, within 1–2 hr of the exchange there will be a rebound rise in the serum bilirubin levels.

VI. THE INFANT OF A DIABETIC MOTHER The infant of a diabetic mother has a greater probability of having hypoglycemia, hypocalcemia, electrolyte abnormalities, renal vein thrombosis, and hyperthyroidism than does the infant of a nondiabetic mother. The relation of some of these problems to the maternal disease is not well established.

A. Evaluation and diagnosis

1. Because of increased fat deposits these infants are larger at birth than normal infants of the same gestational age.

2. Infants of diabetic mothers do not have an increased incidence of RDS, as compared with normal infants of the same *gestational* age, but do have an increased incidence compared to normal infants of the same *weight*. The treatment for these infants formerly included caloric deprivation, which produced acidosis, contributing to the RDS.

3. The infants of diabetic mothers have increased blood glucose at birth. Because of high fetal insulin levels, their blood levels rapidly drop within the first hour to levels that can be less than 40 mg/100 ml if no exogenous glucose is given.

B. Therapy The principal therapy is *good control of known maternal diabetes* during pregnancy and careful screening of all other mothers for gestational diabetes.

1. Hypoglycemia As soon as possible after delivery, the infant of a diabetic mother should be started on early glucose feeding, giving 30 ml of 20% D/W q2h 4 times and then progressing to a regular feeding schedule. Dextrostix or chemical blood sugar values should be obtained before the first feeding. (The same precautions should be taken for infants who are small for gestational age and for premature infants.)

2. Respiratory distress syndrome Here the therapy is identical with that for any other infant with RSD (see Sec. **IV.A.4**), except that increased glucose must be added to the IV fluids.

3. Hypocalcemia

a. Clinical hypocalcemia can be manifested by the presence of Chvostek's and Trousseau's signs, general irritability, and tetany. Prolongation of the QT interval is supportive evidence if serum calcium concentrations are not immediately obtainable.

b. An infusion of 10 ml of 10% calcium gluconate solution, i.e., 1 gm calcium $(Ca++)/10$ ml, can be given slowly IV with ECG monitoring. The infusion is stopped when the infant is clinically improved. Afterward, his daily diet may be supplemented by 1–2 gm calcium lactate PO.

4. Hyperbilirubinemia   The increased frequency of hyperbilirubinemia that is occasionally seen in infants of diabetic mothers is probably secondary to dehydration and to fatty liver change. Sufficient nutrition will thus decrease the frequency of hyperbilirubinemia. Phototherapy is necessary if overt jaundice is present.

5. Renal vein thrombosis

a. The presence of hematuria and an abdominal mass on the second to fifth day of life should suggest the possibility of a renal vein thrombosis. The diagnosis is definitively made by renal artery arteriography.

b. Surgical therapy is not indicated. The patients should be conservatively managed with special attention to the fluid and electrolyte problems caused by the compromised renal function. If conditions warrant it, peritoneal dialysis should be instituted to allow time for the renal veins to recannulize (see Chap. 12, Sec. **III.D**).

VII. ANEMIA

A. Anemia at birth   Anemia in the neonatal period may be due to hemorrhage, hemolysis, or decreased red cell production. If anemia is detected during the first 24 hr of life, it is usually due to hemorrhage or hemolysis related to obstetric complications. If the anemia is diagnosed later in the neonatal period, internal hemorrhage, hemolysis due to external agents, or decreased RBC production must be considered.

1. Hemorrhage

a. Evaluation

(1) During labor and delivery, fetal hemorrhage can occur either from rupture of the umbilical cord or placental vessels, placenta abrupta, or obstetric accidents. In most cases the obstetrician will note the hemorrhage. In some, however, the hemorrhage may take the form of a fetal-maternal transfusion, with no overt signs of blood.

(2) Any infant who is in shock at birth, with or without a history of excessive blood loss, is considered to have hemorrhaged.

b. Diagnosis   If no obstetric history of blood loss is documented, the maternal blood should be examined for the presence of fetal RBC (Betke preparation).

c. Therapy   Neonatal hemorrhage should be treated by volume replacement with whole O Rh negative blood, if available, or with plasma expanders.

2. Hemolysis

a. Evaluation   An infant who at birth is in shock and has *pallor* usually has chronic blood loss from repeated placental hemorrhage or in utero hemolysis, commonly due to hemolytic disease of the newborn.

b. Diagnosis The presence of chronic RBC loss or destruction is best documented by an increased number of reticulocytes (greater than 4 percent) in the infant's blood.

c. Therapy This depends on the assessment of the clinical state of the infant. If the degree of blood loss has produced shock or heart failure in an infant, an exchange transfusion with packed RBC should be done (see Sec. **V.D.2**).

B. Anemia in the neonatal period

1. Etiology The hematocrit of infants decreases over the first 10 weeks of life from a birth value of 60 percent to 30 percent at 3 months, when the effective production of new RBC begins. Infants whose hematocrit drops more rapidly should be examined for sources of internal hemorrhage (e.g., Meckel's diverticulum, cephalohematoma), hemolysis, or decreased RBC production.

2. Evaluation and diagnosis The peripheral blood of these infants should be examined for reticulocytes, positive direct Coombs cells, bilirubin levels, and RBC morphology. If the reticulocyte count is decreased in the presence of anemia, decreased production is contributing to the anemia, due to either primary or secondary bone marrow failure.

a. Hemolytic disease of the newborn A positive Coombs test establishes the diagnosis (see Sec. **V**).

An increased serum bilirubin, increased reticulocytes, and abnormal blood smear can establish the diagnosis of spherocytosis, elliptocytosis, and other manifestations of hemolytic disease. A normal blood smear should be followed by determination of the RBC enzymes G-6-PD and pyruvate kinase. (See Chap. 8.)

b. Failure of red blood cell production Premature infants are born with insufficient stores of iron and vitamin E. The peripheral smear may be hypochromic and microcytic in cases of iron deficiency.

3. Therapy

a. For therapy of hemolytic anemia see Sec. **V.D.**

b. Anemia due to iron and vitamin E deficiencies responds well to increased amounts of iron, vitamin E in the diet, or both (ferrous sulfate elixir, 0.6 ml daily, and vitamin E, 25 U daily). If there is no response to iron and vitamin E therapy, bone marrow aspiration should be performed to determine if there is primary bone marrow red cell aplasia.

VIII. THE INFANT OF A DRUG-ADDICTED MOTHER

A. Etiology of the infant's addiction Most of the common addicting drugs cross the placenta so that the fetus is as drug-dependent as the mother. After birth, the infant may undergo withdrawal symptoms. Mothers known to be addicted may be switched to methadone therapy during pregnancy.

B. **Evaluation**   These infants are often of low birth weight and premature. A maternal history is extremely important. In the delivery room, marked respiratory depression may occur, depending on the time when the mother's last drug usage occurred. In most infants who do not have respiratory depression, symptoms of withdrawal will develop within the first 24 hr if they are to occur.

C. **Diagnosis**   The symptoms of withdrawal in the newborn include crying and sleeplessness, tremors, vomiting and diarrhea, yawning and sneezing, fever, and convulsions.

D. **Therapy**

1. **In the delivery room**   For respiratory depression with a positive history of recent drug usage of either methadone or heroin, give naloxone (Narcan), 0.01 mg/kg IV; nalorphine, 0.1 mg/kg IV; or levallorphan, 0.02 mg/kg IV. Repeat q5–10 min if respirations improve.

2. The antagonist's action lasts only 2–3 hr, while methadone depression may last for 48 hr. Repeated doses of the antagonists should thus be given IM as needed.

3. **For withdrawal symptoms,** give **paregoric** (1 ml contains 0.4 mg morphine), 2–4 drops/kg q4h; *or* phenobarbital, 2 mg/kg q6h PO or IM; *or* chlorpromazine, 0.8 mg/kg q6h PO or IM. The duration of therapy is 4–28 days, with the dosages decreased as tolerated.

IX. JAUNDICE

A. **Physiologic jaundice**

1. **Etiology**

   a. The presence of visible jaundice (a total serum bilirubin of greater than 6 mg/100 ml can be seen by most trained observers) is a normal physiologic occurrence in about 20 percent of full-term infants.

   b. The increase in serum bilirubin is almost totally indirect-reacting, due to a deficiency in the amount of glucuronyl transferase, the enzyme necessary for the conversion of the indirect bilirubin to direct-reacting bilirubin.

   c. In a full-term infant, a serum indirect bilirubin of less than 20 mg/100 ml usually carries no increased morbidity, while in a premature infant, the safe level may be as low as 16–18 mg/100 ml, due to a decrease in the integrity of the blood-brain barrier and lack of albumin binding.

   d. Infants whose indirect serum bilirubin exceeds these levels have an increased incidence of kernicterus, with death occurring in almost half of the affected infants. Infants who survive are deaf and have decreased intelligence quotients and neurologic difficulties.

   e. Jaundice occurring before the third day or prolonged more than a week should not be considered physiologic until all other causes have been eliminated.

2. **Diagnosis of kernicterus** Clinically, the symptoms and signs of kernicterus are decreased sucking, vomiting, decreased muscle tone, and muscle lethargy. Once these occur, they cannot be reversed. All infants with jaundice should be thoroughly evaluated with the Coombs test, bilirubin and hemoglobin determinations, a reticulocyte count, and blood cultures and should be carefully watched.

B. **Hyperbilirubinemia in breast feeding**

1. **Etiology** The presence of pregnane-3α, 20β-diol, which is conjugated by the same enzyme as bilirubin, will produce hyperbilirubinemia in some breast-fed infants.

2. **Therapy** If the bilirubin rises near 20 mg/100 ml, breast-feeding should be stopped temporarily and the infant placed on a commercial formula. The mother should be taught to pump her breasts to keep breast milk flowing.

C. **Effect of toxic drugs on bilirubin levels**

1. Any drug that is excreted by the same route as indirect-reacting bilirubin will cause a competitive inhibition of glucuronyl transferase and lead to an increase in the indirect serum bilirubin.

   Vitamin K and its analogue, menadiol sodium diphosphate (Synkayvite), are competitive inhibitors of the enzyme. Vitamin K_1 (phytonadione) is the safest vitamin K analogue to use.

2. Indirect-reacting bilirubin is bound to serum albumin. Any drug that competes with indirect bilirubin for the albumin-combining sites will increase the free indirect-reacting bilirubin, leading to possible toxic damage to the brain at lower total levels of bilirubin.

3. All sulfonamides, as well as some antibiotics, compete with bilirubin for the albumin-combining sites.

D. **Bile duct atresia**

1. **Etiology** Bile duct atresia may be either intrahepatic or extrahepatic, total or partial. Infants with bile duct atresia have prolonged jaundice with varying degrees of indirect- and direct-reacting bilirubin.

2. **Evaluation** The absence of bile in the clay-colored stools, together with a negative rose bengal excretion test, suggests atresia.

3. **Diagnosis** A liver biopsy is necessary to establish definitively whether or not bile canaliculi are present.

4. **Therapy** Surgery is required for those with extrahepatic biliary defects. No totally successful therapy is at present available for those with intrahepatic hypoplasia or aplasia.

X. **FEEDING** See Chap. 1, Sec. **III.A.**

A. **Routine infant feeding**

1. The infant should first be examined to determine whether or not his esophagus is patent to the stomach and his anus perforate.

2. Four hours after birth the normal near-term infant should be first fed with 10% D/W or plain water so that, if he has a tracheoesophageal fistula or other problem, only water will be aspirated.

Medium and large premature infants and those small for their gestational age should be begun on early glucose feedings in a manner similar to that used in infants of diabetic mothers. *Only after an infant has been successfully fed on a clear solution should whole formula feedings be begun.*

3. Commercial formulas contain 30 ml H_2O per 20 or 24 calories (see Table 1-9). This concentration allows the infant to excrete an isotonic urine. Term infants should receive 100–120 calories/kg/24 hr; premature infants or infants small for their gestational age should receive between 120–150 calories/kg/24 hr. Figure 5-3 shows weight loss and gain for the normal low birth weight infant.

4. Some full-term infants may have poorly developed suck reflexes. The use of soft premature nipples may allow these infants to feed more effectively.

5. Infants weighing below 1200 gm, with poor caloric intakes as a primary or secondary problem, can be gavage-fed by a well-trained nursery staff through a nasogastric tube with gravity feeding. **No pressure should ever be applied to the nasogastric tube.** The routine use of gastrostomy for infants with feeding problems is **contraindicated.**

6. The use of intravenous hyperalimentation for infants with prolonged caloric deprivation or primary gastrointestinal problems is a procedure reserved for referral hospitals at present (Filler, R. M., et al., *N. Engl. J. Med.* 281:589, 1969).

B. **Iron** The use of commercial formulas with 12 mg/L of iron is recommended for all infants, regardless of the prenatal status of their mothers. Because ⅓ of the total iron store is obtained during the last trimester, additional oral iron (0.6 ml of ferrous sulfate elixir daily) should be given to premature infants to compensate for the low iron stores for 3–6 months.

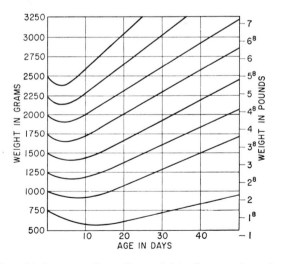

Figure 5-3. A grid for recording the weight of premature infants. (From J. Dancis, J. R. O'Connell, and L. E. Holt, Jr., *J. Pediatr.* 33: 570, 1948, by permission.)

6 Growth and Development

The terms **growth** and **development** are not interchangeable. *Growth* refers to proportionate changes in size, *development* to increase in skill and complexity of function.

I. GROWTH

A. Characteristics of growth Growth is such a conspicuous characteristic of the young of any species that one whose attention is occupied with infants and children may find it easy to take growth for granted.

Observations on growth should be part of every physical examination. Differences in segmental growth rates cause change in the ratio of sitting height to the total height. The sitting height represents about 70 percent of total height at birth, but falls rapidly to about 57 percent at 3 years.

B. Factors influencing growth

1. **Endocrine system**

   a. **Thyroid** Thyroid hormones are important prenatally and during the first year of life, when growth and development are rapid.

   b. **Pituitary** The pituitary growth hormone is essential for normal growth after the second year of life.

   c. **Androgens,** which are produced by the adrenal cortex in both sexes, by the testes in the male, and, to a lesser extent, by the ovaries in the female, can cause the growth spurt at puberty. The androgens stimulate *growth* more than maturation.

2. **Malnutrition** Whether caused by diet or disease, malnutrition retards growth; if sufficiently severe, there may be complete growth arrest. The tendency to grow in length is strong and may continue even when the child is losing weight. When the unfavorable condition is terminated, a sudden spurt of growth usually occurs and may compensate entirely for the growth arrest if its duration has been short.

3. **Illness or privation** Any condition leading to an inadequate caloric intake will lead to growth retardation. This includes any disorder that limits the availability of food, hinders its transport, or interferes with its absorption.

C. Physical measurements Standards for weight, height, width of the hips and circumference of the head and chest in percentiles are listed in any standard pediatric text.

1. **Length** is the measurement of stature taken in the supine position; **height** is the measurement in the erect position.

2. **Hip width** is obtained by obstetric calipers pressed firmly against the most lateral points of the iliac crests.

3. **Head circumference** is obtained by applying a tape over the glabella and supraorbital ridges and the part of the occiput that gives the greatest posterior circumference. Routine measurements of head size should be part of the basic records on infants and young children. This is the age of very rapid growth of the brain, and departures from the normal have both diagnostic and prognostic significance for such problems as microcephaly or hydrocephalus.

D. **Accelerated growth periods** The normal growth of a child is not a uniformly continuous process but has three separate periods of accelerated growth. The velocity of human growth decreases from birth onward, but this decrease is interrupted once and perhaps twice. It is slowed markedly between 6 and 8 years, a period known as the juvenile, or midgrowth, spurt, about which we still have little information, and is entirely reversed from the ages of 13–15, the period known as the adolescent growth spurt and associated with the development of puberty.

E. **Variations in the rate of growth of different tissues** The growth rate of different tissues and body organs varies considerably.

1. **Head** The head is disproportionately large at birth and has attained about 95 percent of its total growth when a child is 8–9 years old.

2. **Lymphatic tissue** The growth of this tissue is remarkable in that the total size of such organs as the thymus reaches its peak in the 5–10-year age group and then gradually regresses. The unique pattern of change exhibited by lymphoid tissue must be kept in mind when assessing tissues such as the tonsils and lymphoid tissue if judged by adult standards. It is likely that what is so often called "hypertrophy" of the tonsils during the preschool and early school years is really a physiologic pattern of growth, since there is an initial spurt in fetal life and in infancy, followed by a long interval of relatively slow growth and then by a second growth spurt in adolescence.

F. **Patterns of growth** Each child grows at his own rate, although all children go through the same stages of growth and development on their way from birth to maturity.

1. **Measurement**

   a. A graphic method of plotting a child's body measurements on standard deviation charts will show how consistently he is maintaining his percentile relationship to other children of his own age and sex.

   b. Repeated measurements of height and weight provide the simplest and still the best index of physical growth. The child should, of course, be assessed not only on his height and weight but also on his rate of growth, relative proportions, and state of maturity in relation to age.

   c. Radiologic examination is often used to determine whether the child's osseous development is delayed or advanced for his age. Dentition will also help to provide confirmatory evidence.

2. **Changes in body proportions**

   a. There is a general cephalocaudal progression of growth at successive age periods. This accounts for the relatively large head and short lower extremities at birth and the progressive changes in these relationships.

b. From the second half of the first year of life to puberty, the extremities grow more rapidly than the trunk, and both more rapidly than the head. At puberty the rates of growth of trunk and extremities are about equal, but the trunk continues to grow after the extremities have ceased their growth in the post-pubescent period.

3. Sex differences in growth At birth and during early childhood, boys are slightly taller and heavier than girls. At about 6 years, girls surpass boys in weight. Boys, maturing about 2 years later on the average than girls, do not catch up in weight until they are a little over 14 years of age. Girls are taller than boys between about 10 and 14 years. Not all measurements follow this pattern. For example, at all ages boys exceed girls in chest circumference, and girls exceed boys in thigh circumference and skeletal maturity. The muscular development of boys exceeds that of girls at all ages.

4. Dentition Individual variation in the date of eruption of the teeth is considerable, although teeth are usually cut in the following order and at the following time.

a. First set of teeth (primary dentition)

(1) Lower central incisors, 5–10 months

(2) Upper central and lateral incisors, 8–12 months

(3) Lower lateral incisors and lower and upper first molars, 12–14 months

(4) Lower and upper canines, 16–22 months

(5) Lower and upper second molars, 24–30 months

b. Second set of teeth (permanent dentition)

(1) First molars, 5 and 7 years

(2) Central incisors, 6½ and 8 years

(3) Lateral incisors, 7 and 9 years

(4) First bicuspids, 9 and 11 years

(5) Second bicuspids, 10 and 12 years

(6) Canines, 10 and 12 years

(7) Cuspids, 11 and 14 years

(8) Second molars, 11 and 13 years

(9) Third molars, 16 and 21 years (or later)

5. Skeletal maturation, or bone age, is a means of classifying the skeletal growth of an individual and should be regarded as a supplement to the general appraisal of the child, just as are measurements of height, weight, and blood pressure.

a. Skeletal maturation is most variable at the onset of ossification.

b. The appearance of primary or secondary centers in the early ages, and the fusion of primary and secondary centers at puberty, determine maturation. The times of onset and completion of various centers, for both sexes, may be found in the tables of maturation and growth in standard textbooks of pediatrics.

6. Growth of the premature infant

a. Weight curves are available for premature infants of varying gestational ages (see Fig. 5-3). The postnatal growth of premature infants resembles the growth pattern of fetuses of the same size rather than that of full-term infants of the same postnatal age.

The most rapid daily weight gain occurs between 2 and 6 months of gestation and levels off to about 20 gm per day thereafter (Table 6-1). Head growth generally exceeds thoracic growth until the fifth month of gestation when their rates of growth become roughly equal.

b. After the first two years of life, differences in height and weight levels between the premature and full-term infants (except for the very smallest premature infants) are not significant.

II. DEVELOPMENT

A. Norms of development All children follow the same pattern of development, although the age at which each development occurs differs within certain limits, even in normal children.

B. Primitive reflexes Many reflexes can be elicited in the newborn, but most are of academic interest only. The reflexes to be discussed are those that may be of clinical importance because they are poorly developed or absent in premature or ill babies, or because they may persist over the age of 3 months, possibly indicating that a neurological abnormality is present.

1. Moro (embrace reflex) reflex This can be elicited, for example, by banging the side of the crib or making some other loud noise. It is best elicited by holding the baby under the back and suddenly allowing the head to drop backward. In *phase 1* the arms and legs are thrown out. In *phase 2* the arms flex as in an embrace.

2. The **grasp reflex** is elicited by the examiner's rubbing his fingers across the baby's palm. The baby grasps the fingers firmly and can be lifted by this means.

3. The **tonic neck reflex** is elicited by turning the baby's head to one side. The baby extends his arm and leg on the same side and flexes on the opposite side.

4. The **walk reflex** is elicited by holding the baby in a standing position. The baby places one foot in front of the other, as though walking.

5. Step reflex If the dorsum of the baby's foot is scraped along the undersurface of a table, he will step up onto the table.

Table 6-1. Average Daily Weight Gain by Birth Weight Groups

Birth Weight (gm)	No. Patients	Age in Months				
		0–2	2–4	4–6	6–8	0–8
1000	4	11.0	19.9	26.5	20.3	19.4
1000–1500	16	10.5	23.5	26.5	19.8	20.1
1500–2000	94	14.5	29.4	25.0	17.2	21.5
2000	49	14.8	30.0	24.7	17.0	21.6
Total	163	14.2	28.6	25.1	17.4	21.3

Adapted from Glaser, K., Parmalee, A. H., and Plattner, E. B. Growth pattern of prematurely born infants. *Pediatrics* 5:130, 1950.

C. Classification of development

1. Motor behavior

    a. Gross Involves the posture and trunk and lower limb movements.

    b. Fine Involves upper limb movements.

2. Vision

3. Hearing and speech

4. Social behavior and play

D. The baby at birth

1. Sleeps most of the time. When awake he is usually crying to be fed. He does not register pleasure.

2. Dislikes looking at light and closes his eyes.

3. Lies immobile. Can flex and extend his legs and arms. When pulled into a sitting position, his head flops back. When lying prone, the infant cannot lift his head from couch.

4. Jaw clonus is usually present, and ankle clonus is occasionally seen.

5. The hands are held clenched, usually with the thumb between the index and middle finger.

E. Importance of development assessment

1. If a **major delay** occurs in all fields of development, this may indicate:

    a. Prematurity—premature baby as (say) 3 months chronological age is not able to perform in the same way as full-term baby of the same age.

    b. Mental retardation.

    c. Cerebral palsy or other neurologic or muscular disorder, e.g., amyotonia congenita.

    d. Severe illness, causing weakness, e.g., gastroenteritis.

    e. Emotional deprivation.

2. If delayed development occurs as **an isolated phenomenon,** it may have resulted from:

    a. Delayed maturation Sometimes, in a particular area (most notably speech, but certainly vision as well), development fails to proceed at the usual rate. Eventually, the child catches up and is completely normal in that area.

    b. Gross motor delay Usually indicates physical disorder; e.g., a dislocated hip prevents the baby from sitting.

    c. Fine motor delay may indicate sensory loss or perhaps blindness.

    d. Delay in vocalizing or speech may indicate deafness.

3. Advanced development

    a. Advanced gross motor development may occur in the black infant and child.

b. Advanced development may occur as an isolated phenomenon. It is of no prognostic significance for future intelligence except in the case of advanced speech development, which may indicate high intelligence.

4. The greatest difficulty in assessment is in the presence of multiple handicaps; e.g., it is hard to assess intelligence in a baby with athetosis and deafness.

F. Predicting height and weight with mnemonics Remember that at 2 years of age the child is about half as tall as he will be at maturity. Remember also that at 3 years the child is 3 ft tall, and at 4 years is 40 in. tall; or at 3½ years the average child weighs 35 lb, and at 7 years weighs 7 times his birth weight. Weech has added several predictive formulas (mnemonics) to those already in use; the values obtained from these formulas (*A.M.A. J. Dis. Child.* 88: 452, 1954) compare reasonably well with published growth charts.

1. Predicted weight from age (3–12 months)

Formula: weight in pounds = age in months + 11

2. Predicted height in inches from age (2–14 years)

Formula: height = (2½ × age) + 30

3. Predicted weight in pounds as function of height (2–12 years)

$$\text{Formula: weight} = 48 + \left(\frac{\text{height}}{2} - 23\right) \times \left(\frac{\text{height}}{10}\right)$$

4. The commonly accepted statement that the child at age 2 has achieved one-half his final height holds up well for boys, but for girls, 10–12 cm (2.54–4 in.) is subtracted from the value obtained. When the length at 3 years is known, an approximation of final height can be obtained by multiplying by 1.87 for boys and 1.73 for girls.

5. Tanner's formula Tanner et al. (*Arch. Dis. Child.* 31: 372, 1956) showed that height at 3 years showed better correlation with height at maturity than it does at any other age.

$$\text{Adult height (cm)} = 1.27 \times H_3 + 54.9 \text{ cm (males)}$$
$$\text{Adult height (cm)} = 1.29 \times H_3 + 42.3 \text{ cm (females)}$$

G. Average level of development from birth to 36 months of age

Age	Accomplishment
Up to 48 weeks:	
0–2 only	When placed in prone position, knees are under abdomen
6	Prone position, legs largely extended
	Ventral suspension (baby held face downward), head in same plane as trunk
	Smiles in response
8	Vocalizes with smile
12	Lying supine, turns head 180° to follow mother or object
	Hands loosely open
	Holds rattle placed in hand for minutes
0–12 only	Grasp reflex; tonic neck reflex

Age	Accomplishment
12–16 only	Hand regard (looks at own hand)
16	Lying prone, takes weight on forearms Turns head to sound Becomes excited at preparation of food
20	When pulled to sitting position, there is no head lag (head may wobble when baby swayed about) Goes for and gets object not placed in hand
24	When lying prone, puts weight on hands and extended arms Rolls from prone to supine Lifts head when pulled to sitting position (no head wobble when swayed)
26	Transfers object from one hand to the other Sits; hands forward for support Chews solid food
28	Lying supine, lifts head up spontaneously Rolls supine to prone Sits 10 sec on solid surface, e.g., floor (must not be tested on bed as mattress gives added support) Standing supported, full weight borne on legs Imitates sounds
36	Stands holding on to playpen Can pick up small object (pellet) with finger and thumb
40	Crawls Can pull up to standing position without help When given small object will approach it with outstretched index finger Waves "bye-bye" Plays simple games, e.g., pat-a-cake
44	Creeps Says one word *with meaning*
48	Cruises (walks around furniture holding on) On request, will give back toy
Up to 36 months:	
12	Says three words *with meaning* Holds out arms or foot to be dressed
0–12 only	Slobbers
13	Walks without support
12–13 only	Casts (throws objects to ground)
15	Can pick up cup, drink, and put it down without help
15–18	Asks mother for potty
18	Dry by day
24	Dry by night Puts on shoes and socks
36	Dresses fully, except for buttoning

7 Psychiatry in Pediatric Practice

The effective application of psychological principles enlarges the pedia-trician's understanding of his work and can be helpful in many aspects of his practice. Education and preventive techniques, as well as support for children and families as they deal with a variety of stresses, are integral aspects of a pediatrician's work. While the usual pediatrician does not practice psychotherapy, much of his work can be psychologically thera-peutic. He also faces the difficult task of determining when and to what extent disturbances in behavior and adjustment should be explored. The extent to which the pediatrician involves himself in these problems is determined by his own interest, knowledge, and skill. However, he should be prepared to offer parents and children the opportunity to discuss with him their concerns in an orderly fashion and provide his assessment.

I. **ETIOLOGY** Knowledge of *child development*, with emphasis on sequential developmental stages (see Table 7-1), provides the best framework for understanding disturbances. From this background, one assesses factors that nurture and support or impede and distort maturation. Disparities between the child's changing *needs*, his growing *capacities*, and the stimu-lation from his *environment* are part of his life experience. Since the child has not reached maturity, the quality, quantity, and reliability of the *nurturing and supportive care* he receives from his parents, family, and others must be understood. Growth and maturation occur when needs are satisfied, capacities supported and enlarged, conflict mastered and inte-grated, and the environment explored, understood, and accepted. Conflict for the child is derived from two sources:

A. **Internal stress** arises when the child's personality structure and capacities deal with his changing biological needs and desires.

B. **External stress** arises when environmental reality confronts the child's needs and his capacity to reconcile them.

II. **EVALUATION** Data include the physician's *previous experiences* with the child and his family; *historical data* derived from past and present con-tacts and enlarged upon as necessary during the assessment; and the physician's own *observations*, past and present, of the child and his family. In considering when and to what extent problems in behavior and de-velopment should be explored, the nature of the problems and the avail-able data provide some guidelines. Parents often request advice about feeding difficulties, bedwetting, or school problems as though these are isolated events in their child's life. *The overt behavioral manifestation is not the problem but only a signal that something is wrong.* The physician should be prepared to evaluate such problems in a more detailed and orderly fashion when appropriate.

A **medical evaluation** is a wise place to begin. Somatic complaints are considered, keeping in mind that they may represent a focal point for a variety of other concerns. Undue attention to physical complaints or medical investigations can disguise important issues and may encourage hypochondriasis. The medical history can provide especially valuable information about births, deaths, illnesses, hospitalizations, or physical handicaps affecting the child or members of his family. Because the physician is frequently involved with families as they deal with stress, he has a unique opportunity to observe and understand constructive methods of coping with adversity as well as with areas of difficulty.

A. Parents The parents should be allowed to express their concerns in their own way. However, it is important to have a structure in mind to organize the data and ensure that important areas are covered. The *physician's attitude* of calm, thoughtful understanding sets the proper tone and will be appreciated by the family. If he is defensive, hurried, or unsure as to how to proceed, the evaluation will not go well. Though parents are usually eager for their physician to listen to their problems, untoward anxiety, defensiveness, or other poorly controlled feelings that interfere with communication and understanding should be dealt with as they arise. Support and reassurance can be helpful but false reassurance, an overly friendly attitude, or excessive sympathy can be disruptive. With experience the physician can assure the parents that their feelings are not unusual and their problems can be understood. Parents may sometimes feel guilty if their child has emotional problems and be fearful of criticism. The physician can cite their coming for help as evidence of their parental concern, defining his role as *working with the parents* to enable them to better understand and help their child. While some parents may invite judgment or criticism, such responses should be avoided.

The **initial discussion** with the parents should be limited to outlining the problems and enlisting the parents' cooperation in discussing them in greater detail on another visit. A formal evaluation should not be attempted without the family's agreement and cooperation. Parents will often appreciate this consideration, utilize the time between appointments to discuss and consider the problem, and use their next appointment time more productively. Resistance on the parents' part to proceeding further should be respected, and the door can be left open for them to return later when they are ready. **Follow-up appointments** are scheduled so that interruptions are avoided and the family can have the physician's full attention. Twenty to thirty minutes is a reasonable length of time, and one should stay within the allotted time and schedule another appointment as necessary.

The mother ordinarily is considered the main source of historical material about her child and usually assumes the major responsibility for his physical care and comfort. However, *it is important that the father be included* since his presence adds to the comprehensive understanding of the family and also involves him in considering his child's problems and participating in making plans to help. If it seems appropriate, the parents may be seen individually in subsequent visits. It is unwise to allow the parents to discuss the child's problem while the child is present as it may cause him distress, shame, guilt, or embarrassment. It is preferable to see the parents for a follow-up visit without the child. Advice, recommendations, referrals, or prescriptions should await completion of the evaluation.

1. History of the child

    a. The **chief complaint** is discussed by the parents in their own way and its history is elaborated. It is important to attend to the parents' exact words, their attitudes, and the degree of their understanding. One mother might angrily say that her child is "stubborn and hateful." Another might say that her child is fine but that "his father and his teacher can't handle him." The reason for seeking help is important to keep in mind as the evaluation proceeds. The duration of the symptom can be especially helpful: "He was always nervous but he seems to be getting worse this year." Circumstances at the onset of the symptom are elicited: "He has seemed upset since my operation." Details about the problem are ascertained: "How often does he wet the bed?" "Has he ever soiled himself in school?" Parents' efforts to deal with the problems should be determined and may include various forms of punishment, shaming, or visits to other physicians, social agencies, or psychiatrists.

    b. The child's **current functioning** is assessed by determining how he deals with the developmental tasks appropriate for his age and family setting (Table 7-1). Fantasies, conflict, and symptomatic behavior are considered within the framework of relevant developmental issues and his ability to deal with them. The emphasis is on overall function, and the child's problems are placed in this perspective. Whatever framework is used should include (*a*) relationships, (*b*) work, (*c*) play, and (*d*) health.

        (1) Relationships with parents, brothers and sisters, friends, teachers, and other adults are assessed: "Does he have a best friend?" "Does he play with children his own age?" "Is he picked on by other children?" "Does he defend himself?" "How does he function in the family?" Observation will tell much here about parent-child relationships and parental attitudes toward the child. Changes in relationships with friends or family can be determined and compared with earlier relationships.

        (2) Work for the child usually includes school performance but also may include responsibilities assigned by his family or social setting. With younger children, one should know if they can dress themselves, bathe themselves, sleep alone, etc. School performance provides valuable data, and school attendance can be a sensitive indicator of difficulties. Frequent or prolonged absence from school may delay academic and social maturation and increase the child's dependency on the family. Earlier school experiences, functioning, and attendance should be determined and compared with present functioning. The age at which the child started school and changes in schools are important.

        (3) Play is an important index of the child's ability to derive pleasure and gratification from life. One asks about the child's interests, sports, and friends, and determines their appropriateness in relation to family, peers, and social setting.

        (4) Physical health and the child's and parents' attitude toward it, are assessed. Acute illness and hospitalization or surgery may

Table 7-1.   Sequential Stages of Development and Behavior

Stage	Relationships	Developmental Tasks	Behavioral Characteristics
Infancy –1 year	Mother or substitutes	Physiologic stability Psychological dependence Attitudes toward self, world Trust, security, optimism	Dependence on mother Urgency of physical needs, e.g., eating, sleeping Responsive to mother's feelings, sensory impressions
Preschool (1–4 years)	Parents or substitutes	Control of gross musculature, bowels, bladder, speech, temper, and behavior Early autonomy Learns meaning of "No"	Physically active Needs frequent limits Temper tantrums, stubborn, messy Separation fears
Nursery school and kindergarten (4–6 years)	Parents and siblings or substitutes	Curiosity, especially about sex differences Play, early social skills Tolerates brief separations Magical thinking	Imitative, imaginative questioning Tries to please Prefers parent of opposite sex Sexual exploration Some separation fears
Grade school (latency) 7–12 years	Family and others, especially of same sex	Learning and mastery in school, play, socialization, physical skills Explores world beyond family Concrete thinking	Friendships, especially with children of same sex Emphasizes rules, fairness Competitive organized play Secrets kept from adults
Junior and senior high school (adolescence) 13–18 years	Family and many others, especially of opposite sex	Sexual development Emancipation from family Concept of self, identity Further learning, mastery, skills Abstract thinking	Erratic, unpredictable, moody Falling in love Competitive, ambivalent, especially with adults Importance of peer groups Transient psychosomatic and psychological distress

result in prolonged concern with the body and cause regressive behavior. Chronic illness or handicaps may be complicated by social, emotional, and educational disability. Concerns about body functions such as appetite, bowel or bladder functions, acne or weight problems are considered, as is overconcern about minor physical complaints such as frequent colds or vague stomachaches.

c. The **developmental history** is elicited, although much of these data may already be available from prior medical contacts. Emotional development is emphasized. Much information can be gathered from such open-ended questions as "What was he like as an infant?" and "How does he compare with his brothers and sisters?"

2. **History of the family** When the child's history has been obtained, the physician inquires into the general functioning of the parents and their background. Some parents may be initially defensive when asked questions about themselves and may wish to continue discussing their child. If this occurs, it should be explained that a general understanding of their functioning and that of other family members is important because of their relationship to their child.

The ability of parents to identify their child's needs and to respond appropriately may be impaired by: (a) other problems or issues in the family, and (b) deficiencies in parenting ability. While these factors are often interrelated, it is best to consider each separately for the purpose of the evaluation. Strengths within the family should also be assessed.

a. **Problems** for families may include a variety of difficulties ranging from financial stress and marital discord to illness or death of one or more members. Issues that may preoccupy the parents but are not considered problems per se include the recent birth of a child, sibling rivalry, the mother's starting to work, or a recent move. Observations made during previous work with the parents may suggest appropriate inquiries. However, each parent should be given a clear opportunity to talk about problems or concerns they may have apart from their child.

b. **Deficiencies** in parenting skills may simply represent a lack of knowledge. However, difficulties in parenting are often acquired in the early upbringing of the parents themselves. General questions about the parents' early background can suggest areas for further elaboration: "What were things like when you were a child?" and "What was your mother like?" One may discover that a mother who herself was too rigidly disciplined is now overindulging her child. One may also discover that one of the parents has had the same symptom their child is now displaying. It is wise to ask mother and father about their past and present relationships with their own parents. They may fail sometimes to see the relevance of maternal grandmother's death last year since their children did not see her often. However, if mother continues to grieve for her own mother, this is of considerable relevance to the child.

c. **Strengths** within the family should be ascertained. The ability of spouses, siblings, and grandparents to support and supplement one another is considered as the evaluation proceeds.

Other sources of information may include school reports, other physicians, social agencies, courts, or other family members. These sources are no substitute for information from the parents, however, and it may be wise as well as time-saving for the physician to ask the parents to collect such outside information for him when possible.

B. Child   Most pediatricians have considerable ability to engage and to enjoy children. The pediatrician's initial approach is that of a friendly adult who wishes to get to know the child. With the patience and composure to wait for children to approach in their own way, the physician is often rewarded with valuable interchanges. This also allows the physician to observe how the child relates to him as well as to others.

The evaluation begins when the child is first seen in the waiting room. His level of functioning is assessed by how he deals with the developmental tasks appropriate for his age and social setting. The question is "How is he doing?" and not "What is he doing wrong?" Special areas of function again include relationships, work, play, and health. Remember that the child is not the person who chooses to come for help and that he may not be able to understand or put his concerns into words.

1. **Preschool child**   Much of the evaluation of the preschool child is done with his parents present, and their ability to separate is assessed. Preliminary discussions of neutral topics and parts of the medical history may take place with parents and child together, while the child plays and becomes accustomed to the physician and office. If unusual behavior is observed, the parents can be asked about it later. Parents and physician should not discuss the child's problems in any detail while the child is present, as it may cause him considerable distress. The physical examination can provide valuable behavioral observations as well as an opportunity for the relationship with the physician to grow. Having the child draw pictures such as Draw-a-Person or Draw-a-Family can be helpful, as can play with simple toys. If a doll house is available in a playroom or waiting room, observations here can be useful. The time-honored question of three magic wishes usually provides valuable data. If the physician chooses to discuss the child's problem with him, it should be done with care and understanding so as not to distress the child unduly. Words such as *worries* or *troubles* can be used. With young children, observation is of more value than questions and answers.

2. **School-age child**   The school-age child should be expected to separate from his mother and to be relatively verbal, especially in areas free from conflict. It is best to begin by inquiring about neutral areas or those of special interest and pleasure to the child: his friends, fun, sports or games, likes and dislikes, and favorite television shows. School functioning, attitudes, and attendance are discussed. These children can usually make comments about family members and relationships, and their views concerning physical health can be discussed. When the child's problem is discussed with him, a special sensitivity to the child's reactions to such a discussion is important in determining how to proceed.

III. **DIAGNOSIS**   Diagnosis is an ongoing consideration of data obtained from historical information and the physician's own observations. It is a working formulation always subject to review as new data accumulate.

When the findings are discussed, it should be kept in mind that the parents have also been thinking about their child during the evaluation if it has proceeded properly. Their conclusions about their child should also be considered. The pediatrician can often use the parents' own words and observations in presenting his findings. It is wise to frame explanations and findings in terms that invite the parents' understanding and agreement.

IV. TREATMENT

A. Preventive techniques

1. **Education** for issues of early infant and child care practices, psychosexual development, somatic concerns, parental attitudes, management, and discipline is part of every pediatrician's practice. Other areas include parental education for such issues as preparation of the child for hospitalization and surgery, genetic counseling, chronic handicapping conditions, adoption, or helping the child to deal with divorce or death of a family member.

2. **Early identification** and intervention with issues of potential difficulty in behavior and development are regularly undertaken. Feeding problems, sleep disturbances, fears, breath-holding, thumbsucking, head-banging, separation problems, enuresis, encopresis, and other somatic concerns are areas where the pediatrician's understanding and counsel are often helpful.

3. **Support in time of crisis** that often involves illness, debility, or death provides a special contribution. The pediatrician can listen to anxieties and misconceptions, provide accurate information, and support constructive methods of coping with adversity. Recuperation from illness is a time when parents and child can often use their physician's support to regain their former adjustment and return to their normal functioning.

B. Comprehensive evaluation

A comprehensive evaluation provides the opportunity for the child and his parents to discuss their problems with the physician and to consider them in an orderly fashion. It provides the best framework for the family and physician should it become appropriate to consider additional help. It can also help the family and physician to provide medical care for a child who is emotionally disturbed. An effective evaluation is a most important therapeutic tool.

C. Parent counseling

Many pediatricians reserve time each week for this work, and patients are generally eager to have more of their physician's time. Most pediatricians have neither the time nor the training for psychotherapy with children but can use their knowledge of children to counsel parents. Empathy with the child underlies an understanding of what life is like for him, especially within his family. However, the pediatrician must be careful not to overidentify with the child to the detriment of work with parents. Such work also requires knowledge of the adult personality with special regard to the function as parents.

1. **Treatment goals** should be determined on the basis of the evaluation. Unrealistic expectations are unfair to both patient and physician. Factors to consider include the degree of psychological disability, the parents' ability to understand the problem and cooperate with the physician, and their motivation to improve the situation. It is important to determine what treatment resources are available in the community and for the physician himself to decide how much he is willing and able to undertake. The aim of treatment is not to change the personality of the child or to satisfy all the family's expectations. Counseling should be an extension of the evaluation process, with the physician collaborating with the parents to see the problems more clearly and to attend to them in a more useful fashion.

2. **The extent of the pediatrician's involvement** should be given careful thought from the beginning. Clear definition of the *length* and *frequency* of interviews is important. A **contract** should be made with the parents for the number of interviews to be undertaken, with an agreement to meet several times or every two weeks for three or four visits and then determine whether further attention is indicated. Such structuring is of great importance, especially with highly troubled families whose needs are great and whose expectations may be unrealistic. Interviews that are unstructured, too long, or held too frequently can encourage dependency, regression, and unrealistic demands and reactions to the physician. A **short-term approach** that focuses on specific issues and can be reinstituted later if necessary is recommended.

3. The **best candidates** for this approach are troubled primarily by misconceptions or lack of knowledge about their child. More-disturbed parents tend to deal with their physician in an unrealistic fashion and to transfer to him exaggerated feelings toward important people in their past. A common example of this phenomenon, called *transference,* is the patient who resents the physician because he has long resented anyone in authority. It is important that the physician recognize transference when it occurs so that his reaction to it can be more appropriate.

   The chief complaint is the point of departure as the physician works with the parents to mobilize their own strengths and resources to improve their function as parents. The primary concern is to define and work on current reality issues. Knowledge gathered from experience with other families is used to support more constructive coping. The physician's active definition of problems, his educational approach, suggestions, support, and encouragement mitigate parents' feelings of hopelessness and failure or overly dependent and regressive behavior.

4. **Restoration of function for the child** is sought and may sometimes obtain despite the persistence of complaints. Every effort is made to restore the child to full activity. *Clearly defined expectations* appropriate to mastery of relevant developmental tasks overcoming symptomatic difficulties are outlined. The child's likes and dislikes and his fears and worries are heard while his active struggle with appropriate expectations is supported. The child's school attendance, school performance, his ability to make friends, to play, and to have fun are usual important areas of function. Other relevant areas may include the ability to separate from parents, physical activities and development of motor skills, bowel or bladder control, control of aggression, and feeding problems.

5. **Problems of the parents** may well relate to difficulties the child is experiencing. If such issues need prolonged attention, the possibility of referring the parents for appropriate help should be discussed with them.

   The pediatrician is the person to whom parents entrust the care of their child's health. He is privy to considerable information about the family and is frequently a person to whom parents and children confide and from whom they seek counsel. He has a special opportunity to use his experience and position to help families with problems of emotional adjustment and development. Attention to this aspect of his work can assist him in determining what he can reasonably undertake and in defining the kind and amount of intervention needed.

V. MEDICATIONS Medications are of well-established therapeutic value in treating emotional problems in adults, but their efficacy in childhood is less clearly established. Parents and schools may sometimes exert pressure on the physician to give medications to a child whose behavior is causing them difficulty. To sedate such children to a more manageable state does not solve the problem and may delay real attention to their difficulties. However, medication can be used as an adjunct to other measures that can produce more long-term benefits.

Hyperactive children with impulsivity, distractibility, and a short attention span may benefit from specific medication. This condition includes children with minimal brain damage as well as with emotional problems. A trial of methylphenidate (Ritalin) is indicated as part of the total management of some patients. Dextroamphetamine sulfate may be tried if methylphenidate is ineffective (see Chap. 14).

Phenobarbital may have a *paradoxical* effect in some children and infants which may lead to increased agitation, hyperactivity, and confusion. **This effect is not always easily ascertained, and increasing dosage or prolonged use can lead to serious difficulty.** Diphenhydramine hydrochloride (Benadryl) has a calming effect but its prolonged use may inhibit learning. Thioridazine (Mellaril) and chlorpromazine (Thorazine) are more potent but also have more side effects. Antidepressants are not effective with children but may be of use with some depressed adolescents.

VI. REFERRAL Referral is discussed with parents in the light of factors considered in the diagnostic assessment and the resources available. A comprehensive assessment may be discouraging for some parents and physicians because of the many factors that can contribute to a child's problems and the absence of some community resources. It should be remembered, however, that improvement in dealing with an important aspect of the problem usually supports a better total adaptation for the child and his family. A comprehensive diagnostic and referral procedure increases opportunities for multilateral approaches to the problems. When **community resources** are considered, it is advisable for the pediatrician to have personal knowledge of the services provided as well as the people who provide them.

In spite of difficulties that are readily apparent to the physician, *a brief contact with the parents is rarely adequate to sustain a referral. Parents should feel that they have had an adequate hearing and have reached some understanding of their problems with their physician.* This mitigates feelings of some patients who see referral as a criticism or rejection. The pediatrician should remember that the family chose to ask him for help with their child and quite likely will have established a relationship of considerable importance to them. Referral elsewhere means the loss of this important relationship; this fact alone accounts for the failure of many referrals. The sustained interest of the physician can often help the family to obtain additional assistance.

When referring a patient to a **psychiatrist,** the physician should not promise more than the psychiatrist can deliver nor attempt to frighten the family by mentioning possible serious consequences if psychiatric help is not obtained. It is preferable to indicate that psychiatrists can be helpful with the kinds of difficulties the family has discussed and that it is worthwhile for the family to meet with the psychiatrist to obtain his opinion.

The pediatrician should also be aware that many of the children and families who consult him prefer to use **somatic** symptoms and concerns or physical explanations to express their psychic conflicts. Such families may have obvious emotional conflicts and even discuss them to some extent with the pediatrician, but they may not understand the implications and their concerns remain focused on somatic issues. Referral of such patients may take considerable preparation and some may persist in their inability to deal with the psychological aspects of their difficulties.

VII. COMMUNITY RESOURCES

A. **Nursery schools and day care centers** can often be used by over-burdened mothers or those wishing to return to work. Such a referral can be a godsend when a mother and her 3- or 4-year-old child are locked into an unhappy relationship at home. Some facilities are able to provide social work services for mothers.

B. **School systems** provide a variety of services. These may include counseling, social work services, psychological testing, individual tutoring, remedial classes for reading and mathematics, special classes for emotionally disturbed or retarded children, speech therapy, and a variety of supervised activities and sports. Individual tutoring can be quite helpful for some children, can provide a useful supportive relationship for the child, and reduce conflict between parent, school, and child.

C. **Visiting nurses and physical therapists** can sometimes help to share with the parents the care and rehabilitation of a chronically ill or physically handicapped child who may also have emotional problems.

D. **Clergymen, lawyers, or legal services** can be helpful, especially when there is a death in the family or when divorce is contemplated or in process.

E. **Supervised group activities** such as scouting, recreational programs, Big Brother and Sister services, and summer camps can be of use. In some areas there are summer camps that specialize in working with diabetic, asthmatic, retarded, or emotionally disturbed children.

F. **Pediatric hospitalization** can relieve family crisis situations relating to emotional problems concerning the care of children with chronic or psychosomatic illnesses as well as undue anxiety about a child's physical health. For certain emotionally disturbed children, the pediatric ward offers opportunities for assistance and observation by nurses, physical therapists, social workers, psychiatrists, and other personnel when parents are unable or reluctant to find help elsewhere.

G. **Institutions and agencies** such as child guidance clinics, drug treatment centers, family service agencies, vocational rehabilitation services, adult psychiatric services and institutions, residential treatment centers, and home-making services can sometimes be helpful.

H. **A clinical psychologist** has special training in the administration and interpretation of psychological tests for evaluating learning problems, mental retardation, brain injury, or psychosis. Many psychologists are also qualified to do psychotherapy with adults and children, and some can provide the same services as a psychiatrist provides.

I. **Social workers** vary considerably in their training and in the kind of work they do. A well-trained, skilled, psychiatric social worker can be of real assistance and some pediatricians are employing them to assist in their practice. The psychiatric social worker can collect complete historical data from the family, assist in providing information about sources of help in the community, coordinate and follow through on referrals, and provide casework services for selected parents; some are also trained to do psychotherapy with children. However, they should not function in lieu of a psychiatrist when one is indicated and is available.

J. **A psychiatrist,** particularly one experienced in pediatric psychiatry, can be used as a *consultant* to the pediatrician. He can be of help with difficult diagnostic problems and may have suggestions regarding management, medications when indicated, and disposition. Collaboration with a psychiatrist is sometimes indicated in managing patients with interlocking physical and emotional problems. Illnesses such as anorexia nervosa and ulcerative colitis may be best managed by the psychiatrist and pediatrician working together. The psychiatrist can also be a source for referral for some parents and children.

VIII. **SUMMARY**   Improvements in medical care plus rising expectations of patients confront the pediatrician increasingly with the emotional concerns and needs of his patients. The etiology of emotional problems is discussed, emphasizing the importance of understanding based on knowledge of child development. An evaluation uses observations of behavior and an orderly collection and assessment of historical data, involving parents in the process. Diagnosis and its use to increase the parents' ability to identify the child's problems, needs, and the factors involved are emphasized. Treatment and preventive approaches, community resources, and the process of making a referral are discussed. A comprehensive approach is presented, with areas for specific intervention outlined.

8 Special Diagnostic Problems

I. HYPOTONIA—THE FLOPPY INFANT Hypotonia as a clinical entity is not rare. One easily remembered anatomic outline of the causes of hypotonia is the following progression from central to peripheral: brain, spinal cord, spinal nerve, myoneuronal junction, muscle (see *Clinics in Developmental Medicine*, No. 31, Spastics International, 1969; *J. Pediatr.* 64: 442, 1964). A few simple questions will help to differentiate the most common causes and provide a functional grouping from which to pursue the diagnosis of the rare causes.

A. Differential features

1. **Is the infant hypotonic?** Hypotonia may be defined as decreased resistance to passive motion.

    a. It may be present when an infant assumes a frog-legged position (except in a newborn of breech presentation). Also, it may be recognized if the muscle is flabby to palpation, there is an increased range of motion, the baby assumes a rag-doll position in ventral suspension, or there is a disproportionate head lag for his age on pulling from supine to sitting position.

    b. To record and follow these movements, a *photograph* in ventral suspension on pulling or sitting, and in the supine position, may be of value.

2. **Is the infant hypotonic, strong, but retarded?**

    a. Central nervous system (CNS) involvement as a cause of hypotonia is usually, *but not always*, accompanied by retardation. To assess retardation, one must ultimately examine fine motor-adaptive or language milestones independently of gross motor skills. Some causes of CNS involvement in hypotonia are listed in Table 8-1, but perhaps the most common are nonspecific mental retardation, perinatal hypoxia, and chromosomal disorders such as Down's syndrome.

    b. Hypotonia in infancy may be the initial manifestation of cerebral palsy; if so, spasticity, ataxia, athetosis, or chorea may develop later in childhood. In this group of infants who are hypotonic but appear strong, the electromyogram is normal and is useful mainly to rule out neuromuscular disorders.

    c. Brisk reflexes are characteristic in this group.

3. **Is the infant hypotonic, weak, but not retarded?** Here, the pathologic condition is in the periphery of the CNS, i.e., in the anterior horn cell, spinal nerves, neuromuscular junction, or muscle. Profound weakness is present if the infant is unable to move his limbs against gravity in the supine position.

Table 8-1.   Causes of Hypotonia

CNS causes

    Nonspecific mental retardation
    Chromosomal abnormalities and syndromes including Down's, Prader-Willi
    Placental insufficiency
    Hypoxia at birth, with respiratory distress, seizures, cardiac arrest, drowning
    Intracranial hemorrhage
    Infections
    Kernicterus
    Hypotonic cerebral palsy
    Metabolic
        Aminoacidopathies
        Mucopolysaccharidoses
        Lipidoses
        Others

Neuropathic causes

    Central
        Todd's postictal paralysis
    Spinal cord
        Acute transverse myelitis
        Epidural abscess
        Trauma to cord, especially in breech delivery
    Anterior horn cell
        Werdnig-Hoffmann spinal muscular atrophy or benign variants
        Acute polyneuritis of Guillain-Barré
        Poliomyelitis
    Peripheral neuropathy
        Congenital idiopathic polyneuropathy
        Diphtheritic polyneuritis
        Tick paralysis
        Poisoning with As, Hg, Tl, Pb
    Myoneural junction
        Myasthenia gravis, either transient, neonatal, or congenital; curare
    Myopathy
        Muscular dystrophy
        Dystrophia myotonica
        Polymyositis
        Mitochondrial abnormalities
        Glycogen storage disease
        Arthrogryposis multiplex congenita, caused by either muscular or neural disease

Other causes

    Benign congenital hypotonia
    Universal hypoplasia of muscle
    Acute illness, fever, dehydration
    Metabolic
        Hypercalcemia
        Renal tubular acidosis
        Rickets
        Celiac disease
        Hypothyroidism

    Congenital heart disease
    Connective tissue disease
        Congenital laxity of ligaments
        Marfan's syndrome
        Ehler-Danlos syndrome
        Osteogenesis imperfecta

B. **Diagnostic techniques**

1. **Biopsy**   In general, a muscle biopsy is useful in differentiating the anterior horn and nerve diseases from the myopathies.

2. **Electroencephalography**   EEG is useful in hypotonia of central origin, primarily epileptiform, toxic, anoxic, and in some space-occupying entities such as porencephalic cyst or chronic subdural effusion.

3. **CPK**   Creatine phosphokinase is the most specific enzyme of muscle but may be abnormal in only a few conditions, such as congenital muscular dystrophy or polymyositis, an acute febrile disease of older children.

4. **A nerve conduction velocity study** can be done on an infant of any size, but the results are abnormal only in peripheral neuropathy or metachromatic leukodystrophy.

5. **Electromyography**   In general, the electromyogram is less useful in children than in adults because small children cannot cooperate voluntarily. It is diagnostic, really, of only one disease, myotonia, a disease usually seen in older children and easily found clinically. The electromyogram can be helpful in confirming neuropathies, where it shows fibrillations, and in anterior horn cell disease, where it reveals fasciculations.

II. **FAILURE TO THRIVE**   *Failure to thrive* is a frequent admitting diagnosis, yet the term is applied to a condition that has many different causes. This ambiguity can be uncomfortable for the physician. In that case, unnecessary tests may be done, time is wasted in uncovering the cause of failure to thrive, and a precise evaluation of the effect of treatment is impossible. The burden falls on the physician to document his impressions with accurate baseline measurements of both developmental and physical variables.

A. **Etiology**   (See Table 8-2.) The following disorders (1–6) are the more common causes of failure to thrive. They require few laboratory tests for diagnosis but may be established by taking measurements of the patient, carefully observing him, and taking a careful history.

1. Observable syndromes, chromosomal abnormalities, and skeletal disorders

2. Intrauterine growth retardation

3. Nutritional deficiency

4. Emotional deprivation

5. CNS disorders

6. Familial short stature, slow maturation, or primordial dwarfism

The rest of the possible differential diagnoses (7–15) includes almost every organ system and require individualized laboratory tests for diagnosis, if indicated after the history and the physical examination.

7. Chronic infection

8. Chronic renal failure, acidosis

9. Congenital heart disease

Table 8-2.   Morphologic Conditions Associated with Failure to Thrive

---

Chromosomal disorders
Down's syndrome, Turner's syndrome, trisomy D or E, cri-du-chat syndrome

Syndromes
Trauma X (or battered child syndrome), hypercalcemia, Cornelia de Lange, Seckel's, Silver's, Bloom's, or Ellis-van Creveld's syndrome, leprechaunism

Others include Smith-Lemli-Opitz syndrome, Menkes' syndrome, ataxia-telangiectasia, Prader-Willi, Fanconi, Hallerman-Streiff, Cockayne's progeria, Rubenstein-Taybi syndromes

Skeletal abnormalities
Achondroplasia, osteogenesis imperfecta, Conradi's rickets, Hunter's, Hurler's, Morquio's diastrophic nanism

Others include cleidocranial dysostosis, metaphyseal dysostosis, cartilage-hair hypoplasia, dyschondrosteosis of Leri, Maroteaux and Lamy pyknodysostosis, Albright's hereditary osteodystrophy

Infections
Congenital rubella

Metabolic disorders
Hypothyroidism, hypopituitarism in the older child, multiglandular syndrome with hypoadrenalism, hypophosphatemia

---

    10. Chronic pulmonary disease

    11. Chronic hepatic disease

    12. Chronic gastrointestinal disease

    13. Endocrine or metabolic disorders

    14. Chronic anemia, congenital or acquired

    15. Immune deficiency disorders

B. Diagnosis

  1. Measurements

    a. Is the patient really failing to thrive?   The answer is found only by taking accurate measurements. Reliability is improved by using methods described in growth and development texts. Parameters include length, skeletal age, weight, head circumference, upper/lower segment ratio, hearing, vision, neurologic findings, gross motor performance, fine motor-adaptive skills, language, and behavior. Many clues to the cause of failure to thrive may be found by carefully comparing the various measurements (see Chap. 6). This is self-evident, but often overlooked.

    b. At what percentile is the patient on a standardized graph?   Length and weight are generally considered abnormal if below the third percentile. *The graph must be standardized for the population to which the individual patient belongs.*

    c. How tall are the parents?   An individual may be expected to achieve the mean parental height. However, he may also follow their slow rate of maturation. For this reason, comparison of height with bone age is necessary.

d. Is the growth failure documented over a satisfactory interval? The yearly weight gain normally decreases after infancy. Growth is intermittent, and a perfectly normal child may have 1 or 2 months with no weight gain. At least a 2-month interval, and preferably a 3-month interval, should be used to evaluate growth. Even then, seasonal variation must be considered.

e. What is the rate of change? Has the patient regressed, fallen below his percentile of expected gain, or is he gaining at a normal rate, although slowly? These are the most important questions to ask, although parental recall of specific milestones is often inaccurate. Measurements from previous clinic visits should be obtained whenever possible.

f. Which specific functions are impaired? Much information can be gained by comparing measurements and skill, and much lost by thinking in terms of an overall D.Q. (development quotient). Evaluation of weight is meaningful only if compared with height. Evaluation of height is meaningful only if compared with bone age and chronologic age.

(1) A bone age more retarded than height suggests hypothyroidism.

(2) A short patient with normal skeletal age probably has impaired growth potential.

(3) A small hand size leads one to suspect CNS involvement.

(4) A lag in all areas of development suggests global CNS involvement.

(5) A disproportionate lag in gross motor skills suggests nutritional, metabolic, muscle, or cord deficit or perhaps neglect in placing the child in a standing position.

(6) Slow fine-motor adaptive development, specifically, is indicative of CNS involvement. The fine motor-adaptive skills develop relatively independently of stimulation, provided vision is intact. They correlate with later I.Q. as well as with the results of the whole developmental examination.

(7) A specific language deficit suggests hearing difficulty, lack of stimulation, or, rarely, a psychiatric disorder.

g. What behavior suggests emotional deprivation? Characteristic behavior includes stereotyped mannerisms, such as rocking, head banging, looking at or waving the hands, and spinning. The patient may fail to prefer the mother as a source of affection, may not cuddle or go to her at all. The mother may not even visit the child in the hospital. The infant may not have learned socially acquired skills such as drinking from a cup or dressing himself. He may have adequate hearing yet not talk. Or in the hospital he may be far more quiet and inactive than a temporary reaction to hospitalization could account for.

h. What are the child's strengths? It may be more important for therapy to determine the patient's areas of strength than to find his weaknesses. Tests of *ability to learn* are of more value than are tests of acquired knowledge.

i. **What are the dynamics of the environment?** The cultural milieu determines to some extent the effect of socioeconomic conditions on the mother. And the mother's interaction with the child is also determined by her problems and the child's individual temperament. Each of these factors bears on the other, and all must be assessed. A standardized home interview and observation of maternal-child interaction is of course far more revealing than hospital observation or a maternal questionnaire alone.

j. **Is the child's withdrawal merely a reaction to hospitalization?** Recovery from a temporary period of inactivity must be considered a therapeutic triumph.

k. **Is catch-up growth present?** A growth spurt may occur in many areas, and sometimes very quickly after hospitalization. Developmental examination findings, as well as weight measurements, should be recorded weekly in the hospital and at regular intervals after discharge. This is especially important in evaluating therapy.

2. **Observation: Can the condition be identified merely by inspection?** See Table 8-2.

3. **History**

a. **Is the birth weight below the 10th percentile for length of gestation?** Patients with intrauterine growth retardation usually continue to be small for their skeletal age. Birth weight should also be compared with that of siblings.

b. **Caloric needs**

   (1) **Is the caloric and protein intake adequate?** A nutritional history and 24-hr diet calculated for calories and protein per kilogram is obtained. This may be more accurate if obtained in the hospital.

   (2) **Does the infant have eating habits suggesting emotional deprivation?** These include eating spoiled foods, inappropriate foods, and garbage, and overeating to the point of vomiting.

   (3) **Is an adequate diet offered but refused?**

   (a) A small intake may be merely the result of decreased growth potential and requirement. One may differentiate this from small intake due to unavailability of food by calculating the calories taken from a free diet in the hospital. This probably should be the first investigation undertaken in the hospital, but it unfortunately is often neglected.

   (b) Anorexia even in infants may be associated with maternal depression, so comparison of the onset with social history is mandatory.

   (c) Patients may be unable to eat because they are preoccupied with other bodily functions, as in diabetes insipidus or dyspnea of chronic pulmonary or congenital cardiac origin.

   (d) There may be a physical problem, such as nasal obstruction, glossoptosis, or cleft palate.

(4) Are adequate calories ingested but lost due to vomiting or regurgitation?

(a) Perhaps the most common cause is maternal feeding difficulty, specifically maternal anxiety, excessive feeding, not burping, or immediately laying the infant down after feeding.

(b) Chalasia is implicated if the condition improves when the baby is supported upright after feeding or when the feedings are thickened.

(c) Neuromuscular incoordination may be the cause. This may be confirmed by barium swallow.

(d) In projectile vomiting, one should of course consider obstruction, especially pyloric stenosis.

(e) Characteristics of rumination include chewing movements of the tongue, pumping the stomach in and out prior to vomiting, and obvious delight after bubbling up the food.

(5) Are ingested calories lost due to malabsorption?   An accurate description of stool number, size, consistency, color, and odor is important. (See Table 8-3 for causes of malabsorption.)

Table 8-3.   Causes of Malabsorption

Common causes	Less frequent causes
Steatorrhea of cystic fibrosis	Hepatic insufficiency
Celiac disease	Biliary atresia
Transient lactase deficiency after gastroenteritis	GI allergy
Chronic diarrhea of infants with anxious mothers	Inflammatory bowel disease
	Megacolon
	Abetalipoproteinemia

Changing formulas is generally fruitless in malabsorption, except for specific sugar intolerance, the most common of which is lactose intolerance, and, rarely, for allergy to milk protein.

(6) Is there any increased caloric need?   This may occur with an enlarged heart in congenital heart disease, spasticity, or hyperthyroidism. Other systemic diseases, such as chronic infection, neoplasm, or conditions associated with fever, may be viewed as causing an increased caloric need.

(7) Are calories being wasted?   Ingested calories cannot be utilized in some metabolic conditions, e.g., diabetes mellitus, glycogen storage disease, hypothyroidism, hypoadrenalism, galactosemia, renal acidosis, and diencephalic syndrome.

c. Emotional factors

(1) Does the infant show symptoms of emotional deprivation?   This diagnosis is not one of exclusion, but has specific findings, as described in **I.g.**

(2) What is the cultural and socioeconomic setting?   The nature of this setting certainly influences the mother.

(3) What is the mother's description of the baby when she first brought him home from the hospital? What kind of baby was he? While most mothers may cry at some time in the first few days after delivery, persistent depression when things are settled at home may be evidence of some pathologic condition. The baby may look abnormal and be rejected by the mother. Other mothers cannot interpret the cues of their children, or understand their needs. This is often seen in mothers whose own childhood was deprived.

(4) Is the child active or passive?

(a) There are individual differences in the infants themselves. Difficult babies are often very active when their diapers are changed, almost falling off the table. They may have irregular sleeping and feeding schedules, cry intensely, and be slow to accept changes in their feeding, bathing, or sleeping environment. Others are passive, and demand little attention.

(b) If the mother does not understand her child's activity, she may either become angry or ignore him. If positive signs of maternal deprivation are present, such a diagnosis should be pursued. It is not wise to blindly order expensive tests that require fasting and impair the patient's rehabilitation or to diagnose maternal deprivation without considering all the possibilities and specifically the nutritional aspect of neglect.

(c) Is the infant retarded, or does he have CNS damage? Here, a history of bleeding, toxemia, placental insufficiency, or infection is relevant, as are difficulties at delivery, such as prolonged labor, cephalopelvic disproportion, meconium staining or other evidence of fetal distress, or need for resuscitation. Neonatal conditions such as cyanosis, jaundice, infection, seizures, hemoconcentration, or vomiting may point to the etiology. Retardation in the fine motor-adaptive areas is significant.

(d) Are the parents small, or were they late to mature?

4. **Physical examination and initial laboratory tests** The common causes may have been determined by observation and history alone. If so, only a few basic tests are needed: CBC, urinalysis, chest and wrist roentgenograms for bone age, stool examination, electrolytes, BUN, calcium, phosphorus. After gathering information from the physical examination and initial laboratory data, one may pursue other diagnoses with appropriate tests.

C. **What can the physician do for the child?**

1. Measuring the child's intake when a free diet is offered in the hospital is perhaps the most productive test. This is an initial step in restoring nutrition, which should come before any tests requiring fasting that might worsen the child's condition. At times IV feeding may be needed.

2. Regular assessment is necessary after discharge. Each area must be reviewed: cultural, socioeconomic, and both the mother's and the child's behavior. Quantitative data should be recorded, rather than merely noting "Doing well" on a return visit chart. With the large

number of variables encountered, the mechanisms of recovery can be understood only by careful attention to individual case studies.

III. THE CHILD WITH RECURRENT INFECTIONS

A. **Evaluation**   "He gets sick all the time. Something must be wrong." This is one of the most common complaints that parents make to the physician caring for their child. In evaluating such a child, taking a careful history and performing a thorough physical examination are essential and should be done before the child receives an extensive series of tests or, even worse, regular injections of gamma globulin.

1. **History**   This should include the age of onset of the first infection and the clinical characteristics, severity, localization, and complications of the succeeding illnesses. It is important to obtain as much objective data as possible: the temperature level, duration of hospitalization, and visible evidence of local infection such as joint swelling and draining ears. The object is to determine in retrospect whether or not the child has had more infections than usual for a child of his age, more severe infections than one would expect, or repetitive infections in one site, suggesting an anatomic or physiologic abnormality (e.g., a foreign body or congenital stenosis of a bronchus).

2. **Family history**   If carefully taken, this may indicate whether or not the pattern of infections in the child is similar to that of his parents as children, or whether evidence suggests autosomal or X-linked inheritance of unusual susceptibility to infection.

3. **Physical examination**

   a. The state of the skin, ears, respiratory tract, and lymphoid system should be assessed.

   b. It should be determined whether the recurrent infections have produced impaired hearing, structural changes in the joints or lungs, or neurologic damage.

   c. Since the lymphoid system is the immunologic system of the body, the size and appearance of the tonsils, the extent and distribution of lymphadenopathy, and the presence or absence of a palpable spleen are important signs of the child's response to his infections.

B. **Factors in recurrent infections**   The rationale for such a careful evaluation of the child is apparent when examining the factors that may lead to the complaint of frequent recurrent infections.

1. **Parental expectation factors**   A certain number of infections are normal in all growing children; an estimated 100 infections occur in the average child before the age of 10. Every child must acquire sufficient immunity to a large number of viral, bacterial, and fungal infections to maintain reasonably good health during adult life. However, parents' emotional responses to their children's illnesses vary greatly. The physician must determine whether the frequency or severity of infections has been unusual and how realistic are the parents' fears about their child's health. Here, the family physician who has observed the child since birth has an enormous advantage over the consultant.

2. **Environmental factors**   The degree of exposure to infection depends on the frequency of close contacts with preschool and school-age

children and particularly on crowded situations at home, especially in the sleeping quarters. Such physical factors as temperature, and particularly humidity, may also affect the respiratory mucosa.

3. Host factors

a. Developmental changes are important. The infant is born with all the antibodies that are in his mother's blood. These usually confer passive protection against most common bacterial infections for a period of 4–6 weeks and against some viral infections (e.g., poliomyelitis, measles) for as long as 8 months. As these passively acquired antibodies gradually disappear from his blood, the infant becomes increasingly susceptible to infection.

b. Anatomic changes also play a role. In the infant the eustachian tube is shorter and more horizontal than in the older child; the laryngeal airway is smaller in relation to tracheal diameter; and the tonsils, adenoids, and their satellite lymph nodes are growing rapidly. Experimental evidence suggests that the blood-brain barrier is more permeable in early life. These developmental anatomic changes undoubtedly play a role in the greater incidence of otitis media, croup, and meningitis in infancy.

c. Physiologic factors may influence the severity and character of respiratory infections. The child with allergy, with his edematous mucosa and tendency to bronchospasm, and the child with cystic fibrosis, whose viscid mucous secretions obstruct the bronchi and interfere with normal ciliary action, are both prone to severe respiratory infections. There is also some evidence that psychologic and physical stress may play a significant role in increasing vulnerability to infection.

d. Immunologic defenses The immunologic system responds to infection in two major ways: by the acquisition of specific delayed hypersensitivity and by the formation of specific antibodies. The intensity of each response varies with different infections.

(1) Delayed hypersensitivity is mediated by sensitized small lymphocytes, so-called T, or thymus-dependent, lymphocytes, which are long-lived and are found in the circulation, subcortical zones of the lymph nodes, and periarterial sheaths to the spleen.

(2) The formation of antibodies depends on another group of lymphoid cells, so-called B lymphocytes, which arise from the lymphoid follicles of the cortex of the lymph nodes, spleen, and gastrointestinal tract and assume the morphology of plasma cells as they develop into antibody-forming cells on antigenic stimulation.

(3) The thymus is necessary, at least in early life, for the development of functionally competent T lymphocytes from the stem cells from which both groups of lymphoid cells originate.

(4) Delayed hypersensitivity (cellular immunity) enhances the intensity of tissue responses to bacteria (e.g., tuberculosis) and seems to mediate immunity to most viruses and fungi, as well as to protect the body against foreign tissue grafts and certain tumors.

(5) Antibodies are essential for immunity to infection by pyogenic bacteria and usually act with complement to promote phagocytosis and intracellular killing of these organisms.

C. Immunologic deficiency diseases (see also Chap. 20, Sec. II). Careful study of children with recurrent or unusually severe infections has uncovered a series of conditions due to defective functioning of the host's defenses. Since all these conditions are potentially disabling and often life-threatening and require prolonged or dangerous specific treatment, the general physician's role should be to suspect such conditions and refer suspect patients to a large medical center for definitive diagnosis and delineation of appropriate treatment.

Each of the wide variety of immunologic deficiency diseases depends for its clinical manifestations on a quantitative deficiency or a qualitative functional disturbance of these immunologically important cells or organs: the granulocyte, spleen, thymus, immunologic stem cells or their progeny, T, or thymus-dependent, lymphocytes, memory cells, and B lymphocytes, which are the precursors of the plasma cells in which antibodies are formed.

1. Recurrent infections in early infancy

a. Congenital thymic agenesis (Di George's syndrome, pharyngeal pouch syndrome) When a congenital malformation affects the third and fourth pharyngeal pouches, from which the thymus and parathyroids are derived in the embryo, the result is a syndrome characterized by hypoparathyroidism, manifested as neonatal tetany, frequent malformations of the mouth, ears, and great vessels, and a tendency to recurrent infections developing in the early months of life.

(1) The infections may be viral, fungal (thrush), or bacterial.

(2) The lymph nodes show normal cortical follicles with plasma cells, but lack the subcortical layer of T lymphocytes.

(3) Antibody formation and immunoglobulins are normal, but there is little response of circulating lymphocytes to phytohemagglutinin stimulation. This is a pure deficiency of cellular immunity due to the lack of a thymus (see Chap. 20, Sec. **II.B.2.d**).

b. Severe combined immunodeficiency (Swiss agammaglobulinemia or alymphocytosis) is the most severe type of immunologic deficiency. It is characterized by complete absence of both cellular immunity and the capacity to form antibodies, although instances have been described in which one or more of the immunoglobulins have been present in the blood.

(1) Pathologically, the thymus consists of a small epithelial structure lacking either small lymphocytes or Hassall's corpuscles; the lymph nodes lack follicles, subcortical T lymphocytes, or plasma cells.

(2) Clinically, stubborn candidiasis, cough with pneumonitis, chronic diarrhea, and runting from the age of a few months develop in these children.

(3) *Absence of clearly defined tonsils, tiny lymph nodes, an absolute lymphocyte count of less than 1500/cu mm, thrush, and failure to thrive should suggest the diagnosis.*

(4) Family history may be helpful. The disease may be inherited either as an autosomal (either sex) or X-linked (boys only) recessive and is invariably fatal by the age of 2 years.

(5) Definitive diagnosis is made by histologic examination of lymph nodes, the lack of immunoglobulins on immunoelectrophoresis (exceptions exist), and failure of the lymphocytes to respond to stimulation with phytohemagglutinin.

(6) Chickenpox and vaccinia are fatal in these children.

2. Recurrent infections in late infancy

a. Recurrent pyogenic bacterial infection This syndrome (pyoderma, purulent conjunctivitis, pharyngitis, otitis media, pneumonia, septic arthritis, meningitis) generally is a manifestation of the *antibody deficiency syndrome*, i.e., inability to synthesize immunoglobulins in response to infection. The common pathologic substratum of this condition is a lack of plasma cells associated with a deficiency of circulating immunoglobulins, especially γG. If cellular immunity is normal, as it usually is, the response to *viral* and *fungal* infections is normal. A number of conditions manifest the antibody deficiency syndrome.

(1) Transient hypogammaglobulinemia In this condition, maturation of immunoglobulin synthesis is delayed. The level of gamma globulins, which usually falls only to 300–500 mg/100 ml before starting to rise in the second or third month of life, continues to decline. In such infants, recurrent attacks of fever (often with wheezing) responsive to antibiotics are common. Diagnosis is made by immunoelectrophoresis, which shows absent γM and γA and low γG. (For therapy, see Chap. 20, Sec. **II.A.3.**)

(2) Congenital X-linked agammaglobulinemia, the most common of the immunologic deficiencies, is confined to males, inherited through the female who is normal, and characterized by the absence of follicles or plasma cells in the lymph nodes. This condition should be suspected in any boy with a history of unusually severe or frequent infections or whose presenting complaint is a swollen joint. Small, smooth tonsils and absence of an adenoid shadow on a lateral pharyngeal x-ray are confirmatory signs. Lymph nodes swell in response to local infection, but are histologically abnormal. Diagnosis is made by immunoelectrophoresis, which shows γM, γA, and γG to be missing by 9 months of age. (For therapy, see Chap. 20, Sec. **II.C.3.**)

(3) Congenital dysgammaglobulinemia Patients have been observed with symptoms similar to X-linked agammaglobulinemia but with one or more of the immunoglobulin classes present, sometimes even in increased amounts. The most common form is characterized by increased γM, with absent or low γA and γG. In such cases, tonsils, lymph nodes, or spleen may be enlarged and may contain many plasmacytoid cells secreting γM globulin.

(4) Partial γG globulin deficiency should be suspected in patients of either sex with a history of recurrent pyogenic infections, but without marked quantitative deficiency of globulin. The normal person has γG globulins of four different subclasses (γG$_1$, γG$_2$, γG$_3$, γG$_4$). One or more of these may be absent, indicating an inability to respond to certain specific antigenic groupings and thus to a particular type of infection.

There is also a syndrome identical to that of antibody deficiency, in which the only immunologic defect is the absence of the third component of complement involved in phagocytosis.

b. Wiskott-Aldrich syndrome   This rare X-linked recessive disease is characterized by eczema, recurrent infections (particularly otitis media), thrombocytopenic purpura, absence of isohemagglutinins, and low γM globulins.

c. Recurrent infections with hypergammaglobulinemia   Defects in the body's defenses that permit chronic recurrent infections in an otherwise normal person can result in lymphadenopathy, hepatosplenomegaly, and hypergammaglobulinemia. Two such conditions are

   (1) Congenital agranulocytosis, in which circulating granulocytes are virtually absent.

   (2) Chronic granulomatous disease, a hereditary disease that is more common in males and in which the number of white blood cells and phagocytosis are normal. The cells, however, are unable to kill certain types of organisms after ingestion.

d. Overwhelming sepsis and meningitis   The spleen has been shown to play the key role in clearing bacteria from the blood in the nonimmune host, just as the liver does, once immunity is established. Thus, absence of the spleen during the first few years of life, when lack of immunity, bacteremia, and meningitis are most common, poses a grave threat to survival. Absence of the spleen occurs with certain rare congenital cardiac malformations. Splenic hypoplasia has been described in two families. The younger the child, the more serious is the risk involved in splenectomy.

e. Immunologic amnesia   One of the striking characteristics of the immune individual is his capacity for a rapid and enhanced immunologic response on reexposure due to the presence of "instructed" lymphocytes or "memory cells" in the body. The term *immunologic amnesia* has been used to describe a condition in children, often in the same family, in which reexposure produces a primary rather than a secondary response due to destruction of the memory cells by an autoantibody against their own lymphocytes. Although the production of immunocompetent lymphocytes continues, infections result in an increase in this lymphocytotoxic substance and a consequent fall in the count of circulating lymphocytes.

3. Infections in late childhood

a. Common variable hypogammaglobulinemia   This condition may develop in patients of either sex at any age. It is characterized by recurrent pyogenic infections, principally sinusitis and pneumonia, sometimes by spruelike symptoms, and by the absence of γM and γA and low γG globulins. Plasma cells are scarce. The lymph nodes may show necrobiosis and atrophy; in some instances, the nodes and spleen are enlarged due to hyperplasia of the reticulum cells.

   (1) The antibody deficiency syndrome, with recurrent pneumonia and sepsis, also may occur as a *secondary* phenomenon in multiple myeloma and in certain lymphomatous tumors in which cellular immunity and antibody formation are depressed either by replacement of functionally normal tissue by tumor cells or by cytotoxic drugs used for chemotherapy of the disease. Similarly, using immunosuppressive therapy (cytotoxic drugs and antilymphocytic serum) in connection with transplantation greatly enhances the risk of infection.

    (2) **Secondary hypogammaglobulinemia** may occur with the nephrotic syndrome because of urinary loss and increased catabolism, resulting in enhanced susceptibility to bacterial infections.

  b. Acquired dysgammaglobulinemia Dysgammaglobulinemia may also occur as an acquired condition, with frequent infections and a disproportion of the immunoglobulins.

  c. Ataxia-telangiectasia In this hereditary disease, ataxia and telangiectasia develop in childhood and are followed by increased susceptibility to infection, usually manifested as sinusitis, bronchitis, and pneumonia. The immunologic defect is not completely clear, but deficiency of γA and γE globulin, lack of local antibody, and a depression of cellular immunity are thought to play a role.

IV. CYANOSIS

A. Physiologic features

  1. Clinical cyanosis is dependent on the absolute concentration of reduced hemoglobin in the blood rather than on the O_2 saturation or partial pressure of O_2 or CO_2. The threshold for visible cyanosis in the skin and mucosa is 4–5 gm/100 ml of reduced hemoglobin. This is of practical importance in that a patient with less than 5 gm/100 ml of total hemoglobin cannot be cyanotic, and a person with polycythemia can exhibit cyanosis with only a small fraction of his total hemoglobin unsaturated.

  2. The first step in the approach to a patient with cyanosis is to determine whether the cyanosis is central or peripheral in origin. The following outline lists the most important considerations in diagnosing central or peripheral cyanosis.

  a. Central cyanosis results from inadequate oxygenation of systemic arterial blood due to an abnormality in cardiac, respiratory, or hematologic mechanisms.

    (1) **Cardiac cyanosis** in congenital heart disease results from an abnormal communication between the right and left side of the heart that permits venous blood to enter the systemic arterial circulation without passing through the lungs.

      (a) Congenital heart disease with a right to left shunt and *decreased* pulmonary blood flow.

      (b) Congenital heart disease with a right to left shunt and *increased* pulmonary blood flow.

      (c) Congenital heart disease with *decreased alveolar ventilation* secondary to congestive heart failure.

      (d) Shock Although there are myriad causes of shock, the common factors resulting in shock are hypovolemia, failure of cardiac output, and a decrease in peripheral resistance (see Chap. 2, Sec. II).

(2) Pulmonary

(a) Primary lung disease, resulting in inequalities of ventilation and perfusion or impairment in the process of diffusion.

(b) Primary pulmonary hypertension, leading to right heart failure and decreased cardiac output.

(c) Mechanical interference with lung function

i. A CNS abnormality resulting in decreased pulmonary ventilation or apnea.

ii. Neuromuscular disorders.

iii. Anatomic problems such as choanal atresia, stenosis, or tracheoesophageal fistula.

(d) In addition to structural abnormalities, keep in mind various drugs such as morphine and valium overdose which can severely decrease respirations.

(3) Hematologic   Cyanosis can be due to abnormal forms of hemoglobin.

(a) Familial methemoglobinemia may occur as a recessive form, due to an abnormality of red blood cell enzyme systems, or as a dominant form associated with the presence of hemoglobin M. The methemoglobin molecules are incapable of carrying O_2 and thus the patient is rendered functionally anemic, with truly unsaturated blood, in that a certain fraction of his red blood cells becomes useless for O_2 transport.

(b) Acquired methemoglobinemia results when the formation of methemoglobin exceeds the rate of reduction because of the action of certain chemical agents, most often nitrates, sulfonamides, and aniline derivatives.

b. Peripheral cyanosis   In this type of cyanosis the cardiac, respiratory, and hematologic systems are functioning normally, and the blood delivered to the tissues is fully saturated. However, the peripheral circulation is sluggish, leading to a wide A-Vo$_2$ difference and capillary hemoglobin reduced more than 4–6 gm/100 ml. Peripheral cyanosis most commonly results from:

(1) Vasomotor instability, common in the neonate

(2) Cold environment

(3) Local venous obstruction

(4) Polycythemia with peripheral sludging of blood

B. Clinical Approach

1. History   The approach to the patient with cyanosis starts with a careful history, keeping in mind the foregoing diagnostic categories. Obviously, a previous history of congenital heart disease is pertinent, but specific questions about the duration of the cyanosis, familial disorders, ingestion of nitrates, use of aniline dyes, and specifics about drug intake are important.

2. Physical examination

a. Observe the patient carefully before touching him. Note the color distribution, because if cyanosis is peripheral, or due to reduced flow, it will usually be more pronounced in the *peripheral* tissues and less pronounced or even absent in such central areas as the oral mucous membranes and the conjunctiva.

b. If cyanosis is present when the patient and his tissues are warm, it is more likely to be of central origin and not the result of reduced flow.

c. Carefully record the blood pressure and pulse rate. Note the respiratory pattern, including respiratory frequency, depth, presence of retractions, grunting, and alar flaring.

d. Differential cyanosis, or unusual body distribution of cyanosis, is usually indicative of serious congenital heart disease.

    (1) With massive pulmonary-aortic shunting through the ductus arteriosus, the upper part of the body will be pinker than the cyanotic lower part, with the line of demarcation usually just below the umbilicus.

    (2) The contrasting situation of pink lower extremities and a cyanotic upper body is pathognomonic of complete transposition of the great vessels with interrupted aortic arch, an indication for urgent surgical intervention.

e. The coexistence of clubbing of the extremities usually indicates that cyanosis is due to long-standing arterial unsaturation.

3. Laboratory studies

The impression as to the cause of cyanosis based on the history and physical examination can be confirmed and better defined by certain laboratory investigations.

a. A chest film and ECG should be part of the basic evaluation if the cardiovascular or pulmonary system appears involved.

b. A warmed heelstick or finger-prick blood can give a great deal of important information. Note the color, and if the blood fails to become red on exposure to room air, consider the possibility of methemoglobinemia (chocolate brown), which can be confirmed by absorption spectrometry. The blood can be checked for the hematocrit and RBC morphology examined.

c. A Dextrostix test and blood sugar should be done to rule out hypoglycemia, which commonly presents with cyanosis, especially in the neonate.

d. Arterial blood gases are essential to the work-up, but heelstick arterial blood gases are *not* reliable for Po_2. In the neonate especially, arterial gases should be drawn from the right extremity or right superficial temporal artery to exclude right-to-left shunting. If an umbilical artery catheter is in place, so much the better (see Chap. 5, Sec. **II.B**). Ear oximetry is also an easy and quick method for checking O_2 saturation.

e. The response of the patient's arterial Po_2 to 100% O_2 inhalation should be tested.

f. If such studies strongly suggest cardiac disease, cardiac catheterization and angiography enable precise anatomic and physiologic diagnosis.

V. ABDOMINAL MASSES   Discovery of an abdominal mass requires careful and thoughtful abdominal palpation at each available opportunity throughout childhood and rigorous use of the rectal examination. Early detection and treatment may be lifesaving. A mass is often found in a completely asymptomatic patient. Normal or normally enlarged organs must be distinguished from problem masses. For example, unusually shaped or positioned kidneys may cause considerable confusion, and a distended urinary bladder may be remarkably enlarged. Differential diagnosis of abdominal masses may be simplified by considering the (1) newborn period and (2) early childhood and beyond.

A. Masses of genitourinary origin   About 50 percent of all abdominal masses found in the neonatal period originate in the genitourinary tract. Initial evaluation should include a hemogram, urinalysis, and chest and abdominal roentgenograms. A skeletal survey and IVP with voiding cystourethrogram are often indicated.

1. **Congenital multicystic kidney** is the most common mass found in the neonate. Usually only one kidney is involved, with the other normal. The mass may be lobulated and extend far anterior into the peritoneum.

2. **Congenital polycystic kidney** is a separate entity and is often not detected until late infancy or childhood. Polycystic kidney disease involves both kidneys and may give rise to hematuria or evidence of urinary tract infections. Patients should be carefully evaluated for polydactyly and hepatic cysts, which are frequently associated with this inheritable condition. The family history may reveal other members similarly affected.

3. **Hydronephrosis** presents as a smoothly rounded mass or masses; one or both kidneys may be affected secondary to a ureteropelvic obstruction, e.g., a ureterocele or aberrant vessel. These kidneys may be so large as to obstruct the vena cava. Hypoplasia of the abdominal wall musculature may accompany such a mass.

4. **Tumor** is most often unilateral, does not cross the midline, and presents as asymptomatic enlargement of the abdomen. Calcification is infrequently found on a KUB film. Intravenous pyelography may show nonvisualization of the affected kidney.

5. **Teratomas** are usually discovered in the first few years of life. Asymptomatic abdominal enlargement is common. These tumors may become enormously enlarged and cross the midline. On x-ray study, calcification within the mass may be irregularly diffuse or spotty; distinct bones or teeth are not uncommon. Such large masses may cause intestinal and ureteral obstruction that prompts consulting the physician.

6. **Congenital malformations** such as aniridia and hemihypertrophy should raise suspicion of possible Wilms' tumor in early infancy. These patients require frequent evaluation for the earliest possible detection.

7. **Ovarian cysts** may be asymptomatic. Torsion produces necrosis and infection, with accompanying fever and pain. The cysts are often much too large to remain in the pelvis and present as a midabdominal mass.

8. **Ovarian granulosa–theca cell tumor** presents a large, deep pelvic and lower abdominal mass. Signs of precocious puberty (breast swelling, vaginal bleeding, pubic and axillary hair) induced by increased estrogen production assist in the diagnosis.

9. **Hydrometrocolpos** develops in a female with an imperforate hymen, but is usually asymptomatic until menses start and drainage is prevented. In the newborn, the distended vagina may present as a lower abdominal mass with a smooth, rounded surface. All lower abdominal masses in young females require evaluation for some form of vaginal atresia, imperforate hymen, or other anomaly by careful identification of orifices.

B. **Gastrointestinal tract** Masses arising from the gastrointestinal tract may be asymptomatic or produce various degrees of intestinal obstruction.

1. **Duplications** occur most often in the terminal ileum. A right lower quadrant mass may be palpable in the newborn period. Symptoms are variable and may include diarrhea or obstruction with proximal distension. The mucosa may be similar to that of adjacent intestine or contain ectopic tissue such as gastric mucosa. As in Meckel's diverticulum, ulceration may result in bleeding or perforation.

2. **Mesenteric cysts** filled with serous or chylous fluid probably result from anomalies of lymphatic development. Cysts are thin, unilocular or multilocular, and may involve the mesentery of the small or large bowel. Mesenteric involvement may be extensive and present as generalized abdominal distension. These cysts may undergo torsion. Rupture leads to serous or chylous peritoneum and possible peritonitis.

3. **Pancreatic cysts** are extremely rare in the newborn. In older children, pancreatitis and blunt abdominal trauma may produce a pseudocyst.

4. **Fecal impaction** in the neonate or infant may be indicated by abdominal distention with single or multiple masses. Atresia or ectopia of the anus should be obvious on examination.

5. **Meconium ileus** may be present in infants with cystic fibrosis. The abdomen is distended, but a distinct mass is uncommon. The typical granular appearance of the bowel contents on x-ray may be helpful; the family history may aid in the diagnosis.

6. **Hirschsprung's disease** presents with impaction of fecal material proximal to the aganglionic segment. Fullness or mass in the left lower quadrant is often palpable. A barium enema defines the dilated proximal bowel.

7. **Midgut volvulus** in the newborn or older child presents as obstruction and midabdominal mass. The child is irritable and experiences considerable intermittent cramplike pain. The temperature may be elevated, as infarction and necrosis may occur. Some degree of malrotation of the gut is often found. Several episodes over days or weeks may be experienced before obstruction occurs.

8. **Intussusception** is rare in the neonate. In infants and older children, sudden severe abdominal pain may be accompanied by vomiting. The pain is characteristically intermittent. Between episodes, the abdomen is soft and easily palpated; a sausage-shaped mass may be detected. Blood in the stool is a useful clinical sign. A barium enema may be both diagnostic and therapeutic. Intussusception may occur transiently over several weeks with minimal discomfort before a severe crisis occurs.

9. **Congenital hypertrophic pyloric stenosis** classically presents as persistent and projectile vomiting during the neonatal period. The characteristic physical finding is a midabdominal olive-shaped tumor. Radiographic examination will visualize a narrow, elongated pyloric channel. There is no apparent increased risk to first-born males, but males are affected five times more often than females. *TTT is surgical pyloroplasty.*

10. **Hepatosplenomegaly** is discussed in Sec. **VI**. Masses may also arise from the liver and biliary tree. **Congenital hepatic cysts** may attain huge proportions, but rarely cause difficulties.

C. Other conditions

1. **Neuroblastoma** Infants with neuroblastoma, the most common solid tumor in childhood and usually arising in the adrenal glands, often present with diarrhea and weight loss. Variable hypertension, tachycardia, sweating, and pallor may result from high levels of catecholamines and their metabolites. A mass may be palpated during an incidental evaluation for various gastrointestinal complaints. Calcification is found in almost 50 percent of the tumors on abdominal x-ray. Peripheral blood and bone marrow aspiration may be useful in diagnosis.

2. **Choledochal cyst** is rare in newborns. In older children, an abdominal mass in the right upper quadrant or midabdomen accompanied by pain and jaundice should elevate suspicions. The size of the cyst may vary over several days, indicating intermittent obstruction of the common duct.

3. **Hydrops of the gallbladder** is a rare cause of a palpable mass at any age.

4. **Inflammatory processes,** such as **appendiceal abscess** or **ileitis,** present as a right lower quadrant mass with fever and leukocytosis. Diarrhea, pain, and irritability are common. A sausage-shaped, indurated mass is characteristic of terminal ileitis. Rectal examination reveals tenderness in the right lower segment, with palpable fullness.

5. **Lymphoma** may present as an abdominal mass, arising in the retroperitoneal space or occasionally in the ileocecal region and sometimes heralded by intussusception. Tumors often arise in the deep pelvis and may be detected only by careful rectal examination.

VI. HEPATOSPLENOMEGALY

By virtue of their large components of reticuloendothelial tissue and in-series venous drainage systems, the liver and spleen tend to share one another's biologic fate. With several well-known exceptions, the broad categories of disease (e.g., cardiac failure, neoplasia, infection) that produce hepatomegaly also tend to cause splenomegaly, and vice versa. Thus it is feasible to consider hepatomegaly and splenomegaly as a single clinical entity.

A. Evaluation

1. First, one must be certain that one is indeed palpating an enlarged liver or spleen and not a different upper quadrant mass such as a kidney, pancreatic or ovarian cysts, thickened omentum (as in tuberculous peritonitis), fecal matter, or a Riedel's lobe. Often, an IVP (with total body opacification in infants) is helpful in making these distinctions.

2. Depression of these organs secondary to emphysema, subdiaphragmatic masses, or laxity of supportive tissues must be ruled out.

3. The patient's age is relevant, since the liver is normally palpable at up to 2 cm below the right costal margin in the neonate and at up to 1 cm in children less than 7 years old; the spleen is normally palpable up to 3–4 years of age.

4. Both the liver and spleen can enlarge without becoming palpable—the liver, by enlarging in its posterior or lateral aspect or both, as sometimes occurs in cirrhosis; and the spleen, by enlarging only a fraction of the 2–3 times required for clinical detection. In such instances, visceromegaly can be reliably shown only by an isotopic scan in two planes.

B. Diagnosis

1. **Geographic factors** The area where the patient has lived is of great relevance. Malaria, for example, is perhaps the commonest cause of hepatosplenomegaly in the world as a whole, but its probability as a cause is much lower in Montana than in Vietnam. The work-up should be varied accordingly.

2. **History** Table 8-4 outlines the various conditions that can cause hepatosplenomegaly. The list can often be narrowed by a careful history and physical examination. The history should include infections, toxic exposures, fevers (their absence being more helpful than their presence), rashes, joint complaints, dietary habits and weight changes, psychomotor development, cardiopulmonary status, familial metabolic dyscrasias or hematologic disease, and close intermarriage.

3. **Physical examination**

   a. The child's nutritional status is assessed for evidence of chronicity and etiology.

   b. The presence of jaundice indicates hemolytic or obstructive and/or hepatocellular disease. Its absence points to cardiac failure, primary tumor, cirrhosis, or amyloidosis.

   c. Characteristic facies are seen in some of the mucopolysaccharidoses, and specific ophthalmologic changes are seen in many of the metabolic storage diseases.

   d. The status of the extremities (edema, adenopathy, arthritis) and the nervous system (psychomotor retardation, extrapyramidal signs) can help to narrow the diagnostic field.

4. **Laboratory studies**

   a. Though often ordered by reflex, **liver enzymes** rarely provide data on hepatic function that cannot be obtained by a careful history and physical examination. If significantly elevated or differentially altered, liver enzymes may elucidate local, ongoing pathologic processes (e.g., hepatocellular necrosis, biliary tract obstruction) without establishing their primary cause. Normal values exclude few entities.

   b. **BSP excretion studies,** though sensitive to discriminations in hepatic parenchymal functional mass, seldom narrow the diagnostic possibilities.

   c. If facilities are available, **a dynamic ^{99}Tc scan** is often extremely helpful in determining liver and spleen size, shape, displacement, and circulatory characteristics, and the relative distribu-

Table 8-4.   Differential Diagnosis of Hepatosplenomegaly

Mechanical
Elevated hepatic postsinusoidal pressure: congestive failure, hepatic vein thrombosis, cirrhosis
Obstruction of bile egress: biliary atresia, gallstones, pancreatitis, duodenal diverticulum, choledochal cyst
Trauma: subcapsular hemorrhages
Cruveilhier-Baumgarten syndrome: congenitally patent umbilical vein with cirrhosis and portal hypertension

Neoplastic
Local: lymphangioma, hemangioma
Metastatic: neuroblastoma, Wilms' tumor, osteogenic sarcoma
General: leukemia, lymphoma, reticulum cell sarcoma, histiocytosis (Letterer-Siwe, Hand-Schüller-Christian)

Infectious   Acute or chronic bacterial or viral infections represent the commonest cause of mild, transient hepatosplenomegaly

Hematologic
Hemolytic anemias: erythroblastosis fetalis and other Coombs-positive anemias, enzymopathy, hemoglobinopathy, spherocytosis
Marrow displacement: myelophthisic anemias with extramedullary hematopoiesis, osteopetrosis
Miscellaneous: pernicious anemia, hemochromatosis, first-degree polycythemia

Endocrine-Metabolic
Endocrine: diabetes mellitus, hyperthyroidism
Nutritional: kwashiorkor
Storage diseases: mucopolysaccharidoses, Niemann-Pick, Gaucher's, neurovisceral lipidosis, Leroy's I-cell, Farber's syndrome, glycogen storage (Von Gierke's), Tangier disease
Cirrhosis producing with secondary splenomegaly: cystinosis, tyrosinosis, galactosemia, hereditary fructose intolerance, cystic fibrosis, α-1 antitrypsin deficiency, amylopectinosis, Indian childhood cirrhosis, ulcerative colitis, regional enteritis, Kunkel's syndrome

Collagenoses
Juvenile rheumatoid arthritis
Lupus erythematosis

Toxic
Carbon tetrachloride
Vitamin A excess
Veno-occlusive disease of Jamaica (*Senecio, Crotalaria* alkaloids)

Miscellaneous
Sarcoid, amyloid, syndrome of the sea-blue histiocyte, Chédiak-Higashi syndrome, chronic granulomatous disease
Wiedemann-Beckwith syndrome

---

tion of radionuclide between the two organs offers a reasonably reliable assessment of liver function.

d. Peripheral smear   A simple peripheral smear is the most revealing single study in hepatosplenomegaly.

(1) Cell numbers and types can indicate a variety of neoplasms, viral infections, and parasitoses; their inclusions may indicate the presence of various storage diseases or other dysmetabolic processes (e.g., Chédiak-Higashi syndrome).

     (2) Red cell morphology may reveal hemolytic anemia, and parasites are sometimes visible within red cells.

     (3) Platelet and white cell counts, in conjunction with red cell morphology, may provide evidence of hypersplenism, consumptive coagulopathy, or both.

e. Bone marrow biopsy and culture often complement and extend peripheral smear data. Many of the bacteria are readily cultured from marrow aspirates, and certain neoplastic and storage diseases display more typical morphologies here than in the peripheral smear.

f. Liver biopsy When hepatosplenomegaly persists and storage, obstructive, inflammatory, or infiltrative has not been identified with certainty, closed or open (preferable) biopsy must be done for histologic diagnosis.

VII. JAUNDICE

A. Bilirubin metabolism

1. Although bilirubin is derived from multiple sources, the bulk of it results from the breakdown of hemoglobin. The porphyrin moiety of hemoglobin is converted to biliverdin, which is further reduced to bilirubin.

2. Unconjugated bilirubin is transported in serum that is bound to albumin.

3. To be excreted in bile, the bilirubin must be made water-soluble, which is accomplished by the conjugation of bilirubin with glucuronic acid.

4. The amount of unconjugated and conjugated bilirubin is approximated by the indirect- and direct-reacting van den Bergh test.

5. Conjugated bilirubin is excreted into the intestine, where the bacterial flora oxidize it to urobilinogen. When conjugated bilirubin accumulates in the intestine, it is capable of degradation to bilirubin by the action of β-glucuronidase in the intestinal wall. The unconjugated bilirubin may then be absorbed into the circulation.

6. In neonates, jaundice is not usually apparent until serum bilirubin exceeds 5.0 mg/100 ml. The jaundiced infant will have a yellow cast in the skin and scleras. Daylight observations are more accurate than those made in artificial light.

B. Jaundice in the newborn

1. Evaluation Physiologic jaundice of the newborn is a common self-limited form of jaundice caused by immaturity of the bilirubin conjugation enzyme systems in the liver and by the presence of β-glucuronidase in the intestinal wall. It reaches an average peak of 6 mg/100 ml during the fifth to seventh day of life in prematures, although values as high as 12 mg/100 ml in full-term infants and 14 mg/100 ml in prematures may still be considered physiologic.

2. Differential diagnosis See Table 8-5.

a. Day of onset Visible jaundice that appears during the first day of life or after the fifth day is definitely *not* physiologic.

b. History Prenatal conditions must be elicited, including diabetes, blood group incompatibility, hereditary anemias, infections during pregnancy, or premature rupture of membranes.

Table 8-5.   Differential Diagnosis of Neonatal Jaundice[a]

First 24 hours
　Blood group incompatibility (ABO, Rh, minor group)
　Congenital infections (toxoplasmosis, rubella, cytomegalic inclusion disease,
　　syphilis)

Day 2 to 4
　Physiologic
　Blood group incompatibility
　Infection (bacterial and viral)
　Hemolytic anemias (spherocytosis, G-6-PD, pyruvic kinase)
　Infant of a diabetic mother

Day 4
　Physiologic
　Infection (bacterial and viral)
　Hemolytic anemias
　Breast-feeding
　Resorbing hematoma (cephalhematoma, hepatic subcapsular)
　Obstructive jaundice
　　Anatomic, includes congenital atresia of the bile ducts, pyloric stenosis,
　　　intestinal atresia, choledochal cyst
　　Neonatal giant cell hepatitis
　Familial nonhemolytic (Crigler-Najjar, Gilbert's)
　Hypothyroidism
　Galactosemia

---

[a] It is best to consider the differential diagnosis of neonatal jaundice from the
day of onset.

    c. A careful **physical examination** should always be made, and the
presence of hepatosplenomegaly, lethargy, petechiae, or hematomas should be noted.

    d. Laboratory studies　In the newborn period, many of the signs and
symptoms of various entities causing jaundice overlap, and
laboratory studies are essential to the diagnosis. Table 8-6 lists
the laboratory tests of most importance. The baseline studies
should be done in every case.

       (1) With an elevated indirect bilirubin, a low hematocrit, and
elevated reticulocyte count, hemolytic anemia is probable,
with blood group incompatibility its most likely cause. Maternal and infant blood typing and a Coombs test will confirm
the diagnosis. In ABO incompatibility, the direct Coombs
test is often negative, and an indirect Coombs test should be
done. Minor blood group incompatibilities (e.g., hR, Kell,
Duffy) may also cause a Coombs-positive hemolytic anemia.

       (2) Peripheral smear and osmotic fragility will confirm the diag-
nosis of spherocytosis. Special tests will be required to diagnose other hemolytic anemias (see Table 8-6 and Chap. 15).

       (3) Elevated direct bilirubin usually indicates obstructive disease,
but mild elevations can occur in sepsis as well. The WBC may
be elevated in sepsis, but often is depressed, as is the platelet
count.

       (4) Occasionally, prolonged hyperbilirubinemia will develop in

Table 8-6. Laboratory Studies in Neonatal Jaundice

Type of Study	Diagnostic Application
Baseline studies	All cases of neonatal jaundice
Maternal and infant blood types	
Direct Coombs test	
Bilirubin, direct and indirect	
WBC, hematocrit, reticulocytes, platelets, peripheral smear	
Indicated clinically or by history	
Indirect Coombs test	ABO incompatibility
Cultures	Bacterial sepsis
IgM, VDRL, specific antibody titers	Congenital infections
Osmotic fragility, RBC enzyme assays, Hb electrophoresis	Hemolytic anemias
T4	Hypothyroidism
Reducing substances in urine	Galactosemia
Abdominal flat plate contrast studies	Pyloric stenosis, intestinal atresia, choledochal cyst
Rose bengal, peroxidase	Biliary atresia
Liver biopsy	Biliary atresia, neonatal giant cell hepatitis

breast-fed infants. Breast milk obtained from mothers of these children contains pregnane-3α, 20β-diol, which inhibits glucuronyl transferase. Cessation of nursing for 3–4 days will usually result in a significant reduction in hyperbilirubinemia. Dehydration will also predispose the newborn to hyperbilirubinemia.

C. Jaundice in older children   After the newborn period the normal total bilirubin is less than 1 mg/100 ml, with a direct fraction of less than 0.5 mg/100 ml. As Table 8-7 shows, the differential diagnosis in this period is different from that in the newborn.

Table 8-7.   Differential Diagnosis of Jaundice in Older Children

1. Hepatitis (infectious and serum)
2. Other infectious agents (infectious mononucleosis, Weil's disease)
3. Drug-induced (e.g., phenothiazine, halothane, anabolic corticosteroids)
4. Poisons (e.g., mushrooms, phosphorus, carbon tetrachloride)
5. Hemolytic anemias (sickle cell, G-6-PD, spherocytosis, thalassemia, autoimmune)
6. Cirrhosis (postinfectious, Wilson's disease, excessive iron, galactosemia, cystic fibrosis, tyrosinosis, antitrypsin)
7. Collagen diseases (lupus erythematosus, polyarteritis nodosa)
8. Familial nonhemolytic (Crigler-Najjar, Gilbert's, Dubin-Johnson, Rotor)
9. Mechanical obstruction of bile duct (calculi, abdominal tumors)
10. Hepatic tumors

1. **Viral hepatitis** is the most common cause of jaundice in this age group. An elevated direct and indirect bilirubin, with a decrease in fecal urobilinogen and an increase in urine bilirubin and urobilinogen as well as a rise in SGOT, SGPT, and alkaline phosphatase occurs in hepatitis. In infectious hepatitis the Australia antigen is negative, and thymol turbidity is elevated. In serum hepatitis, the reverse is true.

2. **Hemolytic anemias** are characterized by a low hematocrit, an elevated reticulocyte count, and a low serum haptoglobin. The peripheral smear may show spherocytes, target cells, or sickle cells.

3. In **obstructive liver disease** there is a predominant elevation of the direct bilirubin. Urine bilirubin will be increased and urine urobilinogen decreased. Stool bilirubin and urobilinogen are both decreased. SGOT and SGPT will be mildly increased. Table 8-8 lists the basic work-up for jaundice in older children, as well as special studies for certain clinical situations.

Table 8-8. Jaundice in Older Children: Laboratory Studies

Type of Study	Diagnostic Application
Baseline studies	In all cases
WBC, hematocrit, reticulocytes count, peripheral smear	
Serum bilirubin, total, direct and indirect	
Urine bilirubin and urobilinogen	
Fecal urobilinogen	
SGOT, SGPT, alkaline phosphatase, prothrombin time	
Australia antigen	
Indicated clinically or by history	
ESR, ANA	Collagen disease
Coombs	Autoimmune hemolytic anemia
Total protein A/G ratio, protein electrophoresis.	Collagen disease, infection
Mono spot, heterophil antibody	Infectious mononucleosis
Blood cultures	Sepsis
Sickle cell preparation, hemoglobin electrophoresis, osmotic fragility, red cell enzyme assays, haptoglobin	Hemolytic anemia
Toxicology screen	Poisonings
Serum copper, ceruloplasmin	Wilson's disease
Abdominal flat plate, cholangiography	Tumors, bile duct stones
Liver biopsy	Cirrhosis, collagen disease
Liver scan	Neoplasm

VIII. ANEMIA See also Chap. 15.

A. **General findings in anemia** Anemia causes decreased transport of O_2 from the lung to the peripheral tissues. It is a result of an inadequate number of red cells or a decrease in their concentration of hemoglobin.

1. **Physical signs**   In moderate degrees of anemia, physical signs include tachycardia, tachypnea, and a widened pulse pressure, which are compensatory mechanisms to increase the flow of blood (and O_2) to the major organs. In addition, pallor and a "hemic" heart murmur are usually present. In mild anemia these findings may be absent; in severe cases "high output" heart failure may occur.

2. **Hemoglobin and hematocrit**   Both the hemoglobin concentration and the hematocrit vary with the age of the patient. For example, values that are normal for a 3-month-old premature infant would suggest anemia in a 7-year-old. Normal values for hemoglobin and hematocrit for various ages are given in Table 8-9; the diagnosis of anemia rests on significant deviations from these figures.

Table 8-9.   Normal Red Cell Values

Age	Hemoglobin (gm/100 ml)	Hematocrit (%)	Reticulocytes (%)	MCV (μ^3)	MCH ($\mu\mu g$)	MCHC (%)
1 day (term)[a]	16–24	47–60	4.1–6.3	106	38	36
2 weeks	13–20	42–66	0.5–1.0	98	33	34
3 months	10–15	31–41	0.5–1.0	82	27	34
6 months– 6 years	11–14	33–42	0.5–1.0	82	27	34
7–12 years	11–16	34–40	0.5–1.0	82	27	34
Adult						
Female	12–16	37–47	0.5–1.6	82–93	27–31	32–36
Male	14–18	42–52	0.5–1.6	82–93	27–31	32–36

[a] Central venous values. Capillary values are higher.

B. **Classification**

1. **Microcytic hypochromic anemia**   Red cell precursors in the marrow undergo multiple rounds of cell divisions and synthesize hemoglobin. Any disorder that interferes with either heme synthesis (e.g., iron deficiency, lead intoxication) or globin synthesis (e.g., the thalassemias) results in cells with decreased concentrations of hemoglobin, causing this type of anemia.

2. **Macrocytic megaloblastic anemia** occurs in disorders that interfere with cellular DNA synthesis, but allow normal hemoglobinization (e.g., folate deficiency, B_{12} deficiency).

3. **Normocytic normochromic anemia** is caused by diseases that interfere both with cell division and hemoglobinization (e.g., aplastic anemias, leukemias), as do many disorders that cause excessive loss of red blood cells (e.g., hemolysis due to G-6-PD deficiency, sickle cell disease, and hemorrhage).

C. **Corpuscular indices**   Corpuscular indices as a function of age are given in Table 8-9.

1. In the **microcytic hypochromic anemias,** both mean corpuscular hemoglobin (MCH) and mean corpuscular volume (MCV) are decreased,

but the decrease in the former is often greater, resulting in a low mean corpuscular hemoglobin concentration (MCHC) (see Table 8-10). Also, in microcytic hypochromic anemias the hemoglobin is less than ⅓ the hematocrit (a useful index past the newborn period).

Table 8-10.   Red Cell Indices in Anemia

Type of Anemia	MCV (μ^3)	MCH ($\mu\mu$g)	MCHC (%)
Hypochromic microcytic	50–80	12–25	25–30
Macrocytic	95–150	32–50	32–36
Normocytic	82–93	27–31	32–36
Normal	82–93	27–31	32–36

2. In the **normocytic normochromic anemias** the corpuscular indexes are normal, and the hemoglobin is ⅓ the hematocrit.

3. In the **macrocytic megaloblastic anemias** the MCV and MCH are increased to the same degree (Table 8-10) resulting in a normal MCHC, and the hemoglobin is ⅓ the hematocrit.

4. The only disorders in which the MCHC may be increased (hemoglobin greater than ⅓ the hematocrit) are the spherocytic anemias, in which there is a decrease in the MCV.

D. Red cell turnover

1. The normal red cell has a life span of 120 days; the reticulocyte can be identified for only 1–2 days. These young cells can be recognized by the presence of polychromasia on Wright's stain, or by the presence of reticulum (ribosomal granules) when stained with brilliant cresyl blue.

2. Reticulocytes usually make up about 1% of the mature red cell population. They are larger than mature red cells, often causing an increase in the MCV when large numbers are present.

3. Reticulocytosis results as a compensation for acute blood loss or for a chronic hemolytic process. Also, appropriate therapy of iron deficiency states (e.g., with iron, folate, or vitamin B_{12}) always results in a rapid reticulocytosis. It should be remembered that a reticulocyte "count" of 1% with a hematocrit of 45 gives the same absolute number of reticulocytes as a "count" of 3% with a hematocrit of 15. The latter is, of course, an inappropriate response to anemia and does not suggest hemolysis.

E. Hemolytic anemia   A hemolytic anemia is suggested by several findings:

1. The reticulocyte count is elevated. When occult bleeding and the inadvertent treatment of deficiency states have been ruled out, a truly elevated reticulocyte count is sufficient to establish the diagnosis.

2. The indirect fraction of the serum bilirubin may be moderately elevated, with cholelithiasis a common complication in a long-standing process.

3. Determination of the serum LDH level is also useful. Since LDH is found in high concentrations in red cells, hemolysis causes significant elevations in the serum levels.

4. In a hemolytic process the serum haptoglobin levels are decreased, since free haptoglobin binds with the hemoglobin from the hemolyzed cells and is no longer detectable. **Interpretation of serum haptoglobin levels is often difficult.** The protein is an acute phase reactant, as are fibrinogen and c-reactive protein, and its value may be falsely elevated in spite of hemolysis. Furthermore, haptoglobin is *absent* in the newborn period, and some people have a congenital lack of it.

5. In delineating the site of hemolysis, determination of the presence of urine hemosiderin is often useful. When present, this indicates that hemolysis is occurring within the renal vasculature. In states with generalized intravascular hemolysis (e.g., sickle cell disease) the results will be positive; in Coombs-positive hemolytic anemias or in the congenital spherocytic anemias, in which hemolysis occurs within the spleen, they will be negative.

F. **Differential diagnosis**   The following is a morphologic classification of anemias, with pertinent diagnostic features:

1. **Microcytic hypochromic anemias**   The cause of this type of anemia is decreased heme or globin synthesis.

   a. **Iron deficiency anemia**

      (1) **Etiology**   Decreased heme synthesis occurs because of insufficient iron. Prenatal iron stores are depleted by 6 months of age. Prematures have even smaller stores.

      (2) **Features**

         (a) The serum is colorless.

         (b) Serum iron is decreased (normal values, 65–175 μg/100 ml) while the serum iron-binding capacity is increased (normal values, 250–420 μg/100 ml).

         (c) Absence of iron stores in the marrow—useful when the child is over 5.

         (d) Rapid reticulocytosis after treatment with oral iron. A rise in hematocrit follows within 2 weeks.

   b. **Plumbism**   In this condition there is decreased heme synthesis.

      (1) **Etiology**   Ingested lead interferes with porphyrin biosynthetic pathways. It is usually associated with iron deficiency. (See also Chap. 3, Sec. **III.D.3.**)

      (2) **Features**

         (a) A large proportion of red cells have basophilic stippling.

         (b) The urine is positive for coproporphyrins, and ALA is elevated.

         (c) The concentration of lead in whole blood is high (> 50 μg/100 ml).

         (d) High erythrocyte protoporphyrin, ALA, and so on.

         (e) The lead mobilization test gives positive results (see Chap. 3, Sec. **III**).

(f) The roentgenogram shows growth arrest lines at the metaphyseal plates of the long bones.

c. Thalassemia major (beta chain variant, A_2 type)

(1) Etiology   In this inherited condition the homozygote has insufficient synthesis of the beta chain of hemoglobin. Overproduction of alpha chain (unbalanced hemoglobin synthesis) causes hemolysis. There are several forms of beta thalassemia. The A_2, which is common, is described. The heterozygote for this condition has a high intracellular concentration of hemoglobin A_2.

(2) Features

(a) Marked anemia, evident by 6 months of age.

(b) Hepatosplenomegaly.

(c) Thickened cranium and prominent cheek bones.

(d) Reticulocytosis, often with nucleated red blood cells.

(e) Marked red cell changes: hypochromia, microcytosis, targeting, anisocytosis, poikilocytosis, basophilic stippling, and teardrop forms.

(f) Normal platelet count; slightly elevated WBC. X-ray evidence: increased marrow cavities; hair-on-end appearance of calvarium.

(g) Hemoglobin electrophoresis shows (1) decreased or absent hemoglobin A, (2) increased hemoglobin F (10–90% of total; normal less than 2%), (3) hemoglobin A_2 may be normal (1.9–3.2%) or increased.

d. Thalassemia minor, or thalassemia trait (beta chain variant, A_2 type)

(1) Etiology   The heterozygote has a mild inadequacy in the production of beta chain of hemoglobin.

(2) Features

(a) Mild anemia is evident at approximately 6 months.

(b) Moderate hypochromia, microcytosis, targeting, and basophilic stippling.

(c) Serum has a normal pale-yellow tinge, and the serum iron is normal or elevated, while the iron-binding capacity is normal or decreased.

(d) The reticulocyte count may be normal or mildly elevated.

(e) The spleen tip may be palpable.

(f) Hemoglobin electrophoresis shows (1) hemoglobin A_2, 3–6% (normal, 1.9–3.2%); (2) hemoglobin F is normal ($< 2\%$) or slightly increased ($< 5\%$).

e. Thalassemia minor, or thalassemia trait (alpha chain variant)

(1) Etiology   The heterozygote has a mild inadequacy in production of the alpha chain of hemoglobin.

(2) Heterozygous forms The heterozygous form is common among blacks (2–7%) in the United States and in inhabitants of Southeast Asia (3–30%). Two forms of the heterozygous condition exist. In one form the patient is a silent carrier, and the condition commonly manifested by the presence of a high (1.2–2.0%) concentration of Bart's hemoglobin (γ_4) at birth; there is no anemia. In the second form there is also a high level of Bart's hemoglobin at birth, but the patient has a mild anemia throughout life [see **(1)**]. This form is common among blacks in the USA. The homozygous condition (alpha thalassemia major) is incompatible with life and has been detected in the newborn period only in infants from Southeast Asia.

(3) Features

  (a) Mild hypochromic, microcytic anemia.

  (b) No evidence of iron deficiency.

  (c) Presence of elevated concentrations of Bart's hemoglobin (γ_4), 3–14% at birth (normal, < 0.5%).

  (d) Peripheral blood reticulocytes have more beta chain synthesis than alpha chain synthesis. The beta/alpha chain ratio is > 1.0 (normal, 1.0). This determination requires a research laboratory and is needed in making the diagnosis after the newborn period.

2. Macrocytic megaloblastic anemias In these anemias the red cells are larger than normal. In the megaloblastic anemias the defect occurs in the marrow because of interference with cellular DNA synthesis. In the macrocytic anemia of liver disease the cells appear large because of excessive membrane cholesterol, and the marrow is *not* megaloblastic.

  a. Folic acid deficiency Tetrahydrofolic acid is a methyl donor needed for the synthesis of DNA precursors. Since the body stores last only 2–3 months, deficiency occurs rapidly. Although in the untreated state the reticulocyte count remains low, erythropoiesis is ineffective, with intramedullary destruction of erythroid precursors.

  (1) Etiology Common causes of deficiency include poor diet, malabsorption syndrome, interference (e.g., diphenylhydantoin) or increased utilization (e.g., active erythropoiesis as a result of chronic hemolytic states, leukemia, or pregnancy). When poor diet is the cause, hospitalization and resumption of adequate intake will result in prompt reticulocytosis, with a rise in the hematocrit.

  (2) Features

   (a) Megaloblastic macrocytic anemia

   (b) Leukopenia

   (c) Presence in the peripheral blood of a large percentage of hypersegmented polymorphonuclear leukocytes having five or more lobes (normally, < 3% have five lobes, and none has six)

   (d) Occasional thrombocytopenia

(e) Elevated serum lactic dehydrogenase (LDH)

(f) Mild elevation of indirect bilirubin

(g) Decreased haptoglobin

(h) Megaloblastic marrow with a delay in nuclear maturation of granulocyte and erythroid precursors (nuclear-cyto-plasmic dissociation)

(i) Low serum folic acid concentrations (normal, 4–16 mμ/ml)

b. Vitamin B$_{12}$ deficiency   Vitamin B$_{12}$ is needed for DNA synthesis. Deficiency usually takes years to develop because of large body stores.

(1) Etiology   Deficiency occurs as a result of inadequate intake, intestinal malabsorption, or lack of gastric intrinsic factor. (usually without gastric atrophy). The adult type of pernicious anemia with gastric atrophy and absent gastric hydrochloride is rare.

(2) Features

(a) Macrocytic, megaloblastic anemia with leukopenia and evidence of ineffective erythropoiesis as described for folic acid deficiency.

(b) Low serum vitamin B$_{12}$ concentration (normal 150–1000 $\mu\mu$g/ml).

(c) Evidence of subacute combined degeneration (ataxia, spasticity, weakness), a late finding.

c. Liver disease

(1) Etiology   The membranes of the erythrocytes accumulate large amounts of cholesterol and become macrocytic. These cells are readily hemolyzed, particularly in the presence of hypersplenism. Spur cells appearing morphologically similar to acanthocytes may be seen in severe obstructive jaundice.

(2) Features   Evidence of liver disease, mild anemia, macrocytosis, elevated reticulocyte count, and nonmegaloblastic bone marrow.

3. Normocytic normochromic anemias

a. Marrow failure   The marrow does not make sufficient cells. The erythroid series may be affected alone, or the granulocytes and thrombocytes may also be involved.

(1) Aplastic anemia   Here, there is decreased production of red cells, white cells, and platelets.

(a) **Etiology**   It may be idiopathic or occur after treatment with chloramphenicol (idiosyncratic), radiation, mustards, and antimetabolites (dose-related).

(b) **Features**

i. Severe anemia with leukopenia and thrombocytopenia.

ii. Bone marrow aplasia found on biopsy.

iii. Fetal hemoglobin is often increased (normal, <20%).

(2) Acute lymphocytic leukemia Here, the effective marrow is "crowded out" by blasts.

(a) Etiology Unknown

(b) Features

   i. Anemia

   ii. Thrombocytopenia

   iii. Nucleated red blood cells on peripheral smear

   iv. Teardrops on peripheral smear

   v. Pelger-Huët anomaly on peripheral smear

   vi. Presence of large number of lymphoblasts in marrow and often in peripheral blood

b. Hemolytic anemia This is a result of increased erythrocyte destruction. There is a high reticulocyte count, elevated serum LDH, indirect bilirubin, and decreased haptoglobin.

(1) Antierythrocyte antibody This is characterized by coating of erythrocytes with antibody, followed by their destruction by the macrophages of the spleen.

(a) Etiology It may be idiopathic or associated with mononucleosis, lupus erythematosis, atypical pneumonia, malignancy, ITP (Evans' syndrome), or dysgammaglobulinemia.

(b) Features

   i. Positive direct γ-Coombs or strongly positive direct non-γ-Coombs (detects complement).

   ii. Warm or cold agglutinins (anti-I) may be present.

   iii. The urine is negative for hemosiderin.

   iv. The peripheral smear may show microspherocytes.

(2) Hereditary spherocytosis There is abnormal leakage of $Na+$ into cells. In the absence of an energy source, osmotic swelling occurs and microspherocytes are formed. This occurs in the spleen, resulting in a hemolytic anemia.

(a) Etiology The condition is inherited as a mendelian dominant, but exceptions are not uncommon.

(b) Features Hemolytic anemia, microspherocytes on smear, urine negative for hemosiderin, increased osmotic fragility, increased autohemolysis (normal is 4% lysis after 48-hr incubation).

(3) Glucose 6-phosphate dehydrogenase (G-6-PD) deficiency In this inherited condition, reduced glutathione is not present in high enough concentrations to protect the cell from oxidant stress. Exposure to oxidants (e.g., sulfonamides, furadantin, or antimalarials) leads to denaturation of hemoglobin and Heinz body formation, with erythrocyte destruction and compensatory reticulocytosis. There are two forms of this X-linked disorder, one found in blacks and the other in Greeks and Jews.

(a) Features in blacks

i. Eleven percent of black males are affected.

ii. Almost normal enzyme activity is present in young cells, with low amounts in old cells. There is low enzyme activity on quantitative assay, but the G-6-PD screen *may be normal.*

(b) Features in Greeks and Jews

i. Enzyme activity is absent in all cells.

ii. The G-6-PD screen is abnormal.

iii. Heterozygote female carriers can be readily detected.

(4) Sickle cell anemia   An abnormal hemoglobin molecule causes sickling of the cell at low oxygen tension. This results in a chronic hemolytic anemia and in thrombotic crises.

(a) Etiology   The condition is hereditary, is confined to blacks, and is considered symptomatic only in the homozygote.

(b) Features   Onset of moderate to severe hemolytic anemia after 6 months of age; positive sickle cell preparation: hemoglobin electrophoresis after 6 months of age: hemoglobin S, 80–100%; hemoglobin A, 0; hemoglobin F, 0–20%.

(5) Vitamin E deficiency   This fat-soluble vitamin prevents oxidation of phospholipids in the red cell membrane. The red cells of premature infants are susceptible to this type of oxidation, resulting in a hemolytic anemia. **Feature**   Positive peroxide hemolysis test (normal is 0% of cells lysed).

IX. FEVER   In 1868, Wunderlich correlated several disease states with changes in body temperature. With this, the measurement of fever became one of the cardinal signs of illness and a common presenting symptom in pediatrics.

A. Definition   As presently defined, fever is an elevation of body temperature from the usual "normal" of 98.6° F. However, the range of normal is some 1.5° F, and activity and emotion, the ambient temperature, dress, and diurnal variation may both raise and lower this core temperature. Similarly, the temperature varies with the route of measurement: **rectal**, 97.2–100.4° F; **oral**, 96.5–99.2° F. Axillary temperatures are generally 2° F *lower* than the rectal route and 1° F *lower* than the oral route.

B. Pathophysiologic mechanisms   Fever is secondary to the activated release of an endogenous pyrogen from polymorphonuclear leukocytes or monocytes, directly or through lymphocyte stimulation. The release is via endotoxin, viruses, bacteria, antigen-antibody complexes, and corticosteroids. The pyrogen acts through the autonomic nervous system to cause vasoconstriction, and through the somatic motor system to produce shivering. Except for disruptions in central motor mechanisms (CNS lesions or infections) or peripheral receptors (heat stroke, ectodermal dysplasia), sweating will usually prevent temperatures from rising over 106° F.

C. **Etiology** Fever has many causes, but in the majority of instances in children, it is of acute infectious origin, nearly always lasts less than 10 days, and is triggered by a viral process in more than 90 percent of cases. More than half are infections of the upper or lower respiratory tract, the remainder involving mainly the gastrointestinal or genito-urinary systems.

D. **Fever patterns** Several types of fever patterns have been felt to be diagnostically important.

1. **Continuous fever** is shown by a temperature curve with a nearly constant level, fluctuations being only 1–1.5° F (e.g., the stepladder picture of typhoid fever).

2. **Remittent fever,** characterized by daily fluctuations of more than 2° F, is found in septicemia, miliary tuberculosis, pyelonephritis, lymphomas, and collagen disorders.

3. **Intermittent fever,** as seen in malaria, is present when the temperature drops to or below normal and then rises to its previous height. (Note that *two* daily temperature spikes may occur in juvenile rheumatoid arthritis or kala azar.)

4. **Relapsing, or recurrent, fever** consists of an initial febrile period followed by normalization for several days, only to rise again to its previous height. This is sometimes encountered in brucellosis and may be the Pel-Ebstein fever of Hodgkin's disease.

E. **Evaluation**

1. **Physiologic concomitants** are sometimes helpful in evaluation.

   a. **The pulse rate** usually increases about 10 beats/min for each degree of fever, though more than this in bacterial processes. Raised intracranial pressure, meningitis, and salmonella infections are exceptions to this rule.

   b. The **respiratory rate** will usually increase 2 cycles/min for each degree of temperature elevation, inappropriate increases suggesting pulmonary pathology, increased intracranial pressure, or acid-base disturbances.

2. **Age group** Evaluation of an acute onset of fever depends to some extent on the age of the child as well as on an estimation of his "toxicity."

   a. **Newborn** It is important to remember that in the newborn with sepsis or serious illness, fever is often absent. In fact, the neonate may be hypothermic in such instances. In this age group, subtle symptoms such as decreased appetite, lethargy, and irritability may be the only indication of serious illness.

   b. **Under 6 months** For the infant under 6 months of age, *the presence of fever requires a systematic and thorough evaluation.* Like the neonate, a child of this age group may only exhibit changes in feeding patterns, lethargy, or irritability as the major sign of such serious illnesses as meningitis. A history of contact or exposure is important, and, although in a majority of cases viral processes are involved, the child with a fever in this age group who appears even slightly ill or in whom a source of infection is not readily apparent should be studied completely. This may include complete blood count, examination of a clean voided urine (if necessary via a suprapubic bladder tap), chest x-ray, cultures of the nose, throat, and stool, and a CSF examination. The yield may be low, but the danger of missing a serious infection justifies a conservative approach and only then makes ambulatory management of these patients possible.

  c. Older infant and child   In these patients, a careful physical examination for an infectious etiology is again the most productive approach.

3. Reducing fever   Unlike adults, children will often run temperatures up to 104–105° F with benign illnesses. It may be helpful to reduce temperatures above 103° F prior to examination with a tepid bath, or antipyretics, or both, since this will often make the child more comfortable, cooperative, and almost invariably, less "toxic-appearing." (See Chap. 1, Sec. **III.B.**)

4. A careful search for rashes, petechiae, adenopathy, and inflamed joints may be helpful, as will upper and lower respiratory or abdominal findings.

5. Laboratory tests

  a. A CBC within the first day or so of an acute viral illness may show both a leukocytosis and a shift to the left and hence be confused with the hematologic picture more often seen with bacterial disease.

  b. In the absence of significant physical findings, a urinalysis (especially gram stain of the unspun specimen) may be helpful.

  c. Tachypnea out of proportion to the fever in an infant or a persistent cough in the child who seems toxic may be clues to explain presence of an infiltrate on the chest x-ray.

  d. The ESR may be helpful, as it will be normal in uncomplicated viral illnesses and elevated in collagen disorders or primary atypical pneumonia.

6. In some cases, especially when the child is seen early in the course of an illness, no cause may be found in spite of careful search. Examination at a later time may then reveal the earlier episode to have been the prodrome of a childhood exanthem.

7. Persistent fever   The intensity of the pediatrician's concern often increases when a child's fever has persisted beyond 10–14 days.

  a. Only about 10 percent of children *admitted* to the hospital for evaluation of unexplained fever have persistent fever. In about 50 percent of these cases of prolonged fever there is some infectious component and hence, as with the fevers of more acute onset, a careful history, physical examination, and screening for infectious agents is the most productive approach.

  b. Another 20 percent of these cases are collagen-inflammatory disorders, half of which are juvenile rheumatoid arthritis.

  c. Malignant disease is initially manifested by persistent fever in only 6 percent of children with prolonged fever.

F. Treatment of fever in children should take a position of secondary importance to attempts to determine its cause. Generally speaking, no specific form of therapy is available. Reduction of the child's fever makes him more comfortable and the physician better able to assess the severity of the illness (see **E.3**).

An intriguing question, still unanswered, is whether we should "treat" the fever of viral illnesses at all, since some data suggest that hyperpyrexia may be important endogenous therapy for halting further viral replication.

X. EDEMA

A. Physiologic features

1. Edema, which may be localized or have a generalized distribution, indicates an abnormal increase in the amount of extravascular fluid.

2. On physical examination the gross generalized form is recognized by puffiness of the face, especially periorbitally, and by persistence of an indentation of the skin following pressure (pitting), especially of the lower legs if the patient is ambulatory, or of the sacrum if he is bedridden.

3. In its subtle form edema can be detected by the persistent indentation of the rim of the stethoscope bell on the chest or abdomen following auscultation.

4. One of the first symptoms a patient may note is that the ring on his finger is fitting more snugly or his shoes are uncomfortably tight. In older adolescents, by the time edema becomes clinically recognizable the volume of the interstitial space may be expanded up to several liters.

5. **Factors in edema formation**

   a. The extracellular space, which comprises the plasma volume and interstitial space, represents about one-third of the total body water. The distribution of fluid between the plasma and interstitial compartments is determined by the balance of the hydrostatic pressure, the colloid osmotic pressure, and the tissue turgor pressure across the capillary endothelium. Damage to the capillary endothelium increases the permeability of these vessels, resulting in transfer from the vascular to interstitial compartment of fluid containing more protein than usual. The basic factors (increased hydrostatic pressure, decreased oncotic pressure, increased capillary permeability) are operative in a variety of edematous states.

   b. In some instances an abnormal retention of salt and water may be the primary disturbance, with edema a secondary manifestation of the generalized increase in the volume of the extracellular fluid.

   Table 8-11 groups the major clinical situations associated with edema formation under the predominant physiologic factor.

B. Clinical approach

1. **History and physical examination**

   a. The approach to the patient with edema must begin with a complete history and physical examination, including a dietary history and blood pressure determination. A history of cardiac, hepatic, or renal disease may be relevant, and the patient's

Table 8-11.   Clinical Syndromes in Edema

Increased hydrostatic pressure

> Constrictive pericarditis
> Portal hypertension
> Congestive heart failure
> Chiari's syndrome
> Thrombophlebitis
> Extrinsic venous compression

Decreased oncotic pressure

> Inadequate intake
>> Impaired alimentation, failure of utilization, loss of protein from the GI tract
>> Hypercatabolic hypoproteinemia
> Impaired production of protein
>> Liver disease
>> Chronic constrictive pericarditis
>> Transient dysproteinemia of infancy
> Loss of protein
>> Nephrosis
>> Ascites
>> Loss via skin
>> Loss via gastrointestinal tract
> Idiopathic hypoproteinemia

Increased capillary permeability

> Allergic reactions
> Inflammatory reactions

Impaired lymphatic drainage

Sodium and water retention

> Primary aldosteronism
> Secondary aldosteronism
>> Congestive heart failure
>> Cirrhosis of liver
>> Chronic anemia
>> Acute glomerulonephritis
>> Nephrotic syndrome
>> Excessive saline administration
>> Prolonged steroids

Tissue tension with localized edema in scrotum, extremities, periorbital areas

Colloid osmotic pressure of tissue fluids

Localized edema such as in gonadal dysgenesis, neonatal tetany

account of the sequence of edema appearance may provide a clue to the underlying problem.

b. Edema of one extremity is usually the result of vascular or lymphatic obstruction; edema secondary to hypoproteinemia is usually generalized. Edema associated with congestive heart failure tends to be more extensive in the legs, with the greatest accumulation at the end of a day of ambulation and upright posture.

    c. The color, thickness, and sensitivity of the skin are important, since local tenderness and erythema suggest inflammation; thickened, hard, and less sensitive skin is seen in patients with repeated episodes of prolonged edema.

2. Laboratory studies

    a. Determination of the total serum protein with an albumin/globulin ratio will clearly differentiate those patients in whom edema is due to diminished intravascular colloid osmotic pressure.

    b. Urinalysis, including specific gravity, a careful sediment examination, if indicated, urinary electrolytes is often very revealing. Slight to moderate proteinuria is frequent in patients with *congestive heart failure;* persistent massive proteinuria usually reflects the presence of the *nephrotic syndrome.* Hematuria, red cell casts, and proteinuria suggest acute poststreptococcal glomerulonephritis, particularly if accompanied by a history of injection.

    c. Liver function studies, serum electrolytes, and baseline renal studies with BUN and creatinine are often of value in differential diagnosis. If hypercholesterolemia is present, the serum may be cloudy on inspection.

3. Most important in dealing with the edematous patient is to keep in mind that his edema may arise from a variety of abnormal conditions and not necessarily from just one of the disorders mentioned. Careful following of the patient's daily weight, the best guide to successful treatment, and continued stepwise investigation lead eventually to success in both diagnosis and treatment.

9 Antibiotics and Infectious Diseases

From an initial, careful history and physical examination and a few simple laboratory tests, a tentative diagnosis can be established and a rational course of management instituted for the patient with an infectious disease. Antimicrobial therapy is based on *identification* of the pathogen and the *site of infection* as well as host factors such as clinical status of the patient, renal impairment, and possible immunologic impairment. *The value of appropriate gram stains and cultures of body fluids or exudates, or both, in the evaluation of the patient cannot be overemphasized.*

I. **PRINCIPLES OF ANTIMICROBIAL THERAPY** Rational therapy is based on the patient's clinical status, the pathogenic bacterium isolated or suspected, its antibiotic sensitivity pattern, the site of infection, and antimicrobial pharmacology. Since any antimicrobial agent must be considered potentially toxic to the host as well as to the parasite, the common and serious side effects of drugs prescribed should be kept in mind.

A. *The decision to administer antimicrobial agents presumes suspected or proved bacterial infection.* Exceptions to this rule include the occasional circumstances when prophylactic antibiotics are indicated (Table 9-1). Antibiotics should not be given to patients with viral infections and those with fevers of unknown etiology without adequate evidence of a suspected bacterial infection.

B. Cultures and, if possible, smears of the infected lesions should be obtained *before* antibiotic therapy is initiated. In the examination of purulent exudates, a technically acceptable preparation can be recognized by the pink (not blue) appearance of the polymorphonuclear leukocyte nucleus. The presence of leukocytes and absence of epithelial cells in a microscopic field helps to identify an adequate sputum specimen. The diagnosis of certain infections, such as tuberculosis, bacterial endocarditis, and cystitis, often requires multiple cultures from the same site. The identification of unusual or fastidious organisms by the diagnostic bacteriology laboratory requires *prompt* delivery of the specimen, with an indication of the organisms suspected.

C. Before the culture results are available, a rational choice of an antimicrobial agent can be made from knowledge of the most likely pathogens at a given site of infection. Recommended choices of antimicrobials for specific pathogens are listed in Table 9-2. When the focus of infection is not clear, repeated physical examination and review of the history will often provide clues.

D. A single drug is usually adequate. Therapy should be directed against the *most likely* pathogen(s); broad-spectrum "shotgun" therapy is

Table 9-1. Some Situations in Which Prophylactic Antimicrobial Drugs May Be Useful

Potential Infection	Drug	Dose
1. Streptococcal (group A) infection, rheumatic fever	(a) Benzathine penicillin G, IM *or*	1.2 million U each month
	(b) Sulfadiazine, PO *or*	1.0 gm qd for patients > 60 lb; 0.5 gm qd for patients < 60 lb
	(c) Penicillin G, PO	200,000–250,000 U bid
2. Meningococcal infection (no method uniformly effective)	(a) Sulfonamides for sensitive strain, PO *or*	100–150 mg/kg daily in 3 divided doses for 3 days (up to 6 gm daily)
	(b) Rifampin[a], PO	5 mg/kg bid for 2 days for children 3 months–1 year; 10 mg/kg bid for 2 days for children 1–12 years; 600 mg bid for 2 days for children > 12 years
3. Syphilis exposure	Penicillin, IM	2–4 million U procaine benzathine penicillin G, IM (test VDRL q3 months for 1 year)
4. Gonorrhea exposure	Penicillin, IM	2–4 million U procaine penicillin (test VDRL q3 months for 1 year)
5. Prevention of bacterial endocarditis		
(a) *S. viridans*	(a) Penicillin	(a) 600,000 U each of aqueous and procaine penicillin 1 hr before dental extraction and 600,000 U procaine penicillin for 2 days after
(b) Enterococcus	(b) Ampicillin, PO and gentamicin, IM	(b) Ampicillin, 25–50 mg/kg 1 hr before UTI manipulation and 25 mg/kg q6h for 2 days after it; gentamicin, 1 mg/kg in q8h for same period
6. Tuberculosis	Isoniazid	5 mg/kg, up to 0.3 gm daily for 12 months
7. Urinary tract infection in patients with indwelling catheters	(a) Neomycin plus polymyxin *or*	Constant bladder rinse via triple lumen catheter (1 L daily); neomycin, 40 mg/L; polymyxin, 20 mg/L
	(b) ¼% acetic acid irrigation	

8. *E. coli* (newborn diarrhea)	Neomycin, PO	50–100 mg/kg daily
9. Grossly contaminated injury, including bites	Penicillin Tetanus toxoid, IM Soap and water	0.6–1.2 million U daily 0.5 ml when indicated Plenty
10. Intravenous polyethylene catheter cutdown (avoid when possible)	Neomycin plus polymyxin B	Topical ointment to entry site
11. Sepsis following splenectomy, especially in children under 4 years of age	Ampicillin	50 mg/kg PO
12. Staphylococcal infection (chronic granulomatous disease)	Dicloxacillin	25 mg/kg PO
13. Pertussis in exposed susceptible	Erythromycin	20 mg/kg daily PO × 7–10 days
14. Diphtheria in exposed susceptible	Penicillin G Procaine penicillin	25,000–50,000 U/kg daily 300,000–600,000 U/kg daily IM for 7 days

---

[a] Dosage and safety for children under 5 years of age has yet to be determined. Its use has been associated with subsequent emergence of resistant organisms.

181

Table 9-2. Choice of Antimicrobial Agents for Specific Pathogens[a]

Organism	Drug	Infection	Pediatric Dose
Gram-positive cocci			
1. Group A streptococcus[b]	Penicillin G (Alt.: erythromycin, cephalothin, clindamycin)	Pharyngitis, impetigo Cellulitis, pneumonia Empyema, bacteremia Meningitis	50,000 U/kg/d PO *or* IM 50,000–100,000 U/kg/d PO, IM, *or* IV 100,000 U/kg/d IV *or* IM 300,000 U/kg/d IV
2. *Strep. viridans*	Penicillin G (Alt.: see 1)	Subacute bacterial endocarditis	250,000 U/kg/d IV
3. Enterococcus	Ampicillin or penicillin G plus an aminoglycoside	Subacute bacterial endocarditis	300 mg/kg/d (ampicillin) 250,000 U/kg/d (penicillin G) 3–7.5 mg/kg/d (gentamicin)
4. Pneumococcus	Penicillin G (Alt.: see 1)	Pneumonia Meningitis, complications (empyema)	25,000–50,000 U/kg/d (penicillin G) PO, IM, *or* IV 300,000 U/kg/d IV
5. *S. aureus* (penicillin-sensitive)	Penicillin G	Soft tissue abscess Endocarditis, pneumonia	50,000 U/kg/d PO, IM, *or* IV 300,000 U/kg/d IV
6. *S. aureus* (penicillin-resistant)	Semisynthetic penicillin (Alt.: cephalothin, erythromycin, clindamycin, vancomycin)	Mild infection Severe infection	50–100 mg/kg/d PO *or* IM 300 mg/kg/d IV
Gram-positive bacilli			
7. *Clostridium perfringens*	Penicillin G (Alt.: chloramphenicol)	Gas gangrene	300,000 U/kg/d
8. *Clostridium tetani*	Penicillin G (Alt.: tetracycline) Human antitoxin	Prevention of tetanus	100,000 U/kg/d PO *or* IM 250 U IM
9. *Listeria monocytogenes*	Ampicillin (Alt.: erythromycin, tetracycline, chloramphenicol)	Meningitis	300 mg/kg/d

10. *Corynebacterium diphtheriae*	Diphtheria	Penicillin G Antitoxin (horse) *or* Erythromycin	25,000 U/kg/d PO *or* IM 20,000–120,000 U IV 30–50 mg/kg/d PO, IM, *or* IV
Gram-negative cocci			
11. Meningococcus	Meningitis Meningococcemia	Penicillin G (Alt.: chloramphenicol, ampicillin, erythromycin)	300,000 U/kg/d IV 150,000 U/kg/d IV
12. Gonococcus (see Table 9-12)	Gonorrhea	Penicillin G (Spectinomycin, tetracycline, ampicillin–plus probenicid)	4.8 million U penicillin IM 2 gm spectinomycin (4 gm in females) IM 2 gm tetracycline daily for 5 days PO 3.5 gm ampicillin IM *or* PO ½ hr after 1 gm probenicid PO
Gram-negative bacillic			
13. *E. coli*	(a) Urinary infection	Sulfisoxazole (*Gantrisin*) *or*	150–200 mg/kg/d
	(b) Urinary infection Sepsis, meningitis Surgical wounds	Ampicillin	50–100 mg/kg/d 300 mg/kg/d 200 mg/kg/d
	(c) Sepsis	Cephalothin *or*	250 mg/kg/d
	(d) Sepsis, meningitis	Kanamycin *or*	15 mg/kg/d (maximum, 1.0 gm/d)
	(e) Sepsis, meningitis	Gentamicin	3–5 mg/kg/d
14. *Klebsiella*	(a) Sepsis, pneumonia	Kanamycin *or*	15 mg/kg/d
	(b) Sepsis, pneumonia	Cephalothin (Alt.: gentamicin, chloramphenicol, colistin)	250 mg/k/d
15. Enterobacteriaceae	(a) Sepsis	Gentamicin *or*	3–7.5 mg/kg/d IM *or* IV
	(b) Sepsis	Chloramphenicol (Alt.: kanamycin, tetracycline, colistin)	50–100 mg/kg/d IM

---

[a] Intended as rough guidelines only.

[b] Always treat for 10 days to prevent postinfection sequelae.

[c] Since sensitivity patterns vary, antibiotic choice should be based on specific sensitivity determination whenever possible.

183

Table 9-2. (*Continued*)

Organism	Infection	Drug	Pediatric Dose
16. *Proteus mirabilis*	Urinary tract infection	Ampicillin (Alt.: cephalothin, gentamicin, kanamycin)	50–100 mg/kg/d PO
17. *Proteus*, indole-positive		Kanamycin (Alt.: gentamicin, carbenicillin, chloramphenicol	15 mg/kg/d (maximum 1.0 gm/d) IM or IV
18. *Pseudomonas aeruginosa*		(a) Gentamicin (b) Carbenicillin (Alt.: Colistimethate)	3–7.5 mg/kg/d IM or IV 400–500 mg/kg/d IV
19. *Salmonella*		Chloramphenicol Ampicillin (if sensitive)	50–100 mg/kg/d IV 200–300 mg/kg/d PO, IM, or IV
20. *Serratia*		Gentamicin (Alt.: kanamycin, chloramphenicol, carbenicillin)	3–7.5 mg/kg/d IM or IV
21. *Shigella*		Ampicillin (Alt.: chloramphenicol, tetracycline)	50–100 mg/kg/d PO, IM, or IV
22. *Bacteroides*	Pulmonary infections Abscess, bacteremia	Penicillin G Chloramphenicol Clindamycin (Alt.: tetracycline, ampicillin)	300,000 U/kg/d IV 50–100 mg/kg/d IV 25 mg/kg/d IV
23. *Pasteurella multocida*		Penicillin G (Alt.: tetracycline)	50,000 U/kg/d PO
24. *Hemophilus influenzae*	Otitis media Meningitis, septic arthritis	Ampicillin *or* sulfonamide Ampicillin *or* Chloramphenicol	50–100 mg/kg/d; 100–200 mg/kg/d PO *or* IM 300–400 mg/kg/d IV 50–100 mg/kg/d IV

Ch. 9 Antibiotics and Infectious Diseases **185**

avoided. Multiple drugs may, however, be indicated before identification of the pathogen in patients with life-threatening infections and in the treatment of relatively resistant organisms in which synergistic antibacterial action can be anticipated.

E. Prophylactic use of broad spectrum antibiotics generally has been unsuccessful and carries the risks of superinfection, toxicity, and allergy. When specific therapy is directed against a specific organism (e.g., penicillin for group A streptococci), prophylaxis is more likely to succeed (see Table 9-1).

F. Mechanism of action Bactericidal antibiotics cause cell death in vitro; bacteriostatic agents inhibit cell growth without killing the organism. When humoral or cellular defenses are of minor importance (e.g., in bacterial endocarditis) or are impaired (e.g., in patients with gamma globulin deficiency, leukemia, or receiving antimetabolite drugs), this difference in mechanism of action of antibiotics may be clinically important, and bactericidal drugs may be preferable to bacteriostatic drugs.

G. *Antimicrobials should be given in adequate doses, by an appropriate route and vehicle, and for an adequate length of time.* Choice of the route of administration is affected by clinical factors such as vomiting or shock and by the site and type of infection. Absorption, diffusion into the site of infection, and route of excretion of the antimicrobial drug also should be considered. The rate of administration of individual IV doses varies with different antibiotics to avoid toxicity at peak levels.

H. Due to the ever-expanding list of drug incompatibilities, antibiotics administered IV should, in general, be mixed in separate IV bottles and administered at the appropriate interval by a "piggy-back" arrangement.

I. Assessment of therapy depends primarily on the response of the patient and secondarily on the laboratory data. Resistance of an organism in laboratory tests does not always correlate with clinical response. This is especially true in urinary tract infections (UTI) in which the antibiotic may be concentrated many fold in the urine. Common reasons for apparent failure of antimicrobial therapy are listed in Table 9-3.

II. OTHER ASPECTS OF THERAPY

A. Adequate supportive treatment requires careful attention to respiration, blood volume, acid-base and electrolyte balance, and the patient's nutritional status.

B. In general, **fever** exceeding 102° F may be treated with antipyretics, but care must be exercised not to obscure fever, since it can be a sign of inadequate therapy or developing complications.

1. The major reason for treatment of fever is usually the patient's comfort, although high fevers place increased metabolic demands on the body, and, in serious infections, control of fever may be an important supportive aspect of therapy (see Chap. 1, Sec. **III.B** and Chap. 8, Sec. **IX**).

2. Above a rectal temperature of 100.4° F, increased body temperature increases the patient's fluid requirements by approximately 8 percent for each degree Fahrenheit (12 percent for each degree centigrade above 38° C).

Table 9-3. Reasons for Antibiotic Failure

Drug factors
  Inadequate dose
  Wrong route of administration
  Interval between doses too long
  Failure to consider penetration and diffusion of drug
  Incompatibility of drugs mixed in IV fluids
  Interference of intestinal absorption of one antibiotic by another drug
  Failure to consider physical properties of the drug (e.g., relationship of
    activity with pH)
  Failure to consider mechanism of action of the drug (e.g., sulfonamide
    competition with para-aminobenzoic acid)
  Drug fever
Pathogen factors
  The bacterial pathogen has become genetically or phenotypically resistant.
  The bacteria are in an inactive or dormant phase. L forms or spheroplasts
    have often been suspected but seldom proved to be mechanisms for per-
    sistent infection.
  Superinfection
Host factors
  Surgical drainage of an abscess or obstructed conduit; or removable foreign
    body has been overlooked.
  Normal variation in expected clinical course
  Defect in humoral or cellular defenses
  The patient has concomitant serious disease.
Human factors
  Wrong diagnosis
  Prescribed antibiotic not given or wrong medicine given
  Contaminated IV equipment
  Phlebitis in IV site or abscess in IM site

C. **Surgery** has a primary role in the management of certain infections.
   The possible need for adequate drainage of loculated pus, removal of
   necrotic tissue, relief of obstruction, and removal of foreign bodies
   should always be considered.

D. Hospitalized patients with certain bacterial and viral diseases should
   be placed in **isolation**. Elective admissions of children harboring communicable diseases constitute a hazard to hospitalized patients and
   should be deferred. Admission of a patient, whether elective or emergency, requires careful recording of the patient's history of communicable diseases (especially mumps, measles, varicella, rubella, and
   hepatitis). Guidelines for hospital precautions and periods of con-
   tagiousness of common communicable diseases of childhood can be
   found in *Pediatrics* 53:663–673, 1974.

E. For certain viral diseases (Table 9-5) the administration of **gamma
   globulin** to close contacts within several days of exposure may modify
   the subsequent clinical appearance of the disease and limit its further
   spread.

III. **SPECIFIC ANTIMICROBIAL AGENTS** Table 9-2 summarizes the drugs of
   choice and dosages for specific bacterial pathogens. Table 9-6 lists major

routes of excretion of antimicrobials and modification in the presence of renal failure. Table 9-7 shows suggested dosage modification of the antimicrobials in neonates.

A. **Penicillin** The penicillins remain the drug of choice for most infections due to gram-positive cocci, gram-positive bacilli (Clostridia), Neisseria, and spirochetes. In addition, they are effective against many anaerobic bacteria gram-negative rods (e.g., *Proteus mirabilis*). The various preparations may be grouped as follows:

1. **Oral penicillin** Penicillin G is acid-labile and is absorbed poorly when given with food, in contrast to **phenoxymethyl penicillin** (penicillin V). The latter preparation is relatively acid-resistant and is absorbed from a full stomach, although higher blood levels are achieved when given 1 hr before or 2 hr after meals.

2. **Parenteral penicillin G** preparations give a wide variation of peak levels and duration of antibiotic effects.

   a. **Aqueous penicillin G** results in rapid attainment of high blood levels. Its rapid excretion in patients with normal renal function (*not* newborns—see Table 9-7) requires that it be administered frequently (usually q4h) for optimal therapy. It is prepared as a potassium or sodium salt (1.7 mEq/10^6 U), which must be taken into consideration when large doses are administered to patients with poor renal function or electrolyte imbalance.

   b. **Procaine penicillin G** is absorbed slowly from IM injection and so produces relatively low but prolonged serum concentrations. It should thus be used only in infections due to highly susceptible organisms (e.g., pneumococcus or group A streptococcus).

   c. **Benzathine penicillin G** produces even lower blood levels, which last for as long as 3–4 weeks. It is used primarily against group A streptococci, prophylactically in patients with rheumatic heart disease, and therapeutically when adherence to a program of oral penicillin seems questionable.

3. **Penicillinase-resistant penicillins** are used primarily in the treatment of penicillin-resistant *Staphylococcus aureus* infections. All are significantly *less* potent than penicillin G against penicillin-sensitive microorganisms. The only clinically significant difference between preparations relates to recommended route of administration.

   a. **Methicillin, oxacillin, and nafcillin** are recommended for parenteral administration.

   b. **Cloxacillin and dicloxacillin** are absorbed significantly better from the gastrointestinal tract than are the other penicillinase-resistant penicillins and are the agents of choice in oral therapy.

4. **Broad spectrum penicillins**

   a. **Ampicillin and amoxicillin** share the gram-positive spectrum of penicillin G. In addition, they are effective against most *Hemophilus influenzae*, but some resistant strains have recently been reported. They are also effective against *Shigella* spp., enterococci, and some gram-negative enteric bacteria (e.g., *Proteus mirabilis* and some strains of *Escherichia coli*).

Table 9-4. Doses of Antimicrobial Agents[a]

Antimicrobial	Dose	Frequency	Route	Usual Maximum Dose
A. Penicillins				
1. Oral penicillin G[b, c]	50,000–100,000 U/kg/d	q6h	PO	6.4 MU
Phenoxymethyl penicillin (V)[c]			PO	6.4 MU
2. Parenteral				
a. Aqueous penicillin G[a]	25,000–400,000 U/kg/d	q2–6h	IV	24 MU
b. Procaine penicillin G[a]	25,000–50,000 U/kg/d	q12–24h	IM	
c. Benthazine penicillin G[c]	600,000–1,200,000 U	single dose	IM	
3. Penicillinase-resistant				
a. Methicillin,[a] oxacillin,[a] nafcillin[a]	100–300 mg/kg/d	q4h	IM or IV	12 gm
b. Cloxacillin,[c] dicloxacillin[c]	25–100 mg/kg/d	q6h	PO	4 gm
4. Broad Spectrum				
a. Ampicillin[a]	50–100 mg/kg/d	q6h	PO	4 gm
	50–400 mg/kg/d	q4–6h	IM or IV	12 gm
Amoxicillin	20–40 mg/kg/d	q8h	PO	3 gm
b. Carbenicillin[a]	50–65 mg/kg/d	q6h	PO	40 gm
	400–600 mg/kg/d	q2–4h	IM or IV	
B. Cephalosporins				
1. Cephalothin[a]	60–250 mg/kg/d	q4–6h	IV	12 gm
2. Cephaloridine[c]	100 mg/kg up to 4 gm	q6h	IM	
3. Cefazolin[c]	25–100 mg/kg/d	q4–6h	IM or IV	6 gm
4. Cephalexin[c]	25–50 mg/kg/d	q6h	PO	4 gm
C. Erythromycins[c]	30–50 mg/kg/d	q6h	PO	4 gm
	50 mg/kg/d	q6h	IV[d]	4 gm
D. Lincomycins[c]	30–60 mg/kg/d	q6–8h	PO	5 gm
	20–100 mg/kg/d	q6–8h	IM or IV	5 gm
Clindamycin[c]	10–25 mg/kg/d	q6h	PO	5 gm
	10–40 mg/kg/d	q6h	IM or IV	5 gm

E. Sulfonamides[c]	150–200 mg/kg/d	q6h	PO	8 gm
	100–120 mg/kg/d	q6h	IV	
F. Aminoglycosides				
1. Streptomycin[c]	20–40 mg/kg/d	q12h	IM	2 gm
2. Kanamycin[a]	50–100 mg/kg/d	q6h	PO	—
	15 mg/kg/d	q12h	IM	1.5 gm
3. Gentamicin[a]	3–7.5 mg/kg/d	q12h	IM or IV	5 mg/kg
4. Neomycin	50–100 mg/kg/d	q4–6h	PO	0
5. Paromomycin	25–30 mg/kg/d	q4–6h	PO	0
G. Nitrofurantoins[c]	5–7 mg/kg/d	q6h	PO	400 mg
H. Polymyxins				
1. Polymyxin B[c]	1.5–2.5 mg/kg/d	q8h	IV or IM	2.5 mg/kg
2. Colistimethate (Polymyxin E, Coly-Mycin M)[a]	2.5–5 mg/kg/d	q8h	IM	5 mg/kg
	5–15 mg/kg/d	q6–8h	PO	0
3. Colistin[a]	10–15 mg/kg/d	q6–8h	PO	0
I. Chloramphenicol[a]	50–100 mg/kg/d	q6h	PO or IV	4 gm
J. Tetracycline,[c] Chlortetracycline,[c] Oxytetracycline[c]	20–40 mg/kg/d	q6h	PO	2 gm
	10–20 mg/kg/d	q12h	IV or IM	2 gm
1. Doxycycline[c]	2–4 mg/kg/d	q12h	PO	4 mg/kg/d
2. Minocycline[c]	4 mg/kg/d	q12h	PO	4 mg/kg/d
K. Methenamines				
1. Mandelamine[c]	75 mg/kg/d	q6h	PO	4 gm
2. Hiprex[c]	75 mg/kg/d	q12h	PO	8 gm

[a] For newborn doses see Table 9-7, p. 192.
[b] 1 mg = 1600 units.
[c] Not recommended for newborns.
[d] May be given in continuous drip.

189

Table 9-5. Gamma Globulin Prophylaxis of Viral Diseases for Exposed Susceptibles[a]

Disease	Indication	Dosage	Efficacy
Measles	Close contact within 5 days	0.04 ml/kg 0.25 ml/kg	Modification Prevention (recommended for high risk patients only)[b]
Hepatitis A (infectious hepatitis)	Close contact (preferably within 1 week of exposure)	0.02 ml/kg	Modification (to anicteric, mild disease)
	Anticipated travel to endemic areas	0.02 ml/kg per months of exposure (up to 0.12 ml/kg for 6 months at which time a repeat dose is recommended)	Modification (to anicteric, mild disease)
Varicella	Close contacts at high risk (within 3 days)	0.6–1.2 ml/kg[b] for patients on corticosteroids for various diseases, on immunosuppressive drugs, with leukemia or other disseminated malignancies, or impaired delayed hypersensitivity	Possible modification

[a] When gamma globulin is indicated it should be given as soon as possible following exposure. It is of no proved value in the prophylaxis of rubella and mumps. In posttransfusion hepatitis hyperimmune gamma globulin, when available, may be beneficial.
[b] Zoster immune globulin (ZIG), if available, is preferable. Request should be directed to the CDC, Atlanta, Georgia or regional representative. Convalescent plasma also may modify the illness, if given immediately after exposure.

Table 9-6. Modification of Antibiotic Dosage in Renal Disease (with Some General Rules of Thumb Based on Fragmentary Evidence)

Antibiotic	Major Excretory Route	Dosage Modification
I. Little or no change		
A. Cloxacillin, dicloxacillin[a]	Kidney (liver)	None
B. Chloramphenicol[b]	Liver	
C. Doxycycline[c]	Liver	
D. Isoniazid[a, d]	Liver (kidney)	
E. Erythromycin[b]	Liver	
F. Oxacillin[b]	Kidney (liver)	
G. Penicillin[b] (low dose)	Kidney	
II. Minor alteration		
A. Ampicillin[e]	Kidney (liver)	In anuric patients give
B. Carbenicillin[a, e]	Kidney (liver)	full dose on first day,
C. Cephalothin[a, e], cephalexin	Kidney and liver	followed by half doses
D. Lincomycin[b], clindamycin	Liver and kidney	thereafter
E. Methicillin[b]	Kidney (liver)	
F. Penicillin[b] G (high dose)	Kidney	
III. Major alteration		
A. Amphotericin B	Liver and kidney	Normal or slightly
B. Cephaloridine[a, e]	Kidney	reduced dose if creatinine clearance > 30 ml/min and BUN < 50
C. Colistimethate[a]	Kidney	Half-dose every day if
D. Gentamicin[d, f]	Kidney	creatinine clearance
E. Kanamycin[a, d, f]	Kidney	10–30 ml/min and BUN 50
F. Polymyxin B[b]	Kidney	Half dose q2–3 days if
G. Streptomycin	Kidney	creatinine clearance
H. Vancomycin[b]	Kidney	< 10 ml/min or BUN > 80
IV. Relatively contraindicated in renal insufficiency		
A. Nitrofurantoin		
B. Nalidixic acid		
C. Absorbable sulfonamides		
D. Methenamine mandelate		
E. PAS		
F. Tetracycline other than doxycycline		

[a] Significant removal by peritoneal dialysis.
[b] Not appreciably removed by dialysis.
[c] Doxycycline is the tetracycline of choice in renal failure.
[d] Significant removal by hemodialysis: 25% a-v difference.
[e] Significant removal by hemodialysis: 15–25% a-v difference.
[f] References: Bennett, W. M., et al., *J.A.M.A.* 223:991, 1973; Bulger, R., and Petersdorf, R. G., *Postgrad. Med.* 47:160, 1970; Kunin, C. M., *Ann. Intern. Med.* 67:151, 1967.

Table 9-7. Recommended Parenteral Dosages for Antimicrobials in Newborns

	1 Week	1–4 Weeks
Ampicillin	50–100 mg/kg/d q12h	100–200 mg/kg/d q8h
Carbenicillin	300 mg/kg/d q8h	100 mg/kg/d q6h
Cephalothin	40 mg/kg/d q12h	60 mg/kg/d q8h
Chloramphenicol[a]	25 mg/kg d q6–8h	50 mg/kg/d q6–8h
Colistimethate,[b] colistin (for oral use only)	15 mg/kg/d PO q6h	15 mg/kg/d q6h
Gentamicin	5.0–7.5 mg/kg/d q8–12h	7.5 mg/kg/d q8h
Kanamycin	15 mg/kg/d q12h	15 mg/kg/d q12h
Neomycin (for oral use only)	50–100 mg/kg/d PO q4–6h	15 mg/kg/d q12h
Oxacillin, Nafcillin, Methicillin	50–100 mg/kg/d q12h	100–200 mg/kg/d q6h
Paromomycin (for oral use only)	25–30 mg/kg/d PO q4–6h	15 mg/kg/d q6h
Penicillin G	50,000–100,000 U/kg/d q12h	50,000–150,000 U/kg/d q6–8h

[a] For premature infants, the dosage is 25 mg/kg/d throughout the first month of life.
[b] See Sec. III, p. 217.

    (1) Due to its limited gram-negative spectrum and its susceptibility to penicillinase, **ampicillin should not be used alone in the treatment of sepsis of undefined etiology.**

    (2) Dose-related diarrhea and maculopapular rash after about 5–7 days of treatment are more common with oral ampicillin than with the other penicillin preparations.

  b. Carbenicillin differs from ampicillin in its bactericidal activity against *Pseudomonas aeruginosa* and ampicillin-resistant Proteus strains and in its high cost. Its usefulness is limited to infections with these organisms.

    (1) High parenteral dosages, usually intravenous, are necessary to achieve therapeutic serum concentrations in most cases.

    (2) The oral preparation provides sufficient drug concentration in the urine and may be effective in the occasional case of localized UTI due to *Pseudomonas* and ampicillin-resistant *Proteus* strains.

    (3) Best results with parenteral carbenicillin have been reported in UTI, but mixed success in *Pseudomonas* pneumonia and in septicemia in leukemia patients has been noted.

    (4) The combination of carbenicillin and gentamicin has been demonstrated to be synergistic against many *Pseudomonas aeruginosa* isolates and probably represents the most effective antibiotic therapy currently available for severe *Pseudomonas* infection. **The drugs should not be mixed** for simultaneous administration, since in aqueous solution (but not in serum) antagonism may occur.

    (5) The high dosages required and the sodium content of carbenicillin (6.2–6.5 mEq/gm) can result in excess sodium load for patients with impaired renal or cardiac function. In addition, the increased motor activity and convulsions occasionally associated with massive doses of penicillin can occur.

5. **Adverse reactions** to penicillins are relatively common. An estimated 1–3 percent of adult patients are allergic to the penicillins, but the incidence is less among children. Because all penicillins share the same basic chemical structure, patients with hypersensitivity to one preparation may react to any of the others.

   a. **Immediate reactions** include anaphylaxis, angioneurotic edema, and urticaria. The single most important method of identifying the patient with penicillin hypersensitivity is the eliciting of a history of atopic reactions to penicillins or their analogues.

   b. **Delayed reactions** include fever, eosinophilia, serum sickness, dermatologic manifestations and occasional autoimmune phenomena.

   c. Neutropenia has been reported with methicillin, ampicillin, and oxacillin.

   d. Convulsive activity may result from intrathecal administration or high doses in patients with marginal renal function.

   e. Hyperkalemia or congestive heart failure from excess cation can result when very large doses of penicillin salt are given in the presence of impaired renal function.

   f. Diarrhea may result from the oral preparations and is usually dose-related.

B. **Cephalosporins** are similar to penicillin in chemical structure and mechanism of action. They are effective against most gram-positive cocci, including penicillinase-producing *S. aureus*, but they appear to be less active against enterococci. In addition, the cephalosporins are bactericidal for most strains of *Klebsiella, Proteus mirabilis, E. coli,* and *Salmonella* and *Shigella* species.

These drugs are used primarily in the treatment of staphylococcal infections in patients allergic to penicillin and in infections caused by sensitive enteric bacteria. Since many gram-negative bacteria are resistant, these drugs alone cannot be expected to give broad spectrum coverage in "gram-negative sepsis" of unknown etiology.

1. **Cephalothin** is used primarily IV; IM administration is very painful.

2. **Cephaloridine** is for IM use only.

3. **Cefazolin** is a new preparation for either IM or IV administration.

4. **Cephalexin** is an oral preparation which gives adequate serum and urine levels. Use is limited to susceptible UTI and treatment of infections in other soft tissues due to susceptible gram-positive cocci. This preparation is well tolerated; its absorption is delayed and reduced by food in the stomach.

5. **Adverse reactions** are summarized as follows:

   a. **Allergic manifestations** are similar to those with penicillin. Although most patients with penicillin allergy tolerate cephalosporins well, there is a small but definite risk of cross-sensitivity.

b. The Coombs test in patients receiving cephalosporins may become positive, but hemolytic anemia is rare.

c. Cephalothin, which must be administered parenterally, is irritating, and phlebitis is commonly associated with its use IV.

d. Renal toxicity may occur with cephaloridine, especially in high doses (greater than 100 mg/kg daily).

C. Erythromycin is used commonly as an alternative oral drug for patients allergic to penicillin and is a drug of choice in the treatment of *Mycoplasma pneumoniae* infections. In addition, its spectrum includes most gram-positive organisms, spirochetes, and some rickettsiae. Its action is primarily bacteriostatic, and it diffuses well into most body fluids.

1. Most *S. aureus* currently isolated are sensitive to erythromycin, but resistance may develop during therapy.

2. No currently available preparation of erythromycin has been demonstrated to be clinically superior to the others.

3. Adverse reactions

  a. Erythromycin estolate (Ilosone) has been associated with cholestatic hepatitis, especially when administered for prolonged periods.

  b. Other adverse reactions are generally limited to mild gastrointestinal upset or rash and are infrequent.

4. Parenteral preparations are available but are seldom used because large volumes must be administered to obtain adequate dosage by the IM route, and phlebitis frequently complicates IV use.

D. Lincomycin and clindamycin are similar to erythromycin in absorption, distribution, and mechanism of action, but not in chemical structure. The antibacterial spectrum is similar, but not identical, to that of erythromycin. Bacteria resistant to the lincomycins frequently are also resistant to erythromycin. Important differences include clindamycin's efficacy against anaerobic bacteria, including *Bacteroides*, and lesser potency of the lincomycins against *Mycoplasma pneumonia*, *Neisseria*, and enterococci.

1. Lincomycins penetrate well into bone and may have special effectiveness in the treatment of osteomyelitis.

2. Both drugs are available in oral and parenteral preparations (IM or IV route). Oral clindamycin is better absorbed and costs less than lincomycin.

3. Clindamycin and lincomycin can cause severe diarrhea and potentially fatal colitis. Although these serious complications have been reported only in patients > 14 years old, these drugs should be used cautiously in children. Diarrhea is less common with oral clindamycin than with oral lincomycin. Less common adverse reactions include jaundice, neutropenia, and rash.

4. Lincomycin preparations are reserved for the treatment of anaerobic infections (clindamycin) and for patients allergic to penicillin where less toxic antimicrobial agents are inappropriate.

E. Sulfonamides have a spectrum of activity that includes the common gram-positive cocci, *H. influenzae*, *Nocardia*, some strains of *Shigella*, and many *E. coli.* Since certain products of tissue necrosis such as para-aminobenzoic acid (PABA) inhibit the action of sulfonamides, clinical effectiveness of these agents is limited to mild and moderate infections with minimal suppuration.

1. Current uses include *E. coli* UTI, prophylaxis against group A streptococcal infections in patients with rheumatic heart disease, and otitis media (in combination with penicillin).

2. In established group A streptococcal infection, sulfonamides *cannot* be relied on to prevent postinfectious sequelae.

3. **Adverse reactions**   A wide variety of adverse reactions have been associated with sulfonamides.

    a. Rash and fever are the most common, but hepatitis, vasculitis, bone marrow depression, and Stevens-Johnson syndrome may occur.

    b. Hemolytic anemia may occur in patients with glucose 6-phosphate dehydrogenase (G-6-PD) deficiency.

    c. Nephrotoxicity is now rare due to the use of more soluble sulfonamides (e.g., sulfisoxazole, trisulfapyrimidines).

    d. Interference with bilirubin metabolism by competition for albumin-binding sites may occur. **Avoid sulfonamides in neonates and in pregnant women at term** in order to prevent the risk of kernicterus.

F. **Aminoglycosides** are bactericidal for most enteric bacilli but are ineffective against *Bacteroides* and other anaerobic organisms. In vitro synergism with penicillin and ampicillin against most strains of enterococci has been demonstrated for streptomycin, kanamycin, and gentamicin. Endocarditis due to enterococcus is usually treated with one of these aminoglycosides and ampicillin (or penicillin G).

Because activity of the aminoglycosides is greatly increased at alkaline pH, the urine can be alkalinized for maximum effect in UTI. Aminoglycoside antibiotics are poorly absorbed from the gastrointestinal tract, and achievement of effective blood levels requires *parenteral* administration.

1. **Streptomycin** has variable effectiveness against the common enteric bacilli and *H. influenzae.*

    a. In view of the rapid development of high-level resistance during therapy, **streptomycin should not be used alone**, even against a sensitive bacterium.

    b. Streptomycin remains an effective first-line drug in the treatment of tuberculosis.

    c. **Adverse reactions** include dose-related 8th nerve damage (vestibular greater than auditory), skin eruptions, fever, and, rarely, nephrotoxicity.

2. **Kanamycin** is effective against most of the commonly isolated Enterobacteriaceae. *Pseudomonas* and *Bacteroides* are generally resistant.

    a. Kanamycin was introduced as an antistaphylococcal drug and remains an effective second-line drug against most strains of *S. aureus.* It also is active against *Mycobacterium tuberculosis.*

b. Adverse reactions

(1) Minor hypersensitivity reactions (rash, eosinophilia, fever) may occur at any dose. However, the serious adverse reactions, renal failure and irreversible deafness, are dose-related and usually preventable if the daily dose is limited to 15 mg/kg and the duration of therapy does not exceed 14 days in patients with normal renal function. Renal function and auditory acuity (especially for high frequencies) should be monitored closely in patients receiving prolonged courses of kanamycin.

(2) Rarely, neuromuscular block with respiratory paralysis has been reported when kanamycin has been administered by the intraperitoneal or IV route, especially in renal failure. The IM route is therefore preferable except in shock.

(3) When toxic levels of kanamycin are present, prompt reduction can be achieved by either peritoneal dialysis or hemodialysis.

3. Gentamicin is bactericidal against most common gram-negative enteric bacilli and *S. aureus.* Success has been reported in a variety of severe infections due to *Pseudomonas, Serratia,* Enterobacteriaceae resistant to kanamycin, and in gram-negative sepsis of unknown etiology.

a. Since gentamicin-resistant *Pseudomonas* has been associated with its extensive use, **the indiscriminate use of gentamicin (including topical preparations) should be avoided.** Guidelines for administration are the same as for kanamycin (see **F.2.,** p. 195).

b. Adverse reactions

(1) Adverse reactions are similar to those of the other aminoglycosides (kanamycin and streptomycin).

(2) Ototoxicity (vestibular greater than cochlear) and nephrotoxicity are dose-related; therefore, auditory and renal function should be monitored closely during therapy. If possible, serum levels of gentamicin should also be monitored.

4. Neomycin and paromomycin are similar to kanamycin in spectrum, but the high incidence of nephrotoxicity and ototoxicity precludes their use as systemic agents.

a. As oral agents, their use is limited to the treatment of non-invasive bacterial gastroenteritis and to the suppression of bowel flora.

b. Malabsorption and intercurrent staphylococcal enterocolitis may complicate the oral use of these drugs.

c. Increased systemic absorption of neomycin through diseased bowel mucosa or from wounds may result in toxic blood levels, particularly in patients with renal failure.

d. Topical neomycin in skin infections and 0.25% neomycin as a bladder irrigant are other frequent uses.

G. Nitrofurantoin affects most common gram-positive and gram-negative pathogens (except *Pseudomonas*). The prompt renal excretion of nitrofurantoin results in adequate urine levels but negligible blood levels. It is therefore used only in the treatment of UTI. It is available only as an oral preparation.

1. **Toxic reactions** occur in about 5 percent of patients (most commonly, nausea, vomiting, and abdominal cramps). Nitrofurantoin macrocrystal preparation may cause less gastrointestinal upset and may result in greater tissue levels of the drug.

2. **Other adverse reactions** include rashes, peripheral neuropathy, allergic pneumonitis, and hemolytic anemia in patients with G-6-PD deficiency.

3. **Nitrofurantoin should not be given to patients with significant renal impairment,** since in these cases urinary concentrations of the drug usually are not sufficient to inhibit susceptible organisms, and blood levels in such patients may be high enough to cause toxicity.

4. **Nitrofurantoin should not be administered to newborns** or to women who are or may be pregnant because it crosses the placenta and competes with bilirubin for albumin-binding sites.

5. Nitrofuranzone, a similar derivative, is widely used as a topical antibacterial agent in burns and other cutaneous wounds.

H. **Polymyxins** are polypeptide agents, which are effective against *Pseudomonas aeruginosa* and the common Enterobacteriaceae (except *Proteus* strains and *Serratia*). *Bacteroides* species and the gram-positive bacteria are resistant.

1. Polymyxins are poorly absorbed from the gastrointestinal tract, penetrate tissues poorly, and do not diffuse into the CSF. They are excreted via the kidneys.

2. Polymyxins have been used primarily to treat known *Pseudomonas* infections and "gram-negative sepsis" when *Pseudomonas* is suspected, but the introduction of gentamicin and carbenicillin have challenged their use in this regard.

3. Poor tissue penetration limits the effectiveness of the polymyxins in the treatment of soft tissue infections outside the urinary tract.

4. The available oral preparations of these drugs are nonabsorbable and may be used in the treatment of gastroenteritis due to enteropathic *E. coli*. Topical preparations are also available.

5. **Adverse reactions**

   a. Parenteral polymyxins are nephrotoxic, and patients receiving these agents should be monitored closely for abnormalities of urine sediment or renal function.

   b. Mild neurologic complaints (circumoral paresthesias, mild ataxia) are common.

   c. Rarely, high blood levels of these drugs result in neuromuscular block with weakness and respiratory insufficiency.

6. **Polymyxin preparations**

   a. **Polymyxin B** is available for IM or IV use.

b. Colistimethate (polymyxin E, Coly-Mycin M)   This agent and *polymyxin B* are essentially interchangeable at their respective recommended doses.

c. Colistin is the parent compound of colistimethate and is available for oral or topical use.

I. Chloramphenicol is effective against most common gram-negative bacilli, including *H. influenzae* and anaerobic bacilli (but not *Pseudomonas*) and most gram-positive organisms, including *S. aureus,* and many rickettsiae. It is well absorbed from the gastrointestinal tract and diffuses well into tissues and the cerebrospinal fluid. It is conjugated in the liver and subsequently excreted in the urine. It can be administered PO or IV; the IM preparation is no longer approved.

1. Restriction of its usage has been urged, due to the rare but often fatal occurrence of aplastic anemias. With the availability of alternative antibiotics, the indications for chloramphenicol have diminished.

2. Chloramphenicol remains the drug of choice in severe *Salmonella* infections, including typhoid fever and severe ampicillin-resistant *H. influenzae* infection.

3. Because of its excellent diffusion into the brain and effectiveness against anaerobic bacteria, chloramphenicol is often used preferentially in the treatment of brain abscesses.

4. **Adverse reactions,** other than aplastic anemia, are usually dose-related and reversible.

   a. Interference with iron metabolism, total iron, vacuolization of erythrocyte precursors in bone marrow, decreased reticulocyte count, and anemia, as well as leukopenia and thrombocytopenia, are common at the dosage of 100 mg/kg/day.

   b. Patients should be followed with serial determinations of the reticulocyte, leukocyte, and differential count (q48–72h) and of the serum iron and iron-binding capacity.

   c. Because the glucuronide transferase system is not fully developed in newborns, the administration of chloramphenicol may produce excessive blood levels and result in the shocklike "gray baby" syndrome, which is potentially lethal unless the condition is recognized and the drug discontinued. For this reason, **chloramphenicol is contraindicated in infections in newborns for which alternative antibiotics are available.** If no alternative drug exists, chloramphenicol should be given in low doses (see Table 9-7).

   d. Other rare reactions include optic neuritis and peripheral neuritis.

J. Tetracycline   The introduction of alternative antibiotics, the increasing prevalence of resistant strains of common pathogenic bacteria, and the numerous side effects of the tetracyclines have limited their usefulness.

1. Tetracyclines are moderately effective against the common Enterobacteriaceae (except *Proteus*), although increasing resistance (often mediated by R factors) has developed among *E. coli* and other previously sensitive bacilli.

2. Although most anaerobic organisms are sensitive, effectiveness against *Clostridia* has not remained uniform.

3. The tetracyclines also may be effective against certain gram-positive organisms, although resistance is common among staphylococcal and streptococcal isolates.

4. While most isolates of *H. influenzae* and *Neisseria* are sensitive to tetracyclines, other drugs are preferred.

5. *Mycoplasma pneumoniae* and many rickettsial species are also sensitive to tetracyclines.

6. **Adverse reactions**

   a. Gastrointestinal irritation resulting in nausea, vomiting, and/or diarrhea is common.

   b. When the drug is administered during the period of dental calcification (from the fifth month of gestation to approximately age 8 years), permanent binding of tetracycline to calcium may produce a dose-related brownish stain on the teeth.

   c. Dermatologic reactions, including photosensitivity, can occur. Photosensitivity reactions have been reported with all preparations, but occur most commonly with demeclocycline.

   d. **Other adverse reactions** include:

      (1) Superinfection (e.g., oral moniliasis).

      (2) Prerenal azotemia (especially in patients with preexisting renal disease).

      (3) Renal tubular acidosis (with outdated preparations).

      (4) Pseudotumor cerebri.

7. At the recommended dosages and frequency of administration, little difference has been demonstrated in the clinical efficacy of the numerous tetracycline preparations available, except:

   a. **Doxycycline,** which is the tetracycline of choice in patients with renal disease, and

   b. **Minocycline,** which may be effective in treatment of meningococcal carriers.

K. **Methenamine** (Mandelamine, Hiprex) has little native antibacterial activity, but at a pH of less than 5.5 it hydrolyzes to produce formaldehyde and mandelic acid, which are antibacterial. Its use is limited to the treatment of UTI, in which it acts as a surface antiseptic agent.

1. In patients receiving methenamine, urine pH must be monitored with indicator paper, and acidifying agents, such as ascorbic acid, methionine, ammonium chloride, or acid ash diet, may be required to maintain urinary acidity. If patients are unable to acidify their urine or if the infection is due to a urea-splitting organism, such as *Proteus,* the drug is generally ineffective.

2. **Adverse reactions** are uncommon and consist of mild gastrointestinal upset, hematuria, and, rarely, ataxia. Metabolic acidosis due to the acidifying agents may occur in patients with impaired renal function.

IV. TREATMENT OF INFECTIOUS DISEASES

A. Impetigo

1. **Etiology**   Usually, group A β-hemolytic streptococci. *S. aureus* is often recovered from cultures of impetiginous lesions, but in many cases appears to be nonpathogenic. An exception is bullous impetigo, which is caused by *S. aureus*, bacteriophage group II (Sec. **VIII,** p. 440).

2. **Evaluation and diagnosis** include careful examination of the skin, scalp, and draining lymph nodes. If the diagnosis is in doubt, a gram stain of the bullous fluid may be helpful.

3. **Therapy**

   a. Benzathine penicillin G (600,000 U) IM or oral penicillin V (250,000 U tid) for 10 days is effective for most patients.

   b. Clindamycin (10–20 mg/kg per day qid) or erythromycin (30–50 mg/kg per day qid) or an oral preparation of a penicillinase-resistant penicillin, such as dicloxacillin (25–50 mg/kg per day qid), are effective alternatives.

   c. Topical antibiotics in place of systemic antibiotics or pHisoHex scrubs alone are less effective.

B. Cellulitis (including erysipelas)

1. **Etiology**   *S. aureus*, β-hemolytic streptococci, and, less commonly, *H. influenzae*, type b.

2. **Evaluation**

   a. Needle aspiration of the advancing border of an active lesion should be carried out for gram stain and culture.

   b. A blood culture should be done in patients with severe cellulitis, high fever, generalized toxicity, or impaired host defenses.

   c. Sinus x-ray studies should be done in patients with facial cellulitis around the eyes (see Chap. 23, Sec. **III.C**).

3. **Diagnosis** is usually established by the characteristic warm, erythematous, tender, edematous, and indurated skin.

   a. Streptococcal cellulitis (erysipelas) is suggested by advancing, well-demarcated, heaped-up borders; facial involvement may assume a butterfly distribution.

   b. *H. influenzae*, type b, although not a common cause, is suggested by a fever greater than 102° F, facial involvement, and the characteristic purple color (which occurs in about half the patients) in a child 6 months–2 years old.

4. **Therapy**

   a. Application of local heat, e.g., warm compresses, 10–20 min qid or more.

   b. If feasible, immobilization and elevation of the affected extremity.

   c. Incision and drainage of any primary suppurative focus.

   d. **Antibiotics**

      (1) **Localized cellulitis without fever** may be treated with oral antibiotics but, if evidence of systemic toxicity is present, paren-

teral antibiotics should be given until sustained clinical improvement has occurred.

(2) Streptococcal disease or erysipelas usually responds to benzathine penicillin G (0.6–1.2 million U IM in 1 dose) or oral penicillin V (250,000–400,000 U qid). More severely ill patients may initially require procaine penicillin G (600,000–900,000 U IM q12h), or even IV penicillin (100,000 U/kg per day q4h). Treatment should be continued for 7–10 days.

(3) Staphylococcal cellulitis is treated either with penicillin or a penicillinase-resistant penicillin, depending on the organisms' in vitro sensitivity; e.g., nafcillin or oxacillin (200–300 mg/kg per day IV q4h) for severe infections, or dicloxacillin (25–50 mg/kg per day qid PO for milder infections). Ampicillin (300 mg/kg per day q4h) IV is recommended for *H. influenzae* cellulitis, in view of the high incidence of positive blood cultures in this disease.

(4) Orbital cellulitis For patients with orbital cellulitis, hospitalization and high doses of antibiotics given IV are indicated. The initial choice should include a penicillinase-resistant penicillin and, if the child is under 6 years of age, an antimicrobial effective against *H. influenzae* B.

C. **Scalded skin syndrome (Ritter's disease or toxic epidermal necrolysis), bullous impetigo,** and **staphylococcal scarlet fever** represent a spectrum of dermatologic manifestations of staphylococcal infection, resulting from release of soluble toxins by *S. aureus*. The most common manifestation is generalized exfoliative dermatitis, known as Ritter's disease when it occurs in newborn infants and as toxic epidermal necrolysis, or Lyell's disease, in older children.

1. **Etiology** The infecting organism is *S. aureus* (usually bacteriophage group II).

2. **Evaluation**

   a. Cultures of the skin, nose, and throat, and often of blood should be made (exceptions include children with any localized bullous impetigo and older children who are afebrile and nontoxic).

   b. Gram stain of the scalded skin, or bullous fluid, or both will differentiate direct staphylococcal skin invasion from the more common toxin-mediated skin changes.

   c. A history of *S. aureus* in the family or nursery and possible drug allergies should be sought, as well as Nikolsky's sign (gentle rubbing of the skin results in sloughing of the epidermis).

3. **Diagnosis** is established by the clinical picture in association with recovery of *S. aureus* from the patient. Nikolsky's sign is usually indicative of the scalded skin syndrome, but its absence does not exclude this diagnosis.

4. **Therapy**

   a. A 7–10-day course of a penicillinase-resistant penicillin (or penicillin if the *S. aureus* is sensitive) usually is sufficient. The antibiotic is usually given parenterally (e.g., oxacillin 300 mg/kg per dose q4h IV) (see Table 9-7 for dosage in infants less than 4 weeks of age).

b. After a good clinical response has been achieved, therapy may be completed with oral dicloxacillin (25–50 mg/kg per day qid). In the patient with a blood culture positive for *S. aureus*, effective antibiotic levels should be maintained for at least 3 weeks.

c. Contact precautions are indicated until the lesions have resolved.

d. Corticosteroids have not been demonstrated to be beneficial.

D. Animal bites Initial management is primarily prophylactic.

1. Potential bacterial complications

a. Etiology Potential pathogens include anaerobic and microaerophilic streptococci, other anaerobic cocci, *Clostridia* species (including tetani), *Pasteurella multocida, Streptobacillus moniliformis,* and *Spirillum minus.* (The latter two cause the two types of rat-bite fever).

b. Evaluation of the patient who has been bitten by an animal includes an assessment of the patient's immunity to tetanus (previous immunizations) as well as the extent of the wound.

c. Diagnosis of a bacterial complication of an animal bite is suggested by the finding of cellulitis (see **B.2**).

d. Therapy Besides local antisepsis and surgical care of the bite, including irrigation and débridement if necessary, the following prophylactic measures should be considered:

(1) Tetanus immunization

(a) Tetanus toxoid (0.5 ml IM) is indicated only if the patient has not received a booster in the previous 5 years or has not completed the basic series of three tetanus immunizations.

(b) In the absence of a history of two documented preceding tetanus immunizations, patients with other than clean, minor wounds should receive passive immunization with human tetanus immune globulin (5 U/kg IM, up to 250 U). In such cases, tetanus toxoid is given but in a separate syringe and site, with subsequent completion of the recommended series at monthly intervals.

(2) Antibiotics Indicated only for severe bites. Since most of the potential bacterial pathogens are sensitive to penicillin, low-dose penicillin V (300,000–600,000 U bid for 3–5 days) is recommended.

2. Rabies prophylaxis The recommendations are based on those of the U.S.P.H.S. Advisory Committee, 1967.

a. Evaluation

(1) Species of biting animal involved Carnivorous animals (especially skunks, foxes, coyotes, raccoons, dogs, cats, and bats) are more likely to be infective than other animals. Bites of rodents seldom, if ever, require specific antirabies prophylaxis.

(2) Vaccination status of the biting animal An adult animal immunized properly with one or more doses of rabies vaccine has only a minimal chance of having rabies and transmitting the virus.

(3) **Circumstances of the biting incident**   An unprovoked attack is more likely to indicate that the animal is rabid than is a provoked attack. Bites during attempts to feed or handle an apparently healthy animal should generally be regarded as provoked.

(4) **Extent and location of bite wound**   The likelihood that rabies will result from a bite varies with its extent and location, as follows:

   (a) **Severe**   Multiple or deep puncture wounds and any bites on the head, face, neck, hands, or fingers.

   (b) **Mild**   Scratches, lacerations, or single bites on areas of the body other than head, face, neck, hands, or fingers. Open wounds, such as abrasions, suspected of being contaminated with saliva also belong in this category.

(5) **Presence of rabies in the region**   If adequate laboratory and field records indicate that there is no rabies infection in a domestic species within a given region, local health officials may be justified in modifying general recommendations concerning antirabies treatment after a bite by that species.

b. **Diagnosis** of animal rabies is based on pathologic examination of the animal's brain.

   (1) A dog or cat that bites a human being should be captured, confined, and observed by a veterinarian for at least 5, preferably 7–10 days. Any illness in the animal should be reported immediately to the local health department.

   (2) If the animal dies, the head should be removed and shipped under refrigeration to a qualified laboratory for examination.

   (3) Because clinical signs of rabies in a wild animal cannot be reliably interpreted, the animal should be killed at once and its brain examined for evidence of rabies.

c. **Therapy**

   (1) Immediate and thorough local treatment of all bite wounds and scratches is perhaps the most effective means of preventing rabies. The wound should be flushed copiously with water and a quarternary ammonium compound such as Zephiran (which has a known antirabies effect).

   (2) Suturing of the wound or other form of primary closure is not advised.

   (3) **Postexposure prophylaxis**   The decision to undertake this must be based on the animal involved, the geographic epidemiology of rabies in that area, the wound itself, and the considerable morbidity and potential mortality of the therapy employed.

      (a) **Hyperimmune antiserum**   Maximum effectiveness of hyperimmune antiserum requires administration within 24 hr of the bite. Human antirabies serum is now available through the Center for Disease Control and will replace equine antisera, which can induce serum sickness.

(b) Vaccine (duck embryo) in addition to antiserum is considered the best postexposure prophylaxis. For vaccine dose, see package insert.

(4) If antirabies serum is indicated, a portion of the total dose should be thoroughly infiltrated around the wound. Tests for hypersensitivity to horse serum should be performed and a careful history taken.

E. Acute otitis media

1. Etiology

a. *D. pneumoniae* is the most common pathogen involved.

b. *H. influenzae* The majority of isolates are from children under 6 years of age.

c. Group A streptococcus.

d. Miscellaneous, infrequent bacterial isolates include *S. aureus, Streptococcus viridans*, gram-negative enteric bacilli, and *P. aeruginosa* (the latter two are usually associated with chronic otitis media and otitis externa).

e. Parainfluenza viruses, respiratory synctial virus, adenovirus, and Coxsackie virus.

2. Evaluation

a. Pneumotoscopy.

b. Nasopharyngeal and throat cultures are unnecessary as they correlate poorly with cultures of the middle ear exudate. In special circumstances, such as otitis media with meningitis or sepsis, the offending pathogen often can be identified by a diagnostic tympanocentesis for gram stain and culture.

3. Diagnosis is established by the characteristic findings on examination of the tympanic membranes: inflammation, distortion of the landmarks, loss of the light reflex, and diminished or absent mobility, or a bulging or even perforated drum, or both.

4. Therapy

a. Antibiotics

(1) Since the differentiation of viral from bacterial otitis media cannot be made on clinical criteria (and tympanocenteses are not routinely performed), antibiotics are prescribed for all patients with symptomatic otitis media. The choice of drugs is influenced by the patient's age, as shown in Table 9-8.

(2) For the child with documented penicillin allergy, erythromycin is substituted for penicillin, but should not be relied on to treat possible *H. influenzae* (i.e., in children under 6).

(3) In choosing antibiotics, the physician should note that prescribing two oral drugs decreases the likelihood of compliance by the family.

(4) Duration of therapy is 7–10 days.

Table 9-8.   Antibiotics in Otitis Media

Age	Antibiotic	Dosage	Route
Under 6 years	1. Ampicillin[a] *or*	50–100 mg/kg/d qid	PO
	2. Penicillin V	80,000 U/kg/d qid up to 1.6 million daily	PO
	+		
	sulfisoxazole (Gantrisin) *or*	150–200 mg/kg/d qid	PO
	3. A-P Bicillin	0.6–1.2 million U XI in one dose	IM
	+		
	sulfisoxazole	See above	
6 years or over	1. Penicillin V *or*	400,000 U tid or qid	PO
	2. Erythromycin	30–50 mg/kg/d qid	PO

[a] Ampicillin-resistant *H. influenzae* b has been reported.

    b. A perforation of the tympanic membrane may give rise to otitis externa, for which a topical antibiotic such as colistimethate (4 drops tid after the ear canal has been rinsed and dried completely) may be helpful in severe cases, but routine use of such drops is not indicated.

    c. Severe pain not relieved by analgesics is the major indication for a myringotomy.

    d. Decongestants, including antihistamines, sympathomimetic nosedrops, systemic sympathomimetics, and saline nosedrops, may provide symptomatic relief, but their efficacy in this regard is unproved.

    e. Follow-up care

        (1) The patient's status should be checked after 3 days of antibiotics (usually a phone call is sufficient). By then most children are afebrile and significantly better. Treatment failures may also become evident between the fifth and seventh days of therapy, with a recrudescense of fever.

        (2) Most important, however, is the evaluation of the patient approximately 3 weeks after institution of therapy, at which time the tympanic membranes should have normal landmarks and mobility. An abnormal tympanic membrane or hearing deficit at this time indicates possible chronic otitis media, or chronic serous otitis ("glue ear") (see Chap. 22, Sec. **II.C.4**).

  F. Sinusitis   See also Chap. 22, Sec. **III.**

    1. Etiology

      a. *H. influenzae*, pneumococci, and group A streptococci in younger children.

      b. In older children *S. aureus* is a major pathogen and *Klebsiella* and other gram-negative bacilli sometimes produce disease.

      c. In brittle diabetic patients and impaired hosts, fungal infection, especially phycomycosis, must be considered.

    2. Evaluation includes examination of the nares, transillumination of the sinuses, culture of the purulent discharge, and sinus x-rays.

3. Diagnosis

a. Pain over the paranasal sinuses, often with accompanying headache, purulent nasal discharge, and fever, constitutes the cardinal finding of acute sinusitis. Pain is often manifest over the bridge of the nose in ethmoid sinusitis, while pain from sphenoid sinusitis may be referred to the palate or to the mastoid area.

b. Chronic sinusitis may not be clinically evident and should be considered in the evaluation of fever of unknown origin.

c. Since the sinuses are poorly developed during the first year of life, sinusitis is rare in this age group.

4. Treatment

a. Fluids and analgesics (see Chaps. 1 and 4).

b. Relief of obstruction by use of sympathomimetic amines administered topically (e.g., phenylephrine, 0.25% drops or spray) or systemically (e.g., phenylpropanolamine hydrochloride, 2.5–10.0 mg PO q6h).

c. Antihistamines are of doubtful value in bacterial sinusitis.

d. Antimicrobial drugs are often not required in the treatment of mild sinusitis. In severe sinusitis, the choice of drugs depends on the age of the patient and the microbiologic evaluation of the nasal discharge. Ampicillin (100 mg/kg per day in divided 6-hr doses) is effective against the commonest agents (*H. influenzae*, pneumococci) in young children; drugs effective against penicillinase-producing *S. aureus* (e.g., dicloxacillin, 25 mg/kg daily in divided 6-hr doses) often are indicated in older patients.

G. Streptococcal pharyngitis (tonsillitis)

1. Etiology   Group A β-hemolytic streptococcus.

2. Evaluation   must include a properly obtained throat culture (vigorous swab of both tonsillar areas and the posterior pharynx, which, if done properly, usually induces a gag reflex).

a. The disease should be suspected in any patient with a sore throat and fever.

b. Any history in the patient or his family of recent streptococcal pharyngitis, scarlet fever, rheumatic fever, or penicillin allergy should be noted.

3. Diagnosis   is established by a positive throat culture.

4. Therapy

a. Penicillin   Prevention of rheumatic fever requires either benzathine penicillin G given IM, or a 10-day course of oral penicillin (see Chap. 11, Sec. **IV.D**). The parenteral route insures treatment for a sufficient length of time, while oral therapy is dependent upon the cooperation of the patient. Treatment schedules recommended by the American Heart Association are as follows:

(1) Intramuscular penicillin (benzathine)   Children should be given a single injection of 600,000–900,000 U. The larger dose is probably preferable for children over 10 years of age, and adults should receive 1.2 million units.

(2) **Oral penicillin** Children and adults are given 200,000 or 250,000 U[1] 3–4 times a day for a full 10 days. Therapy must be continued for the entire 10 days, even though the temperature returns to normal and the patient is asymptomatic.

b. For patients with documented penicillin allergy, oral erythromycin (30–50 mg/kg per day in 3 or 4 divided doses) or clindamycin (10–20 mg/kg per day in 3 or 4 divided doses) for 10 days is recommended. Sulfonamides, while effective in prophylaxis, are ineffective in the treatment of streptococcal infections.

c. Bed rest is not necessary. Children can return to school as soon as the symptoms subside.

d. Throat cultures are indicated for symptomatic family members but are not necessary for others unless recurrent streptococcal pharyngitis occurs in the family. Such recurrences may necessitate antibiotic treatment of the entire family.

H. Cervical adenitis

1. Etiology

a. Group A β-hemolytic streptococci (75–90 percent of cases).

b. *S. aureus.*

c. *M. tuberculosis.*

d. Atypical mycobacteria, especially Battey strain.

e. Cat-scratch fever (agent unknown).

f. Viruses, including rubella, measles, herpes simplex, and adenoviruses.

2. Evaluation

a. **History** This should include assessment of the duration and tempo of the disease, as well as contact with animals and with individuals with tuberculosis.

b. **Laboratory data**

(1) These usually include leukocyte and differential count, tuberculin skin test, ASO titer, and heterophil, or "mono spot" test.

(2) In some cases, additional skin tests with the atypical mycobacterial antigens are indicated.

(3) Needle aspiration or surgical biopsy under local or general anesthesia often is indicated if the diagnosis remains in doubt after the preceding diagnostic steps. Surgical biopsy or drainage, however, should be deferred if atypical mycobacterial disease or cat-scratch fever is seriously suspected, since a chronic, draining fistula may result from incomplete excision. Any surgical or aspirated specimen should be stained and cultured for bacteria, mycobacteria, and fungi.

---

[1] Of the various oral forms available, buffered penicillin G is satisfactory and less expensive. Although higher blood levels may be achieved with α-phenoxymethyl penicillin (penicillin V) or α-phenoxyethyl penicillin (phenethicillin), especially when taken near meals, their superiority in the prevention of rheumatic fever has not been documented.

3. Diagnosis

a. Cervical adenitis of acute onset with pain, fever, and a recent pharyngitis is usually streptococcal. Failure to respond to appropriate penicillin therapy in such a case suggests streptococcal or, more likely, staphylococcal abscess formation, or a nonbacterial cause such as mycobacterial or cat-scratch fever.

b. Tuberculous or atypical mycobacterial adenitis can mimic acute pyogenic lymphadenitis, but these entities generally are insidious in onset and without pain or constitutional symptoms.

(1) Tuberculous adenitis is suspected when a positive tuberculin skin test (see Sec. **VI.V**) is associated with a pulmonary infiltrate, or a history of contact with active tuberculosis, or both.

(2) In patients with atypical mycobacterial adenitis, the intradermal PPD (intermediate strength) generally does not exceed 12 mm induration, and reaction to the atypical intradermal antigen should be at least 2 mm larger in diameter than that to the standard PPD.

(3) A negative reaction to second strength tuberculin virtually excludes the diagnosis of tuberculous or atypical mycobacterial adenitis in patients with intact cellular immunity.

c. Cat-scratch disease is suggested by the history of exposure to a cat, usually a kitten, or an inflamed scratch or papule at the site of the presumed scratch, or both.

4. Therapy

a. Streptococcal adenitis   Penicillin G, either IM (procaine, 600,000–1.2 million U) daily, or IV (aqueous, 100,000–250,000 U kg daily) in severe cases, is given until the fever and localized inflammation have subsided. This response should occur within 2–3 days, after which a 10-day course of penicillin can be completed orally. Hot compresses and aspirin also are prescribed. The adenitis may become fluctuant ("pointing"), necessitating surgical incision and drainage.

b. Staphylococcal adenitis   Since the organism is often penicillin-resistant, one of the penicillinase-resistant semisynthetic penicillins is given initially and continued if the offending pathogen cannot be demonstrated to be sensitive to penicillin. Severity of the illness determines whether or not the IV route and hospitalization are necessary in place of oral cloxacillin or dicloxacillin.

(1) Recommended preparations and doses are as follows:
IV: nafcillin, oxacillin, or methicillin 200 mg/kg per day q4h.
PO: dicloxacillin, 50 mg/kg per day qid.
PO: penicillin, 300,000–600,000 U qid.

(2) Duration of treatment is determined by the patient's response but usually a 10–14-day course is sufficient.

(3) Surgical incision and drainage are often necessary in staphylococcal disease.

c. Tuberculous adenitis   Antituberculous drugs are given (see Table 9-10).

d. Atypical mycobacterial adenitis   Although the natural history of this disease is variable, the adenopathy will often resolve spontaneously. The atypical mycobacteria are not communicable from man to man, and the patient presents no danger to siblings or classmates.

> **(1)** Since atypical strains are frequently resistant in vitro to the usual antituberculous drugs, observation only is usually the preferred management.

> **(2)** Successful treatment of some infections with rifampin alone or in conjunction with other agents has been reported.

> **(3)** When increasing adenopathy or related symptoms indicate more aggressive management, surgical excision of the involved nodes is recommended. The surgical wound should be sutured without a drain to prevent a subsequent fistula.

e. Cat-scratch disease   Symptomatic treatment with hot compresses and aspirin is prescribed. Occasionally, severe pain or fluctuance necessitates needle aspiration or even surgical excision of the involved nodes. These measures should be avoided, if possible, in view of the risk that a fistula and draining sinus may result.

I. Infectious mononucleosis

1. Etiology   Probably Epstein-Barr virus.

2. Evaluation   Liver function tests (alkaline phosphatase and SGOT) are often abnormal.

3. Diagnosis is confirmed by increased atypical lymphocytes (usually 20%) on peripheral blood smear, and serologic demonstration of heterophil antibody (not absorbed by guinea pig kidney antigen) by a mono spot, or heterophil, test. Exudative pharyngitis is common and small petechiae are often evident at the junction of the hard and soft palate.

4. Therapy

> **a.** Supportive (fluids, rest).

> **b.** In patients severely toxic or with marked splenomegaly or respiratory compromise (and threatened rupture), corticosteroids (prednisone, 1–2 mg/kg daily for 5–7 days) may be beneficial. The duration of the disease is generally not affected by corticosteroids, and these drugs should not be used routinely.

> **c.** Sore throats due to infectious mononucleosis should not be treated with ampicillin, since it causes an allergic-type rash in more than half of patients so treated.

> **d.** Due to the risk of splenic rupture, strenuous activity such as athletics should be prohibited as long as significant splenomegaly persists.

J. Upper respiratory infection (URI)

1. Etiology   Over 90 percent of cases are presumably viral.

2. Evaluation usually necessitates only a history and physical examination. Cultures should be obtained only if specific bacterial entities are questioned. White blood count and differential are rarely, if ever, of help in differentiating viral from bacterial disease.

3. **Diagnosis** is usually obvious after exclusion of lower respiratory disease (pneumonia, bronchitis, asthma, bronchiolitis croup, and streptococcal pharyngitis). The diagnosis of bacterial nasopharyngitis requires purulent rhinorrhea and pure growth of the pathogen on nasopharyngeal culture. It occurs primarily in infants.

4. **Therapy** is symptomatic and may include antipyretics, oral fluids, decongestants, cough expectorants or suppressants, and occasionally a cool mist vaporizer.

   a. Antibiotics are not indicated *except* in associated otitis media, sinusitis, and purulent bacterial nasopharyngitis. In the latter case, oral ampicillin (50 mg/kg daily), or penicillin (200,000–400,000 U tid) for 5 days is prescribed.

   b. The use of antibiotics otherwise is of no clinical effectiveness, represents an unnecessary cost, and may induce toxic reactions and the emergence of resistant bacteria.

K. **Croup (epiglottitis and laryngotracheitis)** *Epiglottitis of acute onset represents one of the few true pediatric emergencies.*

   1. **Etiology** *H. influenzae*, type b, causes 90–95 percent of epiglottitis. Other causes include group A streptococcus and pneumococcus.

      a. Diphtheria and infectious mononucleosis can cause a picture similar to epiglottitis.

      b. Laryngotracheitis is usually viral in origin (most commonly, parainfluenza virus), but rare bacterial cases do occur.

   2. **Evaluation** is directed toward differentiation of mild from severe croup and epiglottitis from the more common and usually milder laryngotracheitis.

      a. The degree of respiratory distress is assessed by the patient's color (pale or cyanotic), the presence of retractions, degree of air exchange on chest auscultation, restlessness, heart rate at rest (if possible), and altered mental status.

      b. **Severe laryngospasm can result from too vigorous an attempt to visualize the epiglottis,** and therefore visualization should be attempted only in a controlled situation with emergency airway equipment nearby.

      c. Other diagnostic features include the rapidity of progression of respiratory disease and the patient's state of hydration.

      d. The laboratory work-up should include a throat and blood culture and lateral neck x-ray.

   3. **Diagnosis** of croup is apparent from the patient's barking cough and inspiratory stridor and is confirmed on x-ray.

   4. **Therapy** See Chap. 22, Sec. I, p. 455.

      a. In epiglottitis and severe laryngotracheitis, emergency hospitalization is necessary, and in view of the significant risk in epiglottitis of sudden, unpredictable airway obstruction, tracheostomy or early intubation should be performed. In experienced hands, the use of *early* nasotracheal intubation is safer than tracheostomy even when tracheostomy is performed as an elective procedure. *Postponing intervention until the child becomes severely distressed increases the risks of either procedure many times.*

b. Moisture   Cool, moist air with 100% O_2, as necessary.

c. IPPB   Aerolized 2.5% Vaponefrin by intermittent positive-pressure breathing (IPPB) (diluted in normal saline—0.3 ml Vaponefrin + 2.7 ml normal saline). These treatments may be repeated q30min, under supervision, provided excess tachycardia is not induced. Aerosilized saline alone may produce symptomatic improvement.

d. Hydration.

e. Sedation   A quiet room where a parent may stay with the child and elimination of unnecessary procedures help to reduce the associated anxiety of respiratory distress. In patients in whom excessive apprehension aggravates the respiratory distress, mild sedation (choral hydrate, 10–15 mg/kg q6–8h) may be beneficial (see Chap. 1, Sec. **II.C.2.b**).

f. Steroids   A short course of high-dose corticosteroids (1–3 doses dexamethasone, 1 mg/kg q6h) in severe croup has become commonplace, although controlled studies have failed to show a clearcut benefit.

g. Antibiotics   Ampicillin (300 mg/kg per day IV) or chloramphenicol (100 mg/kg/d IV) is indicated in epiglottitis and in those cases of laryngotracheitis (while awaiting results of the culture) in which the progressive severity suggests secondary bacterial infection. If the blood culture is positive, antibiotics should be given for 7–10 days.

h. Home care   Most cases of croup are mild and, provided epiglottitis has been excluded, can be managed at home. Therapeutic measures include a vaporizer, a steamed-up bathroom, and, occasionally, outdoor air. Parents should be instructed to call a physician if the child's respiratory distress increases or fails to respond to the measures described.

L. Bronchiolitis

1. Etiology   This is usually viral (most commonly, respiratory syncytial virus).

2. Evaluation   This should include assessment of hydration and respiratory exchange.

3. The **diagnosis** is suggested by the abrupt onset of dyspnea in an infant and by prominent wheezing, hyperinflation of the lungs, and retractions. Fever may not be present.

4. Therapy

   a. Humidified O_2 (40% or more). In severe cases, arterial blood gases should be monitored to determine the O_2 requirements of the patient.

   b. Adequate hydration of the patient is important. Whether fluids are administered PO or IV depends on the severity of the respiratory distress. In severe respiratory distress, administration of oral fluids may induce vomiting and aspiration pneumonia and is contraindicated.

c. In severe cases, endotracheal intubation may be required.

d. Congestive heart failure can develop in severely ill patients, necessitating digitalis (see Chap. 11, Sec. **D.1**, p. 260).

e. Antibiotics are not routinely given, but are indicated if associated otitis media, pneumonia, or bacterial infection is present.

f. Glucocorticoids have *not* been demonstrated to be beneficial in controlled studies.

g. Bronchodilators are usually *ineffective*, and their repeated administration may even be harmful.

M. Pneumonia   See also Chaps. 5 and 19.

1. Etiology

a. Viruses probably cause the majority of pediatric pneumonias. Respiratory syncytial virus is a particularly prominent cause in infants. Other common viral pathogens include the parainfluenzas (1, 2, and 3), influenza A and B, and adenoviruses.

b. *Mycoplasma pneumoniae* is a common cause of pneumonia in school-age children and adolescents. Its clinical features include insidious onset, nonproductive cough, fever, sore throat, headache, and unilateral peribronchial infiltrate or lobar consolidation.

c. *D. pneumoniae* is the most frequent cause of bacterial pneumonia. Classically, pneumococcal pneumonia causes lobar or segmental consolidation, but pneumococcal bronchopneumonia is not infrequent in children.

d. Staphylococcal pneumonia is suggested by rapidly evolving respiratory distress, empyema, and the characteristic radiologic features of rapid progression, lobular ectasia, and pneumatoceles in an infant or child less than 3 years old. Even in an extremely ill child, however, the initial x-ray film may only demonstrate faint focal mottling.

e. Streptococcal etiology is suggested by an interstitial bronchopneumonia, resembling a viral pneumonitis, sudden onset of symptoms, chills, leukocytosis, and often a preceding viral infection (e.g., measles). An early serosanguinous pleural effusion is characteristic.

f. *H. influenzae* pneumonia can mimic any of the preceding types of pneumonia and should be suspected in a young child or infant who is toxic or fails to respond to adequate penicillin therapy.

g. Other gram-negative organisms and *Pneumocystis carinii*, fungi, and tuberculosis (**V**, p. 225) are rare causes of pneumonia in children, occurring primarily in neonates, leukemia patients, and other hosts with immunologic deficiencies.

2. Evaluation may include the following:

a. Chest x-ray (posteroanterior and lateral).

b. Tuberculin skin test.

c. Sputum or deep tracheal aspirate for *gram stain* and *culture*. Cultures from the nasopharynx should be interpreted with great caution.

d. *Blood culture*(*s*) in the patient who appears toxic.

e. If pleural fluid is present, a diagnostic thoracentesis should be done.

f. Cold agglutinin titer.

g. ASO titer if group A streptococci are suspected.

h. *Diagnostic lung puncture* in critically ill children in whom a specific etiologic diagnosis is of major importance to guide antimicrobial therapy (see *Pediatrics* 44 : 486, 1969).

i. Leukocyte and differential counts occasionally are helpful but, in general, should not be relied on to distinguish bacterial from other causes.

3. Diagnosis   This is usually established by the chest x-ray study and physical signs of consolidation. Etiologic diagnosis usually is made from the culture, the clinical features described, and, in the case of *M. pneumoniae*, the cold agglutinin titer.

4. Therapy

a. Antibiotics

(1) Children who are mildly ill with features suggestive of viral etiology can be managed *without* antibiotics, provided the patient can be followed closely.

(2) Infants and hospitalized patients should receive antibiotics when pneumonia is diagnosed.

(3) The choice of specific antibiotics is based on interpretation of available gram-stained specimens, age of the patient, and other suggestive clinical features.

(4) Specific recommendations

(a) The toxic, hospitalized patient between the ages of 2 months and 5 years should be treated with both a penicillinase-resistant penicillin (300 mg/kg per day) and ampicillin or chloramphenicol (75 mg/kg/d IV q6h).

(b) Infants < 2 months old should receive a penicillinase-resistant penicillin IV (300 mg/kg per day q4h for infants > 4 weeks old—see Table 9-7 for infants < 4 weeks old), and gentamicin IM (5–7.5 mg/kg per day q8–12h) or kanamycin (15 mg/kg per day q12h).

(c) Nontoxic children with suspected pneumococcal pneumonia should be treated with IM procaine penicillin G (0.6–1.2 million U) daily for 1–3 days, by which time definite clinical improvement with uncomplicated pneumococcal pneumonia should have occurred. Subsequently, a 7-day course can be completed with oral penicillin V (200,000–400,000 U tid). Suspected *Mycoplasma* pneumonia is treated with oral erythromycin, 30–50 mg/kg per day in 4 daily doses for 10 days.

(5) Identification of the pathogen, or failure to respond to these regimens, or both necessitates reevaluation of the choice of antibiotics.

(6) Duration of antimicrobial therapy is based on the individual patient's clinical response, but, in general, staphylococcal pneumonia requires 6 weeks of parenteral therapy, and *H. influenzae* and streptococcal pneumonia usually respond to 2–3 weeks of therapy.

(7) Recommended alternatives to the penicillins in the penicillin-allergic patient are cephalosporins, erythromycin, clindamycin, and chloramphenicol (for *H. influenzae*).

b. Indications for hospitalization include the following: significant respiratory distress or toxicity, cyanosis, age under 6 months, empyema or pleural effusion, possible staphylococcal pneumonia, and inadequate home care.

c. In the case of empyema, drainage by repeated aspiration or insertion of a tube is necessary (Chap. 1, Sec. **5**, p. 4). (Loculated pleural fluid may explain persistent fever in the face of seemingly adequate antibiotic therapy.)

d. Symptomatic care should include O_2 if necessary, high humidity (such as the use of a vaporizer in the home), expectorants, bronchodilators if bronchospasm is present, and deep tracheal suction in patients with ineffectual cough.

e. Postural drainage and physiotherapy may be helpful, particularly with underlying bronchiectesis.

f. Initial follow-up of the ambulatory patient should be on a day-to-day basis until definite clinical improvement has occurred.

g. Although radiologic resolution may lag behind clinical improvement, persistence of radiologic abnormalities without improvement for more than 4–6 weeks should alert the physician to possible underlying pulmonary disease (e.g., tuberculosis, foreign body, cystic fibrosis).

N. Bacterial meningitis   This disease constitutes a true emergency.

1. Etiology   *H. influenzae*, type b (60–65 percent), meningococci, and pneumococci account for most cases of acute bacterial meningitis in children over 2 months of age. Infrequently involved organisms are β-hemolytic streptococci and gram-negative enteric bacteria except in neonatal meningitis, in which *E. coli*, group B streptococci, *Klebsiella*, and other enteric pathogens are common.

2. Evaluation

a. A lumbar puncture (LP) should be performed as soon as the diagnosis is suspected (Chap. 1, Sec. **4**, p. 4). *Before* the LP is performed, a blood glucose, for comparison with the CSF glucose, should be obtained.

   Examination of the fluid includes opening and closing pressures, total leukocyte and differential count (preferably by Wright stain smear as chamber differential counts can be unreliable), evaluation of xanthochromia, glucose and total protein determinations, gram stain, and culture. If tuberculosis is suspected, an acid-fast stain of the CSF may be diagnostic.

b. In infants, the presenting symptoms and signs are nonspecific and include a high-pitched cry, irritability, anorexia, vomiting, lethargy, and/or a full fontanelle. Meningeal signs are *uncommon*, and fever is not invariably present.

c. Papilledema is a relative contraindication to LP, and, if it is present, a neurosurgical consultation should be considered before proceeding. (Papilledema is rare in *acute* bacterial meningitis, and its presence may suggest other diagnostic possibilities, e.g., brain abscess.)

d. Other diagnostic procedures include blood culture, smears and cultures from any purpuric lesions, cultures of any body fluids of possible pathologic significance (e.g., stool, urine, abscess, middle ear), BUN, serum electrolytes, chest x-ray, and a tuberculin test. In infants, transillumination should be performed and the head circumference carefully measured.

3. **Diagnosis** can be established only by the LP. In meningitis, the cerebrospinal fluid is characteristically cloudy and under increased pressure with > 100 WBC/mm^3, predominantly polymorphonuclear cells, elevated total protein, low glucose (less than ½ of the pre-LP blood glucose concentration), and organisms in the CSF gram-stained smear. However, the CSF frequently may not have all of these findings and any abnormality in these parameters must be viewed with suspicion, including the presence of *any* polymorphonuclear leukocytes. The CSF culture usually confirms the diagnosis.

4. **Therapy**   The initial choice of antibiotics usually is based on the CSF gram-stain smear and the patient's age. They are always given IV.

a. In children over 2 months of age in whom no reason exists to suspect an unusual organism, ampicillin is the drug of choice (300 mg/kg daily IV q2–4h after an initial bolus of 150 mg/kg) until the etiologic agent is identified. *In regions where ampicillin-resistant H. influenzae is a consideration,* initial therapy should include penicillin G (300,000 U/kg daily IV q4h) and chloramphenicol (100 mg/kg daily IV q4h). If the culture discloses meningococci or pneumococci, penicillin G is the drug of choice. When *H. influenzae* is recovered, ampicillin is the drug of choice if sensitivity is confirmed in vitro.

b. In infants 2 months old or younger, initial therapy, before the etiologic agent is identified, includes the following

   (1) Penicillin (300,000 U/kg daily) or ampicillin (300 mg/kg daily) q4h IV. Oxacillin (or similar drug) 300 mg/kg per day q4h IV is substituted if staphylococcal meningitis is suspected (e.g., concurrent neonatal impetigo or epidemic staphylococcal sepsis originating from the infant's nursery). *For infants 4 weeks old or younger, these dosages are modified (see Table 9–7).*

   (2) Gentamicin (5–7.5 mg/kg per day q8–12h) or kanamycin (15 mg/kg per day q12h) parenterally.

   (3) If the pathogen is a gram-negative enteric, intrathecal antibiotics are commonly used. Gentamicin, 2 mg (1 mg/ml) is given daily intrathecally until the CSF is sterilized, or for at least 3 days and then every other day during the first 2 weeks of therapy.

c. The duration of antibiotic therapy depends on the infant's clinical course, but should be given for a minimum of 2 weeks.

d. Other aspects of management

(1) During treatment, frequent observations of vital signs should be made. IV fluids should be kept at or just below maintenance. There should also be monitoring of acid-base status, fever control, and treatment of complications (convulsions, shock, hyponatremia from inappropriate ADH, subdural effusions, lateral sinus thrombosis, acute cerebral edema, and disseminated intravascular coagulation [DIC]).

(2) The LP should be repeated after 24–48 hr of therapy and again at the end of therapy, by which time the CSF glucose should be normal and CSF protein and cell count markedly improved. A few mononuclear cells at this time are not abnormal, but polymorphonuclear leukocytes suggest continued inflammation.

(3) Persistence or recrudescence of fever during therapy most commonly results from phlebitis, drug fever, nosocomial infection, or a subdural effusion.

(4) Children should be observed for recurrence of fever for 24–48 hr after discontinuance of antibiotics and before discharge from the hospital.

O. Brain abscess

1. Etiology   Usually mixed anaerobic (streptococci or *Bacteroides*) and aerobic pathogens (such as streptococci, staphylococci, or pneumococci) are involved. Almost any organism, including the Enterobacteriaceae, *Nocardia*, and fungi, can cause a brain abscess.

2. Evaluation   includes a neurologic examination and history. Careful fundoscopic examination for papilledema or diminished venous pulsations is necessary, since LP in the presence of increased intracranial pressure may precipitate herniation. This risk is particularly high in posterior fossa lesions (e.g., cerebellar abscess).

If papilledema is absent, and no other signs of increased CSF pressure are present, LP is recommended. Skull x-rays, brain scan, and an EEG may be useful. An echo encephalogram is helpful in noting displacement of midline structures by unilateral edema. If these examinations suggest an abscess, an arteriogram is indicated.

3. Diagnosis   The diagnosis of brain abscess must be considered whenever an intracranial mass is evident clinically or radiologically, or whenever CSF examination reveals abnormalities consistent with a parameningeal inflammatory process (increased pressure, lymphocytosis, or elevated protein, usually with normal glucose levels).

4. Therapy

a. In the presence of brain swelling, hyperosmotic agents such as mannitol are commonly used. Decadron, 1 mg/kg may also help to reduce cerebral edema (see p. 44).

b. Fluids should be restricted moderately in an effort to keep the patient "dry."

c. Initial antibiotic therapy is generally directed against anaerobic organisms and the common aerobic gram-positive cocci. Chloramphenicol (100 mg/kg daily IV in 4 divided doses) and a penicillin (oxacillin, 300 mg/kg daily IV in 4 divided doses) is a reasonable choice that can be modified after surgical drainage allows bacteriologic evaluation of the abscess contents.

d. Surgical excision or drainage of the abscess is indicated in most cases when the patient is stable and antibiotics have been administered for 12 hr or more.

P. Infectious gastroenteritis   See Chap. 1, Sec. **III.D.**

1. Etiology

a. Bacterial   Salmonella, shigella, and enteropathogenic *E. coli* (EPEC) are the principal agents of this disease in the United States. Salmonella infections are grouped into four principal clinical patterns: asymptomatic carrier, gastroenteritis, enteric fever (including typhoid fever), and bacteremia with or without extraintestinal localization.

b. Viruses   ECHO virus, polioviruses, Coxsackie virus, and adenoviruses have been implicated. The incidence of proved viral gastroenteritis is surprisingly low, however.

c. Parasites   Gastrointestinal infection by parasites can occur, but is uncommon in the United States. Infection by these parasites is discussed in Chap. 10.

d. Food "poisoning" can be caused by toxins from several bacteria, including staphylococci, *Clostridium perfringins*, and *C. botulinum* (Table 9-9).

2. Evaluation includes an epidemiologic history, assessment of the character and duration of the abnormal stools, and careful assessment of the patient's state of hydration.

a. The demonstration of fecal leukocytes in diarrheal stool is well correlated with inflammatory (usually bacterial) disease.

b. Stool cultures need *not* be routinely obtained. Indications are infancy, toxicity, severe diarrhea, chronic disease or impaired host, and epidemic diarrhea. Stool for culture is preferable to a rectal swab. In children under 2 years of age, when enteropathogenic *E. coli* is suspected, *E. coli* typing by the bacteriology laboratory should be requested.

c. Hospitalized patients with fever and diarrhea should have one or more blood cultures.

3. Diagnosis   The presence of bacterial gastroenteritis can be established only by the results of stool cultures.

4. Therapy is directed primarily toward fluid and electrolyte management (see Chap. 4, Sec. **II.E**). Antibiotics are indicated in EPEC diarrhea, shigellosis, and in some cases of salmonellosis. Antidiarrheal agents like Kaopectate are of limited value.

a. Shigella   Ampicillin, 50–100 mg/kg daily PO qid for 7 days.

b. EPEC   Depends on the antibiotic sensitivity of the organisms.

Table 9-9. Bacterial Food Poisoning

Type of Bacterial Toxin	Pathogen	Effect of Heat or Cold	Incubation Period	Source of Agent	Circumstances
Staphylococcal	Toxin	Heat-resistant toxin	2–6 hr	Human	Meat, pastries, and so on, unrefrigerated 4 or more hr
Clostridium perfringens	Unknown	Heat-resistant organism	6–24 hr	Nature	Meat, beans, heated then kept warm 4 or more hr
Botulism	Toxin	Heat-labile toxin Heat-resistant bacterium	Variable (hr–days)	Nature	Usually, home-canned food
Salmonellosis	Infection	Heat-sensitive organism	8–48 hr	Nature	Improperly prepared, unrefrigerated foods
				Human	Human fecal contamination
Typhoid (*Salmonella typhosa*)	Infection	Heat-sensitive organism	1–2 weeks	Human	Human fecal contamination, occasionally water-borne
Shigellosis	Infection	Heat-sensitive organism	1–3 days	Human	Human fecal contamination, occasionally water-borne
Streptococcal (β-hemolytic)	Infection	Heat-sensitive organism	36–72 hr	Human	Usually milk-borne; rare now

(1) Antibiotics are given PO for a minimum of 7 days until negative stool cultures have been obtained on 3 consecutive days.

(2) Agents that have been used include colistin (15 mg/kg daily, tid), neomycin (50–100 mg/kg daily, qid), and kanamycin (50–100 mg/kg daily, qid). For newborns, the lower dose is recommended.

c. Salmonella Since antibiotics only prolong the carrier state, most patients with *Salmonella* in their stool are *not* treated.

(1) Indications for treatment are infancy, impaired host defenses, sickle cell anemia, chronic inflammatory bowel disease, severe toxicity, and positive blood cultures.

(2) Chloramphenicol (50–100 mg/kg daily q6h IV) is the drug of choice, but recent reports of resistant *S. typhi* suggest that this recommendation may require modification.

(3) If the *Salmonella* isolate is sensitive to ampicillin, parenteral ampicillin (200–300 mg/kg daily) is usually effective. Antibiotics are given for 2 weeks.

Q. Urinary tract infections

1. Etiology Primary UTI are most commonly caused by *E. coli*. Other pathogens include *Proteus, Klebsiella,* Enterobacteriaceae, *Pseudomonas, Streptococcus faecalis,* and, rarely, *S. aureus*.

2. Evaluation should include a history, assessment of the patient's toxicity, fever, character of the urinary stream, and a urinalysis.

a. The **history** should cover previous urinary tract symptoms and infections, including the results of past urinary cultures and antibiotic sensitivities and preceding urinary tract instrumentation.

b. Urinalysis

(1) The urinalysis should include a careful examination of the microscopic sediment and should be done on a freshly voided clean specimen.

(2) Multiple (three if possible), clean-voided urine specimens should be sent for quantitative culture and sensitivity.

(3) In children not toilet-trained, contamination of a specimen obtained by bag is a frequent source of error. A specimen may have to be obtained by suprapubic aspiration or sterile catheterization. A single such specimen obviates the need for multiple cultures, but the procedure should be reserved for diagnostic problems.

(4) To prevent false-positive cultures, urine specimens should be cultured immediately or, if this is impossible, stored temporarily (maximum time, several hours) at 4° C before culturing.

c. Other diagnostic procedures

(1) Agar-coated dip slides allow quantitative bacterial culture, with reliable results.

(2) A gram-stained smear of unspun fresh urine that shows ≥ 1 organisms/oil immersion field correlates well with $\geq 10^5$ bacteria/ml urine.

(3) At least one blood culture should be obtained in patients in whom acute pyelonephritis is suspected.

(4) Indications for an IVP and a voiding cystourethrogram are the following: age less than 2 years, toxicity or sepsis (suggestive of pyelonephritis), and first infection in a male and second infection in a female (unless the history, physical findings, and/or the clinical response to the first infection suggests an early work-up). In these circumstances, a serum BUN, creatinine, and creatinine clearance are also indicated.

3. **Diagnosis** of a urinary tract infection is established by positive urine cultures as follows:

   a. Usually $\geq 100,000$ bacteria/ml, for clean-voided specimens, or growth of any pathogen in catheterized urine or a suprapubic aspirate.

   b. Growth of more than one species of bacteria usually indicates contamination rather than infection.

   c. Colony counts from voided urine of $< 10,000$ and 100,000/ml are indeterminate.

4. **Therapy**

   a. Most initial and uncomplicated UTI respond to oral sulfonamides, e.g., sulfisoxazole (Gantrisin) (150–200 mg/kg per day, administered qid). An effective alternative is ampicillin (100 mg/kg per day PO qid) or nitrofurantoin (5–7 mg/kg/d qid).

   b. Children with pyelonephritis require parenteral antibiotics, hydration, and hospitalization. Ampicillin (100–200 mg/kg per day q4h IV) is effective against many urinary tract pathogens, but a previous history of pyelonephritis, or infection with a resistant organism, or both indicates the need for a broad spectrum antibiotic. Kanamycin (15 mg/kg per day up to 1 gm daily, q12h IM) is recommended in such cases; or, if *Pseudomonas* is suspected, gentamicin (3–7.5 mg/kg daily q8–12h IM). The recommended duration of therapy is usually 10–14 days, but clinical improvement should be evident within 48–72 hr.

   c. Infants, especially newborns, with UTI should have prompt urologic evaluation as well as aggressive antibiotic treatment. The presence of chronic pyelonephritis or previous recurrent UTI (including asymptomatic bacteriuria) often indicates the need for subsequent "suppressive" antibiotic therapy (PO) for 4 weeks or more.

   d. Antimicrobial therapy is based on the clinical response of the patient and the results of subsequent urine cultures.

      (1) A culture should be obtained 24–48 hr after therapy has been initiated, and at this time the urine should be sterile (or have less than 10,000 bacteria/ml).

      (2) A gram stain of the unspun specimen should not show organisms, and the sediment should be significantly cleared of leukocytes 24–48 hr after therapy.

(3) Changes in antibiotics are based on clinical response and the drug sensitivities of the pathogen.

(4) Failure to respond to an appropriate drug should increase the physician's suspicion of an underlying anatomic abnormality.

e. Adequate hydration of the patient is important.

f. Continuous bladder drainage by an indwelling catheter should be done only when absolutely necessary and discontinued at the earliest possible time; a *closed* drainage system is preferable. Bladder irrigation with a solution of 40 ml neomycin and 20 ml polymyxin/L normal saline, or ¼% acetic acid, may reduce the incidence of catheter-induced infection. In young adults, the use of a three-way catheter allowing continuous irrigation is possible and recommended. On removal of the catheter, a urine culture should be obtained.

g. After therapy is discontinued, urine cultures are indicated 48–72 hr later, at subsequent 1–2 month intervals for 6 months, and yearly thereafter. Parents should be alerted to watch for recurrent symptoms, since UTI tend to recur.

R. Septic arthritis

1. Etiology Usually *S. aureus*, *H. influenzae* b, and β-hemolytic streptococcus.

a. Beyond 2 years of age, *S. aureus* is most commonly involved.

b. Gram-negative enteric bacteria can cause septic arthritis, principally in neonates.

c. *Neisseria gonorrhoeae*, pneumococci, and *N. meningitidis* are less commonly involved than the other organisms mentioned.

d. Tuberculous arthritis is uncommon in the absence of a primary tuberculous infection at another site.

2. Evaluation includes the following:

a. X-ray films of the joint(s).

b. A search for other sites of infection.

c. One to three blood cultures.

d. Arthrocentesis.

e. Gram stain and culture (including plating on chocolate agar if *Neisseria* or *H. influenzae* is suspected), WBC with differential, and glucose determination (with a simultaneous blood glucose) are performed on the synovial fluid.

3. Diagnosis This can be established only by the presence of bacteria in the synovial fluid.

4. Therapy

a. Aspiration Early aspiration of the affected joint is both diagnostic and therapeutic, since adequate drainage is critical to the prevention of sequelae. Whether or not open surgical drainage or repeated needle aspiration is chosen depends on the *joint involved* (e.g., the hip and shoulder require surgical drainage), *age* (infants and young children usually require surgical drainage), *viscosity* of the synovial exudate, *pathogen* (staphylococcal disease usually necessitates surgical drainage; meningococcal or gonococcal arthritis may require only needle aspiration), and *response* of the patient to antibiotics.

b. Antibiotics The initial choice of antibiotics is based on the gram-stained smear of the synovial fluid and the patient's age.

(1) In the absence of a diagnostic gram stain, the initial choice should include a penicillinase-resistant penicillin (e.g., oxacillin, 300 mg/kg per day q2–4h IV, up to 12 gm per day). For children 2 months–5 years of age, an agent effective against *H. influenzae* should be added. For infants under 2 months of age, gentamicin (5–7.5 mg/kg per day q8–12h IM) or kanamycin (15 mg/kg per day q12h IM) is indicated in addition to the penicillinase-resistant penicillin.

(2) Once the pathogen is identified, therapy may require modification, so as to provide the most effective drug with the least toxicity, e.g., for a penicillin-sensitive *S. aureus*, penicillin (300,000 U/kg per day q2–4h IV) is substituted for the penicillinase-resistant penicillin.

(3) Because antibiotics diffuse well into synovial fluid, local instillation of antibiotics is rarely necessary.

(4) Antibiotic therapy for 2–3 weeks is usually sufficient, but staphylococcal disease requires 6 weeks and gram-negative enteric arthritis, 3–6 weeks.

c. Other therapeutic measures include early immobilization of the joint and physical therapy when the inflammation subsides.

S. Acute osteomyelitis

1. Etiology

a. *S. aureus* is the organism involved in 75–80 percent of the cases.

b. Other organisms include β-hemolytic streptococci, pneumococci, rarely *H. influenzae* b and *Salmonella*, and occasionally *E. coli* in sickle cell anemia and gram-negative enteric pathogens in neonates. *Pseudomonas* osteomyelitis (*P. aeruginosa*) occasionally occurs.

2. Evaluation includes x-ray films of suspected sites, multiple blood cultures, cultures of potential primary sources of infection (e.g., skin, throat), and needle aspiration of the bone for gram stain and culture.

3. Diagnosis is based on the characteristic clinical picture. Although radiologic evidence of bone destruction and new bone formation do not appear until 10 or more days of active disease, soft tissue swelling, which is evident early, *in conjunction with* local bone tenderness is good evidence of osteomyelitis.

4. Therapy Prevention of chronic osteomyelitis and other sequelae depends on early diagnosis and treatment.

a. Administration of a penicillinase-resistant penicillin (e.g., oxacillin, 300 mg/kg per day q2–4h IV, up to 18 gm per day) is started as soon as the appropriate cultures have been obtained.

b. A second antibiotic is chosen if the gram-stained smear of the aspirate, the patient's age, or the presence of sickle cell anemia suggests an organism other than *S. aureus.*

c. Patients with sickle cell anemia should also receive ampicillin (300 mg/kg per day q2–4h IV) while neonates should be given kanamycin (15 mg/kg per day q12h IM), or gentamicin (5–7.5 mg/kg per day q8–12h IM).

d. The treatment of *Pseudomonas* osteomyelitis usually requires surgical intervention as well as antibiotic therapy with gentamicin and carbenicillin. The choice of antibiotics should be reevaluated when culture and sensitivity results become available.

e. Appropriate antibiotics are usually given for 4–6 weeks, with the exception of kanamycin and gentamicin, which may be necessary for only 3 weeks. In patients with a prompt response to therapy this course may be completed with oral antibiotics after 3–4 weeks of the parenteral drug.

f. Documentation of adequate serum concentrations of antibiotic can be obtained by measuring the bactericidal effect of serum against the original pathogen.

g. Continued toxicity and pain despite adequate antibiotics constitute the main indications for surgical decompression.

h. Other therapeutic measures include adequate hydration and initial immobilization of the affected extremity, followed later by traction. Since osteomyelitis usually results from hematogenous spread of the organism, *a careful search for metastatic infections in other bones or soft tissues (e.g., liver, heart valve) is indicated.*

T. Bacterial endocarditis (BE)   See also Chap. 11, Sec. **III.**

1. Etiology   *Streptococcus viridans* and *S. aureus* are the organisms most commonly involved.

a. Other organisms include *Staphylococcus albus,* microaerophilic streptococci, β-hemolytic streptococci, enterococci (group D streptococci), *Candida albicans,* and *D. pneumoniae.* Gram-negative pathogens are uncommon.

b. "Sterile" endocarditis (i.e., negative blood cultures) accounts for 10–15 percent of cases.

2. Evaluation

a. A careful search should be made for extracardiac manifestations, including petechiae, splenomegaly, hematuria, congestive heart failure, splinter hemorrhages, Roth's spots, neurologic signs and symptoms, anemia, Osler's nodes, and Janeway's spots.

b. Three to five *blood cultures* are obtained during a 6–12-hr period, preferably when fever is "spiking." A possible focus for the organism or procedure that led to bacteremia and bacterial invasion of the heart valve also should be sought (e.g., recent dental procedures, cardiovascular surgery, skin infection, UTI).

c. Multiple urine cultures as well as cultures of possible noncardiac foci, multiple microscopic examinations of fresh urine sediment for red blood cells and rell cell casts, a CBC, ESR, chest roentgenogram, serum complement, protein electrophoresis, and serum rheumatoid factor also are recommended. Repeated physical examination often will detect new manifestations.

d. Once isolated, the causative organism should be saved. After appropriate antibiotics have been started, serum inhibitory or bactericidal dilutions should be determined.

3. Diagnosis is established by positive blood cultures in association with a compatible clinical picture.

a. A change in the character of the heart murmur, although not always present, is highly suggestive.

b. The diagnosis of BE can be made in the absence of blood cultures if other diagnostic features are present, such as a new heart murmur, splenomegaly, RBC casts, petechiae, unexplained congestive heart failure, or Osler's nodes.

4. Therapy

a. If the diagnosis is clinically evident, initiation of antibiotics is reasonable while the results of the blood cultures are still pending.

b. In acute BE, therapy with penicillinase-resistant penicillin and gentamicin *should be initiated* within several hours of the patient's admission to the hospital [see **c(2)** and **c(3)**].

c. Once the pathogen has been identified, recommended antibiotics are as follows (see Table 9-2):

(1) *S. viridans,* β-hemolytic streptococcus, and microaerophilic streptococcus: aqueous penicillin G (250,000 U/kg daily q4h IV, up to 6 million U daily).

(2) *Enterococcus:* ampicillin (300 mg/kg per day q2–4h IV) and gentamicin (3–7.5 mg/kg per day q8h IM). Streptomycin (40 mg/kg per day, up to 2.0 gm per day), kanamycin (15 mg/kg per day up to 1.0 gm per day q12h IM) should be substituted for gentamicin if sensitivity of the organism to these drugs can be demonstrated by microbiologic tests.

(3) *S. aureus:* A penicillinase-resistant penicillin (e.g., nafcillin) (300 mg/kg per day q2–4h IV) should be given unless the organism is penicillin-sensitive, in which case aqueous penicillin G (300,000 U/kg per day q2–4h IV) should be used.

d. Drug therapy is individualized on the basis of the organism's in vitro sensitivities and the results of serum bactericidal tests. A minimum serum bactericidal dilution of 1:8 just before a dose is given is recommended. Although subjective improvement (in appetite, for example) may be prompt, fever can remain elevated for several days to weeks after initiation of antibiotic therapy.

e. In general, duration of antibiotic therapy is 4–6 weeks. For staphylococcal disease, 6 weeks is recommended; for *S. viridans,* 4 weeks appear to be adequate.

f. In addition to a daily physical examination, the ESR and urinalyses are useful parameters to follow.

g. Recurrent manifestations attributed to embolization and associated vasculitis (e.g., neurologic manifestations, hematuria, and splinter hemorrhages) do not necessarily indicate failure of treatment.

U. Neonatal sepsis and meningitis

    1. Etiology   The organisms involved may be *E. coli, Klebsiella,* and other gram-negative enteric bacteria, streptococci (including groups A, B, and D), *Salmonella, Pseudomonas,* staphylococci, and *Serratia.* Almost any organism can cause neonatal sepsis.

    2. Evaluation includes the following:

       a. One or more blood cultures (from a peripheral vein if possible).

       b. Examination of the urine and CSF and leukocyte, differential, and platelet counts.

       c. Cultures and gram-stained smears of the ear vernix, axilla, umbilicus, gastric aspirate, and meconium are also helpful, as is pathologic examination of the placenta and of the umbilical cord section for inflammation.

    3. Diagnosis is established by positive noncontaminated blood culture, CSF culture, or both. Gram smears and cultures of gastric aspirate, ear vernix, meconium, and urine may yield significant pathogens but these results should be interpreted cautiously.

    4. Therapy   See Table 9-2 for antimicrobial dosages in the newborn.

       a. Antibiotics must be instituted on suspicion of the diagnosis and before the culture **results** are available.

       b. Since neonatal meningitis is often associated with sepsis and the likely pathogens are the same, the choice of antibiotics is the same for both entities and is discussed in Sec. **IV.N.4.b.**

       c. Supportive care, including maintenance of normal body temperature, circulation, and acid-base balance, as well as adequate oxygenation, is essential.

       d. In some circumstances, particularly anemia, transfusion of fresh whole blood may be beneficial.

V. Tuberculosis (TB)

    1. Etiology   *M. tuberculosis.*

    2. Evaluation

       a. A detailed inquiry into possible contacts with active cases of TB (e.g., grandparents, babysitters), an intermediate tuberculin (5 U) skin test, and a chest x-ray are essential.

       b. Atypical mycobacterial skin testing is indicated when the reaction to an intermediate strength PPD is 5–9 mm of induration.

       c. In suspected pulmonary or miliary TB or both, the following should be done: gastric aspirates (three) in the morning, immediately on the patient's awakening; first-voided morning urine collections (three) for culture; and liver function tests. A liver biopsy, or bone marrow biopsy, or both may be necessary if miliary disease is suspected.

       d. In the presence of neurologic abnormalities, CSF examination, including culture and acid-fast stain, is necessary.

       e. In proved cases of TB, skin tests and chest x-rays of family members and contacts are essential. Children should be routinely skin-tested yearly up to age 4, as well as on entrance to school and at adolescence. For screening, the tine test is adequate but, if it is positive, and in patients in whom TB is suspected, an intermediate strength PPD (5 U) is required.

3. Diagnosis

a. The demonstration of acid-fast bacilli in exudate or tissue is the most direct method of diagnosis. The judicious use of needle biopsy specimens of pleura, liver, or bone marrow often yields the diagnosis.

b. The culture may not become positive for 3–6 weeks, but a presumptive diagnosis of TB is often made on the basis of the clinical presentation, epidemiologic history, and skin test reactivity to tuberculin antigen. Induration ≥ 10 mm from an intermediate strength PPD generally indicates prior infection with the tuberculosis bacillus (symptomatic or asymptomatic).

4. Therapy   See also Tables 9-10 and 9-11.

a. Asymptomatic converter (positive skin test with a negative chest x-ray): oral isoniazid (5–10 mg/kg once daily) for 1 year. Follow-up chest x-rays are obtained at 3–6 month intervals and again on completion of therapy.

b. Primary nonprogressive pulmonary TB (including an effusion) and cervical adenitis: oral isoniazid (10 mg/kg once daily) and para-aminosalicylic acid (PAS) (0.2–0.3 gm/d) or rifampin (10–20 mg/kg/d). Ethambutol (15 mg/kg/d) is given in place of PAS for patients over 13 years of age. (If approved for younger children it probably will replace PAS in most cases.)

c. Tuberculous meningitis, progressive pulmonary disease, miliary tuberculosis, and other forms of extrapulmonary tuberculosis:

Table 9-10.   Specific Therapy in Tuberculosis

Type	Regimen	Duration
Asymptomatic primary, including recent tuberculin converters	INH	1 year
Members of TB household (active case)	INH	1 year
Infant of TB mother	BCG or INH	1 year (if INH)
Primary nonprogressive pulmonary	INH and PAS, or rifampin or ethambutal (if $\geq$ 14 yrs)	2 years
Cervical adenitis	INH and PAS, or rifampin or ethambutal (if $\geq$ 14 yrs)	2 years
Progressive pulmonary, meningitis, miliary, and other extrapulmonary TB	INH and streptomycin. For the critically ill patient, PAS, rifampin, or ethambutal is also given initially. Streptomycin may be discontinued after 1–3 months if course is favorable	2 years

Table 9-11. Drug Therapy in Tuberculosis

Drugs	Daily Dose/Kg Body Weight[a]	Route and Mode of Administration of Daily Dose	Major Adverse Reactions
Isoniazid	5–20 mg, max. 400 mg	PO, IM, or IV in 1, 2, or 3 divided doses	Hepatotoxicity, peripheral neuropathy[b]; skin rashes, fever less commonly
Streptomycin	20–40 mg, max. 1 gm	IM in 1 or 2 divided doses	8th cranial nerve toxicity (primarily vestibular); skin rashes occasionally, rarely nephrotoxicity
Para-aminosalicylic acid	0.2–0.3 gm, max. 12 gm	PO in 3 divided doses	Gastrointestinal irritation (10%); fever, skin rashes less common
Ethambutol	15–25 mg	PO in 1 dose	Retrobulbar optic neuritis (especially with higher doses—ophthalmologic examination recommended before initiating therapy), skin rashes
Rifampin	10–20 mg	PO in 1 dose	Hepatotoxicity, thrombocytopenia

[a] High dose is recommended for critically ill patients; low dose for prophylaxis and long-term therapy after improvement.
[b] Does not occur in young children; see text.

isoniazid (15 mg/kg per day) and, initially, streptomycin 20–40 mg/kg per day to 1 gm daily. After a satisfactory clinical response has occurred (minimum of 6–12 weeks), streptomycin is replaced by PAS or ethambutol. Therapy is continued for a minimum of 24 months. Initially, critically ill patients with meningitis should receive triple therapy (isoniazid, streptomycin, and PAS or ethambutol or rifampin).

d. If the isolated *M. tuberculosis* is resistant in vitro to isoniazid, rifampin (10–20 mg/kg per day PO, given ½–1 hr before breakfast) is usually added to the regimen, and the dosage of isoniazid is increased to 20 mg/kg per day (up to 400 mg per day).

e. The infant of the tuberculous mother is given **BCG vaccination** or isoniazid. BCG is indicated when close medical supervision of the infant in the first year of life cannot be guaranteed (which is usually the case). BCG vaccination *requires* separation of the infant until the infant's tuberculin test becomes positive (6–12 weeks later). Isoniazid for 1 year is probably effective, but its potential neurotoxicity must be borne in mind.

f. Members of the household of a patient with active tuberculosis are given isoniazid (5–10 mg/kg daily for 1 year), regardless of tuberculin status. Periodic tuberculin tests should be done and chest x-ray films taken in such cases.

g. Pyridoxine (25–50 mg once daily) is indicated in children over 8 years of age and in children receiving high-dose isoniazid (more than 20 mg/kg daily).

h. Corticosteriods given in conjunction with antimicrobial therapy appear to lessen the inflammatory complications of tuberculous pericarditis, peritonitis, and possibly meningitis. They are also indicated when large hilar lymph nodes are obstructing the passage of air and when severe respiratory distress complicates diffuse pulmonary tuberculosis.

i. Isoniazid treatment commonly causes a transient asymptomatic elevation of liver enzymes during the first 3 months of therapy. The physician should be alert to signs and symptoms of hepatitis and discontinue the drug if they appear.

W. Venereal disease

1. Gonorrhea   The infecting organism is *Neisseria gonorrhoeae*.

   a. Evaluation

      (1) In **males,** urethral specimens can be obtained by stripping the penis.

      (2) In **females,** pelvic examination allows the physician to evaluate cervical and adnexal tenderness as well as obtain culture material from the cervix.

      (3) The rectum and pharynx should be cultured in both males and females for *N. gonorrhoeae*.

      (4) *N. gonorrhoeae* is relatively fastidious, and specimens should be cultured promptly and placed in a high CO_2 atmosphere (i.e., candle jar). Transgrow medium is an excellent transport medium for *N. gonorrhoeae* and should be used when direct cultures are not practical.

Table 9-12. Recommended Treatment Schedules for Uncomplicated Gonococcal Infection of the Urethra, Cervix, Pharynx, and Rectum[a]

Drug	Advantages	Disadvantages
Parenteral: Aqueous procaine penicillin G 4.8 million U IM with 1.0 gm probenecid PO (preferably given at least 30 min prior to injection)	One session (multiple injections), aborts incubating syphilis	Penicillin allergy, procaine reactions, (?) reactions to probenecid
Oral: Ampicillin 3.5 gm PO with 1.0 gm probenecid PO (may be given simultaneously)	One session, fewer serious immediate reactions	(?) increase in allergic reactions, (?) reactions to probenecid, effect on incubating syphilis unknown
Parenteral[b]: Spectinomycin 2.0 gm IM in males, 4.0 gm IM in females	One session, little short-term toxicity	Not effective against incubating syphilis, resistance may develop, insufficient data on long-term toxicity
Oral[a]: Tetracycline HCl 1.5 gm PO stat, then 0.5 gm PO qid for 4 days (total 9.5 gm). Other tetracyclines offer no proved therapeutic advantage	Lowered rate of postgonococcal urethritis	Not as effective as above regimens, requires good patient cooperation, effect on incubating syphilis unknown

[a] These regimens are recommended for children over 12. In children under 12 the doses should be reduced proportionately.
[b] For patients in whom penicillin is contraindicated (may include allergy to penicillin, asthma, hay fever, etc.) or in whom penicillin or ampicillin has been ineffective.

229

(5) *A serologic test for syphilis should be performed in all patients with gonorrhea.*

(6) The disease is seen with increasing frequency in children *under* 12 years.

b. Diagnosis *N. gonorrhoeae* is identified by demonstration of gram-negative diplococci on gram-stained smears of urethral or cervical discharge or by culture of appropriate specimens on Thayer-Martin media.

c. Treatment Treatment is outlined in Table 9-12. Case contact finding as well as sex education and counseling are as important as the drug therapy.

2. Syphilis The infecting organism is *Treponema pallidum.*

a. Evaluation and diagnosis

(1) Dark-field examination of skin lesions (chancre or rash). **The material is infectious and should be handled with care.**

(2) Serologic tests for syphilis are usually nonreactive when the chancre first appears, but become reactive during the following 1–4 weeks. Biologic false-positive tests with non-specific antigens (VDRL, Wasserman, Hinton, Kolmer) may be caused by a variety of infections and other illnesses and should be confirmed by tests specific for *T. pallidum* (FTA-Abs, TPI).

b. Therapy in primary or secondary syphilis

(1) Procaine penicillin G, 600,000 U IM daily for 10 days, or benzathine penicillin G, 2.4 million U IM, repeated in 7 days.

(2) In patients allergic to penicillin, give tetracycline 500 mg qid for 15 days, or, in the case of pregnancy, erythromycin 75 mg qid for 15 days.

(3) Case contact findings, as well as sex education and counseling, are as important as the drug therapy. Child abuse must be investigated in cases involving younger children.

10   Parasitic Infections

Infections with protozoa and helminths are subject to rational principles of diagnosis and therapy. Most parasitic infections occur in temperate as well as tropical environments. Their prevalence varies with climate, sanitation, and socioeconomic conditions. The frequency with which the clinician in temperate areas encounters parasitic infections is increasing, both as a result of intercontinental travel and the use of immunosuppressive agents.

I. PRINCIPLES OF DIAGNOSIS

A. General

1. *The diagnosis of parasitic infection can rarely be made on clinical grounds alone.* Many parasites may cause an identical clinical picture, and different clinical presentations may be produced by a single parasite. In addition, parasitic infections are often asymptomatic or produce only mild symptoms. A diagnosis of parasitic infection is commonly suspected only because of an abnormal, unexpected laboratory finding combined with a high index of suspicion.

2. *The diagnosis of most helminthic or protozoal infections requires the demonstration of the parasite in body excreta, fluids, or tissue.*

3. Many parasites have an intricate route of migration through the human host and affect several organs successively or simultaneously. The choice of appropriate diagnostic techniques and materials thus rests on some understanding of the life cycles of the possible infecting agents.

4. Knowledge of the geographic distribution of parasitic infections and their mode of acquisition and means of spread often aids diagnosis and therapy. Detailed information is available from standard parasitology texts.

5. *Patients commonly harbor several parasites.* A complete evaluation must be made to avoid overlooking the most important infecting species in each clinical setting.

B. Hematologic changes in parasitic infections

1. **Erythrocytes**   Anemia is an inconstant and nonspecific finding in most parasitic infections. It reflects the general nutritional status of the patient, rather than any direct effect of the infecting parasite. Iron deficiency anemia in hookworm disease and hemolytic anemia in malaria infections are exceptions.

2. **Eosinophils**

   a. Eosinophilia is often the first clue to the presence of a *helminth* infection. *Protozoa*, conversely, do *not* evoke an eosinophilia. The finding of eosinophilia in amebiasis, malaria, toxoplasmosis, or giardiasis suggests an additional helminth infection.

b. *The level of eosinophilia is of diagnostic aid.* In general, tissue-living helminths evoke a profound eosinophilia and those that exist within the lumen of the bowel evoke a mild eosinophilia or none at all (Table 10-1).

C. Direct identification of parasites Many techniques are available to identify parasites in excreta, fluids, and tissue. Examination of specimens is usually done by hospital, public health, or private laboratories. However, there are several simple procedures, requiring little equipment, which the physician can perform when the patient is seen. It is helpful to have charts of diagnostic stages of helminths and protozoa available for accurate interpretation. If more sophisticated procedures are needed, standard texts of parasitology can be consulted.

1. Blood

a. The **thin dry smear** is useful in detecting malarial parasites. The technique is identical to routine blood smears used for hematologic studies. Wright's or Giemsa stain is used in the usual fashion, and parasites are seen within red blood cells. Species differentiation is of therapeutic importance once malaria parasites have been identified.

b. The **thick dry smear** is useful for the detection of malaria parasites, yielding a much higher concentration of parasites than the thin smear and thus useful when the parasites are few and thin smears are negative. However, the thick smear is harder to interpret since the erythrocytes are lysed, and the parasites are seen on a background of stained proteinaceous debris. Perform the technique as follows:

(1) Spread a drop of blood on a clean microscope slide, using an applicator or corner of another slide. (The smear should be about the diameter of a dime and of a thickness sufficient to allow for transparency when the hemoglobin is removed.)

(2) Allow the smear to dry for 1–2 hr at 37° C.

(3) Cover the slide with distilled water until the color of the hemoglobin has disappeared.

(4) Dry the slide and cover it with Wright's stain as for routine blood smears, or with dilute Giemsa stain for 45 min.

(5) Examine for parasites under the oil immersion lens.

2. Stool Examine feces as soon after passage as possible and before barium or cathartics are given. Helminth ova and protozoal cysts can be identified in older specimens, but the identification of free-living, motile forms requires the examination of *freshly passed, warm stool.*

a. Direct examination of stool enables the rapid identification of intestinal parasites. Living, motile forms as well as ova and cysts can be identified, particularly if there is a heavy infestation. The procedure takes a few minutes and makes use of supplies found in all laboratories.

(1) Examine the specimen grossly for flecks of blood and mucus. If present, take a sample from these areas.

(2) Place a match-head size sample on each of two microscope slides with a wooden applicator.

(3) Mix one sample with 2 drops of saline and cover with cover slip.

(4) Add 2 drops of dilute iodine solution to the other sample, mix, and cover similarly.

(5) Observe for the presence of erythrocytes and leukocytes. *Erythrocytes* suggest amebic colitis, and *leukocytes*, bacterial infection or inflammatory bowel disease and *not* parasitic infection.

(6) Examine the stained slide for the presence of helminth eggs under low power and for protozoal cysts under high power and oil immersion.

(7) Examine unstained slide under low and high power for the presence of motile organisms (ameba, trophozoites, larvae).

b. Concentration   A number of techniques are available for examination of larger quantities of feces for parasites. The formalin-ether technique will concentrate ova and cysts more than 20 times. It is performed as follows:

(1) Emulsify 1–2 gm of feces in 10 ml of a 10% formalin-saline solution.

(2) Strain through gauze into a tapered centrifuge tube.

(3) Add 3 ml of ether and shake vigorously for 1 min.

(4) Centrifuge at 2000 rpm for 3 min.

(5) Four distinct layers appear. The upper three layers are loosened and decanted off.

(6) The deposit is examined for ova and cysts.

c. Quantitation   In certain helminthic infections, estimation of the *worm burden* by quantitation of egg excretion is of great importance. The method of Stoll is commonly employed [Belding, D. L., *Textbook of Parasitology* (3rd ed.), New York: Appleton, 1965].

d. Scotch-tape examination is a useful and simple technique for the demonstration of pinworm eggs.

(1) Evert a strip of Scotch tape, gummed side outward, on the edge of a tongue blade.

(2) Dab the perianal area first thing in the morning.

(3) Place on a microscope slide, sticky side down, on a drop of toluene.

(4) Examine under low power for characteristic eggs.

D. Serologic tests in parasitic diseases

1. Immunodiagnostic tests are helpful in several parasitic infections. They are to be used and interpreted *in conjunction with* clinical and laboratory evaluation and should not be relied on alone for diagnosis.

Table 10-1. Diagnostic Features of Commonly Encountered Parasitic Infections

Disease	Mode of Spread	Location in Man	Clinical Features	Laboratory Diagnosis	Eosino-philia[a]	Remarks
Roundworms (Nematodes)						
Ascariasis	Fecal-oral	Adult—small intestine; Larvae—lung	Vague abdominal distress; cough and pneumonia during lung migration	Eggs in feces	Usually mild; moderate to marked during migration	
Hookworm	Larvae in soil, skin penetration	Small intestine	Vague abdominal distress; anemia in heavy infections	Eggs in feces	Mild to moderate	Distinguish infestation from infection
Whipworm	Fecal-oral	Large intestine	Rarely symptomatic	Eggs in feces	Absent to mild	
Strongyloidiasis	Larvae in soil, skin penetration	Upper small intestine	Duodenitis; hyperinfection syndrome rarely	Larvae in *fresh stool*, duodenal aspirate	Moderate to marked	
Pinworm	Fecal-oral	Large intestine, perianal area	Perianal pruritis	Scotch tape swab for eggs, gross examination of area for worms	Absent	Very common
Creeping eruption (Cutaneous larva migrans)	Larvae in soil, skin penetration (larvae from dog, cat feces)	Skin	Intensely pruritic, serpiginous skin lesions	Physical examination	Variable	

Visceral larva migrans	Fecal-oral, via pica (eggs from dog, cat feces)	Liver, lung, muscle	Fever, hepatosplenomegaly	Clinical diagnosis	Marked	
Trichinosis	Ingestion of undercooked pork	Striated muscle	Fever, diarrhea, periorbital edema, muscle pain	Biopsy of muscle, skin and serologic tests	Marked	
Tapeworms (Cestodes)						
Beef tapeworm	Ingestion of undercooked beef	Small intestine	Asymptomatic	Proglottid segments passed with feces	Absent	
Pork tapeworm	Ingestion of undercooked pork	Small intestine	Asymptomatic, rare auto-infection with CNS symptoms (cysticercosis)	Proglottid segments passed with feces	Absent	
Hydatid disease	Fecal-oral (eggs from carnivore feces)	Liver, lung, bone, brain	Usually asymptomatic, occasionally pressure symptoms in affected organ	Removal of cyst, complement-fixation, hemagglutinin assay, skin test	Variable	
Flukes (Trematodes)						
Schistosoma mansoni	Cecaria in streams, skin penetration	Venules of large intestine	Fever, colitis, hepatomegaly, portal hypertension	Eggs in feces, rectal biopsy	Moderate to marked	Africa, S. America; common in Puerto Ricans

[a] Mild, 5–10 percent; moderate, 10–20 percent; marked, greater than 20 percent. Table continues on p. 236.

Table 10-1. (*Continued*)

Disease	Mode of Spread	Location in Man	Clinical Features	Laboratory Diagnosis	Eosino-philia[a]	Remarks
Schistosoma hematobium	Same	Venules of urinary bladder	Fever, malaise, hematuria	Eggs in urine, bladder or rectal biopsy	Moderate to marked	Africa
Schistosoma japonicum	Same	Venules of small intestine	Fever, malaise, abdominal pain, diarrhea, hepatomegaly	Eggs in feces, rectal biopsy	Moderate to marked	S.E. Asia
Protozoa						
Intestinal amebiasis	Fecal-oral	Lumen and wall of large intestine	Bloody diarrhea, fever, abdominal pain, asymptomatic	Trophozoites in *fresh stool* or proctoscopic material, cysts in stool	Absent	
Extraintestinal amebiasis	Fecal-oral	Liver, lung	Hepatomegaly, fever	Trophozoites from abscess or sputum, complement-fixation	Absent	
Giardiasis	Fecal-oral	Upper small intestine	Diarrhea, abdominal pain, mal-absorption	Cysts and trophozoites in *fresh stool*, duodenal aspirate	Absent	
Toxoplasmosis	Congenital, raw meat, cat feces (?)	All organs, blood, reticuloendo-thelial system	Congenital, acute mono-like illness, asympto-matic	Biopsy, complement-fixation, dye test, immuno-fluorescence antibody test, indirect hemag-glutinin assay	Absent	

Malaria	Bite of infected anopheles mosquito, transfusion rarely	Erythrocytes, reticuloendothelial system	Fever, splenomegaly, anemia, collapse, encephalopathy with *P. falciparum*	Repeated blood smears	Absent	Important to distinguish *P. falciparum* from relapsing
Pneumocystosis	Unknown	Lungs	Fever, cough, dyspnea, lung infiltrates in compromised host	Sputum, bronchial brushings, lung biopsy	Absent	Compromised host

a Mild, 5–10 percent; moderate, 10–20 percent; marked, greater than 20 percent.

2. The tests are specifically helpful in invasive amebiasis, trichinosis, toxoplasmosis, and echinococcosis.

3. The serologic tests noted in Table 10-1 and in the text are performed at the Center for Disease Control, Atlanta, Georgia, and by some local health departments.

II. PRINCIPLES OF TREATMENT   See Table 10-2.

A. *Protozoal infections are always treated.* The principles of treatment consist of the identification of the responsible parasite and the selection of an appropriate therapeutic agent, administered in appropriate dosage.

B. *Helminthic infections are not always treated.* After identifying the causative parasite, the clinician must weigh several additional factors before initiating treatment. These include:

1. The number of worms harbored by the patient and the life span of the infecting worm(s)

2. The likelihood and seriousness of personal and public health complications resulting from infection

3. The availability and efficacy of therapeutic agents and their expected side effects and toxicity

C. Treatment must be individualized and arbitrary rules avoided.

D. **Follow-up clinical and laboratory assessment** is always indicated to determine if treatment has been efficacious. Stools should be examined several weeks after the treatment of intestinal parasites is completed, and re-treatment given if cure has not been achieved. In general, re-treatment with the same drug is more desirable than proceeding to an alternate agent that is more toxic, less efficacious, or both.

E. **Patient education**   The physician should always combine treatment with patient education aimed at *prevention* of future parasitic infection. Attention should be given to the environmental circumstances that resulted in the child's acquisition of infection.

III. SPECIFIC PARASITES

A. **Roundworms (nematodes)**

1. **Ascaris**

a. **Etiology**   Fecal-oral passage of infective ova of *Ascaris lumbricoides.* Man is the only susceptible host. The infection is worldwide in distribution.

b. **Evaluation and diagnosis**   Two distinct clinical phases occur:

(1) **Transient blood-lung migration phase of the larvae**   Pneumonia occurs, with cough, blood-tinged sputum, patchy pulmonary infiltrates, and fever. A marked peripheral eosinophilia is typical. Characteristic larvae may be found in the sputum.

(2) **Prolonged intestinal phase of the adults**   The patient is usually asymptomatic, although vague abdominal discomfort may occur. On rare occasions, more serious manifes-

tations may occur, including intestinal obstruction, appendicitis, and regurgitation and aspiration of wandering adult worms.

(3) The **diagnosis** is confirmed by:

(a) Characteristic ova in feces by direct examination or concentration techniques

(b) Regurgitation or stool passage of adult worms

(c) Occasionally, demonstration of adult worms on abdominal x-ray films

c. Treatment The occasional aberrant wanderings of individual worms and subsequent serious consequences require that *all* ascaris infections be treated. Tetrachlorethylene, used in the treatment of hookworm infection, may provoke ascaris wandering. Ascaris intestinal infections should thus be treated first if a combined infection is present.

(1) Ascaris pneumonitis Symptomatic treatment

(2) Intestinal ascariasis:
Piperazine citrate, 75 mg/kg daily for 2 days
Thiabendazole, 25 mg/kg bid for 2 days

d. Prevention Sanitary disposal of feces

2. Hookworm

a. Etiology

(1) Human hookworms belong to two genera, *Necator* and *Ancylostoma*. The former are prevalent in the southern United States, South and Central America, Asia, and Africa. The latter are rarely seen in the United States.

(2) Infections spread by skin penetration of soil-living larvae hatched from eggs passed in infected feces.

b. Evaluation and diagnosis Three clinical phases of hookworm infection are recognized:

(1) Penetration of the skin by larvae A local papulovesicular dermatitis and a history of walking barefoot in feces-contaminated soil suggests the diagnosis.

(2) Transient blood-lung migration by larvae A mild pneumonitis with peripheral eosinophilia is suggestive. Hookworm larvae may be found in the sputum.

(3) Prolonged intestinal phase due to the attachment of blood-feeding adult worms to the small intestinal mucosa of the host.

(a) In **hookworm infection** the number of infecting worms is small, and diarrhea and abdominal cramps may be the only clinical findings. Infection is confirmed by demonstrating hookworm ova in feces.

(b) In **hookworm disease** large numbers of worms are present, and significant blood loss occurs. The disease is confirmed by (turn to p. 242) :

Table 10-2. Treatment of Common Parasitic Infections

Disease	Parasite	Drug of Choice[a]	Alternate Drugs[a]
Roundworms (Nematodes)			
Ascariasis	*A. lumbricoides*	Piperazine citrate	Thiabendazole
Hookworm	*A. duodenale*	Benphenium	Thiabendazole
	N. americanus	Tetrachlorethylene	Thiabendazole
Whipworm	*T. trichiuria*	Hexyresorcinol enema	
Strongyloidiasis	*S. stercoralis*	Thiabendazole	
Pinworm	*E. vermicularis*	Pyrvinium	Piperazine citrate
			Thiabendazole
Creeping eruption	*A. braziliense*	Thiabendazole	
Visceral larva migrans	*T. canis*	Thiabendazole and symptomatic Rx with steroids for severe symptoms	
Tapeworms (Cestodes)			
Beef tapeworm	*T. saginata*	Niclosamide	Quinacrine
Pork tapeworm	*T. solium*	Quinacrine	
Hydatid disease	*E. granulosa*	None	
Trematodes			
Schistosomiasis	*S. mansoni*	Stibophen	Antimony sodium dimercaptosuccinate
			Niridazole
			Lucanthone
S. hematobium		Niridazole	Stibophen
S. japonicum		Antimony potassium tartrate	Stibophen
Protozoa			
Intestinal amebiasis (see text)	*E. histolytica*	Metronidazole	Paromycin, diiodohydroxyquin

Disease	Organism	Drug of choice	Alternative
Extraintestinal amebiasis	*E. histolytica*	Metronidazole	Above, plus dihydroemetine HCl, chloroquine phosphate
Giardiasis	*G. lamblia*	Metronidazole	Quinacrine
Toxoplasmosis	*T. gondii*	Pyrimethamine plus sulfadiazine	
Malaria (see text)	*P. falciparum*	Chloroquine phosphate	Quinine sulfate, pyrimethamine, sulfadiazine
	P. vivax, P. ovale, and P. malariae	Chloroquine phosphate plus primaquine phosphate	
Pneumocystis	*P. carinii*	Pentamidine isothionate[b]	

[a] See text for dosages.
[b] Available through Parasitic Drug Service, Parasitic Diseases Branch, Center for Disease Control, 1600 Clifton Road, NE, Atlanta, Ga. 30333.

  i. Signs and symptoms of anemia

  ii. Documentation of iron deficiency

  iii. The finding of occult blood in the feces

  iv. The demonstration of large numbers of hookworm ova in the feces by the method of Stoll (see reference in Sec. **I.C.2.c** or other standard text for details).

c. Treatment

  (1) Drugs

   (a) *Necator:*
   Tetrachlorethylene, 0.12 ml/kg in 1 dose
   Thiabendazole, 25 mg/kg bid for 2 days

   (b) *Ancylostoma:*
   Bephenium, 2.5 gm if < 20 kg, in 1 dose
   5.0 gm if > 20 kg, in 1 dose
   Thiabendazole, 25 mg/kg bid for 2 days

  (2) Differentiation between *Necator* and *Ancylostoma* infections is difficult. Infections acquired in the Western Hemisphere should be assumed to be due to *Necator* and treated accordingly.

  (3) Moderate to very heavy infections should always be treated with antihelminthics, as should hookworm disease. Light infections need not be specifically treated if the patient is adequately nourished.

  (4) Iron supplementation should be given to patients with hookworm disease.

  (5) If both ascaris and hookworm infections are present, ascaris should be treated first if tetrachlorethylene is to be used to treat the hookworm infection, as this drug may provoke the migration of ascaris adults.

d. Prevention   Sanitary disposal of feces and wearing of shoes to prevent contact of bare feet with contaminated soil.

3. Whipworm

a. Etiology   Fecal-oral spread of *Trichuris trichiura*. The infection is worldwide, and man is the natural reservoir and only susceptible host.

b. Evaluation and diagnosis

  (1) Diarrhea and abdominal pain have been associated with trichuriasis, but the vast majority of infections are asymptomatic.

  (2) The presence of typical ova in feces by direct fecal smear or concentration techniques is diagnostic.

  (3) Eosinophilia is not associated with trichuriasis, and its presence should suggest another parasitic infection.

c. Treatment   Treatment is toxic and rarely indicated since symptoms are so infrequent.

d. Prevention   Sanitary fecal disposal and wearing of shoes to prevent skin penetration by the larvae.

4. Pinworm

- **a. Etiology** Fecal-oral spread of *Enterobius vermicularis*, a 4 mm-worm just visible to the naked eye, and the most common helminth of man found in the United States. Infection often affects entire households, and autoinfection is also common. Man is the only known host.

- **b. Evaluation and diagnosis**

  (1) Perianal itching, vulvitis, and vaginitis in young children suggest the presence of pinworms. Symptoms may be so intense as to cause insomnia, restlessness, and hyperactivity.

  (2) Adult worms may be seen in the perianal area and on the surface of freshly passed feces, particularly in the early morning.

  (3) Characteristic ova are demonstrated by Scotch tape swab (see Sec. **I.C.2.d**). Examination should be made first thing in the morning and repeated on consecutive days if necessary. A single swabbing reveals only about 50 percent of infections; three swabbings will uncover 90 percent; and five examinations should be performed before the patient is considered free from infection. Scrapings from beneath the fingernails may show eggs in 30 percent of infected children.

  (4) If diagnostic procedures fail, a therapeutic trial is reasonable in markedly symptomatic children.

- **c. Treatment**

  Pyrvinium pamoate, 5 mg/kg in a single dose
  Piperazine citrate, 65 mg/kg daily for 7 days
  Thiabendazole, 25 mg/kg bid for 2 days
  If repeated symptomatic infections occur, it is reasonable to treat all members of a household simultaneously.

- **d. Prevention** Boiling of bedsheets, undergarments, pajamas, and the like is of little or no value. Hand-washing and fingernail cleanliness may reduce transmission and autoinfection.

5. Creeping eruption (cutaneous larva migrans)

- **a. Etiology** Skin penetration by larvae of *Ancylostoma braziliense*, a dog and cat hookworm. The infection is worldwide and occurs in children living in close association with dogs and cats.

- **b. Evaluation and diagnosis** The clinical presentation is diagnostic. Typical serpiginous dermal tunnels, which are indurated, pruritic, and elevated, are produced by the migrating larvae. The larvae rarely migrate more than a few inches in the course of the 2–6 weeks before they die.

- **c. Treatment** Thiabendazole, 25 mg/kg bid for 2 days.

- **d. Prevention** Avoidance of contamination of play and work areas by dog and cat feces.

6. Visceral larva migrans

- **a. Etiology** Ingestion of the ova of dog and cat ascarids, *Toxocara canis* and *Toxocara cati*. Larvae emerge in the intestine and migrate extensively throughout the body.

b. Evaluation and diagnosis

(1) Presumptive diagnosis is based on clinical manifestations in a child known to ingest dirt. These include fever, cough, hepatosplenomegaly, and transient pneumonia.

(2) Hypergammaglobulinemia, marked eosinophilia, and leukocytosis are present.

(3) The parasite is rarely demonstrated; if this entity is suspected, stool examination and tissue biopsy are useless.

c. Treatment

(1) The disease is often mild and self-limited, lasting several weeks. Specific treatment is usually unnecessary.

(2) In severe cases antihelminthic therapy may be beneficial (thiabendazole, 25 mg/kg bid for 2 days).

(3) Antiinflammatory therapy with corticosteroids or antihistamines, or both, may offer symptomatic relief.

7. Trichinosis

a. Etiology Ingestion of raw meat containing encysted larvae of *Trichinella spiralis* (pork is the principal source of human infection). The infection is more common in temperate than in tropical environments.

b. Evaluation and diagnosis

(1) A history of uncooked pork ingestion.

(2) The clinical picture may suggest the diagnosis, but is often unclear until the second or third week of infection. At this time the full-blown picture of fever, facial and periorbital edema, headache, photophobia, conjunctivitis, and severe muscle pains and tenderness may occur. Signs of encephalitis, meningitis, and myocarditis may appear.

(3) A muscle biopsy specimen showing characteristic larvae. (Crush a thin slice of muscle between two slides and inspect it under the microscope to verify the presence of larvae.) Histologic examination of tissue for the presence of inflammatory reaction is essential to confirm *recent* infection. A negative biopsy does not rule out the diagnosis.

(4) Marked peripheral eosinophilia (20–80%) after the third week of infection, which may persist for months.

(5) A positive intracutaneous skin test with *Trichinella* larval antigen (85–100% sensitivity). An immediate wheal and flare reaction occurs after injection of 0.1 ml of antigen. The test becomes positive about 3 weeks after infection and remains positive for 5–7 years.

(6) Agglutination or flocculation reactions with rising titer demonstrated on paired samples (tests turn positive in the third week of infection and may remain positive for months to years).

c. Treatment

(1) The efficacy of specific antihelminthic therapy is in question. In severe cases, thiabendazole may be tried.

(2) Corticosteroids may ameliorate severe symptoms, but they are not universally considered beneficial.

d. **Prevention**   Consumption of only well-cooked pork. Pork is *not* inspected for trichinosis in the United States.

B. Tapeworms (cestodes)

1. Beef tapeworm

a. **Etiology**   The disease is transmitted by the ingestion of under-cooked beef containing *Taenia saginata* larval cysts. The infection is worldwide in distribution; man is the definitive host, and cattle are the intermediate host.

b. **Evaluation and diagnosis**   Most patients are asymptomatic, and the infection is noted only when migrating proglottids pass through the anus. Examination of gravid proglottids is diagnostic.

c. **Treatment**

   (1) **Niclosamid**   Achieves a 90 percent cure rate.

   (a) No prior bowel preparation is required. Dosage is as follows:
   < 10 years of age, 1 gm in a single dose
   > 10 years of age, 2 gm in a single dose

   (b) The worm will be macerated, and search for the scolex (head) is thus unprofitable.

   (c) Re-treat if proglottids reappear in subsequent months.

   (2) **Quinacrine**   Achieves a 75 percent cure rate. The total dose is 25 mg/kg. Treatment is as follows:

   (a) Give a cathartic the evening before treatment and a cleansing enema (Fleet's) in morning.

   (b) Quinacrine on an empty stomach is given in 4–5 divided doses q10min until the total dose is given. Each dose is given with 250 mg sodium bicarbonate.

   (c) Give a saline purge several hours later and follow by a stool examination for scolex for the next 24 hr.

   (d) Re-treat if proglottids reappear in subsequent months.

d. **Prevention**   Thorough cooking of beef.

2. Pork tapeworm

a. **Etiology**   Ingestion of uncooked pork containing larval cysts of *Taenia solium*.

b. **Evaluation and diagnosis**   Adult worms rarely produce symptoms. The passage of gravid motile proglottids through the anus raises the suspicion of infection. Confirmation is obtained by laboratory examination of the proglottid.

c. **Treatment   Quinacrine** is the drug of choice (dosage schedule as for *T. saginata*, **I.c**).

d. **Prevention**   Thorough cooking of pork.

3. Hydatid disease

a. Etiology Man acquires the infection by ingesting eggs of *Echinococcus granulosus* passed in the feces of carnivores.

b. Evaluation and diagnosis

(1) A slow-growing, usually asymptomatic cyst in the proper epidemiologic setting suggests the diagnosis. Two-thirds occur in the liver; one-fourth in the lung; and the remainder are widely scattered.

(2) The **x-ray** appearance is typical but not pathognomonic.

(3) Casoni's intradermal skin test An immediate wheal and flare constitute a positive test, specific for *E. granulosis* and 75% sensitive.

(4) Hemagglutination and bentonite flocculation tests are positive in the majority of cases.

(5) Demonstration of characteristic gross and histologic appearance on removal of cyst. **(Aspiration is dangerous and should not be done.)**

c. Treatment Easily accessible cysts are removed surgically. Most cysts are asymptomatic and may, in fact, be left untreated. Freezing of the cyst and subsequent surgical removal have given favorable results (*N. Engl. J. Med.* 284:1346, 1971).

C. Trematodes (flukes): schistosomiasis

1. Etiology Schistosomiasis is caused by one of three species of blood flukes. Each species has a different geographic distribution and anatomic localization in the infected host and produces different clinical manifestations. The human host acquires the infection through schistosomal skin penetration in fresh water streams. The infection is spread through urination or defecation into streams.

a. S. mansoni is found in Africa, South America, and the Caribbean area, including Puerto Rico (5–10 percent of Puerto Ricans residing in the United States are infected). Its pathologic effects are primarily in the gastrointestinal tract.

b. S. japonicum is found in the Far East and also primarily affects the gastrointestinal tract.

c. S. hematobium is found in Africa and causes disease of the genitourinary system.

2. Evaluation and diagnosis

a. Schistosome infections are not acquired or transmitted in the continental United States. A history of residence or travel in an endemic area is thus required if the diagnosis is suspected.

b. The clinical manifestations of schistosomiasis are varied and reflect acute and chronic stages of infection.

(1) In the acute stages, a *localized dermatitis* is produced at the site of skin penetration; this subsides in a few days. In some individuals an *acute illness*, characterized by fever, chills, abdominal pain, urticarial eruptions, and marked eosinophilia may occur 2–4 weeks later.

(2) The deposition of eggs begins 1–3 months after infection. The symptoms reflect the sites of egg deposition. *S. japonicum* causes abscesses and ulceration of the ileum and cecum. *S. mansoni* infections involve the sigmoid colon and rectum. Both result in abdominal pain and bloody diarrhea. *S. hematobium* infections involve the bladder, producing hematuria, dysuria, and suprapubic pain and tenderness.

(3) The process may become chronic and result in granulomatous inflammation and fibrosis of the intestine, or bladder, or both. Eggs carried to the liver via the portal circulation in *S. mansoni* and *S. japonicum* infections may produce periportal cirrhosis with portal hypertension, although liver function is usually not impaired. Eggs carried to the lungs may produce an obliterative endarteritis with cough, hemoptysis, pulmonary hypertension, and cor pulmonale. Eggs carried to the CNS and skin may produce local lesions in these organs.

(4) A moderate eosinophilia is usually found.

(5) Demonstration of typical eggs is required for diagnosis.

    (a) The number of eggs in feces or urine is small and *concentration techniques* are usually required and should be specifically requested if samples are examined by outside laboratories.

    (b) If the clinical picture is suggestive and eggs are not found, a *rectal or bladder biopsy is done.* The sample should be crushed between two slides and examined directly for eggs.

3. Treatment

a. The serious potential consequences of schistosomal infections and the long life span (20–40 years) of egg-laying adults usually require that all schistosome infections be treated. Treatment should not be undertaken lightly; the agents used have significant toxicity and treatment is prolonged.

b. Specific therapy

    (1) *S. hematobium:*
Niridazole (children under 16), 25 mg/kg for 7 days
Lucanthone (children under 16), 5 mg/kg tid for 7 days
Stibophen, 1 ml IM, day 1; 2 ml IM, day 2; 3 ml IM, day 3; 4 ml IM every other day for 18 injections [For age and weight modification see Barnett, H. L. *Pediatrics* (15th ed.), New York: Appleton, 1972, p. 815.]

    (2) *S. mansoni:*
Stibophen, as in **(1)**
Antimony sodium dimercaptosuccinate, 8 mg/kg IM weekly for 5 weeks
Niridazole (children under 16), 25 mg/kg for 7 days

    (3) *S. japonicum:*
Antimony potassium tartrate (see *Medical Letter* 14, no. 2, 1972)
Stibophen, as in **(1)**
Antimony sodium dimercaptosuccinate, as in **(2)**

    c. The patient should have repeat stool or urine exams monthly for 6 months to ensure cure.

4. Prevention Avoidance of infected water; proper disposal of human feces and urine

D. Protozoa

1. Amebiasis

    a. Etiology Fecal-oral passage of cysts of *Entamoeba histolytica*. Amebiasis is worldwide in distribution and man is the only known host. Sporadic localized epidemics occur in the United States, and the disease is endemic in many institutionalized populations.

    b. Evaluation and diagnosis

        (1) Intestinal amebiasis

            (a) Intestinal amebiasis varies in presentation from the asymptomatic carrier state (by far the most common) to fulminant colonic disease.

                i. Mild colonic infection is characterized by alternating diarrhea and constipation.

                ii. Amebic dysentery presents most frequently as subacute illness. Mild tenderness, bloody diarrhea, low-grade fever, weakness, and malaise are characteristic. The tempo of the illness may clinically distinguish it from more acute, bacillary dysentery. Abdominal tenderness is common, particularly over the sigmoid and cecal areas; appendicitis is sometimes erroneously diagnosed.

            (b) Confirmation in acute cases is obtained by demonstrating motile amebic trophozoites in *fresh stool*, or cysts in the carrier state. Proctoscopy may be useful if multiple stool samples are negative.

            (c) Erythrocytes are plentiful and leukocytes are minimal in the stool, which is helpful in distinguishing between amebic and bacillary dysentery.

            (d) Eosinophilia is *not* found.

        (2) Extraintestinal amebiasis most commonly affects the liver.

            (a) Disease may occur without signs or symptoms of intestinal infection. Fever, chills, an enlarged, tender liver, elevated right diaphragm, minimal liver function abnormalities, and the finding of a filling defect on liver scan are highly suggestive. Of all amebic abscesses, 95 percent are single and situated in the upper part of the right lobe of the liver.

            (b) Serologic tests for invasive amebiasis are extremely accurate.

            (c) Percutaneous liver aspiration is recommended in large abscesses only. Aspirated material may show amebae. However, their absence does not rule out hepatic infection as organisms tend to be located at the margins of the abscess.

(d) A therapeutic trial with metronidazole is an accepted diagnostic measure.

c. Treatment

(1) *All* stages of amebiasis are treated.

(a) Asymptomatic carrier state
Metronidazole, 7–10 mg/kg tid PO for 10 days
or
Diiodohydroxyquin, 7–10 mg/kg tid PO for 3 weeks

(b) Intestinal infection
Metronidazole, 7–10 mg/kg tid PO for 10 days
or
Diiodohydroxyquin, as in **(a)**
and
Paromomycin, 25–30 mg/kg PO tid for 10 days; *and if severe*
Dihydroemetine, HCl, 1.0–1.5 mg/kg IM for 10 days

(c) Hepatic infection
Metronidazole, 7–10 mg/kg PO tid for 10 days
or
Chloroquine phosphate, 10 mg/kg PO qid for 10 days
and
Dehydroemetine HCl, as in **(b)**
and
Paromomycin, as in **(b)**
and
Diiodohydroxyquin, as in **(a)**

(2) In addition to specific amebicidal therapy, supportive care is important in invasive amebiasis. Hospitalization, bed rest, and good nutritional intake may contribute to rapid recovery.

(3) Follow-up stool examinations should be performed at 1 and 2 months to ensure that a cure has been achieved.

d. Prevention Sanitary disposal of feces and treatment of asymptomatic cyst passers.

2. Giardiasis

a. Etiology Fecal-oral spread of *Giardia lamblia*. Infection is worldwide and is common in institutionalized populations.

b. Evaluation and diagnosis

(1) There are often no symptoms. Abdominal pain, chronic and recurrent diarrhea, and weight loss may occur. The diarrhea is not bloody; stools may be bulky and offensive. Steatorrhea and malabsorption may occur.

(2) The diagnosis is confirmed by the demonstration of characteristic motile trophozoites in *fresh diarrheal stool* or *duodenal aspirate* by direct examination. Cysts may be seen in formed stool by direct or concentration methods.

c. Treatment

(1) Specific therapy is highly effective.
Metronidazole, 3–5 mg/kg tid for 7 days
Quinacrine, 2–3 mg/kg tid for 5 days

(2) Supportive measures and restoration of nutritional status are important in patients with malabsorption.

d. Prevention Sanitary disposal of feces.

3. Malaria

a. Etiology Malaria, among the most common worldwide infections of man, is transmitted by the bite of an *Anopheles* mosquito infected with *Plasmodium*. Four species of *Plasmodium* infect man: *P. falciparum*, *P. vivax*, *P. ovale*, and *P. malariae*. Transfusion-induced malaria occurs infrequently.

b. Evaluation and diagnosis

(1) The clinical manifestations of malaria infection are non-specific. Fever, rigors, malaise, headaches, myalgias, and arthralgias commonly occur in acute infections. *Splenomegaly* is the most consistent physical finding.

(2) The fever pattern may become periodic after infection is well established: every 48 hr in *P. vivax* and *P. ovale* infections; every 72 hr in *P. malariae* infections; and every 36–48 hr in *P. falciparum* malaria. Typically, the patient appears well between fever paroxysms.

(3) *It is exceedingly important to distinguish between relapsing malaria (vivax, ovale, and malariae) and falciparum malaria* (Table 10-3). The former group usually produce a self-limited illness that may relapse after months or years. The latter species can infect red blood cells of all ages, with resultant heavy parasitemia, serious complications, and possible fatal outcome. Also, *P. falciparum* may be resistant to antimalarial drugs.

(4) The complications of *P. falciparum* infection include cerebral malaria (presenting as coma, delirium, and convulsions), massive hemolysis, disseminated intravascular coagulation, renal failure, pulmonary edema, and cardiovascular collapse.

Table 10-3. Differentiation of Malarial Parasites

Falciparum	Relapsing (*P. vivax, ovale, malariae*)
Small ring forms	Large ring forms
High parasite count (10% of RBCs)	Low parasite count
Only ring forms	Intermediate forms
Parasites at margins of RBCs	Schuffner's stippling
No Schuffner's stippling	
Crescent-shaped gametocyte (pathognomonic if present)	

(5) A history of residence or travel in an endemic area is almost always elicited.

(6) *The diagnosis rests on the demonstration of malaria parasites in the peripheral blood* (see Secs. **I.B** and **I.C**).

   (a) Clinical sequelae reflect the level of parasitemia. In patients with serious complications, 10% or more of red cells are likely to be parasitized and the infection thus is easily diagnosed by thin smear.

   (b) As previously noted, laboratory differentiation between falciparum malaria and the relapsing malarias is of great importance and will affect the choice of antimalarial agents (see Table 10–3). Textbooks of parasitology should be consulted to aid in species differentiation.

c. Treatment   The choice of antimalarial drugs depends on the infecting species and the geographic area of acquisition of infection.

   (1) Falciparum infections acquired in Southeast Asia and localized areas of Central and South America must be assumed to be resistant to chloroquine phosphate. Alternative drugs should be given, as outlined in **(4)(b)**.

   (2) In **relapsing malaria,** therapy must be directed against both the erythrocytic and exoerythrocytic parasites to prevent relapse. There is no resistance to chloroquine, but relapse may occur if this agent is used alone.

   (3) In addition to vigorous antimalarial therapy, complications of falciparum malaria require intensive supportive measures. Transfusions with packed red blood cells are given in severe hemolytic anemia; corticosteroids, mannitol, or both have been used effectively in cerebral malaria; mannitol may be used in renal failure, and dialysis may be necessary. Heparin may be useful in disseminated intravascular coagulation. Careful attention to fluid and electrolyte balance in each of these situations is essential. (See elsewhere in this manual for guides to therapy.)

   (4) Recommended treatment regimens

   (a) Relapsing malaria
   Chloroquine phosphate, 10 mg/kg PO (or IM if necessary), followed by 5 mg/kg q12h for 3 doses.
   Primaquine, 0.3 mg/kg daily for 14 days. Patients deficient in G-6-PD may demonstrate a hemolytic anemia with primaquine.

   (b) Falciparum malaria

   i. Nonchloroquine-resistant area
   Chloroquine phosphate, as in **(a)**

   ii. Chloroquine-resistant area
   Quinine HCl, 10 mg/kg PO q8h for 10 days (IV, if severely ill, with 10 mg/kg diluted to 0.5 mg/ml in saline, administered 1 ml/min, with ECG and blood pressure monitoring).

Table 10-4. Adverse Effects of Antiparasitic Drugs

Drug	Frequent	Infrequent
Antimony potassium tartrate	Cough, vomiting, myalgia, ECG changes	Cardiovascular collapse, hepatic damage
Antimony sodium dimercaptosuccinate (Astiban)	Similar to but less frequent and severe than with antimony potassium tartrate	
Bephenium (Alcopar)	Anorexia, nausea, vomiting	
Chloroquine phosphate (Aralen)	Anorexia, nausea, visual disturbances	Retinopathy—only with prolonged, high dosage
Dehydroemetine	Diarrhea, nausea, vomiting, myalgias, ECG changes	Hypotension
Lucanthone HCl (Miracil D)	Anorexia, nausea, vomiting	Convulsions, psychosis (in adults only)
Metronidazole (Flagyl)	Anorexia, nausea, vomiting, metallic taste	Peripheral neuropathy, ataxia, neutropenia
Niclosamide (Yomesan)		Nausea
Niridazole (Ambilhar)	Anorexia, nausea, vomiting	Convulsions, psychosis (in adults only)
Paromomycin (Humatin)	Anorexia, nausea, vomiting	Nephrotoxicity
Pentamidine isethionate	Dizziness, tachycardia, headache, vomiting, hypotension	Nephrotoxicity, hepatotoxicity
Piperazine citrate (Antepar)		Anorexia, rash
Primaquine phosphate	Anorexia, nausea	Hemolytic anemia in G-6-PD deficient persons, methemoglobinemia
Pyrimethamine (Daraprim)		Folate deficient macrocytic anemia
Pyrvinium pamoate (Povan)	Anorexia, nausea, red-colored stool	
Quinacrine HCl (Atabrine)	Nausea, vomiting, dizziness	Psychoses, exfoliative dermatitis, hepatic necrosis, yellowing of skin
Quinine sulfate	Tinnitus, nausea, vomiting, vertigo	Hypotension, hemolytic anemia
Stibophen (Fuadin)	Similar to but less frequent and severe than with antimony potassium tartrate	
Tetrachlorethylene	Nausea, vertigo, inebriation	
Thiabendazole (Mintezol)	Anorexia, nausea, vomiting, dizziness	Tinnitus, drowsiness

Pyrimethamine, 0.3 mg/kg PO tid for 3 days
Sulfadiazine, 10 mg/kg PO qid for 7 days

(5) Patients treated with pyrimethamine should receive folinic acid supplementation.

(6) Response to therapy is followed by dramatic clinical improvement. Repeated blood smears show disappearance of parasitemia.

d. Prevention   Persons traveling through or residing in malarious areas should receive prophylactic suppressive therapy with chloroquine phosphate, 5 mg/kg weekly. To prevent relapsing malaria, a 14-day course of primaquine should be taken after leaving an endemic area.

4. Toxoplasmosis

a. Etiology   *Toxoplasma gondii*, an obligate intracellular parasite, is responsible for this infection. Congenital transmission has been clearly established. The mode of acquisition of postnatally acquired infection remains obscure. Transmission by meat ingestion and spread by cat feces are strong possibilities.

b. Evaluation and diagnosis

(1) Infection is largely asymptomatic. Serologic evidence of prior infection is demonstrated in 25–40 percent of the population of the United States. Several symptomatic forms are recognized:

(a) Congenital infection is usually the result of asymptomatic acute infection in the mother. Prematurity or spontaneous abortion may occur. Newborns with toxoplasmosis are asymptomatic at birth, and most remain so. In a small number there is development of chorioretinitis, microcephaly, hydrocephaly, mental retardation, cerebral calcification, and seizure disorders.

(b) Acquired infection shows clinical variations ranging from a mild viral-like illness with lymphadenopathy to fatal pneumonia and encephalitis (seen in compromised hosts).

(2) Demonstration of *rising antibody titers* by complement-fixation (CF), hemagglutination (HA), and indirect fluorescent antibody tests (IFA) establishes the diagnosis. Newborn infections can be diagnosed by demonstration of IgM *Toxoplasma* antibodies or the persistence of high titers of CF, HA, or IFA beyond 4 months of age.

(3) Rarely, in special circumstances, the diagnosis may be established by the demonstration of organisms in tissue sections or smears of body fluids. Intraperitoneal mouse inoculation is required for isolation. To determine if an infection is recent, however, rising serologic titers are still required.

c. Treatment

(1) There have been no controlled clinical trials to establish the efficacy of drug therapy.

(2) Infants with active disease should be treated in the hope of preventing further destruction of tissue.

(3) Treatment of acquired toxoplasmosis depends on the clinical severity of the illness. Patients with underlying severe illness and immunoincompetence should be strongly considered for treatment if infection is clinically apparent.

(4) Specific therapy
>Pyrimethamine, 0.5 mg/kg daily for 1 month
>*and*
>Sulfadiazine, 0.15 mg/kg qid for 1 month

(5) Pyrimethamine is a folic acid antagonist, and supplemental folinic acid should be given. **Pyrimethamine is contraindicated in pregnancy.**

d. Prevention Since the mode of spread of infection remains unknown, preventive measures are speculative. Avoidance of ingestion of raw meat and areas of cat feces contamination, particularly during pregnancy, may be of benefit.

5. Pneumocystis

a. Etiology *Pneumocystis carinii*, an organism of uncertain classification, is the etiologic agent. Little is known of the route of infection or the pathogenesis of disease, but the pulmonary focus suggests a respiratory portal of entry.

b. Evaluation and diagnosis

(1) *P. carinii* produces a bilateral diffuse interstitial pneumonia in immunologically compromised hosts. The pneumonia is perihilar in distribution, and symptoms are usually insidious in onset. The diagnosis must be considered when pneumonia develops in patients with leukemia, lymphoma, hypogammaglobulinemia, and those receiving immunosuppressive therapy. Bacterial pathogens should be ruled out by appropriate sputum studies.

(2) Diagnosis requires the demonstration of the parasite by methenamine silver stains in tissue sections obtained at lung biopsy. Rarely, sputum and bronchial brushings may show organisms.

c. Treatment

(1) Pneumocystis carinii pneumonia is usually present as a terminal event in patients with severe underlying illness. Spontaneous recovery has been documented; the effect of therapy is thus difficult to assess.

(2) Recovery from or remission of the underlying illness or withdrawal of immunosuppressive therapy may have a beneficial effect on *P. carinii* infection.

(3) Oxygen and other respiratory supportive measures are of great importance.

(4) Pentamidine isethionate, 4 mg/kg IM daily in a single dose, for 12–15 days should be given in proved cases; IV use is associated with more significant side effects, including hypotension, vomiting, facial flushing, and transitory hallucinations. It is rarely justified to give pentamidine empirically. The side effects and toxicity of the drug and the possibility of misdiagnosis strongly favor proof of infection by lung biopsy before institution of therapy.

(5) Occasional favorable reports on the use of pyrimethamine and sulfadiazine have appeared, but controlled trials are lacking.

11 Disorders of the Heart

I. CARDIAC ARRHYTHMIAS Cardiac arrhythmias are not seen as often in children as they are in adults with atherosclerotic heart disease. Nevertheless, since arrhythmias in pediatric patients may be life-threatening, their prompt recognition and treatment are essential.

A. **General considerations** Cardiac arrhythmias, while most often seen in patients with heart disease, can also be manifestations of other conditions.

1. Metabolic and electrolyte status, hypoxia, or possible drug ingestions should also be considered as potential precipitating causes.

2. The clinical setting may also be important in that newborns are subject to premature atrial beats; hyperthyroid patients can present with episodes of supraventricular arrhythmias; and certain cardiac conditions such as atrial septal defects and Ebstein's anomaly are causes of atrial arrhythmias.

3. Most arrhythmias in children without underlying congenital heart disease are much better tolerated than they are in adults, and therapy should not pose a greater *risk* to the child than does the arrhythmia.

B. **Evaluation of common arrhythmias** An important concept to keep in mind is that diagnosis rests on analyzing the sequence and relationship of *both* atrial and ventricular activity. Atrial activity may be difficult to appreciate, particularly with a tachycardia in which P waves may not be visible in the ECG. Carotid sinus massage is a useful technique to bring out ECG signs of atrial activity. ECG monitoring is necessary, since prolonged sinus bradycardia may result. Alternatively, an esophageal electrode may help establish the diagnosis.

C. **Specific arrhythmias** See Table 11-1.

1. **Sinus bradycardia** Sinus bradycardia is often seen in normal children. In newborns, rates of 30–60 beats per minute may be produced by increased vagal tone, e.g., following intubation.

a. **Therapy**

(1) Sinus bradycardia may be abolished in newborns with 0.005 mg/kg atropine given IV. In older children, the usual dose is 0.01–0.02 mg/kg.

(2) Atropine may be repeated every few hours if necessary, provided there are no signs of an excessive anticholinergic effect (dilatation of the pupil, inhibition of sweating, fever, rash, dryness of the mouth, CNS disturbances).

Table 11-1. Common Arrhythmias

| Rhythm | Rate | | Characteristics | | | Treatment of Choice |
	Atrial	Ventricular	Atrial Activity	Ventricular Activity	AV Conduction	
Supraventricular tachycardia	150–350, regular	150–350, regular	Often not seen, as P wave may be in QRS or T	Normal or right bundle branch block	1:1	Digitalis Cardioversion
Atrial flutter	250–350, regular	125–350, regular	Saw-tooth flutter waves in II, III, AVF, or U	Normal	In children, may be 1:1, 2:1; 3:1, 4:1	Digitalis Cardioversion
Atrial fibrillation	300–600, irregular	100–350, irregular	Irregular fibrillation waves; occasionally no activity seen	Normal, but some beats aberrant	Varying	Digitalis Cardioversion
Paroxysmal atrial tachycardia with block	125–250, regular	Same or less	P waves visible	Normal, usually	1st-degree AV block; fixed or varying 2nd-degree block	Stop digitalis. Potassium given if low
Ventricular tachycardia	Equals ventricular rate or less, regular	150–300, regular	Can be retrograde and inverted or normal	Bizarre	1:1 retrograde, or no relation	Cardioversion Lidocaine

2. **Sinus tachycardia** Treatment should be directed at correcting the underlying condition, e.g., anemia, fever, hyperthyroidism.

3. **Paroxysmal supraventricular tachycardia**

   a. **Etiology** It includes both atrial and nodal tachycardia and occurs both in normal children and in patients with heart disease (particularly Ebstein's anomaly and Wolff-Parkinson-White syndrome). The rate varies from 150–350, and in infants there may be 1:1 conduction, even at high rates. There is an increased frequency of right bundle branch block.

   b. **Therapy** Often, this arrhythmia may be self-limiting.

      (1) Carotid sinus massage may terminate the attack. **This technique may cause severe bradycardia.**

      (2) Digitalization Many patients convert to normal rhythm during acute digitalization. Maintenance digoxin is continued for several months to prevent recurrence. For digitalization schedule, see **D.1.**

      (3) Propranolol, quinidine, procainamide, and edrophonium HCl are very rarely used in children (see **D**).

      (4) Electrical cardioversion is effective in restoring normal sinus rhythm.

4. **Atrial flutter**

   a. **Evaluation** This is characterized by atrial rates of 250–400, with characteristic saw-toothed flutter (F) waves on the ECG, best seen in leads II, III, aVF, and VI. There may be 1:1 conduction or 2:1 or 3:1 AV block.

   b. **Therapy** Digitalis frequently is not effective in children. Cardioversion with 30–50 watt-sec of energy usually restores sinus rhythm. Maintenance digoxin is recommended.

5. **Atrial fibrillation**

   a. **Etiology** Rheumatic mitral valve disease is often the underlying lesion, but atrial fibrillation may be seen in association with atrial septal defects, Ebstein's anomaly, Wolff-Parkinson-White syndrome, or myocarditis. It is also seen in patients with a left atrial volume overload, as in large ventricular septal defects or after palliative systemic-to-pulmonary arterial anastomosis.

   b. **Evaluation and diagnosis** Atrial activity is rapid and chaotic, with an irregular ventricular response of 150–350 beats/min.

   c. **Therapy** Digitalis will cause an increase in AV block and slow the ventricular response to the rapid atrial rate. Occasionally, it may produce conversion to sinus rhythm. Electrical cardioversion is usually indicated, however. Quinidine and procainamide are rarely useful in children.

6. **Paroxysmal atrial tachycardia with block**

   a. **Etiology** It is frequently associated with digitalis toxicity.

   b. **Evaluation and diagnosis** The atrial rate is regular and varies from approximately 175–250, with variable AV block. The ventricular rate may be regular or irregular, depending on the type of AV block.

    c. Therapy Cessation of digitalis therapy and administration of potassium chloride IV (in the absence of concomitant hyperkalemia) is the treatment of choice.

7. Premature ventricular contractions (PVCs) Many healthy children have isolated PVCs, and these do not require treatment. Occasionally, unusual sensitivity to caffeine or nicotine will produce PVCs. In ambulatory patients in whom short runs of PVCs develop, or who experience discomfort, treatment with quinidine, propranolol, or procainamide is indicated (see **D.3,5**). In a hospitalized, postsurgical patient in whom this may be a portent of a more serious arrhythmia, lidocaine (Xylocaine) should be given IV (see **D.4**).

8. Ventricular tachycardia

    a. Etiology It is usually seen in severe heart disease, drug (digitalis) intoxication, or in association with the Wolff-Parkinson-White syndrome.

    b. Evaluation and diagnosis A widened and often bizarre QRS complex is seen on the ECG with a rapid rate of 150/250 min. Inversion of P waves in leads II, III, and aVF often suggests retrograde activation of the atria. Diagnosis is confirmed if ventricular fusion (Dressler) beats of sinus capture is seen.

    c. Therapy Lidocaine, 1 mg/kg IV, rapidly repeated if the initial bolus is not effective. Persistence demands electrical conversion with delivery of 30–50 watt-sec.

9. Cardiac arrest See Chap. 2, Sec. I.

D. Drugs used in the treatment of cardiac arrhythmias

1. Digitalis Digoxin is the preparation of choice. In treating children, **special care should be taken to make sure the correct dose is both requested and given.** Death due to a **misplaced decimal point** is an avoidable tragedy.

    Studies with radioactive digoxin indicate that infants and children absorb and excrete digoxin in the same way as do adults. But therapeutic serum levels of digoxin in newborns and infants are in the range of 1.2–2.4 mg/ml; this level appears to be both required and well tolerated, though it is significantly higher than in adults.

    a. Dose

        (1) Prematures Give 0.035 mg/kg PO over 24 hr, with an initial dose of ½ the digitalizing dose; ¼ the digitalizing dose is a normal maintenance dose and generally given in 2 divided doses q12h. *For parenteral administration, give 75% of the calculated PO dose.*

        (2) Children under 2 years of age The digitalizing dose is 0.04–0.06 mg/kg, with the same rules applying to maintenance dose and parenteral administration as described in **(1).**

        (3) Children over 2 years of age The digitalizing dose is usually 0.03–0.05 mg/kg, with the same rules applying to maintenance doses and parenteral administration as described in **(1).**

        (4) All doses must be individualized with reference to the general condition of the patient, renal function, previous experience with the drug, sensitivity, and other parameters.

(5) Before administering digoxin, a baseline ECG, electrolyte determination (particularly serum potassium), and some estimation of the renal function of the patient should be obtained.

(6) In the presence of renal failure, digoxin must be administered with extreme care (*Ann. Intern. Med.* 68:703, 1968; 72:453, 1970).

b. Signs of digoxin effect

(1) Symptomatic improvement of the patient.

(2) Conversion or control of arrhythmia.

(3) ST and T wave changes on the ECG.

c. Digitalis toxicity

(1) Signs

(a) *Any* cardiac conduction or rhythm disturbance, e.g., AV block, PVCs. Frequent ECGs, particularly during and immediately after digitalization, are essential.

(b) Diarrhea, nausea, vomiting, blurred vision, yellow vision, confusion.

(2) Treatment

(a) Discontinue therapy.

(b) Check electrolytes, particularly potassium. The administration of potassium often corrects digoxin-induced arrhythmias. **Potassium is contraindicated in the presence of high-grade AV block.**

(c) Lidocaine, 1 mg/kg IV, may control ectopic beats secondary to digitalis toxicity. **This is also contraindicated in the presence of high-grade AV block.**

(d) Dilantin, propranolol, and procainamide have all been used to control digitalis toxicity, although experience with this treatment in children is limited.

2. Quinidine

a. Dose Quinidine is supplied as both sulfate and gluconate, with the latter providing a more sustained level of the drug. In children, quinidine is used almost exclusively in the oral form, though quinidine gluconate can be used IM and even IV in rare cases. To convert an arrhythmia with quinidine sulfate, the usual dosage is 4–6 mg/kg q2–3h. Usually 5–6 doses are required for converting an arrhythmia but doses up to 12 mg/kg may rarely be required. The usual dosage of quinidine gluconate is 10–30 mg/kg daily in 2 divided doses. For IM administration, the dose is 2–10 mg/kg q4–6h until control is achieved.

b. Signs of quinidine effect

(1) Control of the arrhythmia.

(2) Prolongation of the QT interval.

c. Quinidine toxicity

(1) Signs

(a) Arrhythmias such as PVCs or AV block.

(b) Widening of the QRS complex by more than 50 percent.

(c) Tinnitus, headache, visual complaints, salivation, muscle paralysis, hypotension.

(d) Thrombocytopenic purpura.

(e) Sudden death is a rare but recognized complication.

(2) Treatment

(a) Discontinue therapy.

(b) Treat the specific reaction appropriately.

3. **Procainamide** has general cardiovascular effects similar to quinidine and can be used as an alternative. Its greatest use is in the treatment of ectopic ventricular arrhythmias, particularly if there is a clinical reason not to use quinidine. It is rarely used parenterally and is contraindicated in patients with AV block.

   a. Dose The usual dose is 40–60 mg/kg daily in 4 divided doses. It is supplied in 250-mg capsules.

   b. Signs of procainamide effect are the same as for quinidine.

   c. Toxic effects

   (1) Nausea, vomiting, rash, and a lupus-like syndrome have been reported.

   (2) Drug fever and agranulocytosis are recognized complications of this therapy.

   (3) QRS widening and sudden death can occur (less likely than with quinidine).

4. **Lidocaine** has electrophysiologic properties that are essentially the same as those of procainamide and quinidine. It is used when short-term control of a specific arrhythmia requires IV therapy. Its half-life is only about 2 hr, and repeated administration by bolus or by constant infusion is necessary.

   a. Dose As a bolus, give 1 mg/kg, which can be repeated q30–60 min as required. Alternatively, an infusion of 0.2–0.3 mg/min is used. The drug is supplied in vials or ampules of 0.5, 1.0, and 2.0%. It is important to realize that lidocaine is metabolized primarily by the liver and therefore **should be used with extreme caution in neonates and in children with liver disease.**

   b. Toxicity

   (1) Signs The major toxic effect is convulsion when doses greater than 3 mg/kg are used. Hypotension is also seen.

   (2) Treatment

   (a) Discontinue therapy.

   (b) Treat the specific reaction symptomatically.

5. **Propranolol** is a beta-adrenergic blocking agent, which causes a decrease in automaticity, prolongation of the refractory period, and slowed conduction velocity. It is a second-line drug (after digitalis) in controlling atrial arrhythmias. It is the *drug of choice* in the control of digitalis-induced arrhythmias and is widely used in the treatment of idiopathic hypertrophic subaortic stenosis. Congestive heart failure and bronchospasms are **contraindications** to its use.

a. **Dose**   Orally, 0.5–1.0 mg/kg per day PO in 3–4 doses. For IV use, 0.1 mg/kg is given over 10 min q8–10h as needed, with limitation to a maximum dose of 10 mg. Special precautions should be observed when this drug is used in the anesthetized patient because of hypotension. The drug is supplied in 10- and 40-mg tablets and in 1 mg/ml vials.

b. **Toxicity**

(1) **Signs**   Hypotension, bronchospasm.

(2) **Treatment**   Discontinue therapy and treat the specific reaction appropriately.

II. CONGESTIVE HEART FAILURE

A. General concepts of management

1. Acute congestive heart failure (CHF) can occur in any condition in which the circulatory demand is greater than the cardiac capacity because of *increased load* (e.g., fluid overload), *obstruction* (e.g., valvular stenosis), or *decreased cardiac muscle strength* (e.g., myocarditis). Therapy is directed at the cause of failure.

2. High output cardiac failure due to thyrotoxicosis, beriberi, systemic AV fistulas, or anemia is best treated by correcting the primary condition.

3. In right ventricular failure associated with pneumonia or cystic fibrosis, treatment of the pulmonary problem is of paramount importance in managing congestive failure. If due to an arrhythmia, this should be corrected first.

B. Treatment

1. **Increase in cardiac output**

   a. Digitalis increases cardiac output by increasing stroke volume and reducing myocardial irritability. For dose, see pp. 260 (**D.1.a**) and 265 (**C.3**).

   b. Morphine is thought to allay anxiety and to decrease peripheral and pulmonary vascular resistance. For dose, see p. 265 (**C.4**).

2. **Decrease in cardiac work**

   a. **Bed rest**   While difficult to manage in infants, this is helpful in older children.

   b. **Adjustment of circulatory blood volume**

   (1) **Diet**   In chronic CHF, sodium restriction may be all that is necessary, but may be difficult to achieve in children. Low-sodium formulas, such as Lonalac, SMA S-26, or Similac PM 60/40 are prescribed for infants (Table 1-7).

   (2) **Fluids** are limited to 50–90 ml/kg daily. This may be impossible in a child with free oral intake, and sodium restriction alone may suffice. During IV therapy, sodium-free or low-sodium solutions are used.

   (3) **Diuretics**   See (**b**). The efficacy of the diuretic is dependent on adequate renal perfusion and therefore to some extent on cardiac output and acid-base status. Also, the effects of

diuretics on electrolytes should be properly understood; special care should be taken to avoid hypokalemia, particularly in the digitalized patient.

(a) **Ethacrynic acid and furosemide** These agents block sodium resorption, increasing excretion of sodium, potassium chloride, and ammonium ions.

   i. **Furosemide (Lasix)** is available in 40-mg tablets and in 2-ml ampules containing 10 mg/ml. The usual dose is 1 mg/kg regardless of the route of administration; the onset of diuresis varies from 5 min IV to 2 hr PO.

   ii. **Ethacrynic acid (Edecrin)** is available in 25- or 50-mg tablets and in vials of 50 mg that must be diluted prior to administration. The daily dose is 0.5–1.0 mg/kg IV and 1–2 mg/kg given PO in 4 doses. The onset of action is approximately the same as that of furosemide.

   iii. **Toxic effects** include problems of uric acid excretion, vertigo, deafness, and agranulocytosis. When taken orally, there may be gastrointestinal irritation. The most common problem is hypokalemia, and supplemental potassium may be required.

(b) **Mercurial diuretics** The mercurial diuretics inhibit resorption of sodium and chloride.

   i. **Mercuhydrin** is available in ampules of 2 ml, containing 40 mg Hg/ml and 5% theophylline. In the immediate newborn period, a dose of 0.1 ml is recommended; in infants under 1 year of age, 0.25 ml, and in children, doses of 0.5–1.5 ml are used (all IM). Onset of action is approximately 2 hr after injection.

   ii. Mercury may produce severe hypersensitivity reactions with rash, bronchospasm, agranulocytosis, and, rarely, anaphylaxis. More often seen are the electrolyte disturbances common to all diuretics such as hypochloremia and hyponatremia. **Mercurial diuretics should not be used in the presence of anuria and in patients with renal insufficiency.**

(c) **Thiazides** The thiazide diuretics, e.g., chlorothiazide (Diuril) and hydrochlorothiazide (Hydrodiuril), inhibit sodium and potassium reabsorption in the tubule and have some carbonic anhydrase inhibiting effect.

   i. Chlorothiazide is available in a syrup of 250 mg/5 ml and tablets of 250 and 500 mg. Dose is 20–40 mg/kg daily PO in 2 divided doses. Hydrochlorothiazide is available in tablets of 25 and 50 mg. The dose is 2.0–3.5 mg/kg daily PO in 2 divided doses.

   ii. Skin rashes, nausea, thrombocytopenia, weakness, muscle cramps, hyperuricemia, hypokalemia, and hypochloremic alkalosis may occur. Potassium supplements such as potassium triplex or potassium gluconate (Kaon Elixir) are advised.

(d) **Spironolactone (Aldactone)** is an aldosterone antagonist, most commonly used in patients with cirrhosis or nephrotic syndrome. Its use in CHF is limited as diuresis may not begin for several days. The drug is supplied in 25-mg tablets; daily dosage is 3 mg/kg PO. Toxic reactions include diarrhea, muscle weakness, and mild adrenergic effects.

(e) **Acetazolamide (Diamox)** is a carbonic anhydrase inhibitor and inhibits urinary excretion of sodium, potassium, and bicarbonate, with a resultant decrease in excretion of ammonia and titratable acid. The drug is supplied in 250-mg tablets, and the dosage is given approximately as a single daily dose of 5 mg/kg PO. Effectiveness is lost after 3–4 days, and it is not commonly used in the treatment of CHF.

C. **Acute pulmonary edema** Pulmonary edema may occur as a manifestation of CHF and in association with such conditions as toxic inhalation, drowning, acute glomerulonephritis, and severe infections. Therapy is directed at reducing the amount of alveolar transudate by adjustment of circulatory volume and by increasing myocardial contractility.

1. Place the patient with his head and chest elevated, and try to place sphygmomanometer cuffs, inflated to less than systolic pressure, on three limbs; rotate them approximately q10–15 min.

2. Give 100% O_2. Use of a positive pressure breathing apparatus may help by increasing intraalveolar pressure, thus decreasing transudation of fluid.

3. Digitalis should be given IV at a dosage of approximately 0.01–0.02 mg/kg as a bolus, if serum K is normal.

4. Morphine is given to decrease tachypnea and anxiety, at a dose of 0.2 mg/kg q4–6h as required.

5. Furosemide or ethacrynic acid, 1 mg/kg IV, is recommended.

III. **INFECTIVE ENDOCARDITIS** See also Chap. 9, Sec. **IV.T.**

A. **Etiology** Infective endocarditis occurs most commonly in persons with preexisting heart disease. Congenital heart disease accounts for 65–70 percent of pediatric cases; the majority of the remainder involve rheumatic valvular lesions.

1. Patients with both cyanotic and acyanotic congenital heart disease (CHD) are prone to infective endocarditis. It is most common among patients with cyanotic CHD and decreased pulmonary blood flow (e.g., tetralogy of Fallot, tricuspid atresia, transposition of the great arteries with ventricular septal defect, and pulmonic stenosis). The disease may develop in those who have undergone systemic-to-pulmonary arterial anastomoses (Blalock-Taussig anastomosis, Waterston-Cooley anastomosis, Potts shunt, Glenn shunt) often at the site of the anastomosis.

2. Probably 90 percent or more of cases of infective endocarditis are caused by streptococci (*S. viridans*, enterococci, microaerophilic, anaerobic, and nonhemolytic) and staphylococci (*S. aureus* and *S.*

albus). Pneumococci and gonococci are now rarely the cause of infective endocarditis. From 5–10 percent of cases are said to be due to unusual organisms such as *Listeria monocytogenes*, bacillus species, and diphtheroids. A large number of gram-negative organisms, including *Pseudomonas, Aerobacter aerogenes, Escherichia coli, Proteus,* and *Hemophilus influenzae,* may be involved.

3. Endocarditis due to fungi occurs in patients receiving long-term antibiotics or corticosteroid therapy, in those undergoing cardiac surgery, and in narcotic addicts using drugs IV. *Candida* species are perhaps the most common, but *Histoplasma, Blastomyces, Coccidioides, Aspergillus, Mucor,* and *Cryptococcus* have also been documented.

B. **Evaluation**

1. **Fever** is the single most frequent sign of infective endocarditis, although periods of normal temperature may last for a few days to several weeks. Administrations of small quantities of antibiotics may mask fever. Fever may be minimal when profound CHF is present.

2. **Murmurs**   A significant murmur is present in the vast majority of patients, and a changing murmur is a valuable diagnostic clue. Occasionally, a patient with infective endocarditis may present with severe CHF and low cardiac output; a murmur may not become audible until the cardiac output is improved.

3. **Cutaneous manifestations**   Petechiae are the most common skin manifestations of infective endocarditis. Subungual splinters, Osler's nodes, and Janeway's lesions are less common in pediatric patients.

4. **Embolic phenomena**   Specific sites include the spleen, lung (in right-sided endocarditis), and the central retinal artery.

5. **Renal manifestations**   Hematuria is common. Renal failure may follow chronic infective endocarditis. In some patients with focal embolic glomerulitis, hematuria, casts, progressive azotemia, and a decrease in the serum complement are ominous.

6. **Nervous system manifestations**   Cerebrovascular accidents and an acute purulent meningitis have been documented. Neuropsychiatric symptoms are more common in patients with subacute bacterial endocarditis; multiple brain abscesses are more frequent in acute endocarditis.

7. **Other manifestations** include splenomegaly and clubbing.

C. **Diagnosis**   The diagnosis of infective endocarditis can be based on the clinical features mentioned earlier. Blood cultures are positive in 70–75 percent of patients if the clinical picture is consistent with endocarditis; therapy may be initiated after five or six blood cultures have been obtained.

D. **Therapy**   Infective endocarditis is potentially a lethal disease, and 6 weeks of parenteral therapy is advised (see Chap. 9, Sec. **IV.T.4**).

IV. ACUTE RHEUMATIC FEVER

A. **Etiology**   Acute rheumatic fever (ARF) is a sequel to a group A β-hemolytic streptococcal infection. The pathogenesis of ARF is not yet clearly understood. It is uncommon in children under 5 and is rarely diagnosed in patients under the age of 2, although cases in the newborn have been documented.

B. **Evaluation**   Manifestations of ARF may be mimicked by transient viral infections, rheumatoid arthritis (see Chap. 20, Sec. **I.A**), leukemia, congenital hemoglobinopathies (specifically sickle cell anemia), and systemic lupus erythematosus.

   1. **Laboratory findings**   None of the serologic tests, including anti-streptolysin O (ASO), streptokinase, or antihyaluronidase, is specific to ARF.

      a. **Throat cultures**   Since many children are chronic carriers of the streptococcus involved it is impossible to be sure that any such streptococci isolated represent a recent infection.

      b. **Immunologic studies**   The ASO determination is useful in establishing evidence of preceding streptococcal infection, but in 20 percent of culture-documented streptococcal infections, no rise in ASO titer occurs.

      c. **Acute phase reactants**   A number of tests measure the presence and degree of inflammation in patients with ARF; leukocyte count, C-reactive protein (CRP), erythrocyte sedimentation rate (ESR), and serum mucoprotein. The two acute phase reactants most commonly used in rheumatic patients are ESR and CPR, but *neither is specific* for rheumatic fever.

C. **Diagnosis**   The modified Jones criteria for the diagnosis of ARF are satisfied by two of the major, or one of the major and two of the minor, manifestations listed in Table 11-2.

D. **Therapy**

   1. **Bed rest** is indicated when the patient is acutely ill, exhibits signs of significant cardiac involvement, or has other signs of progressive rheumatic inflammatory disease. If there is no heart damage, a general practice is to keep the patient in bed until the ESR is normal. If heart damage has been considerable, 2–4 weeks of bed rest after the ESR is normal may be necessary.

   2. **Salicylates** often ameliorate fever, tachycardia, and polyarthritis within 1–2 days. A blood salicylate level of 25–30 mg/100 ml is necessary for maximum antiinflammatory effects. Initially, 75–100

Table 11-2.   Modified Jones Criteria for Diagnosis of Acute Rheumatic Fever

Major Manifestations	Minor Manifestations
Polyarthritis	Fever
Carditis	Prolonged P-R interval
Chorea	Arthralgia
Erythema marginatum	Preceding streptococcal infection
Subcutaneous nodules	History of ARF
	Increased ESR or CRP
	Increased WBC

mg/kg of aspirin administered in 4–6 divided doses over 24 hr will result in an adequate blood level. In patients with minimal or no carditis, aspirin should be continued for 1–2 weeks and the patient then observed for another 1 week–10 days. If symptoms do not recur, no further treatment is needed.

3. **Corticosteroids** may be lifesaving in toxic, acutely ill patients with myocarditis and pericarditis. There is as yet no proof that corticosteroid administration modifies the *duration* of the acute disease or reduces the *incidence* of residual heart damage. Prednisone, 2 mg/kg PO, is given for 3–4 weeks and then tapered slowly.

4. **Treatment of streptococcal infection** (See Chap. 9, Sec. **IV.G**). For most patients a single IM injection of 600,000 to 900,000 U benzathine penicillin G is satisfactory. If oral medication is preferred, 200,000–250,000 U of penicillin qid is given for 10 days. If the patient is allergic to penicillin, oral erythromycin, 30–50 mg/kg in 4 divided doses, for 10 days, must be used.

5. **Prophylaxis** All patients with a well-documented history of rheumatic fever, or who have rheumatic heart disease, should have indefinite prophylaxis against streptococcal infections and recurrences of rheumatic fever. Any of the following regimens may be used:

   a. Benzathine penicillin G, 1,200,000 U IM every 4 weeks.

   b. Oral penicillin: buffered potassium penicillin G, 200,000 or 250,000 U twice daily.

   c. Sulfadiazine, 1.0 gm PO once a day for patients > 60 lb; 0.5 gm PO once a day for patients < 60 lb.

V. **TREATMENT OF HYPOXIC OR CYANOTIC SPELLS** Paroxysmal dyspnea with marked cyanosis occurs most commonly in patients with tetralogy of Fallot and may have serious consequences.

A. **Etiology** The mechanism of cyanotic spells is still unclear. They may result from enhanced reduction of the already decreased blood flow to the lungs due to spasm of the infundibular muscle. Cyanotic spells also may be precipitated in part by relative anemia, and what might appear to be an adequate hemoglobin and hematocrit in a cyanotic patient might actually be considerably lower than the patient's needs (see Chap. 8, Sec. **IV**).

B. **Evaluation and diagnosis** During a spell, there is reduction in arterial O_2 saturation and in pulmonary vascularity, disappearance of the systolic murmur, and increased voltage of the P wave in the standard limb leads of the ECG.

C. **Therapy**

   1. Position the child in the knee-chest position.

   2. Administer O_2 by mask.

   3. Give morphine sulphate, 0.2 mg/kg SQ or IM.

   4. Correct acidosis with sodium bicarbonate, 1–2 mEq/kg as an initial bolus, repeating as determined by arterial blood gases.

5. Administer beta-adrenergic blocking agents such as propranolol, 0.1 mg/kg as an IV bolus.

6. Give ventilatory support with mask or endotracheal intubation, if necessary.

7. If after 30 min or more the spell has not lessened in severity and the state of consciousness has not improved, consider systemic to pulmonary artery anastomosis on an emergency basis.

12 Renal Disorders in Children

I. SERUM CREATININE AND CREATININE CLEARANCE

A. The serum creatinine, creatinine clearance, or both are still the simplest available parameters for the assessment of functioning glomeruli, even though abnormal results are apparent only after a loss of 50 percent of renal function. The normal creatinine clearance is 71 ± 16 ($\pm$ 1 S.D.) ml/min/M^2 (Table 12-1).

Table 12-1. Normal Values for Creatinine Clearance

Age	Creatinine Clearance (approximately in ml/min/1.73M^2)
First week	40
First month	50
Second month	70
Third–sixth month	80
Sixth–eleventh month	100
Twelfth–nineteenth month	120 (normal adult)

B. **Calculation for creatinine clearance**

$$\frac{UV}{P} \times \frac{1.0}{M^2}$$

where U = urine concentration of creatinine in mg/100 ml; V = urine volume/min; P = average of two serum creatinines; and M = surface area (M^2).

C. Since the urinary creatinine remains fairly constant until the renal mass is unable to maintain homeostasis, if serum creatinine doubles, the clearance will fall to 50 percent of normal; if it quadruples, the clearance will be reduced to 25 percent of normal.

D. Such correlation is seen until the clearance is reduced to 10 to 8 percent of normal. From that point on the serum creatinine itself becomes the best indicator of the degree of renal failure.

E. The method of determining the creatinine clearance requires *exact* 24-hr collection, with a blood test for serum creatinine at the beginning and end.

II. SYMPTOMS AND SIGNS OF DECREASED GLOMERULAR FUNCTION

A. **Growth** Normal growth can continue in the presence of a maximal fall of the GFR to 25 percent of normal. From then on, growth is progressively delayed, with complete arrest at a GFR of approximately 10 percent of normal.

B. Water excretion Rapid adjustment to water load is proportionately reduced, and dilutional hypervolemia, or edema, or both produced with or without secondary arterial hypertension.

C. Urea, urate, creatinine, sulfate, organic acid anions These are proportionately retained in the serum and contribute to the appearance of the uremic syndrome and metabolic normochloremic acidosis.

D. Phosphate and calcium

1. Serum inorganic phosphorus increases only after the GFR falls below 20 percent of normal.

2. Further decreases in GFR are followed by hyperphosphoremia, hypocalcemia, and secondary hyperparathyroidism (see Chap. 17, Sec. **IV.B**).

3. Tetany or increased neuromuscular irritability are seldom seen in renal patients. Hypercalcemia may be responsible for nausea, vomiting, and arterial hypertension. The increased parathyroid activity may induce a pancreatitis of variable severity.

E. Hydrogen excretion

1. The decreased phosphate filtration decreases the titratable acidity fraction, with further impairment in the $H+$ excretion and decompensation of the metabolic acidosis already present (see Chap. 4, p. 88).

2. Ammonium (NH_4) production by the distal tubule remains normal, but decreases proportionally with the fall in the GFR. $H+$ excretion is again hampered and metabolic acidosis aggravated.

3. The decreased total ammonium production permits the excretion of undetermined acids bound to sodium, resulting in the development of the characteristic hyperchloremic acidosis seen with moderate uremia. Once the undetermined acids stop filtering because of further compromise of the GFR, the normochloremic pattern of metabolic acidosis returns.

F. Sodium, calcium, and magnesium excretion is affected only in severe renal failure. Changes in *serum* calcium influence decisions concerning bone therapy. The *urinary* calcium levels may now be misleading.

G. Potassium excretion is unaffected until GFR falls below 5 to 10 percent of normal.

H. Primary tubular defects See p. 286.

I. Pericarditis, pleuritis, and pneumonitis

1. **Pericarditis** develops in one-fifth of patients in acute renal failure, but in at least one-half of patients with chronic disease. Pain is present in one-third. The disappearance of pericardial friction rub may suggest fluid accumulation, and all efforts should be made for early detection of tamponade. A fibrinous pleuritis in the left base may simulate the pain of pericarditis, but pleuritic pain is uncommon.

2. The "uremic lung" is characterized by bilateral perihilar infiltration with peripheral emphysema.

III. GENERAL THERAPEUTIC MEASURES

A. Nutrition   Growth may be improved by appropriate dietary management. The limiting factor is the available glomerular filtration.

1. Fluid   The aim is to replace insensible loss and urine output (see Chap. 4, Sec. II). For the patient in chronic renal failure, fluid restriction can be more detrimental than overhydration.

2. Calories

   a. In fasting conditions there is an obligatory loss of 25–35 calories/kg daily. Since 50 percent is normally contributed by carbohydrates, the minimal administration of glucose necessary to avoid increased tissue breakdown is 400 gm/M^2 daily, or 3–4 gm/kg in the small-size patient.

   b. The caloric requirement doubles in normal activity, increasing to 70 calories/kg daily. Ideally this is given as 50% carbohydrates, 35% lipids, and 10–15% protein.

3. Protein

   a. The obligatory excretion of nitrogen through the kidney makes progressive restrictions necessary. While the glomerular filtration rate remains above 25% normal, any reasonable diet is usually tolerated.

   b. The progression of renal disease decreases osmotic tolerance, and protein restriction is necessary. (Each gram of protein contains 6 mOsm urea; as the GFR decreases from 25 to 10% normal, a decrease of urinary concentration ability from 900 to 300 mOsm/L occurs, forcing a restricted protein diet of 1.5–1 gm/kg daily. At these levels, it is imperative to use proteins of high biologic value (egg, meat, milk) in order to satisfy essential amino acid requirements.

   c. For the infant whose diet is basically milk, the use of a maternal-like milk formula is lifesaving, and preferences for one could depend on the degree of GFR available (see Tables 1-7 to 1-9).

   d. As renal function falls below 10 percent normal and approximates zero, further restrictions become necessary or dialysis must be started.

     (1) If dietary management is preferred, the reduction of daily protein intake to 0.5 gm/kg essentially as eggs and protein-free supplements may be effective.

     (2) If hemodialysis is instituted on a 3-times-a-week schedule, liberalization of the protein intake is then possible to a daily average of 1–2 gm protein/kg, 2 gm Na daily, and 2 gm K daily. Diets including electrodialyzed whey and proteins of high biologic value have been devised that are reasonably well tolerated, and, when gradually increased to 2 gm/kg or more of protein daily, can produce growth in a substantial number of children in renal failure.

4. Multivitamins   Daily administration of 1–2 standard multivitamin tablets or equivalent liquid preparations cover the basic requirements. Folic acid (1–2 mg/kg daily) should be added as more severe renal failure supervenes.

5. Salt

a. As arterial hypertension is a usual complication in the early stages of renal disease, limitation of salt intake is necessary, unless significant osmotic diuresis produces renal sodium wasting, as is often the case in the azotemic-polyuric phase of early renal failure. A "no salt added" diet is usually the maximal restriction needed under these circumstances or with the nephrotic syndrome. It provides 40–100 mM Na daily (2–4 gm NaCl), depending on the amount used in cooking.

b. If such a diet is not sufficient, it may be combined with antihypertensive drugs, or diuretics, or both.

c. In renal failure or in interstitial or predominantly tubular nephropathies, "salt-wasting" may occur. In these cases, free salt intake may be necessary both for conservation of the body sodium pool and to preserve the potassium excretion that becomes sodium-dependent. Daily requirements are estimated by monitoring urinary sodium excretion, and by the appearance of pitting edema and hypertension, indicating excessive salt administration.

6. Potassium

a. Hypokalemia   (See also Chap. 4, Sec. **I.A.3.**) Although hypokalemia may not be considered as important in renal disease, it is a common complication in the management of the patient with edema and secondary hyperaldosteronism (especially in the nephrotic patient during spontaneous or corticosteroid-induced diuresis) and the patient with polyuric renal disease complicated by acute gastrointestinal disorders (i.e., polycystic nephronophthisis, cystinosis, and renal tubular acidosis). Unless renal failure supervenes, none of these patients will require any dietary potassium restrictions; rather, they will require potassium supplementation as follows:

(1) Potassium chloride, 300-mg tablet of 4 mM per tablet, or 1 mM/ml solution; enteric-coated tablets should *not* be used because of their intestinal insolubility.

(2) Potassium bicarbonate, 300-mg capsules of 3 mM per capsule, or Shohl's solution, 140 gm citric acid + 100 gm Na citrate or K citrate dissolved in water to 1 liter.

(3) The requirement may range from 1–2 to 2–5 mM/kg daily and even higher in children with long-standing cystinosis.

(4) Prolonged hypokalemia will lead to secondary metabolic alkalosis and *possible paradoxical aciduria if sodium deficit is also present.* If the hypokalemia is severe (less than 2 mM/L serum), IV replacement should be given at 4–5 mM/kg daily as KCl (2 mM/ml), at least in the first 24 hr, and continued according to the laboratory results and urinary output.

(5) In renal tubular acidosis, cystinosis, postobstructive diuresis, and acute tubular necrosis, less than 1 mM/L serum levels may be found *and required replacement may exceed the maximal recommended intravenous fluid K+ concentration of 40–80 mM/L and reach 150–200 mM/L* (extremely caustic to the vessel wall, but lifesaving).

b. Hyperkalemia

(1) Dietary control

(a) While urinary output remains high and secondary hyper-aldosteronism is effective, the usual dietary protein restrictions will correct any excess in potassium administration. Since there is 3 mM potassium per gram of nitrogen, 6.25 gm protein is allowed.

(b) The conditions that usually lead to hyperkalemia are the onset of *terminal* renal failure or sudden oliguria due to vomiting, diarrhea, or both or gastrointestinal bleeding; and the indiscriminate administration of aldosterone antagonists (spironolactone) or drugs containing $K+$ such as potassium penicillin.

(c) Serum levels below 6 mg/100 ml are usually well handled by further restrictions in potassium intake. This is accomplished by eliminating all leguminous vegetables (beans, peas) and fruits (avocados), as well as peanuts and potatoes. Fresh apples, berries, pears, grapes, and pineapples are acceptable.

(2) Cation exchange resins

(a) If these resins are to be used, full control of hyperkalemia may be expected in 12–24 hr after beginning therapy.

(b) One gram of a finely powdered sodium polystyrene sulfonate (Kayexalate) can remove 1 mEq of potassium in exchange for 1 mEq of sodium in vivo when placed in the intestinal tract PO or PR; 1 gm/kg daily is given in 4 divided doses. To increase exchange surface, it should be in suspension and not as paste. Nearly 3–4 gm fluid is needed per gram resin.

(c) If given PO, it should be suspended in sorbitol syrup 70–80% in order to avoid intestinal impaction. If administered PR, an initial cleansing enema should be given and the emulsion (no sorbitol is needed) placed high in the sigmoid by tube and followed after 4 hr by removal with a saline enema.

(d) Impaction, sodium load, hypocalcemia, and hypomagnesemia are possible complications. Kayexalate should be discontinued when serum potassium reaches 4–5 mM/L.

(3) Intravenous therapy

(a) Severe hyperkalemia of 7–8 mM/L or higher requires emergency IV therapy, especially in the presence of the characteristic ECG changes.

(b) Sodium bicarbonate (2.5 mEq/kg) is given rapidly in 30–60 min, as the severity of ECG changes may indicate. If necessary, 10% calcium gluconate at a dose of 0.5–1.0 ml/kg may be given over 2–5 min, with ECG monitoring. This will have only a transient effect.

(c) If hyperkalemia persists, 50% glucose (1 ml/kg) may then be given with insulin (0.5 U/kg) to elevate blood glucose to 200 mg per 100 ml; this is also a temporary measure, as the K+ is now pushed within the cells and not excreted.

7. **Calcium, phosphorus, and vitamin D** Early management of calcium-phosphorus derangements is probably the clue to successful medical management. Once renal function has fallen below 25–20% normal, increased parathyroid activity will not prevent the appearance of hyperphosphoremia, and the serum will reflect the characteristic pattern of chronic renal failure (low calcium and high phosphorus). Restriction of *dietary* phosphorus intake or use of intestinal phosphorus binders (see **a**) will control hyperphosphoremia; use of an oral calcium supplement and vitamin D will prevent hypocalcemia.

a. **Oral phosphate binders** Because of hypermagnesemia already present in the patient with chronic renal failure, the use of plain aluminum hydroxide (Amphojel, 300-mg and 600-mg tablets, 300 mg/tsp) at a dosage of 50–150 mg daily, given immediately after meals, is preferable to preparations containing magnesium (e.g., Gelusil).

b. **Calcium** See also Chap. 4, Sec. **II.E.2.c.**

(1) **Hypocalcemia** True hypocalcemia is seen only in renal disease with alkalosis and hyperphosphoremia.

(a) If acute replacement of calcium is needed, 15 mg calcium/kg/q4h is given IV as 10% calcium gluconate or 22% calcium gluceptate. The correcting effect lasts only a few hours, and a new infusion or further PO administration is required.

(b) Among oral preparations calcium lactate is best tolerated. However, its low calcium content per weight (18%) requires ingestion of many tablets (each 300-mg tablet contains 54 mg calcium) to provide the minimal allowance of 500–1000 mg calcium daily. Approximately 10–20 mg/kg daily concomitant administration of vitamin D will improve intestinal absorption.

(c) In general, good control of serum phosphorus levels should *precede* the administration of calcium, but seizures or other complications may make immediate treatment with calcium unavoidable.

(2) **Hypercalcemia** Although not a common complication in renal disease, hypercalcemia is a possible complication of indiscriminate use of vitamin D, severe secondary hyperparathyroidism, and inappropriate dialyzate concentration of calcium. If acute hypercalcemia occurs and immediate treatment is necessary, carry out the following measures:

(a) Reduce calcium intake to a minimum (less than 100 mg daily; special milk formulas are available with minimal calcium content) and discontinue administration of vitamin D in any form (as such, or in multivitamins, and so on).

(b) Attempt to decrease the reabsorption of calcium from the gut by administration of corticosteroids (prednisone, 1–2 mg/kg daily).

(c) If urinary output is normal and no severe hyperphos-phoremia is present, phosphate IV or PO will control the hypercalcemia without necessarily aggravating the incidence of soft tissue calcification. The recommended adult phosphate dosage is 2 gm daily, administered as Neutra-Phos (5 gm of the concentrated powder or 4 tablets of 1.25 gm each provides 1 gm phosphorus) ; or administered IV as a standard monodibasic salt (1.5 gm diluted in 500–1000 ml 5% D/W) and given in no less than 6–8 hr under close ECG monitoring. Since Neutra-Phos is a K+ salt, the IV route is seldom useful in renal disease unless hypokalemia has occurred. Phosphate may enhance the excretion of H+ by providing more buffer to form titratable acidity.

c. **Vitamin D**   The use of vitamin D_2 (Calciferol) is recommended to improve intestinal reabsorption and increase the parathyroid hormone–end-organ responsiveness, avoiding inappropriate hypertrophy of the parathyroid gland.

(1) Administration should start as soon as the GFR falls below 25–20% normal and the physiologic compensation for the hyperphosphoremia is no longer present; dosage should be cautious (500–1000 U/kg daily), and follow-up should include the urinary calcium/creatinine ratio and serum calcium levels. These will be needed as long as vitamin D is administered and during the 30–90 days thereafter.

(2) If toxicity develops and is recognized early, loss in renal function will probably be reversible.

(3) Patients on vitamin D should be cautioned to decrease vitamin D intake when traveling or moving to areas with higher sun exposure than that where they reside.

B. **Anticonvulsant therapy**

1. Usual causes for seizures in the renal patient with preserved renal function are hypertensive encephalopathy, a severe metabolic alkalosis with *relative* hypocalcemia, or hypomagnesemia following hyponatremia or hypernatremia underlying CNS complications.

2. In chronic renal failure, the appearance of seizures most likely relates to acute acid base and electrolyte changes, and a careful evaluation of those parameters should always be done to provide adequate therapy. If hypomagnesemia is suspected, a load of 15 mg/kg Mg^{2+} given IM or slowly IV will usually correct the deficit (50%, 2.5%, and 1% $MgSO_4$ solutions are usually available).

3. The anticonvulsants of choice are diazepam, diphenylhydantoin, and phenobarbital at standard dosages (see Chap. 14, Sec. **I.A.2.b**). No corrections are necessary for progressive loss of function or dialysis. Long-term use may lead to increased vitamin D requirements.

C. **Antihypertensive therapy**

1. **Hydralazine** reduces hypertension by direct relaxation of the vascular smooth muscle.

   a. The most important side effects are **tachycardia**, nausea, vomiting, headache, diarrhea, and positive lupus erythematosus (LE) and rheumatoid factor (RF) reactions (*very rare in children*).

The drug should be avoided in patients with arrhythmias and heart failure.

b. Hydralazine is given parenterally at an initial dosage of 0.15 mg/kg that is progressively increased to up to 10 times the initial dose q6h, according to the response. Orally, 0.7 mg/kg daily is given in 4 divided doses, which are also freely increased according to response.

2. Reserpine

a. The rauwolfia alkaloids deplete stores of catecholamines and 5-hydroxytryptamine in many organs, depletion starting 1 hr after administrations and becoming maximal by 24 hr. Adrenal medulla depletion is less complete and slower in development. Tissue catecholamines are slowly restored, and repeated doses have a cumulative action even at intervals of a week or longer.

b. Side effects Mental depression is almost never seen in children, but nasal stuffiness is common and is generally well tolerated. However, reserpine should not be used in the neonate who is an obligate nose breather.

c. In acute hypertensive crisis, the recommended IM dosage is 0.07 mg/kg per dose, q4–6h (in patients weighing over 25 kg, an initial dose of 1–2 mg should be given and subsequent doses based on response) to be followed by an oral maintenance dose of 0.02 mg/kg daily. As the cumulative effect of the drug takes place, this dose usually can be reduced to 0.1–0.5 mg daily, given in 1 dose.

3. Methyldopa is an inhibitor of the dopa decarboxylase and is metabolized into alpha-methyl norepinephrine, a weak pressor agent which displaces norepinephrine at nerve endings. Its maximal effect is attained at 4–6 hr and lasts no more than 24 hr after a single dose.

a. Side effects are minimal but include drug fever and hemolytic anemia with a positive Coombs test, positive LE cell reaction, and positive RF, and granulocytopenia and thrombocytopenia. **It is not recommended for patients with pheochromocytoma.**

b. The IV dosage is from 10–50 mg/kg daily, administered in 4 divided doses q6h, beginning with 10 mg/kg/24 hr and doubling each subsequent dose until the desired effect is obtained. It is recommended that it be diluted in 5% D/W and that it be given over 30–60 min. A paradoxical rise in blood pressure can be seen with too rapid injection.

c. The dosages may be given PO q6h, remembering that about 50 percent of the administered dose is absorbed and excreted as inactive metabolites in the urine. *Both* methyldopa and its metabolites *produce false-positive tests for pheochromocytoma, in both blood and urine.*

4. Diazoxide is the third and possibly most effective acute antihypertensive drug now available. A benzothiazide with no diuretic effect, it acts directly over the vessel smooth muscle, promptly and effectively reducing its tone.

a. It is administered only IV (3–5 mg/kg per dose) **by rapid push** to obtain minimum binding to serum protein and maximum action over the smooth muscle. The average fall in both systolic and diastolic pressures is 40 mm Hg in a few minutes and the effect lasts 3–15 hr. If an initial dose proves ineffective, a second can be tried after 15–20 min.

b. Hyperglycemia often occurs and tends to be severe in the patient under corticosteroid therapy; and transient tachycardia often follows its administration.

5. Guanethidine sulfate is an adrenergic neuron-blocking agent with tissue catecholamine store depletion effect. It is a long-acting medication with cumulative effect.

a. Postural hypotension is a serious and common complication. Muscle weakness and diarrhea are less often seen. A rise in BUN thought to be secondary to decreased cardiac output and edema without heart failure can also occur.

b. Dosage is 0.2 mg/kg/24 hr in a single dose PO, increasing by the same at weekly intervals until the desired effect is achieved.

6. Magnesium sulfate is reportedly an effective antihypertensive medication. The recommended dosage is 0.2 ml of a 50% solution per dose IM, repeated q4–6h, diluted with procaine, *as the drug is extremely painful.*

D. Peritoneal dialysis The indications for dialysis in renal failure are intractable congestive heart failure, increasing acidosis, intractable hyperkalemia, and continuing clinical deterioration. Every case should be judged on its own merits. The decision to dialyze should not be made on the basis of one isolated laboratory value.

1. Procedure Disposable catheter sets are now available for pediatric peritoneal dialysis (McGaw, V-4901 for pediatric use).

a. After ensuring that *the bladder is empty*, the abdomen is prepared in a sterile fashion.

b. To make insertion easier and decrease the risk of perforation of intraabdominal contents, distend the abdominal cavity with an initial load of dialysis fluid (approximately 20 ml/kg) by means of a 20- or 21-gauge needle inserted at the catheter site.

c. The catheter is inserted, usually in the midline, one-third of the distance between the umbilicus and the symphysis pubis. It can then be advanced to the left lower quadrant and connected to the tubing.

d. The usual amount of fluid exchanged is 20 ml/kg initially with gradual increase to 40–50 ml/kg/exchange. (The initial loading fluid is not removed. The presence of such a reservoir will ensure that all the holes in the catheter are under water and will prevent air lock.) The fluid is usually warmed to body temperature, then allowed to run in as fast as is tolerated, equilibrated for 15–20 min, and drained for 15–20 min. At every fifth cycle the abdomen is allowed to drain dry, a specimen is sent for culture, and the patient is weighed.

e. The usual dialysis is carried on for 36–72 hr, depending on the indications and the patient's clinical status.

2. Factors affecting dialysis

a. Clearance Urea is cleared at the rate of 14–30 ml/min at 20° C. Creatinine is cleared at a slower rate of 10–15 ml/min.

b. Temperature Warming the solution will decrease heat loss (especially important in small infants) and, more important, will increase urea clearance.

c. Rate Increasing the flow of the dialysis fluid will shorten the time for dialysis, but is expensive and will increase protein loss and aggravate hyperglycemia.

d. Type of solution Hypertonic solutions (i.e., 7.5%) will increase the urea clearance by approximately 50 percent, **but will also result in severe dehydration and hyperglycemia and thus should be used with extreme caution, if at all.**

3. Solutions

a. Usually, 1.5% glucose and water with added electrolytes is used. Prepared solutions are available.

b. *Prepared solutions contain no potassium; K+ should be added as required.* In patients with hyperkalemia, except those on digitalis, no K+ needs to be added to the initial three to five exchanges; subsequently, 2.5–3.5 mEq/L may be added to the dialyzing fluid (see Table 12-2 for the composition of a standard solution).

c. The 1.5% glucose solution as used in dialysis is hyperosmolar (372 mOsm/L and thus can cause appreciable fluid loss up to 200–300 ml/hr). For removal of excess fluid, glucose can be added to increase the osmolarity of the solution as desired. However, the use of solutions of higher osmolality can rapidly dehydrate infants and children (4.25% glucose = 525 mOsm/L; 7.5% glucose = 678 mOsm/L). Thus *all patients being dialyzed should be weighed often and kept in fluid balance.*

d. When dialyzing for certain toxins, various additives such as albumin are useful in increasing removal.

4. Infection is usually due to *Staphylococcus aureus* and gram-negative organisms. Antibiotics are not advised routinely, but culture of fluid every fifth cycle should be done routinely. Treatment should be begun in a symptomatic patient. If intraperitoneal antibiotics are used, they must be given with extreme care, as high blood levels can result from peritoneal absorption.

5. Hyperglycemia is a special problem in diabetic patients, but can also occur in nondiabetic patients and result in nonketotic hyperosmolar coma. Blood sugar should be monitored routinely in patients dialyzed with 4.25 or 7.5% solutions.

6. Hyperproteinemia About 0.5 gm/L of protein is lost in dialysis.

7. Perforation The risk of perforation of abdominal organs (e.g., bladder, bowel) can be reduced appreciably by distending the

Table 12-2. Composition of a Standard Peritoneal Dialysis Solution (McGaw)

Sodium	140 mEq/L
Chloride	101 mEq/L
Calcium	4.0 mEq/L
Magnesium	1.5 mg/L
Acetate	45 mg/L

abdominal cavity with dialysate and emptying the bladder before catheter insertion.

IV. ACUTE RENAL FAILURE

A. Etiology

1. **Prerenal**   Decreased perfusion of renal arteries due to hypotension and/or hypovolemia as occurs in dehydration, burns, shock, etc.

2. **Renal (parenchymal injury)**   Nephritis, hemolytic-uremic syndrome, chronic pyelonephritis, acute tubular necrosis, severe or prolonged prerenal state.

3. **Postrenal (obstructive problems)**   Congenital anomalies, urethral stricture, inflammation, stones, hematoma, tumor.

B. Treatment   See also Sec. III, and Chaps. 2 and 4.

1. **Prerenal**   The recognition of a contracted circulating blood volume is mandatory for adequate therapy. Restoration of circulating blood volume is then attempted, and if urine flow is not promptly re-established, treatment is continued as in **d.**

   a. The presence of oliguria or anuria is determined by insertion of an indwelling bladder catheter and the finding of urine flow less than 20 ml/kg daily. Any urine obtained should be carefully examined and analyzed for Na, K, creatinine, and osmolality. See Table 12-3.

   b. Insertion of central venous line for infusion of fluids and electrolytes and measurement of CVP.

   c. Reexpansion of circulating blood volume if CVP is low with solutions such as Ringer's lactate, normal saline, and saline and bicarbonate mixtures at an initial rate of 20–30 ml/kg over 20–60 min. In clinical circumstances associated with large colloid losses, e.g., burns, an initial infusion using plasma at 10–20 ml/kg is appropriate in aiding restoration of plasma oncotic pressure. (For further details of rehydration, see pp. 92–93).

   d. If after restoration of ECFV, oliguria or anuria persists, an infusion of mannitol, 0.5 gm/kg (2.5 ml/kg of 20% solution) should be administered over 10–20 min. This should result in an increase in urine output of approximately 6–10 ml/kg over the next 1–3 hr. If an increase in urine flow does not occur, no further mannitol should be given. A trial dose of ethacrynic acid or furosemide, 1 mg/kg, IV, may also be administered in an attempt to establish urine flow after ECFV is restored. These agents will cause changes in urine electrolytes and osmolality,

Table 12-3.   Urinary Changes in Acute Renal Failure

Urine	Prerenal	Renal
Volume	↓	↓
Osmolality	↑	Isosmotic with plasma
Urinary Na	↓ (< 10 mEq/L)	↑ (> 40 mEq/L)
Creatinine U/P	↑	↓ < 10/1

making distinction between prerenal and renal oliguria more difficult. In the presence of hemoglobinuria or myoglobinuria after an initial successful diuresis, an infusion of 5% mannitol in 0.2% saline in an amount equal to urine flow may be given over the next 6–8 hr.

e. If oliguria or anuria persists after all of the foregoing measures, treatment should be carried out as outlined in **2.**

2. Renal

a. Insert indwelling cathether and central venous line.

b. Weigh twice daily.

c. Measure intake and output.

d. Fluid replacement.

(1) Fluid replacement should be restricted to insensible losses (see Table 12-4). Urine losses need not be replaced if they represent the loss of edema fluid. Replacement fluid should contain 20–30% glucose to provide as many calories as possible, but should not contain electrolytes. With the addition of heparin (1 U/ml), such solutions may be given via peripheral IV sites.

(2) Higher concentrations of glucose may be given via central lines, and, if tolerated, additional glucose can be given PO as hard candy.

(3) With the fluid restrictions given, weight should decrease by approximately 0.5 percent daily.

(4) When diuresis begins, increasing urine volume must be replaced with a solution containing approximately the same amount of Na as the urine being excreted. No K need be given while the serum K is normal or elevated. Exceptions are patients with diabetic ketoacidosis and salicylism.

e. Hyperkalemia If the serum K is between 5.5 and 7 mEq/L serum, Kayexalate at a daily dose of 1 gm/kg PO or PR may be given [Sec. **III.A.6.b.(2)**]. If the serum K is above 7 mEq/L, or ECG changes or arrhythmias are present, the following therapy is indicated:

(1) Sodium bicarbonate, 2.5 mEq/kg, as an IV push over 10–15 min.

(2) Calcium gluconate 10%, 0.5 ml/kg, IV over 5–10 min with ECG monitoring.

(3) Glucose, 50%, 1 ml/kg. Follow with 30% glucose IV infusion.

Table 12-4. Insensible Fluid Loss

Age (years)	Fluid Loss (ml/kg/hr)
0–3	1.0
4–9	0.8
10 and over	0.5

(4) If hyperkalemia persists, insulin, 0.5 U/kg IV, should be given while infusing 20% glucose. This dose may be repeated in 30–60 min, if necessary.

(5) If there is still no response, or a poor response, dialysis may be necessary.

f. Hypertension If acute and severe (diastolic > 120), treat as follows:

(1) Diazoxide, 2.5 mg/kg IV over 10–20 sec. This dose may be repeated in 20 min if necessary.

(2) If diazoxide is unavailable, give hydralazine, 0.3–0.5 mg/kg IV. This dose may be increased to 10–20 mg and repeated q20 min 3 times if required. (Monitor with ECG as advisable.)

(3) If necessary, Aldomet may be given, 6–20 mg/kg over 5–10 min IV. (For treatment of lower blood pressure levels, see Sec. **III.C.**)

(4) If hypertension is severe and unresponsive to medical management, dialysis should be performed to remove excess fluid.

g. Congestive heart failure (See also Chap. 11, Sec. **II.**) Congestive heart failure (CHF) can usually be prevented by proper fluid restriction. There is no place for diuretics in the *anuric* patient. Digitalis will not produce a dramatic effect but, nevertheless, digitalization should be done slowly and maintenance doses reduced as dictated by serum levels. If CHF is severe, dialysis is indicated.

h. Acidosis can usually be alleviated by providing glucose for calories as well as exogenous bicarbonate, citrate, or lactate. If it is severe and treatment is difficult due to expanded ECFV, dialysis is indicated.

i. Seizures See Chap. 14, Sec. **I.**

3. Postrenal

a. If creatinine is < 5 mg/100 ml or creatinine U/P ratio is > 15, an IVP may be attempted.

b. Urologic consultation.

c. Possible cystoscopy, with unilateral retrograde pyelogram.

d. Surgical correction or bypass as required.

V. ACUTE POSTSTREPTOCOCCAL GLOMERULONEPHRITIS

A. Etiology Infection with a nephritogenic strain of group A, β-hemolytic streptococci.

B. Evaluation Edema, periorbital initially, hematuria, and hypertension are present either singly or in combination. A hypertensive seizure may be the initial presentation. Some children present with abdominal pain, and hypoalbuminemia and hyperlipemia may occasionally be seen early in the course of the disease. In cases of microscopic hematuria, an Addis count should be requested.

C. **Diagnosis** is confirmed by the finding of urine sediment containing red cell casts and protein, elevated BUN and creatinine, decreased C3, and evidence of preceding streptococcal infection. [Antistreptolysin O (ASLO) may not rise if the initial infection is treated early with appropriate antibiotics.]

D. **Treatment** Therapy is entirely symptomatic.

1. Appropriate antibiotics to eradicate the streptococcal infection (see Chap. 9, Sec. **IV.**).

2. A low-salt diet is prescribed until the patient is asymptomatic, when a normal diet is resumed. There is no need for protein restriction in the usual case.

3. Bed rest is maintained until there is clinical improvement; gradual ambulation may then be begun. If recurrent hematuria or proteinuria occurs with ambulation, a further 2–3 weeks of bed rest may be indicated.

4. **Hypertension** This is best treated with a low-sodium diet, reserpine, and the addition of hydralazine if required.

   a. **Reserpine,** 0.02 mg/kg up to 25 kg, and then an initial dose of 1–2 mg should be given IM.

   b. **Hydralazine,** 0.15 mg/kg IV or IM initially, to be increased as required. Edema may be alleviated by the use of diuretics.

E. **Prognosis** The usual course ends in complete recovery. However, up to 5 percent of patients who appear clinically to have acute post-streptococcal glomerulonephritis may have a continuously downhill course and progress to renal insufficiency. These patients on renal biopsy usually show evidence of preexisting underlying chronic glomerular disease. The urine sediment may remain abnormal for a prolonged period; the proteinuria often clears up before the hematuria, which can persist for up to 2–3 years following the illness. However, even these patients make a complete recovery.

VI. **NEPHROTIC SYNDROME** The nephrotic syndrome is characterized by proteinuria, edema, hypoproteinemia, and hyperlipidemia. The incidence is 1.9/100,000 among whites and 2.8/100,000 among nonwhites under 16 years of age. The peak incidence is between 2 and 3 years (75 percent of cases occur in children under 5 years of age).

A. **Etiology** The nephrotic syndrome can occur as part of the clinical course of any progressive glomerulonephritis, but the pathogenesis is unknown.

B. **Evaluation**

1. **History** A history of antecedent infection or nephritis is solicited.

2. **Physical examination** A careful assessment should include weight, blood pressure, sites and extent of edema, and cardiac status.

3. **Laboratory evaluation** includes 24-hr urinary protein, serum protein and A/G ratio, urinary serum protein electrophoresis, serum lipid, BUN, electrolytes, creatinine clearance, and C3 ($\beta_1 C$).

4. An IVP is not usually helpful.

5. The presence of any of the following: gross hematuria, a low C3, an age of presentation below 2 months or over 6–7 years, a failure to respond to steroids, elevated BUN, and elevated BP should cast doubt on the diagnosis of lipoid nephrosis, and *a renal biopsy should be performed* to define glomerular histology and to detect the presence of underlying renal disease, which will alter therapy.

C. **Diagnosis**   A combination of the defined clinical features with proteinuria in excess of 1 gm/M^2/24 hr confirms the diagnosis.

D. **Treatment**

1. **Specific therapy**

   a. **Drugs**

   (1) Corticosteroids are the treatment of choice, usually 1.5–2.0 mg/kg prednisone daily PO in divided doses. This regimen is continued for 28 days. (A maximum dose of 80 mg/M^2 should not be exceeded.) Diuresis usually occurs in 10–20 days, associated with a decrease in urine protein. Following this, a further 1-month course of alternate-day prednisone in a reduced dose (1.0 mg/kg daily as 1 dose q48h) is given, after which it is tapered over 2–3 weeks and discontinued.

   (2) A recurrence is treated in the same manner as the initial presentation. If recurrences are frequent, the alternate-day prednisone may be continued for a prolonged period, i.e., 6–12 months.

   (3) In patients who fail to respond to prednisone, a trial of immunosuppressive therapy may be indicated. Cyclophosphamide appears to be more effective in patients who are frequent "relapsers" and require many or prolonged courses of prednisone and less effective in those who show no response to corticosteroids. Chlorambucil is also helpful in steroid-unresponsive or dependent patients.

   b. **Albumin**

   (1) When the accumulation of the fluid is severe and associated with clinical symptoms of cardiac or respiratory compromise, salt-poor albumin may be given in a dose of 1 gm/kg IV slowly q8–12 hr.

   (2) This may be followed with a diuretic such as ethacrynic acid, 1 mg/kg, although this is not usually necessary. The use of a diuretic alone can be hazardous, as this can aggravate an already existing contraction of the circulating blood volume.

   (3) Paracentesis should be avoided because of the risk of infection.

2. **General measures**

   a. **Diet**   There is no need for dietary restrictions other than a low-salt diet during periods of edema.

   b. **Activity**   No restriction of activity is required.

   c. **Infection**   Early and vigorous treatment of any suspected bacterial infection is important, as these can lead to relapses and were the leading cause of death prior to the advent of antibiotics.

E. Prognosis

1. In the usual type of nephrotic syndrome, 90–95 percent of children will show an initial response to corticosteroids. Of these, only about 15–17 percent will *not* have a further relapse. These relapses are more common in the first year than later, but thereafter can occur up to 15 years later.

2. The rate of relapse in a group of children tends to decrease after the first 10 years. If a child remains free of a relapse for up to 3–4 years, there is a good chance that he will remain free of relapses thereafter. However, if he has one relapse, the subsequent course cannot be predicted.

VII. RENAL TUBULAR ACIDOSIS This syndrome consists of hyperchloremic acidosis associated with normal or slightly decreased glomerular function and inappropriately alkaline urine.

A. Proximal renal tubular acidosis

1. **Etiology** A defect in the proximal reabsorption of $NaHCO_3$ is present, with an abnormally low threshold for $NaHCO_3$ reabsorption in the proximal tubule.

2. **Evaluation and diagnosis**

   a. Growth failure is usually present.

   b. Arterial blood gases and serum electrolytes will reveal a hyperchloremic acidosis with normal K and Ca levels.

   c. Urine pH will vary with the degree of acidemia. All urine for pH should be collected under oil and measured while fresh. A pH of less than 5.5 is seen with severe acidemia and a serum $NaHCO_3$ below the patient's renal threshold.

   d. A **bicarbonate titration test** may be done that consists of infusing $NaHCO_3$ (e.g., 1–2 mEq/kg over 1 hr) slowly when the patient is acidotic and measuring serum $NaHCO_3$ levels, urine pH, titratable acidity, and ammonium excretion. The renal threshold for $NaHCO_3$ reabsorption in proximal renal tubular acidosis will be below the norms for children of comparable age.

   e. **Ammonium chloride loading test** To distinguish disease of the proximal from the distal tubule, an ammonium chloride loading test may be done by administering 5.5 mEq/kg PO ammonium chloride followed by measurement of the urine pH, titratable acidity, and ammonium excretion. The serum $NaHCO_3$ concentration should fall to 17 mEq/L or less; if not, a larger dose of ammonium chloride should be given *cautiously*. Normal values for this test are shown in Table 12-5. This test is not necessary if in

Table 12-5. Ammonium Chloride Loading Test (Normal Values)

Age[a]	Urine pH	Titratable Acid (mEq/min/1.73M²)	Ammonium Excretion (mEq/L)
1–12 months	< 5.0	62 (43–111)	57 (42–79)
4–15 years	< 5.5	52 (33–71)	73 (46–100)

Adapted from C. Edelman et al., *Pediatr. Res.* 1:452, 1967; *J. Clin. Invest.* 46:1309, 1967.
[a] Although current data is sparse, normal values for ages 1 to 4 years appear to approximate those of older children.

the acidemic state the urine pH is 5 or less and if the urine pH becomes > 6 at a low HCO_3 threshold.

3. Therapy

   a. Large doses of bicarbonate (10–15 mEq/kg daily) are required to maintain serum pH. In primary proximal RTA (renal tubular acidosis) this dose may be decreased after 6 months to determine if the threshold is still abnormal and if acidosis develops.

   b. A repeat bicarbonate titration test should be performed, as it appears that the disorder improves spontaneously and most children will recover.

   c. Growth will improve with therapy, but may not reach the 50th percentile in all children with primary proximal renal tubular acidosis.

B. Distal renal tubular acidosis

1. Etiology   A permanent defect in the distal tubule is present, resulting in an inability to establish a hydrogen ion gradient between blood and tubular fluid.

2. Evaluation

   a. The presenting symptoms are usually growth failure, polyuria, and polydipsia.

   b. Arterial blood gases and serum electrolytes reveal a hyper-chloremic acidosis, with hypokalemia seen in a number of patients..

   c. The urine pH is rarely below 6.5, even in the face of severe existing acidemia.

   d. Concentrating ability is markedly impaired, with maximal urine osmolalities of less than 450 mOsm.

   e. Urinary calcium excretion is elevated, above 2 mg/kg daily.

   f. GFR is decreased to a variable degree.

   g. X-rays will reveal nephrocalcinosis in most patients.

3. Diagnosis   This is confirmed by performing an ammonium chloride loading test as previously described (**A.2.e**). There is an inability to acidify the urine below 6.5, with depressed rates of excretion of titratable acid and ammonium.

4. Treatment

   a. Sodium and potassium bicarbonate and citrate in daily doses of 1–3 mEq will correct the acidosis, improve growth, and normalize the GFR. However, they will not reverse nephrocalcinosis or improve concentrating ability.

   b. There is no indication at present that children will recover spontaneously from distal tubular acidification, and therapy must be continued for life.

   c. The dose of sodium and potassium bicarbonate and citrate should be adjusted according to the blood pH, and daily urine calcium excretion should be kept below 2 mg/kg.

13 Acute Hepatic Failure

I. ETIOLOGY   In acute hepatic failure there is often a history of a preceding viral infection and exposure to blood products or one of the substances listed in Table 13-1. Often, the cause cannot be identified with certainty.

II. DIAGNOSIS   The diagnosis relies on a consistent history, identification of a possible cause, demonstrating symptoms and signs of liver disease, documenting specific biochemical abnormalities, and ruling out other causes of coma, shock, hypovolemia, bleeding, and biochemical abnormalities.

A. History   A history of chronic liver disease must be sought. The duration of the acute history may be several hours to a few days, frequently including fevers up to 101–102° F, with malaise and decreased appetite. Nausea and fatigue are common. Often the patient will be ill for 1–2 days, recover and be without complaint for 12–24 hr, and then acutely decompensate into hepatic coma.

B. Laboratory findings

1. Elevated hepatocellular enzymes.

2. Elevated bilirubin (indirect and direct).

Table 13-1.   Possible Etiologies Reported in Association with Acute Hepatic Failure

1. Infectious hepatitis (26/42 cases[a])
2. Serum hepatitis (5/42 cases[a])
3. Reye's syndrome (7/42 cases[a])
4. Toxins
   a. Anesthetic agents: halothane (2/42 cases[a]) methoxyflurane, ethchlorvynol
   b. Antiarthritis agents: phenylbutazone, indomethacin
   c. Antibiotics: tetracyclines, sulfonamides, isoniazid, paraaminosalicylate, ethionamide, proethionamide, chloramphenicol in pregnancy
   d. Anticonvulsants: diphenylhydantoin
   e. Antithyroid agents: methimazole, propylthiouracil
   f. Oral contraceptives: e.g., Enovid
   g. Oral hypoglycemics: chlorpropamide
   h. Tranquilizers: chlorpromazine, phenothiazines
   i. Hormones: methyltestosterone
   j. Mushroom poisoning: *Amanita phalloides*
   k. Industrial chemicals: carbon tetrachloride, benzene derivatives, yellow phosphorus
   l. Trauma

[a] See the references at the end of this chapter.

3. Prolonged prothrombin time, usually not responsive to parenteral vitamin K.

4. Elevated blood ammonia.

5. Decreased serum albumin.

6. Decreased blood sugar.

7. Presence of Australia antigen in serum.

8. Leukocytosis, with "shift-to-the-left" and eosinophilia.

9. Decreased serum copper and ceruloplasmin.

III. TREATMENT

A. **State of consciousness** Hepatic failure can be manifested as any variation in the level of consciousness from mild confusion to decerebrate rigidity.

1. Confusion and restlessness may be a manifestation of hypoglycemia and are not indications for sedation.

2. Because hepatic coma can include depression of the gag reflex and respirations, requiring endotracheal intubation and mechanical ventilation, **sedatives are generally contraindicated** except in the most extreme circumstances.

3. In the rare instance of uncontrollable agitation, mild sedation may be accomplished with drugs *not metabolized by the liver*, such as long-acting barbiturates or meperidine.

4. **Morphine, paraldehyde, and short-acting barbiturates are contraindicated.**

B. **Hepatocellular injury** The initial destructive process must abate, and the patient must be supported while regeneration is allowed to take place.

1. **Removal of cause** In specific instances, further injury may be preventable.

   a. Drugs and agents known to be toxic must not be given or must be discontinued.

   b. Exposure to viral and bacterial infection is to be avoided, preferably with isolation of the patient.

   c. Persons who have contacts with the patient who is suspected of having viral hepatitis should be immunized with gamma globulin (see Table 9-5).

2. **Monitoring the injury** Frequent monitoring of hepatocellular enzymes and bilirubin is helpful. However, once serum enzymes are markedly elevated, variations are at best a rough predictor of hepatic function and residual. Prothrombin time uncorrectable with vitamin K and serum albumin below 2 gm/100 ml indicates hepatic damage.

3. **Promoting regeneration** There is no product known to promote hepatic regeneration rapidly. Although adrenal corticosteroids are given to patients with fulminant hepatic failure, clear evidence for their efficacy in this condition has yet to be forthcoming.

C. Functional hepatic failure   Essentially, function failure can be thought of as failure to *produce* needed substances and failure to *detoxify* threatening substances.

1. **Hypoglycemia** is the major contributing factor in shock, coma, seizures, and death.

   a. Because of failure in both gluconeogenesis and glycogenolysis, the blood glucose may persist at extremely low levels.

   b. Specific therapy is a continuous infusion of maintenance 5% glucose or higher concentrations (10–15% peripherally or 20% centrally with a CVP line). Because of the difficulty maintaining adequate blood sugar levels, frequent blood glucose determinations must be made.

2. **Bleeding disorders**   Defects can be within the coagulation system itself or the result of esophageal varices in the chronically ill patient with acute decompensation.

   a. **Decreased production of vitamin-K–dependent coagulation factors II, VII, IX, and X**   Hepatocellular damage can cause an almost immediate reduction in factor levels, which is demonstrated by a prolonged prothrombin time on admission. Gastrointestinal bleeding (from varices, or oozing from diffuse bleeding points) and edema of the bowel wall (secondary to hypoalbuminemia) reduce oral vitamin K absorption.

      (1) The bleeding diathesis is a contraindication to IM injections. *Intravenous* vitamin K is thus the treatment of choice (see Chap. 15, Sec. **VI.A.1.d**).

      (2) The coagulation disorder and prothrombin time will often not be corrected with vitamin K, and the patient must be given fresh plasma, factor concentrates, or exchange transfusion with fresh whole blood.

      (3) Drugs that inhibit vitamin K are contraindicated (see Chap. 15, Sec. **VI.**).

   b. **Esophageal varices**   Varices are usually present only in chronic liver disease with acute decompensation. Treatment for variceal bleeding is ice-water lavage, compression with a Sengstaken-Blakemore tube, vasopressor infusion (during celiac arteriography if available), and surgery.

   c. **Disseminated intravascular coagulation (DIC)**   DIC can be a part of fulminant hepatic failure, as it can in any other systemic catastrophe (see Chap. 15, Sec. **VI.B**).

3. **Hypoalbuminemia**   Decreased production of albumin leads to low serum albumin, decreased serum osmolality, decreased blood volume, and possible ascites, edema, shock, and low renal plasma flow and urine output.

   a. Hypovolemia and shock must be treated aggressively (see Chap. 2, Sec. **II.C**).

   b. Shock in hepatic failure is usually a primary volume disorder. Vasopressors are of little use until adequate blood volume has been established.

   c. Other causes of shock (e.g., septic, cardiogenic) must be ruled out.

d. Ascites is usually not of great significance unless as a source of infection or a cause of respiratory distress. Unless contraindicated by bleeding, diagnostic peritoneal tap is recommended (5–10 ml) in *all* cases to rule out infection, including tuberculosis. However, removal of *large* volumes of peritoneal fluid has no effect on the primary disorder and is contraindicated.

e. In the patient with respiratory distress secondary to large-volume ascites, only enough fluid should be removed to relieve the respiratory distress.

f. Both ascites and peripheral edema frequently respond to restoration of adequate vascular volume and osmolality, both of which are also needed to maintain renal plasma flow and urine output and to avoid renal failure.

g. Diuretics are of little use until volume is restored and are often contraindicated in the acute phase, as they may further deplete intravascular volume and precipitate shock (see p. 264).

  (1) If the patient is potassium-depleted (see below), this condition will be aggravated by diuretics. If diuretics are used, they must be used with extreme caution.

  (2) Mild diuretics such as spironolactone and chlorthiazide are chosen first.

  (3) Furosemide, ethacrynic acid, and mannitol must be used with caution.

  (4) Acetazolamide will increase renal ammonium production and is **contraindicated** (see p. 265).

4. Detoxification   Hepatic detoxification failure must be approached as follows:

a. Specific drugs and substances known to be hepatotoxic or metabolized by the liver must be avoided.

b. While the specific circulating substances that aggravate CNS or hepatic deterioration have not been identified, it has been well documented that the high-protein diets and ammonium salts precipitate hepatic coma. Therefore the patient must be given no oral protein while in acute decompensation and must be restricted to a minimum of oral protein while in the recovery phase. In addition, protein degradation in the intestinal tract must be reduced to a minimum by:

  (1) Altering intestinal flora with an oral, poorly absorbed antibiotic such as neomycin.

  (2) Removing remaining intestinal products with frequent enemas, or cathartics, or both.

c. Gastrointestinal bleeding must be closely monitored, as blood is a frequent source of intestinal protein and can itself aggravate coma.

5. Exchange transfusion   Several specific treatments for detoxification failure are controversial and under evaluation. The most common approach to a patient who is rapidly deteriorating is exchange transfusion or plasmaphoresis (with return to the patient of red cells, *fresh* plasma and *fresh* platelets).

a. Exchange transfusion should be performed in a patient stable enough to tolerate it and under close supervision by a physician team, with careful monitoring of CVP and vital signs.

b. In the transfusion, 150–200 percent of estimated blood volume is exchanged through a large central line in small aliquots (20–30 ml), using fresh, heparinized whole blood.

c. After the exchange is completed, protamine sulfate (1 mg for each 1 mg of heparin the patient has received during the previous 4 hr) is given to counteract the heparin, with monitoring of clotting time or partial thromboplastin time.

D. Serum electrolytes and renal function   Electrolyte and renal function must be followed closely.

1. Renal function in acute hepatic failure is usually intact if there is no primary renal lesion. However, hypovolemia and shock produce decreased renal perfusion and can cause renal failure in the forms of acute tubular or cortical necrosis or the so-called hepatorenal syndrome.

2. Decreased perfusion of the adrenals can cause partial or complete adrenal insufficiency, salt-losing in nature, and thereby perpetuate the fluid and electrolyte disorder as well as serve as a separate cause for shock.

3. Serum creatinine and creatinine clearances are better indexes of renal function than BUN, which may reflect gastrointestinal bleeding, hydration, or protein intake.

4. Serum electrolytes often reflect the renal response to hypovolemia (see Chap. 4, Sec. I).

a. If renal failure is not present, the patient must be given generous IV potassium supplements, which can be estimated at a *minimum* as the total urinary potassium excretion over 24 hr, plus replacements of estimated deficits.

b. Frequent ECGs and serum electrolyte determinations are mandatory. *Often, the potassium-depleted patient will not show symptoms because the low serum albumin reduces the ratio of bound-to-free potassium, making more cation available for intracellular uses.*

E. Infection   Patients in hepatic failure are susceptible to infection from almost any source. The clinical parameters of infection will often be misleading.

1. With septic or nonseptic hepatic inflammation, the patient can be febrile or hypothermic, will usually have a polymorphonuclear leukocytosis, but can be leukopenic.

2. If the patient is comatose, gag and cough reflexes will be depressed, and improper handling of secretions and vomitus may serve to initiate pulmonary infection. Occasionally the comatose patient requires prophylactic intubation to avoid this circumstance.

3. Patients in shock, or with DIC, or both may have bacterial sepsis. Therefore, thorough culturing should be done in the patient in acute hepatic failure, including culture of the peritoneal fluid (if not contraindicated by a bleeding diathesis) and of the CSF (if also indicated in the evaluation of coma and if *not contraindicated* by increased intracranial pressure). (Note: Cerebral edema can result from low serum albumin and low osmotic pressure.) Microscopic, bacteriologic, and chemical analysis must be made of all available fluids (CSF, peritoneal fluid, sputum, urine, stool) for signs of infection.

4. Antibiotics can occasionally be withheld until sepsis is strongly evident and an organism identified on culture. However, if antibiotics are given on clinical evidence before cultures are available, they must be of a type that is neither hepatotoxic nor metabolized by the liver (see Table 9-6). If such drugs are given, their dosage must be carefully considered and serum levels monitored if it is possible.

REFERENCES

Trey, C., Lipworth, L., Chalmers, T. C., Davidson, C. S., Gothleib, L. S., Popper, H., and Saunders, S. J. Fulminant hepatic failure: Presumable contribution of halothane. *N. Engl. J. Med.* 279:789, 1968.

Trey, C. Acute Hepatic Failure. In Clement A. Smith (Ed.), *The Critically Ill Child*. Philadelphia: Saunders, 1972, p. 106.

14   Disorders of the Nervous System

I. PAROXYSMAL DISORDERS

A. Convulsive disorders—epilepsy Isolated or recurrent seizures are among the most common neurologic disorders of childhood. The term *epilepsy* designates any condition in which loss of consciousness and convulsive movements are recurrent over a period of time.

1. Classification

a. Grand mal convulsions are the most common convulsive disorders, except in infancy. An aura may precede tonic-clonic movements of the extremities and a sudden loss of consciousness. The ictal event usually lasts for 2–4 min, after which the child may be somnolent, confused, and fatigued and may complain of headache.

(1) Etiology Lead intoxication, birth trauma, cryptogenic.

(2) Evaluation History, x-rays, measurement of blood glucose, calcium, phosphorus, and electrolytes, and an electroencephalogram (EEG) are required.

(3) Diagnosis Spike discharges may be seen on the EEG.

(4) Treatment See Table 14-1.

b. Psychomotor (temporal lobe) seizures are seen throughout childhood and early adolescence. The patient may exhibit a variety of automatic behavior, including lip-smacking, staring, grimaces, hand posturing, laughing, and grasping motions. Some patients experience an aura of bewilderment and act irrationally. Episodes of such behavior last longer than grand mal seizures and may be followed by a convulsion. The patient is often aware of his initial symptoms and aura, but is unable to terminate the automatisms.

(1) Etiology Trauma, cryptogenic, or (rarely) due to a mass lesion.

(2) Evaluation The same procedures should be done as for grand mal convulsions. The EEG should include sleep tracing.

(3) Diagnosis Characteristic history and EEG abnormality.

(4) Treatment See Table 14-1.

c. Focal motor seizures and hemiconvulsions are usually related to structural damage of the motor cortex and may not be associated with loss of consciousness.

(1) Evaluation is the same as for grand mal convulsions. A technesium brain scan and cerebral angiography should also be done to rule out a surgically remediable lesion.

(2) Diagnosis A reliable witness and, commonly, a focal spike discharge on the EEG.

(3) Treatment See Table 14-1.

d. **Myoclonic seizures** are sudden, brief jerking movements of the arms and legs and may occur singly or just before rising. The patient does not lose consciousness.

(1) Etiology Cryptogenic.

(2) Evaluation is the same as for grand mal convulsions.

(3) Diagnosis By history. The EEG may be normal.

(4) Treatment usually requires trial of and combinations of anti-convulsants (see Table 14-1).

e. **Petit mal, or centrencephalic, epilepsy** is a term restricted to certain EEG abnormalities of synchronous spike and wave discharges which accompany a clinical picture of staring, loss of consciousness, and blinking or lip-smacking and rarely last more than 10–15 sec. Onset is usually at about age 5–8 years.

(1) Etiology Cryptogenic.

(2) Evaluation Hyperventilation for 1–2 min may produce a spell.

(3) Diagnosis is made by a history of brief lapses of consciousness and the characteristic EEG findings.

(4) Treatment (See Table 14-1.) Treatment is successful when appropriate "anti-spike-wave" medications (e.g., ethosuximide [Zarontin] or trimethadione [Tridione]) are employed. Children with petit mal should also receive *maintenance* doses of phenobarbital or diphenylhydantoin (Dilantin) because convulsions develop in many of these children.

When medications fail to control the seizures and the frequency or severity of the spells interferes with daily life, a ketogenic diet may be necessary (see p. 315).

f. **Akinetic and absence spells** are variants of centrencephalic epilepsy characterized by frequent bouts of staring, head nods, and a blank facial expression for 5–10 sec. Some patients are propelled to the ground with the ictus.

(1) Etiology Cryptogenic.

(2) Evaluation By EEG.

(3) Diagnosis The EEG shows atypical spike and wave discharges, many of which transiently disappear when diazepam (Valium) is injected IV.

(4) Treatment See **e.(4)**, above.

g. **Infantile spasms (massive myoclonic seizures)** represent a syndrome of severe, diffuse CNS malfunction during the first 6 months of age. The spells are massive attacks of flexion of the head and extension of the arms, legs, or both in salaam fashion and occur in series or as isolated events. The frequency may approach 100 times per day. Tactile stimuli may precipitate the spells. They have been mistaken for colic.

(1) Etiology is nonspecific and includes prenatal infection, birth trauma and anoxia, cerebral malformations, porencephaly, and tuberous sclerosis.

(2) Evaluation usually reveals a significant neurologic abnormality (microcephaly, developmental retardation). A search for metabolic etiology and examination with a Wood's light for early cutaneous signs of tuberous sclerosis should be performed.

(3) Diagnosis By history and classic hypsarrhythmia on EEG.

(4) Treatment Untreated, the prognosis is grave, and more than 90 percent of those surviving to 3 years of age are severely retarded.

(a) ACTH gel (150 U/M² IM daily) should be administered. Blood pressure, hematocrit, and electrolytes should be measured and stool guaiac tests done while the patient is receiving ACTH. Antacids should be administered with feedings.

(b) Initial treatment should continue for 10–14 days, with follow-up EEGs each week. If the clinical response is favorable, and the EEG abnormalities are no longer seen, treatment can be terminated after 6 weeks of ACTH.

(c) Oral therapy with hydrocortisone cypionate (liquid Cortef, 10 mg/5 ml) should be continued for 3–4 months. Babies should receive 20 mg PO tid.

(d) When no favorable response, as measured by EEG and clinical evaluation, is evident after 2–3 weeks of ACTH therapy, the drug should be stopped and trials of anticonvulsants begun. Diazepam, in doses up to 30 mg PO per day, has been a useful adjunct to other anticonvulsants for some children who did not respond to ACTH.

h. Breathholding spells are periods of apnea followed by transient unconsciousness, are usually precipitated by emotion or minor injury, and have their onset in children 4–18 months old. The apnea always *follows expiration*.

(1) Two types of breathholding spells are described:

(a) The **pallid breathholding spell** follows a frustrating stimulus in response to which the child becomes apneic and pale and may experience a brief tonic seizure with prompt spontaneous recovery. The EEG may be abnormal during ocular compression, producing bradycardia and > 2 sec of asystole.

(b) In **cyanotic breathholding spells,** violent crying is followed by apnea, cyanosis, and flaccidity. Prompt resolution with return of consciousness is seen, and the child appears normal. Spells of this type are rarely seen after 2–3 years of age. The EEG is normal during ocular compression.

(2) Treatment with anticonvulsants is not indicated. Infants with unprovoked periods of apnea should be evaluated for epilepsy.

i. Febrile convulsions are brief (2–5 min), generalized tonic-clonic seizures with loss of consciousness in an otherwise healthy, febrile child, aged 5 months–3 years.

(1) Etiology A rapid increase in body temperature has been postulated as triggering the convulsion.

(2) Evaluation [See Sec. **I.A.1.a(2)**, p. 295, when no site of infection is evident.] There is little evidence that a lumbar puncture is indicated in a child older than 16–18 months when an extracranial source of fever has been satisfactorily identified *and* no meningeal signs are present.

(3) Diagnosis If the child has any of the following, he is *excluded* from the classification of simple febrile convulsion and must be evaluated for an etiology other than fever.

(a) First seizure when under 6 months or over 3 years old.

(b) Evidence of head trauma.

(c) Abnormal CSF suggestive of infection or hemorrhage.

(d) Prolonged convulsive activity (> 6 min).

(e) *Persistently abnormal* EEG.

(4) Treatment

(a) There is a limited role for *anticonvulsants* in the management of a single febrile convulsion because of the brevity of the spell and the rapid return to normal activity.

(b) Administration of anticonvulsants during subsequent febrile illnesses has little proved value in preventing recurrent simple febrile convulsions, and there is evidence that daily anticonvulsant therapy may be ineffective.

(c) Should the patient have a recurrence of seizures when afebrile, or after age 4 years, or both, anticonvulsant therapy for 2–3 years should be instituted. Phenobarbital is the drug of choice (see Table 14-1).

j. Hysterical fits (psychogenic epilepsy) These spells are occasionally seen as conversion symptoms in children and adolescents with bona fide epilepsy, as well as in previously healthy patients. The spells rarely occur when the patient is alone and lack the true tonic-clonic rhythmic jerking of a grand mal convulsion.

(1) Etiology Overwhelming conversion symptom complex.

(2) Evaluation should include an EEG during a "spell." If temporal lobe seizures are considered, a complete work-up should be initiated.

(3) Diagnosis is confirmed when one witnesses opisthotonic posturing, flailing, beating movements of the arms, tightly closed eyelids, and spitting and crying out with hyperventilation unaccompanied by urinary incontinence or tongue-biting.

(4) Treatment Initially one should be very supportive and understanding. Ultimate therapy is psychiatric.

2. Approach to therapy of convulsive disorders

a. General measures After a detailed evaluation for metabolic, infectious, toxic, degenerative, cerebrovascular, and neoplastic etiologies of recurrent seizures, specific therapy should be instituted.

(1) Treatment is aimed at preventing further seizures and allowing the patient to lead a normal life. This will be the case in the majority of children with seizures.

(2) Treatment of the child with one seizure should be individualized, depending on the severity of the seizure, the child's age, and understanding of the parents.

(3) When there is reasonable doubt as to the authenticity of the seizure, it may be wise to await a second spell and seek out witnesses before initiating treatment.

(4) *Every child who has had a seizure should have an EEG* to establish a baseline of reference to define focal abnormalities. This is most useful if performed at least 5–7 days after the seizure, as nonspecific postictal electrical changes are minimized. If a child *appears* postictal but there are no witnesses to a convulsion, an EEG may be helpful in defining the episode closer to the event. There is no reason to withhold therapy until after the EEG is performed.

(5) The pediatrician, particularly, should consider the impact of both the disease and its management on the developing child and adolescent. This is especially important in evaluating management failures.

b. Anticonvulsant therapy

(1) General principles

(a) The general principle of using the single drug that is most effective and least toxic is stressed when patients fail to respond to recommended therapy. It is advisable to obtain blood levels of the anticonvulsant in question.

(b) When a single drug is used, if seizure control is not optimal initially, the drug should be increased to near-toxic levels before being abandoned. This usually requires 4–6 weeks per drug.

(c) Always continue a medication, decreasing it *gradually*, when a second or replacement preparation is introduced. This lessens the chances of status epilepticus from drug withdrawal.

(d) Medications should be prescribed in capsule or tablet form whenever possible. Tablets may be crushed for infants and disguised with sweets for toddlers. This assures a uniform dose, prevents error in dispensing medication of more than a single concentration (and short shelf life), and is easily transported in a unit dose.

(2) Anticonvulsant drugs   Table 14-1 lists the most commonly used, safest anticonvulsants for each general class of seizure disorder. It is not intended to be exhaustive. The medications are listed in the order of efficacy (balancing anticonvulsant properties with sedative effects and toxic side reactions).

Table 14-1. Maintenance Therapy of Seizure Disorders

Seizure Disorder	Medication	Daily Dose (mg/kg, bid–tid)	Preparations
Grand mal, focal motor, or psychomotor seizures	*Group A:*		
	Phenobarbital	3–5	Tablets, 15, 30, 64[a], 100[a] mg; elixir, 20 mg/5 ml
	Mephobarbital	3–10	Tablets, 30, 50, 200 mg
	Diphenylhydantoin	5–8	Tablets, 50 mg; capsules, 30, 100 mg; suspension, 125 mg/5 ml
	Primidone	5–25	Tablets, 50, 250 mg; suspension, 250 mg/5 ml
Centrencephalic (petit mal), akinetic, or myoclonic seizures	One medication from group A[b] plus one from group B		
	Group B:		
	Ethosuximide	5–25	Capsules, 250 mg
	Methylphenylsuccinimide	20–40	Capsules, 500 mg; suspension 250 mg/5 ml
	Methsuximide	5–20	Capsules, 300 mg
	Diazepam	0.5–2	Tablets, 2, 5, 10 mg
	Trimethadione	15–40	Tablets, 150 mg; capsules, 300 mg; suspension, 150 mg/5 ml
	Paramethadione	15–40	Capsules, 150, 300 mg
	Acetazolamide	5–25	Tablets, 125, 250, 500 mg

[a] As Eskabarb (long-acting phenobarbital).
[b] Diphenylhydantoin may aggravate petit mal seizures.

(a) **Phenobarbital** is perhaps the most widely used and one of the most effective anticonvulsants, alone and in combination with other drugs. It is well tolerated in childhood.

    i. **Side effects** include hyperkinesis, drowsiness, and ataxia.

    ii. **Therapeutic blood levels** are 0.5–1.5 mg/100 ml.

(b) **Mephobarbital (Mebaral)** may be used as a substitute for phenobarbital and causes hyperkinesis infrequently. Side effects are uncommon.

(c) **Diphenylhydantoin** is presently the most effective of all anticonvulsants and has a relatively low incidence of serious side effects. Dosage must be individualized, and blood level determinations in refractory cases are helpful.

    i. The **therapeutic blood level** is 15–25 μg/ 100 ml. Lateral gaze nystagmus is seen when this is reached.

    ii. **Common side effects** include (a) gingival hyperplasia, which is not entirely treatable by good oral hygiene and has required gingivectomy; (b) hypertrichosis of the face, arms, and trunk; (c) megaloblastic anemia, responsive to folic acid therapy; and (d) asymptomatic depression of normal values of PBI, T_4, and RT_4.

    iii. **Toxic effects** are infrequent and include agranulocytosis, ataxia, diplopia, dysarthria, eosinophilia, eliptocytosis, exfoliative dermatitis, hematuria, hepatitis, leukopenia, lymphadenopathy, macrocytosis, peripheral neuropathy, skin rashes, Stevens-Johnson syndrome, thrombocytopenic purpura.

(d) **Primidone (Mysoline)** is used in the treatment of psychomotor and grand mal epilepsy. Its action is believed similar to that of barbiturates.

    i. **Frequent side effects** are noted when the medication is instituted in full dosage. For this reason, starting treatment with $\frac{1}{5}$ to $\frac{1}{10}$ of the full dose and increasing this every 4 days until maximum dosage is achieved is recommended. Behavior changes, irritability, drowsiness, vomiting, and ataxia may cause the patient to discontinue this medication if the dose is not increased gradually.

    ii. **Toxic effects** from long-term therapy are infrequent. Megaloblastic anemia responsive to folic acid has been reported.

(e) **Ethosuximide** is useful for petit mal epilepsy in combination with other drugs. However, it is available only in gelatinous 250-mg capsules, which challenges parental ingenuity in administering it. The medication must usually be removed from the capsules for young children, or the capsule may be frozen and cut into small bits.

    i. The **minimal effective dose** for a toddler may be 125 mg tid.

ii. **Toxic effects** Agranulocytosis is the most serious toxic effect, and an initial CBC and periodic checks should be done. It is less toxic than trimethadione and usually is effective in less than 24 hr after therapy starts. Hiccups are seen as an idiosyncratic reaction.

(f) **Trimethadione (Tridione)** and **paramethadione (Paradione)**, because of their serious toxic effects, should not be used before ethosuximide is tried and is unsuccessful.

i. **Toxic effects** include "yellow vision," leukopenia, and agranulocytosis.

ii. **Side effects** are vomiting, hiccups, rashes, photophobia, and alopecia.

iii. The **minimal effective dose** is probably 150 mg tid.

iv. Initial and weekly CBCs are *mandatory* and thereafter may be performed monthly.

(g) **Methylphenylsuccinimide (Milontin)** and **methsuximide (Celontin)** are not often used, but may be if ethosuximide fails. Toxic effects on bone marrow have been observed. Side effects of gastrointestinal disturbance and drowsiness are seen.

(h) **Acetazolamide (Diamox)** is a carbonic anhydrase inhibitor, useful in conjunction with another anticonvulsant for centrencephalic seizures.

i. There is no minimal effective dosage, and children have been given more than 2 gm daily to control seizures.

ii. **Side effects** are probably dose-related and include anorexia, polyuria, paresthesias, and hyperpnea, when an acidotic state occurs.

(i) **Diazepam (Valium)** has been shown to be an effective oral anticonvulsant. For the poorly controlled centrencephalic seizure disorder, it is a useful drug in combination therapy.

i. The dose should be increased slowly and withheld when toxic symptoms appear. There is a wide safety margin, and children have taken up to 30–40 mg daily with cessation of seizures and minimal side effects.

ii. Drowsiness, amnesia, nystagmus, ataxia, and dysarthria are commonly seen and are dose-related. Amphetamines have successfully counteracted the somnolence.

B. **Neonatal seizures** (See also Chap. 5, Sec. **VI.B.3.**) Convulsive disorders during the first 2–3 weeks of life are a relatively common problem in any special care nursery. Etiology, evaluation, and treatment of seizures in the neonate are unique. Seizures frequently are unrecognized in newborns because of their atypical form.

1. **Etiology** The most common causes are metabolic disturbance, birth injury, and infection (see Table 14-2).

Table 14-2.   Etiology of Neonatal Seizures Grouped According to Response to Therapy

---

I. Metabolic disorders
   A. Hypocalcemia
   B. Hypoglycemia
   C. Hyponatremia, hypernatremia
   D. Pyridoxine dependency
   E. Withdrawal
      1. Barbiturates
      2. Narcotics
II. Infections
   A. Meningitis (bacterial)
   B. Sepsis
   C. Viral meningoencephalitis
III. Traumatic
   A. Intracerebral hemorrhage
   B. Subarachnoid hemorrhage
   C. Skull fracture
   D. Subdural hematoma
   E. Cortical vein thrombosis
IV. Perinatal anoxia
V. Postmaturity
VI. Congenital cerebral defects

---

2. Evaluation and diagnosis

a. Convulsions as such are almost never seen. Instead, the seizure discharges are manifested clinically by apnea, twitching of the eyelids or of one extremity, abnormal crying, deviation of the eyes, or cyanosis. The lack of organization and myelination of the neonatal nervous system is responsible for the poorly differentiated spells.

b. A number of neonatal seizures have a recognizable cause that becomes evident after a thorough evaluation. An accurate and thorough assessment of the etiology and prompt therapy are imperative, as morbidity or mortality for the infant with seizures is significant in about 50 percent.

c. Laboratory studies   Each infant must have appropriate blood chemistry studies to include glucose, calcium, magnesium, electrolytes, protein, phosphate, and BUN. A lumbar puncture, skull x-ray, EEG, evaluation for sepsis, head circumference measurements, transillumination of the skull, and subdural taps when indicated are also required. Urinalysis should include amino acid screening, ferric chloride, dinitrophenylhydrazine, a test for reducing substance with glucose oxidase dipstick, and Benedict's test to rule out galactosemia.

d. Hypocalcemia is the leading cause of seizures in neonates and is most likely to appear between the fourth and eighth days of life. It is more common in prematures and after difficult delivery. Classic signs of tetany are absent, although Erb's sign is usually present. Ionized serum calcium is usually < 7.5 mg/100 ml and phosphate, > 7.5 mg/100 ml. Focal seizures are common, with EEG abnormalities most striking during the ictus. The cause is usually speculative.

e. **Hypoglycemia** is usually noted in the first 72 hr of life and may be seen with sepsis, in intracranial hemorrhage, and in infants of diabetic mothers. It is an infrequent cause of neonatal seizures, occurring in fewer than 10 percent.

f. **Hypomagnesemia** is uncommon and may present with symptoms identical to hypoglycemia.

g. **Pyridoxine dependency** is not accompanied by clinical abnormalities except seizures, and the diagnosis is made by prompt response to pyridoxine given IV. If this diagnosis is made, treatment must be continued indefinitely to prevent recurrence.

h. **Pyridoxine deficiency** is seen after the neonatal period and is caused by a lack of exogenous vitamin B_6.

i. **Hyponatremia** and **hypernatremia** are rare cases of neonatal seizures and may be noted after therapy has been instituted for seizures due to another metabolic etiology. Prognosis is favorable when the electrolyte imbalance is not associated with sepsis.

j. **Meningitis** and **sepsis** account for a significant number of seizures in neonates (see Chap. 9, Sec. **V.N**).

k. **Birth injury** often causes seizures, and these occur on the second to fifth day of life.

(1) **Subarachnoid hemorrhage** is confirmed by the presence in the CSF of blood with xanthochromic supernate and protein usually greater than 250 mg/100 ml. The EEG may be normal in these infants and the prognosis is good.

(2) **Intraventricular hemorrhage** may be recognized by seizures during the first day of life in a desperately ill baby. A bulging anterior fontanelle, enlarging head size, abnormal EEG, and bloody CSF are noted. The prognosis is poor.

(3) **Subdural hematomas** are recognized by the presence of blood in the subdural space. Positive transillumination is usually noted. Treatment consists of daily subdural taps with removal of not more than 5–7 ml of fluid. If after 7–10 days the fluid is still present, the child should be evaluated by a neurosurgeon for craniotomy and stripping of hematoma membranes.

3. **EEG with treatment of metabolic deficiency** Therapeutic trials to correct metabolic deficiency should not be postponed until the results of blood chemistry studies are available. Optimally, these trials should be done while an EEG is being recorded (the doses listed in Table 14-3 are therapeutic). One should wait 10–15 min between IV infusions to begin the next trial. Infusions should begin with the treatment least likely to respond.

4. **Treatment of seizures** Diagnosis is made by epileptogenic electrical activity and arrested clinical seizures. If there is a failure of response in the clinical trial of metabolic therapy, treatment of the seizures should be initiated with diazepam IV (supplied as 5 mg/ml [1 mg/0.2 ml]) in 0.2-mg increments, up to a total of 3 mg, with

Table 14-3.   Intravenous Infusions During Electroencephalography for Diagnosis of Neonatal Seizures

Substance	Amount
Pyridoxine	50 mg
Magnesium sulfate, 3%	5 ml
Glucose, 50%	1–2 ml/kg
Calcium gluconate, 10%	Up to 10 ml given slowly

the dose repeated later if the first has been successful. **Respiration and heart rate** must be closely monitored during administration. Daily maintenance therapy with phenobarbital should also be started, with a dosage of 10–12 mg/kg per day.

C. **Headache**   The child with persistent or recurrent headache presents a challenging diagnostic problem. When the headache is not due to acute infection, systemic illness, or trauma, the physician must consider migraine. The prevalence of migraine is about 3 percent in the general population of children. Most are 6–12 years of age when initial symptoms begin. Girls frequently experience their initial attack with menarche.

1. **Evaluation**   Skull x-rays, blood pressure recordings, and an EEG with strobe stimulation should be done.

2. **Diagnosis**   The diagnosis is made by history. Sometimes, an excessive response to strobe light stimulation is seen on the EEG.

   a. **Common migraine** is the most frequent type of headache seen, and there is usually no prodrome. The pain is a steady, severe ache, which may become throbbing, and lasts 4–6 hr. It is unilateral (not always on the same side) most of the time.

   b. **Classic migraine** often consists of an aura for 20–30 min prior to the pain. Visual symptoms (scotomas, flashing lights, blurred vision, fortification spectra) are followed by a severe unilateral frontal pain that becomes throbbing, and the patient may then vomit. He prefers to sleep in a cool, dark place, and this may terminate the episode. Variants include mild hemiparesis, ophthalmoplegia, and severe abdominal cramps. During an attack of migraine, children may present with an acute confusional state.

   c. **Cluster headaches (histamine or Horton's headaches)** are characterized by severe unilateral neuralgia-like pain in the retroorbital region and are very rarely seen in childhood.

3. **Treatment**   Prophylaxis is the best therapy. Maintenance barbiturates in anticonvulsant dosage are beneficial to children with migraine, and ergot preparations are generally not needed until adolescence (see Table 14-4).

D. **Abdominal epilepsy** is a syndrome of paroxysmal pain, altered state of consciousness, and postictal symptoms. It may occur alone or in association with other convulsive disorders. Psychomotor seizures are frequent accompaniments. Cyclic vomiting may occur.

Table 14-4. Drugs Used for Treatment of Migraine

Medication	Daily Dose	Frequency
Aspirin	65 mg per year of age per dose PO or PR	q4–6h prn
Phenobarbital	3–5 mg/kg per day	Continuous treatment bid
Diphenylhydantoin	5–8 mg/kg per day	Continuous treatment bid
Fiorinal (butalbitol, 50 mg; caffeine, 40 mg; aspirin, 200 mg; phenacetin, 130 mg)	Under age 5: ½ tablet Over age 5: 1 tablet	Qid Qid
Cafergot (ergotamine tartrate, 1.0 mg; caffeine, 100 mg)	1 or 2 tablets with initial symptoms, then 1 q30 min prn up to a total of 4 tablets in 12 hr Suppository: ½ PR initially and ½ q45 min prn up to a total of 3	
Methysergide (prophylaxis only)	2 mg once daily. Small risk of retroperitoneal fibrosis and vascular insufficiency. Use in children should be restricted to those jointly cared for by a pediatrician and neurologist.	

1. **Etiology** Cryptogenic.

2. **Evaluation** Systemic causes of abdominal pain should be ruled out, particularly porphyria and plumbism.

3. **Diagnosis** Abnormal EEG.

4. **Treatment** Anticonvulsants (as for grand mal; see Table 14-1).

E. **Narcolepsy**

   1. **Etiology** Cryptogenic.

   2. **Evaluation** *Hypoglycemia must be ruled out.* Skull x-rays and the EEG are normal interictally. During an attack the EEG will show a rapid transition from waking rhythm to sleep potentials.

   3. **Diagnosis** is made by a history of attacks of uncontrollable daytime sleep, cataplexy (loss of muscle tone with retention of consciousness), hypnagogic hallucinations, and sleep paralysis.

   4. **Treatment** is with methylphenidate (Ritalin) in doses of 5–10 mg 30 min before meals. Dextroamphetamine sulfate 2.5–10 mg after meals should be tried if methylphenidate is not successful. Long-acting capsules of amphetamines are available and are given in the morning as a daily dose. These children may react with excessive somnolence to hypnotics and antihistamines, and the use of these medications should be judicious.

II. ALTERATIONS IN THE STATE OF CONSCIOUSNESS

A. **Nontraumatic alterations** Many children are brought to the pediatrician with altered states of consciousness, from mild confusion and somnolence to severe obtundation and coma. Head trauma must be ruled out in these children and symptomatic evaluation carried out.

   1. **Etiology** The causes may be metabolic, toxic, infectious, postictal, cerebrovascular, mass lesions, and psychiatric.

   2. **Evaluation** should include a history of the chronology of the disease and the progression of signs and symptoms; a detailed neurologic examination; and special attention to vital signs, level of consciousness, and focal deficits. Special reflex testing and the child's response to initial treatment are also required.

   3. **Treatment** An outline of management can be found in Chap. 2, Sec. **IV**, p. 43.

B. **Traumatic alteration**

   1. **Evaluation**

      a. If the child did not lose consciousness following a head trauma and is alert and normally responsive, a careful general evaluation and neurologic examination may be done following the accident and superficial injuries treated.

      b. Evaluation for focal neurologic deficit such as hemiparesis and pupillary abnormalities must be made, and signs of increased intracranial pressure should be sought.

      c. Skull roentgenograms must be done and a search made for basal skull fractures.

d. CSF rhinorrhea may be a clue to a basal fracture, as are "raccoon eyes." Glucose in the nasal secretions (detected by a Dextrostix) is diagnostic of CSF rhinorrhea; blood behind the tympanic membrane is another finding pathognomonic of basal skull fracture.

e. Neurosurgical consultation is necessary for further management and *lumbar puncture should not be performed.*

f. In instances of increased intracranial pressure without focal signs, treatment of cerebral edema should be instituted (see Table 2-6).

g. Regardless of age, any child with a vague or incomplete history of single or repeated bouts of head trauma should be admitted to the hospital and evaluated for signs of the battered child syndrome (see Chap. 2, Sec. **XII**). Roentgenograms of the skull, chest, and long bones should be made, and subdural hematoma must be ruled out.

h. Head trauma syndromes

(1) Cerebral concussion is the most common head trauma syndrome and may occur from mild injury. It is a state of loss of consciousness immediately following the trauma, usually lasts minutes to hours, and is not associated with any recognizable anatomic changes in the CNS.

(a) Retrograde amnesia, which is loss of memory for events immediately preceding the trauma, often occurs.

(b) Anterograde amnesia (memory loss after the trauma) usually lasts longer than retrograde amnesia.

(c) The severity of the injury may be judged by the extent of these two components of posttraumatic amnesia.

(d) Examination should include detailed neurologic examination. In many cases of blunt facial trauma, the sense of smell may be lost. The patient with a mild concussion is usually lethargic and diaphoretic, and vomiting and headache may be seen in the first 24–48 hr. Papilledema will rarely be seen, but the presence of retinal hemorrhage or nuchal rigidity should alert the physician to the possible presence of an intracranial hemorrhage.

(e) Treatment Any scalp lacerations should be treated to prevent infection, and then evaluation should be continued. The patient whose evaluation is negative usually becomes increasingly alert and responsive. Many of these children can be discharged to the care of responsible parents. It is useful to give them a list of guidelines for care. A sample set of such guidelines may be obtained from Emergency Services Department, Children's Hospital Medical Center, Boston.

(2) Epidural hematoma is a neurosurgical emergency and is almost uniformly fatal if unrecognized. It usually results from tearing of the middle meningeal artery in association with an overlying skull fracture of the temporal bone and may cause contralateral hemiparesis, ipsilateral pupillary dilatation, and rapidly progressive obtundation and coma. **Immediate surgery is mandatory.**

(3) Subdural hematoma and effusions

(a) Etiology   The cause is almost always trauma or post-meningitis infection. These hematomas are most commonly seen in children during the first 2 years of life.

(b) Evaluation

    i. A history of irritability, vomiting, poor feeding, apathy, failure to thrive, convulsions, delayed motor milestones, anemia, and an enlarged, "boxy" head should alert the physician.

    ii. One should check for a tense, bulging fontanelle, retinal hemorrhages, decreased percussion note of the skull, positive transillumination, and increase of head size above normal percentiles. In long-standing hematomas the skull roentgenograms may show abnormally split cranial sutures. **Lumbar puncture is contraindicated.**

    iii. This diagnosis in infants is excluded only after bilateral subdural taps have been performed, as 50 percent of affected children are found to have hematomas over both hemispheres. In older children with closed sutures the definitive study is cerebral angiography.

(c) Treatment is by removal of the subdural fluid (alternating hemispheres daily) and may be successful in "drying up" the effusion in 2–3 weeks. In unusually large subdural hematomas—or when signs referable to compression of underlying brain are evident—early consultation with a neurosurgical colleague is necessary.

(4) Posterior fossa subdural hematomas may be present from acute trauma, but are likely to be missed until the child shows signs of increased intracranial pressure.

(a) The presence of cerebellar signs, or positive transillumination over the suboccipital region, or both should warrant investigation with a contrast study (ventriculogram or angiogram).

(b) Treatment is operative intervention. Lumbar puncture is contraindicated. Treatment of increased intracranial pressure with osmotic diuretics is a temporizing measure only [see Sec. **(5)(d)i**].

A. Benign increased intracranial pressure (pseudotumor cerebri)   Affected children may present with the symptoms and signs of intracranial hypertension: headache, vomiting, cranial nerve palsy, and papilledema without an antecedent illness.

1. Etiology includes changes in hormone balance, termination of corticosteroid therapy, administration of fluorinated corticosteroids, administration of tetracycline, penicillin, and vitamin A. Also, a small percentage of these patients are found to have a cerebral venous sinus thrombosis.

2. Evaluation

a. Physical examination may show enlarging head size if sutures are in the process of closing. Papilledema is present, and a VIth nerve palsy is common.

b. Cerebellar signs and meningeal irritation are not present; this should alert the physician that a posterior fossa mass or basilar meningitis may be responsible for such signs. Skull roentgenograms, EEG, and a technesium brain scan are necessary.

(1) Diagnosis A cerebral angiogram or a pneumoencephalogram, or both, will confirm the diagnosis of mild ventricular dilatation without obstruction to the flow of CSF. Cerebral venography may be needed to rule out a sinus thrombosis when focal neurologic signs are not otherwise explained.

(2) Treatment Many patients will show spontaneous recovery after lumbar puncture and pneumoencephalography. Careful follow-up examination is needed, and the patient should be checked for visual changes associated with papilledema. Those who remain symptomatic may be treated as follows:

(a) Acetazolamide (Diamox), 25 mg/kg daily.

(b) Dexamethasone (Decadron), 2–4 mg q8h initially for 3–4 days, then 2–4 mg q12h for 10 days, with a tapering dose.

III. MISCELLANEOUS DISORDERS

A. Myasthenia gravis may present as diffuse weakness at any age and is seen in newborns. Three forms are known in childhood.

Transient neonatal myasthenia gravis occurs at or shortly after birth. An infant of a myasthenic mother may be floppy (p. 141) and have ptosis and stridor, be a poor eater, and have diminished reflexes, which may last 3–4 weeks. Immediate treatment with neostigmine may be lifesaving. The disorder does not recur after symptoms disappear at about age 1 month (see Table 14–5).

Persistent neonatal myasthenia gravis is seen in infants of healthy mothers who do not have myasthenia. Fetal movement may have been decreased during the latter part of the pregnancy. Symptoms are similiar to those in infants who have transient myasthenia gravis, but respiratory distress is usually absent. External ophthalmoplegia is common in this group. It is also seen at birth. Many children are refractory to therapy (see Table 14-5).

Juvenile myasthenia gravis occurs after the first year of life and is seen in girls 5 times as often as in boys. Ptosis (unilateral or bilateral) may be the only presenting sign. Generalized weakness, bulbar muscle weakness, and a flat, expressionless face are seen later.

1. Diagnosis is by a positive response to edrophonium (Tensilon) (see Table 14-5), and an electromyogram (EMG) confirms this finding.

2. Treatment (See Table 14-5.) Anticholinesterase medications usually produce a marked improvement in muscle strength, but long-term results of medical therapy alone are discouraging. A child who becomes unresponsive to medications should be considered for thymectomy, as this may produce a lasting remission. Treatment with ACTH and prednisone is controversial but frequently helpful, although not thoroughly studied in children.

3. Crises Cholinergic or myasthenic crisis (see **a.b.c**) in a myasthenic child is a medical emergency and presents as acute respiratory failure (see Chap. 2, Sec. **VII.C**). **Myasthenic crisis** occurs when the

Table 14-5. Drug Therapy for Myasthenia Gravis

Age of Patient	Diagnostic Dose of Edrophonium (Tensilon, 10 mg/ml)[a]	Oral Maintenance Dose		
		Neostigmine (Prostigmin) 15 mg	= Pyridostigmine (Mestinon) 60 mg	= Ambenomium (Mytelase) 6 mg
Neonatal[b]				
Transient	1 mg IV or 2 mg IM	1–5 mg[c]	6 mg, then is increased	Not to be used for neonates (no blood-brain barrier exists. Convulsions occur with overdose)
Persistent	Same	Same	Same	
Juvenile				
>2 yrs old	<30 kg, 1–5 mg IV or 2–10 mg IM	Initial dose, 3.75 mg	Initial dose, 15 mg	Initial dose, 2 mg
	>30 kg, 5–10 mg IV or 10–20 mg IM	Increase these increments until desired effects are attained or side effects occur. Adjuvant drugs (ephedrine, 12.5–25.0 mg tid) may be used.		

[a] Atropine must be available for cholinergic side effects.

[b] Positive response = improved respirations, good cry, Moro reflex, increased tone.

[c] Oral dose is 30 times parenteral dose. Parenteral neostigmine available as 0.25 mg/ml, 0.5 mg/ml, and 1.0 mg/ml.

patient becomes unresponsive to his regular dose of medication and can be seen with intercurrent infection. **Cholinergic crisis** is due to an overdose of anticholinesterase medication. The symptoms of cholinergic crisis are pallor, bradycardia, increased blood pressure, increased secretions, miosis, fasciculations, severe abdominal cramps, and dysarthria.

a. **Treatment of crises** begins with supported respirations. Assisted ventilation may be needed (see Chap. 2, Sec. **VII.C**). The differentiation between myasthenic and cholinergic crises may be difficult, and IV edrophonium, 1 mg q60sec, up to a total of 4 mg, should be administered. If the symptoms decrease abruptly, one can assume that inadequate medications (myasthenic crisis) are the cause.

b. **Treatment of myasthenic crisis** should proceed with prostigmine IV as needed, not to exceed 2.5 mg/hr. Atropine sulfate should be administered (0.1–0.3 mg IV) to decrease the muscarinic effects of increased bronchial secretions and diarrhea. **Do not give any of the following to patients in myasthenic crisis:** (1) sedatives, (2) hypnotics, (3) quinine—including tonic water, or (4) antibiotics of the neomycin, bacitracin, streptomycin, or kanamycin groups.

c. **Treatment of cholinergic crisis** Atropine sulfate is the drug of choice and should be given in a dose of 0.2–1.0 mg IV as needed to decrease production of copious secretions and prevent further respiratory embarrassment.

B. **Bell's palsy** usually refers to involvement of the 7th nerve at or near the stylomastoid foramen and presents with a sudden onset of ipsilateral weakness of the upper and lower portions of the face. Recognition of an intracranial lesion warrants full investigation of the cause.

1. **Examination** reveals a characteristic deformity that is rarely mistaken. The child has a flat nasolabial fold, cannot close his eyelids, pucker his lips, or wrinkle his brow. Saliva may drool from the corner of his mouth. Speech is abnormal. The deficit is accentuated when the patient smiles.

Almost all children with incomplete Bell's palsy recover in 3–6 weeks. Denervation occurs only when facial paralysis is clinically complete. Such patients should be evaluated for decompressive surgery after EMG has confirmed total denervation.

2. **Treatment** to prevent secondary deformity should begin at onset.

a. **Massage** The facial muscle should be massaged upward by placing the thumb inside the mouth and index finger on the cheek.

b. **Eyedrops** Instillation of methylcellulose eyedrops should be done qid, keeping the lids opposed with the use of an eye pad to prevent corneal injury. Older children should wear clear plastic glasses.

c. **Corticosteroids** The use of corticosteroids for a short time is controversial, but has benefited some patients. (Children 8 years of age or older may be given prednisone, 40 mg daily in divided doses for 4 days, then 5 mg daily to end at 8 days; children under 8 should be given 20 mg daily for 4 days, tapering off to 5 mg, to end at 8 days.)

C. Acute infectious polyneuritis

1. **Etiology**   This syndrome usually follows an acute viral infection by 1–2 weeks, although no causal relationship has been established. The peak incidence is in children 6–9 years of age.

2. **Evaluation and diagnosis** is made when symmetric weakness of the legs (greater distally) ascends to involve the arms in 1–4 days. Paresthesias may also be present. Involvement of cranial nerves (especially the VIIth) may also be seen in 50 percent of patients. Deep tendon reflexes are markedly diminished, and 75 percent of patients have autonomic disturbances such as urinary retention.

    a. **Laboratory evaluation**   A heterophil or rapid mono spot test should be performed. Lumbar puncture usually shows normal protein initially and increased protein after 7–10 days. Lymphocytes are sometimes seen in the CSF, but rarely exceed 50 cells per cubic millimeter.

    b. The major complication is respiratory paralysis and is fatal unless treated vigorously.

3. **Treatment** consists of supportive therapy. Physical therapy is given to prevent contractures. Initially, frequent vital capacity determinations should be made. A bedside tracheostomy set, endotracheal tube, and Ambu bag should accompany the patient. Assisted ventilation should be utilized when decreased vital capacity compromises good aeration.

D. Acute cerebellar ataxia is a syndrome of early childhood (1–4 years of age) manifested by frequent falls due to truncal ataxia, nystagmus, intention tremors, and abnormal cadence of speech. It usually evolves in 1–3 days.

1. **Etiology**   The condition follows a viral illness.

2. **Evaluation and diagnosis**   Accidental drug ingestion should be excluded. When there is no evidence of a brainstem or posterior fossa mass or increased intracranial pressure, a lumbar puncture may be performed and usually shows no evidence of inflammation. When the patient has opsoclonus (darting, jerky eye movements at rest), or myoclonus, or both, a neuroblastoma should be excluded.

3. **Treatment** is supportive, with adequate nutrition stressed, as the child may have to be fed. Corticosteroids or ACTH are useful in symptomatic control of myoclonus and opsoclonus, and may need to be continued for many months. Recovery usually begins in 5–7 days and is usually complete.

E. Sydenham's chorea (St. Vitus' dance, chorea minor)

1. **Etiology**   Antecedent streptococcal infection.

2. **Evaluation** for acute rheumatic fever.

3. **Diagnosis** is made by seeing choreiform movements of the arms, which are brief, abrupt, dancing jerks, usually of one arm. There is a characteristic posture of the outstretched arm in which the hand is hyperextended at the metacarpophalangeal joint and flexed at the wrist. Facial grimacing is prominent and tossing movements of the head are seen. Speech is indistinct, and grunting sounds are uttered involuntarily. Mentation is normal, although most patients are emotionally labile.

4. **Treatment** with phenobarbital (3–5 mg/kg daily) or chlorpromazine (up to 100 mg tid) may decrease the adventitious movements. Sydenham's chorea has been reported in young women taking oral contraceptives and is apparently reversible.

F. **Wilson's disease** In this condition there is hepatolenticular degeneration with abnormal deposits of copper in the brain, liver, cornea, and kidney.

1. **Etiology** This is a hereditary (autosomal recessive) disease. A major defect is an almost total absence of ceruloplasmin in plasma, with resultant decreased copper-binding.

2. **Evaluation and diagnosis**

   a. Onset is usually in the early teens and may begin as a tremor of the hands, ticlike movements under stress, and tremulous speech when the tones are sustained. Hypertonia, "winged-beating" tremors, mental changes, behavior changes, and dysarthria are later manifestations.

   b. Hepatomegaly may be present, and a thorough evaluation of the corneal limbus should be made for Kayser-Fleischer rings. Presumptive laboratory diagnosis is made by finding less than 25 mg/100 ml ceruloplasmin in a child over 6 months of age. Liver biopsy with findings greater than 250 μg copper dry weight is pathognomonic. Sibs of affected children should be screened, although treatment of a carrier is not indicated.

3. **Treatment** Penicillamine, 15–30 mg/kg daily in 3 oral doses, will produce an increased urinary copper excretion. A low copper diet, with avoidance of mushrooms, chocolate, liver, and shellfish should be prescribed.

4. **Prognosis** Patients with mild neurologic symptoms become functionally normal after 6–12 months of penicillamine treatments. Those who are severely affected may not improve. The natural history of the untreated illness is progressive disability with liver failure and death in about 5 years.

G. **The hyperkinetic child syndrome** is seen mostly in boys 4–10 years old. Some consider it as evidence of miminal cerebral dysfunction (i.e., manifestations of a diffuse, mild insult to the brain in early life). However, in many such children, no serologic abnormality can be found.

1. **Evaluation and diagnosis**

   a. Hyperactivity and restlessness, short attention span, attacks of anxiety, impulsive behavior, easy frustration, associated learning problems (perceptual motor handicap), and clumsiness.

   b. On examination, many of these children will be found to be left-handed (and the only left-handed members of their family), and their dominant handedness may not correlate with dominant foot or eye, as is normally the case. Signs of motor incoordination may also be present.

   c. EEG abnormalities are nonspecific.

2. **Therapy** Treatment is with drugs that modify the hyperactive behavior, combined with environmental modification. Drugs should be

Table 14-6.   Drugs for Hyperactivity

Medication	Dose	Preparation
Dextroamphetamine (Dexedrine)	2.5–15 mg bid	5-mg tablets 15-mg capsules
Methylphenidate (Ritalin)	5–20 mg bid	5-, 10-, 20-mg tablets
Thioridazine (Mellaril)	10–30 mg tid	10-, 25-mg tablets

tried in the order listed in Table 14-6, and the second daily dose of medication should be given no later than lunch time to prevent insomnia. Therapeutic doses may seem high, but are well tolerated in childhood. Generally, combinations of medications are not effective when a trial of each drug in high doses has been effective.

APPENDIX
Ketogenic Diet

1. The purpose is formation of ketone bodies.

2. The allowance of food must be weighed using a scale that records the weight in gm.

3. Meals are to be divided into three equal parts and eaten at approximately the same time every day to avoid wide fluctuations in ketogenesis.

4. To avoid fluctuations in ketogenesis, no part of any meal is to be saved and used at another. Patients are to be encouraged to complete a meal.

5. All preparations or foods with sugar, sorbitol, mannitol, hexitol, or alcohol added, or with carbohydrate value, are to be avoided unless specifically included in the list of foods allowed. Antibiotic and anticonvulsant syrups, toothpaste, and mouthwash are also excluded. Labels must be carefully read.

6. Vegetables may be weighed either after cooking or raw. They may be cooked in water with seasonings such as salt, sautéd in allowed fat, or used to prepare soup.

7. Meat should be free of flour, bread crumbs, gravies, or thickened sauces.

8. The following *may* be used in moderate amounts without weighing:

   a. Fat-free clear broth (bouillon)

   b. Juice of ½ lemon or lime

   c. Vinegar

   d. Chicory, endive, lettuce, parsley, and watercress

   e. ½–1 in. slice of a whole sour or dill pickle

   f. 1 or 2 small, red radishes

9. "Low" caloric beverages are not to be used. They may make an appreciable difference in the diet if used in excess because they have some carbohydrate food value.

10. The following may be chosen and used occasionally in addition to the diet:

    a. 1 level teaspoon of plain, powdered cocoa

    b. 1 piece of dietetic chewing gum

    c. Sugar-free Kool-Aid; add Sweet 10 (Pillsbury)

11. The following may be used as desired without weighing:

    a. Herbs, such as basil, thyme, dill weed, parsley flakes

    b. Salt, pepper, and spices for seasoning

    c. Garlic or onion salt

    d. Artificial sweeteners

12. Dietary supplements per day:

    a. Ca lactate, 300 mg PO tid

    b. Multivitamins, 1 capsule

    c. Vitamin C, 250 mg bid

    d. Vitamin B complex, 1 capsule

    e. Fe sulfate 300 mg PO

13. Diet prescription[1]:
    Ketogenic = gm of fat (K)
    Antiketogenic = gm of protein + gm of carbohydrate (AK)
    K/AK = 3/1

14. Meal pattern for toddler[2]:

	Grams	Calories	C (gm)	P (gm)	F (gm)
Breakfast					
Tomato juice, ¼ c	50	11.5	2.1	0.5	0.1
Saltine, 1	3	14.0	2.7	0.3	0.4
Butter, 2 tsp	10	73.3	0.04	0.6	8.1
Cream (36%), ½ c	115	437.0	3.5	2.3	41.4
Lunch					
Hamburger or roast beef, cooked	25	70.0		6.0	4.0
Butter	5	37.0			4.0
Spinach, raw	100	25.0	3.2	2.3	0.3
Butter	10	73.3			8.1
Sliced Tomato	25	5.2	0.9	0.3	0.1
Saltine	3	14.0	2.7	0.3	0.4
Butter	10	73.3			8.1
Cream (36%)	50	190.0	1.5	1.0	18.0

[1] Urine should be checked daily with a Ketostix indicator for presence of ketones.
[2] Infants may be maintained on Portagen formula supplemented with MCT Oil (both available from Mead Johnson).

	Grams	Calories	C (gm)	P (gm)	F (gm)
Supper					
Pork chop (cooked) or plain omelet	50	145.0		8.2	12.5
Egg	50	145.0		8.2	12.5
Cream (36%)	7	27.0	0.2	0.2	2.5
Butter	7	54.0			5.6
Cabbage	100	16.0	2.4	1.4	0.1
Butter	10	73.3	0.04	0.1	8.1
Cucumber	10				
Saltine	3	14.0	2.7	0.3	0.4
Butter	10	73.0		0.1	8.1
Cream (36%)	50	190.0	1.5	1.0	18.0
Frozen peach gelatin dessert (with MCT Oil; K/AK = 3.29/1)	50	51.6	2.15	1.62	4.74
	Totals	1498.4	21.13	23.15	181.89

15 Blood Disorders

I. HYPOCHROMIC MICROCYTIC ANEMIAS See Chap. 8, Sec. **VIII.C.1.**

A. Iron deficiency

  1. Etiology

    a. Inadequate stores provided at birth (prematurity, fetal-maternal bleeding, severely iron-deficient mother).

    b. Failure of dietary iron intake to keep up with increasing requirements of an expanding blood volume as the child grows (usually seen in the first few years of life in children with inordinately high milk intake > 1 quart daily).

    c. Iron loss (hemorrhage).

  2. Evaluation and diagnosis See Table 15-1.

Table 15-1. Findings in Iron Deficiency Anemia and Thalassemia Trait

Iron Deficiency	Thalassemia Trait
Decreased serum iron	Normal or increased serum iron
Increased iron-binding capacity	Normal or increased iron-binding capacity
Clear plasma	Yellowish plasma
Less severe RBC changes for any degree of anemia	More severe RBC changes for any degree of anemia
Decreased A_2 on hemoglobin electrophoresis	Increased A_2 on hemoglobin electrophoresis
Can occur in any ethnic group	Seen predominantly in groups of Mediterranean origin
Responds to iron	No response to iron
Iron replacement and maintenance therapy usually necessary	No therapy indicated or necessary; genetic counseling may be appropriate

    a. Hypochromic, microcytic smear, decreased serum iron, and increased iron-binding capacity; the iron-binding protein (transferrin) is less than 15 percent saturated. A quick and usually reliable bedside test is to look at the patient's serum in a spun hematocrit tube; in iron deficiency, it is strikingly pale.

    b. Hemoglobin electrophoresis shows a low hemoglobin A_2 level, but is otherwise normal.

    c. Bone marrow examination shows absent stainable hemosiderin.

3. **Therapy**   The goal of therapy is to replenish marrow iron stores as well as to achieve a normal hemoglobin value. Therefore treatment should be continued at least 3 months after normal hemoglobin level has been reached. Since dietary iron rarely provides sufficient replacement, a supplement is required. Oral therapy is preferred unless the patient is unable to tolerate it or the family is not considered sufficiently liable to administer the dose regularly.

   a. **Oral therapy**   The recommended therapeutic dose is 4–6 mg/kg daily of elemental $Fe++$. This should be given in 3 daily doses. Ferrous sulfate is probably the most effective and least expensive iron-containing drug. Since it consists of 20% elemental $Fe++$ by weight, the usual daily dose is 30 mg/kg.

   b. **Parenteral therapy**

   (1) The calculated total dose should aim at raising the hemoglobin concentration to 12.5 gm/100 ml and to provide additional iron (20% to replenish depleted body stores. The dose is calculated by using the formula

$$\text{mg } Fe++ = \frac{(\text{blood volume}) \times [12.5 - \text{observed hemoglobin}] \times (3.4) \times (1.2)}{100}$$

   where blood volume = 75 ml/kg and 3.4 = iron content in mg/gm hemoglobin.

   (2) Imferon, an iron-dextran complex containing 50 mg elemental $F++$ per milliliter is used for deep IM injection in the buttock. Since this dark-brown solution tends to stain superficial tissues, separate needles should be used for withdrawing it from vial and injection, and the Z-tract injection technique should be used. Adverse reactions include local pain, headaches, vomiting, fever, urticaria, angioneurotic edema, arthralgias, and anaphylaxis. **The total dosage should be spaced over 2–3 weeks, not to exceed 0.1 ml/kg/dose.**

B. **Lead poisoning**   See Chap. 3, Sec. III for a detailed description.

   1. **Laboratory findings**   Hypochromic microcytic anemia, basophilic stippling of the RBC on the Wright stain smear, and Pappenheimer bodies on Prussian blue stain smear.

   2. **Treatment** of the anemia should be delayed until the body burden of lead is reduced with chelation therapy as outlined in Chap. 3, Sec. **III.** It is important to remember that iron forms a toxic complex with dimercaprol (BAL), and **iron therapy should not be given concomitantly** with it. Replacement therapy following chelation may require administration of iron for up to 6 months.

C. **The thalassemias**   The thalassemias are hereditary defects in globin chain synthesis transmitted as autosomal recessive traits.

   1. **Beta thalassemia (homozygous condition)**   Inadequate production of beta chains in beta thalassemia leads to unbalanced production of alpha chains, and the excess alpha chains precipitate as intracellular inclusions. This leads to destruction of RBCs in the bone marrow (ineffective erythropoiesis) and marked shortening of the RBC life span. The RBCs that manage to reach the peripheral blood contain reduced hemoglobin levels and are therefore hypochromic.

   a. **Evaluation and diagnosis**

   (1) **Clinical manifestations** vary with the age of the patient and

the severity of the anemia. It is clinically undetectable in the early months of life, due to the relatively large amount of fetal hemoglobin present. However, as gamma chain synthesis recedes, normal beta chain production does not occur and anemia and hepatosplenomegaly develop. The characteristic facies is apparent by 1 year of age.

(2) Transfusion therapy leads to increased iron overload, resulting in hemosiderosis of vital organs and a bronzed complexion.

(3) Congestive heart failure due to myocardial hemosiderosis and chronic anemia is an important source of morbidity and mortality in these patients.

b. Treatment

(1) Transfusion with packed RBC (10–20 ml/kg) should be given at sufficiently frequent intervals to maintain a minimal hemoglobin of 7–8 gm/100 ml. Long-term effects of a hypertransfusion regimen started early in life are not yet clear.

(2) Iron chelating agents (e.g., Desferoxamine) have been utilized with varied results in an attempt to mobilize the increased iron stores. At present this is an experimental procedure and should be conducted only under a research protocol.

(3) Splenectomy The indications for this procedure are generally considered to be:

(a) Hypersplenism as manifested by neutropenia, thrombocytopenia, or increasing transfusion requirements.

(b) Symptomatology (e.g., "small stomach syndrome") resulting from marked splenic enlargement.

(c) Hypermetabolism by spleen, with generalized wasting.

(d) After splenectomy, thalassemic patients have a significant increase in risk of *septicemia*, especially if they are under 4 years old. The procedure should be deferred, if possible, until the child is over 4 because of this increased risk. Some advocate antibiotic prophylaxis after splenectomy (see Table 9-1, p. 180).

(4) Folic acid (1 mg daily) is useful in preventing megaloblastic crises induced by the rapid turnover of erythropoetic cells.

(5) These patients should not be treated with iron preparations because they already have increased tissue iron deposition and run the risk of hemosiderosis.

(6) Secondary conditions requiring supportive therapy include congestive heart failure, gallstones, and endocrinopathies.

2. Beta thalassemia trait (heterozygous condition) The major significance of this condition is that its presentation as a mild hypochromic, microcytic anemia frequently causes it to be confused with iron deficiency and mistakenly treated with iron. The major differential points are a normal or increased serum iron level and an increased hemoglobin A_2 on hemoglobin electrophoresis in thalassemia trait (see Table 15-1). Iron therapy is **contraindicated** in this condition unless there is concomitant iron deficiency.

3. **Alpha thalassemia (heterozygous condition)** Patients with this problem may have a hypochromic anemia similar to, but usually milder than, beta thalassemia trait. Anemia is rare.

4. **Alpha thalassemia (hemoglobin H disease)** In this form of alpha thalassemia, the abnormal gene from one parent is combined with a so-called silent carrier gene from the other parent.

   a. Affected patients have a moderately severe anemia (8–12 gm/100 ml) and an abnormal band on hemoglobin electrophoresis. The band corresponds to hemoglobin H (beta tetramer) and may total 12–40 percent of the total hemoglobin.

   b. The need for transfusion therapy will depend on the severity of the anemia.

D. **Chronic disease** is often associated with a mildly microcytic, hypochromic anemia unresponsive to hematinics.

II. **MACROCYTIC ANEMIAS** The most common causes are vitamin B_{12} and folate deficiency. Less common causes are antimetabolite therapy, hereditary orotic aciduria, liver disease, thiamine deficiency, sideroachrestic anemia, and Di Guglielmo's syndrome. Establishment of a correct etiologic diagnosis is of primary importance since incorrect treatment of B_{12} deficiency with folate may result in hematologic improvement, but progressive neurologic damage.

A. **Vitamin B_{12} Deficiency**

1. **Etiology** The causes may be intrinsic factor deficiency (congenital or acquired), congenital transcobalamin deficiencies, generalized intestinal malabsorption, selective B_{12} malabsorption, or resection of the distal ileum.

2. **Evaluation and diagnosis**

   a. Physical examination may demonstrate the neurologic signs associated with subacute combined degeneration of the spinal cord.

   b. Peripheral smear shows macro-ovalocytes, marked variation in RBC size and shape, and a high MCV (> 110). Although nucleated RBC may be present, there is a reticulocytopenia. Neutropenia and thrombocytopenia may also be present, as well as hypersegmentation of the polymorphs.

   c. Bone marrow examination shows megaloblastic erythroid maturation and giant metamyelocytes.

   d. Nonspecific laboratory findings may include a positive Coombs test, hyperbilirubinemia, and elevated LDH. The most specific findings are low serum B_{12} (except in transcobalamin II deficiency), an abnormal Schilling test, and a successful response to a therapeutic trial of vitamin B_{12}.

3. **Treatment**

   a. **Therapeutic trial** Give 1–3 μg vitamin B_{12} daily (IM) for 10 days. If the patient is B_{12}-deficient, his response will be as follows: within 24–48 hr the marrow will convert from megaloblastic to normoblastic morphology. Reticulocytosis should appear within 3 days and peak around the fifth day. Hemoglobin should return to normal levels within 4–8 weeks. (Although folate-deficient patients may respond to very high doses of B_{12}, they will not respond to this very low dose.)

b. Subsequently, 100 μg IM daily for 2 weeks should be given to replenish body stores; then 100–1000 μg IM once monthly for the rest of the patient's life or until the underlying disorder is cured.

c. Life-threatening hypokalemia may occur during early treatment, and serum K+ values should be carefully monitored.

d. A rise in serum uric acid frequently accompanies the reticulocytosis, usually reaching its peak at about the 4th day after the start of treatment. This may be prevented by allopurinol.

B. Folic acid deficiency

1. **Etiology** Body stores of folate are relatively small. Deficiency may be manifested within 1 month of folate deprivation, and full-blown megaloblastic anemia is seen within 3–4 months. Causes include dietary inadequacy, congenital and acquired malabsorption syndrome, antimetabolite therapy, and conditions that create a high folate demand due to increased hematopoiesis (chronic hemolysis, pregnancy, leukemia).

2. **Evaluation** This condition is often seen in infants with a history of poor growth, serious infection, chronic diarrhea, and goat's milk feeding. The neurologic signs associated with B_{12} deficiency are absent.

3. **Diagnosis** Hematologic findings are similar to those associated with B_{12} deficiency. The major differences noted in laboratory studies are a normal B_{12} level, low folate level, and normal Schilling test.

4. **Treatment**

   a. A therapeutic trial of folate consists of 20–200 μg folic acid IM daily for 10 days. If malabsorption does not appear to be a problem, this dose can be given PO. B_{12}-deficient patients do not usually respond to this small dose of folate.

   b. A dose of 1–5 mg PO daily for 4–5 weeks is usually adequate to replenish body stores even in patients with malabsorption. Patients with simple dietary deficiency can usually stop therapy at this point if they are on a proper diet, while patients with malabsorption or increased need for folate may require therapy indefinitely.

III. HEMOLYTIC ANEMIAS

A. Congenital hemolytic anemias

1. **Hereditary spherocytosis**

   a. Etiology This condition results from autosomal dominant inheritance. Erythrocytes are unusually susceptible to splenic sequestration and destruction, and the patient has a chronic hemolytic anemia that may manifest itself as early as the first day of life (neonatal jaundice).

   b. Evaluation

   (1) A peripheral smear shows small, round RBCs that lack the normal areas of central pallor.

(2) There is increased osmotic fragility and high mean corpuscular hemoglobin concentration (MCHC).

c. Treatment

(1) In general, the anemia is rarely severe enough to require transfusion, but, following viral infection, there may be a temporary slowdown of erythropoiesis, causing a sudden drop in hematocrit. Such aplastic crises are associated with an increase in pallor, a drop in bilirubin level and reticulocyte count and, if severe enough, cardiac decompensation. The process is usually self-limited but the patient must be observed closely until the return of reticulocytosis.

(2) Secondary folate deficiency may lead to a megaloblastic crisis unless prevented by a prophylactic administration of folate (1 mg daily).

(3) Splenectomy is the treatment of choice; it results in a decrease in bilirubin and reticulocyte count and a rise in hematocrit, despite persistence of spherocytes and abnormal osmotic fragility. If possible, splenectomy should be deferred until the patient is over 4 to lessen the risk of pneumococcal sepsis. Antibiotic prophylaxis should be considered after splenectomy (see Table 9-1).

2. Congenital nonspherocytic hemolytic anemias

a. Etiology   This is a heterogenous group of hereditary RBC enzyme defects.

(1) **Type of defect**   In some patients the Embden-Meyerhof pathway (e.g., pyruvate kinase [PK], triose phosphate isomerase) may be involved; in others, involvement is in the hexose monophosphate shunt (e.g., glucose 6-phosphate dehydrogenase, glutathione reductase).

(2) **Pattern of inheritance**   This varies with each enzymopathy. PK deficiency has an autosomal recessive pattern, while G-6-PD deficiency follows an X-linked recessive pattern. The latter is most commonly seen in males of Mediterranean origin and black males.

b. Evaluation   These conditions may present with hemolytic jaundice in the neonatal period, hemolytic anemia at any age, or gallstones. Acute hemolytic episodes following infection or exposure to oxidant drugs is characteristic of hexose monophosphate shunt defects (see Table 15-2).

c. Diagnosis   PK deficiency may be associated with burr cells, while hexose monophosphate shunt defects may be associated with Heinz bodies in the RBCs (brilliant cresyl blue staining). The precise diagnosis can only be made by assay for the specific enzyme defect.

d. Treatment

(1) Splenectomy may be useful in increasing the hemoglobin level in patients with Embden-Meyerhof defects. It is best deferred beyond the age of 4 years to reduce the risk of overwhelming sepsis. No treatment is needed in mild cases.

(2) In hexose monophosphate shunt defects, therapy consists mainly of avoidance of the large number of oxidant drugs that precipitate hemolysis.

Table 15-2. Drugs Provoking Hemolysis in G-6-PD–Deficient Red Cells

Acetanilid
Acetophenetidin (phenacetin)
Acetylsalicylic acid (aspirin)
N_2 acetylsulfanilamide
Antipyrine
Colamine
Fava bean
Furazolidone
Isoniazid
Naphthalene (moth balls)
Naphthoate
Nitrofurantoin (Furadantin)
Pamaquine
Para-aminosalicylic acid
Phenacetin
Phenylhydrazine
Primaquine
Probenecid
Pyramidone
Salicylazosulfapyridine
Sulfamethoxypyridazine (Kynex)
Sulfacetamide
Sulfisoxazole (Gantrisin)
Sulfoxone
Synthetic vitamin K compounds
Thiazolsulfone

(3) Occasionally, during a severe infection or after exposure to an oxidant drug, anemias may be sufficiently severe to warrant transfusion of packed RBCs. More commonly, adequate treatment of infection or discontinuation of the offending drug is sufficient.

3. Sickle cell anemia

a. Etiology The RBCs contain hemoglobin S, which consists of two normal alpha chains and two abnormal beta chains ($\alpha_2^A \beta_2^S$).

Hemoglobin S crystallizes on deoxygenation and produces morphologic disfiguration of the RBC. This is a hereditary disorder, affecting mainly blacks. (Approximately 10 percent of black Americans carry the trait, while 0.2 percent have the homozygous form of the disease.)

b. Evaluation

(1) There are no clinical manifestations of the disease until a high proportion of the RBCs contain hemoglobin S (at about 6 months of age).

(2) The earliest clinical presentation is often painful swelling of the dorsum of the hand or foot due to ischemic necrosis of the metacarpal or metatarsal bones.

(3) Other manifestations are hepatosplenomegaly, pallor, cardiomegaly, and icterus. Progressive episodes of infarction and scarring in the spleen cause it to shrink in size as the patient becomes older, and it is usually no longer palpable by adolescence.

(4) Laboratory findings These include severe anemia (hemoglobin 5–9 gm/100 ml), associated with bizarre RBC shapes ($0.5->20\%$ are in the sickled form), reticulocytosis (usually 10–20%), and variable hyperbilirubinemia. Exposure of the blood to a reducing agent (e.g., sodium metabisulfite) produces the characteristic sickling change. Hemoglobin electrophoresis demonstrates the abnormal band corresponding to hemoglobin S; no hemoglobin A is seen.

c. Treatment is palliative and revolves about the various "crises" that afflict these patients.

(1) Painful (thrombotic crises) These are produced by vaso-occlusive episodes due to plugging of vessels with sickled cells. The signs and symptoms depend on which organ's microvasculature is involved (e.g., bone, liver, spleen, gastrointestinal tract). Among the precipitating causes are infections, dehydration, acidosis, and hypoxia. Treatment consists of reversing these factors and providing analgesia.

(a) Adequate hydration is the mainstay of therapy. These patients, even when dehydrated, are frequently unable to concentrate their urine, so urine specific gravity should not be used as a guide to fluid therapy.

(b) Parenteral therapy is preferred if pain or dehydration are severe. Use half-normal saline containing 5% dextrose infused at a rate of 80–100 ml/kg daily. Sodium bicarbonate may be added to the IV fluid in sufficient quantity to raise the urine pH to 6.5–7.0 (see Chap. 4, Sec. II).

(c) Oxygen should be considered in severe crises, especially if there is concomitant pulmonary infection.

(d) In severe vaso-occlusive episodes (especially if the CNS is involved), dilution of the sickle cells with normal RBC has been found to be beneficial. This can be achieved by transfusions of packed RBCs (10 ml/kg), with or without concurrent phlebotomies, q12h until the hemoglobin is increased to 12–13 mg/100 ml or by performing a partial exchange transfusion with packed RBC. The risks are circulatory overload, isoimmunization, hepatitis, and increasing blood viscosity. If the sickle crisis has not terminated, the latter problem can lead to increased severity.

(e) Long-term transfusion therapy (to turn off production of hemoglobin S) should be seriously considered in children with neurologic foci of thrombotic crises. This involves the additional risk of hemosiderosis, however.

(2) Aplastic crises Infections can sometimes result in complete cessation of RBC production for 7–14 days, with disappearance of reticulocytes, a rapid drop in hemoglobin level, and decrease in serum bilirubin.

(a) These episodes are usually self-limited but, when anemia is severe or when symptoms of congestive heart failure are present, the patient should be slowly transfused with relatively fresh packed RBCs at a rate of 2–3 ml/kg q8h until the hemoglobin level reaches 7–8 gm/100 ml, and the cardiac status stabilizes.

(b) Oxygen should be given to dyspneic patients, but digitalization is usually not necessary.

(c) In cases of severe congestive heart failure, transfusion should be monitored by frequent CVP readings.

(3) Sequestration crises Sudden pooling of large amounts of blood in the spleen or liver may result in significant hypovolemia and marked organomegaly. Treatment must be prompt and directed toward correction of hypovolemia with plasma expanders or whole blood transfusion while monitoring the patient's CVP.

(4) Hyperhemolytic crises are probably not a frequent occurrence, but may occur when the patient is coincidentally G-6-PD–deficient and has an infection or is exposed to an oxidant drug. Treatment consists in appropriate antibiotic therapy if a bacterial infection is present, removal of an offending oxidant drug, and correction of dehydration and acidosis. If severe anemia is present, packed RBCs should be given slowly.

(5) Megaloblastic crises are due to the increased folate requirements of rapid erythropoiesis. Treatment with 1 mg folic acid per day is preventive.

(6) Miscellaneous problems

(a) Infection Patients with sickle cell disease have an unusual susceptibilty to pneumococcal sepsis and *Salmonella* osteomyelitis. This should be borne in mind when unexplained fever is present. The risk of overwhelming pneumococcal infection justifies strong consideration of penicillin therapy when unexplained significant fever or toxicity is present.

(b) Gallstones These are common in sickle cell patients after the age of 10. Surgical intervention must be carefully considered in patients with obstructive jaundice, fever, and abdominal pain because this constellation can also be produced by intrahepatic cholestasis secondary to sickling.

(c) Splenectomy is rarely necessary because of autosplenectomy due to multiple infarctions and fibrosis in the spleen. However, recurrent splenic sequestration crises or significant hypersplenism may be indications.

(d) In surgery in patients with sickle cell disease, general anesthesia must be approached with caution and with scrupulous avoidance of hypoventilation, hypoxia, acidosis, and dehydration. It is generally a good idea to increase

O$_2$-carrying capacity and dilute hemoglobin S (to < 40%) by slowly transfusing the patient preoperatively with packed RBCs (10 ml/kg). A sickle screen should be performed on all black patients prior to general anesthesia.

(e) Interactions with other hemoglobins Sickle hemoglobin may interact with other hemoglobins (SC) or thalassemias (S-thal) to produce a hemolytic anemia with milder symptoms. The incidence of crisis is less in these conditions, but sequestration crises of the spleen do occur. Retinopathy should be carefully watched for in older children with hemoglobin SC.

4. Other hemoglobinopathies

a. Hemoglobin C

(1) Evaluation This is a much milder condition than homozygous hemoglobin S disease. Among the symptoms seen are periarticular pain, abdominal pain, and hemorrhagic manifestations. Splenomegaly is present on physical examination.

(2) Diagnosis Laboratory findings include mild normochromic, normocytic anemia with many target cells present and a mild reticulocytosis (1–7%). A very slow-moving band is seen near the origin on hemoglobin electrophoresis.

(3) Treatment is symptomatic and transfusion therapy is rarely required. Splenectomy does not appear to influence the clinical course.

b. Unstable hemoglobins
These patients have a congenital hemolytic anemia associated with Heinz bodies in the RBC and an abnormal hemoglobin heat stability test. In general, these patients exhibit a mild, compensated hemolytic anemia; patients with hemoglobin Zurich can exhibit a marked increase in the hemolytic rate when challenged by an infection or an oxidant drug (see Table 15-2). Splenectomy is useful on some occasions.

B. Acquired hemolytic anemias

1. Autoimmune
The patient with this condition produces antibodies directed against his own erythrocytes that are demonstrable either on his RBC or in his plasma. This may occur secondary to collagen diseases, lymphoma, infections, drug therapy (e.g., penicillin, methyldopa, quinine), or any of a miscellaneous group of diseases. It may also be idiopathic.

a. Evaluation and diagnosis

(1) Routine hematologic studies show anemia associated with reticulocytosis. The *sine qua non* for diagnosis is the Coombs, or antiglobulin, reaction. A positive direct Coombs test indicates antibody coating the erythrocytes, a positive indirect Coombs tests indicates antibody in the patient's plasma.

(2) If the reaction is maximal at about 30° C, a "warm" antibody is present, which is usually of the 7-S globulin variety and requires addition of albumin to the RBC suspension in order to cause agglutination.

(3) "Cold" antibodies are of the 19-S variety, react best at low temperature, fix complement, and agglutinate RBCs in saline suspension.

(4) This differentiation is important for therapy, as patients with cold antibodies respond poorly to corticosteroid therapy or splenectomy and should avoid exposure to low temperature.

b. Therapy

(1) If secondary to a known disease or drug, therapy should be directed at this process.

(2) In addition, corticosteroid therapy is frequently useful in hemolytic anemia associated with warm antibodies. Prednisone 1–2 mg/kg daily up to 60–100 mg daily may be used. Several weeks may elapse before a favorable response is noted, at which time prednisone dosage should be very slowly reduced to the minimum amount necessary to keep the hemoglobin and reticulocyte count within an acceptable range.

(3) If the patient fails to respond to prednisone or requires an unacceptably high dose, splenectomy should be considered. If corticosteroid and splenectomy fail to control the process, immunosuppressive drugs should be considered.

(4) Blood transfusion is hazardous in these patients and should be used only if life-threatening anemia develops because the patient's anti-RBC globulin usually will cross-react with antigens on the donor RBCs and cause a hemolytic transfusion reaction. If the blood bank can identify a specific antigen against which the antibody is directed, blood may be given from a donor whose erythrocytes are negative for this factor. Otherwise, the unit of blood that is *least* reactive with the patient's plasma should be used and should be infused extremely slowly, with close monitoring of the patient for evidence of transfusion reaction.

2. Nonautoimmune

a. Etiology   This condition has multiple causes, including mechanical trauma from prosthetic heart valves, chemical agents and drugs, severe burns, and infections (malaria, *Clostridium welchii*).

b. Diagnosis   The Coombs test is negative. The smear usually contains many fragmented RBCs.

c. Therapy consists in treatment of the primary disease, as well as transfusion with packed RBCs when anemia is severe.

IV. ANEMIAS ASSOCIATED WITH PRIMARY BONE MARROW DISEASE

A. Aplastic anemia (pancytopenia)   There are two general types of aplastic anemia: constitutional and acquired.

1. Constitutional aplastic anemia, or Fanconi's anemia, is commonly associated with skeletal, renal, and pigmentary anomalies and chromosome breaks in lymphocyte culture. Some patients may have the chromosomal anomalies without the phenotypic ones; thus, chromosome studies are mandatory in all patients with aplastic anemia. Although this is a hereditary condition, the patients commonly do not show signs of hematologic disorder until after infancy. The most common presenting age for boys is 4–7 years and for girls, 6–10 years.

a. **Diagnosis** Pancytopenia, reticulocytopenia, and hypoplastic marrow associated with skeletal anomalies and chromosome breaks are diagnostic.

b. **Therapy**

(1) In addition to supportive care with RBCs and platelets when necessary, a combined administration of an androgen and a corticosteroid has been found to be successful in most cases. The usual plan of therapy is to give up to 5 mg/kg daily of oxymethalone and 1 mg/kg daily of prednisone until the hemoglobin is normal.

(2) These medications are then slowly tapered off until the hemoglobin falls below 12 mg/100 ml, at which point they are maintained indefinitely. These patients require continued therapy in order to maintain hematologic stability.

(3) Liver function tests should be monitored in patients on oral androgen therapy.

2. **Acquired aplastic anemia**

a. **Etiology** This condition may be secondary to hepatitis, radiation toxicity, drugs (e.g., chloramphenicol), or chemicals (e.g., benzene).

b. **Evaluation and diagnosis** Pancytopenia, reticulocytopenia, and marrow findings are similar to those in constitutional aplastic anemia. However, there is generally no family history of anemia nor phenotypic or chromosome anomalies.

c. **Therapy**

(1) Supportive therapy with RBCs and platelets as needed.

(2) Androgens and corticosteroids are also used as in constitutional aplastic anemia, but the response rate in acquired disease is much lower. However, when a response is obtained, it is often possible to taper off and then discontinue drugs completely.

(3) In severe cases bone marrow transplantation may be considered. This is still regarded as experimental and fraught with many risks, and it should be performed only in centers where personnel have experience with the technique. If transplantation is even remotely considered, non-RBC transfusions should be limited, related donors avoided, and washed, frozen RBCs used when RBCs are required.

B. **Hypoplastic anemia (pure red cell anemia, Diamond-Blackfan syndrome)**

1. **Etiology** The familial incidence suggests hereditary involvement, but no definite inheritance pattern has been established.

2. **Diagnosis** Anemia is associated with normal leukocyte and platelet counts. Reticulocyte count is low. Red cell indices may show slight macrocytosis. Bone marrow examination is diagnostic (an aspirate of normal cellularity containing normal myeloid elements and megakaryocytes, but with a striking paucity of erythroid cells).

3. **Therapy**

a. Corticosteroid therapy has been very effective in some cases, especially if begun early in the disease.

(1) Allen and Diamond recommend 30 mg prednisone per day as the starting dose. A response is usually seen within 2–4 weeks if the regimen is going to be successful.

(2) This dose should be maintained until the concentration attains normal or near normal levels, at which time, gradual tapering off of the dosage should be attempted. Growth retardation may be ameliorated to some extent by giving the prednisone on alternate days, once remission has been attained.

b. Patients who do not respond to prednisone can be supported with periodic transfusion of packed red cells, although this may lead to hemochromatosis or hepatitis.

V. ACUTE LYMPHOBLASTIC LEUKEMIA is the most common malignant disease of childhood, occurring in approximately 4 children per 100,000. Acute lymphoblastic leukemia accounts for 90 percent of childhood leukemias.

A. Etiology   The cause is unknown, although an association with viruses is common in similar animal models.

B. Diagnosis   There are multiple clinical presentations of acute leukemia in childhood. Whenever it is suspected, a bone marrow aspiration must be performed and the tissue examined by an experienced hematologist or pathologist.

C. Prognosis

1. The prognosis is constantly improving in acute lymphoblastic leukemia in children. At present, the projected 5-year survival is 50 percent for those children who receive optimal therapy. This end can be achieved if all children are treated in cooperation with Acute Leukemia Study Groups A and B or independent leukemia centers at research institutes.

2. A poorer outcome has been associated with the following: initial white blood count greater than 50,000, massive hepatosplenomegaly, CNS involvement at presentation, and age of onset of less than 1 year.

D. Treatment

1. Chemotherapy   There are approximately eight drugs now being used often in acute lymphoblastic leukemia.

a. Vincristine is the most effective single agent for inducing remission in acute lymphoblastic leukemia.

(1) Mechanism   Vincristine arrests blast cells in mitosis during the DNA synthesis phase.

(2) Absorption, metabolism, and excretion   Vincristine is poorly absorbed from the gastrointestinal tract; 90 percent is excreted via the liver into the biliary tract (T $\frac{1}{2} = <$ 10 min).

(3) Dose   Give 1.5–2.0 mg/M^2 IV once every 7 days.

(4) Toxicity   Vincristine is a **neurotoxic** drug and causes severe abdominal pain, constipation, and distention. This can be partially prevented with stool softeners and dietary precautions. Other toxic effects are alopecia, hyponatremia, neuritic pain, paresthesias, loss of deep tendon reflexes, footdrop, and other signs of muscular weakness, and hoarseness. Extravasation can cause severe local reactions.

b. Prednisone and other corticosteroids are second only to vincristine in induction of initial remission.

(1) Mechanism Corticosteroids cause the lysis of lymphocytes and also appear to interrupt cell cycles.

(2) Dose Give 40–60 mg/M² PO.

(3) Toxicity (See Sec. **IV.B.3.a**, p. 330.) A low-salt diet and the addition of an antacid are helpful in preventing some of these problems.

c. Methotrexate is a folic acid inhibitor.

(1) Mechanism Inhibits DNA synthesis.

(2) Absorption, metabolism, and excretion It is well absorbed PO and is excreted unchanged in the urine (T ½ = 2½ hr). This drug will accumulate in renal failure.

(3) Dose Give 3–30 m/M² PO, IV, IM; intrathecal, 12 mg/M² per dose.

(4) Toxicity Methotrexate affects the most rapidly dividing cells and thus causes gastrointestinal and bone marrow toxicity. If mouth ulcers occur, therapy should be interrupted until they have healed. Acute hepatitis has been described, as has a syndrome consisting of dyspnea, bilateral pulmonary infiltrates, and hypoxemia.

d. 6-Mercaptopurine is a purine analog (6-MP).

(1) Mechanism It interferes with DNA production by preventing purine synthesis.

(2) Dose Give 50–90 mg/M² PO daily. Give higher doses if given less often.

(3) Absorption, metabolism, and excretion It is well absorbed PO (T ½ = 90 min). Activated in the liver, excreted 60 percent metabolized and 20 percent unchanged via the kidneys, it slowly accumulates only in renal failure. In the presence of allopurinol, the degradation of 6-MP by xanthine oxidase is markedly inhibited, and the dose should be decreased by 50–75 percent.

(4) Toxicity Bone marrow suppression, occasional hepatitis, and hematuria have been reported.

e. Cyclophosphamide is a synthetic alkylating agent.

(1) Mechanism Active metabolites cause decreased DNA synthesis and a cessation of cellular division.

(2) Dose Give 75–200 mg/M² PO up to 450 mg/M² IV.

(3) Absorption, metabolism, and excretion Absorption PO is incomplete (80%). Activated and inactivated in liver (T ½ = 3–4 hr). Less than 25 percent is excreted unchanged in urine.

(4) Toxicity Bone marrow depression, hemorrhagic cystitis, anorexia, nausea, vomiting, alopecia, bladder fibrosis, and amenorrhea seem to be reversible in most cases. To avoid hemorrhagic cystitis give the drug in the morning, keep patient well hydrated, and encourage frequent voiding.

f. Cytosine arabinoside is a pyrimidine antagonist.

(1) **Mechanism** It interferes with the conversion of cytidilic to deoxycytidilic acid and thus inhibits DNA synthesis. Also, this drug appears to inhibit DNA polymerase and to increase the number of cells in a particular phase of cell division and facilitate their destruction.

(2) **Dose** The dose is variable.

(3) **Absorption, metabolism, and excretion** This preparation is poorly absorbed PO. By IV or the SC route the drug is rapidly metabolized by the liver (T $\frac{1}{2} = < 10$ min). It can be given intrathecally. There may be some renal metabolism, but it is excreted mainly as inactive metabolite.

(4) **Toxicity** Bone marrow depression, nausea, vomiting, diarrhea, stomatitis, and alopecia.

g. L-Asparaginase This is an enzyme obtained from bacteria, usually *Escherichia coli.*

(1) **Mechanism** Some leukemic cells require l-asparagine for growth. By depriving the cells of this amino acid, the susceptible cells will die.

(2) **Dose** Give 5000–10,000 U/kg daily. The dose schedule does not seem critical with this agent.

(3) **Absorption, metabolism, and excretion** This preparation is not absorbed, as it is an enzyme (T $\frac{1}{2} = 20$–44 hr; in the presence of hypersensitivity, this is significantly decreased). L-asparaginase is metabolized and there is no renal excretion.

(4) **Toxicity** may result from inhibition of protein synthesis or from hypersensitivity reactions to either the enzyme or impurities in the preparation.

(a) Toxic effects include fatty change in the liver, serious hypersensitivity in up to 15 percent of patients, hyperglycemia and rare ketoacidosis, pancreatitis, azotemia, hypoalbuminemia, and decreased coagulation factors. Many of these abnormalities will correct themselves as therapy is continued.

(b) By inhibiting the synthesis of liver enzymes, L-asparaginase may enhance the toxicities of other antitumor agents (especially vincristine).

h. Daunorubicin [anathracycline antibiotic (Rubicomycin)]

(1) **Mechanism** It forms complexes with DNA and inhibits DNA-dependent RNA polymerase.

(2) **Dose** Give 1–2 mg/kg per dose.

(3) **Absorption, metabolism, and excretion** It is not absorbed PO (T $\frac{1}{2} =$ about 3 hr). It is probably activated in vivo. Excretion is mainly via the kidney.

(4) Toxicity   This preparation depresses bone marrow, is cardio-toxic in a dose of 20 mg/kg or more, leads to hypotension and dyspnea and can be death. ECG changes are inconsistent and unreliable as guides to toxicity. Adriamycin, a newer derivative, appears to have less toxicity.

2. **Protocols**   Because specific protocols change from year to year, there is no "standard" treatment for leukemia. Children should be treated at a leukemia treatment center according to the protocol currently in use at that center, and no specific protocol will be recommended here. Other aspects of therapy, however, are discussed below.

3. **Emotional support**   Children with acute leukemia and their families require more than medication. It is important for one physician to establish close rapport with the family and be available to answer questions and to support the family through emotional as well as physical crises. Knowledge of the ever-improving prognosis is a constant source of hope to these families.

   After diagnosis and initial induction of remission, as much of the therapy as possible is administered on an outpatient basis, to avoid unnecessary hospitalization and to allow the child to participate in his usual activities. Parents should be advised not to be overly attentive to the patient at the expense of other siblings. When possible, any procedure contemplated is best explained openly and honestly to both patient and parents.

E. Complications

1. **Infections**   Bacterial infection is the most common cause of death in leukemic children in relapse. Gram-negative septicemia is the commonest septicemia seen at our institution and elsewhere. As treatment improves and prolongs life, there is an increasing population of partially and completely immunosuppressed individuals, who are prone to the more opportunistic infecting agents, e.g., viruses and fungi.

   a. Any child who is found to be clinically "septic" should be completely cultured and then started on broad spectrum antibiotics: oxacillin, 300 mg/kg, and gentamicin, 5 mg/kg, until cultures are returned, when only specific therapy need be carried out.

   b. *Pneumocystis carinii* pneumonia is being increasingly recognized in immunosuppressed individuals. Where suspected, a lung biopsy, bronchial washing, or tracheal aspiration should be performed and the specimen appropriately stained and examined (methenamine silver). The treatment is usually pentamidine isothionate, 4 mg/kg (see Chap. 10, Sec. **III.D.5.**).

   c. *Varicella infections can be lethal to immunosuppressed children;* thus susceptible children should avoid others with varicella or herpes zoster. If a susceptible child is exposed to either of these, he should receive zoster immune globulin (ZIG) (Table 9-5) or zoster immune plasma (ZIP) as soon as possible (see **E**, p. 186).

   d. Oral moniliasis should be vigorously treated with nystatin or gentian violet.

   e. In severely neutropenic children with infection, transfusions have been used with some success. These may be associated with transfusion reactions and, rarely, graft versus host disease.

2. **Bleeding** is usually associated with thrombocytopenia and is best treated with platelet transfusions, in a dose of 6 U/M², and given as required. Central nervous system bleeding is more likely to occur when there is a very high white cell count and a low platelet count. Disseminated intravascular coagulation (DIC) can occur "spontaneously" with infections and should be ruled out in any child who suddenly bleeds from multiple sites (see Sec. **VI.B**, p. 339).

3. **Hyperuricemia** can occur before therapy or as a result of it. Children with elevated WBCs and marked organomegaly are more prone to this complication. Uric acid levels should be obtained initially and be followed with treatment.

   a. It is our practice to start allopurinol, 10 mg/kg daily PO, together with initial therapy if the white cell count is elevated above 20,000 and also if massive tumor destruction is anticipated (e.g., massive hepatosplenomegaly).

   b. *Alkalinization of urine may aid in excretion. Uric acid nephropathy has been reported with childhood leukemia and can be fatal.*

4. **Central nervous system leukemia** has become much more prevalent as survival has been prolonged. The incidence is approximately 50 percent in patients who do *not* receive initial CNS prophylaxis as part of the *initial* therapy. The incidence of later CNS involvement has fallen to approximately 5–10 percent. The presentation may be silent or it may appear with increased intracranial pressure and papilledema, cranial nerve palsies, or peripheral neuropathies.

   a. If CNS involvement is suspected, a lumbar puncture should be done and the findings of elevated protein, decreased sugar, and pleocytosis are confirmatory.

   b. Therapy is usually with intrathecal methotrexate, 12 mg/M² q48h, until the CSF is normal. There are many complications of this therapy, such as bleeding and chemical arachnoiditis.

5. Other complications of leukemia are discussed in recent reviews of this topic (*Pediatr. Clin. North Am.* 19:1123, 1972; *Cancer* 30:1480, 1972).

VI. DISORDERS OF THE COAGULATION MECHANISM   Bleeding secondary to abnormalities of the coagulation mechanism may be due to deficiency of clotting factors, or to abnormal consumption of clotting elements.

A. Deficiency of clotting factors

1. Hemorrhagic disease of the newborn

   a. Etiology   Hemorrhage in the first few days of life occurs due to a relative deficiency of factors II, VII, IX, and X (the vitamin K–dependent factors). This follows from the patient's not receiving or being able to utilize vitamin K.

   b. Evaluation

   (1) Check the history for vitamin K administration.

   (2) Evaluate the patient's gestational age.

   (3) Determine the source and extent of bleeding.

(4) Prothrombin time (PT), partial thromboplastin time (PTT), platelet count.

(5) Specific factor assays.

c. Diagnosis

(1) The diagnosis is strongly supported by lack of vitamin K administration.

(2) The condition is more common in prematures than in full-term infants.

(3) Bleeding may occur from any site and with any degree of severity.

(4) The platelet count and fibrinogen are normal; PT and PTT are prolonged.

(5) Factors II, VII, IX, and X are decreased.

d. Treatment

(1) Prophylaxis

(a) Administer 0.5–1.0 mg natural vitamin K_1 IM (Aqua-MEPHYTON) or vitamin K_1 oxide (Konakion) to all newborns at birth.

(b) The synthetic form of vitamin K_1, menadiol, is felt to have less of a margin of safety than natural vitamin K_1.

(2) Corrective treatment

(a) Give 1–2 mg of aqueous colloidal suspension of vitamin K_1 slowly IV. A rise in clotting factors will be noted in 2–4 hr, approaching normal in 24 hr.

(b) For severe hemorrhage, transfuse with *fresh* whole blood.

(c) To replace vitamin K–dependent factors rapidly, administer 10 ml/kg of fresh frozen plasma IV.

2. Hemophilia (hemophilia A; factor VIII deficiency)

a. Etiology   X-linked recessive deficiency of factor VIII.

b. Evaluation

(1) Personal and family history.

(2) Physical examination.

(3) Activated partial thromboplastin time (APTT) and PT.

(4) Factor assay.

(5) Bleeding time.

(6) Platelet adhesiveness.

c. Diagnosis

(1) History and physical examination

(a) In most mild to moderate cases there is positive *family* history, but no *personal* history or stigmata, unless the patient has been exposed to trauma or surgery.

(b) In many severe cases there is no positive family history (de novo mutations), but the patient has a personal bleeding history dating from about 1 year of age or earlier.

(c) Most patients with mild to moderate disease and some with the severe form show no bleeding tendency during the neonatal period and early infancy.

(d) The older patient with severe hemophilia may show chronic joint deformities and contractures secondary to bleeding into joints and muscles.

(2) Laboratory studies

(a) The bleeding time is normal.

(b) The platelet count and platelet adhesiveness are normal.

(c) The PT is normal.

(d) The APTT is prolonged.

(3) Assay for factor VIII

(a) Mild deficiency: 5–30 percent of normal.

(b) Moderate deficiency: 1–5 percent of normal.

(c) Severe deficiency: < 3 percent of normal.

d. Therapy

(1) Factor VIII–containing materials For each U/kg of factor VIII administered, plasma levels will rise by 2 percent. Adequacy of therapy should be monitored with APTT. This becomes prolonged when factor VIII levels fall below 40 percent of normal.

(a) Fresh frozen plasma (must be type-specific or compatible)

i. The amount to be used is limited by volume considerations. Sufficient factor VIII levels to stop closed soft tissue bleeding (10–20% factor VIII) may be obtained, but not enough to stop surface bleeding.

ii. Dose 15 ml/kg initially and then 10 ml/kg q12h.

(b) Cryoprecipitate This plasma fraction is obtained by slow thawing of rapidly frozen plasma and dissolving in 10–20 ml supernatant plasma. It contains factor VIII concentrated approximately 20 times. Factor VIII content (expressed as units) in different containers of cryoprecipitate varies, depending on donor and manufacturer.

(c) Lyophilized factor VIII preparations Concentrations of factor VIII vary from 20 to 100 fold. Preparation from pooled plasma involves a greater risk of hepatitis when compared with cryoprecipitate, which is produced from single units of plasma.

e. Treatment of bleeding

(1) Bleeding into joints

(a) For minor bleeding (incipient hemarthrosis not requiring joint aspiration) a single dose of factor VIII concentrate (20 U/kg) will suffice. Immobilization with plaster splints is not usually necessary. If used, early mobilization is essential.

(b) For hemarthrosis with a swollen painful joint, administer 20 U/kg of factor VIII concentrate followed by ½ this dose q12h for about 2 days. **Aspiration** of the joint should be considered after the first dose of factor VIII. Immobilization for several days with splints may be necessary to prevent contractures. The joint should be slowly rehabilitated with physical therapy, serial splinting to gain full extension, and eventual weight-bearing.

(c) Prednisone (2 mg/kg daily for 3 days, then 1 mg/kg daily for 2 days) has been found useful in the management of hemarthroses by several groups of investigators.

(2) Other soft tissue bleeding

(a) Localized or early bleeding into skin or muscle responds to a single dose of factor VIII concentrate (20 U/kg). Ice packs may also be helpful.

(b) Bleeding into more vital areas such as the mediastinum, floor of the mouth, and retroperitoneum may require additional maintenance doses q12h for up to 48 hr.

(c) The use of traction or splinting must be considered in intramuscular hemorrhage to prevent contracture.

(3) Bleeding in surgery *Plasma alone is inadequate to increase factor VIII levels to a range safe for operation.*

(a) Administer factor VIII concentrate, 50 U/kg loading dose, followed by 25–30 U/kg q12h. Factor VIII must be administered for 7–10 days (the duration of wound healing). The dose may be decreased by ⅓ during the second week. Higher doses are used in brain surgery or in the presence of infection.

(b) EACA (antifibrinolytic) therapy is helpful in dental procedures (*Br. J. Haematol.* 20:463, 1971).

(c) Therapy should be monitored with APTT determinations.

(4) Bleeding from surface wounds

(a) Small skin wounds and minor epistaxis may respond to ice packs and pressure.

(b) The patient with severe lacerations should be treated like the patient with surgical wounds [see **(3)**].

(c) Gastrointestinal bleeding not involving the mesentery or retroperitoneum usually responds to 3 or 4 doses of factor VIII concentrate in amounts used for enclosed soft tissue bleeding. However, consider the need for diagnostic work-up for the cause of gastrointestinal bleeding.

(d) Hematuria, if mild, may stop spontaneously over a few days. Severe or persistent hematuria requires replacement therapy for 1–2 days with high doses of factor VIII sufficient to attain levels 50 percent of normal. **EACA is**

contraindicated in renal bleeding because of the risk of calyceal and ureteral clotting.

f. Complications

(1) Patients with hemophilia should avoid salicylates, antihistamines, and other drugs that interfere with platelet function.

(2) Inhibitors Antibodies against factor VIII develop in about 8–16 percent of patients receiving factor VIII transfusions.

(a) *Inhibitors rarely develop in patients who have had more than 100 days of replacement therapy without developing them.*

(b) The presence of inhibitors is suggested by failure of apparently adequate therapy.

(c) Patients with inhibitors should *not* receive factor VIII except in life-threatening situations when amounts of inhibitors are such that they can be overwhelmed temporarily with huge doses of factor VIII and when a hematologist familiar with this complication is available. Exchange transfusion or plasmapheresis may help lower inhibitor levels prior to replacement therapy.

(d) The use of antimetabolites to prevent or mitigate anamnestic antibody responses is still experimental.

3. Factor IX deficiency (Christmas disease, hemophilia B) is one-fifth as common as factor VIII deficiency. Clinically, the two diseases are very similar. Plasma levels can be raised from 0.5–1.5 percent with 1 U/kg of factor IX. Therapy should be monitored with APTT.

a. Plasma Regular bank plasma or fresh frozen plasma may be used, but is adequate only for treatment of enclosed soft tissue bleeding. The dose is 15 ml/kg loading with 10 ml/kg q12h.

b. Lyophilized factor IX concentrates

(1) These are made from pooled plasma and thus increase the risk that hepatitis will develop.

(2) For surgery, administer a loading dose of 40 U/kg, followed by 15 U q12h.

B. Disseminated intravascular coagulation (DIC)

1. Etiology

a. There is abnormal consumption of clotting elements, leading to their decrease and to thrombosis and bleeding.

b. Consumption may be initiated by any pathologic state that triggers the cascade of clotting elements at some point in its course.

2. Evaluation

a. In the setting of any conditions known to produce DIC, **unexplained bleeding** requires laboratory investigation with the tests listed in Table 15-3.

b. Physical examination should reveal evidence of bleeding, peripheral thrombosis, or both.

3. Diagnosis See Table 15-3.

Table 15-3.   Laboratory Evidence of Disseminated Intravascular Coagulation

1. Platelets decreased
2. Prothrombin time prolonged
3. Partial thromboplastin time prolonged
4. Fibrinogen decreased
5. Thrombin time prolonged
6. Fibrin split products: elevated titers
7. Microangiopathic changes on blood smear

4. Therapy

a. Treat the underlying disease.

b. Usually treat only if there is evidence of active bleeding in addition to abnormal laboratory values.

c. Heparin   Give 50–150 U/kg IV q4h until the patient is clinically stable and laboratory studies are approaching normal levels. Begin with lower doses. In refractory cases, constant infusion instead of administration by push may be helpful. **Note the following:**

(1) Heparin breaks the chain of consumption primarily by inhibiting activated factor X and thrombin.

(2) Adequate heparinization is usually characterized by a whole blood clotting time 2–3 times normal or an APTT of 60–80 sec 4 hr after the last dose of heparin (or at any time during constant infusion).

(3) Success of heparinization (cessation of DIC) is best monitored by following fibrinogen levels by a modified thrombin time. Platelet levels can also be followed, but their return is usually slower than that of fibrinogen.

d. Clotting elements may be administered as fresh frozen plasma, or platelets, or both, as needed, only *after* adequate heparinization has been begun.

16   Gastrointestinal Disorders

I. GENERAL PRINCIPLES

A. Socioeconomic factors Improvements in public health measures, knowledge of the physiology of fluid and electrolyte imbalance, and the advent of antibiotics have all contributed to a reduction in infant mortality from gastroenteritis in developed countries. However, in developing countries, antenatal care is still inadequate, and thus the incidence of prematurity and neonatal sepsis remains high. The decline in breast-feeding, as well as overcrowding, lack of refrigeration, and poor personal hygiene contribute to a high incidence of diarrheal disease. Inadequate medical facilities and delay in seeking medical attention further increase the mortality and morbidity of gastroenteritis by such serious sequelae as renal failure or permanent brain damage (cortical thrombosis). And poverty, ignorance, and other stresses of life can further depress maternal functioning in any setting.

B. Differential diagnosis Diseases of other systems (e.g., urinary infection) that may be characterized predominantly by gastrointestinal symptoms and nutritional failure must be excluded. Surgical conditions have to be differentiated from the medical diseases they may mimic (e.g., enterocolitis in Hirschsprung's disease or paralytic ileus in celiac disease). Last, one must question whether or not the therapy itself is responsible for the symptoms (e.g., superinfection following long-term use of antibiotics or nosocomial infections from indwelling catheters).

II. NONINFECTIOUS GASTROINTESTINAL DISORDERS

A. Malabsorption syndrome Differential diagnosis includes generalized disease states (e.g., cystic fibrosis or acrodermatitis enteropathica), specific enzyme defects (e.g., disaccharidase deficiencies or abetalipoproteinemia), and diarrheal disorders precipitated by foods (e.g., gluten intolerance and milk allergy). Congenital or acquired structural bowel abnormalities may lead to malabsorption. Malabsorption secondary to parasitic infection (e.g., *Giardia lamblia,* hookworm) may be seen in endemic areas or in travelers from such areas. Maternal deprivation may also result in a clinical picture difficult to differentiate from malabsorption. In older children, malabsorption may be associated with regional enteritis or ulcerative colitis.

The infant or child with malabsorption usually shows failure to thrive and abdominal distention and passes foul-smelling, pale, bulky stools (steatorrhea). At other times, when sugar intolerance predominates, the stools may be more watery (osmotic diarrhea).

1. Cystic fibrosis (See also Chap. 19, Sec. **VI.**) Cystic fibrosis is a common cause of maldigestion in children, with an incidence of approximately 1 in 1000.

a. Diagnosis is confirmed by analysis of sweat induced by pilocarpine iontophoresis that shows an excess amount of both sodium and chloride. [See Sec. **(4)a,** below.]

(1) The sweat test should always be performed on all siblings even though symptom-free, as cystic fibrosis is a genetic disease with an autosomal recessive mode of inheritance.

(2) Both the sodium and chloride are determined. Large discrepancies between the sodium and chloride should make one suspicious of the accuracy of the analysis.

(3) The average weight of sweat collected is close to 250 mg (S.D., ± 125). A sample weighing less than 40 mg would be considered too small for an accurate assay.

(4) Interpretation of sweat test

(a) In the presence of clinical symptoms, the finding of sweat chloride above 60 mEq/L or sodium above 60 mEq/L is consistent with the diagnosis of cystic fibrosis.

(b) Borderline patients A small number of children suspected of having cystic fibrosis fall into a borderline range with sweat chloride or sodium levels between 50 and 70 mEq/L. These children require repeated sweat tests and continued clinical observation, as well as a variety of other laboratory tests. If the result obtained is inconsistent with the clinical picture, the test should be repeated.

b. Therapy The aim of therapy for the digestive disorder in cystic fibrosis is threefold.[1]

(1) Adequate dietary and vitamin supplements

(a) Infants Adequate caloric intake must be provided; as many as 200 calories/kg/day may be necessary, since absorption is incomplete. The protein intake may be around 4 gm/kg per day. In severe malnutrition, Pregestimil (glucose, medium chain triglycerides, and casein hydrolysate) may be advisable. At other times a formula such as Nutramigen (lactose-free, with casein hydrolysate) is necessary.

(b) Older children Moderate restriction of fatty foods (butter, oils, peanut butter, potato chips, pastry, fried foods, ice cream) and use of skimmed (99% fat-free) milk is recommended. Preferably, the diet should also be high in protein.

(c) Salt intake (See also Chap. 4, Sec. **II.E.**) Hyponatremia and hypochloremia may develop when sweating is profuse, especially during hot weather, febrile episodes, or prolonged physical exertion. During these periods salt supplements are advised: first year, 1 gm per day; 2–3 years, 2 gm per day; over 4 years, 3–4 gm per day. (For

---

[1] *Guide to Diagnosis and Management of Cystic Fibrosis,* 1971; *Guide to Drug Therapy in Patients with Cystic Fibrosis,* 1972. National Cystic Fibrosis Research Foundation, 3379 Peachtree Road, N.E., Atlanta, Georgia 30326.

treatment of heat prostration, see Chap. 2, Sec. **IX.**) *If cor pulmonale is present, excessive salt is contraindicated.*

(2) Pancreatic enzyme replacement   Pancreatin is prescribed for a significant defect in fat absorption, and the amount of pancreatin prescribed may vary with each patient. Adequate replacement will produce a good growth pattern, a decrease in the number of bowel movements, and an improvement in stool consistency.

  (a) Small babies require approximately ¼–1 tsp of Viokase per feeding, or the contents of ¼–1 packet of Cotazyme. The powder is mixed with applesauce and given at the beginning of the meal.

  (b) In older children the dosage varies from 5–10 tablets of Viokase or 2–5 capsules of Cotazym per meal.

(3) Prevention and treatment of the secondary complications of pancreatic insufficiency

  (a) Meconium ileus   In approximately 10–15 percent of newborns with cystic fibrosis intestinal obstruction will develop at birth—so-called meconium ileus. **This is a surgical emergency** and requires relief either by Gastrografin enemas together with IV plasma if uncomplicated or by resection and end-to-side ileoileostomy if volvulus or atresia is present.

  (b) Rectal prolapse   Untreated cystic fibrosis is the commonest cause of rectal prolapse in children in the United States. Immediate treatment is symptomatic, and the prolapsed rectum should be replaced manually with a lubricated glove. Dietary therapy as described and measures to improve the pulmonary condition should prevent recurrence.

  (c) Hypoproteinemia, anemia, and hypoprothrombinemia may occur in small infants. Plasma infusions can be given, but improvement generally follows the addition of pancreatin and substitution of a protein hydrolysate formula (Nutramigen). Hypoprothrombinemia results from lack of the fat soluble vitamin K and sometimes occurs in infants on broad spectrum antibiotics and those fed on soybean formulas. **Treatment** is with vitamin K_1, 5 mg IM or IV. The prothrombin time can be repeated in 8 hr and if still prolonged, a further dose of 5 mg is given. Transfusion is rarely required.

  (d) Fecal masses and abdominal cramps   Small, hard, nontender fecal masses are sometimes found in the large intestine of patients with cystic fibrosis, most often in the right iliac fossa.

    i. Differential diagnosis includes intussusception and an appendiceal abscess masked by the broad spectrum antibiotics these patients take for prolonged periods.

    ii. Treatment is either with mineral oil, 2 tsp bid for children weighing over 25 kg, or dioctyl sodium sulfosuccinate (Colace), 5 mg/kg daily in 3 divided doses; and a standardized extract of senna fruit (Senokot) is given bid as follows: 1 month–1 year, ½ tsp; 1–5 years, 1 tsp; 5–15 years, 2 tsp. We have also used 10% *N*-acetyl cysteine PO as well as PR and, rarely, in refractory cases, a mixture of 50% Gastrografin and normal saline under the supervision of a surgeon and radiologist.

(e) Cirrhosis of the liver   Multilobular biliary cirrhosis occurs in 2–3 percent of patients with cystic fibrosis and leads to hypersplenism, varices, hypoproteinemia, and ascites. Should portal hypertension result in bleeding from esophageal varices, a shunt operation of the portal vein is indicated. Hypersplenism with leukopenia and thrombocytopenia may require splenectomy. The decision to operate will be dependent on the pulmonary status. A preoperative prophylactic tracheostomy is usually advisable.

(f) Diabetes mellitus   In over 1 percent of patients with cystic fibrosis, clinically significant diabetes mellitus develops. Management should follow normal therapeutic measures, except that allowance must be made for the poor absorption of ingested food (see Chap. 18, Sec. **V,** p. 397).

2. Celiac disease (gluten-induced enteropathy)   The incidence of celiac disease is about 1 in 3000. Typically, these infants thrive initially, and the onset of symptoms is rarely before 6 months of age. Irritability is common and, in contrast to cystic fibrosis, the appetite is poor. Older children may present with anemia and growth retardation.

a. Diagnosis   This is established by demonstrating malabsorption, characteristic changes in the small bowel mucosa and the subsidence of symptoms with a gluten-free diet.

Most authorities now believe that celiac disease is a lifelong condition and recommend a gluten-free diet permanently. In view of this restriction it is important to establish a definitive diagnosis initially. The evaluation should include biopsy of the small intestine.

b. Treatment

(1) Severe onset (celiac crisis)   The infant is usually admitted to the hospital with malnutrition and hypoproteinemia and sometimes with explosive gastroenteritis that has resulted in dehydration and electrolyte imbalance (*celiac crisis*). *Paralytic ileus* develops, aggravated by coincident hypokalemia, and hypovolemic shock results from dehydration. This is a critical situation requiring urgent therapy.

(a) Correction of *shock* by plasma expanders (see Chap. 2, Sec. **II.C.1,** p. 36).

(b) Intravenous fluids for correction of acidosis and electrolyte imbalance (see Chap. 4, Sec. **II**).

(c) Treatment for tetany, if present, with 2–5 ml 10% calcium gluconate, slowly (see Chap. 4, Sec. **C,** p. 93).

(d) Vitamin K, 5–10 mg IV to correct hypoprothrombinemia.

(e) **Corticosteroids** Hydrocortisone is given IV (10 mg/kg/24 hr); or oral prednisone (2 mg/kg/24 hr) may be given. Reduction should be slow—over 2–4 weeks, depending on clinical response.

(f) Several cultures of the blood, stools, and urine should be done over a 24-hr period, as *infection* usually precipitates a celiac crisis. *Antibiotics* should not be withheld if the child is critically ill.

(g) No food should be given by mouth for 24–48 hr. A *gastric tube* may be required if abdominal distention or ileus is marked.

(h) Low-fat, lactose-free **feedings** are started after 48 hours. Initially, milk is excluded. Pedialyte fluids and Jell-O can be supplemented with glucose and ripe bananas. The feedings are given at frequent intervals. A high-protein (4 gm/kg/24 hr), high-calorie (150 calories/kg/24 hr) intake is given as soon as it can be tolerated, using Pregestimil formula either ¼ or ½ strength; the strength and amount are increased as tolerated.

(i) Later, other foods are added, one at a time, including meat, cottage cheese, rice cereal, and fruit.

(j) Within 2–3 weeks regular milk can be slowly introduced. Fat restriction is no longer necessary. Multivitamins (0.6 ml daily) and folic acid (5 mg daily) are given for 4 weeks. A gluten-free diet (see Sec. **III.A**) is then continued and vitamins given according to normal requirements.

(2) **Nonsevere onset** Close medical follow-up is advisable initially, as anxieties and difficulties are frequent at this time. Several excellent diet books can be recommended for the mothers of celiac children.[1]

3. **Malabsorption of sugars** There are two types of sugar malabsorption: deficiency of one or more intestinal disaccharidases and disturbance in the transport of monosaccharides across the intestinal mucosa. Each type has a *primary* (congenital) form, as well as *secondary* (acquired) form (Table 16-1).

a. **Clinical features**

(1) Disaccharide and monosaccharide malabsorption show the same clinical findings, the main symptom being watery diarrhea.

(2) The onset of symptoms occurs when the offending sugar is introduced into the diet.

(3) In infants, the condition leads to dehydration and malnutrition. In older children, the symptoms are less severe, colic, flatulence, and diarrhea occurring when excess carbohydrate is eaten.

[1] *Celiac Disease Recipes.* The Hospital for Sick Children, Toronto, Canada; Sheedy, C. B., and Keifetz, N. *Cooking for Your Celiac Child.* New York: Dial Press, 1969; *Low Gluten Diet with Treated Recipes.* Clinical Research Unit, W. 4644, University Hospital, Ann Arbor, Michigan 48104.

Table 16-1. Clinical Forms of Sugar Malabsorption

Type of Malabsorption	Monosaccharide Malabsorption	Disaccharide Malabsorption
Primary (Congenital)	Glucose-galactose	Alactasia Sucrase isomaltase deficiency
Secondary (Acquired)	Enteritis (infancy) Celiac disease Malnutrition Surgical resection	Enteritis Malnutrition Celiac disease Cystic fibrosis Surgical resection

(4) Secondary disaccharidase deficiency accounts for the majority of cases of sugar intolerance seen clinically in infants. *Lactase* is the most important enzyme to be affected and the last to recover. Secondary disaccharide intolerance is possible in a variety of conditions (Table 16-1).

b. **Diagnosis** of sugar intolerance is by:

(1) Estimation of fecal sugar (15 drops of an equal mixture of liquid stool and water with 1 Clinitest tablet where greater than 0.5% sugar is abnormal).

(2) Oral sugar-loading tests with different mono- and disaccharides. Loading with the offending sugar (2 gm/kg) will result in a flat curve. **Caution: This test may provoke severe diarrhea.**

(3) Quantitative measurements of disaccharidase activity in biopsy specimens of the intestinal mucosa.

c. **Treatment**

(1) **Disaccharide intolerance**

(a) In **lactose intolerance,** all milk and milk products should be eliminated in the diet and a lactose-free formula such as Nutramigen or Isomil may be tried. Alternative formulas include Cho-Free[1] (a carbohydrate-free formula base; glucose can be added) or Pregestimil (glucose, medium chain triglycerides, and casein hydrolysate). Recovery usually occurs within a few weeks in the acquired type of lactose deficiency.

(b) In **primary sucrase, isomaltase deficiency,** the diet is more complicated, as sucrose is found in so many fruits, vegetables, and medications (Sec. **III.B**, p. 356).

(c) **Starch intolerance** is rarely of clinical significance.

(2) **Monosaccharide intolerance**

(a) In congenital glucose-galactose malabsorption, a fructose-containing formula should be devised.

(b) If the intolerance is *secondary,* a carbohydrate-free formula (Cho-Free) can be tried, with glucose given IV

[1] Syntex Laboratories, Inc., Palo Alto, California 94304.

initially to prevent hypoglycemia. Oral glucose can be slowly added to the carbohydrate-free formula as soon as glucose is tolerated.

(c) There is evidence that secondary monosaccharide malabsorption is related to the presence of abnormal bacterial flora in the small intestine. Thus duodenal intubation is advised to obtain intestinal fluid for bacterial culture and antibiotic sensitivities. If an abnormal flora is cultured, antibiotics are indicated. The drugs of choice are colistin sulfate (Coly-Mycin S), 5–15 mg/kg daily PO in 3 divided doses, or kanamycin sulfate (Kantrex), 50 mg/kg daily PO in 4–6 divided doses. Care must be taken to maintain normal renal function.

(d) Intolerance of all monosaccharides is sometimes persistent; if so, IV *hyperalimentation* should be considered.

4. Milk allergy

a. Clinical features

(1) Gastrointestinal allergy to cow's milk proteins becomes apparent in early infancy and is usually characterized by vomiting, failure to thrive, and diarrhea. A family history of extraintestinal allergy is often found. The degree of severity may range from relatively mild symptoms to fulminant diarrhea and circulatory collapse. The stools are often positive for gross or occult blood and contain mucus. Allergy to cow's milk protein is usually of limited duration, most patients recovering by the age of 2 years.

(2) Manifestations are not necessarily limited to the gastrointestinal tract. Atopic dermatitis, urticaria, angioedema, nasal allergy, bronchial asthma, and circulatory shock may also be caused by food hypersensitivity.

b. Diagnosis Laboratory investigations are often unrewarding,, but the following can be tried:

(1) Scratch testing and, if negative, intracutaneous testing. The reliability of testing in infants is poor, and skin irritability and dermographism commonly result.

(2) Serologic testing for milk antibodies. Their presence is not diagnostic and may be unrelated to milk allergy.

(3) Oral challenge with milk, or purified milk proteins (casein, bovine serum albumin, bovine gamma globulin, beta lactoglobulins, lactalbumin), or both. *These tests are not without risk,* and very small amounts of the challenge substance should be given, as **anaphylaxis** may ensue.

c. Treatment

(1) Infants with clinical allergic manifestations or with a family history of atopy should be introduced to new foods *slowly* and cautiously.

(2) Elimination of cow's milk from the diet (see **C**, p. 358) and substitution of a protein hydrolysate or soybean formula.

(3) Occasionally, multiple food allergies will be present and milk, wheat, and eggs should be excluded (see Sec. **III.A. C–E**).

(4) Corticosteroids (prednisone 1 mg/kg daily) may be required for short periods in resistant cases.

5. **Protein-losing enteropathy** is characterized by excessive loss of plasma proteins in the stools, with resultant hypoproteinemia. Mild or moderate malabsorption is usually present with intermittent diarrhea, steatorrhea, and malnutrition.

   a. **Evaluation** Although the list of causes is long, the following conditions are of special importance:

   (1) In acute enteritis, gluten-induced enteropathy, or giant hypertrophy of the gastric mucosa, the deficits are transitory and self-limited.

   (2) *Intestinal lymphangiectasia* may be accompanied by edema, chylous effusions, and ascites.

   (3) In patients with milk-related allergic gastroenteropathy, the protein loss is accompanied by anemia from stool blood loss and responds to an elimination diet (see **III.C**, p. 358).

   (4) A protein-losing enteropathy is sometimes found in iron deficiency anemia and will respond to treatment with oral iron.

   (5) Constrictive pericarditis and chronic volvulus are rarer causes.

   b. **Diagnosis** The diagnosis can be confirmed by degradation studies of albumin ^{131}I, using the PVP test with ^{131}I polyvinylpyrrolidine or ^{51}Cr-labeled albumin. These tests are often unreliable in small infants.

   c. **Treatment**

   (1) Plasma infusions may be helpful, but protein loss often continues unless the primary cause can be identified.

   (2) The primary disease should be treated by surgery, dietary elimination, or drugs, as indicated.

   (3) The patient should be given a low-fat diet (see Sec. **III.F**) and long-chain triglycerides should be replaced with *medium-chain triglycerides* (MCT Oil and Portagen milk formula).

B. **Irritable colon (chronic nonspecific diarrhea)** This syndrome is characterized by persistent or recurrent episodes of loose stools, occurring in children between the ages of 1 and 3 years. A family history of functional bowel symptoms is common. Often, one medication or dietary change will prove helpful, but only for a short period, after which relapse occurs. However, the prognosis is excellent, most cases resolving by 4 years of age.

   1. **Evaluation and diagnosis** *Differential diagnosis* is important and includes infective gastroenteritis and malabsorption syndromes such as cystic fibrosis and sugar intolerance. Stool culture and a sweat test are advisable and malabsorption must be excluded; if growth is normal, investigation should be minimal.

2. **Treatment**

   a. **Reassurance** should be given that the condition is benign and of *self-limited duration*. Precipitating factors and family tension should be discussed and explained.

   b. **Dietary alterations** are usually ineffective and if unsuccessful may further increase anxiety. Avoidance of excessive chilling of fluids can be tried.

   c. **Medications** (costives, antispasmotics, and opiates) are usually ineffective.

   d. A 10–21 day course of sulfisoxazole (150 mg/kg/24 hr in 4 divided doses) is sometimes beneficial. Diiodohydroxyquin (40 mg/kg/24 hr in 3 divided doses) is an alternative.

C. **Crohn's disease (regional enteritis)**

   1. **Clinical features**   Crohn's disease is a chronic inflammatory bowel disease, characterized by transmural involvement with granulomatous reaction, usually affecting the terminal ileum, but sometimes involving any section from duodenum to rectum. Complications such as adhesions, fistulas, intestinal obstruction, perienteric abscesses, and perianal involvement are frequent. Recurrent attacks of abdominal pain and diarrhea are common symptoms, but periodic fever, growth retardation, hypoproteinemia, anorexia nervosa, rheumatic fever, rheumatoid arthritis, and lupus erythematosus are also seen.

      The cause of Crohn's disease is still unknown, but immunological abnormalities and alterations in bowel flora are the subject of extensive research. Psychiatric factors are of importance, and children with this disorder are sometimes depressed with obsessive-compulsive traits and unresolved dependency conflicts.

   2. **Differential diagnosis** is mainly from ulcerative colitis, and Table 16-2 shows some of the main differentiating features. However, there is some overlap, and a minority of cases are impossible to classify distinctly.

   3. **Diagnosis**   Physical examination may reveal abdominal tenderness, palpable masses in the abdomen, or both, usually in the region of the right iliac fossa. Careful scrunity for perianal involvement is important. An upper gastrointestinal series with follow-through usually shows a characteristic radiologic change. A barium enema may also show colonic or terminal ileal involvement. Sigmoidoscopy is sometimes helpful.

   4. **Treatment**

      a. **Bed rest**, with avoidance of emotional tension and improvement in nutrition. Psychiatric assessment is informative, but psychotherapy alone is rarely curative.

      b. **A low-residue diet** is instituted. If marked involvement or longstanding malnutrition is present, the bowel can be *rested* either by parenteral nutrition or by an elemental diet consisting of monosaccharides, amino acids, vitamins, and minerals (Vivonex Elemental Standard Diet).

      c. **Multivitamins, iron, folic acid, and vitamin B_{12}** are given when there is clinical or laboratory evidence of deficiency or extensive intestinal involvement, or after ileal resection.

Table 16-2. Some Differentiating Features Between Crohn's Disease and Ulcerative Colitis in Childhood

Features	Crohn's Disease	Ulcerative Colitis
Fever	Often unassociated with other symptoms	Associated with other symptoms
Diarrhea	Usually *without* blood	Usually with blood
Abdominal pain and tenderness	Usually right-sided Mass in right iliac fossa (12%)	Usually left-sided No mass
Sigmoidoscopy	Normal in 70–90%	Abnormal in 95–100%
Complications:		
Fulminating disease	Rare	In 10%
Perienteric abscess	Common	Uncommon
Fistulas	In 25–50%	Rare
Perianal involvement	In 25–40%	In 8%
Growth retardation	In 25%	In 10%
Carcinoma	Rare	In (?) 10%
Treatment		
Favorable response to steroids and Azulfidine	In 25–50%	In 75%
Curative results of definitive surgery	Fair	Excellent

d. Corticosteroids Prednisone, 2 mg/kg daily, results in subjective improvement in over 90 percent of patients. Unfortunately, relapses can occur and may require increasing dosages. Alternate-day therapy can be tried. ACTH gel (0.8 U/kg/24 hr) can be used. The duration of therapy must be adjusted to the clinical response and the dose tapered off to the minimum that will control the disease; then, if possible, corticosteroids should be discontinued.

e. Salicylazosulfapiridine (Azulfidine) is sometimes beneficial (75–100 mg/kg/24 hr in 4–6 divided doses initially, followed by 40 mg/kg/24 hr in 3 divided dosages as maintenance), but side effects (nausea, headache, rash, and hematologic abnormalities) can occur. The drug is less effective than in ulcerative colitis [see **D.3.a.(3)**].

f. Antibiotics should be given parenterally if there is evidence of perienteric abscess formation: IV penicillin G (50,000 U/kg/24 hr in 6 doses) and IM kanamycin sulfate (6–15 mg/kg/24 hr). (See Table 9-2, p. 182.)

g. Surgery still appears to be necessary for the majority of patients with Crohn's disease. However, long-term follow-up studies on children operated on show that well over 50 percent have a recurrence. Prime indications for surgery are:

(1) Intestinal obstruction.

(2) Fistula formation or perforation.

(3) Abscess formation that fails to respond to antibiotics.

(4) Severe growth retardation may be a relative indication for removal of a localized lesion.

(5) Compression of the ureter.

h. **Immunosuppressive drugs** such as **azathioprine (Imuran)** are at present undergoing trials in this disease.

D. Ulcerative colitis

1. **Clinical features**   Ulcerative colitis, an inflammatory disease with an unknown cause, is characterized by recurrent attacks of bloody diarrhea and diffuse inflammation and ulceration of the mucosa and submucosa of the colon and rectum. Systemic complications include vascular phenomena, growth retardation, inflammation of the liver, renal stones, and arthritis. Local complications include hemorrhage, perforation, toxic dilatation, pericolitis, and increased incidence of carcinoma of the colon and rectum after 10 years.

2. The **diagnostic criteria** and some of the more important features differentiating it from Crohn's disease are summarized in Table 16-2.

3. **Treatment**   At present, the only certain cure for ulcerative colitis is surgical removal of the entire large bowel (panproctocolectomy), with establishment of a permanent ileostomy. However, most patients can be well managed by medical treatment. Attacks of ulcerative colitis vary in severity. As a general rule, an attack should be investigated as quickly as possible.

   a. **Severe attacks**

   (1) Hospitalization is imperative for correction of dehydration and electrolyte losses (especially potassium) by IV fluids (see Chap. 4, Secs. **II.E.2** and **III**).

   (2) Correction of anemia by blood transfusions. These should be repeated, if necessary, to maintain a normal hematocrit. Intramuscular iron dextran (Imferon) can be given if the serum iron is low (less than 65 mg/100 ml) (see Chap. 15, Sec. **I.A.3.a**).

   (3) **Corticosteroids,** although not curative, are highly effective, especially in the first attack.

   (a) Hydrocortisone is given IV 10 mg/kg/24 hr; then oral prednisone PO 2 mg/kg/24 hr, in 3 divided doses. Alternatives are ACTH (1.6 U/kg/24 hr IV in 4 divided doses and ACTH gel 0.8 U/kg daily IM).

   (b) Steroids are continued until the patient has been symptom-free for 1–2 weeks and then gradually tapered off by 5–10 mg per week to the minimum that controls the disease. If large doses of corticosteroids are required, consideration should be given to other forms of therapy.

   (c) Hydrocortisone (100 mg in 120 ml normal saline bid for 7–10 days) in retention enemas effectively controls ulcerative colitis limited to the rectum and the sigmoid and may relieve the rectal tenesmus associated with more extensive disease. **(Approximately 30–40 percent of hydrocortisone administered PR is absorbed systemically.)**

   (4) **Salicylazosulfapyridine (Azulfidine),** 75–150 mg/kg/24 hr, divided into 3–6 doses, is less effective than corticosteroid

therapy in controlling severe attacks, but is one of the main-stays of therapy in milder attacks and in prevention.

(a) Periodic sigmoidoscopy during administration is advisable. When endoscopic examination confirms satisfactory improvement, the dosage is reduced to a maintenance level (40 mg/kg/24 hr in 4 divided doses).

(b) If diarrhea recurs, the dosage should be increased to previous effective levels.

(c) With continued improvement, intermittent therapy can be tried—2 weeks on medication alternating with 1 week off medication. The intervals without medication are gradually increased, and salicylazosulfapyridine may sometimes be discontinued when remission from active disease has persisted from 1–3 years.

(d) Toxic effects include fever, rash, arthritis, thrombocytopenia, agranulocytosis, and aplastic anemia (see also **C.4.e**).

(5) Diet

(a) During the initial phase of intensive treatment, parenteral nutrition may be indicated.

(b) After a few days, a low-roughage, milk-free, high-calorie, high-protein diet is started. Vivonex 100 is sometimes beneficial (see **C.4.b**). Multivitamins are added.

(c) Folic acid (5 mg daily IM) and Imferon IM plus vitamin B_{12} (15 μg daily for 3 days, 7–15 μg weekly, and then 15–30 μg monthly) should be given if serum values are low (see Chap. 15, Sec. **II.A.B**, pp. 322, 333).

(6) Psychiatric problems Attention to the psychiatric problems of the illness and the relationship of the parents to the child are especially important.

b. Mild to moderate attacks

(1) Attempts should be made to **allay anxiety**, with particular attention to avoidance of the stress situation that may have precipitated the attack.

(2) A low-roughage diet is advisable.

(3) Salicylazosulfapyridine (Azulfidine) is indicated (75–150 mg/kg/24 hr in 3 divided doses). If bleeding continues, multivitamins (1 tablet daily), folic acid (5 mg daily), and oral ferrous gluconate (320–960 mg daily for children, 960–1920 mg daily for young adults) are prescribed.

(4) Failure to respond requires treatment as for severe attacks (see **3.a**, p. 351).

c. Preventing relapse

(1) Long-term maintenance therapy with oral corticosteroids in doses small enough to be safe are usually ineffective in preventing relapse. As a general rule, after an attack has been treated with corticosteroids, the dosage should be slowly reduced and then stopped completely.

(2) Maintenance therapy with salicylazosulfapyridine sharply reduces the relapse rate. If this drug is well tolerated, it is usual to continue treatment for up to 2 years.

d. Indications for surgery

(1) In the acute attack

(a) Perforation of the colon

(b) Toxic megacolon (usually)

(c) Massive hemorrhage (sometimes)

(d) Failure of improvement with intensive medical therapy, which may be for only a few days or for some weeks, depending on the clinical circumstance

(2) Chronic disease

(a) Frequent disabling attacks of chronic continuous symptoms leading to chronic invalidism or severe retardation of growth

(b) Carcinoma of the colon

(c) Risk of carcinoma of the colon

E. Constipation   Constipation is a common symptom in childhood and is usually the result of either faulty dietary habits or psychological problems, including those following toilet training (see also p. 23). Differential diagnosis includes anatomic defects (Hirschsprung's disease), local causes (anal fissures), metabolic disorders (hypothyroidism), or neurologic abnormalities (paraplegia). Diagnosis requires an accurate and detailed history, with special emphasis on the onset of symptoms and details of the neonatal period. Social data and psychological difficulties in the family may be of considerable relevance. An abdominal examination may reveal distention, or palpable masses (feces), or both and should always include a rectal examination.

1. Hirschsprung's disease (congenital megacolon)   This condition has an incidence of 1 in 10,000 individuals and has a high mortality when diagnosis is missed or delayed. Onset is usually in the neonatal period, with the presenting symptoms of abdominal distention and vomiting as a result of intestinal obstruction. In older children, constipation is the predominant symptom. Rectal examination reveals an *empty* rectum in contrast to acquired megacolon. Fecal soiling is unusual.

a. Diagnosis is by barium enema, which may demonstrate an aganglionic segment of large bowel; but a rectal biopsy is usually required for confirmation.

b. Treatment   Surgical referral is required for a *colostomy* to relieve obstruction. A *corrective surgical procedure* may be done at a later date when nutrition is satisfactory.

c. Complications

(1) Malnutrition is frequent as a result of intestinal obstruction, electrolyte imbalance, and poor caloric intake (see **A.3**).

(2) Enterocolitis is a serious complication, related to delay in diagnosis. *Colostomy* is the treatment of choice. Immediate supportive treatment includes IV fluids and antibiotics.

2. **Chronic constipation (acquired megacolon)** Patients with this condition are usually toddlers in whom chronic constipation leads to fecal impaction **(obstipation)** and later to fecal incontinence or soiling **(encopresis)**. Often, there is a history of constipation and colic going back to infancy. At other times, an anal fissure is the precipitating factor, or the onset may be related to attempts at bowel training. Psychological upsets, although sometimes difficult to elicit, are common and may be related to such events as the birth of a sibling or the absence of a parent.

   a. **Diagnosis** A careful history and physical examination excludes other causes of constipation. Abdominal examination may reveal mobile masses (feces), while on rectal examination the rectum is full of feces (in contrast to Hirschsprung's disease). Barium enema and rectal biopsy are usually not essential at the initial visit.

   b. **Treatment**

      (1) **Dietary advice** Increased roughage, fruits, and fluids.

      (2) **Psychotherapy** Explanation of bowel-training practices, sibling rivalry, and removal of precipitating factors.

      (3) **Stool softeners** Dioctyl sodium sulfosuccinate (Colace) 5 mg/kg/24 hr in 3 divided doses.

      (4) **Laxatives or bowel stimulants** Standardized extract of senna fruit (Senokot): 1 month–1 year, ½ tsp bid; 1–5 years, 1 tsp bid; 5–15 years, 2 tsp bid.

      (5) **Mineral oil** 1 tbsp bid is a satisfactory alternative to **(3)** and **(4)**.

      (6) Initially, large doses are essential until the stools are soft; the dosage can then be reduced. Regular daily dosage is continued for about 2–3 months and slowly reduced as tone and regular bowel habits are acquired. Relapses are common, and prolonged follow-up is advisable.

   c. **Complications**

      (1) **Fecal impaction** This usually requires enemas, although these are best avoided, if possible. Fleet enemas are effective (twice daily to start), and Colace and Senokot are begun at the same time.

      (2) **Failure of therapy (after 2–3 months)**

         (a) **Psychiatric problems** may be the cause, requiring psychiatric referral. Soiling is usually an indication for earlier psychiatric referral.

         (b) Occasionally, a **short segment form of Hirschsprung's disease** is present, and referral to a pediatric surgeon for rectal biopsy is advisable. This disease is clinically indistinguishable from acquired megacolon, except that response to medical therapy is poor.

III. DIETS

A. Gluten-free diet In addition to avoiding "gluten-containing" foods, foods containing large amounts of fat, roughage (such as raw fruits, vegetables) or gas-forming vegetables (such as cabbage, turnip, onions, peppers, Brussels sprouts) should also be avoided when beginning treatment. These foods may be added slowly to the diet as tolerated when symptoms begin to subside.

Type of Food	Foods Allowed	Foods Avoided
Beverages	Milk (skim milk may be better tolerated initially), fruit juice, cocoa (read label to see that no wheat flour has been added) Slowly add carbonated beverages (for adults, coffee and tea)	Postum, malted milk, Ovaltine, instant coffee, beer
Bread and crackers	Only those made from rice, corn, soybean, wheat-starch (gluten-free), potato, lima bean flours	All bread, rolls, and crackers made from wheat, oats, rye, barley, buckwheat, graham flours; muffins, biscuits, waffles, and pancake and other prepared mixes, dumplings, rusks, zwieback, breaded foods, bread crumbs
Cereals	Cornflakes, corn meal; hominy rice, Rice Krispies, puffed rice, precooked rice cereals	All wheat, rye, oat, barley, buckwheat cereals, Grapenuts, bran, kasha
Desserts	Gelatin, fruit gelatin, ice or sherbet, homemade ice cream, custard, junket, rice pudding, homemade cornstarch pudding, tapioca, cakes and cookies made from allowed flours	Commercial pies, cakes, cookies, pastries, ice cream, ice cream cones, prepared mixes, puddings
Fats	Oil, corn margarine, olive oil (unsaturated fats may be better tolerated initially) Later additions: butter, cream, vegetable shortening, bacon, lard	Commercial salad dressings except pure mayonnaise (read labels)
Fruits	All cooked and canned juices and fruit (include citrus fruit at least once a day) Initially avoid raw fruit, skins, seeds, frozen fruits, prunes, plums and their juices	

Type of Food	Foods Allowed	Foods Avoided
Meat, fish, poultry	All lean cuts (better tolerated if not fried)	Breaded, creamed croquettes; unless 100% pure meat, all processed or canned meats (e.g., cold meats such as bologna, meat-loaf, liverwurst, frank-furts, sausage); chili con carne; stuffings containing meat, fish, or poultry
Eggs	As desired. Avoid fried eggs	
Cheese	All types (add slowly to diet)	
Potato/potato substitute	Potato, rice	Noodles, spaghetti, macaroni, barley
Soups	All clear and vegetable soups; cream soups if thickened with corn-starch or allowed flours	Commercially prepared soups, soups containing barley or noodles, soups thickened with wheat, rye, oat, barley flours
Sweets	For good dental hygiene limit amounts of sugar, jams, jellies, marsh-mallows, molasses, corn syrup Slowly add chocolate or chocolate candy	Candy containing cereal products (read labels)
Vegetables	All cooked and canned Slowly add raw vegetables	Creamed, if thickened with wheat, oat, rye, barley products; strongly flavored vege-tables if they produce discomfort (e.g., baked beans, broccoli, Brussels sprouts, cabbage, cucumber, lentils, onions, peppers, radishes, turnips)
Miscellaneous	Gravies and sauces thick-ened with cornstarch or allowed gravy Slowly add peanut butter, olives, pickles, potato chips, nuts	Gravies and sauces thickened with flours

B. Diet for primary sucrase isomaltase deficiency

   1. Popular foods and the amount of sucrose they contain (in gm)

      a. Fruits

Banana	8.9–11.0	Apricot	5.5
Apple	3.1	Grape	0.2

Grapefruit	2.9	Pears	1.5
Cantaloupe	4.4	Pineapple	7.9
Honeydew melon	7.4	Plums (Italian)	5.4
Orange	4.2	Sweet	4.4
Orange juice		Prunes	2.0
(fresh)	4.7	Strawberries	1.4
Passion fruit		Tangerine	9.0
(frozen)	3.2	Tomatoes, canned	0.3
Passion fruit		seedless pulp	0.4
juice	3.8	Watermelon, firm	4.0
		Overripe	4.9

b. Vegetables

Beets	12.9	Onions	2.9
Cabbage	0.3 (raw)	Parsnips	3.5
Carrots	1.7 (raw)	Green peas	5.5
Cauliflower	0.3	Potato	0.1
Celery	0.3	Pumpkin	0.6
Corn	0.3	Radishes	0.3
Cucumber	0.1	Butternut squash	0.4
Eggplant	0.6	Sweet potatoes,	
Lettuce	0.2	raw	4.1
		Baked	7.2

c. Miscellaneous

Soybean flour	6.8	Almonds	2.3
Meal	6.8	Chestnuts	3.6–8.1
Ice Cream	16.6	Coconut milk	2.6
Sweet condensed		Peanuts	4.5
milk	43.5	Pecans	1.1

d. Cereals

Barley flour	3.1
Rice bran	10.6
Wheat flour	0.2
Wheat germ	8.3
Wheat grain	1.5

e. Packaged dried cereals are oven-roasted in sugar.

f. Bread   White bread contains ¾–1 oz of sucrose per loaf.

g. Peanut butter contains sucrose, but the amount is undetermined.

h. Syrups

Chocolate (dry)	56.4
Honey	1.9
Jellies, pectin	40–65
Starch	25–60
Maple syrup	62.9
Molasses	53.6

i. Canned foods contain sucrose as a preservative. Presweetened products, e.g., Kool-Aid and low-calorie beverages and foods, contain calcium cyclamate and sodium saccharin, an artificial sweetener. Taken in large amounts these foods can produce diarrhea.

j. Dietetic foods such as fruits and vegetables are unsatisfactory, as their natural sugar might be sucrose. Sugarless gum may be given.

k. Cheese products such as Cheese Whiz, cheese spreads, and cheese with additives contain sucrose. Margarine contains vegetable disaccharides. Bacon and ham and cold meats contain sucrose (they are sugar-cured). Mustard, relishes, catsup, Worcestershire sauce contain sucrose.

l. Cough syrups Most brands contain sucrose. (Cerose-DM is sugar-free and nonnarcotic.)

2. Foods allowed

Cheese	Spinach
Butter	Pretzels
Meats	Potato chips
Milk	Popcorn
Oatmeal	Salt
Bread "cassones" (Italian	Pepper
bread has no sugar)	Macaroni
Eggs	Saltine crackers
Potato	Fish
Asparagus	Tea
Broccoli	Buttermilk
Brussels sprouts	Tortellinis (in chicken broth)
Mushrooms	

a. Vitamins A multivitamin preparation containing sodium fluoride (1 daily).

b. Antibiotics Oral antibiotics, pediatric suspensions, contain approximately 2.5 mg sucrose per teaspoon. Given over a period of 3 or more days, they produce severe diarrhea and severe diaper rash. Penicillin (200,000 U and 400,000 U) is distasteful and cannot be disguised in anything sweet. Pediamycin Chewables containing erythromycin sulfate with cherry flavoring have no side effects.

c. Aspirin Baby aspirin has orange flavoring that contains sucrose. Given continually, it can produce diarrhea. Two given at the onset of fever and twice more in an 8-hr period are usually tolerated. Aspirin suppositories may be used in place of oral aspirin.

C. Milk-free diet

Type of Food	Foods Allowed	Foods Avoided
Beverages	Fruit juices, carbonated beverages, Kool-aid, cocoa without added milk solids, nondairy cream/milk substitutes For adults: coffee, tea	Milk: fresh, evaporated, condensed, dried, buttermilk; frappes, ice cream soda, "Great Shakes," Instant Breakfast
Bread and crackers	French, Italian, or Vienna Homemade French toast without added milk Uneeda Biscuits, saltines, graham, oyster, soda crackers, Triscuits	Breads, rolls, biscuits, muffins made with or enriched with milk solids (hamburg and frankfurt rolls), pancakes, waffles, dough-

Type of Food	Foods Allowed	Foods Avoided
		nuts, Pop-Tarts, milk-lunch crackers
Cereals	All types	
Desserts	Jell-O, water ice, popsicles, fruit pie (pie crust made without butter or regular margarine), tapioca, homemade cornstarch pudding, or junket made with fruit juice or milk substitute Milk-free cookies, such as fig bars, gingersnaps, lemonsnaps	Cakes, cream pie, cookies made with milk, ice cream, milk ice, sherbet, custard, commercial pudding mixes
Fats	Kosher margarine, lard, vegetable oil, cream substitutes such as Coffee Rich, Coffee-mate	Butter, margarine, sour cream, whipped cream, salad dressing made with milk, mayonnaise
Fruits	All types	None
Meat, fish, poultry	All types	Creamed meats, gravies, processed or canned meats such as luncheon meat, sausage, hash, frankfurts (unless 100% pure meat), commercial hamburgers
Eggs	All	
Cheese	None	All types
Potato or substitute (macaroni, rice, spaghetti)	All	Potatoes mashed with milk, butter
Soups	Clear soups, broth	Creamed soups
Sweets	For good dental care, limit amounts of sugar, jams, jellies, syrups, honey, candies such as gumdrops, Canada Mints, Planter's Jumbo Block, Good n' Fruity, Dots, Necco Wafers, Mason's Black Crows	Candies made with milk, chocolate, butter, or cream; butterscotch
Vegetables	All types	Those in butter or creamed sauce
Miscellaneous	Mustard, relish, catsup, salt, pepper, spices, peanut butter, gravy without added milk or cream, potato chips, pretzels, pickles, olives	Yogurt

Recipes may be obtained from:
125 Great Recipes for Allergy Diets
Good Housekeeping Bulletin Service
959 Eighth Avenue
New York City 10019 ($0.50)

Allergy Recipes
American Dietetic Assn.
620 North Michigan Avenue
Chicago, Illinois 60611 ($1.00)

D. Egg-free diet

Type of Food	Foods to Include	Foods to Omit
Beverages	Milk, cocoa, fruit juices, carbonated beverages, Kool-Aid	Eggnog, malted drinks
Breads	White, rye, or whole wheat bread; hot breads prepared without egg; saltines, graham, oyster, and soda crackers, Triscuits	Egg-enriched bread or rolls; doughnuts, waffles, pancakes, muffins
Cereals	All	None
Desserts	Fruit ices, sherbet, gelatin desserts; homemade desserts prepared without egg, such as puddings, junket, tapioca, fruit pies; gingersnaps, sugar crisps	Ice cream, custard, cakes, ready-mix puddings, meringue, icings, and cookies made with eggs
Fats	Butter, margarine, cream, lard, vegetable oil, special mayonnaise, gravy	Mayonnaise, salad dressings (check label)
Fruits	All	None
Meat, cheese, fish, or poultry	All	Meat, fish, or poultry processed with egg, or egg-coated; hash, fish sticks
Potato or potato substitute	Potatoes; macaroni, spaghetti, rice	Egg noodles
Soups	All	Soups with egg noodles
Sweets	Candy without eggs,[1] such as hard candy, lollipops; jam, jelly, sugar, syrups, honey	Marshmallows, fondants, nougats
Vegetables	All	Vegetables with egg sauce

---

[1] Examples of candy allowed on egg-free diet: gumdrops, Canada Mints, Planter's Jumbo Block, Jujy Fruit, Good n' Fruity, Dots, Mason's Black Crows, Hershey's Semi-Sweet Chocolate Bar, Mint Juleps, Banana Splits, Necco Wafers, Sugar Babies, Lifesavers.

Type of Food	Foods to Include	Foods to Omit
Miscellaneous	Salt, pepper, catsup, mustard, relish, steak sauce, pickles, olives	
	Potato chips, corn chips, nuts, peanut butter, pretzels, raisins	
	Royal Baking Powder	All other baking powder

E. Egg- and milk-free diet

Type of Food	Foods to Include	Foods to Omit
Meat, fish, or poultry	All except those with added eggs, cheese, or milk	Eggs, cheese; meat, fish, or poultry prepared or coated with egg or cheese; hash, fish sticks; processed meats such as frankfurters, sausage, and luncheon meats (unless guaranteed 100% meat)
Potato or substitute	Potatoes; macaroni, spaghetti, rice	Egg noodles
Soups	Tomato, vegetable and meat stock soups	Creamed soups; soups with egg noodles
Sweets	Candy without eggs or milk, such as hard candy, lollipops; jam, jelly, sugar, syrups, honey (for list of candies permitted, see **D**)	Marshmallows, fondants, nougats, milk chocolate, butterscotch
Vegetables	All	Buttered, creamed, or breaded vegetables; vegetables with egg sauce
Miscellaneous	Salt, pepper, catsup, mustard, relish, steak sauce, pickles, olives	
	Potato chips, corn chips, nuts, peanut butter, pretzels, raisins	
	Royal Baking Powder	All other baking powder

F. Low-fat guidelines

Type of Food	↓ Fat Foods (lower)	↑ Fat Foods (higher)
Beverages	Skim milk, cocoa powder, carbonated beverages, Kool-Aid, coffee, tea	Buttermilk, whole milk (evaporated, condensed), substitutes for coffee cream, cream
Bread	All types	Biscuits, muffins, cornbread, coffee cake, doughnuts, sweet rolls, pastries, griddle cakes, waffles, fritters

Type of Food	↓ Fat Foods (lower)	↑ Fat Foods (higher)
Crackers	Saltines,[1] oyster crackers,[1] Holland Rusk, Crown Pilot, Uneeda Biscuit, wheat wafers, sesame crackers, zwieback, Banquet crackers	Ritz, Triscuits, Triangle Thins, Vegetable Thins, Waverly Wafers, Wheat Thins, Royal Lunch
Cereal	All types	
Dessert	Boiled frostings or confectioner's sugar mixed with skim milk; popsicles, sherbet, water ice; tapioca or cornstarch pudding made with skim milk; fruit juice, fruit whip, Jell-O; angel cake; Dream Whip mixed with skim milk	Ice cream, pies, cakes and frostings, filled cookies, whipped cream, puddings, custards, prepared whipped toppings such as Cool Whip
Cookies	Arrowroot, gingersnaps, animal crackers, vanilla wafers, fig bars, Cowboy and Indians, Fruitana Raisin Biscuit, Iced Fruit Cookies, Golden Fruit, Cinnamon Wafers, Toy Cookies	
Fruit	All	Coconut, avocado
Fat	None	Butter, margarine, solid shortenings, lard, salt pork, oils, salad dressings, mayonnaise, sour cream
Meat	Lean cuts	Bacon, salt pork, spareribs, frankfurts, sausage, cold cuts, canned or processed meats
Fish	All	Fish canned in oil
Poultry	All	Duck, goose, skin of turkey or chicken
Eggs	3–4 per week	
Cheese	Skim milk cottage cheese	All other types (e.g., regular cottage cheese, Cheddar, American, spreads, dips)
Potato or potato substitute	Potato, macaroni, rice, spaghetti	Egg noodles
Soup	Clear broth,[1] bouillon,[1] fat-free soups (canned or homemade)	Creamed soups

Type of Food	↓ Fat Foods (lower)	↑ Fat Foods (higher)
	If soup contains fat leave refrigerated to remove solid fat	
Sweets	For good dental hygiene limit amount of gum, jam, jellies, syrups, molasses, honey, gum-drops, marshmallows	Fudge, chocolate; candies made with chocolate, butter, or cream
Vegetables	All	Vegetables in butter or creamed sauce and others that cause discomfort (e.g., cabbage, turnip, cauli-flower, onions)
Miscellaneous	Seasonings, soy sauce,[1] salt, relishes, vinegar, pepper, mustard, catsup, Worcester-shire,[1] chili sauce	Peanut butter
Snack foods	Pickles,[1] pretzels, plain salted popcorn,[1] fat-free gravy	Olives, potato chips, Fritos, corn chips, nuts, gravies, creamed sauces, yogurt, frozen packaged dinners, stuffings

[1] A good salt source. During the hot weather, add additional salt to food. Use in cooking to help replace sodium lost in sweat.

17 Endocrine Disorders

I. GENERAL PROBLEMS

A. Obesity

1. Etiology

a. Diet Total caloric intake is less important than caloric intake in relation to caloric requirements. The daily distribution of caloric intake is important, as some obese patients eat large quantities of food during times of stress, or eat without satiation.

b. Familial factors Often one or both parents are obese.

c. Psychological factors Both individual and family psychodynamics are important.

d. Metabolism Although many metabolic factors may be abnormal in obesity, their importance in its cause and treatment remains undetermined. Obese patients have a peripheral insensitivity to insulin, with a diabetic response to a glucose load, a compensatory hyperinsulinism, and increased lipogenesis with decreased lipolysis; some have impaired growth hormone release; and 17-hydroxycorticosteroids are in the high normal range in two-thirds, reverting to normal with weight loss.

2. Evaluation and diagnosis

a. Exogenous obesity This is a diagnosis of exclusion. It is supported by a history of abnormal diet, inactivity, or psychological problems and a finding of normal height.

b. Endocrine disorders These are rarely found in obesity, but may include the following:

(1) Cerebrohypothalamic lesions such as tumor, injury, or encephalitis may be diagnosed by other manifestations.

(2) Patients with Cushing's syndrome may exhibit centripetal obesity.

(3) Congenital and juvenile hypothyroidism may be diagnosed by history, physical growth, bone age retardation, or low thyroid function.

c. Syndromes The Prader-Willi syndrome, Pickwickian syndrome, and Laurence-Moon-Biedl syndrome include obesity as one of the parameters.

3. Treatment

a. Prevention is the best form of treatment. Since the number as well as the size of cells increases in obesity, lost weight is rapidly regained. Full parental cooperation and patient motivation are necessary. Frequent visits are required (biweekly is possible), and preferably to the primary physician.

b. Diet Most children will lose weight on a 1000-calorie diet. The meals should be balanced and properly spaced, attractive, and contain adequate protein.

c. Physical activity should be encouraged in all patients.

d. Psychological counseling, with attention to the patient's self-image, should be provided.

e. Hospitalization may be required at the onset in extremely obese children.

f. Medications Amphetamines and thyroid hormone administration are not of proved value and should not be used.

g. Goal Once weight loss has occurred, patients should be cautioned that continued effort is necessary to prevent regain.

B. Problems of growth and development Clinical measurements of growth and development include the measurement of changes in skeleton, such as length, body proportions, and epiphyseal development; changes in body composition, such as weight or the relative amount of muscle and adipose tissue; and changes in the sex organs and secondary sex characteristics.

1. Evaluation

a. Methods of measurement

(1) Length is measured up to 6 years of age and height after 6 years, using the Stuart growth charts. Height is measured with an anthropometer or with the patient standing against a wall, looking straight ahead. To be precise, longitudinal measurements should be made by the same person.

(2) Skeletal maturation is recorded by x-rays of epiphyseal centers for bone age (wrist and hand) and recording of head size, span, and upper/lower segment ratio. The lower segment is measured from the center of the pubic bone to the floor.

(3) Sexual development is recorded by measurements of the perpendicular diameters of the areola and breasts in females, or length and breadth of the penis and testes in males; by recording the presence of axillary, facial, or pubic hair; and by noting such estrogenic effects as pigmentation of the nipples, development of the labia minora, and paleness and type of secretions of the vaginal mucosa.

b. Sequence of sexual development See Table 17-1.

(1) It is important for diagnostic reasons to know that the first stage of puberty seen in boys is enlarging testes and that penis enlargement may not follow for a year or more. In girls, breast development is usually the first sign of puberty.

(2) Genital development correlates more closely with skeletal than with chronological age.

Table 17-1. Sequence of Sexual Development in Boys and Girls[a]

Boys		Girls	
Change	Average Age	Change	Average Age
Growth of testes and penis	10–11	Budding of nipples	9–10
Prostatic activity	11–12	Budding of breasts and growth of pubic hair	11–12
Pubic hair	12–13	Development of breasts, pigmentation of areolae, axillary hair	12–13
Rapid growth of testes and penis and subareolar nodules	13–14	Menarche	13–14
Axillary hair and voice change	14–15	Acne, deepening of voice	14–16
Mature spermatozoa and down on upper lip	15–16	Skeletal growth arrest	16–17
Acne, facial, and body hair	16–17		
Skeletal growth arrest	21		

[a] Adapted from *Arch. Dis. Child.* 44:291, 1969; 45:13, 1970. By permission.

2. Abnormal stature

a. Short stature This may be defined as a height below the third percentile.

(1) Etiology See Table 17-2.

(2) Evaluation

(a) The history includes an accurate perinatal history; parental and sibling heights; significant developmental milestones; past heights (from the private physician or school records); socioeconomic history; past illnesses and surgical operations; complete 24-hr dietary history; and a review of systems.

(b) **Screening tests** include a CBC, urinalysis, examination of stools for fat, chest x-rays; electrolytes, calcium, phosphorus, and alkaline phosphatase measurements; BUN, urine amino acid screen, and wrist x-ray for bone age. The need for more specific tests depends on the individual case.

(c) Observation of catch-up growth or development after a few weeks of hospitalization may reveal findings of diagnostic import.

(3) Diagnosis of constitutional short stature is based on the following:

(a) A height velocity that follows the percentile curves of a standard chart, even though the height attained is below the third percentile.

Table 17-2. Some Causes of Short Stature

Familial factors
  Constitution
Congenital factors
  Pseudohypoparathyroidism
  Prader-Willi syndrome
  Male Turner's, or Noonan's, syndrome
  Progeria
  Laurence-Moon-Biedl syndrome
Chromosomal disorders
  Down's syndrome
  Turner's syndrome
Intrauterine growth retardation
  Infection: rubella
  Environmental: placental insufficiency
  Congenital anomalies: Russell-Silver, Seckel's, Bloom's
  Congenital without associated anomalies
Skeletal disorders
  Achondroplasia
  Osteogenesis imperfecta
  Hurler's syndrome
  Hunter's syndrome
  Morquio's syndrome
  Rickets

Nutritional factors
  Low caloric or protein intake
  Persistent vomiting
  Malabsorption: celiac disease, cystic fibrosis
Endocrine factors
  Congenital or acquired hypothyroidism
  Growth hormone deficiency
  Corticosteroid excess
  Diabetes insipidus
Metabolic disorders
  Acidosis
  Unavailability of glucose
  Altered mineralization
  Fanconi's syndrome
  Galactosemia
  Glycogen storage disease
  Vitamin D-resistant rickets
  Aminoacidurias
  Inborn errors of metabolism
Chronic infection
  Tuberculosis

CNS disorders
  Microcephaly
  Mental retardation
  Diencephalic syndrome
Systemic disorders
  Hematologic causes:
    Chronic anemia
    Fanconi's anemia
  Cardiovascular abnormalities:
    Cyanotic congenital heart disease
  Pulmonary conditions:
    Asthma or bronchiectasis
  Gastrointestinal diseases:
    Regional enteritis or ulcerative colitis
  Renal diseases:
    Renal acidosis
    Chronic renal failure

(b) A family history of short stature.

(c) A bone age equivalent to height age and a negative history, physical examination, and, if indicated, laboratory evidence of other causes of short stature.

(d) The diagnosis of specific endocrine or systemic etiologies as determined by individualized laboratory tests in each case.

(4) Treatment of constitutional short stature There is no specific treatment. Many have a prolonged period of growth in adolescence and attain the predicted adult height. In all cases, counseling may be advisable, and, if maternal deprivation is associated, social service referral is made.

b. Tall stature

(1) Etiology Constitutional or familial tallness is the most common etiology. Pathologic etiologies that may be involved include acromegaly, cerebral gigantism, hyperthyroidism, testicular feminization syndrome, anovarism, Marfan's syndrome, homocystinuria, lipodystrophy, and neurofibromatosis.

(2) Evaluation follows the same guidelines as for short stature.

(3) Diagnosis A growth curve that follows the percentiles and has a normal velocity is supportive of a nonpathologic diagnosis, that is, of constitutional tall stature.

(4) Treatment of constitutional tall stature. Treatment is usually requested in girls. Parents must participate in the decision and must be willing to continue the treatment for at least 1–2 years.

(a) Treatment is started when the height reached is 2 in. less than desired.

(b) A conjugated equine estrogen such as Premarin is used at a dose of 10–15 mg daily. The oral progesterone, medroxyprogesterone (Provera), 5–10 mg daily, is given on the last 5 days of the menstrual cycle to effect withdrawal bleeding. Treatment is continued until complete epiphyseal fusion occurs, usually at a bone age of 16 years.

(c) Hormonal therapy has the associated effects of sudden development of secondary sex characteristics, amelioration of acne, and, occasionally, metrorrhagia and pigmentation of the areolar and nipple.

3. Abnormal sexual development

a. Delayed puberty and hypogonadism

(1) Etiology See Table 17-3.

(2) Evaluation

(a) History includes details of sexual development, age of sexual maturation of each parent, evaluation of previous growth data for the presence or absence of growth spurt, and CNS symptoms.

Table 17-3. Etiology of Delayed Puberty and Hypogonadism

Diagnosis	Females	Males
Idiopathic delayed puberty	Most common cause	Less frequent than in females
CNS-pituitary involvement	Tumor Congenital hypopituitarism Congenital lack of gonadotropins	Tumor such as craniopharyngioma Congenital hypopituitarism Congenital lack of gonadotropins
Fertile eunuch	. . .	Idiopathic Feminizing adrenal tumor Estrogen ingestion
Gonadal disorders: Primary hypogonadism	Congenital failure of development Surgical removal of ovaries Irradiation of pelvic area Gonadal dysgenesis, Turner's Mixed gonadal dysgenesis Pure gonadal dysgenesis Testicular feminization Stein-Leventhal polycystic ovaries	Traumatic or surgical castration Atrophy due to compromised vascular supply Acute orchitis of mumps after puberty, with functioning Leydig's cells Tubular failure with normal Leydig's cell function (cryptoorchidism, "Sertoli's cell only" syndrome) Failure of tubular and Leydig's cells (Kleinfelter's, Reifenstein's, male Turner's, anorchism)
Secondary to systemic disease	Congenital heart disease Chronic renal disease Chronic anemia, such as thalassemia, sickle cell Malnutrition, anorexia nervosa	Same systemic causes as in females

(b) Examination includes staging of sexual development.

(c) Investigations include bone age, skull x-ray, serum luteinizing hormone (LH) and follicle-stimulating hormone (FSH), serum estradiol, 24-hr urinary gonadotropins, 17-ketosteroids (KS), and estradiol.

(d) In females, a vaginal smear for estrogen effect is indicated, and exploratory laparatomy and biopsy of gonadal structures may be needed.

(e) In males, serum testosterone and testicular biopsy may be indicated.

(f) Evaluation of pituitary function is indicated and includes tests of human growth hormone (HGH) release, metyrapone test, and thyroid function tests.

(g) A buccal smear and chromosome analysis are indicated, the latter to diagnose the mosaics XXY and XYY.

(3) Diagnosis in the female

(a) **Idiopathic delayed puberty** is diagnosed when there is no secondary sexual development by about 16 years; no stigmata of the other entities in Table 17-3; FSH, LH, and 24-hr gonadotropins are in the prepubertal range; and there is no estrogen effect on the vaginal smear.

(b) **CNS tumors** may show, in addition to delayed puberty, growth retardation, headaches, nausea, vomiting, visual field defects, an enlarged sella, or suprasellar calcification.

(c) In **congenital hypopituitarism** there is no puberty and there is decreased function of the other pituitary hormones, but no evidence of CNS tumor.

(d) **Turner's syndrome (XO)** may be recognized in infancy by short stature, lymphedema over the dorsum of the hands and feet, and skin folds on the neck. Later characteristics are widely spaced nipples, broad carrying angle of the forearms, low posterior hairline, epicanthal folds, small mandible, and short, spadelike hands. The diagnosis is confirmed by finding XO or XO/XX on chromosomal analysis. The serum FSH and LS and urinary gonadotropins are elevated.

(e) In **primary hypogonadism** there is tall stature, no menarche, infantile external and internal genitalia, and scanty pubic hairs. Bone age is delayed, estrogen absent, vaginal smear infantile, and gonadotropin elevated, but the karyotype is that of a normal female.

(f) **Mixed gonadal dysgenesis** is diagnosed when the adolescent phenotypic female with primary amenorrhea has an enlarged clitoris, labial fusion, hirsutism, excessive masculinity, unusual acne, and a deepening voice. The karyotype may be XO or mosaic. Exploration for gonads and biopsy are indicated.

(g) **Pure gonadal dysgenesis** is diagnosed when the phenotypic female has normal or tall stature but absence of breast

maturation and primary amenorrhea with elevated gonadotropins. Exploration for gonads and biopsy are indicated.

(h) **Testicular feminization** patients are normal in stature or
tall, usually have a positive family history, normal breast
development but absent hair, no uterus, and a short or
absent vagina. The buccal smear is negative and gonadotropins are elevated. Exploration for gonads and biopsy
are indicated.

(i) **Stein-Leventhal syndrome** patients exhibit primary
amenorrhea or normal puberty, followed by amenorrhea
or menstrual irregularity, with hirsutism, obesity, and
sterility. On bimanual examination, enlarged ovaries are
found. Histologic examination shows enlarged ovaries
covered by a thickened collagenous capsule, beneath
which are many small follicular cysts.

(4) Diagnosis in the male

(a) **Idiopathic delayed puberty** is diagnosed when there is
failure of sexual development by about 16 years. As in
females, skull roentgenograms are normal, gonadotropins
prepuberal, and 17-ketosteroids normal. However, testosterone above 0.1 μg/ml is indicative of impending puberty.

(b) The diagnosis of **CNS tumors** and isolated gonadotropin
deficiency is the same as in females.

(c) **Idiopathic fertile eunuchism** is a rare disorder characterized by a eunuchoid appearance, small penis but testes
of normal size, sparse beard, scant body hair, high voice,
and decreased libido. Testicular biopsy shows active
spermatogenesis but a severe decrease in Leydig's cells.

(d) **Fertile eunuchism due to feminizing adrenal tumor** is extremely rare. Testicular biopsy confirms the diagnosis.

(e) **Cryptorchidism** is usually diagnosed before adolescence
by finding an empty scrotum. The testes may be palpable
in the inguinal canal. The buccal smear is negative and
the karyotype is consistent with that of a male. Exploration for gonads when testes are not found is indicated.

(f) A patient with **Klinefelter's syndrome** has the phenotype of
tall stature, and upper/lower segment ratio of less than
1:1, span greater than height, small testes but normal-
size phallus, and normal sexual hair. Associated findings
may include antisocial behavior, mental retardation, an
increased incidence of pulmonary disease, breast cancer,
and varicosities. The buccal smear is positive. Cytogenetic
studies are indicated to detect mosaicism. Serum and
urinary gonadotropins are elevated. Testosterone is low
or low normal. Bone age is retarded.

(g) A patient with **Reifenstein's syndrome** is a male herma-
phrodite who is a phenotypic male but with gynecomastia
and mild hypospadias. This entity is familial. The buccal
smear is negative, urinary gonadotropins are normal or
slightly elevated, and serum testosterone is decreased.

(h) A patient with **male Turner's, or Noonan's, syndrome** has the phenotype of Turner's syndrome but a small penis and small testes and no pubic, facial, or axillary hair. The buccal smear is negative.

(i) Patients with **anorchism** have eunuchoid proportions but no palpable testes and no secondary sex characteristics. On exploratory laparotomy, no testes are found.

(5) Treatment in the female

(a) Idiopathic delayed puberty is treated by reassuring both the patient and the parents.

(b) With **CNS tumor** the treatment is removal of the tumor and postoperative hormonal replacement as indicated.

(c) In **congenital hypopituitarism** treatment is started after a satisfactory linear growth has been achieved, usually at age 15 or 16. Premarin, 0.3 mg, is given PO every day for 6 weeks–3 months and gradually increased to 1.25 mg daily for 6–9 months. This produces development of the breasts and uterus. Subsequently, estrogen is given on days 1–21 and progesterone is added, 5–10 mg, on days 17–21, to induce cyclic withdrawal bleeding.

(d) Isolated lack of gonadotropin, gonadal dysgenesis, primary hypogonadism, secondary hypogonadism, mixed gonadal dysgenesis, pure gonadal dysgenesis, and testicular feminization   Estrogen replacement as in **(c)**.

(e) The following conditions require prophylactic gonadectomy to prevent malignancy: *gonadal dysgenesis, mixed gonadal dysgenesis, pure gonadal dysgenesis,* and *testicular feminization.* Patients with Stein-Leventhal syndrome are treated first with clomiphene, 50 mg PO daily for 5 days; after waiting one month for withdrawal bleeding, a second course is given if the first was not effective; or, finally, by wedge resection of the ovaries.

(6) Treatment in the male

(a) Idiopathic delayed puberty and **CNS tumor**   Treatment is as in females.

(b) Isolated deficiency of gonadotropin is treated by replacement with human chorionic gonadotropin (HCG), starting with small doses of 500–1000 U IM 2–3 times a week. After a few months, 25–50 mg testosterone enanthate IM every 2 weeks is started. This is subsequently increased to 200 mg IM every 2 weeks. Indexes of the success of this treatment are linear growth increase, enlargement of the testes and penis, and advancement of bone age.

(c) The **idiopathic fertile eunuch** is treated with 1000–4000 U HCG for 6–9 months as a single course, to stimulate interstitial cells.

(d) Cryptorchidism is treated by orchiopexy at about age 6. If the gonad cannot be brought down due to adhesions or small size, it should be removed to avoid malignancy. If the testes cannot be brought into the scrotum, prostheses may be inserted. If there is a failure of secondary sex characteristics, testosterone may be administered, 25–50 mg IM every 2 weeks.

(e) Klinefelter's syndrome patients should undergo laparotomy if the testes are not palpable in the scrotum. After a satisfactory linear growth has been achieved, testosterone therapy is started. Depot testosterone (enanthate, phenylacetate, or cyclopentyl proprionate) is started at a dose of 50 mg IM every 2 weeks; after epiphyseal fusion, it is increased to 200 mg IM every 2 weeks. The adult maintenance dose is 200 mg IM every 4 weeks. Signs of overdosage are acne, edema, and personality change.

(f) In **Reifenstein's syndrome, male Turner's syndrome, anorchism patients,** and **primary hypogonadism** treatment is testosterone.

b. Sexual precocity

(1) Etiology See Table 17-4.

(2) Evaluation This includes the following:

(a) A detailed family history with respect to the age of sexual maturation.

Table 17-4. Etiology of Sexual Precocity

Premature pubarche
Premature thelarche (in females)
Precocious puberty:
  Idiopathic
  Cerebral lesions causing pressure on or invasion of the thalamus:
    Brain tumor
    Pineal tumor
    Postencephalitic scar
    Tuberous sclerosis
    Neurofibromatosis
    Hypothalamic hamartoma
    Hydrocephalus
  Syndromes:
    Albright-McCune-Sternberg
    Silver's
    Precocious puberty and hypothyroidism
  Nonendocrine tumors producing gonadotropin:
    Hepatoblastoma
    Choriocarcinoma
  Medication, e.g.:
    Androgen (males)
    Estrogen (females)
  Genital, e.g.:
    Ovarian granulosa-theca cell tumor (females)
    Testicular tumor of Leydig's cells (males)
  Adrenogenital syndrome (in males), *adrenal hyperplasia, adrenocortical tumor*

(b) Physical examination, including staging of sexual development and investigation of CNS involvement.

(c) Laboratory tests include skull and wrist roentgenograms to determine bone age; determination of serum LH and FSH, estradiol, urine KS, and gonadotropins; a vaginal smear for estrogen effect and a pregnancy test in females, and serum testosterone in males.

(d) If indicated, a pelvic examination under anesthesia or culdoscopy may be done in females to rule out ovarian tumor, and a testicular biopsy may be done in males.

(3) Diagnosis

(a) Premature pubarche This is precocious development of sexual hair. No other secondary sexual characteristics develop. Adrenal hyperplasia or tumor must be ruled out.

(b) Premature thelarche is precocious development of one or both breasts. No sexual hair is present. Rectal examination is negative for masses, and menarche occurs at a normal age.

(c) Idiopathic precocious puberty is the most common diagnosis in precocious puberty, especially in females. The bone age is advanced, and gonadotropins are elevated. Pelvic examination reveals normal findings.

(d) In **precocious puberty due to cerebral lesions** there may be a history of convulsions, motor retardation, polyuria, obesity, cachexia, hypothermia, emotional lability, or evidence of visual, neurologic, or systemic involvement.

(e) McCune-Albright syndrome is precocious puberty with polyostotic fibrous dysplasia and café-au-lait spots.

(f) Silver's syndrome is precocious puberty in children of low birth weight and short stature, with congenital hemihypertrophy, a small mandible, and incurvation of the fifth finger.

(g) The syndrome of **precocious puberty** and **hypothyroidism** includes increased pigmentation, papilledema, an enlarged sella, and galactorrhea in some cases.

(h) Gonadotropin-producing hepatoblastoma is a rare cause of precocious puberty and presents with a mass in the liver.

(i) Gonadotropin-producing choriocarcinoma may be found in the pineal gland in prepubertal males or in the ovary. The pregnancy test is highly positive. Testicular biopsy shows hyperplasia of Leydig's cells and tubular maturation with spermatogenesis. Ovarian biopsy shows immature follicular cysts.

(j) Precocious puberty due to drugs may be diagnosed by the history. In females the areola may be darkly pigmented due to exogenous estrogen.

(k) Ovarian granulosa–theca cell tumor is diagnosed in females when an ovarian mass is palpable rectally and is confirmed by abdominal x-ray, an IVP, culdoscopy, and laparotomy.

(l) A **testicular tumor of Leydig's cells** presents an asymmetric mass in the testis and premature puberty. Testicular biopsy confirms the diagnosis.

(m) **Adrenogenital syndrome** is discussed in Sec. **IV.A.3.a.**

(4) Treatment

(a) In **premature pubarche and thelarche, idiopathic precocious puberty, McCune-Albright syndrome, and Silver's syndrome,** the treatment is reassurance that the child will be a normal adult. The parents are encouraged to treat the patient as a normal child. These children are otherwise immature, and care must be taken not to regard them as adult because of their sexual appearance.

(b) For **precocious puberty due to cerebral lesions**, treatment is directed to the lesion.

(c) In **precocious puberty with hypothyroidism**, treatment of the hypothyroidism usually results in regression of the puberty.

(d) With **drug-induced puberty**, withdrawal of the medication results in cessation of pubertal development and sometimes in regression of the puberty.

c. **Ambiguous genitalia** A newborn with ambiguous genitalia should not be assigned a sex without a diagnosis and determination of the most functional sex for that child. Changing the sex after a few years produces severe psychological and family problems.

(1) Etiology Ambiguous genitalia may be due to end-organ anomalies of the genitalia; the virilizing effects of exogenous hormones or congenital virilizing adrenal hyperplasia; or gonadal disorders such as Turner's syndrome, true hermaphroditism, male pseudohermaphroditism, or female pseudohermaphroditism.

(2) Evaluation

(a) Evaluation includes a careful history of maternal hormone ingestion or production, a genetic history, a buccal smear or cytogenetic studies, and 24-hr KS.

(b) If indicated, further studies include 24-hr pregnanediol and dehydroepiandosterone, retrograde contrast x-ray studies, surgical exploration if extragonadal causes are excluded, daily sodium and potassium determinations, and dermatoglyphics.

(3) Diagnosis The diagnostic approach is outlined in Table 17-5.

(4) Treatment

(a) **Sex assignment** In general, the sex assigned should be that most functional for the individual.

i. All female and most male pseudohermaphrodites and all true hermaphrodites should be given a *female* sex assignment, since they are capable of functioning as a

Table 17-5. Etiology of Ambiguous Genitalia. [Primary Abnormality Gonadal (A), Extragonadal (B).]

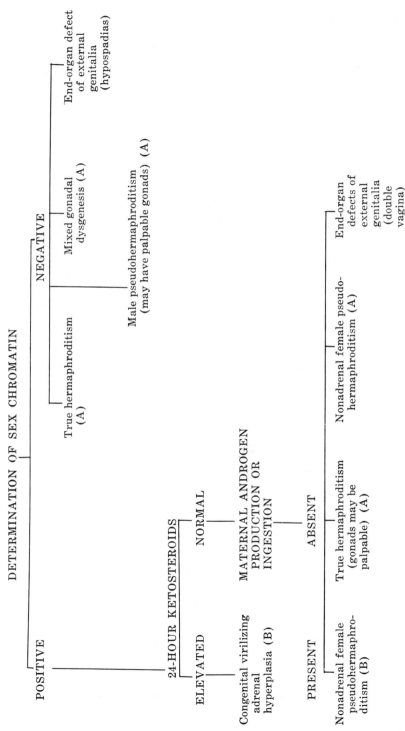

DETERMINATION OF SEX CHROMATIN

POSITIVE

NEGATIVE

True hermaphroditism (A)

Mixed gonadal dysgenesis (A)

Male pseudohermaphroditism (may have palpable gonads) (A)

End-organ defect of external genitalia (hypospadias)

24-HOUR KETOSTEROIDS

ELEVATED

NORMAL

Congenital virilizing adrenal hyperplasia (B)

MATERNAL ANDROGEN PRODUCTION OR INGESTION

PRESENT

ABSENT

Nonadrenal female pseudohermaphroditism (B)

True hermaphroditism (gonads may be palpable) (A)

Nonadrenal female pseudohermaphroditism (A)

End-organ defects of external genitalia (double vagina)

normal female after surgical correction of the external genitalia and removal of the testes.

ii. In **gonadal dysgenesis,** sex assignment depends on the development of the ducts and external genitalia. Such patients are most often reared as females, especially if there is an inadequate phallus, or if a vagina is present. Male sex assignment is given only if there is a penile urethra with complete fusion of labioscrotal folds and no female internal genitalia. If even a rudimentary vagina is present, the infant is reared as female.

(b) Surgery

i. In **female pseudohermaphrodites,** surgical correction is indicated if the defect will interfere with function. Clitoridectomy and preliminary vaginoplasty should be done when the child is between 3–6 months of age, in order to minimize psychological stress on both parents and child. When the patient is 16–20 years old, further vaginoplasty is done as needed.

ii. In **male pseudohermaphrodites** reared as males, devoloped breasts should be surgically removed, as testosterone therapy does not suppress such development.

iii. In **gonadal dysgenesis,** surgical therapy consists of correction of hypospadias and undescended testes, with removal of inappropriate female organs; or, alternatively, removal of the phallus and reconstruction of the vagina.

(c) Hormonal therapy

i. **Male pseudohermaphrodites** with scrotal testes, reared as males, require no treatment if virilization occurs. If they become feminized, testosterone enanthate, 50–100 mg IM every 2 weeks, is given after surgical removal of the breasts. A few may not respond because of an abnormality of extragonadal steroid metabolism or end-organ resistance.

ii. Patients with **structural gonadal defects, reared as males,** may also be treated with testosterone.

iii. Patients with **gonadal defects, reared as females,** should be given estrogen at adolescence. If the uterus is absent, Premarin is given PO in daily doses of 0.625–1.25 mg, continuously. If the uterus is present, cyclic therapy with the same dose for 21 days each month is given. If menstruation does not occur, or intermittent bleeding is a problem, progesterone may be added during the last 5 days of estrogen therapy.

(d) Psychological management Appropriate diagnosis and management is most important to minimize psychological problems. Parents should be fully aware of the therapy to be given and of its limitations. Some patients require psychotherapy during adolescence, to help them adjust to family or social life.

II. DISORDERS OF THE THYROID

A. Hypothyroidism

1. Etiology

  a. Congenital hypothyroidism may be due to agenesis or dysgenesis of the thyroid gland, a defect in hormone transport, or, rarely, thyroid-binding globulin deficiency syndrome. Hormone transport may be interfered with by an inborn enzymatic defect at the level of iodine trapping, organification, coupling, deiodination, or secretion; or transport may be interfered with by iodine deficiency or maternal ingestion of antithyroid drugs or iodides.

  b. Acquired hypothyroidism may be idiopathic, iatrogenic after thyroidectomy or radioactive iodine (RAI) treatment, due to thyroiditis, associated with isolated TSH deficiency or with hypopituitarism, or due to medications such as iodides, cobalt, fluorine, PAS, and resorcinol.

2. Evaluation of thyroid function

  a. Evaluation includes special emphasis on previous height and weight, determination of mental status, activity, pulse rate, and cold tolerance.

  b. Laboratory studies include roentgenograms to determine bone age and the presence of wormian bones and enlarged sella, T_3 and T_4 uptake, cholesterol, TSH, thyroid antibodies, carotene, RAI, and an ECG.

3. Diagnosis Hypothyroidism may present insidiously.

  a. In the **neonatal period,** one may find a prolonged physiologic jaundice, somnolence, lethargy, dyspnea, or feeding difficulty. There may be constipation, a protuberant abdomen and umbilical hernia, subnormal temperature, cold, mottled, and pale skin, a slow pulse, cardiomegaly, and a large tongue.

  b. In **infancy and childhood,** growth and developmental retardation become apparent. Delayed maturation is evident by an infantile facies, an upper/lower segment ratio inappropriate for the height age, delayed closure of the anterior fontanelle, depressed bridge of the nose, delayed dentition, and delayed sexual maturation. Myxedema becomes apparent in the thick tongue, hoarseness, and subcutaneous thickening about the neck, eyelids, genitalia, and the backs of the hands. The skin becomes dry and carotenemic, although the scleras are clear. The hair is coarse and brittle and the muscles hypotonic.

  c. The diagnosis is confirmed by a low PBI, T_3, T_4, and a low RAI uptake, and a high cholesterol.

  d. Hypothyroidism secondary to hypopituitarism is diagnosed if the TSH is low or absent.

4. Treatment The initial dose of desiccated thyroid is 15 mg PO, increased in 15-mg increments every 2 weeks to a full maintenance dose, which must be individualized. However, in children it is about 120 mg/M^2. The response to thyroid is indicated by an increased activity and appetite, slight weight reduction, improved circulation and warmer skin, and acceleration in linear growth.

L-Thyroxine is a product of more uniform potency, and this should be the *drug of choice* in equivalent potency of desiccated thyroid.

B. Simple nontoxic goiter   This consists of a diffuse thyroid enlargement, often found in girls at puberty, in clinically euthyroid patients.

   1. Etiology   The etiology is multifactorial and may include iodine deficiency, influence of goitrogen in the diet, genetic influences, and possibly an increased physiologic requirement for thyroid hormone, overstimulation by increased TSH at puberty, or ovarian hormones with a goitrogenic effect.

   2. Evaluation includes investigation for a history of possible goitrogen ingestion, a physical examination, and measurement of thyroid antibodies and T_4.

   3. Treatment   Treatment is reassurance, but, if the gland is very large, T_4, 0.1–0.15 mg daily, is given, resulting in a decrease in the output of TSH. Excision has the *disadvantage* of recurrence, scar, possible hypoparathyroidism, and hypothyroidism.

C. Thyroiditis

   1. Etiology   The etiology of thyroiditis most commonly includes chronic lymphocytic thyroiditis (Hashimoto's), a probable autoimmune disease; subacute thyroiditis (De Quervain's), probably a viral process; and acute bacterial thyroiditis, due to β-hemolytic streptococcus.

   2. Evaluation of thyroiditis includes determination of T_4, PBI, thyroid antibody titers (colloid and microsomal), and serum gamma globulin, and a WBC, ESR, and possible biopsy of the thyroid.

   3. Diagnosis

   a. Hashimoto's thyroiditis

   (1) The diagnosis is made clinically when a pebbly, firm, enlarged thyroid is found, with signs of either hyper- or hypothyroidism, predominantly in females age 6–16, with a positive family history of lymphocytic thyroiditis or other thyroid disease. It is sometimes associated with rheumatoid arthritis, diabetes mellitus, Addison's disease, myasthenia gravis, or ovarian dysgenesis.

   (2) The diagnosis is confirmed by thyroid antibodies in significant titer, needle biopsy evidence of lymphocytic infiltration between the thyroid follicles, and a PBI-T_4 disparity of 1–2 μg/100 ml. The RAI uptake is normal or borderline high.

   b. Subacute thyroiditis is diagnosed when the patient has a sore throat, malaise, fever, chills, and a tender thyroid with pain that radiates to the back and neck. It is confirmed by a high ESR but normal WBC, a low or absent RAI uptake, and edema, hyperemia, and lymphocytic infiltration on thyroid biopsy.

   c. Acute bacterial thyroiditis is diagnosed when the patient is febrile and has an untreated pharyngitis, an acute enlargement of the thyroid with extreme tenderness, and an elevated WBC but low RAI uptake.

4. Treatment

a. Hashimoto's thyroiditis is treated by total thyroid hormone replacement with 1–3 grains of desiccated thyroid daily to suppress TSH, continued indefinitely in the majority of cases. In a few cases, spontaneous remission may occur.

b. In **subacute thyroiditis,** the process is self-limited and lasts a few days to a month. The treatment is symptomatic, to relieve local symptoms.

c. In **bacterial thyroiditis,** treatment is with penicillin G (see Table 9-2, p. 182). The response is dramatic, with a decrease in size of the gland and disappearance of the symptoms.

D. Hyperthyroidism (Graves' disease, diffuse toxic goiter, exophthalmic goiter, thyrotoxocosis)

1. Etiology
These conditions are caused by excessive thyroid hormone secretion. The role of TSH and long-acting thyroid-stimulating hormone (LATS) is controversial. Extremely rare causes of hyperthyroidism include an autonomously functioning thyroid adenoma and hyperfunctioning thyroid carcinoma.

2. Diagnosis

a. The diagnosis is established by a history of increased appetite, weight loss, diarrhea, amenorrhea, irritability, restlessness, and findings of exophthalmos, lid lag (von Graefe's sign), inability of convergence (Möbius' sign), retraction of the upper eyelid and infrequent blinking (Stellwag's sign), tremors, sweating, smooth and flushed skin, muscle weakness, tachycardia, dyspnea, increased pulse pressure, and a firm, enlarged thyroid with increased neck circumference.

b. Laboratory tests confirming the diagnosis are elevated T_3 and T_4, and increased metabolic rate and radioiodine uptake.

3. Treatment

a. Antithyroid medication

(1) Propylthiouracil, 100 mg tid, or methimazol (Tapazole), 10 mg tid is given PO for 6 weeks, at which time the clinical evaluation and T_4 determination are repeated. If the child is euthyroid or hypothyroid, the frequency is reduced to bid. The child is reevaluated at 3 months and subsequently at intervals of 4–6 months, or whenever there is clinical indication of hypo- or hyperthyroidism.

(2) If, after 2 years of therapy, the patient is clinically euthyroid and has normal thyroid function tests, a T_3 suppression test is done. After 10 days of T_3 (75–100 μg), reduction of the RAI to less than half the initial value indicates that the disease is inactive. If so, antithyroid medication is discontinued.

b. Surgery is indicated if the patient is not taking medication, or if medication fails to control the symptoms. Complications of surgery include a transient or permanent hypoparathyroidism, paralysis of the vocal cords, hypothyroidism, and recurrence of thyrotoxicosis.

   c. Radioactive iodine is not recommended in children because of isolated cases of thyroid carcinoma following such treatment.

III. DISORDERS OF THE PITUITARY

A. Hypopituitarism

1. Etiology Hypopituitarism may be idiopathic or may result from craniopharyngiomas or other hypothalamic or pituitary tumors; the maternal deprivation syndrome; irradiation for tumors of soft tissue of the head, skull, or brain; infiltrations such as histiocytosis; or isolated pituitary hormone deficiencies.

2. Evaluation

   a. History This includes previous growth measurements, social development, previous irradiation or steroid administration, and CNS involvement such as headaches or vomiting.

   b. Physical examination includes fundoscopy and estimation of visual fields and, if indicated, an EEG, pneumoencephalogram (PEG), Sonar-B scan, and carotid angiogram.

   c. Laboratory tests include lateral skull and wrist roentgenograms for bone age, fasting blood sugar, HGH response either to arginine or to glucagon and propranolol, tests of thyroid function, serum FSH and LH, urinary gonadotropins, metyrapone test of ACTH release and adrenal reserve, serum osmolarity, and urine specific gravity.

3. Diagnosis

   a. Idiopathic The patient often presents with gradual growth retardation after 1 year of age and has a small triangular face, protuberant abdomen, and increased pectoral tissue. Later, puberty will be delayed. On skull x-ray, the sella may be small. The bone age is moderately retarded if there is deficiency of TSH, gonadotropins, or both. HGH is low or undetectable by radioimmunoassay.

   b. Maternal deprivation is diagnosed by history, an inadequate HGH release, and poor metyrapone response of ACTH, all of which improve with environmental changes.

   c. Other underlying conditions, such as developmental defect, infiltration, or tumor, are diagnosed by the systemic findings.

   d. Craniopharyngioma causes cessation of growth in a child whose previous growth curve was normal. The signs vary with the location, but often include headaches, nausea and vomiting, papilledema, scalp vein engorgement, VIth nerve weakness, and visual difficulty. It is diagnosed by calcification above an enlarged sella.

   e. Isolated growth hormone deficiency syndrome Patients with this syndrome have a normal birth weight and length, but impaired linear growth in the first year, with a final height of 125–145 cm. A tendency to spontaneous hypoglycemia may disappear by age 2–5 years. Features include normal proportions, protruding frontal bones, saddle nose, small hands and feet, thin sparse hair, slow nail growth, high-pitched voice, slow motor development, but normal intelligence unless severe hypoglycemia occurs. Puberty is delayed but normal.

f. Isolated FSH and LH deficiency   This may occur in developmental disorders of the CNS such as arhinencephaly, Friedreich's ataxia, or Laurence-Moon-Biedl syndrome, with primary adrenal insufficiency, or with Kallmann's syndrome. At puberty the secondary sex characteristics fail to develop, and linear growth continues unchecked, as there is no epiphyseal closure.

g. Isolated deficiency of ACTH is rare and presents with addisonian features and delayed, sparse, or absent sexual hair.

4. Treatment

a. HGH deficiency can be treated with HGH, 2 mg IM 3 times weekly, with evaluations every 3 months. However, this preparation is available only on a limited basis.

b. TSH deficiency is presently treated with thyroid replacement.

c. Gonadotropin deficiency is treated with chorionic gonadotropin, as described in Sec. **(5)**, p. 373.

d. ACTH deficiency is usually asymptomatic, and no corticosteroids are needed. However, in acute stress or major illness, hydrocortisone or an equivalent is given 2–3 times the normal cortisol secretion rate of 13 mg/M^2/24 hr, and during surgery the dose should be 10 times the secretion rate.

B. Hyperpituitarism

1. Etiology

a. Gigantism   This occurs when the epiphyses are open, whereas acromegaly, a disproportionate enlargement of the hands, face, and feet, occurs after epiphyseal closure. The cause is stimulation by excessive growth hormone. The lesion may be anterior pituitary hyperplasia, eosinophilic granuloma (most commonly), or amphophilic or chromophobe adenoma. It must be differentiated from cerebral gigantism.

b. Pituitary Cushing's, or Nelson's, syndrome   This is due to basophilic adenoma secondary to bilateral adrenalectomy for adrenal Cushing's disease.

2. Diagnosis

a. Gigantism

(1) Diagnosis is made when excessive growth or acral enlargement, prognathia, widely spaced teeth, and coarse and leathery skin are associated with persistent HGH over 15 µg/ml. Serum phosphate over 5 mg/100 ml is found. The x-ray films show an enlarged sella, enlarged mandible, hands, and feet, tufting of the terminal phalanges, and thickening of the vertebrae.

(2) Differential diagnosis must be made from *cerebral gigantism*, in which height, weight, and head size are above the 97th percentile, and the patient is mentally retarded, but with normal HGH as presently measured. The skull x-ray shows a high orbital roof, increased intraorbital distance, but normal-sized sella. The bone age corresponds to the height age. The EEG is abnormal, and the PEG usually shows somewhat dilated ventricles.

   b. Nelson's syndrome is diagnosed when an enlarging sella is found after bilateral adrenalectomy for adrenal Cushing's syndrome, on skull x-ray, arteriography, and PEG. Findings may include visual field defects, nerve palsies, and hyperpigmentation. The diurnal variation in the plasma cortisol and urinary 17-OH steroids disappears; ACTH secretion is elevated in the plasma and is not suppressed by dexamethasone.

   3. Treatment of hyperpituitarism is surgical removal, or stereotactic implantation of 90 yttrium or 192 iridium, cryosurgery, or irradiation of 3000–4000 r in 6–8 weeks. The treatment is followed by serial HGH measurement. Replacement therapy of other pituitary hormones may be required.

C. Diabetes insipidus

   1. Etiology   See Table 17-6.

Table 17-6.   Etiology of Diabetes Insipidus

A. *Insufficient secretion of ADH (neurohypophyseal DI):*
   1. *Idiopathic*
   2. *Infections:*
      a. Meningitis
      b. Encephalitis
      c. Measles, mumps, chickenpox, pertussis, tuberculosis
   3. *Tumors involving:*
      a. Suprasellar area
      b. Third ventricle
      c. Pineal gland
   4. *After surgical removal* of pituitary or hypothalamic tumors
   5. *Head trauma,* especially basal skull fractures
   6. *Reticuloendotheliosis*
   7. *Delay of maturation of the osmoreceptor mechanism* in infants
   8. *Hereditary:*
      a. Autosomal dominant
      b. X-linked
B. *Unresponsiveness of the renal tubules to* ADH *(nephrogenic DI)*
C. *Compulsive water-drinking (psychogenic DI)*

---

   2. Evaluation

   a. Patients with diabetes insipidus (DI) have a history of polyuria, diurnal enuresis, polydipsia, and a preference for water over milk. Constipation is common.

   b. Laboratory tests include determination of creatinine and BUN to rule out renal disease; fasting and 2-hr postprandial blood sugar to rule out diabetes mellitus; 24-hr fluid intake and output; a urine concentration test over several hours with simultaneous osmolalitis on the serum sodium and urine specific gravity or simultaneous osmolalities on the serum and urine, followed by a trial of aqueous vasopressin (Pitressin).

c. If DI occurs in a postoperative patient, follow-up includes an accurate intake and output balance, daily weights, specific gravity on every urine specimen, and frequent serum electrolytes and osmolarity determinations. A baseline developmental or I.Q. test should be performed.

3. Diagnosis

a. Neurohypophyseal DI is diagnosed when the history of polyuria and polydipsia is documented by failure to concentrate urine after water-withholding but ability to concentrate after vasopressin is administered. In nephrogenic DI there is no response to vasopressin. Compulsive water-drinking must be ruled out. These patients concentrate urine above 1.010 on water-withholding.

4. Treatment

a. Fluid replacement only may be sufficient treatment for all patients under 2 years of age, for patients with a partial antidiuretic hormone (ADH) insufficiency, and for patients with nephrogenic DI.

b. Reducing the solute load is helpful. This is done by limiting protein intake to 1 gm/kg daily, using a low-sodium milk, and low-sodium foods.

c. Vasopressin dosage must be individualized by the response.

(1) Vasopressin tannate (Pitressin tannate in oil), 1–5 U (0.1–0.5) IM every 3–5 days.

(2) Lysine vasopressin (Diapid) nasal spray is given at bedtime or as often as q4h, with the frequency determined by urine volume.

d. In postoperative DI, Pitressin tannate in oil may be used every other day, but signs and symptoms of water intoxication and cerebral edema should be carefully observed.

e. Chlorothiazide, 1 gm/M^2 daily, divided tid, is helpful in nephrogenic diabetes.

f. Chlorpropramide has been used in a few cases of nephrogenic DI.

IV. GYNECOMASTIA

A. Etiology

1. Idiopathic gynecomastia is the most common type and is benign.

2. Iatrogenic gynecomastia Percutaneous absorption, inhalation, or ingestion of even small amounts of estrogen may cause gynecomastia.

3. Pathologic gynecomastia may be due to interstitial tumors of the testis, feminizing tumors of the adrenal gland, Kleinfelter's syndrome, other types of testicular failure, chorioepithelioma, hepatic disease, or paraplegia.

B. Evaluation Evaluation includes a history of estrogen exposure, physical examination with observation of pigmentation on the areola and staging of sexual maturation, and individualized laboratory studies.

C. Diagnosis

1. In **idiopathic gynecomastia,** the buccal smear, karyotype, and sexual development are normal, but serum estradiol is elevated.

2. **Iatrogenic gynecomastia** is diagnosed from the history. Serum estradiol is elevated.

D. Treatment

1. **Idiopathic** Treatment is reassurance of spontaneous regression in a few months to a year. If massive enlargement or severe emotional disturbance results, surgical removal may be indicated.

2. **Iatrogenic** Estrogen withdrawal results in regression of breast enlargement.

V. DISORDERS OF THE PARATHYROID

A. Hypoparathyroidism

1. **Etiology**

   a. **Neonatal tetany** is described in Chap. 5, Sec. **VI.B.3,** p. 114.

   b. **Idiopathic hypoparathyroidism** may be seen in the neonatal period or at any time in childhood.

   c. **Di George's syndrome** is a developmental defect of the structures arising from the pharyngeal pouches and branchial arches.

   d. **Iatrogenic hypoparathyroidism** may result from thyroid surgery and may be transient or permanent.

   e. **Pseudohypoparathyroidism** is failure of the end-organs, the kidney and skeletal systems, to respond to parathyroid hormone.

   f. **Pseudopseudohypoparathyroidism** is a variant of pseudohypoparathyroidism, an X-linked dominant.

2. **Evaluation**

   a. **History** A complete history should be elicited, including a family history of similar symptoms and a maternal history of renal disease.

   b. **Physical examination** Special emphasis should be placed on neuromuscular irritability, examination of the lens for cataracts, the presence of loose teeth, and evaluation of mental status.

   c. **Laboratory studies** include x-rays, determination of total protein, pH, Mg (as some neonatal forms of tetanus respond clinically only when Mg returns to normal), Ca, P, alkaline phosphatase, BUN, urinary P and Ca, and, if needed, a Ca infusion and parathyroid hormone (PTH) infusion test. Hypocalcemia may cause a prolonged QT interval on the ECG. The following investigations are indicated because multiple glands may be involved.

3. **Diagnosis**

   a. **Hypoparathyroidism** in the older child presents with signs of irritability such as Chvostek's sign (a twitching of the facial muscles when a sharp tap is given over the facial nerve anterior to the ear) or Trousseau's sign (carpal spasm produced after 3–4 min of application of a blood pressure cuff slightly over the systolic pressure); laryngospasm, which may mimic croup; muscular cramps, numbness, stiffness, tingling of the hands and feet; and headache, vomiting, signs of increased intracranial pressure, and convulsions.

b. Associated findings may include mental retardation, seizures, mucocutaneous candidiasis, soft, irregular teeth, dry skin, cataracts, alopecia, steatorrhea, Addison's disease, Hashimoto's thyroiditis, pernicious anemia, primary gonadal insufficiency, or hepatitis.

c. Confirmatory laboratory tests include low serum Ca (below 9 mg/100 ml), normal Mg (1.9–2.5 mg/100 ml), and elevated P (over 4.5 mg/100 ml). On Ca infusion of 30 mg/kg over 8 hr, a marked phosphate diuresis is seen in every 8-hr urine collection, with a transient rise in serum calcium and fall in serum phosphate. The PTH infusion test of 5 mg/kg over an hour followed by PTH IM q8h for 3 days results in a 10-fold rise in urinary phosphate excretion, a rise in serum Ca, and a fall of serum phosphate.

d. Di George's syndrome is recognized by the susceptibility to viral and mycotic infections, absent cellular immunity, lack of phytohemagglutination stimulation of the lymphocytes, and absent thymus, seen on x-ray. There may be malformation of the great vessels, and a double aortic arch.

e. Pseudohypoparathyroidism is a failure of the end-organs to respond to parathyroid hormone, as seen by the failure of response to the PTH infusion test. These patients have profound growth failure, with obesity, round face, shortened first, fourth, and fifth metacarpals and first and fifth metatarsals, thickening of the calvaria, exostoses, bowing, generalized demineralization, calcification of the basal ganglia, lenticular calcification, and mental retardation.

f. Pseudopseudohypoparathyroidism has the phenotype of pseudohypoparathyroidism but a normal serum Ca and P level and is inherited as an X-linked dominant.

4. Treatment   See also Chap. 4, Sec. I.

a. Acute **hypocalcemia** is treated with 1 ml/kg 10% calcium gluconate slowly IV, monitored by ECG. Slow continuous infusion is also used (15 mg/kg over 4 hr or 30 mg/kg over 8 hr). This infusion must not be allowed to infiltrate subcutaneous tissue. Calcium gluconate may also be given via a gavage tube in 1 or 2% solutions at a dose of 100 mg/kg.

b. In **idiopathic hypoparathyroidism, Di George's syndrome, postoperative hypoparathyroidism,** and **pseudohypoparathyroidism,** the treatment of choice is vitamin D_2. The dose is 6–16 mg daily PO (1 mg = 40,000 U). Patients should be checked every 1–3 months for evidence of hypercalcemia or vitamin D toxicity such as weight loss, vomiting, polyuria, and polydipsia. They should also be checked for metastatic calcification by the following: serum Ca and P, 24-hr urine Ca or calcium/creatinine ratio on any sample of urine (normal is 0.03–0.17). Periodic ophthalmologic evaluation for cataracts should be carried out. If hypercalcemia or toxicity occurs, vitamin D is temporarily discontinued.

B. Hyperparathyroidism

   1. Etiology

      a. Primary hyperparathyroidism Hyperplasia of the parathyroids and parathyroid adenoma.

      b. Secondary hyperparathyroidism The causes include chronic renal disease, vitamin D–deficiency rickets, vitamin D–resistant rickets, osteogenesis imperfecta, malabsorption, and sprue.

   2. Evaluation includes history; physical examination; serum Ca, P, alkaline phosphatase, Mg, and PTH; urinary Ca, P, and creatinine clearance; urinalysis, urine culture, BUN; tuberculosis skin test (PPD); IVP; and skeletal x-ray studies.

   3. Diagnosis

      a. Primary hyperparathyroidism is uncommon in childhood.

         (1) Physical signs include anorexia, constipation, abdominal pain, lethargy, and weight loss. Urinary findings include polyuria and polydipsia, renal colic, and hematuria. Headache, confusion, delusions, hallucinations, mental retardation, alopecia, pitting and thickening of the nails, and clubbing may also be found.

         (2) Roentgenograms show subperiosteal erosion in the short tubular bones and absence of dura around the teeth.

         (3) Confirmatory tests include elevated Ca, decreased P, elevated alkaline phosphatase, decreased Mg, elevated pH, and increased 24-hr urinary Ca and P.

         (4) In idiopathic hypercalcemia, the serum P is normal or elevated and the serum Ca is unresponsive to corticosteroid administration. Roentgenograms show increased mineralization and no subperiosteal demineralization, although there may be submetaphyseal demineralization.

      b. In secondary hyperparathyroidism, the presenting symptoms are predominantly either those of the primary disease, or of short stature with pathologic fractures.

   4. Treatment

      a. In primary hyperparathyroidism, treatment is surgical removal of the adenoma of hyperplastic parathyroids, preceded by angiographic visualization.

      b. In secondary hyperparathyroidism, treatment is directed to the primary disease. This may include correction of acidosis by sodium bicarbonate or citrate, 2–3 mEq/kg daily; vitamin D_2, 25–50,000 U, or 0.5–1.0 mg dihydrotachysterol per day to increase the absorption of calcium; a low-protein or low-phosphorus diet; and calcium lactate or aluminum hydroxide to precipitate phosphate in the gut and delay absorption.

VI. DISORDERS OF THE ADRENALS

   A. Adrenocortical disorders The principal hormones secreted by the adrenal cortex are the estrogens and androgens, hydrocortisone, and aldosterone.

1. **Adrenocortical insufficiency (adrenal crisis, Addison's disease)** may appear abruptly or insidiously, and the deficiency may be temporary or permanent, depending on the cause.

    a. **Etiology**   It may result from the following:

    (1) Adrenal hypoplasia or aplasia of the adrenal glands.

    (2) Trauma or bleeding into the adrenal gland.

    (3) Fulminating infections causing hemorrhage or necrosis; meningococcemia is usually the underlying disease (e.g., Waterhouse-Friderichsen syndrome). However, it may occur in the course of other fulminating infections.

    (4) A salt-losing crisis with congenital adrenal hyperplasia.

    (5) Insufficient adrenal steroid therapy during stress (e.g., surgery and infections) in patients who are receiving or have recently received steroids.

    b. **Evaluation**   The symptoms in the acute form are vomiting, dehydration, hypotension, hypoglycemia, and coma.

    c. **Diagnosis**

    (1) **Laboratory findings**   The serum Na and Cl levels are low (they may be normal in the early stages). The K is high (but may be normal in the early stages); serum $NaHCO_3$ is low. Urinary Na and Cl are elevated. There is eosinophilia and moderate neutropenia.

    (2) **Confirmatory tests**   The following tests measure the functional capacity of the adrenal cortex:

    (a) Corticotropin (ACTH) test.

    (b) **Prolonged corticotropin (ACTH) test**   A positive test consists of failure of circulating eosinophils to be depressed by 50 percent or more following an infusion of aqueous corticotropin IV over an 8-hr period.

    (c) Plasma 17-hydroxycorticosteroid and cortisol levels are low.

    (d) Urinary 17-hydroxycorticosteroid excretion is decreased.

    (e) Urinary 17-ketosteroid excretion is decreased.

    d. **Therapy**

    (1) IV transfusion of 50% glucose in water, 1–2 ml/kg, rapidly if the patient is severely hypoglycemic and oral administration of glucose is not effective.

    (2) Normal saline in 5% dextrose IV, 150 ml/kg/24 hr.

    (3) Hydrocortisone hemisuccinate (Solu-Cortef), 50 mg/kg IM in 4 divided doses.

    (4) Maintenance therapy with cortisone acetate, 1–2 mg/kg daily PO, and possibly fludrocortisone (Florinef), 0.1–0.2 mg daily.

2. **Chronic adrenal insufficiency (Addison's disease)**

    a. **Etiology**   Tuberculosis, once the most frequent cause, is no longer so. Hereditary enzymatic defects with congenital adrenal atrophy or hyperplasia, lesions secondary to infection, and neoplasms are now more common causes. Addison's disease may be familial and has been described in association with diseases such as hypoparathyroidism, candidiasis, diabetes mellitus, and Hashimoto's lymphocytic thyroiditis.

b. Evaluation

(1) There is a gradual onset of weakness, anorexia, and weight loss. Attacks of vomiting, diarrhea, and abdominal pain commonly occur during the course of the disease and may simulate an acute abdominal condition.

(2) Chronic adrenocortical insufficiency must be differentiated from anorexia nervosa, certain muscular disorders such as myasthenia gravis, salt-losing nephritis, debilitating infections, and recurrent spontaneous hypoglycemia.

c. Diagnosis Usually, the serum Na and Cl are low and K elevated. Hypoglycemia may be present. The most definitive test is the measurement of the 24-hr output of urinary 17-hydroxycorticosteroids before and after the administration of ACTH (they do not increase when ACTH is given).

d. Therapy

(1) Most children with this disease are kept in good health on oral glucocorticoid medication alone. All should be encouraged to use table salt liberally, especially during the summer months. The most convenient glucocorticoid to use is cortisone acetate, the dose varying from 1–2 mg/kg daily, given preferably at intervals of about 8–12 hr.

(2) Because the disease easily escapes control and the addisonian crisis develops rapidly, **all patients should be treated promptly with appropriate antibiotics for even mild infections.** Intramuscular cortisone acetate, as well as antibiotics, should be given prior to dental extractions and elective surgery (see Sec. **(d)**, p. 392).

(3) Parents must be made aware of the dangers of intercurrent illness—in particular, vomiting.

3. Hyperadrenocorticism The disorders caused by excessive production of adrenocortical hormones are usually divided into those in which the predominant manifestations are related to a hypersecretion of androgenic hormone (adrenogenital syndrome), cortisol (Cushing's syndrome), aldosterone (primary hyperaldosteronism), or estrogens.

a. The adrenogenital syndrome (congenital adrenal hyperplasia) results from an inherited lack or deficiency of an enzyme required for cortisol synthesis and is inherited as an autosomal recessive. In an attempt to supply physiologic amounts of cortisol, there is an overproduction of ACTH by the pituitary gland, which in turn results in adrenocorticol hyperplasia and overproduction of androgens and precursors of cortisol. Four distinct enzymatic defects in the synthesis of cortisol are known: (1) deficiency of 21-hydroxylase (the most common), (2) 11-β-hydroxylase, (3) 3-β-hydroxysteroid dehydrogenase, and (4) 20,22 desmolase defect.

(1) Evaluation

    (a) Prenatal onset   The condition has been diagnosed on amniocentesis.

    (b) Pseudohermaphroditism in girls   The masculinization is confined to the external genitalia. The infant is born with an enlarged clitoris and variable degrees of labial fusion.

    (c) Sexual precocity in boys   This is not obvious at birth.

    (d) About one-third of infants with the 21-hydroxylase defect show signs and symptoms of **adrenal insufficiency,** which generally appear during the first weeks of life and consist of anorexia, vomiting, diarrhea, failure to thrive, and eventual dehydration and circulatory collapse—the so-called salt-losing crisis. The aldosterone production in these infants is inadequate and probably accounts for the sodium loss.

    (e) In salt-losing, virilizing adrenal hyperplasia, the infant is usually between 1–3 weeks of age with a history of vomiting and weight loss. Dehydration, hyponatremia, and hyperkalemia are often present.

    (f) Patients with the 11-β-hydroxylase defect have hypertension that returns to normal with cortisone administration. The hypertension is believed to result from excessive production of desoxycorticosterone.

    (g) Males with the 3-β-hydroxysteroid dehydrogenase defect usually show incomplete masculinization (hypospadias, with or without cryptorchidism of the external genitalia) and salt-losing manifestations are often present in both sexes.

    (h) Patients with 20,22 desmolase defect may also be salt losers.

(2) Diagnosis

    (a) The urinary 17-ketosteroid levels are elevated.

    (b) Urine

        i. 21-hydroxylase deficiency: 17-ketosteroids, pregnanediol, and testosterone levels are elevated. Aldosterone is reduced.

        ii. 11-β-hydroxylase deficiency: 11-desoxycortisol (compound S), tetrahydrocompound S, desoxycorticosterone, 17-ketosteroids, and testosterone levels are elevated. Urinary pregnanediol is normal.

        iii. 3-β-hydroxysteroid deficiency: 17-ketosteroid levels are moderately elevated but may be normal. Urinary dehydroepiandrosterone is raised.

(3) Therapy

    (a) A solution of 0.9% NaCl in 5% D/W, 150 ml/kg per day, is administered IV.

(b) Hydrocortisone hemisuccinate is added to the IV solution in a dose of 50 mg/kg/24 hr. It is then given IM qid for the first 7–10 days in order to bring about a maximum degree of suppression of the urinary 17-ketosteroids. Children under 2 years of age are given 25 mg daily and older patients, 50–75 mg daily.

(c) After obtaining maximum suppression, a maintenance dose of oral cortisone is given in the following daily doses: children under 2, 15–25 mg; children 2–6, 15–50 mg; children over 6, 50–75 mg.

(d) During stressful situations such as infections and operative procedures, the dose of cortisone should be tripled. The daily dose of oral cortisone should be given at 8-hr intervals because it is absorbed rapidly and is effective for only about 6 hr. In addition to cortisone, varying amounts of NaCl (2–5 gm daily) and fludrocortisone (0.05–0.2 mg daily) are given to infants with the salt-losing type of disorder.

(e) Surgical removal is indicated when adrenal tumors are associated with virilization.

b. Cushing's syndrome

(1) Etiology Tumors of the adrenals, adrenal hyperplasia, ACTH-producing pituitary tumors, and iatrogenic (too much corticosteroid for too long a period of time).

(2) Evaluation Clinical manifestations are the result of abnormally high blood levels of hydrocortisone. In addition, manifestations caused by the excessive secretion of other adrenal hormones are sometimes present. The signs and symptoms include obesity that characteristically spares the extremities, hypertension, hirsutism, plethora, purple striae, acne, easy bruising, and weakness.

(3) Diagnosis

(a) There may be glycosuria and hyperglycemia, with a diabetic glucose tolerance curve and a hypokalemic, hypochloremic alkalosis.

(b) The plasma and urinary levels of 17-hydroxycorticosteroids are usually elevated. Administration of dexamethasone, 1.25 mg/22 kg of body weight daily, at 6-hr intervals causes their output to fall to less than 2.5 mg daily on the second day of the test in normal subjects, but not in patients with Cushing's syndrome.

(4) Therapy It is often difficult to differentiate adrenal tumor and hyperplasia. Surgical exploration may be necessary to establish the cause, with removal of the tumor if one is encountered. When Cushing's syndrome is associated with a demonstrable pituitary tumor, hypophysectomy, x-ray therapy, or the implantation of radioactive gold or yttrium should be considered.

c. Primary hyperaldosteronism

(1) Etiology Adrenal hyperplasia or tumor.

(2) **Evaluation**   Clinical manifestations are hypertension, muscular weakness, polyuria and polydipsia, paresthesias, periodic paralysis, tetany, and edema.

(3) **Diagnosis**   Serum pH, CO_2 content, and Na levels are elevated, and the serum K and Cl concentrations are decreased. The urinary excretion of aldosterone is increased, with normal levels of 17-ketosteroids and 17-hydroxycorticosteroids. The kidneys are unable to concentrate urine.

(4) **Therapy**   Surgical removal of the tumor. Subtotal or total adrenalectomy for hyperplasia.

B. **Pheochromocytoma**   The adrenal medulla is derived from the ectoderm of the neural crest and secretes the hormones epinephrine and norepinephrine into the circulation. Overproduction of adrenal medullary hormones (hyperadrenalism) is caused by tumors of the adrenal medulla or of accessory chromaffin tissue. Almost all of the latter are pheochromocytomas. These functionally active tumors consist of chromaffin tissue and secrete large amounts of epinephrine, or norepinephrine, or both. In children, as many as 20 percent of such tumors are extraadrenal in location.

1. **Evaluation**   Clinical manifestations most commonly noted are hypertension, headache, hyperhidrosis, anxiety, weight loss, tachycardia, and fatigue.

2. **Diagnosis**   Typically, symptoms and signs are intermittent. The diagnosis of a functionally active pheochromocytoma is usually made by the detection of an increased concentration of catecholamines, either in the blood or urine, or of an increase in the urinary output of 3-methoxyhydroxymandelic acid (also called vanillylmandelic acid, or VMA), which is the major metabolite of epinephrine and norepinephrine metabolism.

3. **Therapy**   Surgical removal with careful control of blood pressure.

18 Juvenile Diabetes Mellitus

I. GENERAL FEATURES OF DIABETES Diabetes mellitus is characterized by a metabolic derangement secondary to partial or complete insulin deficiency. In mild cases of insulin lack, the metabolic consequence is a decreased capacity to assimilate ingested foodstuffs, resulting in glucose "intolerance." In severe failure of the insulin-producing system, there is hyperglycemia, ketogenesis, and protein-wasting.

The most recently reported (1969) incidence of diabetes in the United States is 1.25/1000 population under age 25. In about 5 percent of the total diabetic population, the diagnosis is made before 16 years of age.

Diabetes in the young is considered to be hereditary. The mode of inheritance is probably polygenic.

II. NATURAL HISTORY See Table 18-1.

III. CLINICAL COURSE

    A. The **initial phase** begins from the onset of clinical symptoms to the time of diagnosis, lasting anywhere from 1 day to several weeks. It is often precipitated by infection, emotional upset, or physical trauma.

    B. The **recovery phase** usually occurs a few days following therapy, when the stress is controlled and the tissues become more sensitive to insulin.

    C. The **remission phase** is typical of juvenile diabetes. It usually occurs 1–3 months following the introduction of insulin. The duration is variable, lasting anywhere from a few weeks to several months.

    D. The **intensification phase** follows the remission phase and occurs about 6–18 months after the initial diagnosis. Endogenous insulin is depleted. About one-third of the total juvenile diabetic population bypasses the remission phase.

IV. DIAGNOSIS

    A. Clinical presentation Suspicion of diabetes is usually brought to medical attention by one or more of the following situations:

        1. A strong family history of diabetes mellitus, e.g., parents with diabetes mellitus.

        2. Positive urine sugar on routine physical examination.

        3. Symptoms suggestive of diabetes mellitus without glycosuria.

Table 18-1. Stages in the Natural History of Diabetes Mellitus[a]

Stage	Fasting Blood Sugar	Glucose Tolerance Test	Cortisone-Glucose Tolerance Test[b]	Delayed and/or Decreased Insulin Response to Glucose	Clinical Features
Prediabetes	Normal	Normal	Normal	+	Asymptomatic
Subclinical diabetes	Normal	Normal; abnormal during pregnancy, stress	Abnormal	++	Asymptomatic
Chemical diabetes	Normal or increased	Abnormal	Not necessary for diagnosis	+++	Asymptomatic
Overt diabetes	Increased	Not necessary for diagnosis	Not necessary for diagnosis	++++	Classical signs and symptoms of diabetes mellitus

a Modified from Fajans, S. F. *Med. Clin. North Am.* 55:794, 1971. By permission.
b Has not been adequately evaluated in the pediatric age group to confirm its diagnostic or prognostic value.

4. A history of polydipsia, polyuria, recent weight loss, and enuresis, and, subsequently, glycosuria and hyperglycemia.

5. Severe ketoacidosis and coma.

B. **Diagnostic tests** It would be easy to make the diagnosis in the last two situations, but in the asymptomatic patient the diagnosis of diabetes mellitus, particularly of the prediabetic, subclinical, or chemical type, is dependent on the demonstration of carbohydrate intolerance. A series of carbohydrate function tests, namely, the oral glucose tolerance test (OGTT), intravenous glucose tolerance test (IVGTT), and the tolbutamide test, may be necessary to make the definite diagnosis. For the standardization of testing conditions the subject should be on a diet high in carbohydrate for 3 days prior to the test. The subject is then tested in a fasting and basal state.

1. **Oral glucose tolerance test** The OGTT is still generally accepted as a standard test for the initial work-up of asymptomatic diabetes mellitus.

   a. A loading dose of 1.75 gm glucose/kg of body weight is given.

   b. Blood samples are obtained at 0, ½, 1, 1½, 2, and 3 hr for glucose determination by the Somogyi-Nelson or ferrocyanide method and for insulin by immunoassay. When possible, urine is obtained simultaneously for glucose determination.

2. **Intravenous glucose tolerance test**

   a. A loading dose of 0.5 gm glucose/kg of body weight at "0" time is given by IV push.

   b. Blood samples are obtained at -30, 0, 1, 3, 5, 10, 15, 30, 45, 60, 90, 120, 150, and 180 min for the determination of sugar and immunoreactive insulin (IRI). The result of blood sugar is expressed by the glucose disappearance rate ("K-rate"). A K-rate higher than 1.2%/min is usually suggestive of carbohydrate intolerance. A blunted and decreased response of insulin is suggestive of the early diabetic state.

3. **Tolbutamide stimulation test**

   a. Tolbutamide, 25 mg/kg of body weight (maximum dose, 1 gm), is given by IV push at "0" time.

   b. Blood samples are obtained at -30, 0, 1, 3, 5, 10, 15, 30, 45, 60, 90, 120 min for the determination of sugar and IRI. Asymptomatic diabetes is usually found to produce a blunted and decreased IRI response.

4. **Individual variations in tolerance and response to carbohydrate function tests** The carbohydrate tolerance in the same person may vary from time to time. Also, different responses may be elicited from different tests. Some patients are thus required to go through multiple and repeated tests in order to elicit carbohydrate intolerance.

V. THERAPY

A. **General objectives in management**

1. Maintenance or establishment of optimal physical health, with emphasis on normal growth and development.

2. Control of metabolic alterations, including avoidance of hyperglycemia, ketoacidosis, abnormal serum lipid concentration, and excessive glycosuria.

3. Education of both patient and family to a full understanding of the disease and their role in its management.

4. Adequate and prompt control of ketoacidosis and coma.

5. Prevention of, or delay in, the onset of complications.

B. Management of diabetic acidosis and coma Here, the basic principles involve an adequate insulin administration program, proper handling of precipitating factors (e.g., infection), prompt correction of dehydration, and the prevention and control of complications such as shock, oliguria, cardiac arrhythmias, and potassium deficiency.

There is no rigid guide for insulin or fluid and electrolyte therapy. The clinical response and the improvement of biochemical status dictate further management in the individual patient.

1. **Guidelines for the treatment of severely acidotic and dehydrated comatose children**

   a. Sufficient history (particularly of the events leading to the onset, recent weight, the last insulin administration in the known diabetic patient) and physical examination (signs of infection and physical trauma).

   b. Accurate body weight.

   c. **Baseline studies,** including CBC, platelet count, pH, CO_2, acetone, electrolytes, BUN, glucose, urinalysis, and cultures.

   d. Urine bagging for constant collection to avoid catheterization except in the comatose patient. Urine samples should be collected q1–2h for sugar and acetone determination.

   e. Determination of blood sugar, acetone, pH, CO_2, and electrolytes q2–3h until the patient is out of danger.

   f. A **flow sheet,** containing hourly intake and output, insulin administered, urinary sugar and acetone, and blood chemistry.

   g. An **intravenous infusion** should be started (a cut-down or central venous catheter if the patient is in shock) (see Chap. 2, Sec. II.C).

   h. Serial monitoring with an ECG (lead 2) to detect T wave changes (especially if serum K+ determinations are not feasible).

   i. **Administration of regular (crystalline) insulin,** 0.5–2 U/kg (½ IV and ½ SQ) (see **C.3.a**). Repeat 2 U/kg SQ q2h in severe cases according to the clinical state and the sugar and acetone in blood and urine. *IV insulin drip is not recommended.*

   j. Treat infection if present.

2. **Fluid and electrolyte program for the first 24 hours** (See also Chap. 4, Sec. **E**, p. 92). The fluid deficit in severe diabetic acidosis is about 10–15% of ideal body weight (100–150 ml/kg). The amount of fluid replacement for the first 24 hr consists of 75% of the estimated loss, plus the daily maintenance and continuing losses.

   a. **First hour** Give normal saline, 20–30 ml/kg; or, if the patient is in shock, give blood, dextran or albumin.

   b. **Second hour** Give normal saline, 15–20 ml/kg.

c. Third–eighth hour   Give 10 ml/kg/hr ($\frac{1}{2}$ normal saline). Use $\frac{1}{2}$ normal saline in 5% D/W when blood sugar falls to 250 mg/100 ml.

d. Ninth–twenty-fourth hour   Give remainder of calculated fluid requirement ($\frac{1}{3}$ normal saline, $\frac{2}{3}$–5% D/W).

e. If the blood pH is below 7.15 at any time, give 0.3 mEq/kg sodium bicarbonate stat. Then give 20 mEq in each 500 ml of IV solution for the next 1000 ml.

f. When urinary output is established, give K+ 40–80 mEq/L as equal amounts of potassium chloride and potassium phosphate.

3. Calculation of electrolyte deficit

a. Sodium deficit: (140–serum sodium) $\times$ 0.6 (diffusion constant) $\times$ weight in kg; or estimate on the basis of 70–80 mEq/1000 ml of fluid loss.

b. Potassium deficit can be estimated in the same manner as sodium. Too rapid a correction of potassium deficit should be avoided.

c. Sodium bicarbonate: 0.7 mEq $NaHCO_3$/kg of body weight raises the CO_2 content 1 mM/L.

C. Insulin

1. Insulin preparations are divided into three categories according to promptness, duration, and intensity of action following SQ administration. They are classified as fast, intermediate, and long-acting types (see Table 18-2).

2. Insulin selection   In general, NPH is preferred as the intermediate-acting insulin. In patients in whom a little longer action is needed, Lente insulin may be used.

a. The majority of preadolescent patients are given a single injection of NPH before breakfast, and adequate control is usually achieved, although some patients require added regular insulin.

b. Adolescent patients are usually better controlled on a combination of NPH and regular insulin.

c. A small number of children, primarily adolescents requiring a large dose of insulin, are better treated with NPH injections twice daily, with $\frac{3}{4}$ of the total daily requirement before breakfast and $\frac{1}{4}$ before supper.

d. Regular insulin is required during acidosis and other acute situations in which the patient's food intake is variable.

e. Long-acting insulin (Ultralente) is not recommended in pediatric patients; hypoglycemic reactions following its administration often occur during sleeping hours and hence may be prolonged and severe.

3. Insulin therapy   The administration of insulin therapy is based upon the various phases of the clinical course of diabetes mellitus.

a. Initial phase (newly diagnosed patient with moderate to severe ketoacidosis or coma)   The administration of adequate quantities of rapidly acting insulin (regular) is essential for recovery from diabetic ketoacidosis.

Table 18-2. Insulin Preparations

Type	Appearance	Action	Peak Activity (hr)	Duration (hr)	Composition[a]	Compatible in Use with Regular Insulin
Regular (crystalline)	Clear	Rapid	2–4	5–7	—	· · ·
NPH (neutral protamine Hagedorn)	Turbid	Intermediate	6–12	24–28	Protamine, zinc, insulin	Yes
PZI (protamine zinc)	Turbid	Prolonged	14–24	36+	Same as NPH	No
Semilente	Turbid	Rapid	2–4	12–16	Zince, acetate buffer, insulin (no protein modifier)	· · ·
Lente (30% Semilente, 70% Ultralente)	Turbid	Intermediate	6–12	24–28	Same as Semilente	Yes
Ultralente	Turbid	Prolonged	18–24	36+	Same as Semilente	No

[a] Available as 40, 80, and 100 U/ml (U40, U80, and U100).

(1) Roughly approximate initial dosage

  (a) Give 1–2 U/kg of body weight stat.

  (b) Then give 1 U/kg SQ q1–2h until the blood sugar is less than 300 mg/100 ml, with diminishing ketonuria and acidosis.

  (c) Sliding scale Then give insulin q4h (the amount depending on the clinical and chemical response), using a sliding scale based on urinary sugar and acetone level, as follows:

    i. For children over 4 years of age use this rule of thumb: 2–4 U insulin per + for 3+ and 4+ urinary sugar spillage if no acetone is present; 4–5 U insulin per + for 3+ and 4+ urinary sugar if acetone is present.

    ii. For children under 4 years of age, reduce the sliding scale by 25 to 33 percent.

(2) Adjustment in insulin dosage is made until the total daily requirement can be estimated moderately well, which is usually after 48 hr of initial therapy. Then ⅔ of the total daily requirement is given as a single dose of an intermediate preparation.

(3) Further adjustment in dosage and addition or substitution of another preparation may be necessary if indicated by the patient's "chemical" response.

(4) In mild to moderate ketoacidosis, insulin therapy should be less vigorous because of the danger of inducing hypoglycemia. After an initial dose of 0.5–1.0 U/kg, the sliding scale can then be followed.

(5) For patients presenting with mild or moderate diabetes, without significant ketosis, treatment may be started with an arbitrary amount (0.5 U/kg daily) of an intermediate preparation; further adjustments are made as dictated by response.

b. Remission phase This usually occurs after the patient's discharge from the hospital. At this stage the insulin requirement decreases and the patient should be on a gradually decreasing dosage to avoid hypoglycemia. If there is no glycosuria, consider maintenance on a minimum dose of intermediate-acting insulin (2–4 U daily) and prescribe a dietary regimen to avoid the emotional trauma of discontinuing and then reintroducing insulin.

c. Stabilized phase (intensification phase)

(1) In general, the range of the average requirement for exogenous insulin as the patient approaches the stage of "total" diabetes usually rises slowly and unevenly, eventually stabilizing between 0.6 and 1.0 U/kg daily of an intermediate-acting insulin.

(2) Sexual maturation and the adolescent growth spurt increase the requirement for insulin in many children, up to between 0.8 and 1.2 U/kg daily. There is a variable decline in the requirement for exogenous insulin after attainment of full growth and sexual maturation.

4. Insulin regulation

a. Spot urine (second voiding) and block urine tests assist in the adjustment and dosage of insulin during follow-up care.

b. Generally, spot urine sugar tests are maintained at negative to 1+. If the 24-hr urine sugar falls between 5–10% of the daily carbohydrate intake, it is accepted as good regulation.

5. Problems in insulin therapy

a. Hypoglycemia (See Table 18-3.) Hypoglycemia is a major and common complication of therapy and can result from:

(1) Excessive dosage of insulin due to visual failure; mismatching potency of insulin and syringe; inappropriate site of injection or deliberate overdose.

(2) A reduced need for insulin resulting from increased exercise, diminished caloric intake, development of concomitant endocrinologic or systemic disease, recovery from "stress states" (infection, ketoacidosis, surgery), and the use of drugs with hypoglycemic effect.

(3) Treatment

(a) Simple sugars such as orange juice and soft drinks should be given if the patient can swallow. If not, glucagon (0.03 mg/kg body weight SQ; maximum, 1 mg) or epinephrine (0.005 ml/kg of 1:200 suspension) are useful drugs to elevate the blood sugar temporarily at home.

(b) Carbohydrate input should be continued till sugar appears in the urine. In severe cases, it is necessary to administer 50% glucose IV.

Table 18-3. Hypoglycemic Reactions

Type	Pathophysiologic Changes	Clinical Manifestations
Mild	Diminished glucose for cerebral function Acute increased systemic epinephrine	Behavior changes; inattention in school (e.g., daydreaming); subtle changes in character noted by family; hyperactivity in some children
Moderate	Decreased cerebral arteriovenous differences of both glucose and oxygen	Headache, mental confusion, and visual disturbances
Severe	Hypoxia and markedly decreased glucose for cerebral function	Convulsions and coma

b. Lipodystrophy Fat atrophy at the site of injections develops in about a third of juvenile diabetic patients. There is no specific therapy for lipodystrophy but rotation of sites is recommended.

c. Allergic reaction Transient localized urticarial lesions may occur during the first few weeks of insulin therapy and later disappear. Generally, no change in regimen is needed. Occasionally, pure pork insulin may be useful.

d. The **Somogyi phenomenon** is the establishment of a pattern of inapparent hypoglycemia, followed by reactive hyperglycemia and ketonuria. It results from an excessive administration of insulin.

> **(1)** The mechanism of hyperglycemia and ketonuria is an increased concentration of hormones (catecholamine, glucocorticoid, growth hormone) with actions antagonistic to insulin, so that insulin hyposensitivity develops.
>
> **(2)** The Somogyi phenomenon should be suspected when continually increasing the dose of insulin does not produce beneficial results. This factor is also considered if the total insulin dose exceeds 2.0 U/kg per day. To stabilize the situation, reduction in insulin dosage is necessary.

e. **Insulin resistance** is a rare event in the treatment of diabetes mellitus. In the adult, it is defined as an insulin requirement in excess of 200 U per day in the absence of acidosis. A change from beef to pork insulin may be effective in reducing the requirement, and adrenal corticosteroids may dramatically reduce insulin needs in some children.

D. Oral hypoglycemic agents   Two types commonly used in the treatment of adult onset diabetes, sulfonylurea compounds and the biguanides, have no place in the treatment of juvenile diabetes and are probably not even required in the management of young patients with adult-type diabetes. Dietary regulation, with emphasis on the maintenance of normal weight, will suffice in the latter case.

E. Guidelines for the diabetic diet

1. The aim of the diabetic diet is to permit the patient to lead a comfortable, asymptomatic life and to attain normal growth and development. The nutritional needs of diabetic children are essentially no different from those of nondiabetic children. The diabetic diet is thus essentially a normal, well-balanced diet with concentrated carbohydrates eliminated. Dietary manipulation is sometimes used as an adjunct to the insulin adjustment in the regulation of urinary sugar.

The emphasis of the diabetic diet is on the regularity of meals and snacks and the consistency of quantity of foods eaten, rather than on a strictly controlled regimen. It is not recommended that foods be weighed, but rather that the food exchange and diabetic food list commonly available be followed. The simplicity of this approach seems to lead to better acceptance of the disease by the patient and his family.

2. Planning the diabetic diet   A normal, well-balanced diet should have representative proportions of each of the following four basic food groups: **milk,** 3 or more glasses per day for children (small glasses for those under age 6) and 4 or more glasses for teen-agers; **meat,** 2 or more servings; **vegetables and fruit,** 4 or more servings; **bread and cereals,** 4 or more servings. These foods should be taken in sufficient amounts to provide the following:

a. Calories   It is desirable to keep the diabetic's weight in an ideal range for height and body build. The rule of thumb in caloric estimation is by age: 1000 calories daily at 1 year, plus 100 for each additional year up to 20 years.

b. Protein   In view of fat restriction in the diabetic patient, protein intake is usually increased to approximately 20% of the calories.

c. Carbohydrates   Carbohydrates are maintained to about 45–50% of the calories. This is largely accomplished through the avoidance of sweets and foods containing concentrated sugars.

d. Fat   The fat allowance is moderately restricted, to about 30–35% of the dietary calories to make up the balance of daily caloric needs.

e. Snacks   The daily diet is usually planned to include three meals and two or three snacks. The main purpose of snacks in a diabetic diet is to provide additional carbohydrate coverage at the peak of the insulin reaction and to aid in the prevention of possible nighttime hypoglycemia. Snacks are usually scheduled at 3:00 P.M. and at bedtime, with an additional mid-morning snack for young children. The food value for each snack is approximately 10 gm of carbohydrate, but extra food exchange is sometimes used as an adjunct to the insulin adjustment.

VI. EDUCATION   Patients and parents are taught the fundamentals of pathophysiology and management. Insulin preparation, injection technique, and a program for the management of acute illness are introduced. They are also made aware of the symptoms of hypoglycemia, its oral treatment, and the use of glucagon. Qualitative tests for sugar with Clinitest or "2" drop method and acetone are taught. Patients are encouraged to participate in activities normal for their age. The importance of understanding of the dietary instructions, exchange lists, food preparation guidelines, and diabetic foods should be pointed out. All patients are advised to carry a diabetic card or "dog tag."

VII. SPECIAL PROBLEMS OF DIABETES MELLITUS

A. Diabetes and physical growth and maturation   In general, diabetic children follow the normal growth pattern. However, there may be a diminished growth rate in those whose diabetes is poorly controlled.

B. Diabetes and problems in emotional adjustment   Diabetic patients often become overly dependent and demonstrate anxiety and hostility. Understanding, patience, education of both patient and family, and, occasionally, psychiatric counseling are necessary in these cases. Heavy responsibilities, e.g., the administration of insulin, should not be levied on a diabetic child when he is not mature enough to accept them.

C. Infection and diabetes   Urinary tract infections, subcutaneous abscesses, monilial vulvitis and cystitis in teen-age girls, and pyelonephritis occur with higher prevalence in diabetic patients than in nondiabetic individuals. Appropriate and adequate dosage of antibiotics and antifungal agents should be administered promptly, and the establishment of good diabetic control should be emphasized.

19 Pulmonary Disorders

I. GENERAL PRINCIPLES OF THERAPEUTICS

A. Smoking If possible, one should convince the patient and those in the immediate environment to break the habit. This applies to *all* pulmonary diseases (and to good health in general).

B. Environmental control

1. Control should be most vigorous where the child spends most time. Feather-containing products should be avoided, particularly in the bedroom. Airtight plastic covers should be put on bedding not already stuffed with a polyester fiber. It is best to keep furry pets out of the immediate environment. Furniture should be easily cleanable. Hot air heating should be avoided, as should chronic moisture that encourages mold growth.

2. The best mechanical aids are the electrostatic precipitators, because they remove particles, including those smaller than 5μ in diameter.

3. In extreme situations, the physician may be forced to recommend a change in geographic location for the patient.

4. These recommendations should be applied judiciously. When a child has mild or only questionable atopic disease, it is not helpful to disrupt the home environment with expensive and difficult changes that may only lead to increased emotional strain and ultimate deterioration of the child's condition.

C. Chest physical therapy (postural drainage)

1. **Indications** Chest physical therapy is useful in any clinical situation when excess fluid is not removed by the normal cough or ciliary action of the airways. It is sometimes recommended prophylactically for conditions in which future difficulties are anticipated, as in cystic fibrosis without marked clinical pulmonary disease.

2. **Frequency** depends on the severity of the illness as well as the family's daily routine. Expecting a child and his parents to spend unlimited hours each day on such activity can lead to resentment and ultimate termination of a useful technique.

3. **Learning the technique** is best when the parents and child are taught by a qualified physical therapist.

4. **Instructions** Specifically request that the greatest effort be placed on the most involved areas. It is useful to have physical therapy follow aerosol administration (see **D**).

D. Aerosol therapy Particles 5μ are best, since they are most likely to enter the small airways when inhaled through the mouth. Aerosol therapy should be given just prior to chest physical therapy, particularly in patients who have difficulty raising sputum. Saline, mucolytic agents, bronchodilators, and antibiotics may be delivered by aerosol.

E. Desensitization   See Sec. **V.C.7.**

F. Antibiotics   See Chap. 9, Sec. **III.**

G. Psychiatric support   (See also Chap. 7.) The severe and demanding nature of many childhood chronic respiratory diseases virtually requires that the physician, often with the help of the social worker, psychiatrist, or both, give added support to the family.

II. PHARMACOLOGIC AGENTS USED IN CHRONIC RESPIRATORY DISEASES

A. Adrenergic drugs   The sections discussing treatment for a specific condition will indicate which, if any, of these agents are appropriate. **Caution: epinephrine, aminophylline, and isoproterenol are potent cardiotonic agents. They should always be used with caution, particularly if used in combination.**

1. Epinephrine

a. Action   It activates adenyl cyclase, causing an increase of cyclic adenosine monophosphate (AMP) concentration. This produces a relaxation of bronchial smooth muscle and a decrease of bronchial hypersecretion. There is a concomitant increase in heart rate, cardiac output, and O_2 utilization.

b. Side effects include cardiac arrhythmias, especially in hypoxemic patients, drying of secretions, anxiety, restlessness, headache, dizziness, pallor, and vomiting.

c. Administration and dosage   Epinephrine is most useful during acute episodes of bronchospasm. If using 1:1000 aqueous epinephrine, give 0.01 ml/kg per dose SQ or IM (not more than 0.4 ml in a single dose). Repeat at intervals of 15–30 min. If using 1:200 epinephrine aqueous suspension (Sus-Phrine), the dosage is 0.005 ml/kg per dose, with a maximum dose of 0.3 ml in children. Do not repeat before 4 hr as this is a long-acting preparation.

2. Ephedrine sulfate

a. Action   Similar to that of epinephrine.

b. Side effects   CNS stimulation and palpitations.

c. Administration and dosage   0.5–1.0 mg/kg per dose q4h PO. The tablets are available in 15, 25, 30, and 50 mg; the syrup contains 4 mg/ml.

Note: Ephedrine sulfate may be given in combination with a xanthine and a sedative, as in Tedral and Marax (see Table 19-2).

3. Isoproterenol (Isuprel)

a. Action   Similar to that of epinephrine.

b. Side effects   Similar to those of epinephrine. It has been demonstrated to cause a fall of 5–10 mm Hg in Po_2. It thus may be dangerous to have the patient use hand-held precharged nebulizers during a severe attack, especially if O_2 is not being administered. Also, an occasional patient actually has an increase of bronchospasm following isoproterenol by aerosol. This is rare, but may be detected using pulmonary function tests before and after isoproterenol is administered by aerosol.

   c. Administration and dosage Isoproterenol for aerosol use is supplied in a 1:200 solution. 0.25–0.5 ml of this 1:200 solution is combined with 0.5 ml–4 ml saline for use in either a hand spray or O_2-driven nebulizer.

4. Beta-2 stimulants

   a. Action This class of drugs has the advantage of causing bronchodilation without significant cardiovascular effects.

   b. Preparations Thus far, only isoetharine (Bronkometer, Bronkosol) is available in the United States as a component in an aerosol.

B. Xanthines: Aminophylline The xanthines are phosphodiesterase inhibitors, which result in an increase of cyclic AMP.

   1. Action Stimulates CNS and cardiac muscle and relaxes smooth muscle. When used in combination with beta stimulators, aminophylline potentiates their action.

   2. Side effects Nausea and vomiting, hypotension, arrhythmias.

   3. Administration and dosage

      a. Intravenous aminophylline, 4–6 mg/kg per dose (not more than 16 mg/kg/24 hr). It is more effective if given over 10–15 min rather than over 1 hr, but the patient must be observed more closely if this method is used.

      b. Aminophylline can also be given PR. The suppositories contain 125, 250, or 500 mg. They are occasionally useful, but absorption is irregular and unreliable and they must therefore be prescribed cautiously and preferably *not for small children*. This route may also be particularly irritating to the gastrointestinal tract.

C. Corticosteroids See Table 19-1.

Table 19-1. Equivalent Glucocorticoid Effects of Various Corticosteroids

Cortisone	100 mg
Hydrocortisone	80 mg
Prednisone	20 mg
Prednisolone	16 mg
Triamcinolone	8 mg
9α-fluorocortisol	5 mg
Dexamethasone	2 mg

   1. Action Antiinflammatory. They activate the release of cyclic AMP by stimulating adenyl cyclase.

   2. Side effects Cushing's syndrome, osteoporosis, immunosuppression in high doses, ulcers, growth delay. Corticosteroids have less toxicity if given on an alternate day, A.M. dose program. When possible, the child should have a skin test for tuberculosis before corticosteroids are administered.

3. Route and dosage For acute attacks, intravenous hydrocortisone, 4 mg/kg/q4–6h, is given. By the oral route, 1–2 mg/kg/24 hr prednisone is given initially in a single A.M. dose. As soon as the patient's condition permits, he may be switched to an alternate-day A.M. dose program. A child with chronic asthma may be aided by minute amounts on this basis.

Note: Some recent evidence has come to light indicating that phenobarbital, when administered along with dexamethasone, causes a decrease in the half-life and an increase in the metabolic clearance of corticosteroid (*N. Engl. J. Med.* 286:125, 1972). Although this is not the final word, it is a *theoretical* reason to avoid giving preparations containing phenobarbital when using corticosteroids. Hydroxyzine apparently does not produce this effect.

D. Expectorants

1. Iodides

    a. Action Iodides liquify thick, tenacious sputum.

    b. Side effects Goiter, salivary gland inflammation, and gastric irritation. Iodides may provoke acne in teen-agers.

    c. Dosage

        (1) Sodium iodide, IV, 25 mg/kg/24 hr; *or*

        (2) Supersaturated potassium iodide (SSKI), 2–10 gtts per glass of water PO, tid.

2. Glyceryl guaiacolate
This is of questionable value. The dosage is 5 ml q4–6h.

E. Mucolytic agents

1. Acetylcysteine (Mucomyst)
is perhaps the most effective of the mucolytic agents.

    a. Action Its mucolytic action is due to breakage of disulfide bonds in the mucoid secretions. However, it may cause bronchospasm, especially in patients with asthma.

    b. Administration Acetylcysteine loses activity rapidly if in solution of less than 10% concentration, or if in contact with rubber or metal, and it inactivates many antibiotics given by aerosol. Properly administered, it often results in a great outpouring of secretions, which may require mechanical suctioning if the patient has an inadequate cough, or inadequate ciliary action, or both. Many children object to the taste and odor. It often works best if given with a bronchodilator.

    c. The **dose** is 3–5 ml 20% solution q4–6h by aerosol.

2. Saline
given directly as an ultrasonic aerosol liquifies secretions. It has been reported to cause bronchospasm on occasion. It is of questionable value when delivered by a mist tent.

F. Fixed combinations
About 80 bronchodilators, either alone or in fixed combinations, are listed in the *Physicians' Desk Reference.* They have the advantage of convenience in often combining an agent that stimulates the buildup of cyclic AMP and one that retards its breakdown. They also provide a sedative or tranquilizer to counteract the CNS-stimulating effect of the bronchodilators. The disadvantages are increased cost and the inflexibility of fixed combinations. In prescribing

Table 19-2. Fixed Combination Bronchodilators

Brand Name	Composition	Tablet (mg)	Syrup (5 ml) (mg)
Marax	Hydroxyzine HCl	10	2.5
	Ephedrine sulfate	25	6.25
	Theophylline	130	32.5
Tedral	Phenobarbital	8	4
	Ephedrine hydrochloride	24	12
	Theophylline	130	65
Quadrinal	Phenobarbital	24	12
	Theophylline	130	65
	Potassium iodide	320	110
	Ephedrine hydrochloride	24	
Bronkotabs (Hafs)	Ephedrine sulfate	12	
	Glyceryl guaiacolate	50	
	Phenobarbital	4	
	Theophylline	50	
Bronkolixir	Ephedrine sulfate	12	12
	Theophylline	15	50
	Glyceryl guaiacolate	50	50
	Phenobarbital	4	50

fixed combinations the dosage calculated should be based on that of the *bronchodilator* (see Table 19-2).

G. **Newer drugs** See Sec. **V.C.10**, p. 415.

III. VENTILATORS

A. **General principles** The flow of respiratory gases results from the development of a pressure gradient between the mouth and alveoli. Respiration may result either from raising the mouth pressure (artificial ventilation by intermittent positive pressure breathing [IPPB]) or from lowering the alveolar pressure (e.g., spontaneous breathing and negative pressure ventilation). In either case, the pressure gradient is developed in the same direction, and the resultant flow is similar.

In general, expiration is passive and largely dependent on the dynamics of the patient's respiratory tract. An exception to the latter is the "belt respirator," a device that surrounds the lower chest and abdomen and intermittently inflates, producing an active expiratory phase only.

If able to understand, the patient should be informed as to the nature of his disease, and the reasons for the therapeutic regimen shoud be explained to him.

1. **Assisted ventilation** The ventilator will respond to an inspiratory effort *initiated by the patient* (a sudden reduction in the airway pressure). This method of ventilation will usually improve alveolar ventilation and oxygenation but does not completely relieve the work of breathing, especially when the "sensitivity control," which regulates the pressure needed to initiate flow, is set at high pressure. It helps in patients with some degree of reserve or when trying to wean a patient from the respirator.

    2. In controlled ventilation a triggering device regulates the operation during *all* phases of the respiratory cycle.

B. Types of ventilators

    1. Pressure-cycled ventilators   The Bird (Mark 8) is gas-powered (either by compressed air or O_2). In this machine the inspiration ends when the pressure in the system (and thus in the airway) rises to a preselected value.

        a. Operating the Bird respirator   If you are facing the dials:

            (1) On the left end   The sensitivity switch (marked by dot #4) controls the amount of effort the patient must exert to trigger the unit. (The smaller numbers correspond to the greatest sensitivity. They do *not* indicate pressure in cm H_2O.)

            (2) On the middle top   The inspiratory time flow rate switch is at dot #5. A high flow rate results in a rapid termination of inspiration since the predetermined pressure is reached more quickly than at low flow rates.

            (3) Below   The time flow rate switch, a push-pull knob (dot #2), mixes air to vary the concentration of O_2.

            (4) Lowermost on the middle   The apnea switch (dot #3) determines the respiratory rate; e.g., if the machine is to control ventilation completely, and the *duration* of apnea is to be shortened (to increase the respiratory rate), turn this knob counterclockwise (CCW). If assisted ventilation is used, this knob should be set to cycle at approximately 12 breaths/min, so that if the patient becomes apneic the machine takes over automatically.

            (5) On the right end   Pressure control switch (dot #1).

            (6) On top   Negative pressure generator and O_2 mixing valve.

        b. To give IPPB in the average child with asthma, use the rule of thumb, 15-15-15, as follows:

            (1) Set the position of the pressure control at *15.*

            (2) Set the sensitivity control at *15.* If it becomes difficult for the patient to start the inspiration, turn the control counterclockwise to a lower number (less effort).

            (3) Turn the flow rate knob to *15,* and from this setting make adjustments to have a ratio of 1:2 for inspiration/expiration time. If the flow rate is too fast, the tidal volume delivered to the patient will be too small. To measure the expired tidal volume that comes out through the exhalation valve, attach a Wright respirometer to this valve. By manipulation of the pressure control and flow rate control, the tidal volume the patient requires may be obtained.

            (4) When used to deliver IPPB treatment, the apnea switch should *be in the clockwise direction:* **off.**

    2. Volume-cycled ventilators

        a. These machines are more complex than pressure-cycled ventilators. The tidal volume is delivered to the patient irrespective of airway resistance or patient's compliance. Thus *the function of the airway safety valve should always be checked before use.* (This may be done by obstructing the inflow tubing so that a characteristic noise is heard when the air leaks through the safety valve.)

b. In general, the switches on these machines are self-explanatory. They contain the following: tidal volume, duration of inspiration and expiration, selection of assisted-control respiration, concentration of inspired O_2, humidity, frequency of sighs, and end-expiratory pressure.

c. The tidal volume delivered by this respirator can be calculated by the use of Boyle's law if the compressible volume and the peak pressures (reached at the time the volume is delivered) are known. In practice and to monitor the patient, a respirometer is attached to the exhalation valve to obtain actual measurements of tidal volume.

d. A volume-cycled ventilator depends on a closed airway system. It is thus essential to use endotracheal tubes in babies or cuffed endotracheal tubes in older children.

3. Negative pressure ventilators These include tank and chest respirators of various configurations in which pressure and inspiration-expiration time are the determinants of tidal volume and respiratory rate. These respirators may be considered for patients who have relatively normal lungs and airways and who have a defect in the neuromuscular component of respiration.

C. Continuous positive pressure ventilation (See also Chap. 5, Sec. **IV.A.4.c.**) This technique has proved useful in improving the oxygenation of patients who fail to maintain an adequate arterial Po_2 on IPPB despite high concentrations of inspired oxygen. Recruitment of gas exchange units and prevention of terminal airway closure appear to be the physiologic reasons for the beneficial effects.

D. Complications of mechanical ventilation

1. Infection.

2. Pneumothorax, pneumomediastinum, and subcutaneous emphysema.

3. Overcorrection of hypercapnea, with sudden changes in pH, cardiac arrhythmias, tetany, and so on.

4. Interference with venous return and a drop in cardiac output and blood pressure (sometimes as a consequence of a previously borderline hypervolemic condition).

5. Positive fluid balance.

6. Inappropriate ADH secretion.

7. "Stiff" lung.

8. Accidental kinking or accidental displacement of the endotracheal tube into the right main bronchus.

9. Tracheal inflammation, erosion, granuloma formation, and, later, stenosis.

10. Oxygen toxicity: impairment of the defense mechanisms of the lung.

11. Retention of secretions above the "cuff." (Orotracheal suction before deflating the cuff should be done to prevent aspiration.)

12. Gastrointestinal: dilatation, or bleeding, or both.

13. Psychological: e.g., dependence on mechanical respiration.

14. Exhaustion: lack of sleep due to constant "intensive" care.

IV. RESPIRATORY FAILURE   (For respiratory failure in status asthmaticus, see Chap. 2, Sec. **VI.**)

A. Definition   Respiratory failure results from the inability of the pulmonary system to maintain normal blood gas tensions either as a result of respiratory disease or of the failure of the respiratory muscles to function properly.

B. Inadequate oxygenation

1. Hypoxemia is the most serious consequence of acute respiratory failure and is generally the earliest manifestation of impending difficulty. In the absence of an intracardiac shunt, it is caused by one or more of the following:

a. Low concentration of inspired O_2.

b. Hypoventilation.

c. Diffusion defect.

d. Ventilation/perfusion imbalance.

e. Right-to-left shunt at the pulmonary level.

2. Calculation of right-to-left shunts

a. The quantity of the right-to-left shunt is calculated using a modification of Bergren's equation, which assumes a normal arteriovenous O_2 difference (see Table 19-3 for the meaning of the abbreviations):

$$\frac{\dot{Q}s}{\dot{Q}t} = \frac{(PA_{O_2} - Pa_{O_2}) \times 0.03}{4.5 + (PA_{O_2} - Pa_{O_2}) \times 0.03}$$

Table 19-3.   Abbreviations Used in Pulmonary Physiology

f	=	respiratory frequency
Vd	=	dead space (anatomic, dead space in ml = weight in lb)
Vt	=	tidal volume
P_A	=	alveolar tension of gas
Pa	=	arterial tension of gas
R	=	respiratory quotient $\dfrac{(\dot{V}_{CO_2})}{(\dot{V}_{O_2})}$
F_iO_2	=	fractional inspired concentration of O_2
V	=	ventilation
$\dot{Q}s$	=	cardiac output shunt fraction
$\dot{Q}t$	=	cardiac output total
0.03	=	solubility coefficient of O_2 in plasma
P_iO_2	=	inspired tension of O_2
$\dot{V}/\dot{Q}$	=	ventilation/perfusion ratio
$\dot{V}_{CO_2}$	=	carbon dioxide output
$\dot{V}_{O_2}$	=	oxygen uptake

where $4.5 =$ the assumed O_2 difference between arterial and mixed venous blood and 0.03 is the solubility coefficient of O_2 in plasma.

b. A quick method for bedside estimation of right-to-left shunt requires the patient to breathe 100% O_2 for at least 10 min at which time the Pa_{O_2} is obtained:

Then

$$\% R \to L \text{ shunt} = \frac{650 - Pa_{O_2}}{14}$$

with 650 and 14 as constants.

3. Alveoloarterial oxygen difference $(A\text{-}a_{DO_2})$. The $A\text{-}a_{DO_2}$ is a useful method for determining and following defects in blood-gas equilibrium between the alveoli and pulmonary capillaries. It reflects non-uniformity of ventilation-perfusion ratios, diffusion defects, and right-to-left shunting through the lungs. The first two factors are generally eliminated when the patient breathes 100% O_2. Under normal circumstances the $A\text{-}a_{DO_2}$ is 10 mm Hg in a young person.

It may be approximated as follows:

a. The inspired O_2 tension is determined using the "rule of sevens" (see Table 19-4).

Table 19-4. "Rule of Sevens"

Patient breaths	Required O_2 Tension (mm Hg)
20% $O_2 \times 7$	140
30% $O_2 \times 7$	210
40% $O_2 \times 7$	280
50% $O_2 \times 7$	350 (and so on)

b. $A\text{-}a_{DO_2} \cong F_iO_2 - (Pa_{O_2} + Pa_{CO_2})$

This formula is devised from the alveolar-air equation

$$PA_{O_2} = PI_{O_2} - (PA_{CO_2} \times 1/R)$$

and it assumes that $R = 1$.

V. MANAGEMENT OF CHRONIC CHILDHOOD ASTHMA (For management of acute asthma, see Chap. 2, Sec. **V.**)

A. Etiology   This is unknown. There is an increase in the responsiveness of the bronchi of the asthmatic patient to histamine and acetylcholine and a decreased responsiveness of beta receptors. Precipitating factors include infection, environmental allergens, emotional upset, exercise, exposure to cold, and drugs (notably aspirin).

B. Evaluation and diagnosis   In the acute situation, the dyspnea of asthma is generally obvious. Evaluation of the "subclinical" case is often more complex and includes the following:

1. History   Often there are repeated episodes of bronchitis or pneumonia as infants. Cough symptoms linger longer than in other children after URIs. The child is heard to be wheezing by parents after exercise, colds, or while asleep. Symptoms tend to be seasonal and, occasionally, date from changes in geographic area, a new pet, or some other environmental factor. Often there is a family history of atopic disease.

2. **Physical examination** It is often possible to induce a wheeze or an increase in the expiratory phase by having the patient take a deep breath and forcefully expire through a *wide open mouth*. An increase in the anterior-posterior (A-P) diameter of the chest and clubbing should be looked for. In the case of the latter, other problems such as bronchiectasis, cystic fibrosis, immunologic deficiency disease, and congenital heart disease must be considered, since *clubbing is extremely rare in simple asthma*.

3. **Laboratory studies**

   a. **Chest x-ray studies** should be done.

   b. **Pulmonary function test** In more severe cases there is a decrease in the peak flow rate, forced expiratory volume in one second (FEV_1), and vital capacity (VC), along with an increase in the residual volume and total lung capacity. However, maximal mid-expiratory flow rate (MMFR) and flow volume curves may be required to demonstrate abnormalities in mild cases. Inhalation of isoproterenol will generally increase the vital capacity and FEV_1 more than 20 percent in the asthmatic patient. Occasionally, a patient will demonstrate bronchospasm only after exercise.

   c. **Skin testing** is occasionally helpful if combined with careful atopic history.

   d. **Examination of sputum** Eosinophilia is seen on Wright's stain.

   e. A **peripheral eosinophil count** of over 500/mm³ is suggestive of atopic and/or parasitic disease. (See Chap. 10, Sec. **I.B.2**, p. 231).

C. **Treatment** A spectrum of therapeutic maneuvers is available to the physician but they must be organized in a manner that avoids enslavement of the child and family to the disease process. The goal is normal school attendance and unlimited activity, with few, if any, hospitalizations.

1. **Environmental control** See Sec. **I.B.**

2. **Bronchodilators** See Secs. **II.A.14** and **II.B** for pharmacology and dosages.

   a. If the patient has moderate to severe disease, bronchodilators should be used on a long-term basis, although they may be required only during particular seasons. Occasionally, a bedtime dose is sufficient.

   b. In the mildly ill patient who has no difficulty with recurrent atelectasis and who has normal or near-normal pulmonary function tests, there is little need for continual administrations of these agents. However, oral bronchodilators may be kept at home and be started by the parents at the first sign of a cold, cough, or wheezing. By early administration of effective agents, a visit to the emergency room or even hospitalization may sometimes be avoided. Time must be set aside to educate the family about the potential side effects and toxicity of bronchodilators.

3. **Corticosteroids** Only outpatient long-term administration will be discussed here (for dose, administration, and side effects, see Secs. **II.C.2** and **3**). One of the most difficult decisions to be made in the management of the chronic asthmatic child is when and if to begin treatment with these agents.

   a. In general, corticosteroids should be used only after *vigorous* treatment with the more benign program fails to keep the child well and relatively active. The side effects must be weighed against the problems caused by poorly controlled asthma.

   b. Once it is felt that there is no choice, corticosteroids should be titrated to the *minimum effective dose* on an alternate-day A.M. schedule.

   c. It is better to maintain a child on low dosages of prednisone and leading a full life than to have him missing school or in the hospital frequently because such medication is withheld.

4. **Chest physical therapy** See Sec. **I.C.**

5. **Expectorants** may aid some chronic asthmatic patients (see Sec. **II.D**).

6. **Antibiotics** There is little evidence that chronic or prophylactic administration of antibiotics is useful unless there are signs of infection such as increasing sputum production or fever.

7. **Desensitization** seems to help occasional asthmatic patients when relatively few specific antigens can be identified.

8. **Aerosols** (See Sec. **I.D.**) The use of Freon-propelled aerosols has been associated with **overdosages and fatal cardiac arrhythmias,** particularly in the presence of hypoxia. If these devices are prescribed in the pediatric age group, *it is best to have the specific dosage administered by a parent.*

9. **Psychotherapy** (See Sec. **I.G.**) Generally, the pediatrician or social worker who develops an ongoing relationship with the patient can give the needed support. Occasionally, the psychiatrist will be useful in coping with more severe behavior problems. It is also important to remember that some of the behavioral changes seen are induced by the drugs used in the treatment of asthma.

10. **Newer drugs** include the following: beta stimulants (Salbutamol, not available in the United States); isoetharine (see Sec. **II.A.4**), with which there is limited experience thus far, given by aerosol, induces bronchodilation without the side effects of isoproterenol.

    Disodium cromoglycate (Aarane, Intal) has recently been licensed in the United States. It presumably acts as a mast-cell stabilizer. The patient is instructed to inhale a 20-mg capsule, using a device supplied by the company, qid as a prophylactic measure. Thus far about 25–50 percent of severe asthmatics are afforded some relief using this drug. The major disadvantage is cost, which is about $1.00 per day.

VI. CYSTIC FIBROSIS (See also Chap. 16, Sec. **II.A.1.**)

A. Evaluation

1. **Physical examination** Findings vary according to the time at which the diagnosis is made. In the infant, tachypnea, retractions, and a

prominent tympanitic abdomen are typical. Often the infant presents with the picture of bronchiolitis. Later in childhood or adolescence, isolated pulmonary disease may be the only manifestation. Diffuse rhonchi and rales and clubbing of the extremities may be found. Nasal polyps and sinusitis are associated findings.

B. Diagnosis   See also Chap. 16, Sec. **VI.A.**

1. **The chest x-ray picture** may vary from normal to that of extreme "fibrosis," hyperinflation, and hilar adenopathy. Often, the findings tend to be confined to one or two areas of the lung.

2. **Pulmonary function tests**   These vary from normal to the pattern of obstructive disease with overinflation, as demonstrated by an increase in the residual volume (RV), in RV/TLC (total lung capacity), and a decrease in VC. Expiratory flow rates are decreased. Blood gases also vary from normal to the extremes of hypoxemia and finally hypercapnia.

3. **Sputum analysis**   Typical thick, viscous secretions are present. In patients on continuous antimicrobial agents, gram-negative rods (*Pseudomonas*), or gram-positive cocci (staphylococcus), or both are almost routine findings. Hemoptysis is also frequent.

4. **Other laboratory studies**   A vectorcardiogram demonstrates right ventricular hypertrophy due to cor pulmonale in patients with a normal ECG. This correlates with the degree of hypoxemia.

C. Treatment of pulmonary disorder

1. **Adequate hydration** is of primary importance, and mobilization and loosening of secretions is essential.

2. **To decrease the viscosity of sputum,** some centers used the experimental alpha-blocking agent tolazine PO in progressive doses (to minimize the side effects) until the third day, when the therapeutic dose of 2 mg/kg daily is achieved.

3. **Humidification of inspired air** in the form of a mist tent is used in many centers; however, its efficacy has not yet been proved.

4. **Aerosol drugs**   Any generator properly suited to deliver medications can be used. Most of the preparations include normal saline as the base solution.

5. **Acetylcysteine**   See Sec. **II.E.1.**

6. **Bronchodilators**   See Secs. **II.A.3** and **II.B.**

7. **Expectorants**   See Sec. **II.D.**

8. **Chest physiotherapy** can be carried out by the patient, by a therapist, or by electric vibrator.

9. **Antimicrobial agents**   (See Chap. 9, Secs. **III.A.4.b** and **III.F.3.**) Hospitalized patients receive IV therapy (carbenicillin, gentamicin). Aerosol administration of colistin sulfate (2.5 mg/ml) is used in patients who have *Pseudomonas aeruginosa* in their sputum (2 ml of solution bid).

VII. PNEUMOTHORAX

A. Etiology   Spontaneous pneumothorax may be an idiopathic occurrence in a previously healthy person, or it may result as a complication of underlying pulmonary disease.

B. Evaluation and diagnosis

1. **History** A high index of suspicion is present whenever a patient with known lung disease experiences the *acute* onset of severe respiratory distress.

2. **Physical examination** Decreased fremitus, decreased breath sounds, and hyperresonance are present on the affected side. Percussion over the clavicles on opposite sides shows minor differences in percussion tones. In the infant the physical findings may be minimal, even in the face of extensive collapse.

3. **Chest roentgenogram** Sometimes an expired posteroanterior view will aid diagnosis when the pneumothorax is small.

4. **Classification** Generally, a pneumothorax is well tolerated after an initial period of distress because of an adjustment of perfusion to ventilation. (It should be remembered that *pneumothorax can enlarge during reduced in-flight cabin pressures,* which can be a problem when transporting sick infants.)

   a. **Minor to moderate** Less than 30 percent collapse.

   b. **Major** 30–70 percent collapse.

   c. **Complete collapse** If this occurs, the possibility of tension pneumothorax should be suspected.

C. Treatment (For infants, see Chap. 5, Sec. **IV.B.4.**) The following points should be observed:

1. *If the clinical condition is critical, immediate lifesaving maneuvers become more important than diagnostic procedures.*

2. If the leak is in *visceral* pleura, **positive pressure breathing** can aggravate the situation. If there is a leak in the *parietal* pleura (flail chest), on the other hand, positive pressure may be lifesaving.

3. **Simple observation** will suffice if the patient can be watched, the clinical condition is stable, there is no evidence of an "open" leak, and the radiologic diagnosis is "minor."

4. **Cough suppression** If necessary, dextromethorphan, codeine, or morphine should be used to suppress coughing.

5. **Thoracentesis** Needle aspiration of air at the 2nd anterior intercostal space, midclavicular line (see Chap. 1, Sec. **II.B.5**). This procedure may be lifesaving whenever tension pneumothorax is present. There is no need to wait for special equipment; a simple 18-gauge needle can be used to decompress the pleural cavity. Later, a closed thoracostomy drainage system will be in order.

6. **Thoracostomy** Tube thoracostomy is indicated when the pneumothorax is likely to reaccumulate. *Closed thoracostomy* is used to designate a thoracostomy tube connected to a water seal bottle. With the water seal (which can be improvised by placing the end of the tube under the surface of some sterile normal saline contained in anything with an air vent), air (and also fluid) drain from the chest, but air cannot reenter the submerged tube tip *if the end of*

the tube and water seal are below the level of the patient's chest. It is customary to place the "bottle" on the floor. If the system is functioning well, the fluid will be lifted a few centimeters up the tube as the patient breathes and produces negative (subatmospheric) inspiratory pressure. Later, when the visceral and parietal pleura are adherent, this will not be seen.

20 Inflammatory and Immunodeficiency Disorders

I. INFLAMMATORY DISORDERS

A. **Juvenile rheumatoid arthritis (JRA)** is the primary cause of childhood crippling due to a musculoskeletal disorder and is a major cause of blindness in childhood. The youngest reported patient was 1 week old at the time of presentation.

1. **Etiology** This is unknown.

2. **Evaluation** JRA must be considered in all children with arthralgia or arthritis, even if it is confined to one joint. It is also part of the differential diagnosis of unexplained fever and of anterior uveitis. Clinical differentiation from acute rheumatic fever may be difficult (see Table 20-1). There are three modes of onset: acute febrile, polyarthritic, and oligoarthritic.

Table 20-1. Clinical Features of Rheumatoid Arthritis and Acute Rheumatic Fever

Factors that may be common to both diseases:
Migratory polyarthropathy
Myocarditis and pericarditis
Raised antitstreptolysin O titer

Factors that may assist in differentiation:	*Juvenile Rheumatoid Arthritis*	*Acute Rheumatic Fever*
Age	Any	Rare under 4
Rash	Evanescent, migratory, consists of macules	Open rings with distinct edges, lasting 1–2 weeks
Joint pain	May be absent	Present
Fever	Quotidian or double quotidian (but may be remittent)	Remittent or sustained

a. **Acute febrile onset** Irritability, listlessness, weight loss, hyperpyrexia, arthritis, lymphadenopathy, and abdominal pain are usual. Patients frequently have a rash and splenomegaly. Other manifestations include myocarditis, pericarditis, pneumonia, and pleurisy.

(1) The **fever pattern** may be diagnostically of value, being quotidian or double quotidian with wide diurnal swings, peaking

at about 102° F, with a range of 4–9° F. Fever may be the sole manifestation.

(2) Rash The characteristic rash is evanescent and recurrent and consists of salmon-colored macules. The lesions can be made to appear by scratching the skin (Koebner's phenomenon).

b. Polyarthritic onset These children are febrile, ill, and anorectic, and there is usually painful swelling of several joints, but tenderness and redness may be absent. Early cervical spine involvement is a clue to diagnosis. Systemic disease is rare, but not unknown, nor are lymphadenopathy and splenomegaly. Iridocyclitis occurs in about 2 percent.

c. Oligoarthritic onset The joint most commonly involved is the knee, but the ankle, hip, elbow, and wrists may also be involved; tendonitis or bursitis may be present. These patients may be afebrile and not seem ill. The major associated problem is *iridocyclitis*, which may develop in as many as 20 percent, and which may even be the presenting feature.

3. Diagnosis The criteria for the positive diagnosis of JRA include the following:

a. Onset under age 16.

b. Swelling or pain in two or more joints for at least 3 months.

c. Swelling or pain in one joint for at least 3 months and biopsy evidence of synovial cell hyperplasia with lymphocyte and plasma cell infiltration.

d. Either **b** or **c** for 6 weeks with one of the following: x-ray changes, positive Rh factor, typical rash, typical fever for 1 week, iridocyclitis, neck stiffness.

e. Laboratory findings Elevated ESR, anemia, and elevated alpha 2 and gamma globulins are usual except in oligarthritic disease. The presence of rheumatoid factor or positive antinuclear antibody (ANA) is rare. X-ray findings may be normal but also may show soft tissue radiodensity, demineralization, premature closure of epiphyses, or periosteal proliferation.

f. Joint aspiration in oligoarthritic disease is mandatory to exclude septic arthritis.

4. Therapy For a full discussion, see *J. Pediatr.* 77:355, 1970.

a. Rest Bed rest is contraindicated except in an acute painful flare-up, or if heart disease is present. Continued activity, to avoid muscle-wasting and joint deformity, is vital.

b. Physical therapy During exacerbations, involved joints should be passively put through their range of motion 2–3 times daily. One may have to await pain relief before starting. Subsequently, daily active exercises, initially of the extension type and then of the resistant type, are required.

c. Splinting In acute episodes, involved joints are supported by plastic splints or sandbags to avoid flexion deformity. Splints are kept on at night and at variable times during the day, according to the severity of disease. Advanced deformity may require serial corrective splinting.

d. Drugs

   (1) Aspirin is the drug of choice.

      (a) The dose is usually in the range of 90–130 mg/kg daily given at intervals of 4–6 hr. Dosage must be regulated by measuring plasma levels, which should reach 25–35 mg/100 ml.

      (b) If gastritis is a problem, enteric-coated or PR aspirin may be used, but absorption is erratic, and a therapeutic level may be difficult to attain.

      (c) Aspirin is continued until there are no signs of acute disease.

   (2) Corticosteroids are indicated in severe systemic disease not responding to aspirin, serious eye involvement, and myocarditis or pericarditis.

      (a) Prednisone   Maintenance dosage, 0.1–0.4 mg/kg daily.

      (b) Intraarticular triamcinolone is useful in oligoarthritic disease. Injections of 5–20 mg are repeated at intervals of not less than 3 months.

   (3) Gold   In unresponsive polyarthritis, this relatively toxic mode of therapy may be useful.

      (a) Gold thiomalate is given monthly by deep IM injection of 1 mg/kg. It may be 3–6 months before any response is noted.

      (b) Toxic effects include dermatitis, toxic nephritis, and blood dyscrasias. Therapy should be interrupted in the presence of albuminuria, hematuria, pruritis, or granulocytopenia.

      (c) Gold salts should not be used in patients under 12 years of age.

   (4) Hydroxychloroquine has been used successfully in some patients. It should be used only by physicians familiar with it (dose is 10–15 mg/kg daily). Careful ophthalmologic examinations should be done every 3 months.

5. Prognosis   The overall outcome in JRA includes a mortality rate of 4–5 percent due to myocarditis, steroid toxicity, and amyloidosis. Cataracts develop in about 3–4 percent; one-half are induced and one-half are due to uveitis.

B. Systemic lupus erythematosus (SLE)

1. Etiology   In the majority of cases the etiology is unknown, but there are a number of known associations. There is a family history of connective tissue disease in 25 percent of patients; the rash is light-sensitive, and the systemic disease sometimes dates from, or is exacerbated by, exposure to the sun. About 10 percent of cases are drug-induced (see Table 20-2). Of all patients, 80 percent are female, with peak onset in the teen-age years.

2. Evaluation

   a. The classic presentation is with a facial rash of butterfly distribution, polyarthritis, fever, malaise, and generalized weakness. However, the initial features may be rash alone, intermittent

Table 20-2. Drugs Involved in Systemic Lupus Erythematosus

Hydralazine	Sulfonamides
Procainamide	Phenylbutazone
Trimethadione	Para-aminosalicylic acid
Diphenylhydantoin	Isoniazid
Penicillin	

arthralgia, or renal disease—with a nephrotic or chronic nephritic pattern. During the course of the disease, numerous other manifestations may appear. These are detailed in Table 20-3.

Table 20-3. Manifestations Appearing During the Course of Systemic Lupus Erythematosus

Manifestation	Case Incidence (%)
Fever	100
Arthritis	80
Rash	80
Pneumonitis	70
Glomerulonephritis	65
Myositis	60
Pleurisy	60
Oral ulceration	55
Lymphadenopathy	50
Hypertension	40
Peritonitis	30
Petechiae	30
Endocarditis	25–50
Myocarditis	25–50
Pericarditis	25–50
Hepatosplenomegaly	25–40
Seizures	25
Raynaud's phenomenon	20
Psychoses	10–20
Neuropathy	10

    b. Laboratory investigations indicate a high incidence of positive LE cell preparations and ANA, with elevated ESR, anemia, and low serum complement (see Table 20-4); albuminuria, hematuria, leukopenia, and a positive Coombs test occur less commonly. Thrombocytopenia, rheumatoid factor, and a positive STS are rarely seen.

3. Diagnosis Needed are a compatible history of multisystem involvement, with the presence of antinuclear antibodies, or positive LE cell preparation, or both. Skin manifestations are usual but not essential for diagnosis. A renal or skin biopsy may be required.

4. Therapy

    a. General measures Rest, physical therapy, and splinting (A.4.a–c).

Table 20-4.   Laboratory Investigations in Systemic Lupus Erythematosus

Test	Incidence of Positives (%)
ANA	100
LE cell preparation	90
ESR > 25	80
Serum complement low	80
Anemia	60
Inverted albumin/globulin ratio	55
Albuminuria	45
Hematuria	45
Leukopenia	45
Positive Coombs test	35
Thrombocytopenia	25
False-positive STS	25
Rheumatoid factor	15

b. Drugs

   (1) Aspirin to relieve pain and fever (30–60 mg/kg daily).

   (2) Corticosteroids   Patients with active renal, hematologic, or severe skin disease should be treated with prednisone, 1–2 mg/kg/24 hr, until the disease is under control. Then the dosage should be tapered off to the minimum at which the disease remains quiescent; fever and toxicity sometimes then return, but usually subside in 24–48 hr. Alternate-day dosage may be required. Local corticosteroid preparations are used on skin lesions, with an occlusive dressing if practicable.

   (3) Hydroxychloroquine   There is little information on the use of this drug in children, but a lower corticosteroid dosage may be possible with concomitant use of hydroxychloroquine, 10–15 mg/kg/24 hr. For side effects and precautions, see **A.4.d.**

   (4) Immunosuppressive agents   The prognosis of SLE depends on the type of renal involvement, if any. If the renal lesion is basically proliferative glomerulonephritis, rapid progression is likely; in these circumstances successful results have been obtained using azathioprine. (For a discussion of azathioprine, see *Medicine* [Baltimore] 51:393, 1972.)

C. Dermatomyositis

   1. Etiology   Unknown.

   2. Evaluation

   a. The presenting symptoms are progressive muscle weakness and tenderness of the legs. Later the arms, trunk, and neck are involved. Typically there is a violaceous heliotrope discoloration of the upper lids, with scaly erythema in a butterfly distribution over the malar area. Symmetric erythematous atrophic changes over the extensor aspect of the joints develops in most patients. Periorbital edema is not uncommon.

b. Dyspepsia, melena, and hematemesis may be late signs even in patients not treated with corticosteroids.

c. Laboratory findings   Serum LDH and SGOT are commonly elevated. Serum creatine phosphokinase (CPK) and aldolase may be elevated. Alpha 2 and gamma globulins may be high, and, rarely, there may be elevated ANA in low titer.

3. Diagnosis

   a. Rash and myopathy.

   b. Elevation of muscle enzymes (not necessarily all).

   c. Electromyographic changes of myopathic units.

   d. Muscle biopsy if the diagnosis is questionable.

4. Therapy

   a. General measures   Rest, physiotherapy, and splinting as in JRA (see **A.4.a–c**).

   b. Drugs

   (1) Aspirin   This may be used to relieve pain and fever in a daily dose of 30–60 mg/kg.

   (2) Corticosteroids   Almost invariably toxic signs remit after 48 hr of therapy with prednisone (1–2 mg/kg/24 hr in 4 divided doses). Treatment is tapered off when symptoms and signs subside, usually in 2–3 weeks. Corticosteroids should be continued at the lowest controlling dose, probably for up to 2 years. Alternate-day dosage may be indicated.

   (3) Methotrexate   Sporadic case reports demonstrate possible advantages from this drug in dermatomyositis that does not respond to corticosteroids, but experience with its use in children is very limited.

D. Polyarteritis nodosa (PAN)

1. Etiology   PAN is a rare immune-complex disease. Immunofluorescent studies demonstrate deposition of IgM, antigen, and complement in small and medium arteries. Serum sickness, drug hypersensitivity, and Australia antigenemia have been incriminated as etiologic factors.

2. Evaluation

   a. There is multisystem involvement. The frequency of signs is shown in Table 20-5.

   b. Laboratory findings that may be present are shown in Table 20-6. The rash may be nonspecific or basically macular. Frequently there are recurrent tender subcutaneous nodules and patchy skin mottling of livedo reticularis type.

3. Diagnosis   The diagnosis is basically clinical, but sometimes can be confirmed by rectal or skin biopsy to show vasculitis and immune complex disease. Renal arteriography may reveal the typical vascular lesions.

4. Therapy

   a. Fever and pain relief with aspirin, 30–60 mg/kg daily.

Table 20-5.   Frequency of Signs in Polyarteritis Nodosa

Sign	Frequency (%)
Prolonged or recurrent fever	90
Macular rash	60
Conjunctivitis	50
Cough	50
Hypertension	? 50
CNS abnormalities	30
Congestive heart failure	30
Erythema multiforme	15
Ischemia of extremities	10
Pericarditis	< 10

Table 20-6.   Laboratory Findings in Polyarteritis Nodosa

Abnormal urinary sediment	Leukocytosis
Chest x-ray infiltrates	Eosinophilia
Cardiomegaly	Elevated ESR
Abnormal ECG (ischemia or	Antinuclear antibody
left ventricular hypertrophy)	Rheumatoid factor negative

b. Appropriate treatment of congestive heart failure, pericardial effusion, or hypertension if present.

c. Corticosteroids are indicated, but the results are disappointing. The usual dose is prednisone 2 mg/kg/24 hr, tapered off when there is clinical improvement.

E. Serum sickness

1. Etiology   Serum sickness is commonly seen as a manifestation of drug hypersensitivity. The mechanism is probably the deposition of antigen-antibody complement complexes that are formed in moderate antigen excess. Almost every drug has been cited as a cause, particularly penicillin and sulfonamides. Sera still used that may cause the disease include antitetanus serum (ATS), snake antivenom, and gas-gangrene, rabies, and diphtheria antisera.

2. Evaluation   In serum sickness, there is a stereotyped response of fever, urticaria, lymphadenopathy, and, more rarely, arthralgia and variable rashes occurring 7–12 days after the first exposure to drug or serum, or 1–5 days after repeat exposure.

3. Diagnosis

a. Diagnosis is by typical history, but, if the illness is mild and due to an antibiotic, it must be differentiated from a recurrence of the original infection.

b. A Forssman-type heterophil antibody may be found, i.e., one that agglutinates sheep cells, but not if previously absorbed onto guinea-pig cells.

4. Therapy

a. If urticaria is severe, 0.01 ml/kg of a 1:1000 dilution of aqueous epinephrine is given SQ. Otherwise, an antihistamine such as chlorpheniramine maleate should be given (0.35 mg/kg daily in 4 divided doses). Rarely, a brief course of prednisone is needed. This should be started at 2 mg/kg/24 hr and tapered off as soon as symptoms subside. The patient should be advised to avoid the suspected precipitating cause.

b. Antisera from animal sources should be used only when essential. A previous scratch test with a 1:100 dilution is **mandatory**. Preferably, hyperimmune sera from human sources should be used.

F. Angioneurotic edema Two distinct diseases with similar manifestations are included under this head: simple angioneurotic edema and hereditary angioneurotic edema.

1. Simple angioneurotic edema

a. Etiology A reagin-mediated hypersensitivity reaction resulting in release of histamine, which alters capillary permeability.

b. Evaluation and diagnosis There is usually rapid development of elevated, extensive, and spreading skin lesions, often involving the eyes, lips, genitalia, hands, and feet. The lesions are much larger than those of urticaria. Rarely, there may be laryngeal edema. Eosinophilia may be present. If episodes are repeated, the hereditary type of disease should be excluded by measuring serum C1 esterase inhibitor.

c. Therapy is the same as for serum sickness (see **E.4**). Suspicion of laryngeal involvement requires the alerting of anesthesia and surgical services, the placement *at the bedside* of a resuscitation set, including equipment for tracheostomy, and constant observation.

2. Hereditary angioneurotic edema

a. Etiology The cause is an inborn error in the biosynthesis of alpha 2 globulin that inhibits activity of the first component of complement. Thus C1 is unopposed, and C4 and C2 therefore consumed. Activation of C1 seems to be related to attacks of angioneurotic edema. The condition is inherited in an autosomal dominant fashion, but some patients with no family history of the condition have been described.

b. Evaluation This is one of the periodic diseases of childhood and presents with recurrent nonpruritic edema of the skin; other manifestations include arthralgia, thirst and polyuria, headache, psychological symptoms, and, usually, severe abdominal pain, nausea, vomiting, and diarrhea. Laryngeal obstruction may occur. Some patients describe a rash identical to erythema marginatum. Episodes typically last 1–5 days and recur at irregular intervals. Some patients have only edema, others only recurrent abdominal pain.

c. Diagnosis This is confirmed by estimating serum C1 esterase inhibitor (C1INH) and C4 levels. In these patients C1INH is less than 30 percent of normal. (Rare patients have normal amounts of nonfunctioning C1INH and C4 is less than 25 percent of normal.)

d. Therapy

(1) Corticosteroids and epinephrine are, in general, ineffective.

(2) Epsilon aminocaproic acid (EACA) and its analogue, trans

4-aminoethyl-cyclohexane-1-carboxylic acid (tranexamic acid) are the drugs of choice. Tranexamic acid is probably the most effective and least toxic; however, it is investigational and not currently available for general use.

(3) EACA has been used at an *adult* dose of 7–12 gm daily in 4 divided doses. Its use is limited by side effects of myopathy, nasal congestion, and hypotension. It should be tried if tranexamic acid fails.

(4) Fresh frozen plasma has been reported to have been used successfully to treat life-threatening illness. It presumably acts by supplying the inhibitor, but has the theoretical *disadvantage* of also supplying the substrate.

(5) As with the simple form of disease, one should be prepared to deal with glottic obstruction (see **F.1.c**).

G. Henoch-Schönlein purpura

1. Etiology   This is basically unknown.

2. Evaluation   Patients most commonly present with rash or rash and joint swelling, but vomiting or abdominal colic, or both, are sometimes the initial features.

a. Rash   See **3**.

b. Joints   Involvement varies from transient puffiness to recurrent painful periarticular swelling in multiple sites. Soft tissue swelling occurs, particularly of the hands, feet, and scalp.

c. Gastrointestinal tract   Colicky abdominal pain occurs in 50–75 percent of patients, and most of these have blood in the stools. Intussusception is a rare complication. A small number of patients have massive gastrointestinal bleeding. Intestinal perforation has been described.

d. Hemorrhage   Rarely, cerebral and/or gastrointestinal hemorrhage may occur, and bleeding into the eyelids, conjunctivas, and scrotum.

e. Renal disease   Onset is within 1 month of the onset of the purpura and ranges from microscopic hematuria to nephrotic syndrome or acute nephritis progressing to nephrosis.

3. Diagnosis   This is purely clinical and depends on the stereotyped nature of the rash, a detailed description of which follows (see also *Q. J. Med.* 17:95, 1948).

a. Initial lesions are small and urticarial and change within a few hours to pink maculopapules. After 6–12 hr these become dusky-red macules, which measure 0.5–2.0 cm in diameter and do not blanch. Some may coalesce; the color becomes purple, and petechiae and ecchymoses may be seen at this stage. Eventually, the lesions fade to brown and disappear in about 2 weeks.

b. The most common sites are the buttocks and extensor surfaces of the limbs. The lesions are generally symmetrical.

4. Therapy

a. General measures   Rest is recommended while the discomfort is severe. IV fluids are indicated in severe gastrointestinal disease. A blood transfusion may be needed if extensive bleeding occurs.

      b. Analgesics The arthropathy responds to aspirin. Usually only antipyretic doses are required, but occasionally doses may have to be increased to 100 mg/kg/day.

      c. Corticosteroids There has been no controlled study of corticosteroid use in this condition. Corticosteroids probably do not affect the duration of the illness, the frequency of recurrence, or the renal complications. However, some physicians believe that in this condition corticosteroids are useful for severe abdominal pain, severe gastrointestinal hemorrhage, and for severe, uncomfortable localized soft tissue swelling, or very painful joints, or both. For dose, see **D.4.c**, p. 425.

II. IMMUNODEFICIENCY DISORDERS Defects of the immune system (Table 20-7) may involve either humoral or cellular components or both (Chap. 8, Sec. **C**, p. 151).

A. Humoral defects

  1. Etiology

      a. Infants are born with IgG levels equal to maternal levels due to selective placental transfer and with low levels of IgM and IgA.

      b. The infant's IgG level decreases to a minimum at 3–4 months and then slowly rises with increased synthesis until adult levels are reached after 1 year of life.

      c. The absence of normal immunoglobulin levels predisposes to recurrent infections with encapsulated bacteria, such as streptococci, staphylococci, and *Hemophilus influenzae*, since opsonization of the organisms with specific antibody is necessary before phagocytosis and killing can occur.

      d. A defect in immunoglobulin product does *not* manifest itself by an increased incidence of viral or fungal infections.

  2. Diagnosis The clinical presentation of a child with recurrent *bacterial* infection should require quantitation of his specific immunoglobulin levels and serum immunoelectrophoresis. The results must be judged in relation to the patient's age (Fig. 20-1). Patients more than 2 years old who have IgG levels of less than 300 mg/100 ml have immunoglobulin deficiency.

      a. Transient hypogammaglobulinemia of infancy In some infants the normal onset of immunoglobulin synthesis is delayed beyond 2–3 months. These patients may have IgG levels of less than 200 mg/100 ml. Their clinical symptoms may be somewhat milder than the more severe genetic forms of immunoglobulin deficiency. They may manifest symptoms of bronchospasm that clear when immunoglobulin therapy is instituted.

      b. X-linked agammaglobulinemia of childhood In this condition there is almost complete absence of immunoglobulin production and total immunoglobulin levels of less than 100 mg/100 ml. The onset of symptoms is usually in the first year of life.

      c. Common variable forms of immunoglobulin deficiency This comprises a heterogenous group of patients who have a later onset of clinical symptoms and deficiency of all classes of immunoglobulins. These patients have cells capable of synthesizing immunoglobulin, but it is not released into the circulation.

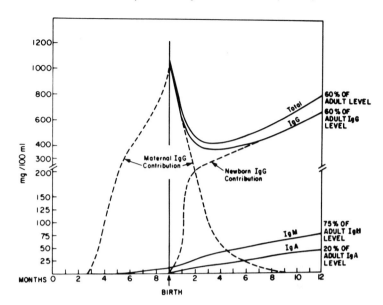

Figure 20-1. Immunoglobulin (IgG, IgM, and IgA) levels in the fetus and infant in the first year of life. The IgG of the fetus and newborn infant is solely of maternal origin. The maternal IgG disappears by the age of nine months, by which time the endogenous synthesis of IgG by the infant is well established. The IgM and IgA of the neonate are entirely endogenously synthesized, since maternal IgM and IgA do *not* cross the placenta. (From E. R. Stiehm and V. A. Fulginiti. *Immunologic Disorders in Infants and Children.* Philadelphia, W. B. Saunders Company, 1973. Reproduced by permission.)

    d. Dysgammaglobulinemia Almost all combinations have been noted. Among the most common are increased IgM, decreased IgG and IgA, and absent IgM or IgA.

   3. Therapy Any patient with clinical disease and reduced immunoglobulin levels, especially of IgG, may benefit from replacement therapy. Pooled gamma globulin contains IgG almost exclusively, with no significant IgM or IgA. The initial dose of pooled gamma globulin is 1.8 ml/kg IM. For maintenance therapy, 0.6 ml/kg is given IM every 3–4 weeks.

B. Cellular deficiency

   1. Etiology Cellular immunocompetence is vested in the circulating small lymphocytes. Absence of these cells causes increased susceptibility to fungal and viral infections without an increased frequency of bacterial infections. The incidence of true cellular deficiency states is very low. Most children with recurrent upper respiratory (viral) infections do *not* have a primary cellular defect.

   2. Evaluation and diagnosis

    a. The hallmark of cellular immunodeficiency states is moniliasis, which may temporarily respond to antifungal agents but recurs.

    b. The total lymphocyte count and the ability of these lymphocytes

Table 20-7. Biologic Properties of the Immunoglobulin Classes

	IgG	IgM	IgA	IgD	IgE	Secretory IgA
First detectable antibody	0	+	0	0	0	0
Major part of secondary response	+	0	0	0	0	0
Binds complement	+	+	0	0	0	0
Active placental transport	+	0	0	0	0	0
Reacts with rheumatoid factor	+	0	0	0	0	0
Agglutination	+	++	0	0	0	0
Opsonization	+	++	0	0	0	+
Virus neutralization	+	+	0	0	0	+
Hemolysis	+	++	0	0	0	0
Anaphylactic activity	0	0	0	0	+	0
Present in body secretions	+	0	+	0	+	++
Antibody (Ab) function	Major antitoxic, antiviral, and antibacterial Ab	Major Ab to polysaccharides and gram-negative bacteria	No unique Ab function	No unique Ab function	Anaphylactic (reaginic) Ab	Major Ab of secretions

Blocking Ab in allergy	Natural iso-agglutinins, saline anti-Rh Ab	Some Ab to polio virus	Protects mucous surfaces
Incomplete Rh & immune anti-A and anti-B isoagglutinins	Heterophile Ab, rheumatoid factor	May prevent development of auto-immune Ab and milk precipitins	Resists digestion

From E. R. Stiehm and V. A. Fulginiti. *Immunologic Disorders in Infants and Children.* Philadelphia: W. B. Saunders Company, 1973. Reproduced by permission.

to undergo mitosis when stimulated in vitro by phytohemagglutinin (PHA) are the two easiest determinations of cellular immunity. Most routine genetics laboratories can do a qualitative PHA stimulation.

    c. The inability to respond to specific antigens can be measured either by intradermal skin tests or in vitro stimulation of lymphocytes.

    d. Di George's syndrome This is a developmental abnormality causing the absence of the thymus gland and parathyroid glands, a right-sided aortic arch, cardiac defects, high-arched palate, and typical facies. Any infant who presents with tetany, a cardiac defect, an absent thymus shadow on x-ray, and lymphopenia should be considered to have this syndrome.

    e. Mucocutaneous candidiasis is characterized by recurrent monilial infections. The total lymphocyte count and PHA stimulation are normal.

    f. Drug immunosuppression There are recurrent fungal infections and unusually severe common viral illnesses such as varicella, rubeola, and herpes simplex.

3. Therapy For gamma globulin prophylaxis in viral exposure, see Table 9-5, p. 190.

    a. Di George's syndrome Correction of the immunologic defect is by transplantation of a fetal thymus gland.

    b. Mucocutaneous candidiasis Transfer factor is presently an experimental form of therapy in this condition.

    c. Drug immunosuppression Transfer factor and white cell infusions are still experimental forms of therapy.

C. Combined immune deficiency syndrome

1. Etiology These patients have a defect that leads to absence of both hormonal and cellular immunity.

2. Evaluation and diagnosis Onset is at 3–6 months of age. Moniliasis, failure to thrive, diarrhea, and recurrent infections are the presenting symptoms.

3. Therapy Histocompatible bone marrow transplantation is the only curative therapy. In the absence of a compatible donor, this disease is uniformly fatal. Measures for maximum support are the following:

    a. A **sterile environment** should be provided, including *reverse precautions* (gown, gloves, mask, hat, and boots), sterilization of the gut with nonabsorbable antimicrobials (see Sec. **4**, p. 196) and antimycotics (Nystatin 400,000 U/24 hr qid PO), sterile food, regular washing of the skin with antibacterial solutions, and regular *re*sterilization of the room.

    b. Antibiotics should be used only for proved infections *except*

    c. Because of the possibility of pneumocystis infestation, patients at this institution receive prophylactic sulfadiazine (150 mg/kg PO) *and* pyrimethamine (1 mg/kg), *and* folinic acid (0.15 mg/kg) daily, although adequate evidence for the efficacy of these agents is lacking.

21 Skin Disorders

I. ACNE

A. Etiology At puberty, increased blood levels of androgenic steroids stimulate activity of the pilosebaceous apparatus. Sebum becomes trapped, and bacterial (*Corynebacterium acnes*) enzymes hydrolyze sebaceous lipids to free fatty acids. The sebaceous ducts distended by inspissated sebaceous material rupture and release irritating free fatty acids into the dermis, where an inflammatory reaction occurs. *Diet is not thought to play a role in the pathophysiology of the disease.*

B. Evaluation Determine the social problem presented by the disease. Ask if flares of disease activity are associated with periods of emotional stress or with menstruation.

C. Diagnosis

1. Subjective findings Flares of activity may be associated with emotional stress or with menstrual periods.

2. Objective findings The skin is oily. Scattered over the face, chest, and back are comedones, inflammatory papules and pustules, and, in some cases, deep, interconnecting, fluctuant cysts. Scarring may be disfiguring.

D. Therapy

1. Soaps Drying and abrasive soaps promote superficial desquamation and opening of plugged follicular orifices. They should be used 2 or 3 times daily. Representative products are Pernox, Fostex, and Brāsivol.

2. Lotions and creams Drying lotions should be applied after washing in the morning and at night. If excess drying and inflammation result, the lotions should be used less often. Representative products are Benoxyl, Microsyn, Transact, Komed, and Fostril.

3. Ultraviolet light Either sunlight or artificial ultraviolet light (UVL) will promote faster and more complete control of the disease. Commercially available UV lamps must be used regularly (3 times weekly at least) with stepwise increases in exposure time.

4. Antibiotics *C. acnes* organisms are exquisitely sensitive to tetracycline. For pustular and cystic acne, start tetracycline at a dosage of 250 mg PO qid until control is obtained. Then decrease the dosage to a maintenance level, which may be 250 mg twice daily.

5. Estrogens Anovulatory drugs with a high estrogen content (0.1 mg mestranol) may be helpful in girls with severe acne. However, 2 or 3 months may pass before significant improvement is seen. A gynecologic consultation should be obtained before starting a patient on anovulatory drugs.

II. ATOPIC DERMATITIS

A. Etiology   Features of the atopic syndrome are mediated by tissue-fixed IgE antibody. The role these mediators play in the eczematous phase of atopic dermatitis is still unknown.

B. Evaluation   Allergy testing with scratch or intradermal skin tests is unrewarding. Thus a careful history to determine precipitants (foods, pollens, dusts, dander) of pruritus or dermatitis is much more helpful.

C. Diagnosis

   1. Subjective findings

   a. Atopic dermatitis evolves in three stages: (1) the infantile stage, 2 months–3 years; (2) the childhood stage, 3 years–puberty; and (3) the adolescent stage, puberty–25 years. Pruritus is common to all.

   b. Extremes of heat or cold, soap and water, alkalis, chemical irritants, infection, wool, inhalants (pollens, dust, dander), particular foods, and psychic stress worsen atopic dermatitis.

   c. The family history is positive for some feature of the atopic syndrome in over 70 percent of cases.

   2. Objective findings

   a. Infantile stage   Erythematous papules with microvesicles, oozing, and crusting involve the scalp, face, neck, the extensor aspects of the arms, and the ankles. Scattered patches occur on the trunk. Antecubital and popliteal fossae are often spared.

   b. Childhood stage   Erythematous papules with less vesiculation and crusting than in the infantile stage, but with more scaling and lichenification, occur commonly on the trunk and extremities. There is less facial involvement than in the earlier stage. Papules and lichenification may be present in the antecubital and popliteal fossae.

   c. Adolescent-adult stage   The face, neck, and upper chest are dry and scaly. Transverse, parallel lines of ruga-like lichenificaton of the antecubital and popliteal fossae are the hallmarks of this stage.

D. Treatment

   1. Topical corticosteroids (see Sec. **XV.A**) are the single most effective therapeutic agents. Applied 2–4 times daily, they rapidly suppress inflammation and pruritus.

   2. Emollients (Eucerin, hydrated petrolatum, Lubriderm) are applied as often as needed for control of cracking and fissuring of dry, lichenified areas. Emollients should always be applied *immediately* after bathing to maintain the benefits of hydration.

   3. Soap and water are irritants to already dried, cracked, and scaling skin. The patient should bathe only to keep reasonably clean, and use of soap should be restricted to such areas as the axillae, groin, and feet. Bland, superfatted, or oil-containing soaps (Basis soap, Oilatum soap, Aveeno Oilated soap) are useful.

   4. Antihistamines (see Sec. **XV.B**) are useful because of their sedative effects. The dosage should thus be raised until the patient is less

active than usual and somewhat drowsy. Double doses are recommended at bedtime, when most pruritus occurs.

III. CONTACT DERMATITIS

A. Etiology Sensitization to contact allergens. To cause contact sensitization, an antigen must penetrate the epidermis and contain reactive
groups that conjugate with tissue proteins. Many substances satisfy
these criteria.

B. Evaluation The location, distribution, and shape of the lesions are the
most useful features in determining the cause of a contact dermatitis.

C. Diagnosis

    1. Subjective findings A history of contact allergy to several different
substances is often obtainable. Pruritus is an early distressing symptom of the eruption.

    2. Objective findings The earliest change is erythema. Edema, vesicu-
lation, and bullous formation follow in rapid succession. *Linearly
distributed vesicles* are pathognomonic of contact dermatitis.

D. Therapy

    1. Acute vesicular contact dermatitis

        a. Aluminum acetate (Burow's) solution, 1:20, used as a cool, wet
compress for 15 min q1–2h relieves pruritus and loosens crusts.

        b. When oozing and crusting begin to resolve, compresses are de-
creased to qid and a topical fluorinated corticosteroid cream (see
Sec. **XV.A**) is applied after each compress is removed.

        c. In mild cases *without* oozing and crusting, calamine lotion with
0.25% phenol relieves pruritus.

        d. In severe, widespread dermatitis, prednisone PO quickly relieves
symptoms and prevents progression of the eruption.

            (1) To prevent generalized eczematous dermatitis, a 10-day
course of corticosteroid therapy as described in Table 21-1

Table 21-1. Ten-Day Oral Prednisone Regimen in Contact Dermatitis[a]

Day of Therapy	Number of 5-Milligram Tablets to be Taken QID				Total Dose (mg)
	Breakfast	Lunch	Dinner	Bedtime	
1	2	2	2	2	40
2	2	2	2	2	40
3	2	2	2	2	40
4	2	1	2	2	35
5	2	1	2	1	30
6	2	1	1	1	25
7	1	1	1	1	20
8	1	1	0	1	15
9	1	0	0	1	10
10	1	0	0	0	5

[a] Should be modified proportionately for younger children.

should be given. A similar schedule should be given to the patient with a warning that prematurely stopping the medication may cause exacerbation.

(2) Prednisone must be avoided if the usual contraindications (i.e., hypertension, gastrointestinal ulcers, diabetes mellitus) are present. After the dermatitis has resolved, patch testing may be done to define the sensitizing allergen clearly. (Patch testing during the active phase of the process can cause exacerbation.)

2. Chronic, lichenified contact dermatitis

a. A fluorinated corticosteroid cream is applied to the lesions at bedtime and occluded with a plastic wrap overnight (see Sec. **XV.A.1**).

b. A lubricating, hydrophilic ointment (hydrated petrolatum, Eucerin) is applied during the day as needed for dryness and scaling.

c. After the dermatitis has resolved, patch testing is done to define the etiology clearly.

IV. DIAPER DERMATITIS

A. Etiology   Diaper dermatitis is the result of dampness, maceration, and chemical irritation.

B. Evaluation   Question parents regarding the use of plastic or rubber occlusive pants and detergents or disinfectants. Examine the scalp, retroauricular areas, face, and axillae for evidence of seborrhea or atopic dermatitis. Scrape the moist, erythematous lesion in the diaper area and examine the material for *Candida albicans.*

C. Diagnosis   Erythema, scaling, and often erosion and ulceration affect primarily convex surfaces, i.e., the buttocks, genitalia, lower abdomen, and upper thighs. The flexural folds may be spared.

D. Therapy   Instructions are as follows:

1. Stop the use of bulky diapers and occlusive plastic or rubber pants.

2. Use disposable paper diapers, or rinse cloth diapers well to remove detergent, enzymes, and chemical irritants.

3. Change diapers more often.

4. With each diaper change, cleanse the diaper area with tepid water.

5. Apply a corticosteroid cream (see Sec. **XV.A**).

6. If *C. albicans* is present, add nystatin cream tid.

V. ERYTHEMA MULTIFORME

A. Etiology   Among the common precipitants are infections with herpes simplex, *Mycoplasma pneumoniae*, vaccinia, adenovirus, *Histoplasma*, and exposures to penicillin, sulfonamides, barbiturates, and butazones. However, in 50 percent of cases an etiologic factor cannot be elicited. Severe erythema multiforme is referred to as the Stevens-Johnson syndrome.

B. Evaluation Review the events of the previous 3 weeks for evidence of the recognized precipitants. Determine if a similar eruption has occurred in the past.

C. Diagnosis

1. **Subjective findings** Successive crops of lesions may appear for from 10 to 14 days. Mucous membrane erosions are extremely painful and debilitating.

2. **Objective findings**

   a. Painful erosions with hemorrhagic crusts involve the mucous membranes of the mouth, lip, nose, eyes, urethra, vagina, and anus. On the dorsa of the hands, palms, wrists, forearms, feet, and legs are erythematous plaques 1–2 cm in diameter, with violaceous or purpuric centers (so-called *target* lesions) that may become bullous. Hyperpigmented spots are left as the lesions resolve.

   b. Corneal ulcerations with subsequent opacities occur in severe disease.

D. Therapy

1. **Mild and moderately severe disease**

   a. Simple topical care with hexachlorophene (pHisoHex) and water prevents secondary bacterial invasion of denuded skin lesions.

   b. Topical anesthetics such as diclonine (Dyclone) mouthwash or lidocaine (Xylocaine) ointments are applied to painful, denuded mucous membranes.

2. **Severe disease**

   a. Prednisone, 1–2 mg/kg/day in divided doses, or IV hydrocortisone in severe cases, will shorten the duration of the disease process.

   b. If skin lesions are extensive, 1:20 aluminum acetate (Burow's) solution as wet compresses should be applied for 30 min q3–4h while the patient is awake.

   c. If oral lesions preclude fluid intake, maintain fluid and electrolyte balance with IV replacement.

   d. If an infectious disease is the underlying cause, treat the infection appropriately.

VI. FUNGAL INFECTIONS

A. Etiology

1. Tinea capitis, tinea corporis (ringworm), tinea versicolor, tinea cruris, tinea pedis (athlete's foot), and tinea unguium (onychomycosis) are superficial infections of the skin, hair, and nails due to keratinophilic fungi.

2. A nonpyogenic, localized hypersensitivity response to inflammatory tinea capitis results in a pustular, follicular eruption termed a *kerion*. A dry, follicular hyperkeratotic eruption on the trunk and proximal extremity may accompany kerion formation.

3. Associated with inflammatory tinea pedis is a vesicular "id" eruption of the fingers and palms.

B. **Evaluation**

1. **Demonstration of fungi** Scrape the active border of skin lesions and collect fine scales on a glass microscope slide. Apply one drop of 15% potassium hydroxide (KOH) or Swartz-Lamkin stain (Muro Pharmacal Laboratories), cover with a glass coverslip, and heat without boiling over an open flame or boiling water. Invert the slide and press onto a paper towel or gauze to express KOH or stain. Examine under "high-dry" ($\times$ 40). The proximal ends of plucked hairs and scrapings from beneath nails are similarly prepared for examination.

2. **Culture of fungi** Scrapings or hairs are planted on Sabouraud's agar or Dermatophyte Test Media (Pfizer, Difco) and incubated for 2–4 weeks at room temperature.

3. **Wood's light examination** In a darkened room, shine a Wood's light on the scalp. Involved hairs show *brilliant green* fluorescence at their bases when *Microsporum* is the agent responsible.

C. **Specific infections**

1. **Tinea capitis**

   a. **Diagnosis**

      (1) **Subjective findings** The incubation time to clinically apparent disease is 2–3 weeks. Except in the case of painful kerion formation, the infection is slightly pruritic or asymptomatic.

      (2) **Objective findings** Tinea capitis causes a patchy, scaling alopecia with dull, lusterless hairs broken off 1–2 mm above the skin ("gray patch"). Inflammation and erythema are mild or moderate. In actively enlarging lesions, vesicles may be seen in the advancing border. Kerion formation is characterized by the appearance of one or more boggy, edematous, raised plaques with nonpyogenic, purulent material crusting on the surface of the lesion. Infected hairs pull out easily without pain.

   b. **Treatment**

      (1) **For children under 10 years of age** Microcrystalline griseofulvin, 10 mg/kg/24 hr PO bid after meals for 4–6 weeks.

      (2) **For children over 10 years of age and adults** Microcrystalline griseofulvin, 500 mg PO bid after meals for 4–6 weeks

2. **Tinea corporis**

   a. **Diagnosis**

      (1) **Subjective findings** Incubation time is 1–3 weeks.

      (2) **Objective findings** Lesions begin as erythematous papules and expand centrifugally with a raised, papular, scaling and sometimes vesicular border. They clear from the center outward and resolve spontaneously after several weeks. Occasionally a deep, inflammatory, nodular reaction occurs (Majocchi's granuloma).

   b. **Treatment**

      (1) **For mild to moderate involvement,** apply 1% tolnaftate solution (Tinactin) bid to the lesions. To prevent recurrence, con-

tinue this treatment for 10 days after the lesions have resolved.

(2) For extensive or deep involvement, give microcrystalline griseofulvin, 10 mg/kg/24 hr PO bid after meals for 2–3 weeks.

3. Tinea versicolor

a. Diagnosis

(1) Subjective findings Disease activity is exacerbated by warm, humid weather. The eruption is slightly pruritic or asymptomatic. Hypopigmentation of affected areas has been attributed to sun-screening by overlying scales. After treatment, 3–6 months may be required for complete repigmentation.

(2) Objective findings A capelike area over the neck, shoulders, and proximal upper extremities is involved by round, finely scaling, hypopigmented or tan macules. The lesions coalesce into extensive, confluent areas over the posterior shoulders. Scraping with a tongue blade or surgical blade raises an abundance of fine white scales.

b. Treatment
Instructions are as follows: Apply selenium disulfide (Selsun) directly to affected areas. After 1 hr, bathe and scrub vigorously with more of the medication, which lathers like a shampoo. Repeat this process daily for 4 days. During warm weather, use of the medication every other week in the bath will prevent recurrence.

4. Tinea cruris

a. Diagnosis

(1) Subjective findings Inflammation and pruritus may be intense.

(2) Objective findings Sharply marginated, erythematous, and scaling areas with elevated borders and little central clearing extend down the medial thighs from the inguinal folds. The scrotum, penis, and labia are commonly spared. Candidiasis, on the other hand, is characterized by a brightly erythematous eruption above and below the inguinal fold, by involvement of the scrotum and labia, and by satellite pustules scattered beyond the poorly marginated central lesions.

b. Treatment

(1) For mild to moderate involvement, 1% tolnaftate (Tinactin) solution or cream is applied bid until the eruption clears, and then continued bid for 10 days more to prevent recurrence.

(2) For severe involvement, give microcrystalline griseofulvin, 10 mg/kg/24 hr PO bid after meals for 3–4 weeks. Initially, if inflammation is severe, cool Burow's solution (Domeboro powder) compresses are applied 3–4 times daily.

5. Tinea pedis

a. Diagnosis
Tinea pedis is rare before puberty. Scaling, erythematous changes on the feet of children are most likely to be *noninfectious* eruptions due to sweating and maceration ("sneaker dermatitis"), especially in children with an atopic diathesis, i.e., hay fever, asthma, eczema, urticaria by history.

b. Treatment

(1) For mild involvement, apply 1% tolnaftate (Tinactin) solution or cream tid.

(2) For moderate involvement with scaling and hyperkeratosis, 1% tolnaftate solution or cream is applied tid on even days. On alternate days, 6% sulfur and 6% salicylic acid in petrolatum is applied bid.

(3) For severe or recurrent involvement, give microcrystalline griseofulvin, 10 mg/kg/24 hr PO bid after meals for 4–6 weeks. Alternate tolnaftate and sulfur-salicylic acid ointment are applied as described in **(2).**

6. Tinea unguium

a. Diagnosis

(1) Subjective findings Acquisition of nail infection is probably from antecedent skin dermatophytosis. Thus tinea pedis or tinea manus usually coexists. The dystrophic nails are asymptomatic.

(2) Objective findings Usually, only one or two nails on one hand are involved. Early white-to-yellow discoloration of the lateral nail tip is seen. With progression of the infection, the nail becomes yellow or brown, thick, and friable. Keratinous debris collects beneath the distal nail plate.

b. Treatment is extraordinarily difficult. High doses of griseofulvin are required for long periods, and the recurrence rate is approximately 50 percent. Surgically removing involved nails at the onset of therapy results in a somewhat better cure rate. Microcrystalline griseofulvin, 20 mg/kg/24 hr PO bid after meals for 6–12 months, is required.

VII. IMPETIGO See also Chap. 9, Sec. **IV.A.**

A. Etiology Impetigo is clinically and bacteriologically classified into two distinct types. The *nonbullous* type is characterized by crusted lesions caused primarily by **streptococci** and sometimes secondarily infected by staphylococci. *Bullous impetigo* is associated with a bulla or a relatively clean, eroded lesion caused by **staphylococci,** usually bacteriophage group II. Glomerulonephritis may result from nonbullous impetigo caused by **streptococci M-type 49 or 12.** Rheumatic fever is not a sequela of cutaneous infection. A primary cutaneous disease may underlie the impetiginous process.

B. Evaluation

1. Gram stain is helpful in bullous but not in nonbullous impetigo, as secondary infection of the latter is frequent.

2. Laboratory evaluation CBC and ASO titer are not helpful. Since nephritogenic strains are propagated by direct contact, throat and skin cultures should be done on family members and close contacts of a patient with impetigo.

C. Diagnosis

1. Subjective findings There is often a history of antecedent minor trauma, or insect bites, or exposure to other affected children. The lesions are relatively asymptomatic. Pruritus is not a prominent feature.

2. Objective findings

a. Nonbullous impetigo Multiple lesions, more numerous on the face and extremities than elsewhere, are characterized by a thick, adherent, yellowish-brown (honey-colored) crust. Involved areas spread centrifugally and coalesce into large, irregularly shaped lesions with no tendency for central clearing. Regional lymphadenopathy is common.

b. Bullous impetigo Flaccid bullae, 1–2 cm in diameter and containing turbid fluid, occur anywhere on the body. After 2–3 days they rupture, leaving discrete, round lesions and coalescent, polycyclic areas that tend to clear centrally. On gram stain, fluid contains gram-positive cocci in clusters.

D. Treatment

1. Nonbullous impetigo

a. Minimal disease may be treated by local cool water soaks to remove crusts. This is followed by hexachlorophene scrubs and the application of a topical antibiotic 2–3 times daily. However, if the lesions do not resolve quickly with topical care, systemic antibiotic therapy is indicated.

b. Moderate or extensive disease Benzathine penicillin G (Bicillin), 600,000 U IM in a single dose, usually is effective therapy. Even if a penicillin-resistant staphylococcus is present in the lesion, treatment of the streptococci with penicillin induces cure. In rare cases, specific antistaphylococcal therapy may be indicated.

2. Bullous impetigo
Since the causative organism, bacteriophage group II staphylococcus, is generally penicillin-resistant, a semisynthetic, penicillinase-resistant penicillin must be employed (see Chap. 9, Sec. III.A.3).

3. Penicillin allergy
Erythromycin is the alternative drug of choice for bullous or nonbullous impetigo in patients allergic to penicillin.

VIII. INFESTATIONS

A. Scabies

1. Etiology Secondary colonization of the lesions with staphylococci and streptococci occurs early and often. Transmission is usually by direct personal contact; however, fomite (bedclothes, towels) transmission is possible.

2. Evaluation With a needle point or the tip of a #11 surgical blade, attempt to extract a mite from the advancing end of a burrow. Scrape the top from a burrow tract and examine under low power for mites, larvae, or ova. Organisms or ova are often difficult to demonstrate. Thus the clinical pattern (symptoms, distribution of eruption, and morphology of individual lesions) must be the basis for diagnosis.

3. Diagnosis

a. Subjective findings Crowded and unhygienic living conditions are frequently, but not necessarily, associated with infestation.

Characteristically, pruritus intensifies soon after retiring to bed, and remits 1 to 2 hr thereafter.

b. Objective findings   The most frequent areas of involvement are the interdigital webs of the fingers, hypothenar eminences, volar surface of the wrists, extensor elbows, periareolar skin, anterior axillary folds, intergluteal fold, penis, scrotum, and, in infants, the soles. The lesions are of three types:

(1) Seen most often on the sides of the fingers are 1–2 cm, curving of S-shaped or subcorneal burrows, which may terminate in a small vesicle.

(2) Firm, indurated, erythematous, ½ cm, excoriated nodules occur most frequently on the interdigital webs, volar surface of the wrists, and the penis and scrotum.

(3) On the lower abdomen, buttocks, and thighs are numerous 0.2–0.5 cm urticarial papules, many of which are capped by a pinpoint crusted excoriation.

(4) Secondary bacterial infection (impetigo) often dominates the clinical picture and obscures the individual lesions.

4. Treatment is as follows:

a. Bathe and scrub thoroughly with soap and water.

b. Apply a scabicide cream or lotion to all skin from the neck down; 12 hr later, without rebathing, repeat the application. Effective scabicides include 1% gamma benzene hexachloride (Kwell), 10% crotonotoluide (Eurax), and 12% benzyl benzoate, 1% DDT, and 2% benzoin (Totocide).

c. Wash bedclothes, towels, and underwear in detergent and hot water.

d. It is wise to treat contacts prophylactically.

B. Pediculosis

1. Etiology   *Pediculus humanus*, the body louse, and *Phthirus pubis*, the pubic "crab" louse. *P. humanus* occurs in two distinct populations. *P. humanus capitis* is transmitted via hats, combs, hairbrushes, and the backs of theater seats. *P. humanus corporus* transmission is via shared clothing and bedding. Although *P. pubis* transmission is most commonly through sexual contact, infestation is possible via clothing, bedding, and towels.

2. Diagnosis

a. Subjective findings

(1) Infestation with *P. humanus* is associated with intractable **pruritus** on the scalp or trunk. Secondary infection, especially of the scalp, frequently follows the onset of pruritus. Persons affected by *P. humanus* often live in a crowded, unhygienic environment, but members of all social groups may be infected.

(2) *P. pubis* in particular is common in adolescents and young adults and is associated with the more commonly recognized venereal diseases. Every patient with *P. pubis* should be questioned about sexual contacts, urethritis, vaginitis, and genital ulcers. A serologic test for syphilis should be obtained.

b. Objective findings

(1) **Pediculosis capitis** Oval egg capsules ("nits") appear along the hair shafts as highlights that are fixed in position and do not brush away easily. Adult lice are seen on the scalp. Purulence and matting of the hair often occurs over the occiput and nape of the neck. Occipital and posterior cervical adenitis may be present.

(2) **Pediculosis corporis** Excoriated papules, parallel linear excoriations, and, in chronic cases, scaling, lichenification, and hyperpigmentation are seen across the shoulders, in the interscapular area, and around the waist. The initial lesion is a pinpoint red macule. After 7–10 days, the time required for sensitization to the louse salivary antigens, the bites become urticarial and papular. Lice and ova are found in the seams of clothing.

(3) **Pediculosis pubis** Pruritus dominates the clinical picture. The yellow, translucent 1–3 mm adult louse is seen on close examination of the skin. Oval egg capsules (nits) are firmly attached to hair shafts 1–2 cm above the skin surface. Reddish-brown, particulate accumulations of excreted heme pigment deposited on the skin about hair shafts are the most apparent clinical sign. Discrete, round, bluish-gray macules (maculae caerulae), measuring 0.5–1.5 cm in diameter, are occasionally seen on the lower abdomen and inguinal areas.

3. Therapy

a. Pediculosis capitis

(1) If secondary bacterial infecton is prominent, prescribe an appropriate antibiotic directed against gram-positive organisms (see Table 9-2).

(2) Instruct the patient to shampoo the hair and scrub the scalp thoroughly with 1% gamma benzene hexachloride (Kwell) shampoo. Repeat in 24 hr.

(3) Towels, bedclothes, caps, and head scarfs should be washed in detergent and hot water.

(4) Prophylactic treatment of family members and close contacts is indicated.

b. Pediculosis corporis

(1) The patient should bathe and scrub thoroughly with soap and water.

(2) Clothing and bedding should be decontaminated by boiling or by pressing with a hot iron, especially along seams.

c. Pediculosis pubis

(1) The patient should bathe and scrub thoroughly with soap and water.

(2) A pediculocidal cream or lotion should be applied to all skin from the neck down; 12 hr later, without rebathing, the application is repeated. Effective pediculocides include 1%

gamma benzene hexachloride (Kwell), and 12% benzyl benzoate, 1% DDT, and 2% benzoin (Topocide).

(3) If eyebrows and eyelashes are involved, 0.25% physostigmine
(Eserine) or $\frac{1}{16}$% phospholene iodide should be applied until
the infestation is eliminated.

(4) Bedclothes, towels, and underwear should be washed in detergent and hot water.

(5) Treat contacts prophylactically.

IX. PITYRIASIS ROSEA

A. Etiology   Pityriasis rosea is a superficial, scaling, self-limited eruption of unknown etiology.

B. Evaluation   Ask about a coryza-like prodrome. Pityriasis rosea may be
virtually indistinguishable from the generalized eruption of secondary
syphilis. Thus a serologic test for syphilis is sometimes indicated.

C. Diagnosis

1. Subjective findings   Pruritus is generally absent or mild. However,
a small percentage of patients complain of significant itching.

2. Objective findings

a. In about 50 percent of cases, a single, primary lesion, the "herald
patch," precedes the generalized eruption by 7–10 days. The
herald patch is round, 2–4 cm in diameter, slightly raised, scaly,
and yellowish-brown in color. It occurs on the trunk or proximal
extremities.

b. The generalized eruption involves the neck, trunk, and proximal
extremities and spares the face and distal extremities. The
lesions form a "Christmas-tree" pattern on the back, where they
are oriented along skin cleavage lines.

c. The individual lesions are round or oval, 0.5–1.0 cm in diameter,
yellowish-tan in color, and characterized by a central "cigarette-
paper" crinkling of the skin, and by a fine, peripheral collarette
of scale. In darkly pigmented skin, the lesions may be papular
and more inflammatory than in lighter skin.

D. Therapy   Generally, no therapy is indicated. If bothersome, the pruritus is treated with oral antihistamines and with intermittent, cool water compresses. Corticosteroid creams are of no use. Exposure to
artificial UV light or sun-tanning occasionally speeds resolution of
the eruption.

X. PSORIASIS is a disease of the skin characterized by thick, scaling, ery-
thematous plaques associated with a marked increase in the rate of epidermal turnover.

A. Etiology   Polygenic inheritance is the etiological factor, but is subject
to environmental influences. Onset or exacerbation of the disease in
children may follow pharyngeal streptococcal infection. Local lesions

may be provoked by simple abrasions and thermal burns (Koebner's phenomenon).

B. Diagnosis

1. Subjective findings   The family history is positive for psoriasis in 50 percent of childhood cases. Emotional stress may be associated with exacerbation of disease activity. Pruritus may be present.

2. Objective findings

a. The lesions are elevated, moderately erythematous papules and plaques which are covered with thick, silvery, loosely adherent, micaceous scale. Punctate bleeding points occur when the scale is removed (Auspitz's sign). Extensor surfaces (elbows, knees, buttocks) and the scalp are the areas most often involved. Scalp lesions stop abruptly at the hairline.

b. An erosive, polyarticular arthritis of the distal interphalangeal joints is associated with psoriasis in 10–30 percent of patients.

C. Therapy

1. Limited disease with isolated plaques   Instructions are as follows:

a. Paint full-strength Zetar emulsion on lesions 1 hr before bathing in water containing 2–4 capfuls of the same emulsion.

b. Apply a fluorinated corticosteroid cream under plastic occlusion at bedtime overnight (see Sec. **XV.A**).

c. Arrange to have careful, graded sunlight or artificial UVL exposure.

d. Cover resistant plaques with 0.2% anthralin paste (Lasan 2, Anthra-Derm) at bedtime. (In such cases, corticosteroid cream under plastic occlusion for 3 or 4 hr during the day will further speed resolution of the lesions.)

2. Scalp

a. Shampoos containing salicylic acid, sulfur, and tar (Zetar, Sebutone, Ionil T) are used daily until scaling is controlled.

b. If the scale is thick and adherent, warm mineral oil should be applied to the scalp and the head wrapped turban fashion with a warm, wet towel for 3 hr before shampooing.

c. Fluorinated corticosteroid *solutions* (see Sec. **XV.A**) may be applied to the scalp after shampooing.

d. In resistant cases, anthralin pomade (Lasan pomade) may be applied to the scalp at bedtime and removed with shampoo in the morning.

3. Acute, generalized disease   The following instructions should be given:

a. Mix a fluorinated corticosteroid cream half and half with Eucerin cream, apply to the affected skin at bedtime, and occlude with plastic wrap overnight (see Sec. **XV.A.1**).

b. As the disease activity decreases (in 2–3 days) add a daily tar bath (Zetar, Balnetar) to the treatment regimen.

c. Avoid UVL exposure, anthralin, and other tar preparations in acute inflammatory disease.

XI. SEBORRHEIC DERMATITIS

A. **Etiology** Disease activity is chronologically coincident with androgenic stimulation of sebaceous glands. Hence seborrheic dermatitis is seen in infancy while transplacentally acquired maternal androgens are still present and is also seen after the onset of puberty.

B. **Infantile seborrhea** This begins in the second or third month of life and resolves spontaneously by the fifth or sixth month. Ordinarily, the disease is limited to the scalp (cradle cap), axillae, and diaper area. Occasionally, it extends to the forehead, ears, trunk, and proximal extremities. Rarely, it erupts into a generalized exfoliative erythroderma (Leiner's disease).

1. **Subjective findings** There is little discomfort or pruritus. Even with widespread dermatitis, an infant will continue to eat and sleep well. Diarrhea may be associated with generalized, erythrodermic disease.

2. **Objective findings** A thick, yellow, greasy scale (cradle cap) is present on the scalp. Confluent, scaling erythema involves the intertriginous areas (axillae, inguinal and intergluteal folds, umbilicus). Individual lesions on the extremities and trunk are erythematous papules 0.5–1.0 cm in diameter, capped by an easily removed, yellowish-tan, greasy scale.

C. **Adult-type postpubertal seborrhea** is limited to areas of high sebaceous gland concentration.

D. **Therapy**

1. **Scalp**

   a. Shampoos containing sulfur, salicylic acid, and hexachlorophene (Sebulex, Ionil, Meted, Sebaveen) are used every 2–3 days until scaling is controlled. Subsequently, shampooing once or twice weekly is sufficient.

   b. If the cradle cap is thick and adherent, warm mineral oil should be applied and the head wrapped with a cloth wet with water for 3–4 hr before shampooing.

   c. In resistant cases, a corticosteroid lotion (see Sec. **XV.A.**) applied tid is useful. Usually, 1% hydrocortisone (Hytone, Cort-Dome) lotion is adequate for most cases. Occasionally a fluorinated corticosteroid (Valisone) may be necessary.

2. **Intertriginous areas** should be left open and dry. Rubber or plastic diaper pants should not be used, and wet diapers should be changed promptly. A fluorinated corticosteroid cream should be applied qid (see Sec. **XV.A**). If staphylococci or *Candida* are present, an appropriate topical antibiotic cream (neomycin, gramicidin, polymyxin) or nystatin cream is added.

3. **Generalized disease** The patient should bathe twice daily in a colloidal oatmeal bath (Aveeno). Topical corticosteroid and antibiotic nystatin are indicated as in **2.**

XII. SUNBURN, PHOTOSENSITIVITY, AND SUNSCREENS

A. Etiology Overexposure to UVL of wavelengths 290–320 mμ.

B. Evaluation

1. Inquire about the ingestion of photosensitizing drugs such as the sulfonamides, sulfonylureas (Orinase, Diabenese), thiazide diuretics, phenothiazines, griseofulvin, tetracyclines, and psoralens.

2. Other causes of photosensitivity are nutritional deficiency (kwashiorkor, pellagra), vitiligo, albinism, porphyria, phenylketonuria, SLE, dermatomyositis, xeroderma pigmentosum, and Rothmund's, Cockayne's, and Bloom's syndromes.

C. Diagnosis

1. **Subjective findings** The initial, transient erythema is relatively asymptomatic; 6–12 hr later, burning and stinging accompany the appearance of the delayed, prolonged erythema. Malaise, chills, and headache are frequent if sunburn is severe.

2. **Objective findings** The initial erythema limited to sun-exposed areas fades in 1–2 hr. Prolonged erythema and edema appear at 6–12 hr and reach maximum intensity (bulla formation) at 24 hr. Low-grade fever is not unusual. Hypohidrosis, hyperpyrexia, and hypotension may ensue in severe cases.

D. Therapy

1. **Treatment of sunburn**

   a. Cool baths with colloidal oatmeal (Aveeno) are soothing.

   b. Damp compresses with cool water relieve burning and stinging.

   c. Aspirin in the usual doses provides symptomatic relief.

   d. Severely affected patients, if treated early, respond rapidly to prednisone, 1–2 mg/kg PO per day in divided doses. The duration of therapy should be no longer than 2 days. Prednisone must not be given if the usual contraindications (hypertension, gastrointestinal ulcers, diabetes mellitus) are present.

2. **Prevention of sunburn**

   a. Para-aminobenzoic acid (5%) in alcohol (Pabanol, PreSun) provides maximum screening for the sunburn wavelengths of the spectrum (290–320 mμ). However, the preparation photooxidizes to a water-washable, brown pigment, which colors skin and clothing.

   b. Para-aminobenzoic acid esters (Block-Out, PABA-film) do not stain clothing or skin, but are somewhat less effective as a sunscreen. However, PABA esters provide adequate protection for the usual lightly pigmented, sun-sensitive skin.

   c. Benzophenone (10%) (Uval, Solbar) provides screening over a broader spectrum (250–360 mμ), but does not protect so adequately in the sunburn part of the spectrum.

   d. Markedly sun-sensitive skin (vitiligo, albinism, porphyria) may require an opaque screen such as titanium dioxide or zinc oxide in a hydrophilic ointment (Reflecta, Covermark).

XIII. URTICARIA

A. Etiology   In most instances of urticaria, the mediators are released by antigen-antibody reactions. Urticaria often accompanies systemic viral illnesses, excitement, heat, cold, and sunlight.

B. Evaluation   In evaluating patients with one isolated episode of urticaria, a careful drug history is most rewarding. In determining the etiology of recurrent urticaria, it is useful to have the patient or parent keep a careful diary of activities and food ingestion and then attempt to correlate episodes of urticaria with a given activity or food.

C. Diagnosis

1. Subjective findings

    a. Following exposure to the causative antigen, the onset of urticaria is within minutes to hours in persons previously exposed and sensitized, and within 10–14 days in persons undergoing primary sensitization. Any single lesion will appear and resolve within minutes to hours. Pruritus is the outstanding subjective feature.

    b. If the urticarial eruption is part of the symptom complex of serum sickness, arthralgias, malaise, and low-grade fever will be associated.

    c. In patients with recurrent urticaria, other features of the atopic diathesis, i.e., rhinitis, asthma, eczema, are often in the history.

2. Objective findings   Urticarial wheals may be limited to the palms, soles, or pressure points or may be generalized. The individual lesions are raised, edematous plaques with erythematous, serpiginous borders and with dusky centers. Lesions may become confluent and cover extensive areas.

D. Therapy

1. Antihistamines are the mainstay of therapy. Diphenhydramine IM is useful for rapid suppression of symptoms. Thereafter, oral antihistamines in doses sufficiently high to suppress urticarial lesions are employed for maintenance (see Sec. **XV.B**).

2. Aqueous epinephrine 1:1000 SQ (0.01 ml/kg) may provide rapid relief of acute symptoms.

3. Avoidance of the responsible antigens is the definitive therapy. Unfortunately, the search for these is often frustrating.

XIV. WARTS

A. Etiology   Warts are caused by a DNA-containing virus of the papovavirus group. The localized viral infection can be spread to other sites by autoinoculation and to other people by direct contact.

B. Evaluation   The amount of pain and degree of disability experienced from a plantar lesion are important in deciding what treatment, if any, should be employed. Genital and perianal lesions may be spread during sexual contact. Thus sex partners should be treated simultaneously to prevent "ping-pong" reinfection.

C. Diagnosis

1. Subjective findings   Plantar warts on weight-bearing surfaces may be painful. Perianal and genital condyloma acuminatum (venereal warts) may be friable and tender.

2. Objective findings

a. Common warts are firm, hyperkeratotic papules containing black specks of hemosiderin pigment in thrombosed capillary loops.

b. Periungual warts involve the lateral and proximal nailfolds but usually do not cause nail plate abnormalities. Punctate, black, thrombosed capillary loops are usually apparent.

c. Plantar warts are hyperkeratotic, dome-shaped, or flat lesions, which may be distinguished from calluses by paring down the lesions and looking for thrombosed capillaries.

d. A mosaic wart is a superficial, nontender, confluent plaque, which may involve a large area of the plantar surface.

e. Filiform warts are small finger-like growths seen primarily on the face and neck.

f. Condylomata acuminata (venereal warts) are soft, friable, pink, elongated, and filiform lesions, which may be seen in any intertriginous area, but are most often found under the prepuce, on the vaginal and labial mucosa, in the urethral meatus, and around the anal mucocutaneous junction. They are often hemorrhagic and the site of secondary infection.

D. Therapy

1. Common warts

a. Apply liquid nitrogen with a cotton-tipped applicator. Keep the lesion frozen for 20 sec. In 6–10 hr a hemorrhagic bulla will form, with the wart in the blister roof, *or*

b. Paint the lesion with cantharidin (Cantharone), apply a patch of 40% salicyclic acid plaster, and occlude with Blenderm plastic tape for 1–2 days. Although no initial pain results, significant distress may occur within 4 hr, *or*

c. Electrodessicate and curette the lesion. This method may leave more noticeable hypopigmentation and scarring than other techniques, *or*

d. In young children who will not tolerate pain induced by the foregoing techniques, lesions may be painted once or twice daily with 10% lactic acid in flexible collodion.

2. Periungual warts   Cantharidin used as previously described is helpful for periungual lesions. Trichloroacetic or monochloroacetic acid may be substituted for cantharidin. Two or three treatments at 2-week intervals may be required. Liquid nitrogen should be used with caution about the nails, since freezing the nail matrix that lies beneath the proximal fold may result in permanent nail plate dystrophy.

3. Plantar warts

a. Plantar lesions are extraordinarily difficult to eradicate. Recurrence after repeated and painful treatments is frequent. Therefore, unless the patient is suffering significant pain or disability, he is best advised to use only repeated daily applications of 40% salicylic acid plaster under ordinary adhesive tape. This treatment reduces the hyperkeratotic mass of the wart and thus relieves weight-bearing tenderness, but it will not permanently destroy the lesion. If more definitive treatment is desired, trichloroacetic acid or the method in **1.b** is recommended. Repeated treatments will probably be required.

b. Liquid nitrogen freezing of the plantar surface often results in a painful, tense, hemorrhagic bulla. Electrodesiccation or surgical excision may leave a tender hyperplastic scar.

4. Mosaic warts Mosaic lesions are best treated with repeated applications of 40% salicylic acid plaster (see **3.a**). They are too extensive to use the more destructive methods.

5. Filiform warts Small filiform warts may be treated as in **1**.

6. Condyloma acuminatum The patient should apply 25% podophyllin in compound tincture of benzoin to lesions in moist, intertriginous areas. The areas should be powdered with talc to prevent smearing of podophyllin onto surrounding normal skin. **The medication should be thoroughly washed off in 4–6 hr;** otherwise a painful primary irritant dermatitis will follow. The recurrence rate is high, and repeated weekly applications may be required. Podophyllin will not induce resolution of verrucae on dry, nonintertriginous skin such as the penile shaft.

XV. TOPICAL CORTICOSTEROIDS, ANTIHISTAMINES, AND DRESSINGS

A. Topical corticosteroids These are the most effective topical antiinflammatory preparations available for a broad array of dermatologic conditions. Commonly used corticosteroids are listed in Table 21-2.

1. Application

a. Topical corticosteroids are applied sparingly but often throughout the day. Their effectiveness is enormously increased by occluding the treated area with polyethylene plastic wrap (Saran Wrap, Handi-Wrap). On the extremities, the plastic is wrapped entirely around the limb in sleevelike fashion and fixed in place at either end with tape. Plastic bags (Baggies) are useful on the feet, and disposable, lightweight plastic gloves (Dispos-A-Glov) are available for use on the hands. The occlusive wrappings are applied at bedtime and removed in the morning.

b. Occlusion is useful in subacute, dry, nonexudative lesions, as seen in psoriasis, lichen planus, and neurodermatitis. **Do not occlude** acute, weeping, exudative processes (e.g., poison ivy contact dermatitis).

c. Ointments that are partially occlusive by their greasy nature are used on dry, nonexudative lesions when plastic occlusion is undesirable or impractical. **Do not use plastic occlusion over an ointment,** because excessive maceration may result.

2. Complications The fluorinated use of topical corticosteroids under occlusion or in intertriginous areas effectively occluded by skin folds can result in the development of atrophic striae or vascular dilatation and telangiectasia. For this reason, 1% hydrocortisone will suffice for most cases of mild-to-moderate inflammation, and fluorinated agents should be reserved for more severe cases and used for short periods, if possible. *Percutaneous absorption of corticosteroids*

Table 21-2. Commonly Used Topical Corticosteroids

Chemical Name	Trade Name	Preparations Available	Sizes Available
Betamethasone	Valisone	Cream 0.1% Ointment 0.1% Aerosol, 0.15%	Tube, 5 gm, 15 gm, 45 gm Tube, 5 gm, 15 gm, 45 gm Container, 85 gm
Fluocinolone	Synalar, Fluonid	Cream 0.025%/0.01% Ointment 0.025%, 0.01% Emollient 0.025% (Synalar only) Solution 0.01%	Tube, 5 gm, 15 gm, 60 gm, 120 gm Tube, 15 gm, 60 gm Tube, 15 gm Bottle, 20 ml, 60 ml
Fluocinonide	Lidex	Cream 0.05%	Tube, 15 gm, 60 gm
Flurandrenolide	Cordran	Cream 0.05%, 0.025% Ointment 0.05%, 0.025% Lotion 0.05% Medicated tape 4 μg/sq cm	Tube, 7.5 gm, 15 gm, 60 gm Tube, 7.5 gm, 15 gm, 60 gm Bottle, 15 ml, 60 ml Roll, 7.5 × 200 cm
Hydrocortisone	Hytone Cort-Dome	Cream 0.1%, ½%, ¼% Cream ½%	Tube, 1 oz Jar, 4 oz Tube, ½ oz, 1 oz Dispensajar, 4 oz Jar, 4 oz
Triamcinolone	Aristocort Kenalog	Cream 0.1%, 0.025% Ointment 0.1%, 0.025% Lotion 0.1% (Kenalog) Spray 0.1% (Kenalog) Foam 0.1% (Aristoderm)	Tube, 5 gm, 15 gm, 60 gm Tube, 5 gm, 15 gm, 60 gm Bottle, 15 ml, 60 ml Spray can, 50 gm, 150 gm Pressurized bottle, 15 gm

in sufficient concentration to suppress elaboration of corticotropin can occur. However, clinically significant pituitary suppression with deleterious effects on the patient is virtually unheard of, even after long-term, extensive therapy with occlusion.

B. Antihistamines The antihistamines are competitive antagonists of histamine, CNS depressants, and local anesthetics. They act specifically in the suppression of urticaria, in which histamine induces increased vascular permeability. However, in the majority of pruritic skin conditions for which antihistamines are prescribed, histamine has little, if anything, to do with the disease process. In these instances, the beneficial effects of antihistamines are due to their sedative action. Antihistamines should never be used topically, because they are potent contact sensitizers. Commonly used antihistamines are listed in Table 21-3.

1. Administration

a. The oral route is the usual means of administration. IM injection is useful for rapid relief of generalized urticaria.

b. Since sedation is an important facet of the effectiveness of these drugs in pruritic skin disease, the usually suggested dose may have to be increased toward the recommended maximum daily dose in order to achieve the desired therapeutic result.

2. Side effects include dizziness, tinnitus, blurred vision, nervousness, insomnia, tremors, dry mouth, nausea, tingling of the hands, and hypotension.

C. Wet dressings are useful in suppressing pruritus, in drying moist, oozing lesions, and in removing crusts. Towels, washcloths, strips of bed sheets, or gauze rolls (Kerlix) are satisfactory materials for open, nonoccluded wet dressings, which allow evaporation of water and hence cool and soothe inflamed surfaces.

1. Application Strips of cotton material are soaked in the dressing solutions and wrung out to a point just short of dripping wet. The dressing is wrapped about an extremity or laid on the area to be treated. Dressings are removed and remoistened q10–15 min to prevent drying. This process is continued for 1–2 hr periods 3 or 4 times per day, depending on the degree of pruritus, oozing, or crusting.

2. Precautions Dressings should not be left in place and remoistened simply by pouring additional solution over them. The process of removal and redressing is instrumental in cooling and debriding. Wet dressings should not be wrapped with plastic or rubber sheets to prevent wetting the bedclothes. If wet dressings are occluded, they *raise* the surface temperature rather than lower it. Also, occlusion prevents evaporation and leads to maceration of tissues.

3. Commonly used solutions

a. Saline One level teaspoon of table salt in 1 pint of tap water approximates normal saline in concentration. It is a physiologic preparation for use on mild to moderate inflammation.

b. Aluminum acetate (Burow's solution) Burow's solution 1:20 is prepared by adding 1 Domeboro packet or tablet to 1 pint of tap water. The only advantage over saline is a mild antibacterial effect. Hence the solution is useful in secondarily infected dermatoses.

Table 21-3. Commonly Used Antihistamines

Chemical Name	Trade Name	Preparations Available	Dosage
Brompheniramine	Dimetane	Tablet, 4 mg Extentab, 8 mg, 12 mg Elixir, 2 mg/5 ml Parenteral, 10 mg/ml, 100 mg/ml	2–4 mg q4–6h 0.5 mg/kg daily maximum
Chlorpheniramine	Chlor-Trimeton	Tablet, 4 mg Repetab, 8 mg, 12 mg Syrup, 2 mg/5 ml Parenteral, 10 mg/ml	2–4 mg q4–6h 0.5 mg/kg daily maximum
Cyproheptadine	Periactin	Tablet, 4 mg Syrup 2 mg/5 ml	2–4 mg q4–6h 0.5 mg/kg daily maximum
Diphenhydramine	Benadryl	Capsule, 25 mg, 50 mg Elixir, 12.5 mg/5 ml Parenteral, 10 mg/ml	25–50 mg q4–6h 5 mg/kg daily maximum
Tripelennamine	Pyribenzamine	Tablet, 25 mg, 50 mg Lontab, 50 mg, 100 mg Elixir, 30 mg/4 ml	25–50 mg q4–6h 5 mg/kg daily maximum
Hydroxyzine	Atarax Vistaril	Tablet, 10 mg, 25 mg, 50 mg, 100 mg Syrup, 10 mg/5 ml Capsule, 25 mg, 50 mg, 100 mg Suspension, 25 mg/5 ml	25–50 mg q4–6h 5 mg/kg daily maximum

   c. Silver nitrate   A 0.5% solution is very effective as a topical bac-
   teriacidal agent. It is useful on widely denuded areas such as
   burns, or on chronic, infected ulcers. A significant disadvantage
   is that it stains cloth, floors, cabinet tops, skin, and fingernails.

22 Disorders of the Ear, Nose, and Throat

I. GENERAL PRINCIPLES OF THERAPY

A. Techniques for establishing an emergency airway

1. Endotracheal intubation

a. A **laryngoscope** is passed into the right side of the mouth, the epiglottis is lifted up, and the arytenoid masses are seen. Usually the glottis (open space between the vocal cords) is seen, and an endotracheal tube is passed between the vocal cords under direct vision. The bevel at the tip of the endotracheal tube is turned sideways so that it will fit easily into the upside-down V-shaped glottis. If the glottis cannot be seen, the tube should be passed anterior to the arytenoid masses. The tip is inserted only 5–10 mm below the vocal cords, and then the tube is taped to the lower face to secure it in place. For recommended sizes for infants of various ages, see Table 2-1.

Table 22-1. Bronchoscope Sizes for Various Ages

Age	Internal Diameter (mm)
Premature	3.0
0–6 months	3.5
6 months–3 years	4.0
3 years–12 years	5.0
12 years and over	6.0

b. A **bronchoscope** may also be passed to establish an emergency airway. Table 22-1 lists the appropriate sizes. In some cases, passing a bronchoscope has these advantages:

(1) A rigid instrument may be easier to pass around an obstructing mass.

(2) The larynx, trachea, and bronchi can be examined (to see if a tumor mass is present).

(3) Therapy may be carried out through the bronchoscope (i.e., removal of a foreign body).

(4) The light from the bronchoscope can illuminate the tracheal rings for later tracheostomy.

2. Tracheostomy
An emergency tracheostomy is often necessary, but, when possible, it would be best if an endotracheal tube or broncho-

scope were in position to convert the emergency tracheostomy into a more leisurely and thus less hazardous procedure, since the airway is already established (see **K.4**, p. 210).

a. A towel is placed under the shoulder, and the head is hyper-extended. The midline of the neck is palpated to identify the cricoid cartilage. A vertical midline incision is made through the skin and subcutaneous tissue from the cricoid to the suprasternal notch. A hemostat is spread vertically in the midline between the strap muscles, and the muscles are retracted laterally. The pretracheal fascia is divided with a small scissors, and the retractors are placed deeper to hold the fascia laterally. The midline is best identified superiorly by finding an inverted "V" where the cricothyroid muscles meet in the midline, or inferiorly, by finding the isthmus of the thyroid gland. Then the trachea is seen, and a midline vertical incision made through two adjacent rings (#2 and 3, or #3 and 4). No dissection lateral to the trachea is needed since it only causes more bleeding. No cartilage is removed in the infant or small child since the trachea is small and stenosis could develop.

b. A safety suture of #0 silk is placed through each cut edge of the trachea incision, and at the end of the procedure the long ends of the silk are taped to the chest. (The sutures are needed if the tube is inadvertently removed, since the soft tissue usually falls over the stoma, making reinsertion difficult or impossible. With the safety silk, one can pull on it, lift the trachea into view, and reinsert the tracheostomy tube.)

c. The skin incision is not sutured, so that any leaking air can escape, instead of being trapped under the skin, dissecting down the neck into the mediastinum, and rupturing the pleura to cause a pneumothorax.

d. The tracheostomy ties are tied around the neck firmly to prevent inadvertent extubation. The tension should be tested by pulling the tracheostomy tube to make certain it will not be too loose and fall out postoperatively. A tracheostomy dressing is placed over the incision to soak up drainage.

e. Postoperatively, special nursing is needed for 24 hr. A postoperative chest x-ray is obtained to rule out pneumothorax and to see that the tip of the tracheostomy tube is cephalad to the carina. Humidification in a croup tent or steam room is needed. Instructions are given to suction the tracheostomy tube every 15 min for 3 hr and then as often as needed. The correct sizes of tracheostomy tubes for various ages are listed in Table 22-2.

3. Large bore needles One or more large bore needles (#12 or #14) or a large Intracath may be placed transcutaneously into the trachea to provide **emergency, temporary aeration.** A definitive procedure will still be needed, but this alone might be lifesaving.

4. Cricothyrotomy

a. When intubation is not possible, and a tracheostomy is being considered, cricothyrotomy is preferred to a tracheostomy in the hands of someone with limited surgical experience. The cricothyroid membrane is located just under the skin, so that dissection and retraction is minimized, compared with a tracheostomy.

Table 22-2.   Tracheostomy Tube Sizes for Various Ages

Age	Tracheostomy Tube Size
Premature	000 or 00
0–6 months	0
6–18 months	1
18 months–4-5 years	1 or 2
4-5–10 years	2 or 3
10 years and over	3 to 5

    b. Cricothyrotomy cannot be done in an infant since its cricothyroid membrane is too small.

    c. If a cricothyrotomy is performed, it must be replaced in 24 hr by a standard lower tracheostomy since erosion of the cricoid might occur, leading to a severe stenosis of the larynx.

    d. A cricothyrotomy is performed by incising the skin horizontally just below the cricoid prominence. The cricoid is the most prominent structure of the larynx in children. The incision is carried through the cricothyroid membrane, and a tracheostomy tube is inserted.

B. Myringotomy technique   An urgent myringotomy may be needed for an acute, painful, bulging eardrum that fails to improve after 48 hr on an antibiotic, or to obtain material for culture if intracranial complications occur from otitis media. General principles for performing myringotomy are as follows:

    1. The infant or child must be well restrained by sheets or other restraining devices.

    2. Good lighting is essential, either by light reflected from a head-mirror or an otoscope, or by an operating microscope.

    3. The myringotomy knife tip should be inspected to rule out a bent tip. (**Note:** A Beaver handle (#3H) with Beaver blades (#71) is recommended; Beaver blades are disposable, sharp, and inexpensive.)

    4. The myringotomy site must be carefully understood:

        a. It should *not* be in the posterior portion of the tympanic membrane (TM), where the incus, stapes, and facial nerve are located. Improper myringotomies have produced conductive losses due to incus injury, sensorineural losses due to pushing the stapes into the inner ear, and facial paralysis due to cutting an exposed facial nerve in the middle ear.

        b. It should *not* touch the margin of the TM or the malleus handle, since in-growth of epithelium with later cholesteatoma formation is possible at these sites.

        c. It is safest inferiorly between the tip of the malleus handle and the margin of the TM at the inferior canal wall.

        d. The myringotomy may also be performed anterior to the malleus handle, but often there is a bulge of the anterior canal wall that obscures this area.

5. The myringotomy incision need only be large enough to allow drainage (1–2 mm).

6. Sedation with meperidine (Demerol) (1 mg/kg) and pentobarbital (Nembutal) (1–2 mg/kg) is needed. In agitated or difficult children a general anesthetic may be required, but the need for the procedure must be weighed against the risks (see Chap. 1, Sec. II.C.2, p. 9).

C. **Management of congenital malformations of the head and neck**

1. **Airway obstruction**

   a. Upper airway obstruction is found in bilateral posterior choanal atresia, glossoptosis with micrognathia (Pierre-Robin syndrome), and macroglossia. Emergency relief can be achieved with an oral airway or an endotracheal tube passed through the mouth, into the oropharynx, and taped to the cheek. *In these examples there is no need to pass the tube into the larynx, which only increases the risk of laryngeal trauma.* Surgical correction can then be performed as an elective procedure with much less risk.

   b. Lower airway obstruction is found in congenital anomalies of the larynx. A tracheostomy may be needed.

2. **Feeding problems** In the group of infants with congenital anomalies, feeding problems are found in infants with cleft palate. A bottle with a regular nipple in which a large hole is cut is effective. Boiling is advisable to soften it. (Soft nipples are commercially available.) The use of special devices such as cleft-lip feeders or squeeze-bottle ketchup dispensers adds another handicap to the cleft-palate infant that can often be avoided. Even breast-feeding is sometimes possible if the infant is tilted to the noncleft side. With all methods, slow feeding with time for burping is advised.

II. DISORDERS OF THE EAR

A. **Removal of cerumen** Whether the dry or the wet techniques to be described are used, the infant or young child should be held securely. The child sits on the adult's lap. The adult holds the child's legs between his crossed legs. The adult holds both hands of the child with the left hand, while the right hand presses the child's left forehead to hold the head firmly against the adult's chest. The left ear can then be cleaned. The hands are then reversed and the other ear cleaned.

1. **Dry techniques**

   a. A #00 blunt ear curet is tiny and can be used to clean out cerumen in children of any age. (Do not use the sharp curet, which looks similar. Test it first on your own skin.) To gain his trust and cooperation, show the child the instrument, and stroke the curet lightly and sequentially over the back of the hand, cheek, and pinna.

   b. The ear canal should be cleaned only under direct vision. The curet can be passed through the otoscope and the speculum, so that the canal is well seen. If the wax is clinging to the walls of the canal, the curet can be passed beyond it and gently withdrawn, with light pressure on the ear canal skin. Usually, when a large mass of wax is seen in the ear canal, there will be a space behind it separating the wax from the TM. The curet (bend curet about 10 degrees at the junction of the shaft and the ring) is passed superior to the mass and positioned just behind the mass, and the wax ball is "pulled" or "slid" out of the canal.

c. On occasion, the canal wall is scratched and bleeds. To prevent a later otitis externa, an eardrop with antibiotic can be prescribed (Cortisporin otic, 3 drops tid for 2 days). If the wax is very hard, it may be softened with hydrogen peroxide or mineral oil for 15 min to allow the wax mass to be moved more easily. The dry technique is successful in 95 percent of children.

2. Wet techniques

a. Irrigation with water is needed if the wax is firmly pushed against the TM, or if the physician does not like using a blunt curet in the ear canal. The water should be body temperature (lukewarm to the touch) to avoid caloric stimulation, causing vertigo and nystagmus.

b. A special metal ear syringe may be used, which has a deflector plate to prevent the water's splashing over the patient or physician. A dental water pick may also be used to irrigate the canal. Once children become used to the sound of the water and having the water splashed on their fingers, acceptance is high.

c. The disadvantages of the wet technique are that it is messier than the dry technique, may frighten some children, and should not be used if a TM perforation is suspected, since the wax may inadvertently be blown into the middle ear.

B. Hearing loss is a common problem in children. It is important to detect it early, so that early treatment can be instituted to alleviate speech defects, learning disabilities, and behavioral changes. Many forms of therapy are available. The following points are stressed:

1. Hearing tests can be performed by audiologists in children at any age, including the first day of life.

2. Any newborn with the following should have an immediate referral for a hearing test: a family history of deafness, rubella during pregnancy, kernicterus, cleft palate, malformed pinna, or any structural anomaly of the head or neck (like Crouzon's disease or Turner's syndrome).

3. If a parent suspects a hearing loss, it is safer and wiser to refer the child for an otologic examination and an audiogram than to wait in the hope the child "will outgrow it." Delaying the identification of deafness may be harmful.

4. Crude tests for hearings can be performed in the office or at home, depending on the age of the child:

a. Newborn   A newborn should startle to a loud sound such as a bell or a beeper. (Avoid vibrations of the crib, such as those produced by slapping the crib, since the newborn may react to the vibratory sensation, not the auditory stimulus, giving a false-positive reaction.)

b. Age 6 months–3 years   Children in this age range should localize a sound produced on one side by turning to the side of the sound.

Squeaky toys or bells may be used, but should be kept out of the child's visual range. Be certain to test each ear separately and from the side.

c. Age over 3 years   These children should hear a soft whisper in each ear when the examiner's lips are close to the pinna. Use words like *cowboy, hot dog,* and *baseball*. It is not appropriate to stand 6 feet away and speak, since a child with one deaf ear will still hear the sound in his good ear, or to use a ticking watch, which only tests the higher frequencies. The human voice is a convenient and important test, since our ears are primarily used to receive communications.

5. Conductive versus sensorineural hearing loss   When the child can cooperate, tuning fork tests are helpful. The 512-cps tuning fork should be used. Normally, the tuning fork is heard louder near the ear canal than on the mastoid bone (a positive Rinne). When it is heard best on the mastoid bone, it is called a negative Rinne. Normally, the sound of a tuning fork pushed on the midline of the teeth does not lateralize to one ear more than the other (Weber Midline). If the tuning fork lateralizes to one ear, this is a significant finding.

a. Conductive hearing losses are due to an ear canal or middle ear disorder. The Rinne test will be negative, and the Weber test will lateralize to the poor hearing ear.

b. Sensorineural hearing losses are due to damage to the cochlea (sensory, or hair, cell) or damage to the 8th nerve (neural, or retrocochlear). The Rinne test will be positive, and the Weber test will lateralize to the good ear.

c. An audiogram is needed to verify the clinical assessment.

C. Specific disorders

1. Abscess of external auditory canal

a. Etiology   *Staphylococcus aureus* is the most common bacterium found in these abscesses.

b. Evaluation   This should include x-ray studies of the mastoid.

c. Diagnosis   A painful mass is seen in the ear canal. Incision with identification of pus confirms the diagnosis.

d. Treatment   See also Chap. 9, Sec. **IV.E.**

(1) If mild, cloxacillin, 50 mg/kg daily PO in 4 equal doses. **If severe,** oxacillin, 100 mg/kg daily IV in 4 equal doses.

(2) Local heat, wet or dry, q1h for 10 min each time.

(3) Incision and drainage when the abscess is ready. This is done under local anesthesia if child is cooperative, or under general anesthesia, if needed.

(4) Culture and sensitivity of pus.

(5) Analgesics: codeine (1 mg/kg) q3h prn.

2. External otitis (acute, diffuse) (swimmer's ear)

a. Etiology   *Pseudomonas aeruginosa* is usually cultured in this infection. Rarely, other bacteria and fungi are found.

b. Evaluation When the TM is involved it is difficult to tell if one is dealing with widespread external otitis, or an otitis media with a secondary external otitis. If the latter occurs and the differentiation is not clear, it is safest to treat for both otitis media and external otitis simultaneously.

c. Diagnosis External otitis is characteristically a diffuse inflammation of the ear canal with or without involvement of the TM.

d. Treatment

  (1) Eardrops: 3 drops 3 times a day for 1–2 weeks (containing cortisone and antibiotics effective against *Pseudomonas* and *Staphylococcus*. See Table 9-2).

  (2) Swimming is not permitted.

  (3) Cleaning of the ear canal as needed, e.g., 1–2 times a week.

  (4) Cotton in the ear canal when there is drainage, to prevent dermatitis of the pinna.

  (5) Analgesics (ASA, codeine) (see Chap. 1, p. 7).

  (6) Systemic antibiotics should be given if facial cellulitis, pinna chondritis, or fever occurs (see Chap. 9).

  (7) If treatment fails after 2 weeks, a culture and a sensitivity test are needed, and if the results so indicate, different eardrops should be selected.

  (8) An ear canal "wick" is occasionally used, but is painful.

3. Bullous myringitis

  a. Etiology *Mycoplasma pneumoniae* is the common agent, but influenza viruses are sometimes suspected.

  b. Diagnosis A blister can be seen on the TM, with the adjacent part of the TM usually normal.

  c. Treatment

  (1) Analgesics (ASA, codeine and Auralgan eardrops).

  (2) Application of a heating pad to the ear.

  (3) Resolution or rupture of the bulla should be awaited.

  (4) No antibiotics are needed.

  (5) No myringotomy is needed.

4. Serous otitis media (SOM)

  a. Etiology SOM may occur in a number of ways.

  (1) SOM may follow an acute otitis media if the pus from the otitis media becomes sterile, yet the fluid persists in the middle ear.

  (2) SOM may form as a transudate if reduced middle ear pressure occurs secondary to eustachian tube obstruction, as seen with large adenoids, URI, allergies, cleft palate, or a submucous cleft palate.

  (3) SOM may form as a result of middle ear mucosal disease if increased mucous glands in the middle ear produce excess fluid.

b. Evaluation   Pneumatic otoscopy reveals that the TM will not move inward on positive pressure (although it might move outward on negative pressure). The child might hear a soft or moderate whisper in each ear. An audiogram confirms a conductive hearing loss.

c. Diagnosis   An immobile TM is found on pneumatic otoscopy, or air fluid bubbles can be seen behind the TM. A myringotomy reveals watery mucoid or viscous fluid ("glue") in the middle ear.

d. Treatment   A combination decongestant and antihistamine for 1–2 weeks.

(1) Under 2 years, 2.5 ml tid; age 2–4, 5 ml tid; age 5 or over, 5 ml qid.
   Note: If antihistamine makes the child sleepy, affecting school performance, the early morning dose should be omitted. If the child becomes hyperactive, the drug should be stopped and a change to pseudoephedrine (Sudafed), 5 ml/kg qid, should be made.

(2) On the child's return visit in 2 weeks, stop the drug if there is improvement but continue it if SOM is still present.

(3) Follow the same procedure on the return visit in 4 weeks.

(4) If on the return visit in 6 weeks SOM persists, the patient should be referred to an otolaryngologist. However, the presence of air bubbles in the fluid is a good sign since it means that air is passing through the eustachian tube. Wait for 3 months before referral.

(5) If nasal obstruction is present, the patient should use a nasal decongestant (Afrin, Otrivin) 2 sprays bid in each nostril for 2 weeks.

(6) Surgical treatment depends on the size of the adenoids or the presence of an allergy or a cleft palate. Sometimes, myringotomy alone is needed. With thick fluid, tympanotomy tubes usually are also used.

5. Hemotympanum

a. Etiology   Chronic otitis media or mastoiditis is the usual cause of a hemotympanum. Barotrauma and head trauma are two other frequent causes.

b. Evaluation   Blood is present behind an intact TM and may appear blue, bluish-black, or reddish-blue. On pneumatic otoscopy the TM is poorly mobile. A hearing loss is present.

c. Diagnosis   A bluish coloration is present behind a poorly mobile TM.

d. Treatment

(1) If secondary to chronic otitis or mastoiditis   Give antibiotics as for acute otitis media (see Table 9-1).

(2) If secondary to barotrauma   2 weeks of pseudoephedrine (5 mg/kg PO in 3 or 4 divided doses).

(3) If secondary to head trauma   Refer the patient to an otolaryngologist for evaluation to rule out ossicular or cochlear damage, or CSF leak.

6. Acute otitis media   See Chap. 9, Sec. **IV.E.4.**

7. Acute otitis media with perforation

    a. Etiology   In acute viral URIs in children under 3 years of age there is often secondary infection by gram-positive bacteria or *H. influenza.* When the purulent material develops, pressure necrosis breaks the TM.

    b. Evaluation   The perforation will be seen if the pus is suctioned out with a #5 ear sucker or wiped with a small cotton-tipped applicator. A hearing loss is present in the infected ear.

        Note: If there is one "uninvolved" ear, there will be no obvious loss of hearing. Each ear must be tested separately to detect a unilateral hearing loss (see **B**).

    c. Diagnosis   The short process of the malleus is obscured by the thick TM. A perforation is seen varying in size from pinpoint to a total perforation. The tympanic membrane is thick, pink, and opaque.

    d. Therapy

        (1) Antibiotics are given as in acute otitis media (see Table 9-2).

        (2) Cotton is placed in the meatus of the ear canal to prevent pus from running down the pinna or onto the face, causing a secondary infection.

        (3) The hearing should be checked when the infection is resolved.

8. Chronic suppurative otitis media

    a. Etiology

        (1) Chronic eustachian tube obstruction or malfunction, as seen with large adenoids, allergy, or palate anomalies.

        (2) Chronic mastoiditis.

        (3) Irreversible middle ear or mastoid disease, e.g., cholesteatoma, osteitis, granulation tissue, or polyps.

        (4) Chronic infections of the nose or sinuses.

    b. Evaluation

        (1) When irreversible middle ear or mastoid disease is present, drainage is chronic despite local treatment, drugs, or systemic antibiotics.

        (2) On TM examination, perforation is seen, which may vary in size from 1 mm up to total perforation of the TM. The middle ear mucosa can be seen through the perforation and may be white (inactive or not infected) or pink and thick (active infection). In the active state, pus or mucopus is seen in the ear canal or middle ear. A cholesteatoma may be seen behind the TM and appears as a white, waxy mass. A polyp may be seen coming through the perforation or from the attic.

        (3) A whispered voice test is performed and usually is abnormal. An audiogram confirms a conductive loss. Look for rhinitis, sinusitis, a history of allergy, or large adenoids.

c. Diagnosis The key finding is a perforation of the TM that fails to heal in 4 weeks.

d. Treatment

(1) Active infection

(a) Eardrops, 3 drops tid for 2 weeks (as in **d(1)**, p. 461).

(b) Clean the ear once a week or more often if needed.

(c) If there is profuse drainage, mix 1 packet of Domeboro powder in 1 pint of water and irrigate the ear with ⅓ pint tid to clean out the discharge, using a bulb syringe. Follow with antibiotic drops.

(d) The patient should keep water out of the ear and should not go swimming.

(e) Refer the patient to an otolaryngologist when the middle ear is dry and inactive or if drainage persists over 6 weeks.

(2) Inactive infection Refer the patient to an otolaryngologist for a tympanoplasty.

9. Acute mastoiditis

a. Etiology Primarily, β-hemolytic steptococcus, pneumococcus, and *H. influenzae.*

b. Evaluation

(1) Medical mastoiditis is an infection of the mastoid that accompanies almost all cases of acute otitis media and can be treated medically. Unless roentgenograms are needed for other reasons, they need not be ordered during an attack of acute otitis media.

(2) Surgical mastoiditis is a more severe form in which surgical intervention is necessary. The severity of the symptoms is due to pus under pressure, so that tenderness and swelling occur over the mastoid region (see other signs in **C.2**). Roentgenograms show that the bony walls of the air cells become decalcified after 2 weeks of mastoiditis.

(3) Masked mastoiditis is an acute mastoiditis that has been rendered "quiet" by antibiotics. However, the infection continues unsuspected and destroys the air cell bony walls. A mild chronic headache may occur. Progression to intracranial complications seems to arise without warning.

c. Diagnosis

(1) Medical mastoiditis shows the following features:

(a) It occurs with otitis media.

(b) No tenderness or swelling occurs over the mastoid.

(c) X-rays reveal clouding of air cells without air cell bony wall destruction.

(2) Surgical mastoiditis shows the following features:

(a) It occurs with, or 1–2 weeks after, an acute otitis media.

(b) Severe tenderness is present over the mastoid tip.

(c) Induration is seen over the mastoid tip, obliterating the normal bony tip (compared with the normal side).

(d) Swelling behind the pinna causes the pinna to stand out from the side of the head (subperiosteal abscess).

(e) It is associated with middle ear complications (facial paralysis and ossicle erosion).

(f) It is associated with intracranial complications (sigmoid sinus thrombosis, extradural or subdural abscess, cerebral abscess, or meningitis).

(g) X-rays reveal clouding of mastoid cells and, after 14 days, destruction of the bony walls of the mastoid air cells.

(3) Masked mastoiditis shows the following features:

(a) The disease follows incomplete antibiotic therapy for acute otitis media.

(b) There is mild unilateral headache and, occasionally, mild tenderness over the mastoid.

(c) Middle ear effusion or infection may be present.

(d) X-rays reveal destruction of the bony walls of the mastoid air cells.

(e) Intracranial complications may occur (see **2.f** above).

d. Therapy

(1) Medical mastoiditis   Treat similarly to acute otitis media.

(a) Antibiotics   See Chap. 9, Sec. **III.A.4.a**, p. 187.

(b) Analgesics   See Chap. 1, Sec. **II.C**, p. 6.

(c) Warm compresses.

(2) Surgical mastoiditis

(a) Admit the child to the hospital.

(b) Start antibiotics IV.

(c) Refer the child to an otolaryngologist for incision and drainage of subperiosteal abscess and simple mastoidectomy.

(3) Masked mastoiditis   Refer the child to an otolaryngologist for simple mastoidectomy.

10. Protruding or prominent ear

a. Etiology   Congenital malformation of the pinna.

b. Therapy Taping the pinna back at birth does not work and should be prevented because it gives the parents false hope. An otoplasty is needed, and the child should be referred to an otolaryngologist or a plastic surgeon.

11. Acute labyrinthitis

a. Etiology Usually a viral upper respiratory infection.

b. Evaluation and diagnosis

(1) Vertigo is the hallmark of acute labyrinthitis. It is of sudden onset and accompanies or follows URI.

(2) When the inner ear involvement is mild, there may be only positional vertigo (e.g., dizziness when rolling over in bed or turning quickly). When labyrinthitis is severe, there is whirling vertigo, nausea, and vomiting. Neither should be confused with the light-headedness or dizziness associated with orthostatic vertigo. The vertigo may last seconds, minutes, hours, or days.

(3) Typically, the symptoms of acute viral labyrinthitis or vestibular neuronitis (vertigo, nausea, and vomiting) reach their maximum on the first day and then slowly improve in 2–14 days.

(4) Benign paroxysmal vertigo of childhood is a milder and more protracted form of labyrinthitis. Horizontal or a slight rotatory nystagmus with an alternating fast and slow rhythmic pattern is typical of inner ear nystagmus, but can be seen during the acute stage only.

(5) Caloric testing is normal in acute viral labyrinthitis. Middle ear disease must be ruled out. When a hearing loss or tinnitus accompanies the vertigo, an audiogram should be be made.

(6) In infants or young children a regression in walking or a staggering gait may indicate vertigo.

c. Therapy

(1) Reassurance that the symptoms will slowly but definitely improve.

(2) In **mild or moderate vertigo** without nausea or vomiting:

(a) Meclizine and niacin (Antivert), 1 tablet tid before meals.

(b) Meclizine (Bonine), 1 tablet qd for children 5–10 years old; 1 chewable tablet bid for children over 10 years.

(3) In **severe vertigo** with nausea and vomiting:

(a) Cyclizine (Marezine) For children under 6, ½ pediatric suppository (25 mg) q4h; 6 to 10 years, 1 pediatric suppository (50 mg) q4h; over 10 years, 1 adult suppository (100 mg) q4h.

(b) Diazepam (Valium), IV; titrate slowly (1 ml/min), 2–5 mg q3–4h (see Chap. 14, Sec. **I.A.b**).

III. DISORDERS OF THE NOSE

A. Allergic rhinitis

1. Etiology   This is caused by various allergens, including dust, ragweed, pets, and food.

2. Evaluation and diagnosis

  a. The symptoms of nasal stuffiness and watery mucoid discharge may occur at specific times of the year (spring for grasses and fall for ragweed) or perennially. There is often a strong family history of allergy.

  b. The symptoms include prolonged paroxysms of sneezing, itchy eyes, and rhinorrhea. The "allergic salute" may be seen (palm pushed against nasal tip with transverse lines on the nose), as well as "allergic shiners" (black eyes). Swollen bluish nasal mucosa can be seen in the inferior nasal turbinates.

  c. Eosinophils are found in the nasal smear, and specific scratch tests may be positive.

3. Therapy   The following three categories of treatment are advised:

  a. Environmental control   The patient should avoid pets and dust, use an air conditioner, and avoid foods that give eczema.

  b. Antihistamines   See Chap. 21, Sec. **B**, p. 452.

  c. Hyposensitization may be of value. An allergist should be consulted.

B. Foreign body

1. Evaluation   Look for a chronic unilateral nasal discharge that is purulent and unresponsive to antibiotics. Good visualization will require a bright light from an otoscope, penlight, or head mirror. Suction may be needed to clean out the mucus or mucopus.

2. Therapy   It is important to succeed in removing the foreign body the first time because the child's patience runs out. If struggling begins, the foreign body can be pushed in more posteriorly, and nasal bleeding may occur. One should thus be prepared to work quickly on a cooperative child or to restrain the uncooperative child. The following guidelines are recommended:

  a. First assemble all equipment (bright light, nasal speculum, suction apparatus and suction tip, a small forceps [avoid large Kelly clamps], a cotton-tipped applicator, and aqueous epinephrine [2 ml of 1:1000]).

  b. Avoid traumatizing the mucosa; once it bleeds, removal of the foreign body is difficult.

  c. Constrict the vessels of the mucosa with epinephrine on a cotton-tipped applicator.

  d. Suction the nasal discharge if present.

  e. Remove the foreign body with forceps.

  f. Refer the patient to an otolaryngologist if he is very resistant, if bleeding is a problem, or if the foreign body is difficult to remove. A short-acting general anesthetic may be needed for removal in the operating room.

C. Epistaxis

1. Etiology   Most commonly, epistaxis is secondary to a URI or nose-picking. It may also be due to bleeding diatheses, including leukemia, and nasopharyngeal angiofibroma in adolescent males.

2. Evaluation

a. The key issue is to identify the bleeding site. The most common site is the nasal septum anteriorly; therefore, look there first. If no bleeding site is seen, then it is posterior bleeding.

b. With children, swift but gentle treatment is critical. Therefore, all equipment must be ready before the evaluation begins.

3. Therapy   Methods of treatment for epistaxis depend on where the bleeding arises.

a. Anterior bleeding   Treatment is easier than in posterior bleeding.

(1) A cooperative child may sit up in chair; an infant must be restrained and kept on the back.

(2) Prepare a mixture of ½ cocaine 4% (or topical Pontocaine 4%) and ½ epinephrine 1:1000.

(3) Place the mixture on a cotton applicator and hold on a prominent or bleeding vessel for 15 sec.

(4) Touch the vessel with a silver nitrate stick and hold in place for 15 sec.

(5) If the bleeding is easy to control, no pack is needed. If it is difficult to control, place a large cotton pack with bacitracin or neomycin ointment into the nostril, against the bleeding vessel. Make the pack large to avoid aspiration. Remove in 24 hr.

b. Posterior bleeding

(1) Restrain the child, keeping him on his back and restraining his arms.

(2) Keep a large suction tip available to suck blood from the mouth and pharynx.

(3) Pass #14 red rubber catheters into each nostril until they are seen in the oropharynx. Use tongue blades and a strong overhead light to view the oropharynx.

(4) Grasp the catheters in the oropharynx with a hemostat, and pull them out of the child's mouth.

(5) Obtain a posterior pack or make one with a rolled-up, 3- by 3-in. gauze pad tied with three silk sutures. Two sutures should point up and one should point down.

(6) Tie one string to each of the catheters coming from the mouth, and withdraw the nasal end of the catheter, pulling the pack into the nasopharynx.

(7) Push the pack securely into the nasopharynx, using the index finger. (To avoid being bitten, place cotton-wrapped blades between the molar teeth and hold securely.)

(8) Roll up a 2- by 2-in. gauze pad, place it vertically over the columella, and tie the two ends of the sutures firmly around the gauze pad. Do not make it too tight, to avoid cutting the columella.

(9) Bring the third string out of the mouth and tape to the cheek.

(10) Pack ½-in. plain gauze packing coated with bacitracin or neomycin ointment (which may cut down bacterial growth and a bad nasal odor) into the bleeding nostril, using a bayonet forceps.

(11) Tape a folded 3- by 3-in. gauze pad under the nostrils to act as a drip pad.

(12) Sedate the child to decrease anxiety, activity, and bleeding.

(13) Give prophylactic penicillin PO to avoid sinusitis.

(14) Leave the pack in for 5 days. First remove the anterior packs. If no bleeding occurs, remove the posterior pack by cutting the strings anteriorly and pulling the pack from the mouth by grasping the third string that was taped to the cheek.

IV. DISORDERS OF THE PARANASAL SINUSES

A. Acute sinusitis

1. Etiology   Acute sinusitis is usually secondary to pneumococcal, streptococcal, or staphylococcal infection; or, in children under 4 years, *H. influenzae* infection (see Chap. 9, Sec. **IV.F**).

2. Evaluation   Acute sinusitis is usually preceded by a URI or swimming.

a. Maxillary sinusitis presents with cheek pain, upper teeth pain, fever, and swelling of the lower eyelid. On intranasal examination, mucopurulent material is seen.

b. Ethmoid and **sphenoid sinusitis** present with localized headache, fever, and nasal discharge.

c. Frontal sinusitis presents with headache, fever, and nasal discharge, and with increased pain on bending the head forward.

d. The most important clinical finding of acute sinusitis is pus in the nose. Gram stain and culture of the purulent material may be helpful. X-rays will identify the site and severity of the infection.

3. Diagnosis   Purulent material in the nose associated with cheek, orbital, or frontal headache makes sinusitis a likely diagnosis. Decreased transillumination or x-ray findings of thickened mucosa and clouding confirm the diagnosis.

4. Treatment   See also Chap. 9, Sec. **IV.F.4.**

a. Antibiotics for 10 days (according to the culture results; see Table 9-2, p. 182.

b. Nasal decongestant until the nose is normal.

    c. Local heat to relieve pain.

    d. Analgesics as needed.

  5. Complications

    a. Evaluation

      (1) Frontal sinus complications

        (a) Pott's puffy tumor, a localized tender swelling of upper eyebrow and forehead.

        (b) Intracranial spread, as in meningitis, extradural abscess, subdural abscess, or frontal lobe abscess.

      (2) Ethmoid sinusitis complications

        (a) Orbital cellulitis, a moderate swelling of the upper eyelid (see Chap. 23, Sec. **III.C.1**).

        (b) Orbital abscess, a pronounced tender swelling of the upper eyelid, sometimes with chemosis of the conjunctiva and diplopia.

        (c) Cavernous sinus thrombosis, with spiking fevers, retinal venous congestion, and papilledema.

        (d) Intracranial spread, as in meningitis, extradural abscess, subdural abscess, or frontal lobe abscess.

      (3) Maxillary sinusitis complication Cheek cellulitis.

B. Subacute or chronic sinusitis All types of acute sinusitis may become subacute or chronic infections. Headaches, nasal obstruction, nasal discharge, postnasal drip, eustachian tube irritation with otitis media, and chronic bronchitis may all result from chronic sinusitis.

  1. Diagnosis X-ray findings of cloudy sinuses or air fluid levels in the sinuses. Cultures of purulent material are helpful.

  2. Treatment

    a. Subacute sinusitis Refer the patient to an otolaryngologist for irrigation or Proetz displacement, as indicated.

    b. Chronic sinusitis Refer the patient to an otolaryngologist for surgical intervention.

      (1) Cellulitis (See Chap. 9, Sec. **IV.B.4.**) Intravenous antibiotics.

      (2) Abscesses Give antibiotics and refer the patient to an otolaryngologist for incision and drainage and possible sinus surgery.

      (3) Intracranial spread Give an antibiotic IV and refer the patient to an otolaryngologist for possible sinus surgery.

V. DISORDERS OF THE MOUTH

A. Herpetic stomatitis (herpetic gingivostomatitis)

  1. Etiology Herpes simplex virus.

  2. Evaluation

    a. Initially, the lesions are yellow and irregular; later a red ring surrounds each lesion; and, by 7–14 days, the lesions are gone.

b. Recurrent vesicles (fever blisters) occur at the vermilion border of the lips after a latent period.

3. Diagnosis Painful characteristic oral lesions associated with a URI. The mucosal lesions are irregular and yellow, with a red base.

4. Therapy The following treatment is suggested:

a. Chloraseptic mouthwash q2h prn *or* diclonine HCl (Dyclone) mouthwash, 1 tsp q2h prn.

b. Nonspicy foods.

c. Glyoxide on the lips.

d. IV fluids may be required in severe cases.

B. Aphthous stomatitis (canker sores)

1. Etiology Unknown.

2. Evaluation The history reveals recurrent episodes of painful internal multiple oral lesions occurring for months. The lesions may coincide with physical or emotional stress. Look for ulcers elsewhere to exclude Reiter's syndrome and Behçet's disease.

3. Diagnosis The recurrent painful oral lesions are small, oval, and light yellow, with a red margin.

4. Therapy Treatment is usually palliative until spontaneous remission.

a. Chloraseptic mouthwash q2h or diclonine HCl; or topical 4% cocaine or 4% topical Pontocaine q2h.

b. Silver nitrate stick to cauterize each lesion. Precede cauterization with topical 4% Pontocaine or cocaine. (**Note:** This may have to be repeated every 2–4 weeks. The relief is dramatic.)

c. An oral suspension of tetracycline (Achromycin) (50 mg/ml) 5 ml held in the mouth for 30 min qid, and then swallowed, may reduce secondary infection and oral discomfort.

C. Tonguetie (ankyloglossia)

1. Etiology Congenital.

2. Evaluation Tonguetie is uncommon and overdiagnosed.

a. Infant The tip of the tongue is often small, and tonguetie is therefore inadvertently overdiagnosed. As the infant grows, this apparent tonguetie disappears.

b. Child Tonguetie may cause a speech defect, as an articulation disorder. Confirmation by a speech pathologist is recommended. Open-bite deformity of the jaws and mandibular prognathism may also be due to tonguetie.

3. Diagnosis

a. In the infant Elevation of the tongue tip reveals a short frenulum, and palpation of the genioglossus muscle under the tongue reveals a tight band, and the infant may also suck poorly.

b. In the child Examination reveals inability to protrude the tongue. Bimanual palpation beyond the lower incisor teeth and under the tongue reveals a tight band. Functionally, the child cannot repeat "ta-ta-ta" with the incisor teeth separated ¼–½ in.

4. Therapy

a. Frenulectomy   The mucosa is incised and sutured either directly or with a Z-plasty repair to avoid postoperative scarring and contracture.

b. Genioglossus myotomy   The muscle is cut to insure freedom of tongue mobility in more severe cases.

c. Postoperative care in either type of operation consists of the following:

(1) A liquid diet for 1–3 days.

(2) A saline mouthwash after eating.

(3) Mild analgesics as needed.

(4) Speech therapy postoperatively to correct an abnormal articulation habit if it was present preoperatively.

VI. DISORDERS OF THE PHARYNX

A. Peritonsillar abscess

1. Etiology   Gram-positive bacteria, especially staphylococci.

2. Evaluation   When an acute tonsillitis occurs, there may be a peritonsillar cellulitis, identified as a slight redness and swelling of the soft palate on the side of the tonsillitis. If the infection progresses, the peritonsillar abscess forms lateral to the tonsil, pushing it medially toward the uvula, and also in the soft palate, causing it to bulge. These abscesses usually occur in children over the age of 2 years. If spontaneous rupture occurs, aspiration pneumonia or death may follow.

3. Diagnosis   The following signs are typical:

a. A soft palate bulge is seen.

b. The tonsil is inflamed and pushed medially.

c. Drooling of saliva occurs due to severe sore throat.

d. "Hot potato" voice is characteristic (as though the patient has a hot potato in his mouth).

e. There are signs and symptoms of infection (increased WBC, pain, fever).

4. Therapy   Hospitalization is required in all cases.

a. IV antibiotics: oxacillin, 100 mg/kg daily in 4 divided doses.

b. Nothing by mouth.

c. IV fluids.

d. Moist steam via face mask or croupette.

e. Meperidine IM, 1 mg/kg q3–4h prn.

f. Elevation of the head of the bed 45–90 degrees.

g. Needle aspiration of the abscess, or incision and drainage in the soft palate area (not lateral to the tonsil to avoid injuring the internal carotid artery).

B. Retropharyngeal abscess

1. **Etiology**   Gram-positive bacteria, especially staphylococci.

2. **Evaluation**   The presenting symptom may be an enlarged neck mass (cervical adenitis or abscess, or both) and, occasionally, hyperextension of the head to increase the airway diameter. If the abscess should rupture, aspiration of pus could result in pneumonia or death.

3. **Diagnosis**   Palpation of the pharynx reveals a fluctuant mass in the posterior wall of the oropharynx or hypopharynx.

4. **Therapy**   Treatment consists of the following:

   a. IV antibiotics: oxacillin, 100 mg/kg daily in 4 divided doses.

   b. Incision and drainage under general anesthesia.

   (1) The anesthesiologist must be very careful not to rupture the abscess during intubation.

   (2) The head should be hyperextended and hanging down so that the pus that wells up in the nasopharynx and mouth is not draining into the larynx, trachea, and lungs.

VII. DISORDERS OF THE LARYNX   See Chap. 9, Sec. **IV.K.**

VIII. ESOPHAGEAL BURNS FROM LYE INGESTION   See also Chap. 3.

A. Evaluation and diagnosis

1. The most important decision to make in any suspected or actual case of lye ingestion is which patients need esophagoscopy and later therapy. This conflict is critical, since failure to identify esophageal burns early will lead to an esophageal stenosis that is difficult to treat and might have been avoided (see Chap. 3, Sec. **II.A**). Esophagoscopy can be performed within 72 hr of ingestion.

2. Esophagoscopy is advisable if the child vomits after drinking lye (e.g., Drano, Liquid Plumber), is observed drinking lye, or if a lye burn is seen in the mouth. At the first sign of a burn of the esophagus, the esophagoscopy stops and treatment begins. If no burn is seen in the esophagus, no therapy is needed.

3. A chest x-ray may detect associated complications of mediastinal widening, pericarditis, or aspiration or chemical pneumonitis (pulmonary edema). Abnormalities detected on x-ray may include gastrointestinal perforation (free air).

B. Treatment   Neutralization with lemon juice or vinegar is effective only if given within 1 min of ingestion. Feeding might induce vomiting of lye, would prevent early surgery, and cause food to trap in the burned areas, leading to esophageal irritation. Therapy should consist of the following:

1. The patient should be hospitalized. **This is an emergency.**

2. Intravenous fluids are needed to prepare for surgery and to avoid esophageal irritation due to trapped food particles.

3. Intravenous ampicillin is given (100 mg/kg/day).

4. Intravenous corticosteroids should be given as follows: hydrocortisone (Solu-Cortef), 100 mg stat and 100 mg q8h for 3 days, then methylprednisolone (Solu-Medrol) IV or IM, 40 mg tid for 12 days, 20 mg tid for 3 days, 10 mg tid for 2 days, and 5 mg tid for 1 day.

5. Esophagoscopy is performed. Stop at the first sign of a burn.

6. If an esophageal burn is present, and the patient is able to swallow saliva, have him swallow 3 feet of fishing line with an opaque, soft lead weight at the end. Allow 24 hr for the weight attached to fishing line to pass, and then x-ray to see if the weight is past the esophagus. If the child is unable to swallow saliva, a gastrostomy will be needed for retrograde dilation.

7. **Dilation**

   a. None is needed if the burn is mild.

   b. Dilation should be *prograde* if the string is down as a guide but *retrograde* if the burn is severe.

   c. The frequency is determined by the response to therapy and must be individualized.

23 Eye Disorders

I. **VISION TESTING** Vision testing is probably the most important part of an eye examination and certainly the most neglected by physicians in general. Some estimate of a child's vision can be obtained at any age, even though quantitative determinations cannot be done until age 2 or 3. The stages of visual development in children are shown in Table 23-1.

Table 23-1. Stages in Visual Development

Age	Visual Reactions[a]
Newborn	Pupils respond to light Optokinetic nystagmus in 50 percent
4–6 weeks	Follows light or large object held close to face over short range
3 months	Follows light or large object over wide range Social responses to mother's face
5–6 months	Sustained deviation from parallel position is abnormal; may indicate poor vision in deviating eye
8–10 months	Grasps small object between thumb and forefinger
2–3 years	Can identify standardized pictures (Allen cards, Osterberg chart) Subjective acuity can be measured
3½–4 years	Snellen illiterate "E" chart can be used

[a] In all of these maneuvers, each eye should be tested separately, since, with both eyes open, the visual behavior may appear completely normal, despite vision in only one eye.

II. **STRABISMUS** The term *strabismus* refers to any abnormal deviation of the eyes from the parallel position. The eyes may be turned in (esotropia) or out (exotropia), or one eye may be higher than the other (hypertropia). *Amblyopia*, a loss of vision without evident organic defect in the visual system, will develop in over one-third of patients with strabismus. In strabismus, amblyopia occurs in the deviating eye, when one eye is preferred. Amblyopia may also occur in an eye that has a worse refractive error than its fellow, as well as in visual deprivation early in infancy, as in congenital cataracts or corneal opacities.

A. **Evaluation**

1. Strabismus can be detected in infancy by observing the corneal light reflex when the patient fixes on a pocket flashlight. The reflexes should be approximately centered in each pupil.

475

2. Depending on cooperation, the *cover-uncover test* can be used in children as young as 1 year. If, when one eye is covered, the other must move to fix on a light, the patient has strabismus. This and the corneal light reflex test will reveal many cases of strabismus not obvious to gross inspection.

3. The most important single test in patients with strabismus is *visual acuity*. Amblyopia is *not* related to the amplitude of the deviation, so that a very small, inapparent strabismus may lead to profound loss of vision.

B. Therapy

1. Amblyopia

a. The most effective treatment of amblyopia is total occlusion of the preferred eye with an Elastoplast patch. The earlier this treatment is begun, the easier and more effective it is and the least inconvenient to the patient. A young infant may learn to use his two eyes equally well with only a few days of occlusion of the preferred eye.

b. The usual period of patching in a 3-year-old is several weeks, and previously untreated amblyopia in a 4- or 5-year-old child typically requires several months of patching.

c. Beyond the age of 6, although many patients will no longer respond at all to any form of treatment for amblyopia, some older children may still achieve near-normal vision in the amblyopic eye with prolonged occlusion of the preferred eye.

d. Amblyopic patients need to be followed into adolescence to detect and treat any recurrence of amblyopia in the successfully treated eye.

e. Parents should never be reassured that strabismus will resolve spontaneously. Although the angle of the deviation may become less over the years, so that the patient's eyes are cosmetically straight, he may still be left with a profoundly amblyopic eye.

2. Strabismus

a. Esotropia may be accommodative or partially accommodative. A hyperopic (farsighted) person must accommodate in order to achieve clear vision, even in the distance. His eyes may be made straight by prescribing spectacles to correct his hyperopia.

b. Surgery may be required to make the patient's eyes straight in nonaccommodative esotropia or in exotropia.

c. In a small minority of patients normal binocular vision can be restored by manipulation with glasses or surgery. These are usually patients whose eyes have begun to deviate later in childhood. In the vast majority of patients with strabismus, straightening the eyes will be primarily of cosmetic significance, although many will achieve some partial binocularity.

d. The most difficult period for the child with cosmetically objectionable strabismus is in the early school years. Correction should be done by the time the child starts school.

III. **INFLAMMATION** Inflammation may be infectious (bacterial, viral, or fungal) or secondary to systemic inflammatory disease.

A. **Eyelids**

1. **Hordeolum (sty)**

   a. **Etiology** *Staphylococcus aureus.*

   b. **Evaluation and diagnosis** A painful swelling that points at the eyelid margin, involving the sebaceous glands of the eyelash follicle.

   c. **Therapy** Frequent hot soaks. Antibiotics are generally not indicated, and incision and drainage are rarely required.

2. **Chalazion**

   a. **Etiology** Foreign body granulomatous reaction to retained meibomian gland secretion.

   b. **Evaluation and diagnosis** A mass anywhere in the tarsus of the eyelid.

   c. **Therapy** If the lesion is small, it may involute with hot soaks or spontaneously; but, if it is large, it will usually require incision and curettage. In an older child, this can be performed under local anesthesia, but general anesthesia is required in younger children.

3. **Marginal blepharitis**

   a. **Etiology** Seborrhea, *S. aureus.*

   b. **Evaluation and diagnosis** Characteristic accumulation of yellowish scales on the eyelashes associated with erythema and thickening of the eye margins, sometimes associated with seborrhea elsewhere.

   c. **Therapy** Although it generally recurs, this lesion can be temporarily relieved by application of sulfacetamide eye ointment to the lid margins at bedtime—or more often if there is much inflammation—and application of hot soaks to the eyes to soften the crusts so that they can be removed as often as necessary. Treatment of seborrhea should be carried out at the same time (see Chap. 21, Sec. **XI.C**, p. 446).

   It is important to reassure the patient that although it is an annoying, chronic, recurrent condition, it will not damage his eyes.

4. **Cellulitis** See Chap. 9, Sec. **IV.B.4.**

5. **Insect bite**

   a. **Evaluation and diagnosis** A history of bite and swelling out of proportion to the mild tenderness and erythema can usually be obtained. The patient may also complain of itching.

   b. **Therapy** Oral antihistamines (p. 453) and cool compresses to the affected area.

6. **Contact dermatitis** See also Chap. 21, Sec. **III.**

a. Etiology Topical medications (e.g., atropine and eyedrops or ointments containing neomycin), soaps, eye makeup, and the like; staphylococcal conjunctivitis.

b. Evaluation and diagnosis Thickening, crusting, and lichenification of the skin of the lids, often extending in streaks down the cheeks where the tears have run down the face. A careful history should be taken to identify the agent involved.

c. Therapy Attempts should be made to remove the offending agent. Topical corticosteroid ointment such as dexamethasone (Decadron) ophthalmic ointment can be applied to the eyelids.

7. Vaccinia

a. Etiology Self-inoculation from scratching of a vaccination site; generalized vaccinia.

b. Evaluation and diagnosis A history of recent vaccination and the presence of typical crusted vesicles and ulcerations.

c. Therapy Hyperimmune globulin has been advocated by some, but by the time the diagnosis is made it is usually too late to have any effect. The globe itself is rarely involved.

8. Herpes simplex blepharitis

a. Evaluation and diagnosis Finding of either a primary or secondary infection, or a viral culture, or both.

b. Therapy Idoxuridine (IDU) eye ointment should be applied to the conjunctival sac prophylactically to prevent the occurrence of herpes simplex keratitis (see **E.4**). **Corticosteroids are contraindicated.**

9. Herpes zoster ophthalmicus

a. Evaluation and diagnosis Rash in the distribution of the first division of the Vth nerve. Patients with lesions on the tip of the nose are likely to have involvement of the globe itself.

b. Therapy Treatment of ocular involvement is discussed in **F.3.** Treatment of the cutaneous involvement with hyperimmune globulin is controversial. In cases of severe pain, the patient may be treated with systemic corticosteroids (prednisone, 100 mg every other day), in addition to analgesics.

B. Lacrimal drainage system

1. Congenital dacryostenosis

a. Etiology Congenital.

b. Diagnosis The presence of dacryostenosis is confirmed by chronic tearing, with or without discharge, from the eye in the absence of conjunctivitis. A gush of tears, or mucus (white), or both may be observed through the lacrimal canaliculi on digital pressure over the lacrimal sac, along the side of the nose just medial to the medial canthus of the eye.

c. Treatment

(1) If infection is present (see **B.2**) it should be treated. In any case, the mother should be taught to perform massage several times a day, with firm pressure over the lacrimal sac to empty it of accumulated tears and mucus, which form an ideal culture medium for bacteria. Massage may also help the membrane at the lower end of the nasolacrimal duct to break down.

(2) Congenital dacryostenosis will resolve spontaneously or with massage in the first few weeks or months of life in most infants. If it has not resolved by a few months of age, or certainly by 8 months of age, probing of the involved nasolacrimal duct should be performed by an ophthalmologist. In younger infants this can be done under topical anesthesia. Older infants will require brief general anesthesia, but the procedure can still be done on an ambulatory basis.

2. Dacryocystitis

a. Etiology Stasis of tears and mucus in the lacrimal sac due to dacryostenosis; pneumococci; staphylococci.

b. Evaluation and diagnosis There is a purulent (yellow or green) regurgitation from the tear sac. If edema of the canaliculi prevents regurgitation, the sac is enlarged and may point to the skin surface inferomedial to the medial canthus of the eye. Pressure over the inflamed sac will often cause a gush of purulent material through the canaliculi and temporary relief of the swelling and discomfort. The infection is almost always localized to the area of the lacrimal sac.

c. Therapy

(1) Every attempt should be made to drain the sac through the normal orifices. Incision and drainage directly over the pointing area should be avoided, since this may result in a permanent lacrimal fistula to the skin. Local heat and systemic antibiotics may be indicated if the infection is severe (see Chap. 9, Table 9-2, p. 182).

(2) If only purulent drainage from the canaliculi is present, without local signs of inflammation of the lacrimal sac, topical antibiotics applied to the conjunctiva and lacrimal massage will suffice. In nasolacrimal obstruction that has not responded to probing, resulting in recurrent dacryocystitis and chronic epiphora, dacryocystorhinostomy (surgical anastomosis of the lacrimal sac directly to the nasal mucosa) is indicated.

3. Dacryoadenitis This is a rare condition.

a. Etiology Mumps, sarcoid, or, rarely, bacterial infection.

b. Evaluation and diagnosis A tender swelling in the lateral portion of the upper eyelid, giving a characteristic S-shaped curve to the upper lid.

c. Therapy Resolution occurs spontaneously in mumps; with treatment of the systemic disease in sarcoid; or with systemic antibiotics in the case of bacterial infection (see Table 9-2).

C. Orbital cellulitis This is a serious and potentially life-threatening infection, usually occurring as a direct spread from infection of the paranasal sinuses, most commonly the ethmoids.

1. **Etiology** *S. aureus, Hemophilus influenzae,* streptococcus, pneumococcus, phycomycosis.

2. **Evaluation** should include a complete eye examination and a history, physical examination, and sinus x-rays to determine the presence of sinusitis. Phycomycosis should be suspected in young infants with severe dehydration and acidosis from diarrhea or vomiting, and older children with diabetic acidosis, leukemia, or a history of immunosuppressive drugs. Careful examination of the palate in these patients may reveal ulceration; if so, a scraping or biopsy is indicated. Laboratory evaluation should include blood, sinus drainage, and oropharynx cultures.

3. **Diagnosis** Edema and inflammation of the lids, but especially proptosis of the globe with chemosis of the conjunctiva, are the diagnostic features. Vision may be decreased and there may be extraocular muscle palsies secondary to the involvement of the nerves to the orbit. Thrombophlebitis of the orbital veins may lead to cavernous sinus thrombosis, which is difficult to distinguish from severe orbital cellulitis, but often involves the Vth nerve in addition to cranial nerves II, III, IV, and VI and usually causes signs of CNS inflammation.

4. **Therapy** See **(4)**, p. 201.

D. Conjunctivitis

1. Ophthalmia neonatorum

a. **Etiology** *Neisseria gonorrhoeae.* Any conjunctivitis beginning within the first three days of life should be considered gonococcal, although staphylococci, streptococci, pneumococci, and fecal organisms may occasionally cause conjunctivitis during this period.

b. **Evaluation** The chemical conjunctivitis from the silver nitrate prophylactic drops may occasionally be confused with gonococcal conjunctivitis, but the inflammation is rarely so severe, and the characteristic copious yellow pus of gonorrheal conjunctivitis is absent. Serologic test for syphilis should be obtained.

c. **Diagnosis** This can be made by smear of the pus and identification of the gram-negative intracellular diplococci. In addition, culture on Thayer-Martin medium should yield positive identification.

d. **Therapy** If untreated, corneal ulceration with permanent loss of vision or loss of the eye may occur. Treatment with systemic penicillin and frequent instillations of topical sulfacetamide drops will relieve the infection and prevent corneal ulceration and scarring (see also Chap. 9, Sec. **W**, p. 228).

2. Inclusion blennorrhea

a. **Etiology** Chlamydia or so-called large virus.

b. **Evaluation**

(1) In newborn infants it starts between 5 and 15 days of life and is characterized by acute inflammation of the conjunctiva with swelling of the eyelids; 3–4 weeks later there is enlargement of the lymphoid follicles in the conjunctiva of the lower eyelid, with mucopurulent discharge.

(2) It may also occur in older children, in which case the follicles in the lower palpebral conjunctiva enlarge early. The infection may be contracted by swimming in a contaminated swimming pool.

(3) The natural course of inclusion blennorrhea is about 3 months. Permanent loss of vision does not occur.

c. Diagnosis is made by staining scrapings of the lower conjunctiva with Wright's or Giemsa stain and observing the typical paranuclear red- or blue (or both red and blue)-staining inclusions in epithelial cells.

d. Therapy   Treatment with oral sulfonamides and topical sulfacetamide or tetracycline eye ointment 4 times a day will cause resolution within a week.

3. Staphylococcal conjunctivitis   This is probably the most common conjunctivitis of infants and children.

a. Etiology   *S. aureus.*

b. Evaluation and diagnosis   There is usually thick, creamy, yellowish-white pus, often drying on the eyelashes as crust. Superficial infiltrates or ulcerations frequently occur around the periphery of the cornea. The eyelid margins may become ulcerated, and contact dermatitis of the lids may occur. Occasionally, there is impetigo of the face, especially in infants.

c. Therapy   Topical sulfacetamide drops or ointment tid, or erythromycin eye ointment tid, will be effective in almost all cases.

4. Acute catarrhal conjunctivitis

a. Etiology   Common pathogens, including *S. aureus,* pneumococci, streptococci, *H. influenzae,* and *H. aegyptius;* rarely, meningococci.

b. Evaluation and diagnosis   reveals conjunctival injection and a mucopurulent discharge, which may accumulate on the lashes during sleep, causing them to stick together, but is never so thick and crusting as in typical staphylococcal conjunctivitis. *A gram-stained smear and culture of the conjunctival sac should be obtained before beginning therapy in any variety of bacterial conjunctivitis.* (The culture swab should be immediately placed in a tube of broth because the amount of material is very small and rapidly desiccates. If eye cultures are handled in the routine way, the organism will not grow in most cases.)

c. Treatment

(1) In general, sulfacetamide eyedrops or ointment will be effective. Since most of the causative organisms are gram-positive, erythromycin is also useful.

(2) Treatment should not be delayed until the results of the culture are known.

(3) Drops or ointment containing neomycin should generally be avoided because of the toxicity of neomycin to the cornea after prolonged usage and the tendency for allergies to develop. Antibiotic-corticosteroid combinations are especially to be avoided because of the side effects of topical steroids (see **E.4** and Sec. **IV**).

(4) Depending on the severity of the infection, the conjunctivitis will usually show some improvement within 2–3 days and generally be completely cleared in a week. If there is no improvement, the results of the previously obtained culture will then be available, and more specific treatment can be directed at the offending organisms.

(5) If the conjunctivitis is severe, topical antibiotics or chemotherapeutic agents should be given frequently, perhaps q1–2h and then reduced to qid when the conjunctivitis is improved. The topical treatment should be continued for a full week or at least for 72 hr after the signs and symptoms of conjunctivitis have resolved. Otherwise, the infection is likely to recur.

(6) Actual failure of therapy due to bacterial resistance is unusual. The concentrations of antibiotic or chemotherapeutic agent achieved by topical therapy in the conjunctival sac are several orders of magnitude higher than that achieved by systemic treatment, so that apparently resistant staphylococci, for example, will respond to topical erythromycin or sulfonamides. However, *systemic* antibiotics should be added in conjunctivitis due to pneumococci, β-hemolytic streptococci, and meningococci.

5. Viral conjunctivitis

a. Etiology Adenovirus type 8; possibly other viruses.

b. Evaluation and diagnosis

(1) This disease may be distinguished from bacterial conjunctivitis in most cases. However, the diagnosis is often made when a bacterial conjunctivitis does not respond to antibiotics.

(2) In epidemic keratoconjunctivitis (EKC) due to adenovirus type 8 there is an acute onset of injection of the bulbar and lower palpebral conjunctiva, with mucopurulent discharge and swelling of the lower lids. Grayish, subepithelial corneal infiltrates occur early and cause pain and photophobia. Lymphoid follicles appear early in the lower palpebral conjunctiva and there is a large, tender, preauricular lymph node.

(3) Other adenoviruses may cause a less severe and prolonged conjunctivitis, frequently in association with pharyngitis. Signs and symptoms are similar except that the corneal lesions are usually on the surface of the epithelium and cause stippled staining with fluorescein. Other less well defined varieties of follicular conjunctivitis are probably also viral[1] in etiology. These are all somewhat contagious, and precautions should be taken in the handling of the patient.

c. Therapy

(1) EKC *is extremely contagious, and hand precautions should be used by the examining physician.* Many epidemics have been initiated by careless nurses and physicians.

---

[1] Conjunctivitis frequently accompanies the acute exanthema. Unless secondary infections with bacteria are suspected, only symptomatic treatment should be given.

(2) If photophobia is severe, the pupils can be kept dilated by a mydriatic-cyclopedic agent such as 0.3% scopolamine hydrobromide. After the acute phase is over, mild conjunctival injection and corneal infiltrates with continued feeling of irritation in the eye may persist from weeks to months.

(3) Topical antibiotics are of no value. Treatment with topical corticosteroids is controversial and can be considered only after herpes simplex has been ruled out. At best, they will relieve the symptoms and cause disappearance of corneal infiltrates temporarily, only to have both recur when treatment is discontinued.

6. Trachoma

a. Etiology   *Chlamydia.*

b. Evaluation   Trachoma is a follicular conjunctivitis that involves the upper lid and upper portion of the globe more severely than the lower. If untreated, infiltration and vascularization of the cornea occur. There may be scarring of the eyelids, with trichiasis (inversion of the lashes rubbing against the globe), and severe visual loss may occur.

c. Diagnosis   This is made from the clinical picture and from finding typical cytoplasmic inclusion bodies in epithelial cells from conjunctival scrapings stained by Wright's or Giemsa stain.

d. Therapy   Oral sulfonamides are given for at least 10 days (see Sec. **E**, p. 195) and topical tetracycline eye ointment is applied 4 times a day until 72 hr after the inflammation has subsided. If photophobia is severe, the pupil may be dilated with 0.3% scopolamine eyedrops.

7. Allergic conjunctivitis   See Sec. **IV.A**, p. 467.

a. Vernal conjunctivitis

(1) Etiology   Presumably hypersensitivity to various pollens.

(2) Evaluation   This entity generally occurs in older children or adolescents and is seasonal. Symptoms include intense itching of the eyelids, with the patient often rubbing his eyes uncontrollably. There is a thick, stringy mucoid secretion.

(3) Diagnosis   Characteristic are papillae on the tarsal conjunctiva of both upper and lower lids, which give a cobblestone appearance (palpebral type), or marked hypertrophy of the conjunctival epithelium adjacent to the cornea (limbal type), or both. A smear of the mucoid discharge usually shows many eosinophils.

(4) Therapy

(a) The most effective treatment is with topical corticosteroids, which usually relieve the symptoms rapidly. Medrysone, a newer corticosteroid that is not absorbed into the interior of the eye, will avoid the complication of corticosteroid-induced glaucoma. However, **exacerbation** of herpes simplex keratitis is still a danger, and the latter should be ruled out by slit lamp examination before any topical corticosteroids are administered.

(b) Dilute solutions of phenylephrine will temporarily relieve symptoms, but reactive hyperemia will occur, so its continued use is not recommended.

b. Acute allergic conjunctivitis

(1) Etiology Common allergens; occurs with allergic rhinitis.

(2) Evaluation and diagnosis

(a) Chemosis (edema) of the conjunctiva, excess lacrimation, itching, and sometimes allergic edema of the eyelids are characteristic. The conjunctiva may be somewhat injected, but the symptoms are out of proportion to the apparent inflammation.

(b) Allergic reaction of the conjunctiva to topical medication may also occur, as well as contact dermatitis of the lids. The most common offender is neomycin, usually administered in a drop or ointment in combination with other antibiotics for conjunctivitis.

(3) Therapy

(a) Treatment of the underlying allergy is usually effective in relieving the eye manifestations, and oral antihistamines are frequently beneficial.

(b) Topical administration of proprietary eyedrops, commonly self-administered by patients, should be discouraged, since the patient is likely to become allergic to some of the ingredients.

(c) On occasion, the symptoms may be severe enough to warrant short-term topical corticosteroid treatment, but cold compresses will usually relieve the symptoms sufficiently.

(d) In a patient whose conjunctivitis initially responds to treatment but in whom conjunctival inflammation recurs while treatment is still being continued, allergy to the topical medication should be considered. Treatment of the allergy consists in discontinuing the medication.

c. Phlyctenular conjunctivitis

(1) Etiology Allergic inflammation, generally associated with remote bacterial infection, typically tuberculosis or local staphylococcal infection.

(2) Evaluation and diagnosis This is a localized inflammation of the conjunctiva, characterized by a small vesicle with surrounding injection which becomes ulcerated. If it is adjacent to the cornea, it may progress across the cornea with vascular reaction. It results in corneal scarring, which may lead to loss of vision if it involves the pupillary area.

(3) Therapy The underlying cause should be discovered and treated. The eye should be treated topically with corticosteroids and the pupil kept dilated with scopolamine 0.3% eyedrops.

8. **Stevens-Johnson syndrome (erythema multiforme exudativum)**

   a. **Etiology** Unknown.

   b. **Evaluation** In the conjunctiva this is usually associated with inflammation as part of the general involvement of mucous membranes. The conjunctivitis is typically purulent or mucopurulent, often with pseudomembrane formation in the fornices. There may be secondary bacterial infection. In severe cases, symblepharon (adhesions between the palpebral and bulbar conjunctiva) may form.

   c. **Diagnosis** This is confirmed by the presence of the characteristic skin lesions of the Stevens-Johnson syndrome.

   d. **Therapy** Erythromycin eye ointment will effectively treat most common secondary bacterial infections and will also make the patient's eyes more comfortable. If herpes simplex infection is ruled out, topical corticosteroids should be used to control the inflammation.

E. **Corneal inflammation**

   1. **Bacterial corneal ulcers**

      a. **Etiology** Common gram-positive or gram-negative pathogens.

      b. **Evaluation**

         (1) These lesions are usually associated with infections of the lids, lacrimal sac, or conjunctiva.

         (2) Peripheral superficial conjunctival staphylococcal corneal ulcers have been mentioned (**D.3.b**). On occasion, these will progress to involve the entire circumference of the cornea adjacent to the limbus and, rarely, will produce a ring abscess of the cornea.

         (3) Pneumococci often cause a severe corneal ulcer with hypopyon (collection of white blood cells in the inferior anterior chamber). It is usually a discrete, round white opacity covered with purulent exudate, which may spread rapidly into the deeper layers of the cornea, causing a corneal perforation and prolapse of intraocular structures, sometimes with loss of the eye.

         (4) *Moraxella,* a diplobacillus that infects only the eye, may cause a picture similar to that of pneumococcal corneal ulcer.

         (5) *Pseudomonas* corneal ulcer usually occurs as the result of irrigation of a traumatized cornea with contaminated solutions. *P. aeruginosa* does not cause conjunctivitis or infect the intact cornea. Since the organism can grow in dilute solutions, bottles of irrigating saline or fluorescein should not be reused for more than one day after they are opened. The ulcer is rapidly progressive and may spread to involve the entire cornea within a few hours. A hypopyon is usually present, and the entire cornea may become necrotic and slough. **The eye will be lost unless treatment is rapidly instituted.**

         (6) Various other bacteria, including streptococci and fecal organisms, may also cause corneal infections in children.

    c. Diagnosis may be attempted from a gram stain and smear of direct scraping from the corneal ulcer itself. Cultures of the ulcer and of the conjunctival sac should also be taken.

    d. Therapy Topical and systemic treatment should be directed to the suspected organism.

        (1) In no case should treatment be deferred until the organism has been positively identified on culture.

        (2) When the organism cannot be reasonably identified immediately, *"shotgun" therapy with antibiotics is completely justified.*

        (3) Pneumococcal corneal ulcers should be treated with systemic penicillin in addition to frequent applications of topical erythromycin or sulfonamide.

        (4) *Pseudomonas* corneal ulcers should be treated with frequent instillations of polymixin B eyedrops and systemic gentamicin until sensitivities can be obtained. Once the organism has been positively identified, systemic and topical treatment can be altered if necessary (see Table 9-2).

2. Interstitial keratitis

    a. Etiology Usually, congenital syphilis or tuberculosis; noninfectious varieties have been described.

    b. Evaluation and diagnosis It is usually a late manifestation of congenital syphilis occurring in preadolescent and adolescent children. The cornea assumes a ground-glass appearance from edema and infiltration, and corneal vascularization proceeds rapidly.

    c. Therapy Treatment of luetic interstitial keratitis is with systemic penicillin, topical corticosteroids, and mydriatic-cyclopegic drops.

3. Fungal keratitis occurs following trauma.

    a. Etiology Most common organisms involved are *Cephalosporium* and *Fusarium* species.

    b. Evaluation These lesions may be difficult to distinguish from bacterial ulcers, but they tend to have more raised borders with radiating lines of infiltrate in the corneal stroma, and satellite lesions often develop around the primary infection.

    c. Diagnosis This can be made by scrapings stained for fungi and fungal cultures.

    d. Therapy Topical treatment with pimaricin is most effective. Topical amphotericin B is not very effective and is irritating to the eye. Topical potassium iodide drops may have some effect in some cases. Nystatin is effective only in *Candida* infections. The patients are often left with severe scarring and may require corneal transplant.

4. Herpetic keratitis This is the most important corneal inflammation.

    a. Etiology Herpes simplex virus.

    b. Evaluation and diagnosis The disease is confirmed by the characteristic appearance of a dendritic figure, which stains with fluorescein. It is a branching, jagged linear infiltrate on the surface of the epithelium, which may resemble branching coral. The patient may be uncomfortable and photophobic, but without much evidence of inflammation.

c. Therapy Whenever epithelial herpes simplex keratitis is present, topical corticosteroid treatment is contraindicated. In most cases the infection can be controlled with topical applications of idoxuridine ointment. If drops are used, they must be put in around the clock. Thus the use of the ointment is much more convenient.

5. Other viral involvement

a. Etiology Adenovirus, trachoma, and varicella–herpes zoster virus. (On rare occasions varicella may cause keratitis, but involvement of the cornea is more common in herpes zoster ophthalmicus.)

b. Evaluation and diagnosis Conjunctival injection and corneal staining with fluorescein will identify the problem. Involvement of the cornea in measles is usually due to secondary infection.

c. Therapy Treatment is topical corticosteroid drops and dilation of the pupil with mydriatic-cycloplegics.

6. Familial dysautonomia (Riley-Day syndrome)

a. Etiology Unknown.

b. Evaluation and diagnosis This syndrome includes deficiency of tears, corneal hypesthesia, and recurrent episodes of high fever and dehydration. These conditions tend to produce a superficial keratitis of the exposure type, during which the corneal epithelium is lost, with opacification and permanent scarring of stroma. Occasionally, severe necrotizing keratopathy occurs. The severity of the systemic illness should not distract the physician's attention from the severe corneal problem, which occurs very rapidly during these febrile episodes.

c. Therapy The corneas can be protected with methyl cellulose drops, bland eye ointment, and by using butterfly adhesive to close the lids, which tend to remain open during sleep.

F. Uveitis This may be *anterior*, involving primarily the iris and ciliary body; or *posterior*, involving the choroid.

1. Anterior uveitis (iritis, iridocyclitis)

a. Etiology Juvenile rheumatoid arthritis (JRA). Reiter's syndrome, Behçet's disease, sarcoid, and idiopathic.

b. Evaluation

(1) In JRA the inflammation is insidious and the first symptom is usually visual loss. Because of the insidious course and ultimately severe complications of the iritis in JRA, every child with this illness should be examined carefully with the slit lamp every 4 months in the absence of symptoms.

(2) Sarcoid may cause a granulomatous iritis. The diagnosis depends on diagnosing the systemic illness.

(3) Herpes zoster ophthalmicus may also cause a severe iritis. Many patients will have a much more acute and symptomatic onset of iritis than those with JRA. The eye will generally be injected, more immediately around the cornea than elsewhere, and the patient often complains of severe pain and photophobia.

(4) Secondary glaucoma is frequently seen in iritis. (Patients with iritis should be examined carefully for inflammation elsewhere in the body and have serologic tests for syphilis, a tuberculin test, and a chest x-ray.)

c. Therapy Treatment is dilation of the pupils with scopolamine 0.3% eyedrops to prevent the formation of posterior synechiae (adhesions of the iris to the lens) and topical corticosteroid drops to control the inflammation. If the band keratopathy becomes severe, the calcium can be removed with disodium edetate (EDTA) drops. Do not use Versenate, which is the calcium salt of EDTA.) Cataracts may eventually require operation.

2. Posterior uveitis (choroiditis and chorioretinitis) The etiology is most commonly *Toxoplasma*, congenital syphilis, rubella, cytomegalic inclusion disease, visceral larva migrans, sarcoid, tuberculosis, and sympathetic ophthalmia. The cause can be determined in about 50 percent of cases.

a. Toxoplasmosis

(1) Evaluation and diagnosis

(a) It is usually a prenatal infection, and the lesions are discrete, atrophic areas with pigmented borders and pigmented lines running through them. They may be anywhere in the retina, but are often found in the macular area in congenital toxoplasmosis.

(b) Most commonly, the chorioretinitis is healed when the patient is first seen in the newborn period. These healed lesions contain viable parasites, and reactivation of the chorioretinitis may occur any time during life.

(c) When active inflammation is present, the vitreous becomes cloudy, and fluffy white lesions appear, usually at the border of an old healed scar.

(d) Presumptive diagnosis of toxoplasmic chorioretinitis may be made from the clinical appearance and from the Sabin-Feldman dye test or the *Toxoplasma* complement fixation test.

(2) Therapy Treatment of active toxoplasmic chorioretinitis consists of systemic and topical corticosteroids and topical mydriatic-cycloplegic drops. Treatment with combined pyrimethamine (Daraprim) and sulfonamide (p. 254), although lethal to the organisms, is of questionable benefit clinically. If it is undertaken, the patient must be given folinic acid concurrently.

b. Congenital syphilis

(1) Evaluation consists in systemic examination and serologic tests. Syphilis typically causes a diffuse fine pigmentary disturbance througout the fundus.

(2) Therapy Systemic penicillin (p. 230).

c. **Rubella** This is not a treatable cause of chorioretinitis.

d. **Cytomegalic inclusion disease** is not a treatable cause of chorioretinitis.

e. **Sarcoidosis**

(1) **Evaluation** The posterior uveitis may have the characteristic "candle-wax droppings" or periphlebitis or both.

(2) **Therapy** Treatment is with topical and systemic corticosteroids as well as with mydriatic-cycloplegic drops.

f. **Tuberculosis** (See Chap. 9, Sec. **IV.V.**) This is now a rare cause of posterior uveitis in children.

g. **Histoplasmosis**

(1) **Evaluation** In posterior uveitis in older children that is presumed to be due to histoplasmosis, there are characteristically peripheral choroidal infiltrates and often hemorrhage in the macula. Other fungus infections, as well as brucellosis and amebiasis, are presumed causes of posterior uveitis.

(2) **Therapy** Diagnosis and treatment of the systemic disease is indicated, but treatment of the uveitis is nonspecific antiinflammatory therapy with systemic corticosteroids.

h. **Sympathetic ophthalmia**

(1) **Etiology** This is an uncommon complication of penetrating ocular injury with uveal prolapse. Presumably, an autoimmune response occurs to the injured uveal tissue, which causes a bilateral posterior and anterior uveitis.

(2) **Treatment** Prevention is by enucleation of a hopelessly injured eye within the first week after injury and careful excision of all prolapsed uveal material in eyes that can be repaired. Once sympathetic ophthalmia is established, removal of the inciting eye is of no benefit. The illness responds to systemic corticosteroid treatment in most cases, but this may have to be continued for years.

3. **Endophthalmitis**

a. **Etiology** Bacterial or fungal contamination of a perforating injury of the eye, corneal ulcer, intraocular surgery, or, rarely, generalized sepsis.

b. **Evaluation** Vision is lost, and the eye becomes painful and intensely inflamed, with chemosis of the conjunctiva, corneal haze, hypopyon, and vitreous opacity.

c. **Therapy** If untreated, the infection may spread to the orbit. Occasionally, the globe, and even some vision, may be preserved by prompt antibiotic therapy early in the course of the disease. However, enucleation or evisceration (removal of the cornea and the contents of the globe, leaving the sclera) is usually necessary.

IV. GLAUCOMA (increased intraocular pressure)

A. **Etiology** Glaucoma may be inherited, due to trauma, or secondary to inflammation, or due to topical corticosteroid application.

B. Evaluation

1. A general pediatric examination to rule out associated primary disease.

2. A complete ophthalmic examination, with specific attention to photophobia and excess lacrimation. It should also include measurement of the corneal diameters to rule out abnormal enlargement, inspection of the corneas for cloudiness, inspection of the optic nerve heads for cupping produced by an elevated intraocular pressure, and measurement of the intraocular pressures.

C. Diagnosis is confirmed by presence of increased intraocular pressure.

D. Therapy

1. **Medical** Acetazolamide (Diamox) 15 mg/kg PO daily; pilocarpine HCl, 2–4%, applied topically q6h.

2. **Surgical** Goniotomy for infantile glaucoma, filtration surgery, and cyclocryotherapy.

V. OCULAR TRAUMA

A. Mechanical injury

1. **Etiology** Sharp tools (e.g., scissors), missiles, blunt trauma (e.g., automobile accidents, blows from fists, falls).

2. **Evaluation and diagnosis**

   a. In all cases the suspected injury is approached with extreme care to prevent further injury. Swelling of the lids and injection of the conjunctiva is a feature of all eye injuries.

   b. The history usually suggests the possible extent of the injury; examination of the anterior segment, posterior segment, lids, and conjunctiva and measurement of vision, eye pressure, and eye movements establish its extent.

   c. A corneal abrasion is demonstrated by the instillation of fluorescein into the conjunctival sac. A suspected external foreign body is looked for on the cornea or on the bulbar and lid conjunctiva.

   d. Suspected penetrating injury is established by evaluating the clarity of the media and measurement of the eye pressure.

   e. Blunt trauma requires slit lamp examination for blood in the anterior chamber (hyphema) and evaluation of the extraocular movements for muscle entrapment.

   f. X-rays are often indicated to detect intraocular or orbital foreign bodies and to evaluate the bony orbit.

3. **Therapy**

   a. Corneal or conjunctival foreign bodies are removed with a small instrument following the instillation of a topical anesthetic (proparacaine 0.5%).

   b. Corneal abrasions are treated by applying a pressure patch to the eye following the instillation of an antibiotic ointment.

c. Penetrating injuries to the eye require repair under general anesthesia. First aid should include protection of the eye from further injury.

d. Orbital fractures may require surgical repair within the first week following the injury.

e. Bleeding into the anterior chamber following blunt trauma requires bed rest and careful observation. Secondary hemorrhage may occur and be associated with the onset of glaucoma.

B. Chemical injury

1. Etiology Often, household liquids.

2. Evaluation and diagnosis The history will often reveal the cause of injury. Examination should focus on the conjunctiva and anterior segment, especially the cornea. Fluorescein may be used to appraise the injury to the cornea.

3. Therapy

a. Initial first aid consisting of copious and prolonged (10–20 min) irrigation with tepid water is the most important step in the prevention of serious complications. This should be done promptly and is facilitated by instillation of a topical anesthetic (proparacaine 0.5%).

b. Further treatment will vary with the extent of the injury. Mild chemical conjunctivitis and corneal abrasion may be treated with topical antibiotic ointment and patching. Strong alkalies are especially prone to cause progressive ophthalmic injury. Injuries from these substances require careful continued ophthalmic care.

Index

Note: To avoid unnecessary repetition most major discussions of medical entities indexed include information on etiology, evaluation, diagnosis, and therapy, e.g., as under Abscess(es), brain.

Hypovolemia, in hepatic failure, 291, 293
Hypoxemia, in respiratory failure, 412
Hypoxia, 268–269
  in hypothermia of infants, 102
Hysterical fits. *See* Epilepsy, psychogenic

Idoxyuridine (IDU) eye ointment, 478
IgA. *See* Immunoglobulin levels
IgE antibody, in atopic dermatitis, 434
IgG. *See* Immunoglobulin levels
IgM. *See* Immunoglobulin levels
Ileitis, and abdominal masses, 159
Ileum, terminal, and abdominal mass, 158
Ileus, meconium, in the newborn, 158
Immersion foot frostbite, 52–53
Immobilization, in osteomyelitis, 223
Immune deficiency syndrome, combined,
    151, 152
  and failure to thrive, 144
Immunization, 26–28
  active, revised schedule for, U.S., 27
Immunoglobulin classes, biologic prop-
    erties of, 430–431
Immunoglobulin deficiency, common
    variable forms of, 428–429
Immunoglobulin levels, in fetus and
    newborn, 429
Immunologic deficiency diseases, and
    recurrent infections, 150–154
Immunosuppressed individuals, and
    bacterial infections, 334
Immunosuppressive therapy
  in acquired hemolytic anemias, 329
  in Crohn's disease, 351
  and pneumocystis, 254
  and risk of infection, 154
  in systemic lupus erythematosus, 423
Impaction, fecal
  in chronic constipation, 354
  in neonate or infant, 158
Impetigo, 200, 440–441
  and scabies, 442
Infancy, early and late, recurrent in-
    fections in, 151–153
Infantile spasms. *See* Spasms, infantile
Infant(s). *See also* Newborn; Prematures
  of addicted mothers, 9, 11
  and alcohol as sedative, 10
  antibiotics for, in pneumonia, 213
  feeding of. *See* Feeding (of infants)
  hypotonia in, 141
  urinary tract infection in, 220
  venipuncture in, 2, 3
Infection(s)
  bacterial, vs. parasitic, 233
  and diabetes insipidus, 384
  and diabetes mellitus, 404
  in dialysis, 280
  and erythema multiforme, 436
  and etiology of fever, 174
  in failure to thrive, 144
  hepatic, in amebiasis, 249
  and hepatic failure, 293
  intestinal, in amebiasis, 249
  in leukemia, 334
  location of site of, 179

and nephrotic syndrome, 285
parasitic, 231–255
prenatal, and neonatal morbidity, 104
recurrent
  as diagnostic problem, 149–154
  in hormonal defects, 428
  and sickle cell crises, 327
  types of, and choice and dosage of
    drugs, 180–181
  upper respiratory, 209–210
    and acute labyrinthitis, 466
    and acute otitis media, 463
  urinary tract, 219–220
    therapy for, 185, 199, 220–221
      prophylactic antimicrobials, 180
Infectious diseases, antibiotics and, 179–
    230
Infestations, 441–444
Inflammatory disorders, 419–432
  and abdominal masses, 159
  of the eye, 477–488
Infusion, intravenous, indications, site,
    and technique, 2–3
Ingestions, common, of low toxicity, 72.
    See also Poison(s)
Inhibitors, in hemophilia. *See* Antibodies
Injury
  grossly contaminated, prophylactic
    antimicrobials in, 181
  mechanical, and ocular trauma, 490
Insulin
  administration in juvenile diabetes, 398
  in hyperkalemia of acute renal failure,
    275–276, 283
  Lente, 399, 400
  neutral protamine Hagedorn, 399, 400
  protamine zinc, in diabetes mellitus,
    400
  Semilente, 400
  Ultralente, 399, 400
Insulin resistance, 403
Insulin therapy, and phases of diabetes
    mellitus, 399, 401
  problems in, 402–403
Intermittent positive pressure breathing
    (IPPB), 409 ·
  in asthma therapy, 46, 51, 410
  in croup, 211
Interstitial keratitis, 486
Intestinal bacteria, in monosaccharide
    malabsorption, 347
Intracranial pressure, benign increased,
    309–310
Intracranial spread, in sinusitis, 470
Intraocular pressure, increased. *See*
    Glaucoma
Intravenous therapy, in hyperkalemia,
    275–276
Intubation
  in controlled ventilation, 49
    for resuscitation of newborn, 107, 110
  for empyema, 214
  endotracheal, in emergency airway,
    455
  nasotracheal, in croup, 210
  in retropharyngeal abscess, 473

Little, Brown's Paperback Book Series

Basic Medical Sciences

Albers, Agranoff, Katzman, & Siegel	Basic Neurochemistry
Colton	Statistics in Medicine
Hine & Pfeiffer	Behavioral Science
Levine	Pharmacology
Peery & Miller	Pathology, 2nd Ed.
Selkurt	Physiology, 3rd Ed.
Sidman & Sidman	Neuroanatomy
Snell	Clinical Anatomy for Medical Students
Snell	Clinical Embryology for Medical Students, 2nd Ed.
Valtin	Renal Function
Watson	Basic Human Neuroanatomy

Clinical Medical Sciences

Clark & MacMahon	Preventive Medicine
Eckert	Emergency-Room Care, 2nd Ed.
Grabb & Smith	Plastic Surgery, 2nd Ed.
Green	Gynecology, 2nd Ed.
Judge & Zuidema	Methods of Clinical Examination, 3rd Ed.
Keefer & Wilkins	Medicine
MacAusland & Mayo	Orthopedics
Nardi & Zuidema	Surgery, 3rd Ed.
Thompson	Primer of Clinical Radiology
Ziai	Pediatrics, 2nd Ed.

Nursing Sciences

DeAngelis	Basic Pediatrics for the Primary Health Care Provider
Sana & Judge	Physical Appraisal Methods in Nursing Practice
Selkurt	Basic Physiology for the Health Sciences

Manuals and Handbooks

Arndt	Manual of Dermatologic Therapeutics
Children's Hospital Medical Center, Boston	Manual of Pediatric Therapeutics
Condon & Nyhus	Manual of Surgical Therapeutics, 3rd Ed.
Friedman & Papper	Problem-Oriented Medical Diagnosis
Massachusetts General Hospital	Manual of Nursing Procedures
Neelon & Ellis	A Syllabus of Problem-Oriented Patient Care
Spivak & Barnes	Manual of Clinical Problems in Internal Medicine: Annotated with Key References
Wallach	Interpretation of Diagnostic Tests, 2nd Ed.
Washington University Department of Medicine	Manual of Medical Therapeutics, 21st Ed.
Zimmerman	Techniques of Patient Care

Little, Brown and Company
34 Beacon Street
Boston, Massachusetts 02106

THE LITTLE, BROWN
MANUAL SERIES

Titles in Little, Brown's Manual Series are readily available at all medical bookstores throughout the United States and abroad. You may also order copies directly from Little, Brown and Company, 34 Beacon Street, Boston, Massachusetts 02106, by simply tearing out, filling in, and mailing this postage-free card.

☐ MANUAL OF DERMATOLOGIC THERAPEUTICS — Arndt (#051802-93AD1). $8.95

☐ MANUAL OF PEDIATRIC THERAPEUTICS — Children's Hospital Medical Center, Boston; Graef & Cone, Editors (#139122-88AC1) $8.95

☐ MANUAL OF SURGICAL THERAPEUTICS, 3rd Edition — Condon & Nyhus, Editors (#152838) $8.95

☐ PROBLEM-ORIENTED MEDICAL DIAGNOSIS — Friedman & Papper, Editors, (#293547-88AB1) $8.95

☐ MANUAL OF ACUTE BACTERIAL INFECTIONS: EARLY DIAGNOSIS AND TREATMENT — Gardner & Provine (#303275) $9.95

☐ DIET MANUAL — Massachusetts General Hospital Dietary Department (#549568) .... Due Spring 1976

☐ MASSACHUSETTS GENERAL HOSPITAL MANUAL OF NURSING PROCEDURES — Massachusetts General Hospital Department of Nursing (#549541-88X1) $8.95

☐ A SYLLABUS OF PROBLEM-ORIENTED PATIENT CARE — Neelon & Ellis (#599808-88W1) $4.95

☐ MANUAL OF MEDICAL CARE OF THE SURGICAL PATIENT — Papper, Editor (#690473) $8.95

☐ MANUAL OF PSYCHIATRIC THERAPEUTICS — Shader, Editor (#782203) $8.95

☐ MANUAL OF CLINICAL PROBLEMS IN INTERNAL MEDICINE: ANNOTATED WITH KEY REFERENCES – Spivak & Barnes (#807133-88Y1) $9.95

☐ INTERPRETATION OF DIAGNOSTIC TESTS: A HANDBOOK SYNOPSIS OF LABORATORY MEDICINE, 2nd Edition — Wallach (#920436-88Z1) ... $7.95

☐ MANUAL OF MEDICAL THERAPEUTICS, 21st Edition — Washington University Department of Medicine; Boedeker & Dauber, Editors (#924024-88AD1) $7.95

NAME_____
(Please print)

STREET_____

CITY_____ STATE_____

ZIP CODE_____

ORDERS FOR LESS THAN $10.00 MUST BE PREPAID. PUBLISHER PAYS POSTAGE AND HANDLING CHARGES ON ALL ORDERS ACCOM-PANIED BY A CHECK. (Please add sales tax if applicable.)

☐ Bill me.
☐ Check enclosed.